Street by Street

READING, BASINGSTOKE
BRACKNELL
FLEET, HENLEY-ON-THAMES, NEWBURY, WOKINGHAM

Ascot, Goring, Hook, Kingsclere, Odiham, Overton, Pangbourne, Sonning Common, Tadley, Twyford

Ist edition May 2001

© Automobile Association Developments Limited 2001

This product includes map data licensed from Ordnance Survey® with the permission of the Controller of Her Majesty's Stationery Office. © Crown copyright 2000. All rights reserved. Licence No: 399221.

Published by AA Publishing (a trading name of Automobile Association Developments Limited, whose registered office is Norfolk House, Priestley Road, Basingstoke, Hampshire, RG24 9NY. Registered number 1878835).

Mapping produced by the Cartographic Department of The Automobile Association.

A CIP Catalogue record for this book is available from the British Library.

Printed by G. Canale & C. S.P.A., Torino, Italy

Ref: MX056

Key to map pages	ii-iii
Key to map symbols	iv-1
Enlarged scale pages	2-15
Street by Street	16-183
Index – towns & villages	184
Index – streets	185-199
Index – featured places	199-201

ii

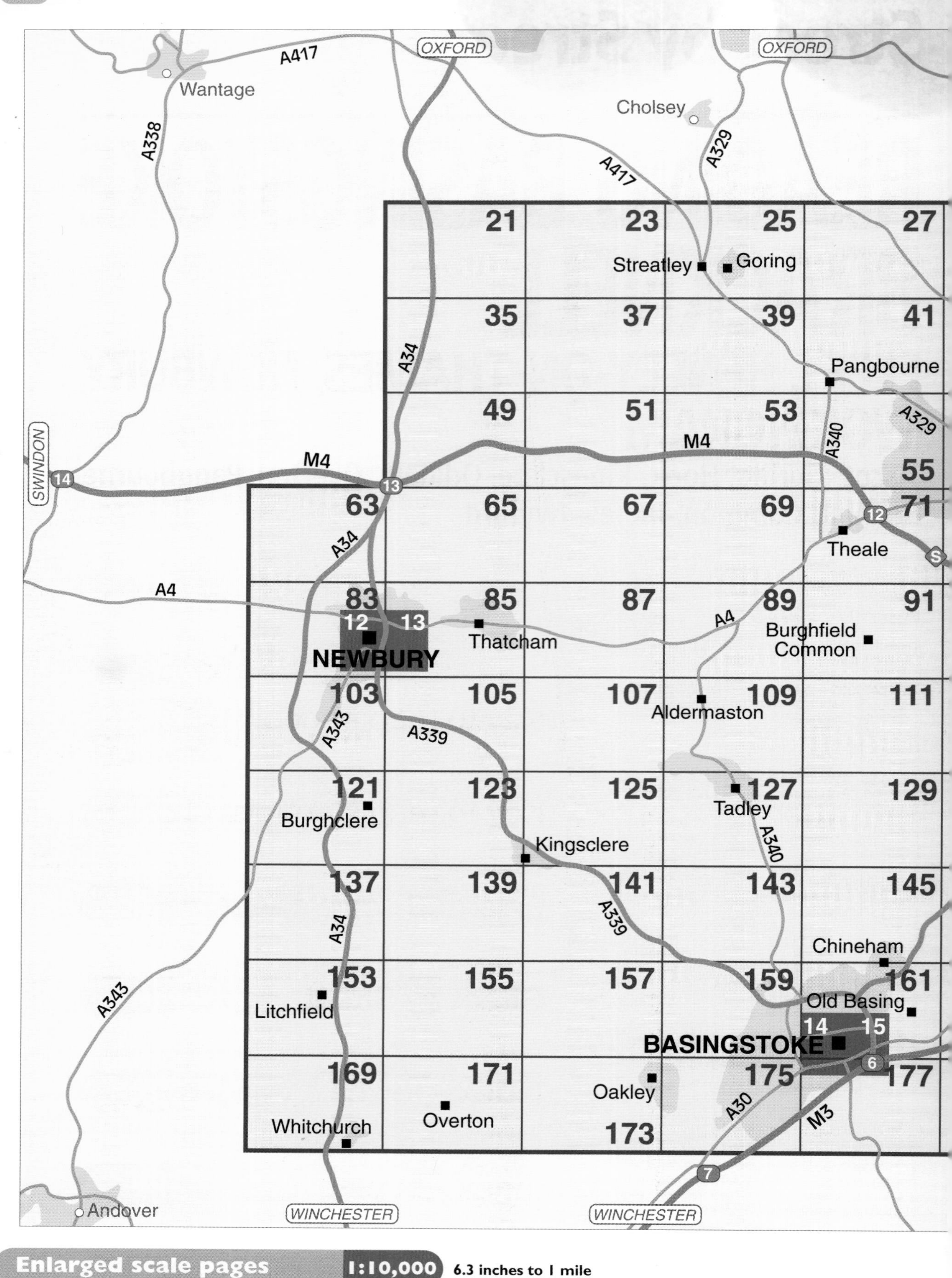

A417
Wantage
A338
OXFORD
Cholsey
A417
A329
OXFORD

| 21 | 23 | 25 | 27 |
Streatley • • Goring

| 35 | 37 | 39 | 41 |
A34
Pangbourne

| 49 | 51 | 53 | |
M4
A340
A329
| | | | 55 |

M4
SWINDON
14
13
| 63 | 65 | 67 | 69 | 71 |
A34
12
Theale
S

A4
| 83 | 85 | 87 | 89 | 91 |
12 13
Thatcham
A4
Burghfield Common
NEWBURY

| 103 | 105 | 107 | 109 | 111 |
A343
A339
Aldermaston

| 121 | 123 | 125 | 127 | 129 |
Burghclere
Tadley
A340

Kingsclere

| 137 | 139 | 141 | 143 | 145 |
A34
A339
Chineham

| 153 | 155 | 157 | 159 | 161 |
Litchfield
Old Basing
14 15
BASINGSTOKE
6

| 169 | 171 | | 175 | 177 |
Oakley
A30
M3
Whitchurch
Overton
| | | 173 | | |

A343
7
Andover
WINCHESTER
WINCHESTER

Enlarged scale pages   **1:10,000**   6.3 inches to 1 mile

0   1/4   miles   1/2   3/4
0   1/4   1/2   kilometres   3/4   1   1 1/4

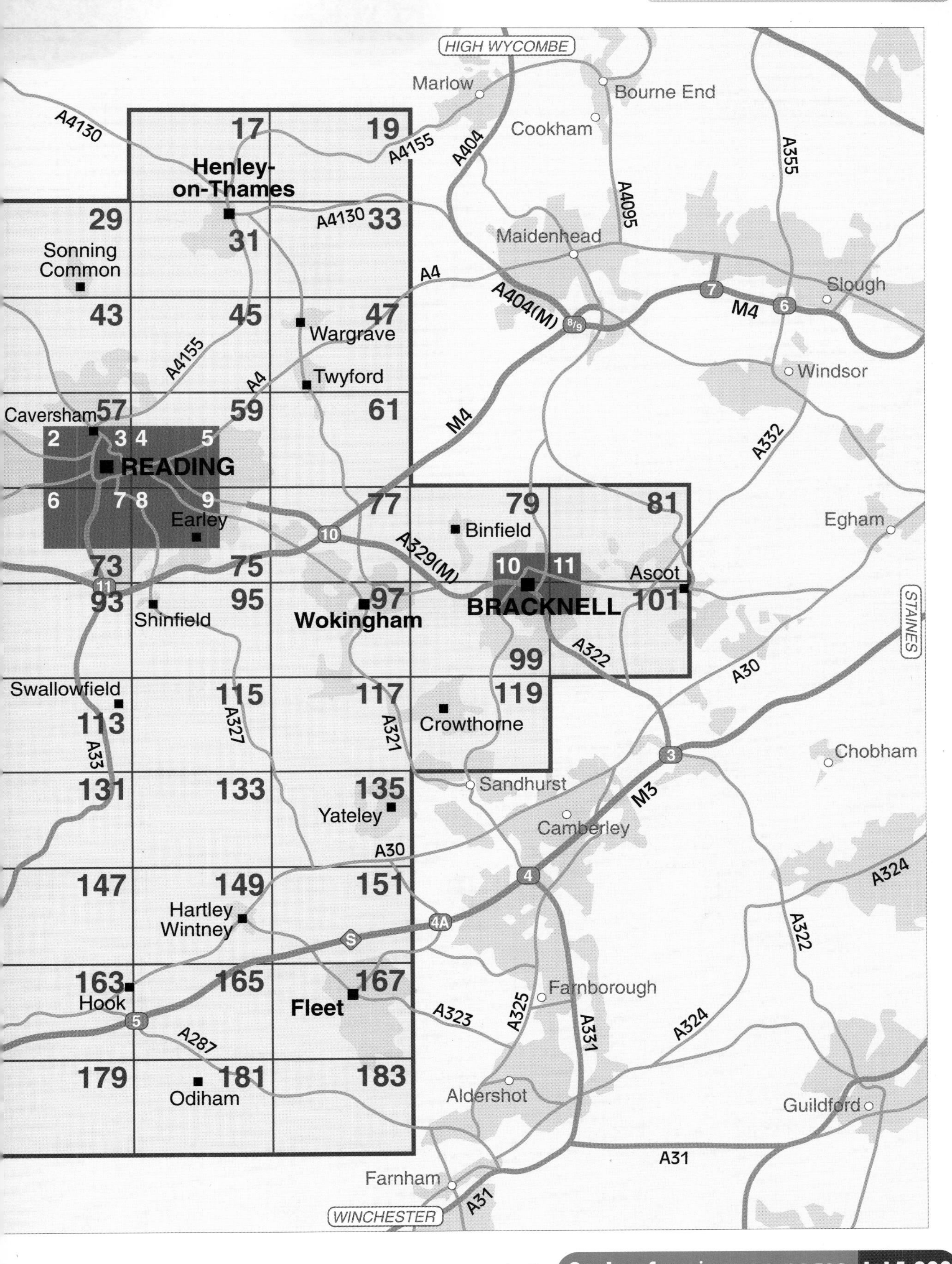

HIGH WYCOMBE

Marlow

Bourne End

Cookham

A4130

17

19

A4155

Henley-on-Thames

A404

A4095

A355

29

A4130

33

Maidenhead

Sonning Common

31

Slough

M4

7

6

43

45

47

A4

A404(M)

Wargrave

8/9

Windsor

A4155

A4

Twyford

A332

Caversham

57

59

61

M4

2 **3** **4** **5**

READING

6 **7** **8** **9**

77

79

81

Earley

Binfield

Egham

A329(M)

73

75

10 **11**

Ascot

101

STAINES

11

93

95

97

BRACKNELL

A322

Shinfield

Wokingham

A30

99

Swallowfield

115

117

119

3

Chobham

113

A327

A321

Crowthorne

A33

M3

131

133

135

Sandhurst

A324

Yateley

Camberley

A30

147

149

151

4

A322

Hartley Wintney

4A

163

165

167

Farnborough

Hook

5

Fleet

A323

A325

A324

A287

A331

179

181

183

Aldershot

Guildford

Odiham

A31

Farnham

WINCHESTER

A31

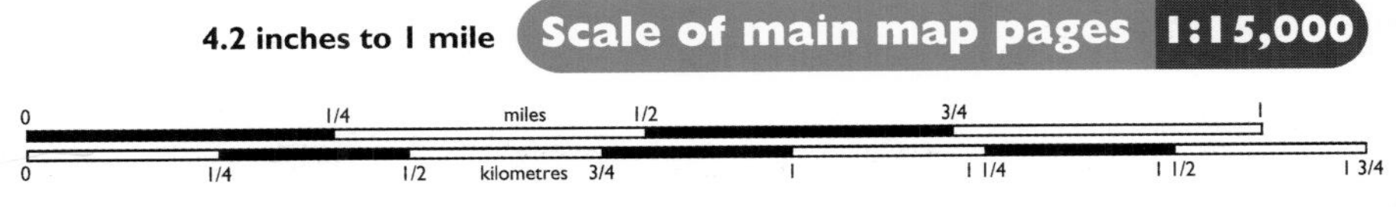

4.2 inches to 1 mile   **Scale of main map pages** **1:15,000**

Junction 9	Motorway & junction
Services	Motorway service area
	Primary road single/dual carriageway
Services	Primary road service area
	A road single/dual carriageway
	B road single/dual carriageway
	Other road single/dual carriageway
	Restricted road
	Private road
← ←	One way street
	Pedestrian street
	Track/ footpath
	Road under construction
	Road tunnel
P	Parking

P+	Park & Ride
	Bus/coach station
⇄	Railway & main railway station
⇄	Railway & minor railway station
⊖	Underground station
⊖	Light railway & station
+++++++++++	Preserved private railway
LC	Level crossing
•—•—•—•—•	Tramway
------------	Ferry route
....	Airport runway
—·—·—·—·	Boundaries- borough/ district
⋁⋁⋁⋁⋁⋁⋁⋁	Mounds
93	Page continuation 1:15,000
7	Page continuation to enlarged scale 1:10,000

River/canal lake, pier	Toilet with disabled facilities
Aqueduct lock, weir	Petrol station
Peak (with height in metres) 465 Winter Hill	Public house PH
Beach	Post Office PO
Coniferous woodland	Public library
Broadleaved woodland	Tourist Information Centre
Mixed woodland	Castle
Park	Historic house/ building
Cemetery	National Trust property Wakehurst Place NT
Built-up area	Museum/ art gallery M
Featured building	Church/chapel
City wall	Country park
Accident & Emergency hospital A&E	Theatre/ performing arts
Toilet	Cinema

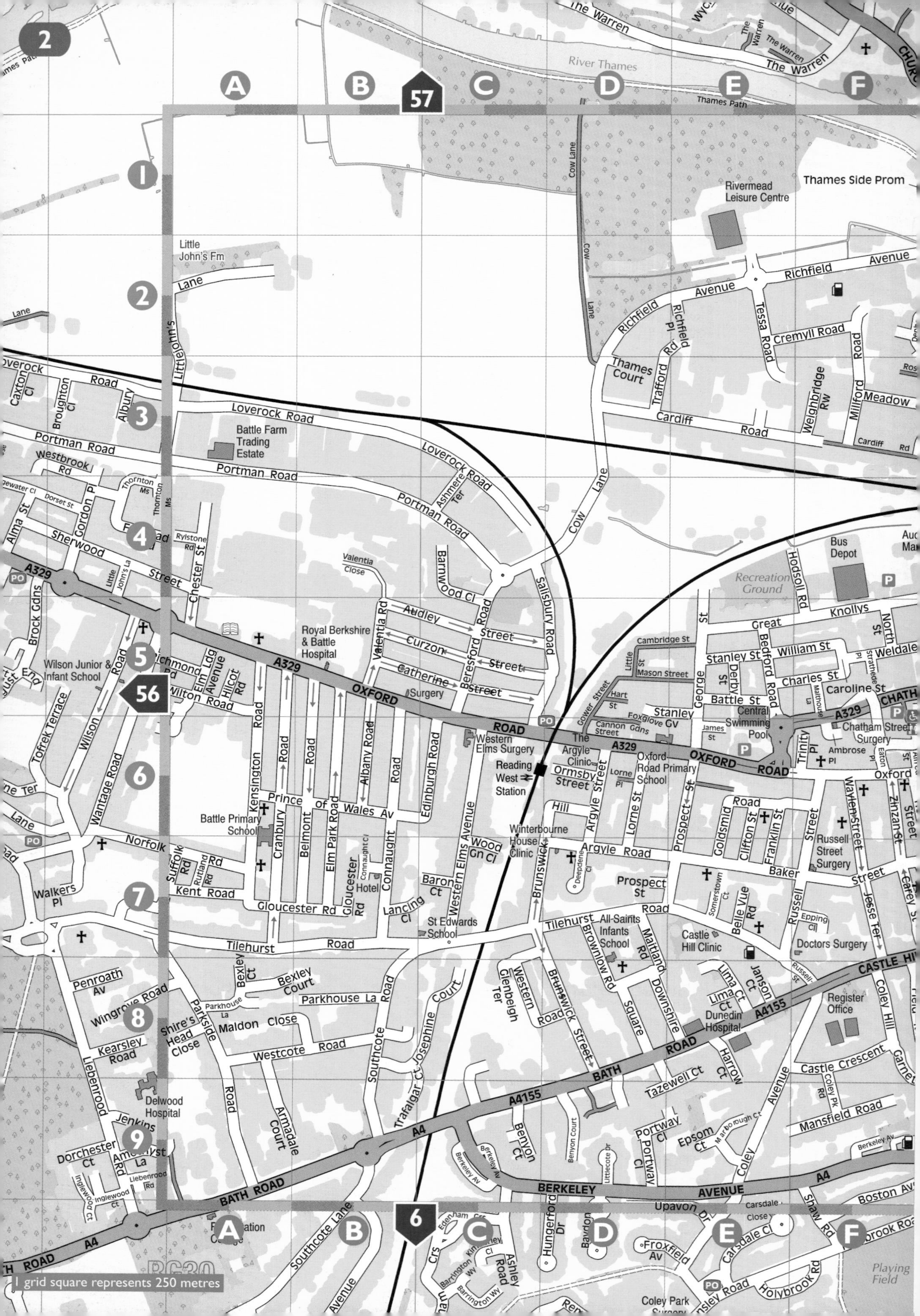
2
A
B
57
C
D
E
F
The Warren
River Thames
Thames Path
Thames Side Prom
Rivermead Leisure Centre
Cow Lane
Little John's Fm
Littlejohn's Lane
Richfield Avenue
Richfield Pl
Tessa Road
Cremyll Road
Thames Court
Trafford Rd
Weighbridge Rw
Milford Road
Meadow
Cardiff Road
Loverock Road
Caxton Ct
Broughton Cl
Albury
Portman Road
Battle Farm Trading Estate
Westbrook Rd
Thornton Ms
Ashmere Ter
Gordon Pl
Alma St
Dorset St
Sherwood Street
Little John's La
Rylstone Rd
Chester St
A329
Valentia Close
Barnwood Cl
Salisbury Road
Recreation Ground
Bus Depot
Hodsoll Rd
Knollys
Great
North St
Brock Gdns
Audley Street
Curzon Street
Catherine Street
Beresford Road
Royal Berkshire & Battle Hospital
Valentia Rd
Wilson Junior & Infant School
Richmond Rd
Elm Ldg Avenue
Hilcot Rd
Wilton Road
56
Oxford Road
Surgery
Western Elms Surgery
Reading West Station
Cambridge St
Mason Street
Little St
Hart St
Gower Street
Cannon Street
Foxglove Gdns
Stanley Gv
Stanley St
Derby St
George St
Battle St
William St
Charles St
Bedford Road
Caroline St
Weldale
Central Swimming Pool
James St
Chatham Street
Chatham Street Surgery
Ambrose Pl
Trinity Pl
Eaton Pl
Malthouse La
Strathede Pl
The Argyle Clinic
Ormsby Street
Argyle Street
Lorne Pl
Lorne St
Oxford Road Primary School
Prospect St
Tofrek Terrace
Wilson Road
Wantage Road
Kensington Road
Cranbury Road
Belmont Road
Elm Park Road
Albany Road
Connaught Road
Edinburgh Road
Western Elms Avenue
Prince of Wales Av
Battle Primary School
Lane
Norfolk Rd
Suffolk Rd
Rutland Rd
Walkers Pl
Kent Road
Gloucester Rd
Connaught Cl
Hotel
Baron Ct
Wood Gn Cl
Winterbourne House Clinic
Hill
Brunswick Hill
Deepdene Cl
Argyle Road
Goldsmid Road
Clifton St
Franklin St
Russell Street Surgery
Baker Street
Waylen Street
Zinzan St
Carey St
Prospect St
Somerstown Ct
Belle Vue Rd
Epping Cl
Russell St
Jesse Ter
Lancing Cl
St Edwards School
Tilehurst Road
All Saints Infants School
Maitland Rd
Brownlow Rd
Castle Hill Clinic
Doctors Surgery
Penroath Av
Bexley Ct
Bexley Court
Parkhouse La
Parkhouse Lane
Wingrove Road
Shire's Head Close
Maldon Close
Parkside Road
Southcote Road
Josephine Court
Glenbeigh Ter
Western Road
Brunswick Street
Square
Downshire
Lima Ct
Janson Ct
Dunedin Hospital
A4155
Castle Hill
Register Office
Coley Hill
Kearsley Road
Westcote Road
Liebenrood Road
Delwood Hospital
Armadale Court
Trafalgar Ct
Bath Road
Tazewell Ct
Harrow Ct
Castle Crescent
Coley Pk Rd
Mansfield Road
Jenkins
Dorchester Ct
Amethyst La
Inglewood Ct
Liebenrood Rd
A4
Benyon Ct
Benyon Court
Littlecote Dr
Portway Cl
Epsom Ct
Marlborough Ct
Coley Avenue
Berkeley Av
Berkeley Avenue
Boston Av
6
Upavon Dr
Carsdale Close
Southcote Lane
Hungerford Dr
Froxfield Av
Shaw Rd
Holybrook Rd
Playing Field
Coley Park Surgery
Ashley Road
Barrington Wy
1 grid square represents 250 metres

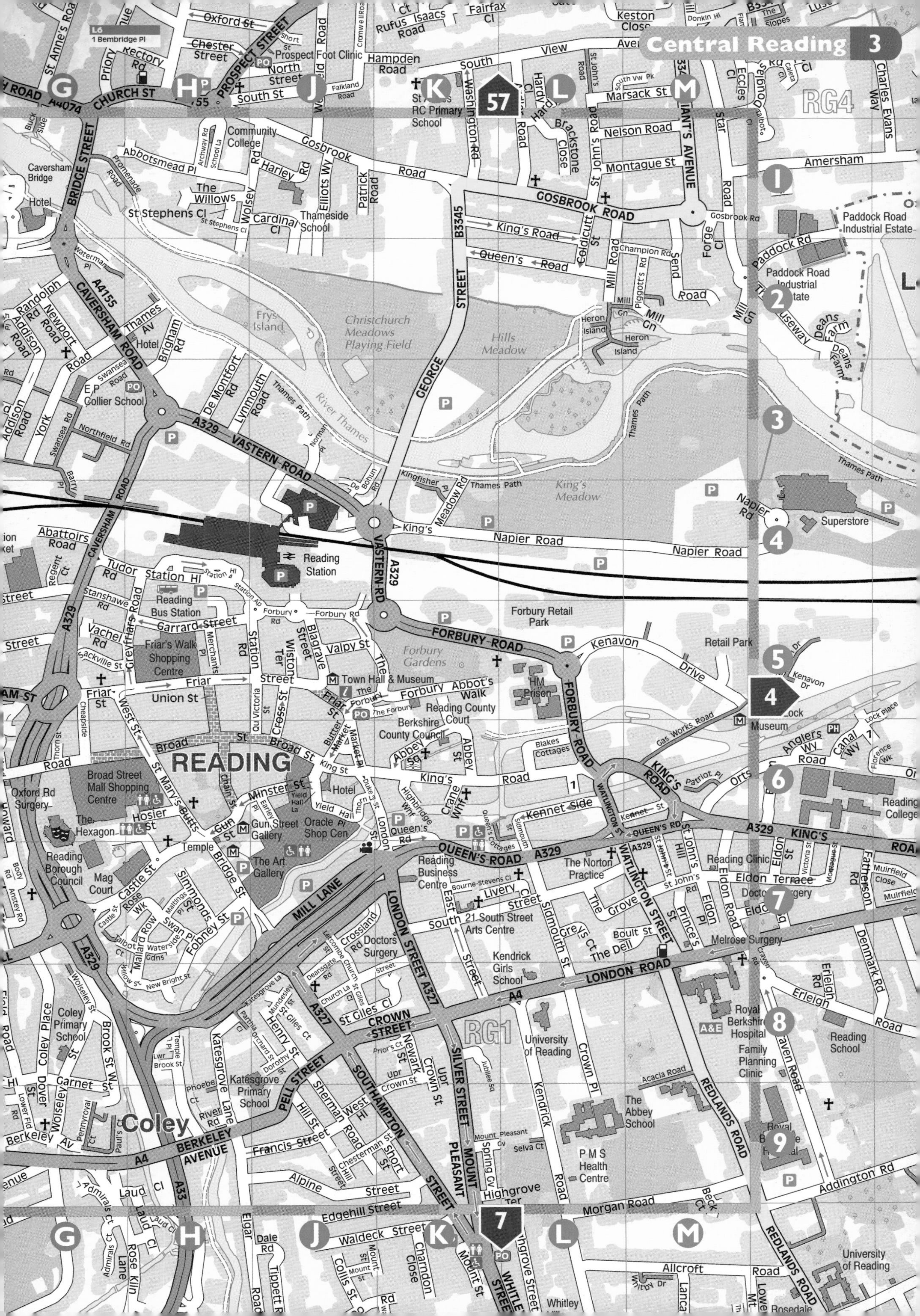

L6
1 Bembridge Pl
Oxford St
Chester Street
Rectory Rd
Prospect Street
Prospect Foot Clinic
Hampden Road
North Street
South St
Church St
A4074
A4155
Rufus Isaacs Road
Fairfax Cl
Keston Close
View Ave
South View
St Anne's Rd
Priory Av
G
H
J
K
L
M
57
St Anne's RC Primary School
Washington Rd
Marsack St
St John's Road
Nelson Road
Montague St
Brackstone Close
Hardy Cl
Gosbrook Road
Gosbrook Rd
Amersham
Charles Evans Way
RG4
I
Community College
Abbotsmead Pl
Promenade Road
Caversham Bridge
Hotel
Bridge Street
The Willows
St Stephens Cl
Wolsey Rd
Harley Rd
Cardinal Cl
Thameside School
Elliots Wy
Patrick Road
B3345
King's Road
Queen's Road
Coldicutt St
Mill Road
Champion Rd
Piggott's Rd
Send Road
Forge Cl
Paddock Rd
Paddock Road Industrial Estate
Mill Gn
Heron Island
Deans Farm
Waterman Pl
Randolph Rd
Addison Road
Newport Road
Caversham Road
Thames Av
Hotel
Brigham Rd
Frys Island
Christchurch Meadows Playing Field
George Street
Hills Meadow
River Thames
Thames Path
Swansea Road
E P Collier School
De Montfort Rd
Lynmouth Road
York Road
Northfield Rd
A329
Vastern Road
Norman Pl
Barry Pl
De Bohun Rd
Kingfisher Pl
Meadow Rd
King's Meadow
Napier Rd
Napier Road
Superstore
Abattoirs Road
Reading Station
Station Hl
Tudor Rd
Regent Ct
Reading Bus Station
Stanshawe Rd
Garrard Street
Forbury Rd
Forbury Retail Park
Forbury Road
Kenavon Drive
Retail Park
Kenavon Dr
Vachel Rd
Greyfriars Road
Friar's Walk Shopping Centre
Merchants Pl
Station Rd
Wiston Ter
Blagrave Street
Valpy St
Forbury Gardens
Sackville St
Friar Street
Union St
Town Hall & Museum
Abbot's Walk
HM Prison
Reading County Court
Berkshire County Council
Gas Works Road
Museum
Lock
Lock Place
Anglers Wy
Canal Wy
Florence Wk
Broad Street
Broad St
READING
Cross St
Butter Market
Market Pl
Abbey Sq
Abbey St
Blakes Cottages
King's Road
Patriot Pl
Orts Road
Reading College
Oxford Road
Broad Street Mall Shopping Centre
Oxford Rd Surgery
The Hexagon
Hosier St
St Mary's Butts
Minster St
Hotel
Yield Hall
Oracle Shop Cen
Gun Street Gallery
Queen's Rd
Kennet Side
Crane Wharf
Highbridge Whf
Watlington St
Kennet St
A329 King's Road
Reading Borough Council
Mag Court
Castle St
Temple
The Art Gallery
Queen's Road
Reading Business Centre
The Norton Practice
Watlington Street
St John's Hill
Reading Clinic
Eldon Terrace
Eldon Road
Doctors Surgery
Fatherson Rd
Muirfield Close
Simmonds St
Swan Pl
Fobney St
Mill Lane
London Street A327
Livery Cl
East Street
South Street
21 South Street Arts Centre
Sidmouth St
Greys Ct
The Grove
The Dell
Boult St
Prince's St
Melrose Surgery
Crossland Rd
Doctors Surgery
Kendrick Girls School
London Road
A4
Erleigh Road
Denmark Rd
Coley Place
Coley Primary School
Brook St W
Garnet St
Katesgrove La
Henry St
St Giles Cl
Crown Street
RG1
University of Reading
Crown Pl
Royal Berkshire Hospital
A&E
Family Planning Clinic
Craven Road
Reading School
Kendrick Road
Acacia Road
The Abbey School
Redlands Road
Coley
Berkeley Av
Berkeley Avenue
Pell Street
Katesgrove Primary School
Southampton Street
Silver Street
Mount Pleasant
Francis Street
Sherman Road
West Hl
Hill St
Short St
Chesterman St
Alpine Street
Spring Gv
Highgrove Ter
PMS Health Centre
Royal Berkshire Hospital
Addington Rd
Morgan Road
Edgehill Street
Waldeck Street
Charndon Close
Laud Cl
Rose Kiln Lane
Admirals Ct
Dale Rd
Elgar Road
Tippett Rd
Collis St
Mount St
Whitley Street
Allcroft Road
Redlands Road
University of Reading
Rosedale
1 2 3 4 5 6 7 8 9

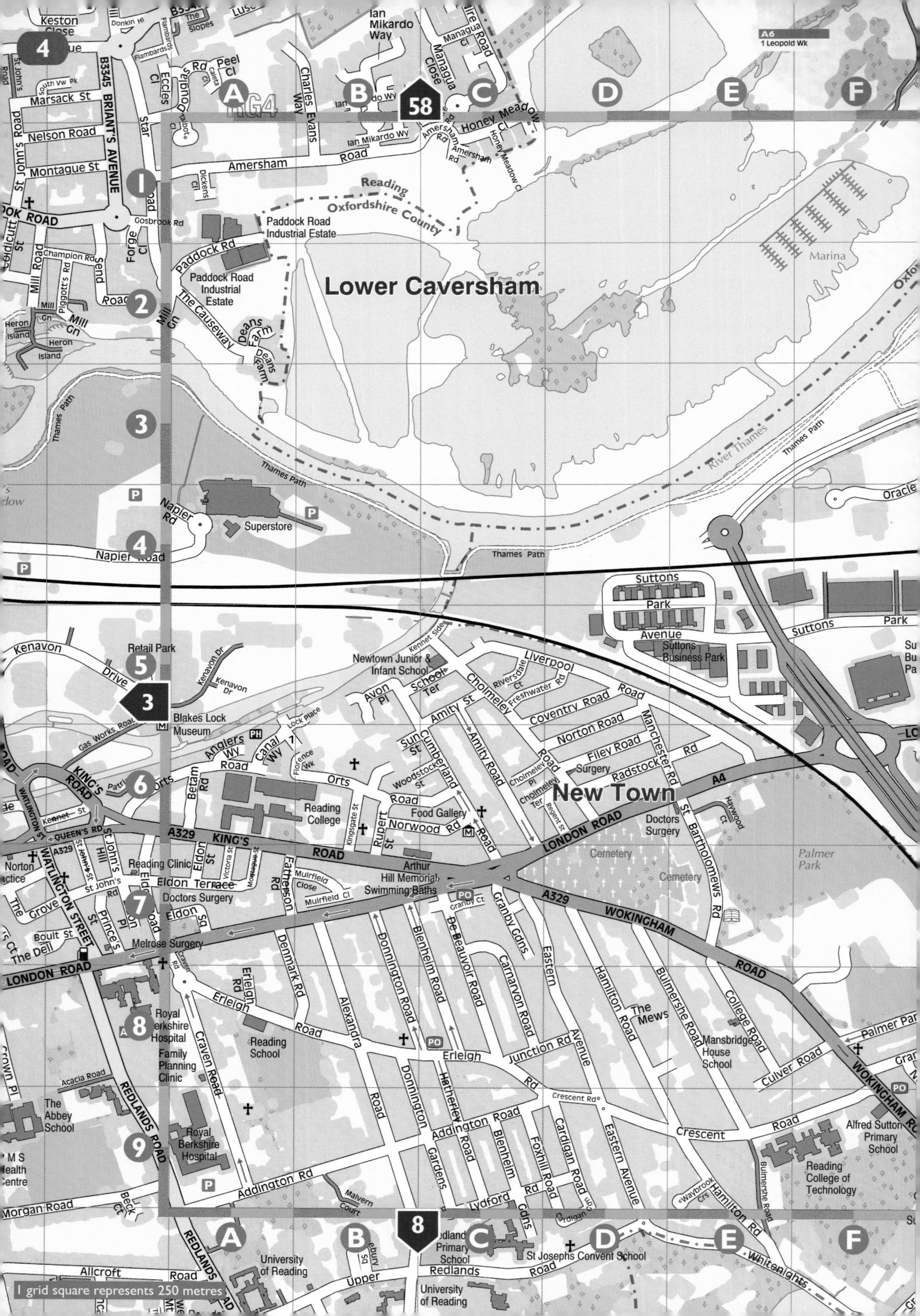

4
A6
1 Leopold Wk
A
B
C
D
E
F
58
Lower Caversham
Reading
Oxfordshire County
Paddock Road
Industrial Estate
Marina
River Thames
Thames Path
Oracle
Superstore
Napier Road
Napier Rd
Suttons
Park
Avenue
Suttons Business Park
Retail Park
Kenavon
Drive
Blakes Lock
Museum
Newtown Junior &
Infant School
New Town
Reading College
Food Gallery
Arthur
Hill Memorial
Swimming Baths
Reading Clinic
Doctors Surgery
Melrose Surgery
Cemetery
Palmer
Park
Royal
Berkshire
Hospital
Family
Planning
Clinic
Reading
School
The
Abbey
School
Mansbridge
House
School
Alfred Sutton
Primary
School
Reading
College of
Technology
St Josephs Convent School
University
of Reading
A329 KING'S ROAD
A329 WOKINGHAM ROAD
LONDON ROAD
A4
BRIANT'S AVENUE
WATLINGTON STREET
REDLANDS ROAD
Amersham Road
Honey Meadow Cl
Liverpool Road
Cholmeley Road
Coventry Road
Norton Road
Filey Road
Radstock Rd
Manchester Rd
St Bartholomews Rd
Erleigh Road
Addington Road
Crescent Road
Whiteknights
Upper Redlands Road
Allcroft Road
Morgan Road
3
8
1 grid square represents 250 metres

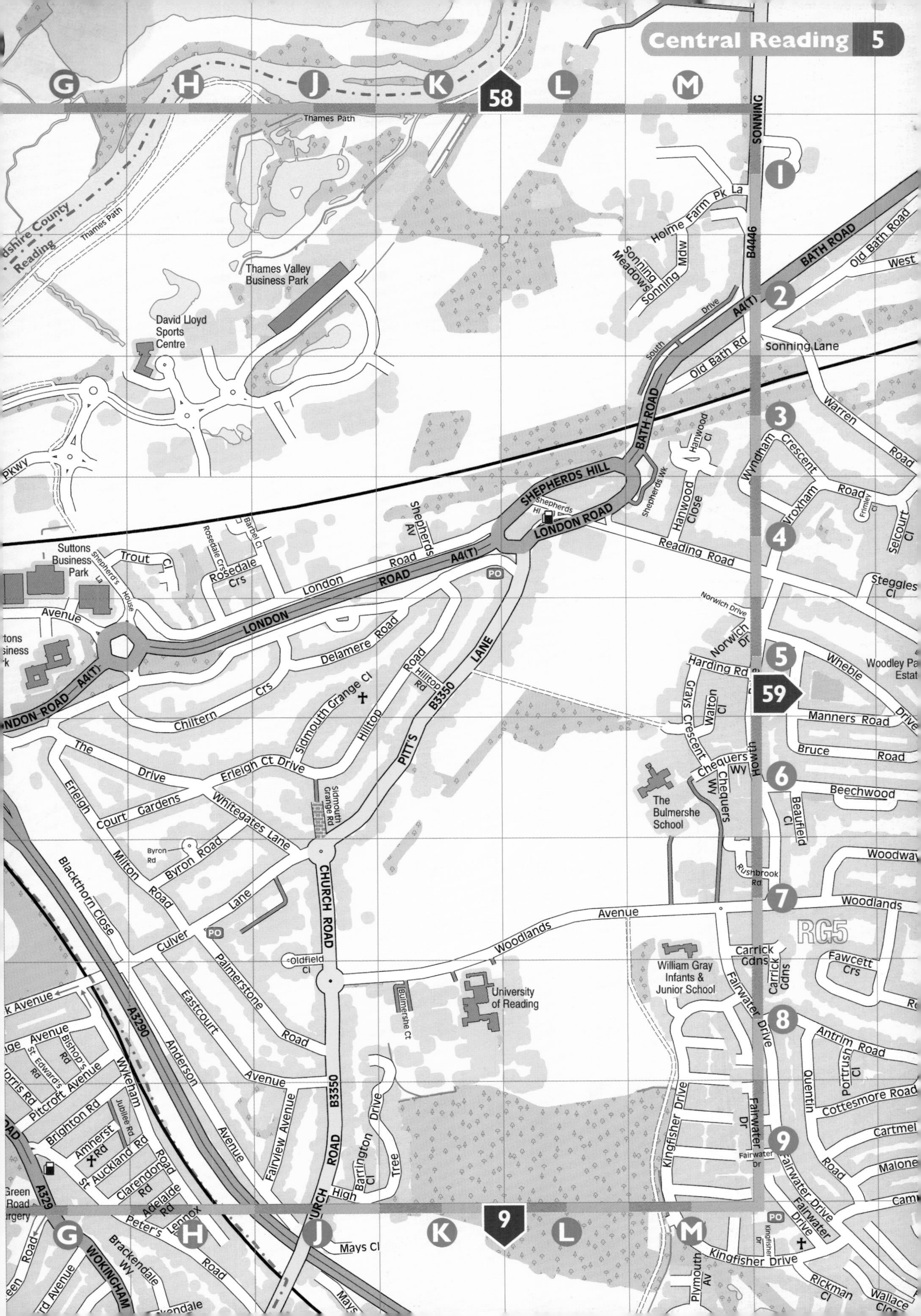

Grid references (top): G H J K 58 L M

I

SONNING

B4446

BATH ROAD

Old Bath Road

West

2

Holme Farm Pk La

Sonning Mdw

Sonning Meadows

Sonning Lane

A4(T)

south

Drive

Warren Road

3

Wyndham

Crescent Road

Vroxham

Frimley Cl

Selcourt

Hanwood Cl

Hanwood Close

Shepherds Wk

Reading Road

Steggles Cl

SHEPHERDS HILL

Shepherds Hl

LONDON ROAD

BATH ROAD

Thames Path

Thames Valley
Business Park

David Lloyd
Sports
Centre

...shire County
Reading

Suttons
Business
Park

Shepherd's House

Shepherd's La

Trout Cl

Avenue

Bartlett Cl

Rosedale Crs

Rosedale
Crs

London Road

LONDON ROAD A4(T)

A4(T)

Norwich Drive

Norwich Dr

4

Harding Rd

5

Wheble

Woodley Pk
Estate

59

Manners Road

Bruce Road

6

Beechwood

Woodway

7

Woodlands

Grays Crescent

Walton Cl

Chequers Wy

Chequers

Howth

Beaufield Cl

Rushbrook Rd

PO

Delamere Road

Chiltern

Crs

Sidmouth Grange Cl

Hilltop
Rd

Hilltop

Road

PITT'S

B3350

LANE

The

Drive

Erleigh Ct Drive

Whitegates Lane

Sidmouth
Grange Rd

The Bulmershe
School

Erleigh

Court

Gardens

Milton

Road

Byron Road

Lane

Byron
Rd

CHURCH ROAD

Woodlands   Avenue

RG5

Carrick
Gdns

Carrick Gdns

Fawcett
Crs

8

Antrim Road

Portrush Cl

Cottesmore Road

9

Cartmel

Malone

William Gray
Infants &
Junior School

Fairwater Drive

Fairwater Dr

Blackthorn Close

A3290

Culver

PO

Oldfield
Cl

Palmerstone

Road

Eastcourt

Anderson

Avenue

B3350

Fairview Avenue

Bulmershe Ct

University
of Reading

Barrington
Cl

Tree Drive

High

CHURCH ROAD

Kingfisher Drive

Quentin

Fairwater Drive

Fairwater
Dr

Fairwater
Drive

PO

Kingfisher
Dr

Plymouth
Av

Rickman
Cl

Wallace
Clo...

Kingfisher Drive

... Avenue

... Avenue

Bishop's Rd

St Edward's

Morris Rd

Pitcroft Rd

Brighton Rd

Amherst Rd

Jubilee Rd

Wykeham Road

Auckland Rd

Clarendon Rd

Adelaide Rd

Lennox

Peter's

Brackendale Wy

WOKINGHAM

...kendale Road

Mays Cl

Mays

A329

Green
Road

...gery

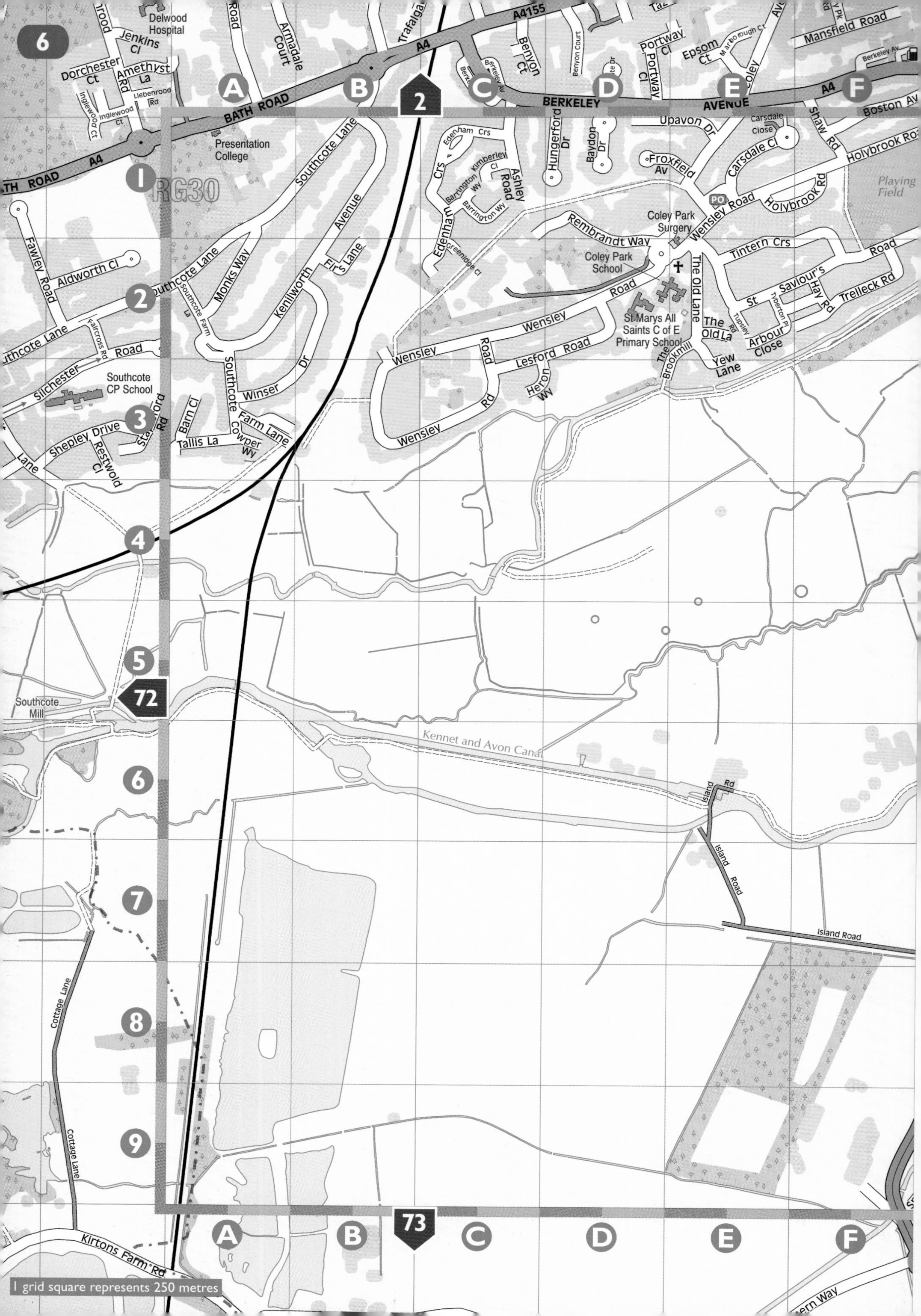

Delwood Hospital
Jenkins Cl
Dorchester Ct
Amethyst La
Liebenrood Rd
Inglewood Ct
Armadale Court
Trafalgar
A4155
A4
BATH ROAD
Benyon Ct
Benyon Court
Portway Cl
Epsom Ct
Marlborough Ct
Coley
Mansfield Road
Berkeley Av
BERKELEY
AVENUE
Upavon Dr
Carsdale Close
Shaw Rd
Boston Av
Holybrook Rd
Presentation College
Southcote Lane
Edenham Crs
Kimberley Cl
Barrington Wy
Ashley Road
Hungerford Dr
Baydon Dr
Froxfield Av
Carsdale Cl
Playing Field
RG30
Fawley Road
Aldworth Cl
Monks Way
Avenue
Firs Lane
Kenilworth
Edenham
Greenidge Cl
Rembrandt Way
Coley Park Surgery
Wensley Road
Holybrook Rd
PO
Coley Park School
Tintern Crs
The Old Lane
St Saviour's Road
Hay Rd
Trelleck Rd
Tyberton Pl
Southcote Farm La
Faircross Rd
Silchester Road
Southcote CP School
Wensley
Road
Lesford Road
St Marys All Saints C of E Primary School
The Old La
The Brookmill
Tupsley
Arbour Close
Yew Lane
Heron Wy
Winser Dr
Southcote Farm Lane
Cowper Wy
Barn Cl
Tallis La
Stanford Rd
Shepley Drive
Restwold Cl
Wensley Rd
Southcote Mill
72
Kennet and Avon Canal
Island Rd
Island Road
Cottage Lane
Kirtons Farm Rd
73
Tern Way
A B C D E F
1 2 3 4 5 6 7 8 9
1 grid square represents 250 metres

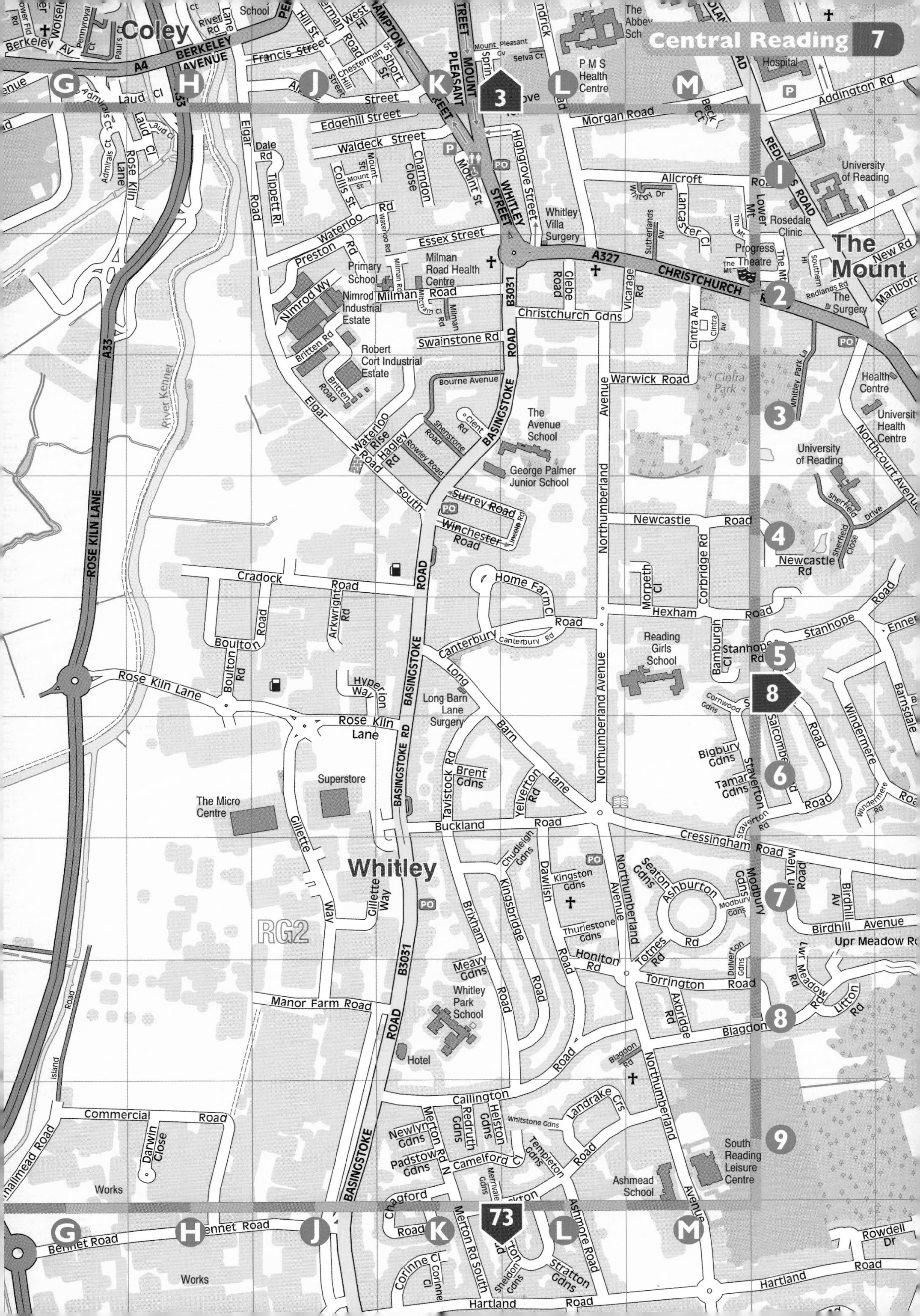

Coley
Whitley
The Mount
RG2
Berkeley Avenue
Francis Street
Edgehill Street
Waldeck Street
Morgan Road
Allcroft Road
Essex Street
Christchurch Road
Milman Road
Christchurch Gdns
Swainstone Rd
Warwick Road
Bourne Avenue
Basingstoke Road
Whitley Street
Mount Pleasant
Elgar Road
Rose Kiln Lane
Cradock Road
Boulton Road
Newcastle Road
Hexham Road
Stanhope Road
Canterbury Road
Long Barn Lane
Northumberland Avenue
Buckland Road
Cressingham Road
Ashburton Rd
Birdhill Avenue
Torrington Road
Blagdon Road
Manor Farm Road
Callington Rd
Commercial Road
Bennet Road
Hartland Road
Ashmore Road
University of Reading
Rosedale Clinic
Progress Theatre
Whitley Villa Surgery
Milman Road Health Centre
Primary School
Nimrod Industrial Estate
Robert Cort Industrial Estate
The Avenue School
George Palmer Junior School
Reading Girls School
Long Barn Lane Surgery
Superstore
The Micro Centre
Whitley Park School
Hotel
South Reading Leisure Centre
Ashmead School
Works
Cintra Park
Health Centre
University Health Centre
PMS Health Centre
Hospital
River Kennet
A33
A327
B3031

3
8
73

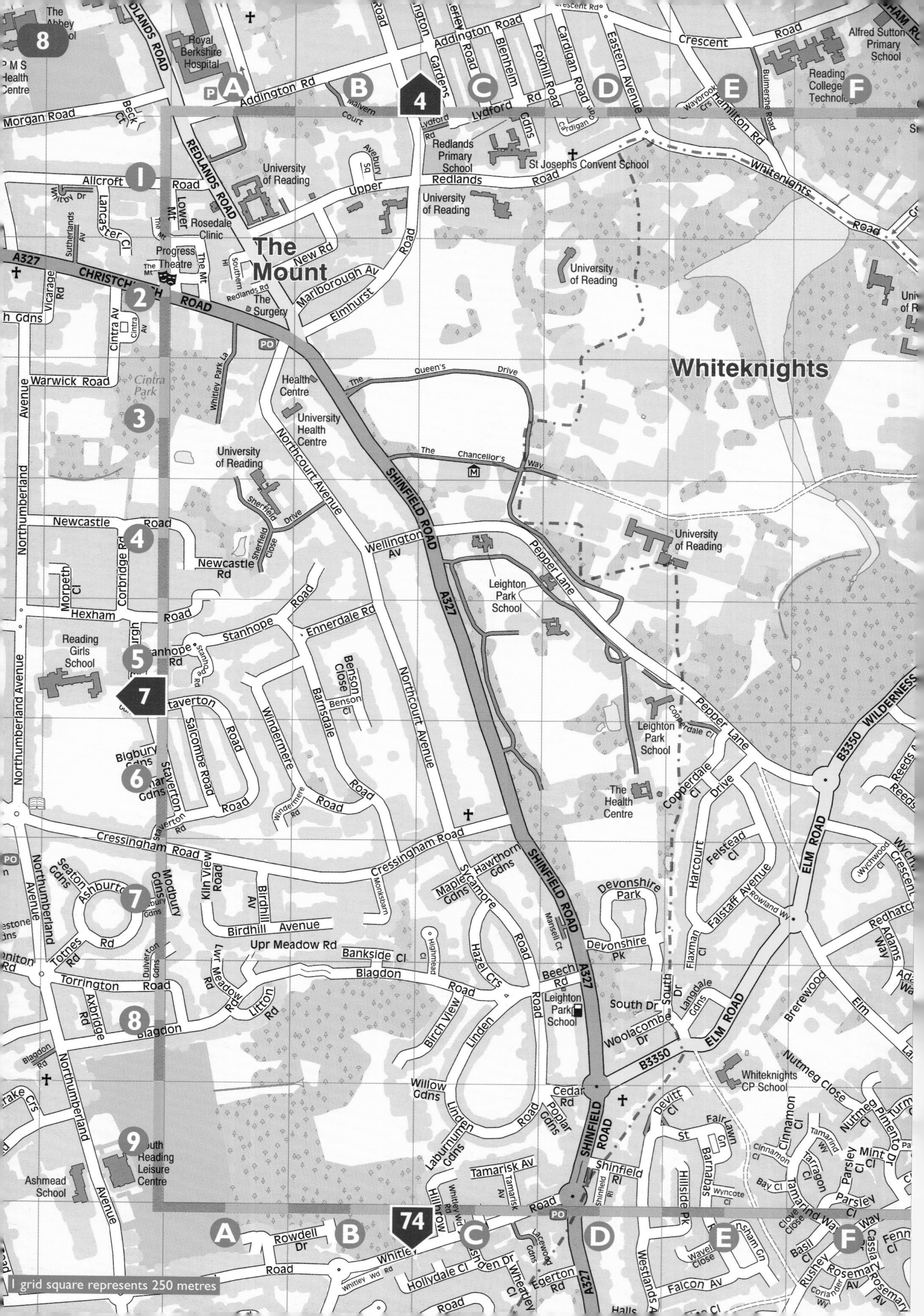
8
4
7
74
A
B
C
D
E
F
The Mount
Whiteknights
Royal Berkshire Hospital
University of Reading
Redlands Primary School
St Josephs Convent School
Alfred Sutton Primary School
Reading College of Technology
Rosedale Clinic
Progress Theatre
The Surgery
Health Centre
University Health Centre
Cintra Park
Reading Girls School
Leighton Park School
The Health Centre
Whiteknights CP School
South Reading Leisure Centre
Ashmead School
Addington Road
Addington Rd
Morgan Road
Allcroft Road
Redlands Road
Upper Redlands Road
Christchurch Road
A327
Shinfield Road
Northcourt Avenue
Northumberland Avenue
Warwick Road
Newcastle Road
Hexham Road
Stanhope Road
Ennerdale Rd
Windermere Road
Barnsdale Road
Staverton Road
Salcombe Road
Cressingham Road
Birdhill Avenue
Upr Meadow Rd
Blagdon Road
Torrington Road
Pepper Lane
Elm Road
B3350
Wilderness
Eastern Avenue
Crescent Road
Hamilton Rd
Whiteknights Road
The Queen's Drive
The Chancellor's Way
Wellington Av
Elmhurst
Marlborough Av
Devonshire Park
Falstaff Avenue
South Dr
Woolacombe Dr
Whitley Road
1 grid square represents 250 metres

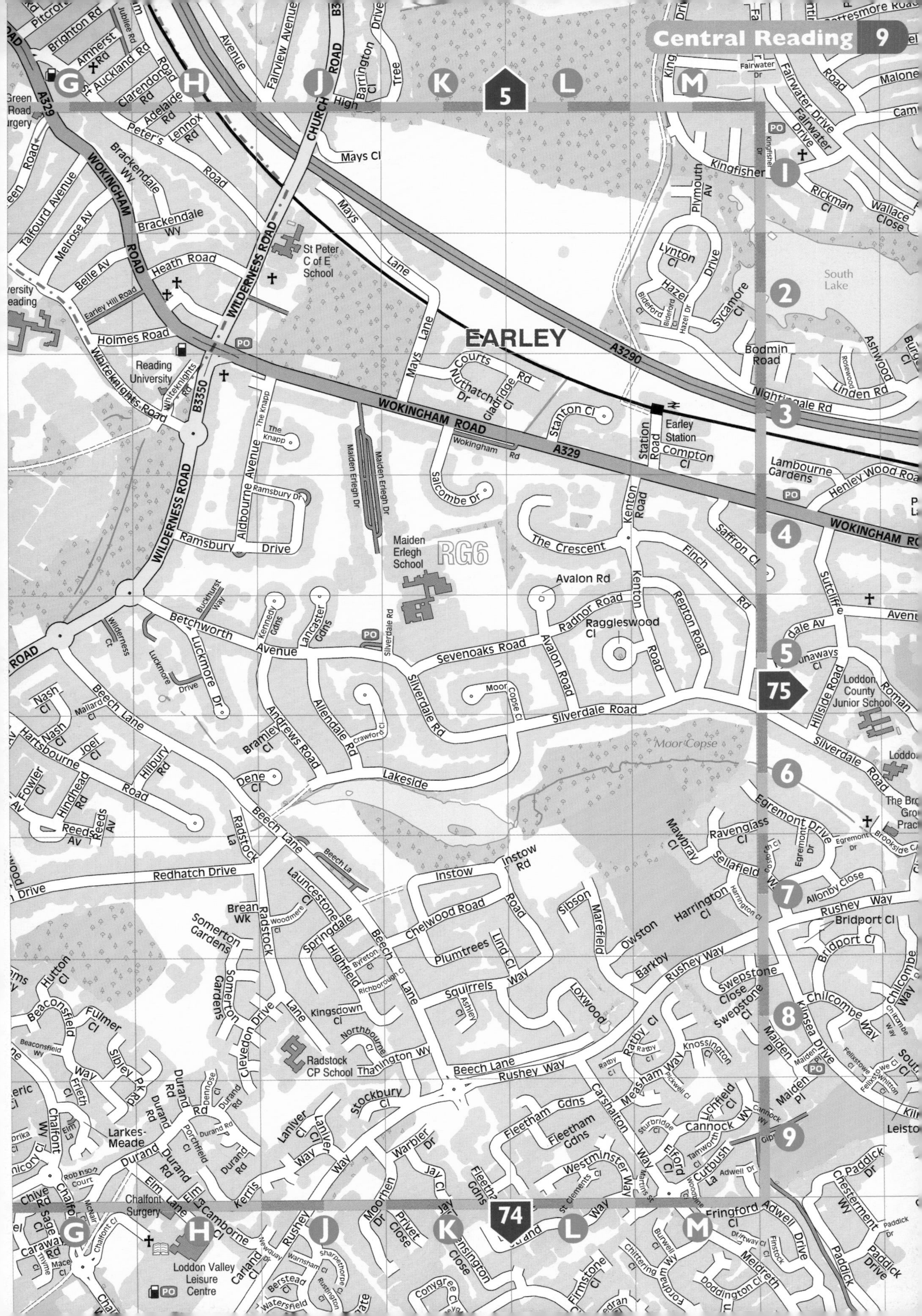
G
H
J
K
L
M
5
1
2
3
4
5
6
7
8
9
75
74
EARLEY
RG6
A329
A3290
B3350
WOKINGHAM ROAD
WILDERNESS ROAD
CHURCH ROAD
Brighton Rd
Amherst Rd
Auckland Rd
Jubilee Rd
Clarendon Rd
Adelaide Rd
Lennox Rd
Peter's Road
Fairview Avenue
Barrington Cl
High
Mays Cl
Mays Lane
Green Road Surgery
Brackendale Wy
Talfourd Avenue
Melrose Av
Belle Av
Heath Road
Earley Hill Road
Holmes Road
Whiteknights Road
Whiteknights Rd
Reading University
St Peter C of E School
Courts Rd
Nuthatch Dr
Gladridge Cl
Stanton Cl
Station Road
Earley Station
Compton Cl
Wokingham Rd
The Knapp
Aldbourne Avenue
Ramsbury Dr
Ramsbury Drive
Maiden Erlegh Dr
Maiden Erlegh School
Salcombe Dr
The Crescent
Kenton Road
Finch Rd
Saffron Cl
Avalon Rd
Radnor Road
Raggleswood Cl
Repton Road
Sevenoaks Road
Avalon Road
Moor Copse Cl
Silverdale Road
Silverdale Rd
Buckhurst Way
Betchworth Avenue
Kennedy Gdns
Lancaster Gdns
Wilderness Ct
Luckmore Drive
Luckmore Dr
Allendale Rd
Crawford Cl
Andrews Road
Bramley Cl
Dene Cl
Lakeside
Moor Copse
Beech Lane
Mallard Cl
Nash Cl
Hartsbourne Road
Joel Cl
Hilbury Rd
Fowler Cl
Hindhead Rd
Reeds Av
Radstock La
Redhatch Drive
Beech La
Launcestone Cl
Instow Rd
Chelwood Road
Sibson
Marefield
Harrington Cl
Owston
Barkby
Rushey Way
Bream Wk
Woodmere Cl
Somerton Gardens
Springdale
Highfield
Byreton Cl
Richborough Cl
Plumtrees
Lind Cl
Squirrels Way
Ashley Cl
Loxwood
Swepstone Close
Swepstone Cl
Kingsdown Cl
Northbourne Cl
Thanington Wy
Radstock CP School
Clevedon Drive
Hutton Cl
Beaconsfield Way
Fulmer Cl
Sibley Pk Rd
Frieth Cl
Chalfont Wy
Durand Rd
Dennose Cl
Porchfield Cl
Larkes-Meade
Elm La
Elm Lane
Camborne
Kerris
Chalfont Surgery
Loddon Valley Leisure Centre
Carland Cl
Laniver Cl
Stockbury Cl
Warbler Dr
Jay Cl
Moorhen Dr
Privet Close
Kensington Close
Fleetham Gdns
Westminster Way
Carshalton Way
Measham Way
Ratby Cl
Knossington Cl
Pickwell Cl
Lichfield Cl
Cannock Wy
Sturbridge Cl
Tamworth Cl
Cutbush La
Elford Cl
Adwell Dr
Fringford Cl
Meldreth Wy
Chittering Cl
Doddington Cl
Firmstone Cl
Convgree Cl
Berstead Cl
Watersfield
Warnsham Cl
Sharpethorpe Cl
Rustington Cl
Chive Rd
Sage Cl
Caraway Rd
Thyme Cl
Mace Cl
Chalfont Cl
Robinson Court
Kingfisher
Kingfisher Dr
Fairwater Dr
Fairwater Drive
Plymouth Av
Lynton Cl
Hazel Dr
Bideford Cl
Sycamore Cl
Bodmin Road
Nightingale Rd
Rickman Cl
Wallace Close
Malone
South Lake
Ashwood
Rosewood
Linden Rd
Lambourne Gardens
Henley Wood Road
Sutcliffe
Loddon County Junior School
Hillside Road
Roman
Egremont Drive
Egremont Dr
Brookside
Ravenglass Cl
Mawbray Cl
Sellafield Way
Allonby Close
Harrington Cl
Bridport Cl
Chilcombe Way
Kinsea Drive
Maiden Pl
Felixstowe Cl
Whitton
Paddick Drive
Chesterment Wy
Paddick Dr
PO

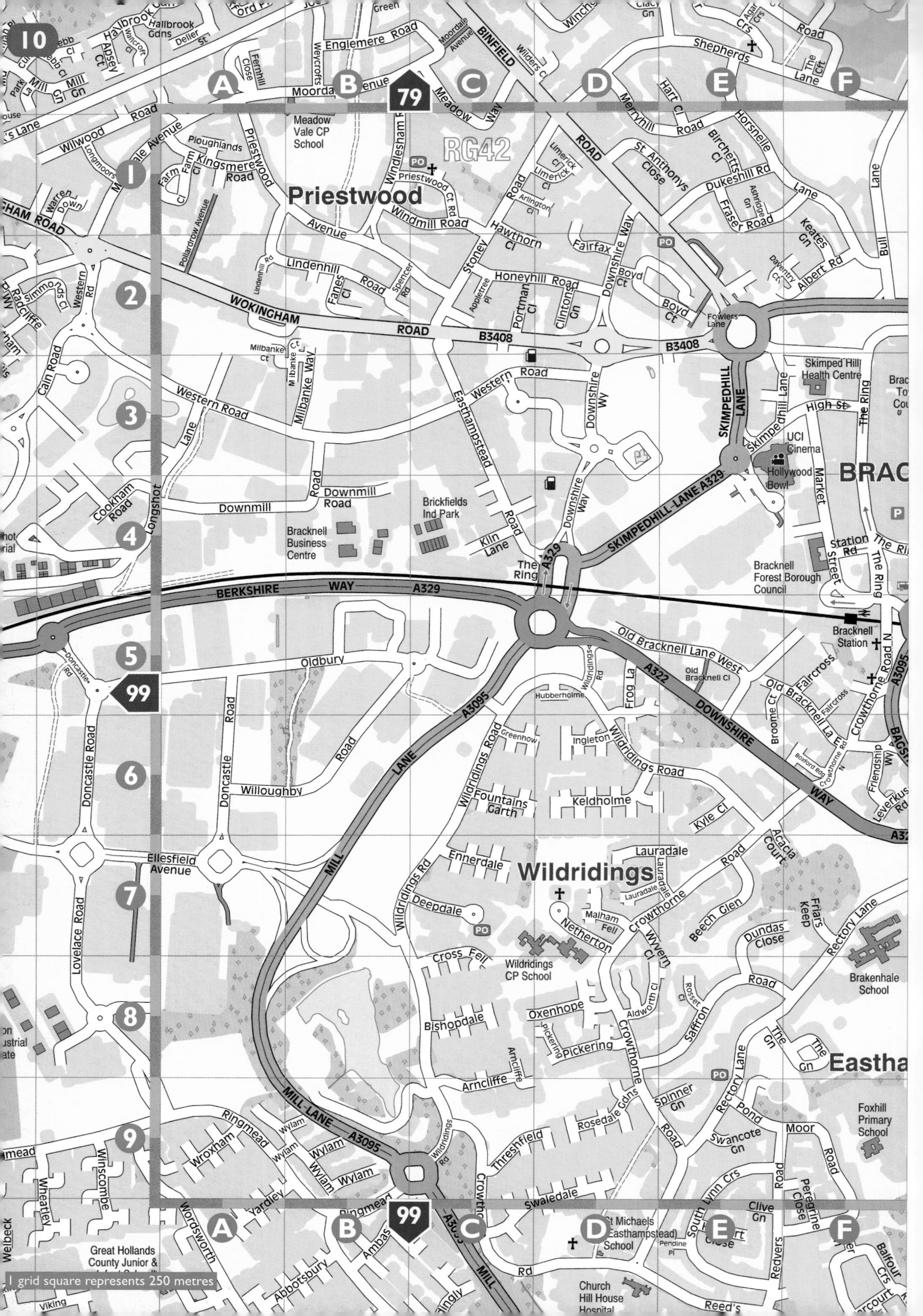
Priestwood
Wildridings
RG42
Wokingham Road
Berkshire Way
Mill Lane
Downshire Way
Skimpedhill Lane
Western Road
Downmill Road
Oldbury
Willoughby
Doncastle Road
Ellesfield Avenue
Lovelace Road
Longshot
Meadow Vale CP School
Bracknell Business Centre
Brickfields Ind Park
Skimped Hill Health Centre
UCI Cinema
Hollywood Bowl
Bracknell Forest Borough Council
Bracknell Station
Wildridings CP School
Brakenhale School
Foxhill Primary School
St Michaels (Easthampstead) School
Church Hill House Hospital
Great Hollands County Junior & Infant Schools
1 grid square represents 250 metres

79
99
99

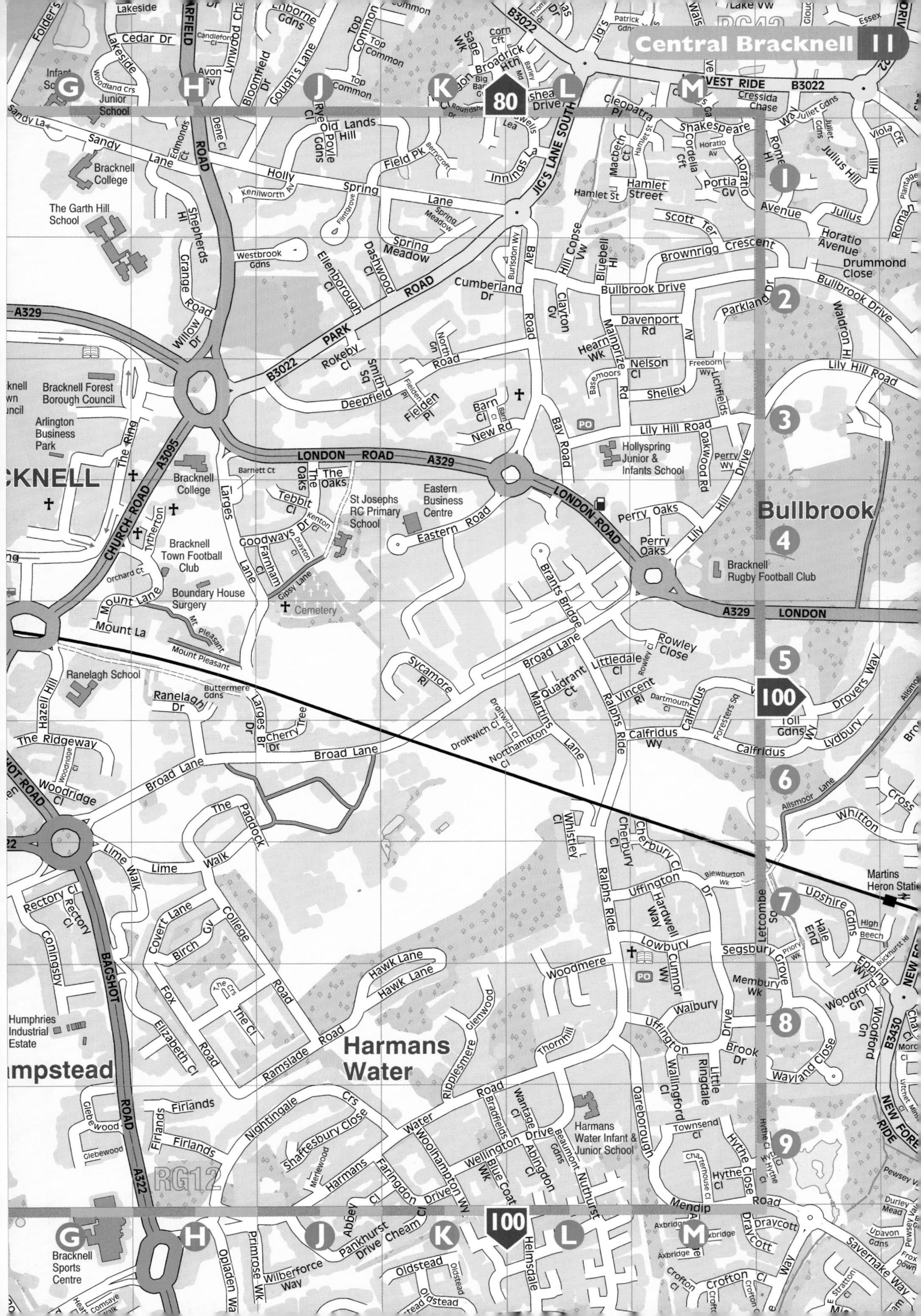
Bracknell College
The Garth Hill School
Bracknell Forest Borough Council
Arlington Business Park
Bracknell College
Bracknell Town Football Club
Boundary House Surgery
Cemetery
St Josephs RC Primary School
Eastern Business Centre
Hollyspring Junior & Infants School
Bullbrook
Bracknell Rugby Football Club
Ranelagh School
Martins Heron Station
Harmans Water
Harmans Water Infant & Junior School
Humphries Industrial Estate
Bracknell Sports Centre
RG12
LONDON ROAD
A329
A3095
CHURCH ROAD
BAGSHOT ROAD
A322
B3022
PARK ROAD
JIG'S LANE SOUTH
HARVEST RIDE
NEW FOREST RIDE
B3430
Sandy Lane
Holly Spring Lane
Spring Meadow
Bullbrook Drive
Brownrigg Crescent
Lily Hill Road
Broad Lane
Ralphs Ride
Uffington Dr
Letcombe Sq
Lime Walk
Ramslade Road
Nightingale Crs
Harmans Water Road
Wellington Dr
Mendip Road
Horatio Avenue
Hamlet Street
Shakespeare Way
Deepfield Road
Eastern Road
Goodways Dr
Larges Lane
Brants Bridge
Calfridus Wy
Drovers Way
Allsmoor Lane
College Road
Hawk Lane
Woodmere
Lowbury
Segsbury Grove
Wayland Close
Hythe Close
Faringdon Drive
Woolhampton Wy
Blue Coat Wk
Nuthurst
Oareborough
Pankhurst Drive
Wilberforce Way
Crofton Cl
Savernake Way
80
100

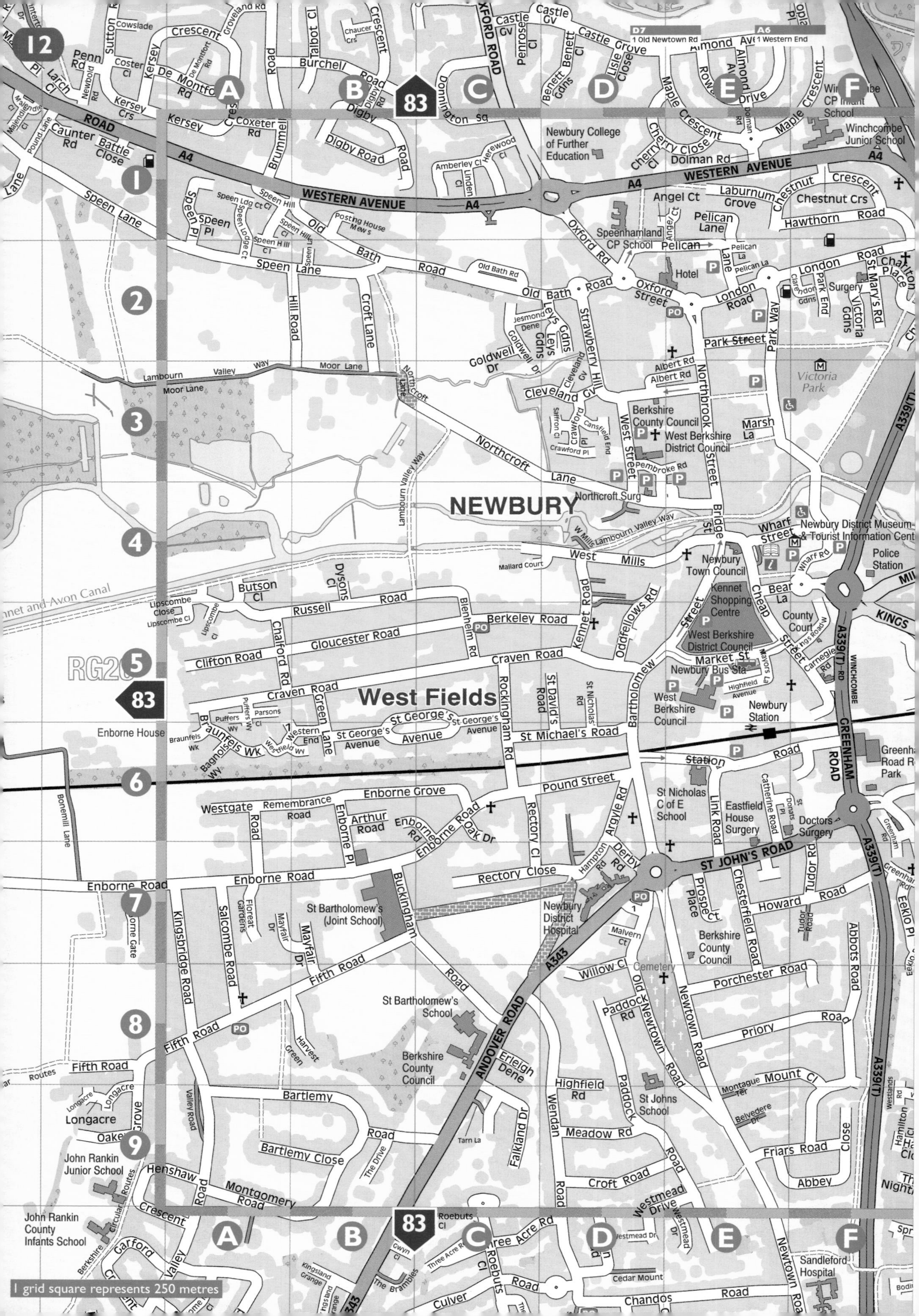
NEWBURY
West Fields
RG20
83
A
B
C
D
E
F
1
2
3
4
5
6
7
8
9
D7 1 Old Newtown Rd
A6 1 Western End
WESTERN AVENUE
A4
ROAD
Speen Lane
Bath Road
Old Bath Road
Oxford Road
Oxford Street
London Road
Cowslade
Crescent
Groveland Rd
Sutton Rd
Talbot Cl
Chaucer Crs
Castle Gv
Castle Grove
Penrose Cl
Benett Cl
Benett Gdns
Lisle Close
Almond Ave
Almond Drive
Penn Rd
Coster Cl
Kersey Crescent
Kersey Crs
De Montfort Rd
Burchell Road
Digby Road
Donnington Sq
Maple Crescent
Cherry Close
Dolman Rd
Winchcombe CP Infant School
Winchcombe Junior School
Newbury College of Further Education
Larch Cl
Newbold Rd
Coxeter Rd
Brummell Road
Counter Rd
Battle Close
Pound Lane
Amberley Cl
Linden Cl
Herewood Cl
Laburnum Grove
Chestnut Crescent
Chestnut Crs
Hawthorn Road
Angel Ct
Pelican Lane
Pelican La
Speenhamland CP School
Hotel
Speen Pl
Speen Lodge Ct
Speen Hill
Speen Hill Cl
Posting House Mews
Hill Road
Croft Lane
Strawberry Hill
Leys Gdns
Jesmond Dene
Goldwell Dr
Park Street
Park Way
Park End
Surgery
Victoria Gdns
St Mary's Rd
Charlton Place
Victoria Park
Lambourn Valley Way
Moor Lane
Northcroft Lane
Northcroft Surg
Cleveland Gv
Albert Rd
Northbrook Street
Berkshire County Council
West Berkshire District Council
West Street
Pembroke Rd
Crawford Pl
Cansfield End
Saffron Cl
Marsh La
Bridge St
W Mills
West Mills
Mallard Court
Wharf Street
Wharf Rd
Newbury District Museum & Tourist Information Centre
Police Station
Newbury Town Council
Kennet Shopping Centre
Cheap Street
Bear La
County Court
Kings Road W
KINGS
Kennet and Avon Canal
Butson Cl
Dysons Cl
Russell Road
Lipscombe Close
Lipscombe Cl
Berkeley Road
Blenheim Rd
Kennet Road
Oddfellows Rd
West Berkshire District Council
Market St
Newbury Bus Sta
Mayors La
Highfield Avenue
Carnegie Rd
Gloucester Road
Clifton Road
Chalford Rd
Craven Road
Rockingham Rd
St David's Road
St Nicholas' Rd
Bartholomew Street
West Berkshire Council
Newbury Station
WINCHCOMBE RD
Puffers Wy
Parsons Cl
Green Lane
St George's Avenue
St Michael's Road
Braunfels Wk
Bagnols Wy
Western End
Westfield Wy
Enborne House
Station Road
Greenham Road Retail Park
GREENHAM ROAD
A339(T)
Bonemill Lane
Westgate Road
Remembrance Road
Enborne Grove
Arthur Road
Enborne Pl
Enborne Rd
Enborne Road
Oak Dr
Pound Street
Rectory Cl
Rectory Close
Argyle Rd
St Nicholas C of E School
Link Road
Eastfield House Surgery
Catherine Road
St Donats Pl
Doctors Surgery
Hampton Rd
Derby Rd
ST JOHN'S ROAD
Chesterfield Road
Tudor Rd
Prospect Place
Howard Road
Kingsbridge Road
Salcombe Road
Floreat Gardens
Mayfair Dr
St Bartholomew's (Joint School)
Buckingham Road
Newbury District Hospital
A343
ANDOVER ROAD
Malvern Ct
Willow Cl
Cemetery
Berkshire County Council
Porchester Road
Abbots Road
Fifth Road
St Bartholomew's School
Harvest Green
Paddock Rd
Old Newtown Rd
Newtown Road
Priory Road
Mount Cl
Montague Ter
Erleigh Dene
Highfield Rd
St Johns School
Belvedere Dr
Bartlemy Road
Bartlemy Close
The Drive
Tarn La
Falkland Dr
Wendan Road
Meadow Rd
Friars Road
Abbey Close
Longacre
Oaken Grove
John Rankin Junior School
John Rankin County Infants School
Henshaw Crescent
Montgomery Road
Valley Road
Carford
Circular Routes
Croft Road
Westmead Drive
Westmead Dr
Roebuts Cl
Three Acre Rd
Gwyn Cl
Kingsland Grange
The Brambles
Culver
Cedar Mount
Chandos Road
Sandleford Hospital
Eeklo Pl
Hamilton

1 grid square represents 250 metres

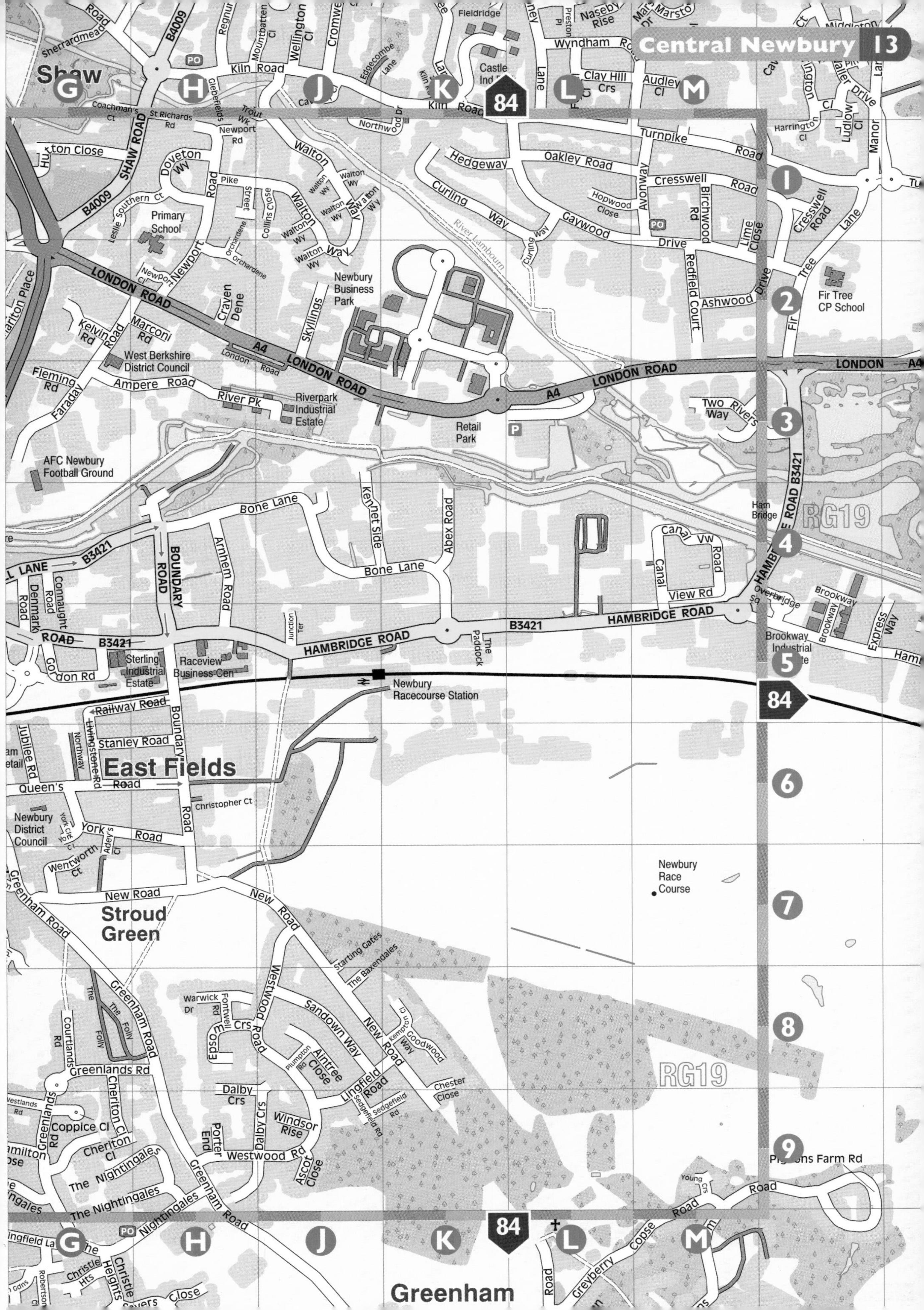
Shaw
East Fields
Stroud Green
Greenham
Newbury Business Park
West Berkshire District Council
Riverpark Industrial Estate
Retail Park
AFC Newbury Football Ground
Primary School
Fir Tree CP School
Newbury Racecourse Station
Newbury Race Course
Sterling Industrial Estate
Raceview Business Cen
Brookway Industrial Estate
Newbury District Council
Castle Ind Est
Ham Bridge
RG19
LONDON ROAD
A4
SHAW ROAD
B4009
HAMBRIDGE ROAD
B3421
BOUNDARY ROAD
Kiln Road
Turnpike Road
Oakley Road
Hedgeway
Curling Way
Gaywood Drive
Cresswell Road
Fir Tree Lane
Bone Lane
Kennet Side
Abex Road
Arnhem Road
Canal View Road
Ampere Road
Faraday Road
Kelvin Rd
Marconi Rd
Fleming Rd
Hutton Close
Doveton Wy
Newport Road
Pike Street
Walton Way
Craven Dene
Skyllings
River Lambourn
Railway Road
Stanley Road
Queen's Road
York Road
Christopher Ct
New Road
Greenham Road
Westwood Road
Sandown Way
Lingfield Road
Aintree Close
Windsor Rise
Dalby Crs
Greenlands Rd
Cheriton Cl
Coppice Cl
The Nightingales
Nightingales
Pigeons Farm Rd
Copse Road
Greybery
Starting Gates
The Baxendales
Chester Close
Sedgefield Rd
Westwood Rd
Ascot Close
Porter End
Epsom Crs
Warwick Dr
Fontwell Rd
Goodwood Way
Kempton Cl
Plumpton Rd
The Folly
Courtlands Rd
Junction Ter
The Paddock
Two Rivers Way
Overbridge Sq
Brookway
Express Way
Redfield Court
Birchwood Rd
Ashwood Drive
Lime Close
Avonway
Hopwood Close
Harrington Cl
Ludlow Cl
Manor Lane
Wyndham Road
Clay Hill Crs
Audley Cl
Naseby Rise
Preston Pl
Fieldridge
Northwood Dr
Edgecombe Lane
Wellington Cl
Mountbatten Cl
Glebefields
Trout Wk
Newport Rd
St Richards Rd
Coachman's Ct
Sherrardmead
Leslie Southern Ct
Orchardene
Collins Close
Gordon Rd
Denmark Road
Connaught Road
Jubilee Rd
Livingstone Rd
Northway
Adey's Cl
Wentworth Ct
Young Crs
Christie Heights
Christie Hts
84

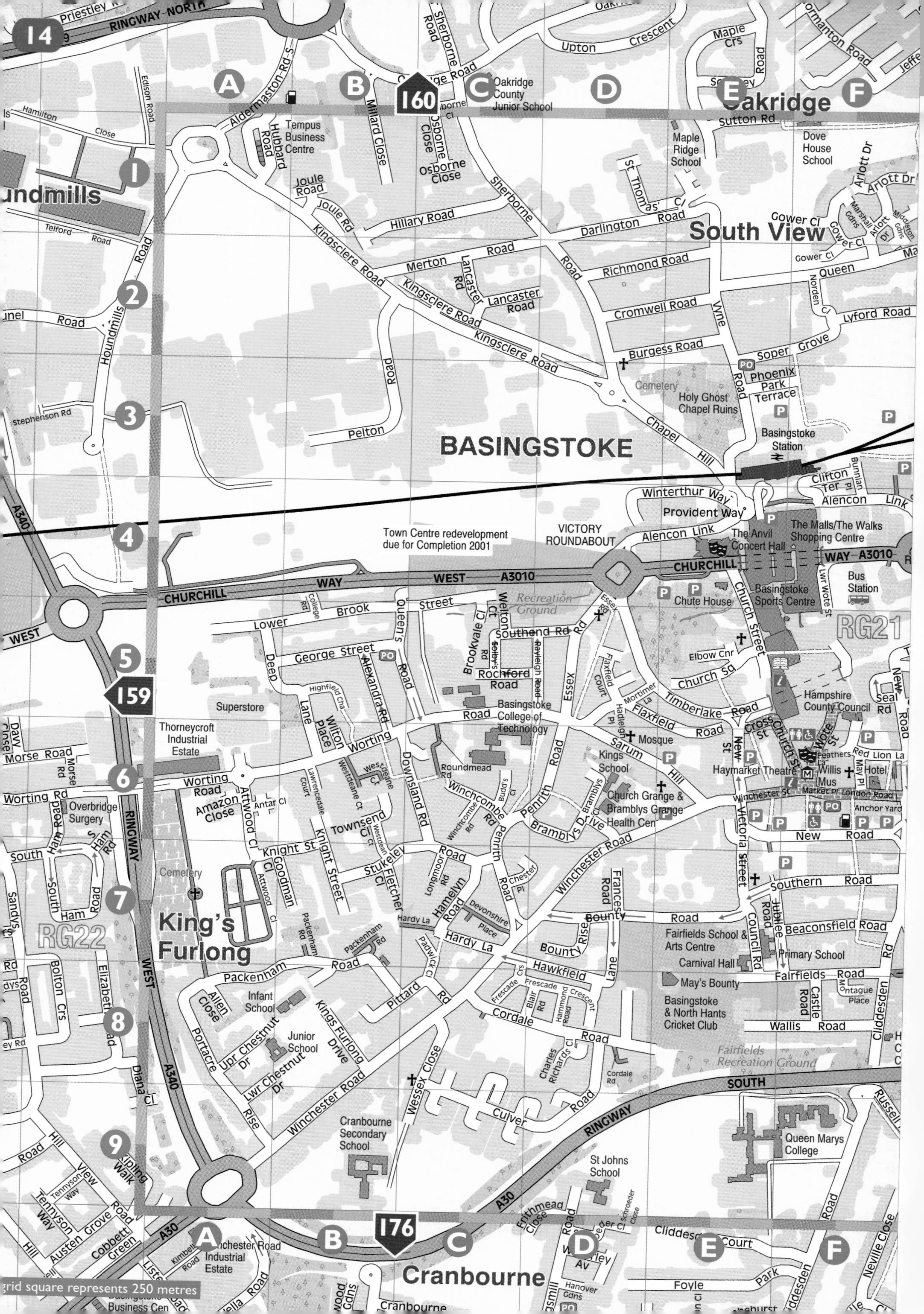

14
160
159
176
A
B
C
D
E
F
1
2
3
4
5
6
7
8
9
Oakridge
South View
BASINGSTOKE
King's Furlong
Cranbourne
RG21
RG22
RINGWAY NORTH
CHURCHILL WAY WEST A3010
CHURCHILL WAY A3010
RINGWAY WEST
RINGWAY SOUTH
A340
A30
Priestley
Upton Crescent
Maple Crs
Ormanton Road
Oakridge County Junior School
Sutton Rd
Dove House School
Arlott Dr
Aldermaston Rd S
Sherborne Road
Hubbard Road
Tempus Business Centre
Millard Close
Osborne Close
Joule Road
Joule Rd
Hillary Road
Kingsclere Road
Darlington Road
St Thomas' Cl
Maple Ridge School
Gower Cl
Marshall Gdns
Middleton Gdns
Merton Road
Lancaster Rd
Lancaster Road
Richmond Road
Cromwell Road
Vyne Road
Norden Cl
Queen
Lyford Road
Burgess Road
Soper Grove
Phoenix Park Terrace
Cemetery
Holy Ghost Chapel Ruins
Chapel Hill
Pelton Road
Basingstoke Station
Clifton Ter
Bunnian Pl
Alencon Link
Winterthur Way
Provident Way
Town Centre redevelopment due for Completion 2001
VICTORY ROUNDABOUT
The Anvil Concert Hall
The Malls/The Walks Shopping Centre
Bus Station
Lwr Wote St
Basingstoke Sports Centre
Chute House
Church Street
Recreation Ground
Essex Rd
Welton Ct
Brookvale Cl
Southend Rd
Rochford Road
Raleigh Road
Lower Brook Street
College Rd
Queen's Road
George Street
Deep Lane
Alexandra Rd
Highfield Cha
Flaxfield Court
Elbow Cnr
Church Sq
Timberlake Road
Hampshire County Council
Seal Rd
New Road
Superstore
Wilton Place
Worting Road
Basingstoke College of Technology
Mortimer La
Hadleigh Pl
Flaxfield Road
Mosque
Sarum Hill
Cross St
Church St
Wote St
Feathers La
Red Lion La
May Pl
Hotel
Willis Mus
Haymarket Theatre
Kings School
Thorneycroft Industrial Estate
Davy Close
Morse Road
Morse Rd
Worting Rd
Westdeane Ct
Downsland Rd
Roundmead Rd
Budd's Cl
Penrith Road
Bramblys Drive
Church Grange & Bramblys Grange Health Cen
Winchester St
Market Pl
London Road
Anchor Yard
Overbridge Surgery
Amazon Close
Antar Cl
Attwood Cl
Lawrencedale Court
Townsend Cl
Winchcombe Road
Winchester Road
New Road
Victoria Street
Southern Road
Ham Road
South Ham Road
Sandy's
Knight St
Goodman Cl
Knight Street
Stukeley Road
Fletcher Cl
Longmoor Rd
Hamelyn Road
Chester Pl
Frances Road
Bounty Road
Bounty Rise
Council Rd
Jubilee Road
Beaconsfield Road
Fairfields School & Arts Centre
Carnival Hall
Primary School
Devonshire Place
Hardy La
Packenham Rd
Padwick Cl
Hawkfield Lane
May's Bounty
Fairfields Road
Montague Place
Castle Road
Cliddesden Road
Bolton Crs
Elizabeth Rd
Packenham Road
Allen Close
Infant School
Pittard Rd
Frescade Crs
Frescade Crescent
Blair Rd
Hammond Road
Cordale Road
Basingstoke & North Hants Cricket Club
Wallis Road
Portacre Rise
Upr Chestnut Dr
Junior School
Kings Furlong Drive
Lwr Chestnut Dr
Wessex Close
Charles Richards Cl
Cordale Rd
Fairfields Recreation Ground
Diana Cl
Culver Road
Queen Marys College
Hill Road
View Road
Tennyson Way
Kipling Walk
Cranbourne Secondary School
St Johns School
Frithmead Close
Schroeder Close
Cliddesden Court
Austen Grove
Cobbett Green
Kimbell Road
Winchester Road Industrial Estate
Neville Close
Foyle Park
Hanover Gdns
Business Cen
Cranbourne
grid square represents 250 metres

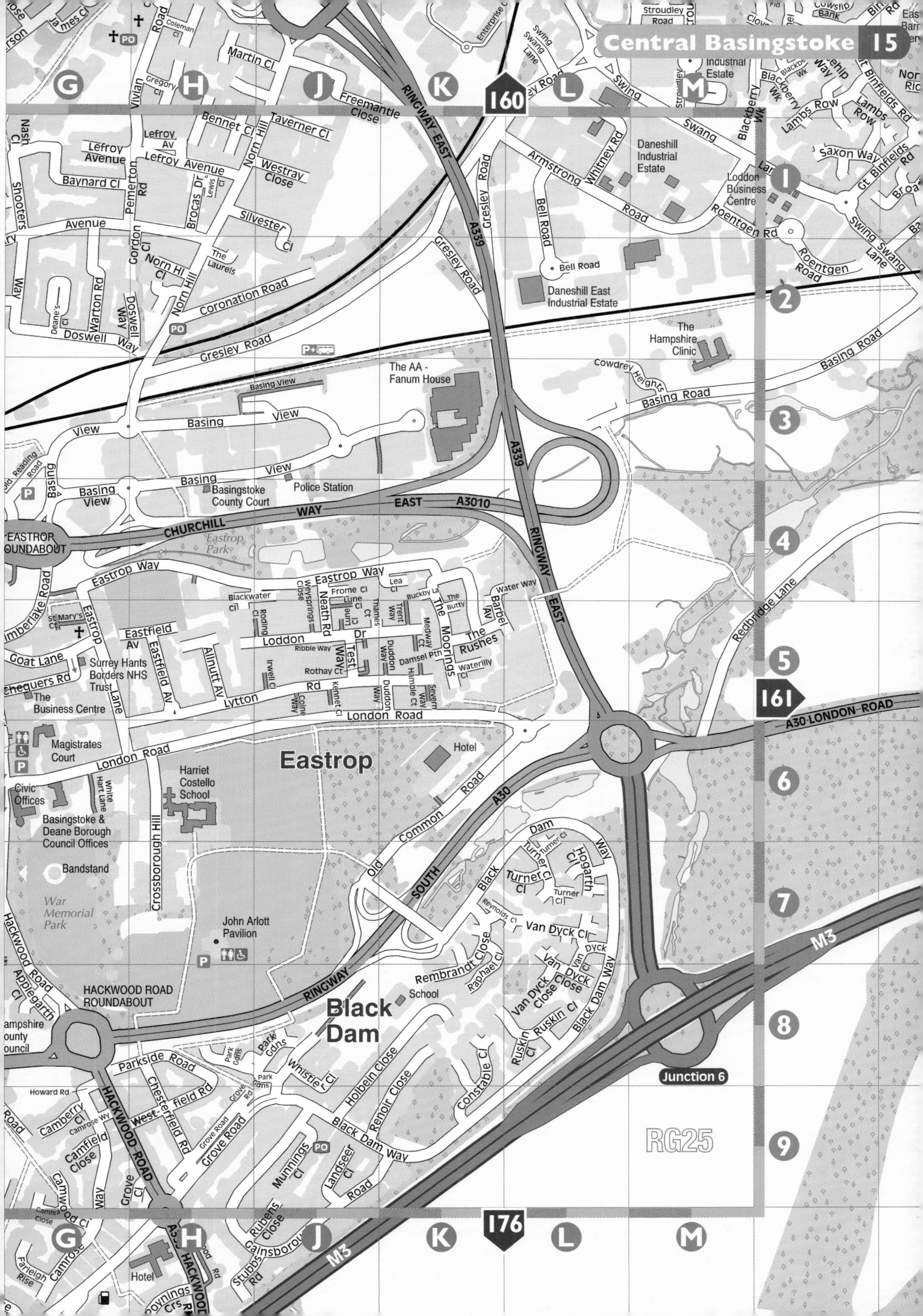
Central Basingstoke
15
160
161
176
RINGWAY EAST
A339
CHURCHILL WAY EAST A3010
RINGWAY SOUTH
A30 LONDON ROAD
M3
Junction 6
HACKWOOD ROAD
HACKWOOD ROAD ROUNDABOUT
EASTROP ROUNDABOUT
Eastrop
Black Dam
Daneshill Industrial Estate
Daneshill East Industrial Estate
Loddon Business Centre
The Hampshire Clinic
The AA - Fanum House
Police Station
Basingstoke County Court
Eastrop Park
Magistrates Court
Civic Offices
Basingstoke & Deane Borough Council Offices
Harriet Costello School
Bandstand
War Memorial Park
John Arlott Pavilion
Surrey Hants Borders NHS Trust
The Business Centre
Hotel
School
RG25
Basing Road
Basing View
London Road
Eastrop Way
Loddon Dr
Lytton Rd
Old Common Road
Black Dam Way
Redbridge Lane
Gresley Road
Armstrong Road
Roentgen Rd
Swing Swang Lane
Coronation Road
Norn Hill
Crossborough Hill
Hackwood Road
Parkside Road
Grove Road
Chesterfield Rd
Doswell Way
Lefroy Avenue
Vivian Road
Freemantle Close
Taverner Cl
Bennet Cl
Westray Close
Silvester Cl
Whitney Rd
Bell Road
Cowdrey Heights
Eastfield Av
Allnutt Av
Goat Lane
Chequers Rd
Eastrop Lane
Timberlake Road
Van Dyck Cl
Turner Cl
Hogarth Cl
Rembrandt Close
Ruskin Cl
Constable Cl
Holbein Close
Renoir Close
Whistler Cl
Landseer Cl
Munnings Cl
Rubens Close
Gainsborough Rd
Stubbs Rd
Camfield Close
Camberry Cl
Applegarth Cl

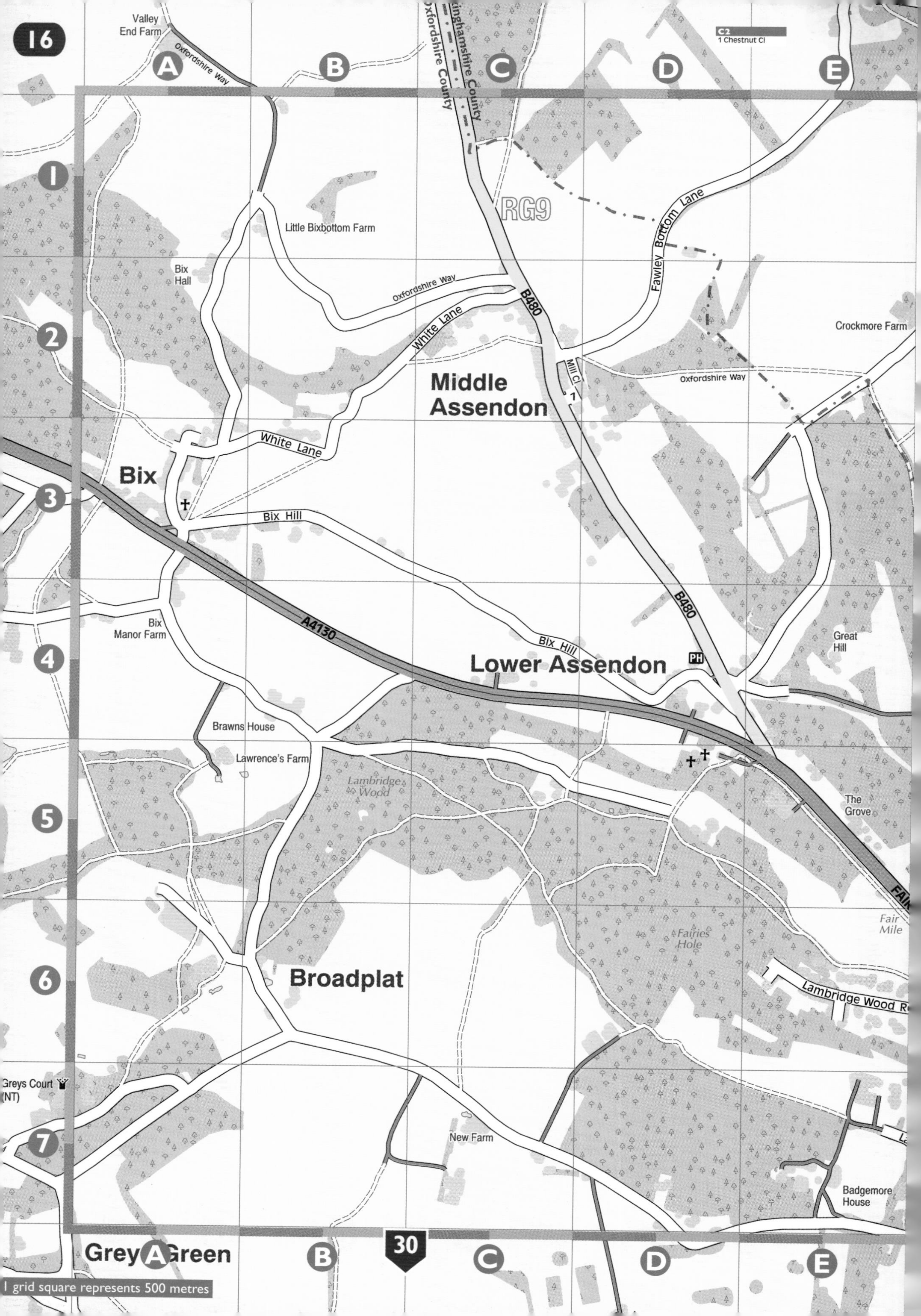

Valley End Farm
Oxfordshire Way
C2
1 Chestnut Cl
Oxfordshire County
RG9
Little Bixbottom Farm
Bix Hall
Oxfordshire Way
White Lane
B480
Fawley Bottom Lane
Crockmore Farm
Mill Cl
Oxfordshire Way
Middle Assendon
White Lane
Bix
Bix Hill
A4130
Bix Manor Farm
Bix Hill
B480
Great Hill
Lower Assendon
PH
Brawns House
Lawrence's Farm
Lambridge Wood
The Grove
Fair Mile
Fairies Hole
Broadplat
Lambridge Wood Rd
Greys Court (NT)
New Farm
Badgemore House
Grey Green
1 grid square represents 500 metres

30

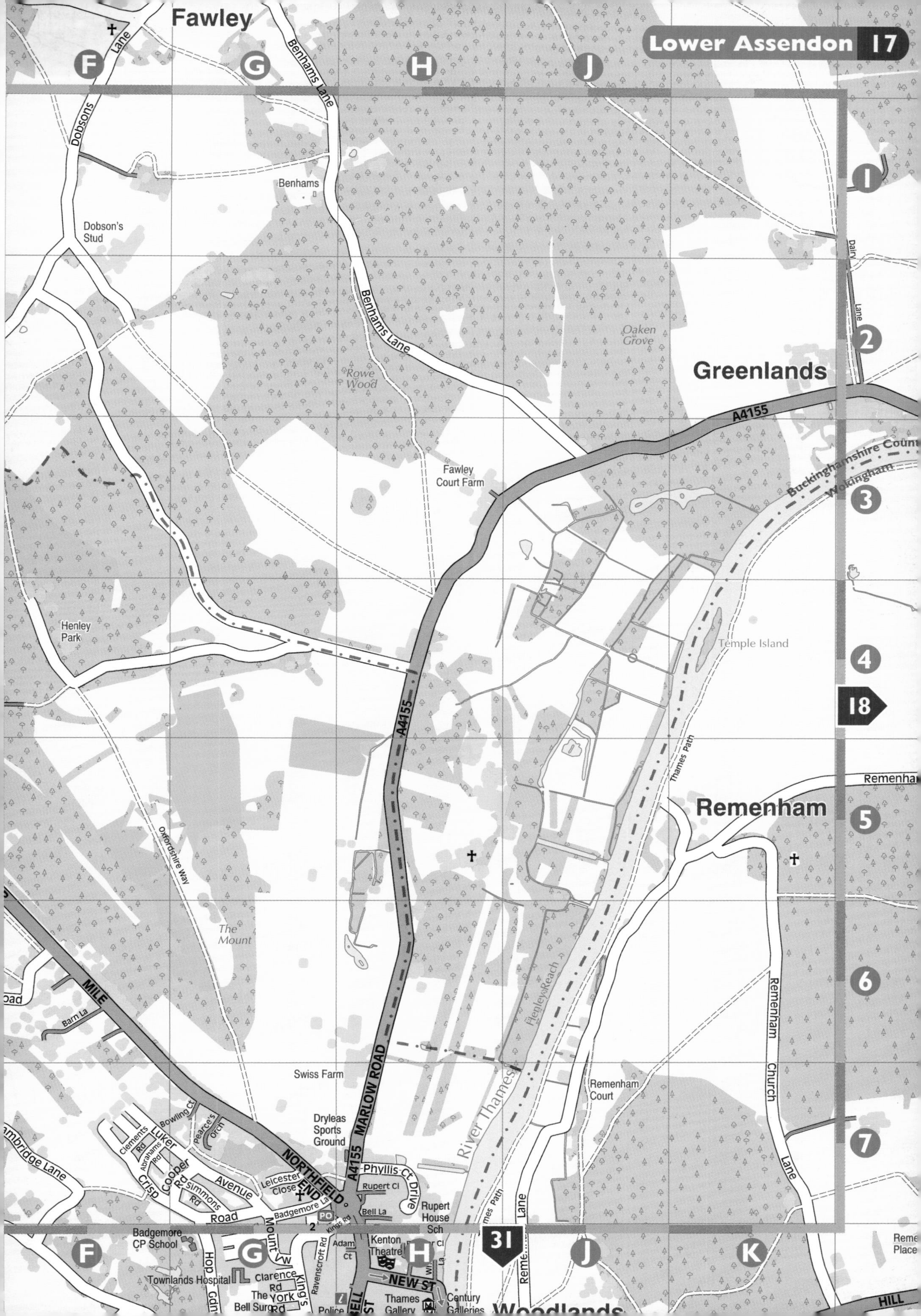

Fawley

F   G   H   J

Benhams

Dobson's
Stud

Benhams Lane

Rowe
Wood

Oaken
Grove

Greenlands

A4155

Buckinghamshire Coun

Woldingham

Fawley
Court Farm

Henley
Park

Temple Island

18

Remenham

Remenha

Oxfordshire Way

The
Mount

Henley Reach

River Thames

Thames Path

Remenham
Court

Remenham Church Lane

MILE

Barn La

Swiss Farm

Dryleas
Sports
Ground

Clements Rd
Abrahams Rd
Luker
Bowling Ct
Pearce's Orch
Cooper Rd
Simmons Rd
Crisp
Road
Avenue

Badgemore
CP School

Townlands Hospital

Clarence Rd
The York
Bell Surg Rd
Bell

NORTHFIELD END
Mount
Kings Rd
Leicester Close
Badgemore La
PO
2

MARLOW ROAD
A4155

Phyllis Ct Drive

Rupert Cl
Rupert Cl
Bell La

Rupert
House
Sch

Ravenscroft Rd
Adam Ct
Kenton
Theatre

NEW ST

Thames
Gallery

Century
Galleries

Police

Woodlands

31

Rem
Lane

Thames Path

HILL

Reme
Place

F   G   H   J   K

1
2
3
4
5
6
7

Dobsons Lane
Lane

Dairy Lane

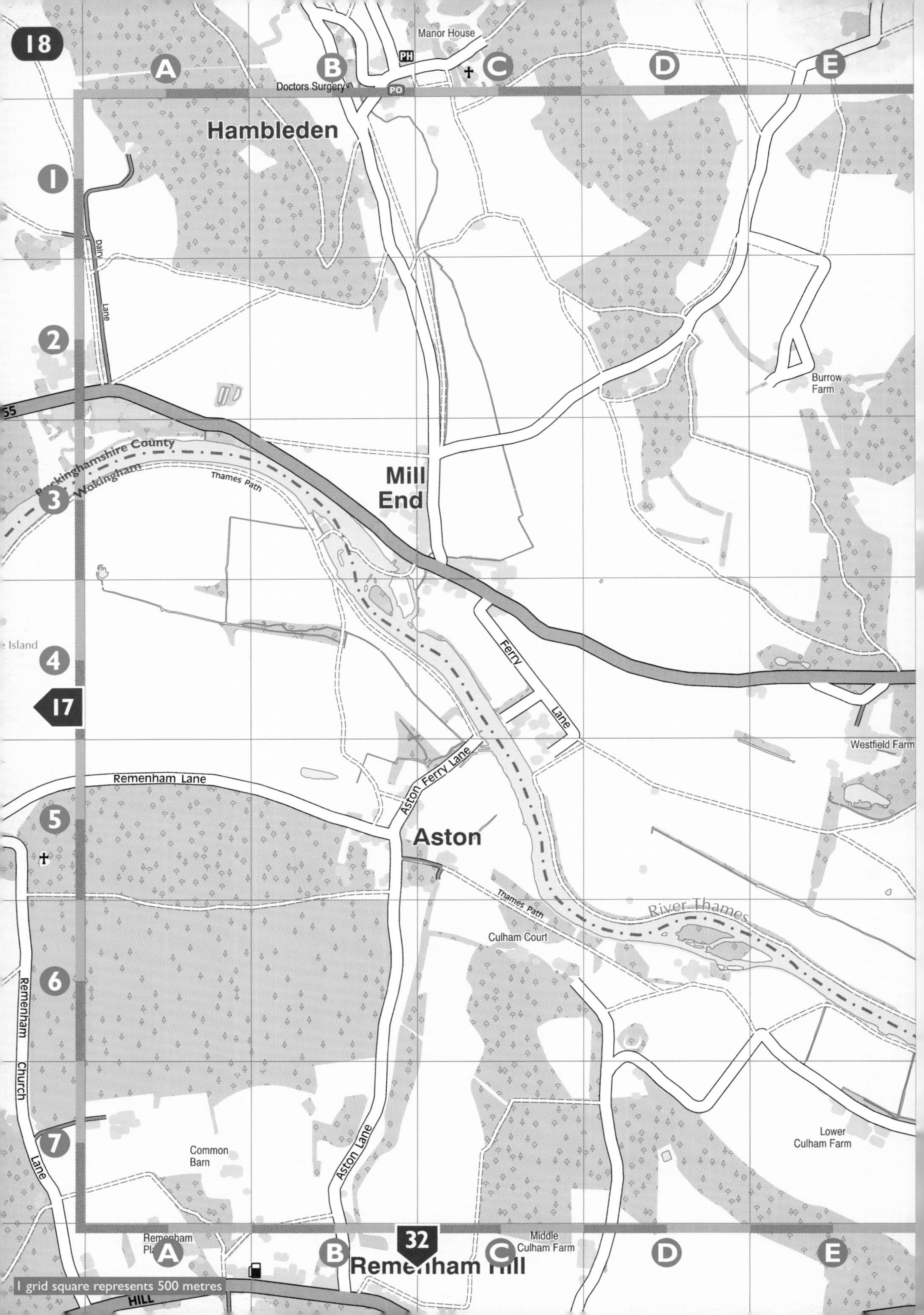

18

A   B   PH   C   D   E

Hambleden

Manor House

Doctors Surgery

PO

†

1

Dairy Lane

2

55

3   Buckinghamshire County
Wokingham

Thames Path

**Mill
End**

Burrow
Farm

Island

4

17

Ferry Lane

Westfield Farm

Remenham Lane

5

†

Aston

Aston Ferry Lane

Thames Path

River Thames

Culham Court

6

Remenham Church Lane

Common
Barn

Aston Lane

Lower
Culham Farm

7

Remenham
Place

A   B   **32**   C   Middle
Culham Farm   D   E

Remenham Hill

HILL

1 grid square represents 500 metres

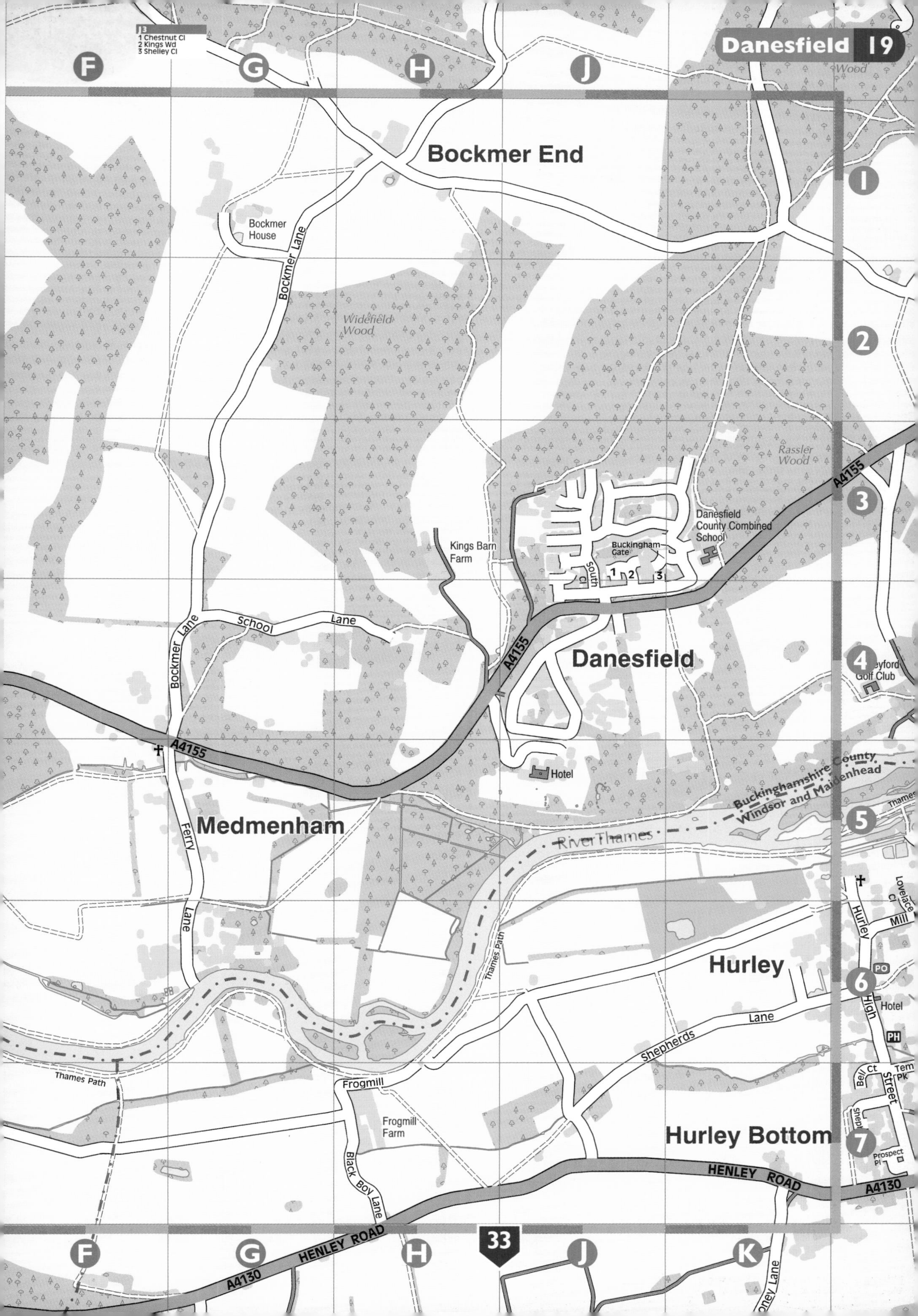

F G H J

1 Chestnut Cl
2 Kings Wd
3 Shelley Cl

Bockmer End

Bockmer
House

Bockmer Lane

Widefield
Wood

Rassler
Wood

A4155

Kings Barn
Farm

Danesfield
County Combined
School

Buckingham
Gate

South Cl

1 2 3

Danesfield

Bockmer Lane

school

Lane

Lane

A4155

A4155

Hotel

Reyford
Golf Club

Buckinghamshire County
Windsor and Maidenhead

Medmenham

River Thames

Thames

Ferry

Lane

Thames Path

Lovelace Cl

Mill

Hurley

Hurley

High

Hotel

PO

PH

Shepherds

Lane

Bell Ct

Street

Tem Pk

Steph

Thames Path

Frogmill

Frogmill
Farm

Black Boy Lane

Hurley Bottom

Prospect Pl

HENLEY ROAD

A4130

F G H J K

HENLEY ROAD

A4130

33

oney Lane

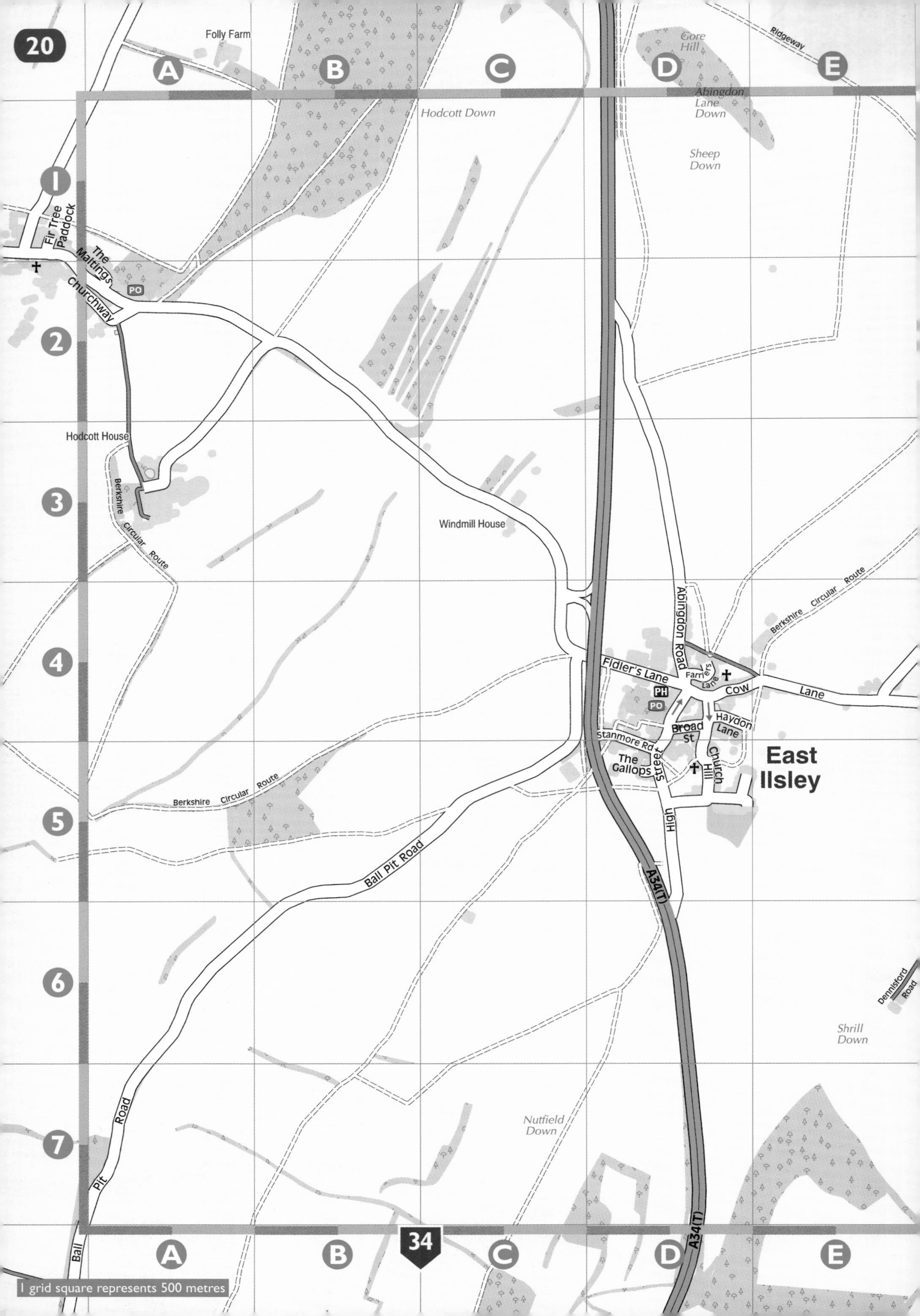

Folly Farm

A   B   C   D   E

Gore Hill

Ridgeway

Hodcott Down

Abingdon Lane Down

Sheep Down

1

Fir Tree Paddock

The Maltings

Churchway

PO

2

Hodcott House

Berkshire Circular Route

3

Windmill House

Abingdon Road

Berkshire Circular Route

Fidler's Lane

Farmers Lane

4

PH

PO

Cow Lane

Stanmore Rd

Broad St

Haydon Lane

Berkshire Circular Route

The Gallops

Street

Church Hill

East Ilsley

5

Ball Pit Road

High

A34(T)

Dennisford Road

6

Shrill Down

Ball Pit Road

Nutfield Down

7

A34(T)

A   B   **34**   C   D   E

1 grid square represents 500 metres

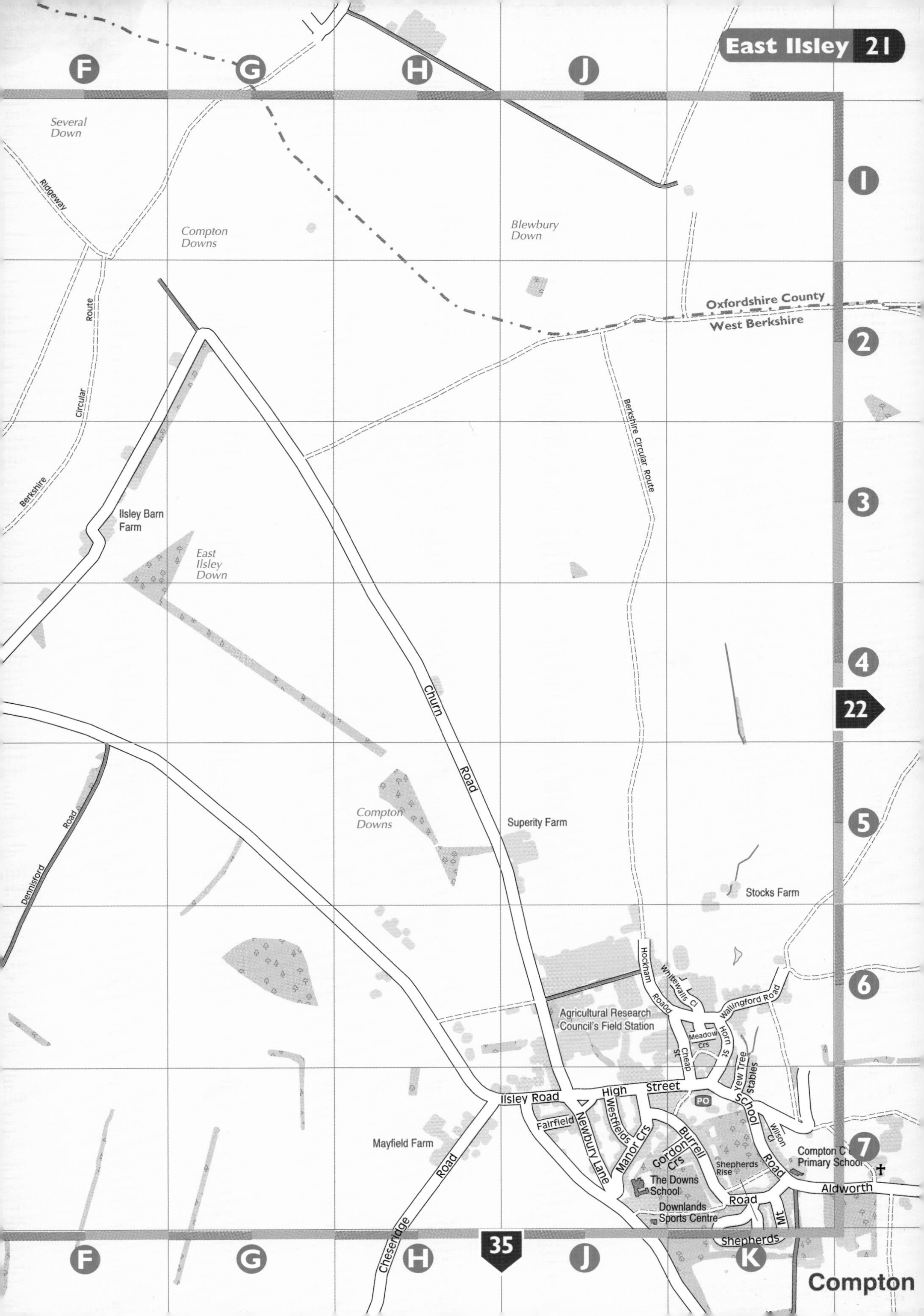

Several
Down

Ridgeway

Compton
Downs

Blewbury
Down

Berkshire
Circular
Route

I

Oxfordshire County

West Berkshire

2

Berkshire Circular Route

3

Ilsley Barn
Farm

East
Ilsley
Down

Churn Road

4

22

Dennsford Road

Compton
Downs

Superity Farm

5

Stocks Farm

6

Agricultural Research
Council's Field Station

Hockham Road

Whitewalls Cl

Wallingford Road

Meadow
Crs

Horn St

Cheap St

Yew Tree
Stables

Ilsley Road

High Street

PO

School Road

Wilson
Cl

Compton C
Primary School

7

Fairfield

Newbury Lane

Westfields

Manor Crs

Gordon
Crs

Burrell
Crs

Shepherds
Rise

Aldworth

Mayfield Farm

Cheseridge Road

The Downs
School

Downlands
Sports Centre

Road

Mt

Shepherds

Compton

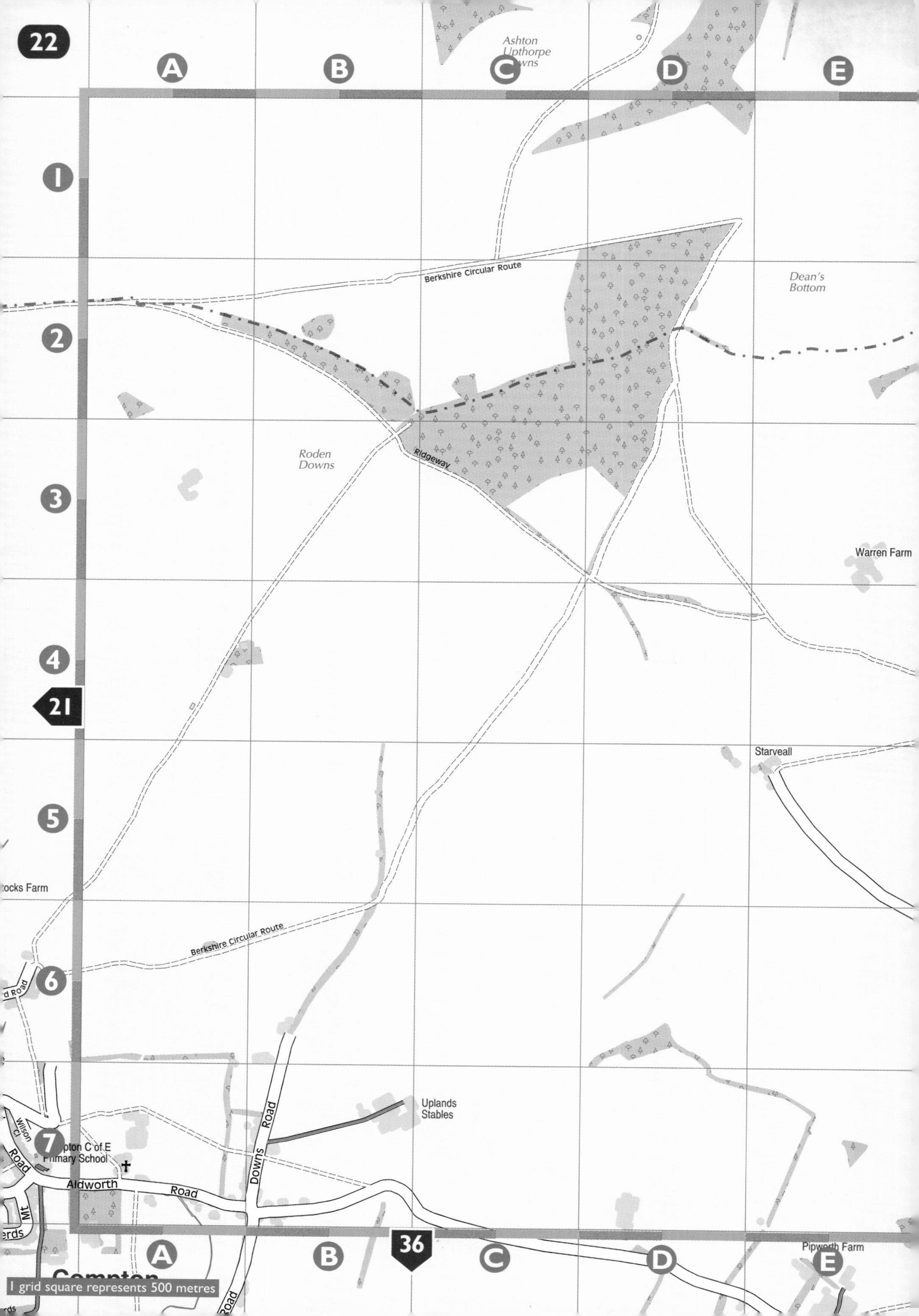

A   B   C   D   E

1

Berkshire Circular Route

Dean's Bottom

2

Roden Downs

Ridgeway

3

Warren Farm

4

21

Starveall

5

...ocks Farm

Berkshire Circular Route

6

...d Road

Ashton Upthorpe Downs

Wilson Cl

7   ...pton C of E Primary School

...ds

Aldworth   Road

Downs   Road

Uplands Stables

Pipworth Farm

Compton

A   B   C   D   E

1 grid square represents 500 metres

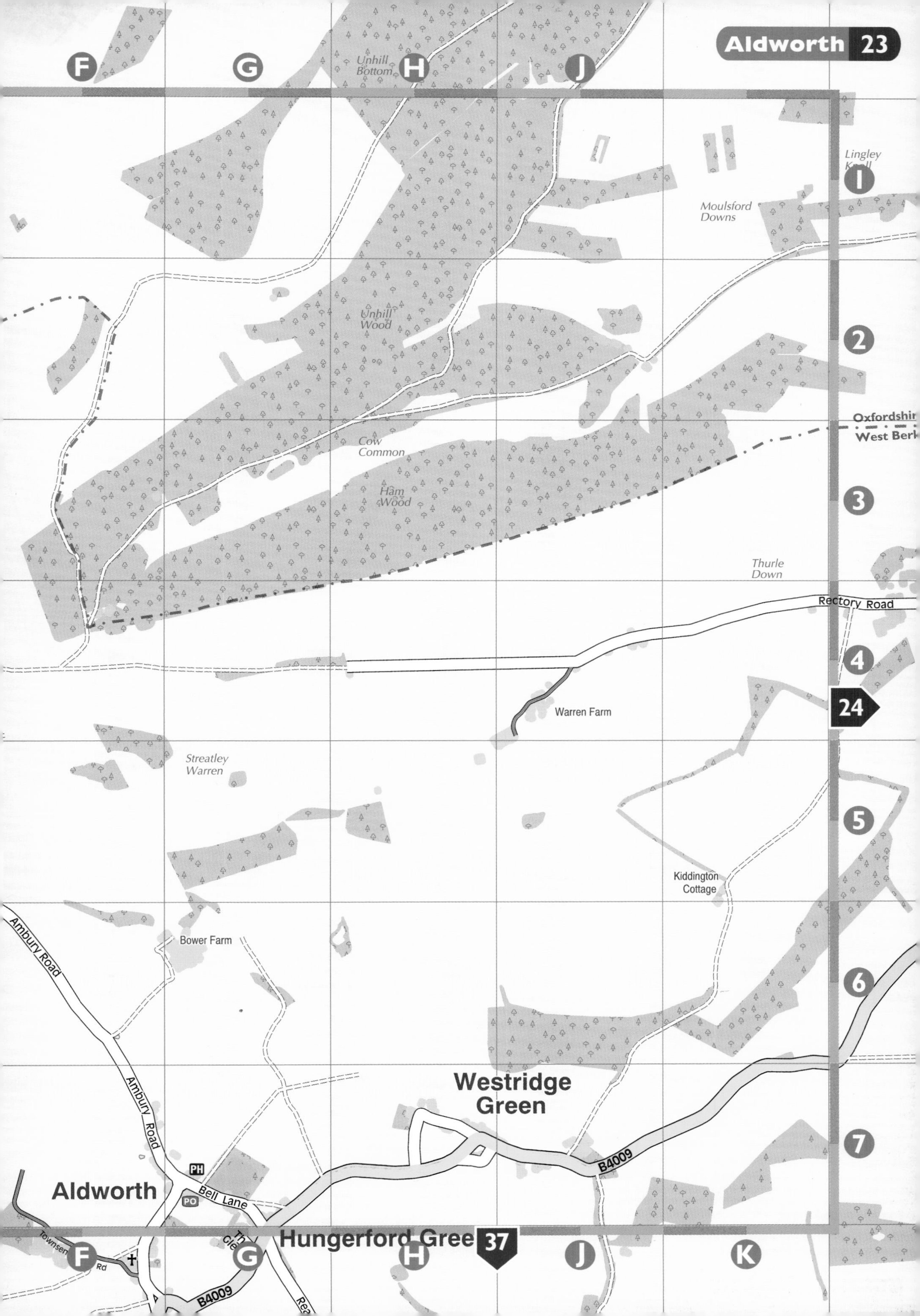
F
G
H
J
Unhill Bottom
Lingley Knoll
1
Moulsford Downs
Unhill Wood
2
Oxfordshire
West Berks
Cow Common
Ham Wood
3
Thurle Down
Rectory Road
4
24
Warren Farm
Streatley Warren
5
Kiddington Cottage
Ambury Road
Bower Farm
6
Ambury Road
Westridge Green
7
B4009
PH
Aldworth
PO
Bell Lane
Townsend Rd
Hungerford Gree
37
F
G
H
J
K
B4009

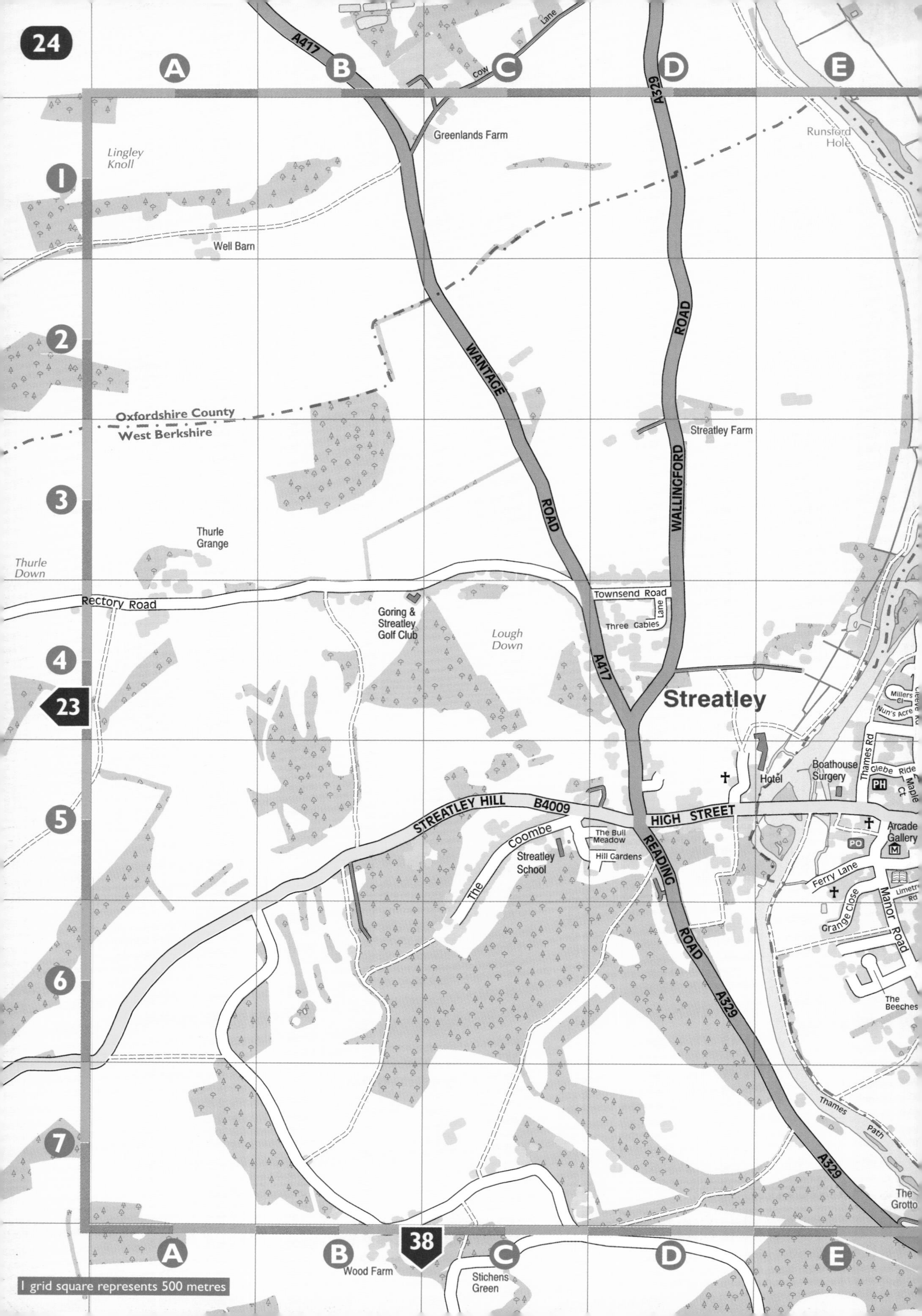
A
B
C
D
E
A417
Cow Lane
A329
Greenlands Farm
Runsford Hole
Lingley Knoll
Well Barn
WANTAGE ROAD
WALLINGFORD ROAD
Oxfordshire County
West Berkshire
Streatley Farm
Thurle Grange
Thurle Down
Rectory Road
Townsend Road
Lane
Three Gables
Goring & Streatley Golf Club
Lough Down
A417
Streatley
Millers Cl
Nun's Acre
Thames Rd
Boathouse Surgery
Hotel
Glebe Ride
PH
Maple Ct
STREATLEY HILL
B4009
HIGH STREET
The Bull Meadow
The Coombe
Streatley School
Hill Gardens
READING ROAD
Arcade Gallery
PO
Ferry Lane
Limetree Rd
Grange Close
Manor Road
The Beeches
A329
Thames Path
The Grotto
Wood Farm
Stichens Green
1
2
3
4
5
6
7
1 grid square represents 500 metres

23
38

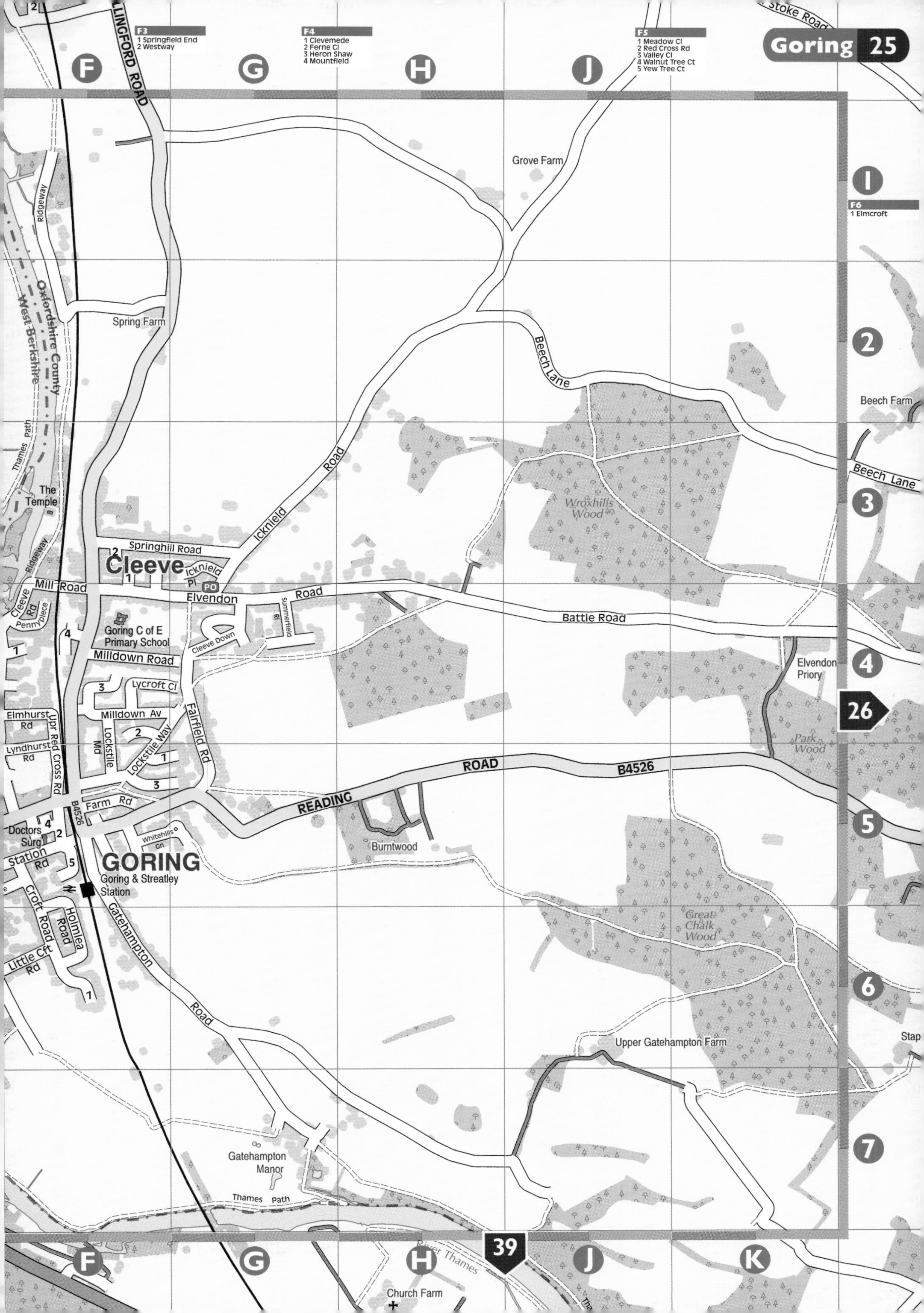

F
G
H
J

F3
1 Springfield End
2 Westway

F4
1 Clevemede
2 Ferne Cl
3 Heron Shaw
4 Mountfield

F5
1 Meadow Cl
2 Red Cross Rd
3 Valley Cl
4 Walnut Tree Ct
5 Yew Tree Ct

Stoke Road

1

Grove Farm

2

Beech Farm

Beech Lane

3

Wroxhills Wood

Spring Farm

Oxfordshire County
West Berkshire

Ridgeway

Thames Path

The Temple

Icknield Road

Springhill Road

Cleeve

Icknield Pl

PO

Elvendon Road

Summerfield Rd

Battle Road

Mill Road

Cleeve Rd

Penny piece

Goring C of E Primary School

Cleeve Down

Milldown Road

Lycroft Cl

Milldown Av

Fairfield Rd

Lockstile Way

Lockstile Rd

4

Elvendon Priory

26

Park Wood

Elmhurst Rd

Lyndhurst Rd

Upr Red Cross Rd

Farm Rd

READING ROAD B4526

5

Doctors Surg

B4526

Station Rd

GORING

Whitehills Gdn

Burntwood

Goring & Streatley Station

Croft Road

Holmlea Road

Little Crft Rd

Gatehampton Road

Great Chalk Wood

6

Upper Gatehampton Farm

Stap

7

Gatehampton Manor

Thames Path

F
G

River Thames

39

H

J

K

Church Farm

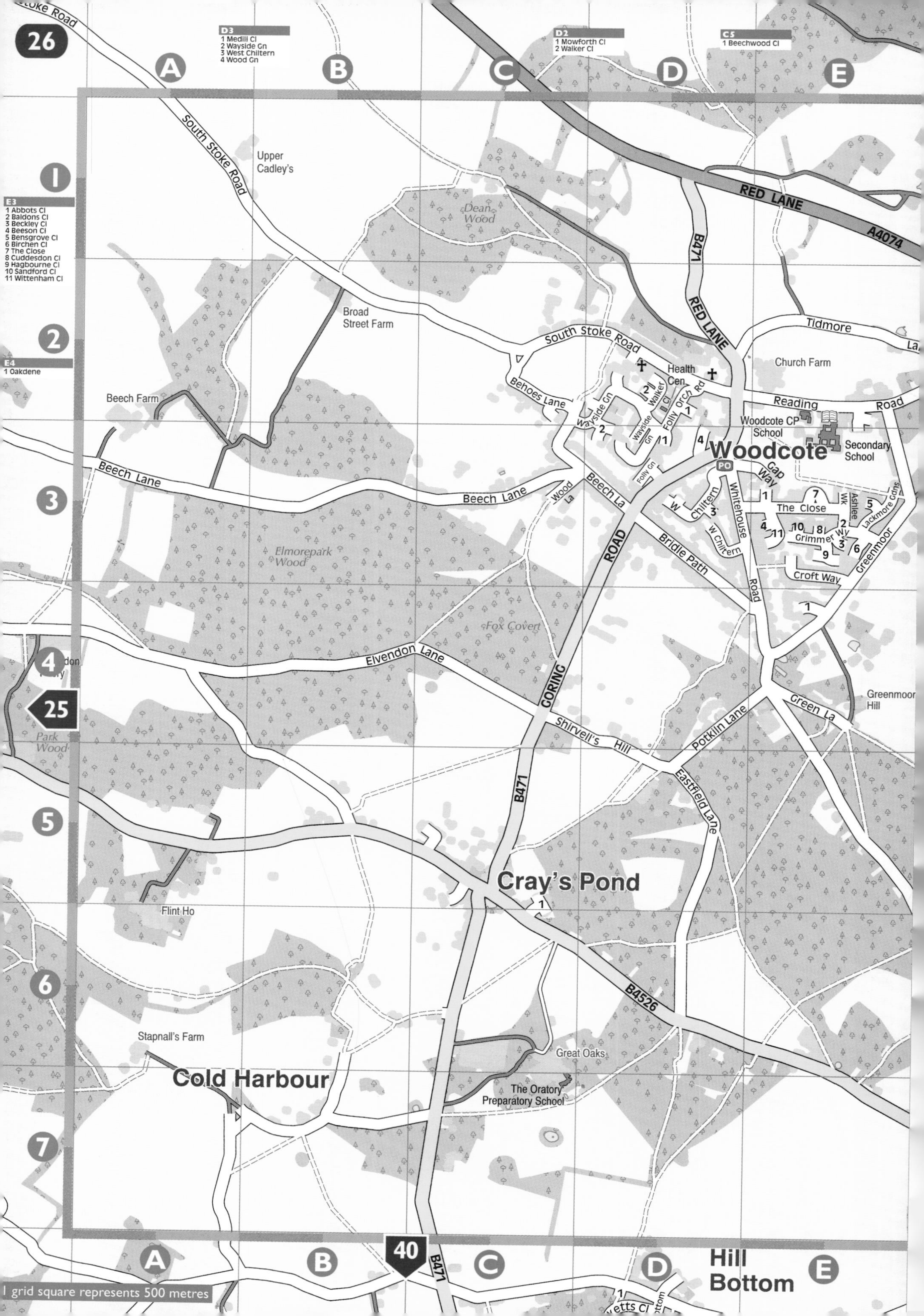

A B C D E

1

2

3

4

25

5

6

7

Upper Cadley's

South Stoke Road

RED LANE

A4074

B471

RED LANE

Tidmore La

Church Farm

South Stoke Road

Broad Street Farm

Health Cen.

Reading Road

Behoes Lane

Beech Farm

Wayside Gn

Walker Cl

Folly Orch Rd

Woodcote CP School

Woodcote

Secondary School

Beech Lane

Folly Gn

PO

Gap Way

Beech Lane

Wood La

Beech La

Chiltern

Whitehouse Road

The Close

Ashlee

Lackmore Gdns

Greenmoor

Elmorepark Wood

GORING ROAD

Bridle Path

W Chiltern

Grimmer

Croft Way

Fox Covert

Elvendon Lane

Greenmoor Hill

don

Park Wood

Shirvell's Hill

Green La

B471

Potkiln Lane

Eastfield Lane

Flint Ho

Cray's Pond

B4526

Stapnall's Farm

Great Oaks

Cold Harbour

The Oratory Preparatory School

A B 40 C D Hill Bottom

B471

E

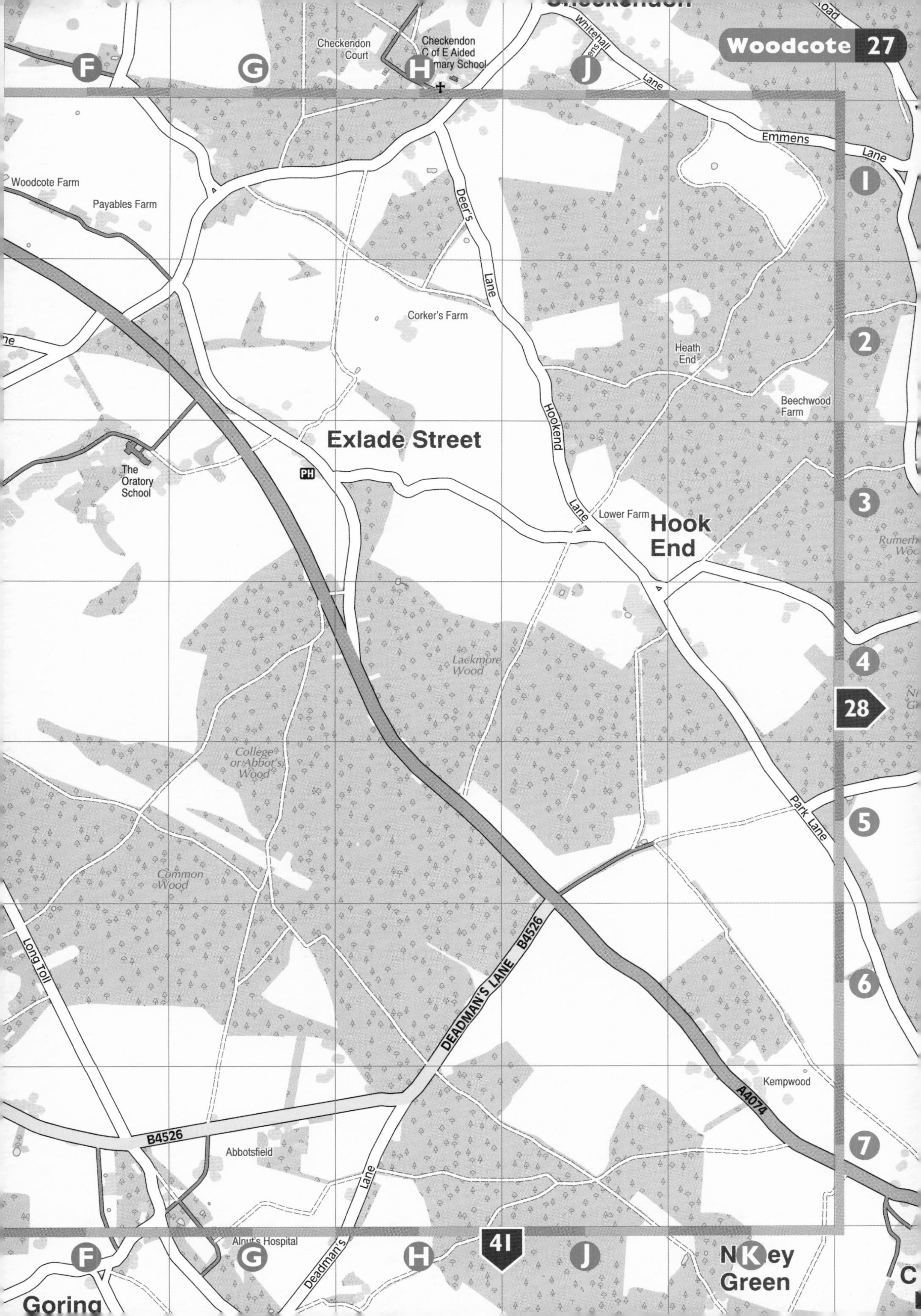

Checkendon

Checkendon Court

Checkendon C of E Aided Primary School

Whitehall Lane

F G H J

Emmens Lane

I

Woodcote Farm

Payables Farm

Deer's Lane

Corker's Farm

Heath End

2

Beechwood Farm

Exlade Street

Hookend Lane

3

The Oratory School

PH

Lower Farm

Hook End

Rumerh Woo

4

28

Lackmore Wood

Park Lane

5

College or Abbot's Wood

Common Wood

6

Long Toll

DEADMAN'S LANE B4526

Kempwood

A4074

7

B4526

Abbotsfield

Deadman's Lane

Alnut's Hospital

F G H 41 J

N Key Green

Goring

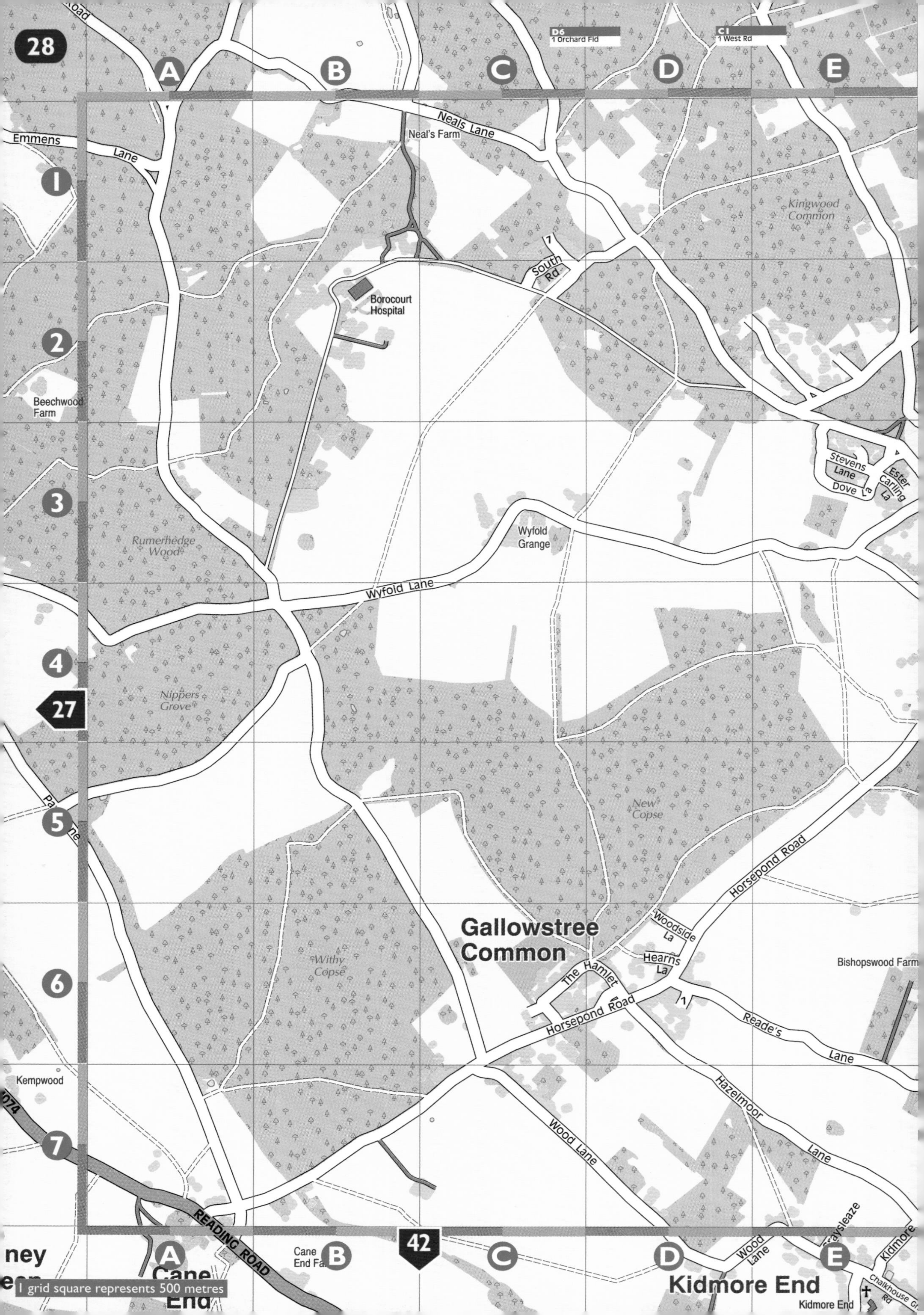

A B C D E

D6
1 Orchard Fld

C1
1 West Rd

Emmens

Lane

Neals Lane

Neal's Farm

1

Kingwood
Common

South
Rd

7

Borocourt
Hospital

2

Beechwood
Farm

Stevens
Lane

Ester
Carling
La

Dove

3

Rumerhedge
Wood

Wyfold
Grange

Wyfold Lane

4

Nippers
Grove

27

New
Copse

5

Pa   ne

Horsepond Road

Gallowstree
Common

Woodside
La

Bishopswood Farm

Hearns
La

The Hamlet

6

Withy
Copse

1

Reade's
Lane

Horsepond Road

Kempwood

M074

Hazelmoor
Lane

7

Wood Lane

READING ROAD

ney
ean

Cane
End

Cane
End Fa

42

Wood
Lane

Kidmore

Kidmore End

Chalkhouse G   Rd

Faksleaze

Kidmore End

1 grid square represents 500 metres

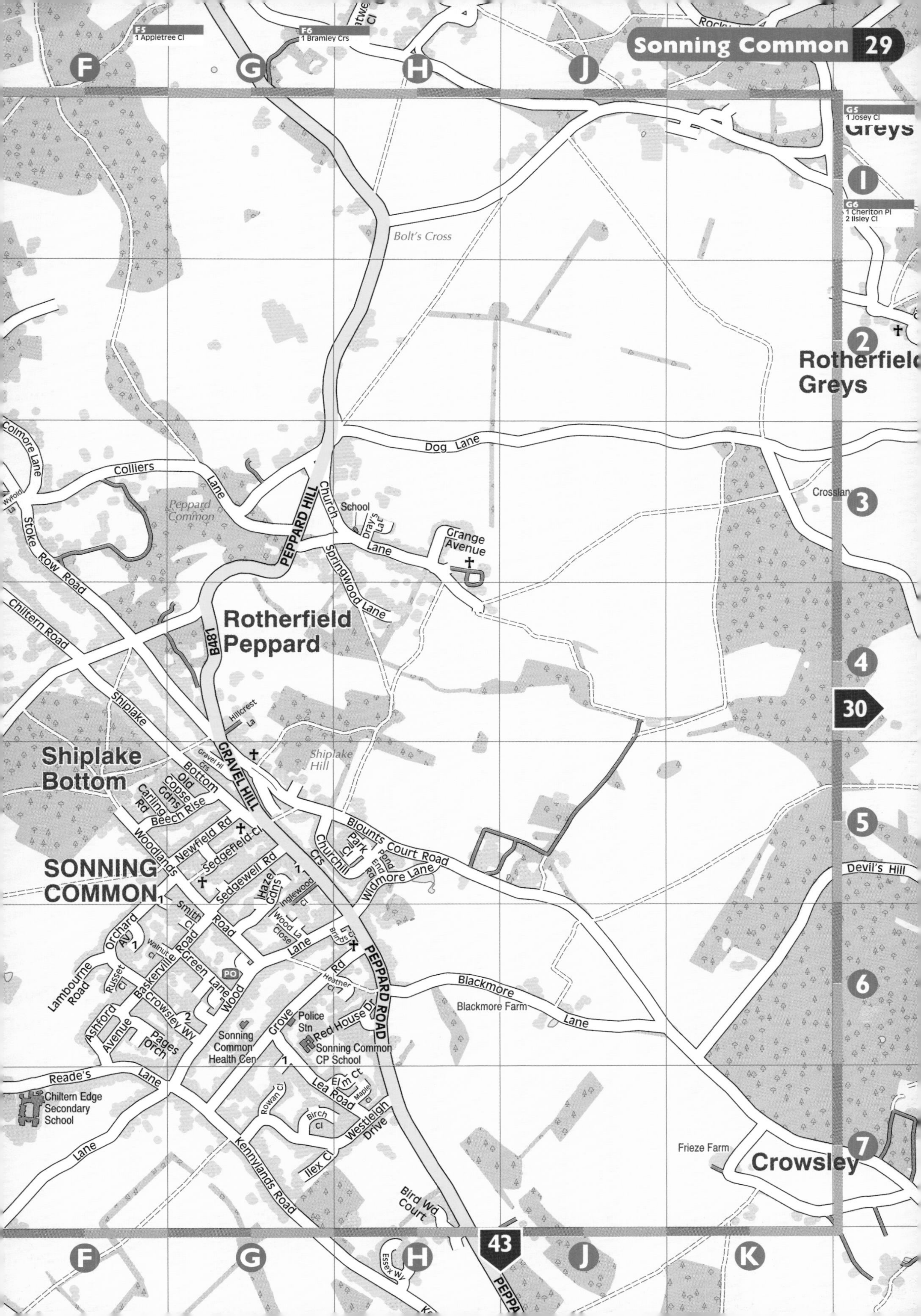

F5
1 Appletree Cl

F6
1 Bramley Crs

F **G** **H** **J**

G5
1 Josey Cl

Greys

I

G6
1 Cheriton Pl
2 Ilsley Cl

Bolt's Cross

2

**Rotherfield
Greys**

Dog Lane

Crosslan

3

Coldmore Lane

Colliers

Lane

Peppard
Common

PEPPARD HILL

Church

Lane

School

Drays La

Springwood Lane

Grange
Avenue

Wyfold

Stoke Row Road

Chiltern Road

**Rotherfield
Peppard**

B481

Shiplake

Hillcrest La

4

30

**Shiplake
Bottom**

Gravel Hl Cl

GRAVEL HILL

Shiplake
Hill

5

Devil's Hill

Bottom

Old
Copse
Gdns

Carling
Rd

Beech Rise

Woodlands

Newfield Rd

Sedgefield Cl

Blounts Court Road

Park
End

Pond
End

Widmore Lane

**SONNING
COMMON**

Sedgewell Rd

Hazel
Gdns

Inglewood

Churchill Crs

Smith

Road

Green Lane

Wood
Close

Wood

Lane

Briants Rd

PEPPARD ROAD

6

Orchard Av

Russet Cl

Baskerville Road

Walnut Cl

PO

Crowsley Wy

Pages
Orch

Lambourne
Road

Ashford
Avenue

Reade's

Lane

Sonning
Common
Health Cen

Grove

Heather
Cl

Police
Stn

Red House Dr

Sonning Common
CP School

Blackmore

Blackmore Farm

Lane

Chiltern Edge
Secondary
School

Rowan Cl

Birch
Cl

Lea Road

Elm Ct

Maple

Westleigh
Drive

Kennylands Road

Ilex Cl

Bird Wd
Court

43

Frieze Farm

7

Crowsley

PEPPA

Essex Wy

F **G** **H** **J** **K**

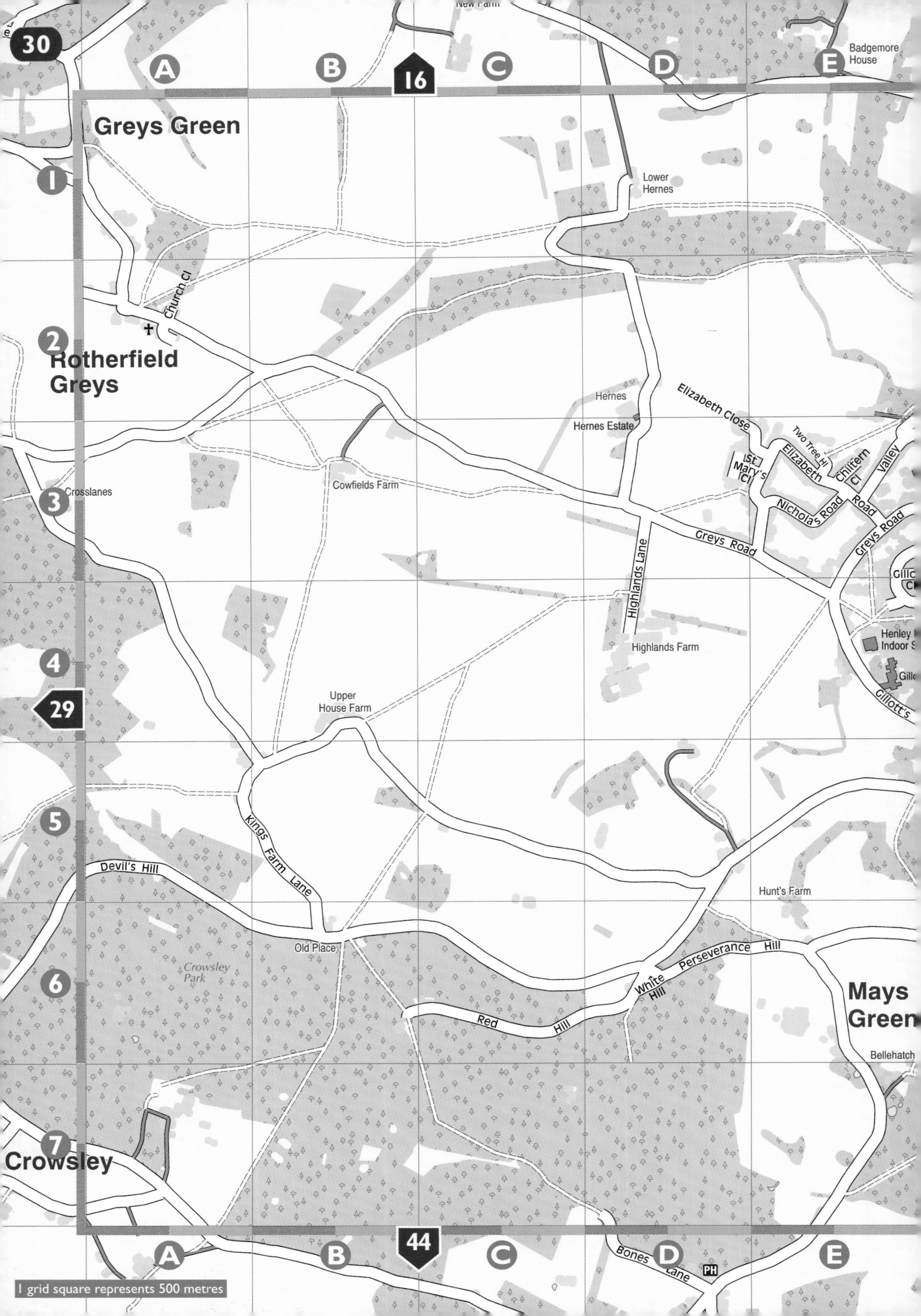

30

Ⓐ Ⓑ **16** Ⓒ Ⓓ Ⓔ

Badgemore House

Greys Green

❶

Lower Hernes

Church Cl

❷ **Rotherfield Greys**

＋

Hernes

Hernes Estate

Elizabeth Close

Two Tree Hl

St. Mary's (Ch)

Elizabeth

Chiltern Cl

Valley

❸ Crosslanes

Cowfields Farm

Nicholas Road

Greys Road

Greys Road

Highlands Lane

Gill

❹

Highlands Farm

Henley
Indoor S

29

Gillo

Gillott's

Upper House Farm

Kings Farm Lane

Hunt's Farm

❺

Devil's Hill

Perseverance Hill

Mays Green

❻ Crowsley Park

Old Place

White Hill

Red Hill

Bellehatch

❼ **Crowsley**

Ⓐ Ⓑ **44** Ⓒ Bones Lane Ⓓ PH Ⓔ

1 grid square represents 500 metres

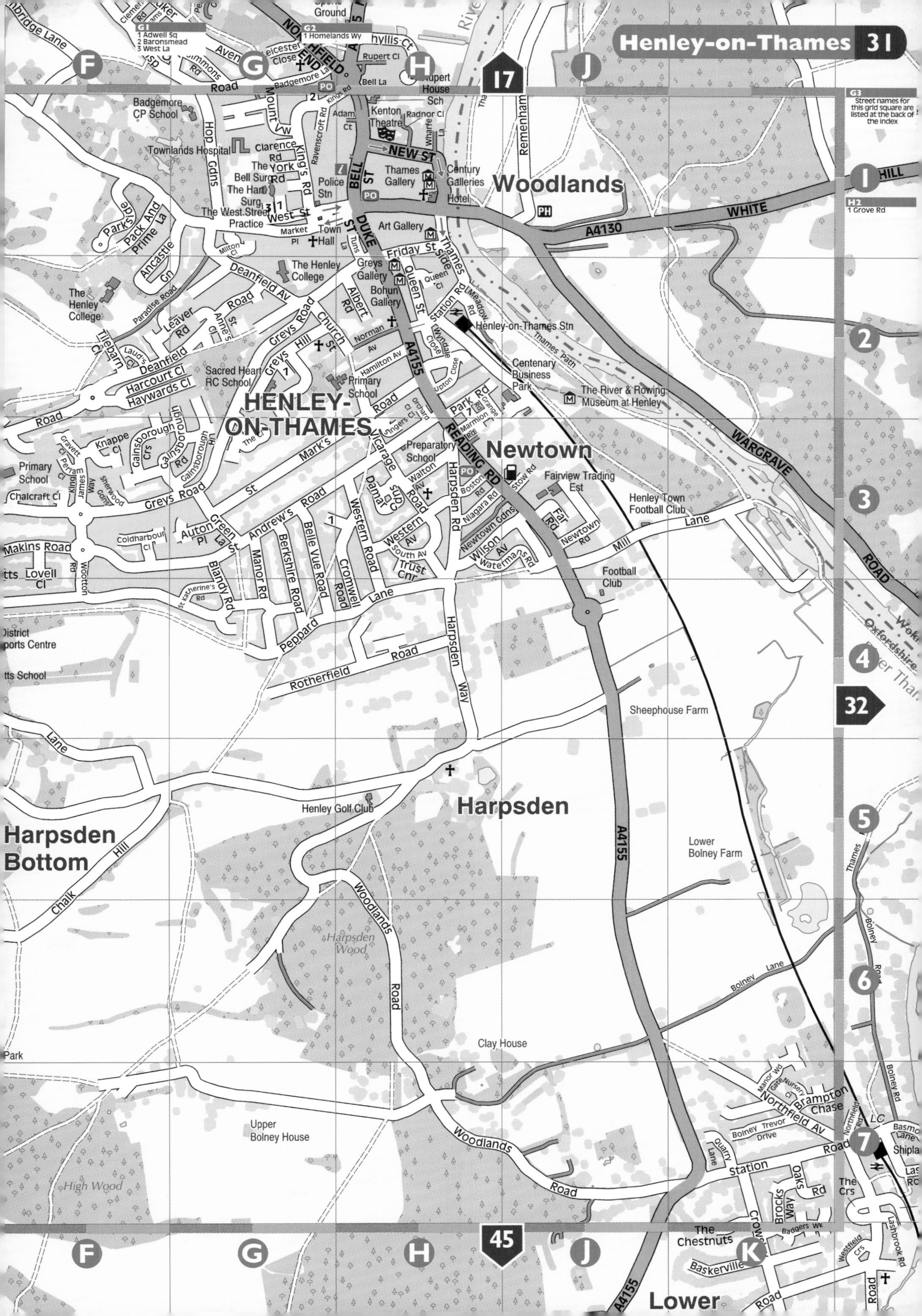
Woodlands
HENLEY-ON-THAMES
Newtown
Harpsden
Harpsden Bottom
Lower
Henley-on-Thames Stn
Townlands Hospital
Badgemore CP School
The Henley College
Sacred Heart RC School
Primary School
Preparatory School
Kenton Theatre
Thames Gallery
Century Galleries
Art Gallery
Town Hall
Police Stn
Greys Gallery
Bohun Gallery
The River & Rowing Museum at Henley
Centenary Business Park
Fairview Trading Est
Henley Town Football Club
Football Club
Sheephouse Farm
Henley Golf Club
Lower Bolney Farm
Clay House
Upper Bolney House
Harpsden Wood
High Wood
The West Street Practice
Bell Surg
The Hart Surg
Hotel
A4130
A4155
WHITE HILL
WARGRAVE ROAD
READING RD
DUKE ST
BELL ST
NEW ST
NORTHFIELD END
Greys Road
Peppard Lane
Rotherfield Road
Harpsden Way
Woodlands Road
Chalk Hill
Bolney Lane
Bolney Rd
Station Road
Northfield Av
Mill Lane
G1 1 Adwell Sq 2 Baronsmead 3 West La
G2 1 Homelands Wy
G3 Street names for this grid square are listed at the back of the index
H2 1 Grove Rd
17
32
45
F G H J K
1 2 3 4 5 6 7

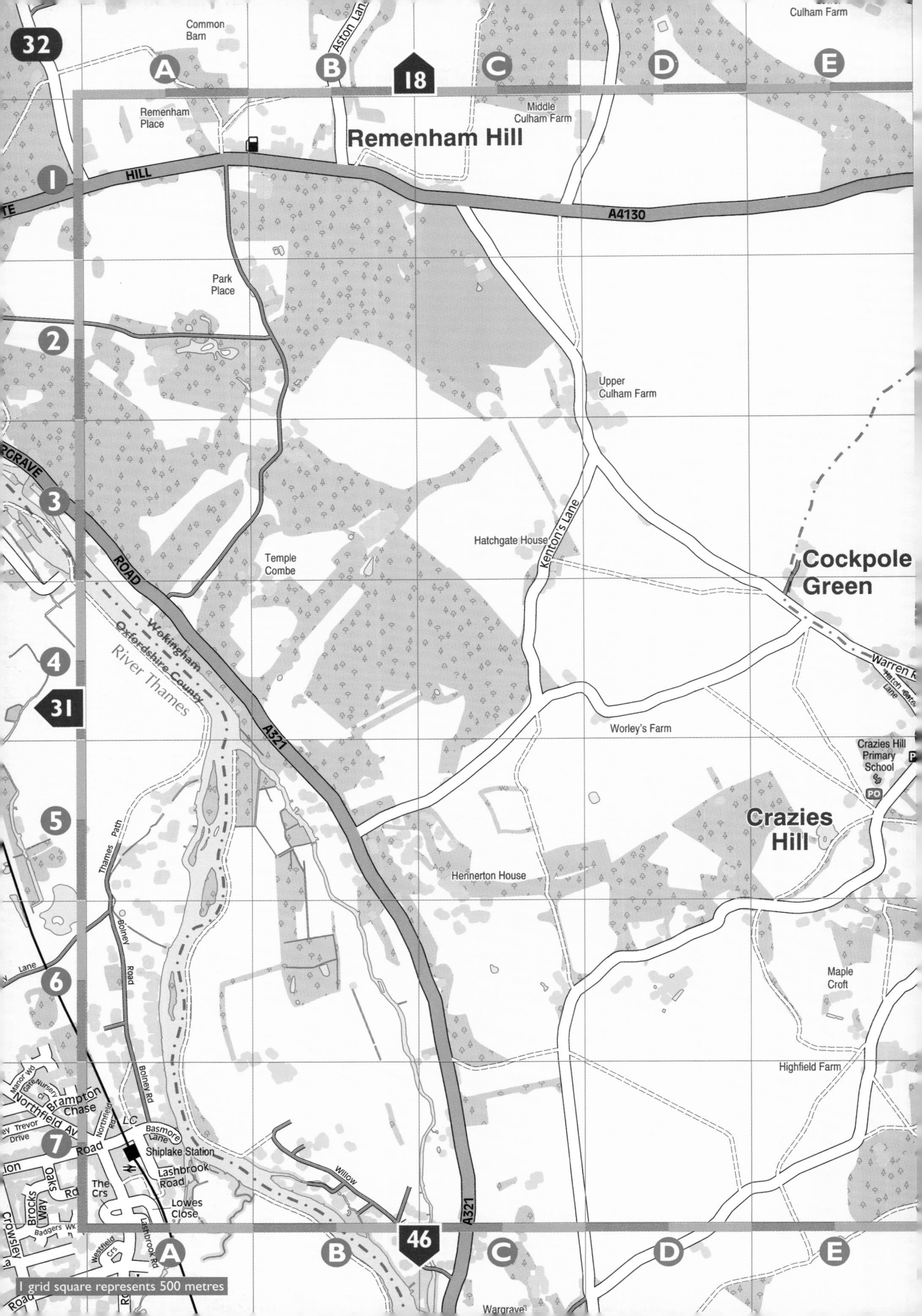

32

A
B
18
C
D
E

Common Barn

Remenham Place

Middle Culham Farm

Culham Farm

Remenham Hill

1

HILL

A4130

Park Place

2

Upper Culham Farm

GRAVE

3

ROAD

Hatchgate House

Kenton's Lane

Cockpole Green

Temple Combe

Wokingham

Oxfordshire County

River Thames

4

31

Worley's Farm

Warren

Crazies Hill Primary School

P

PO

5

Thames Path

Crazies Hill

Bolney Road

Hennerton House

6

Maple Croft

Lane

Highfield Farm

Manor Wd

Brampton Chase

Northfield

Bolney Rd

Northfield Av

Trevor Drive

7

Road

LC

Basmore Lane

Shiplake Station

Lashbrook Road

Willow

The Crs

Lowes Close

Oaks Rd

Brocks Way

Baggers Wk

Westfield Crs

Lashbrook Rd

A321

A
B
46
C
D
E

Wargrave

I grid square represents 500 metres

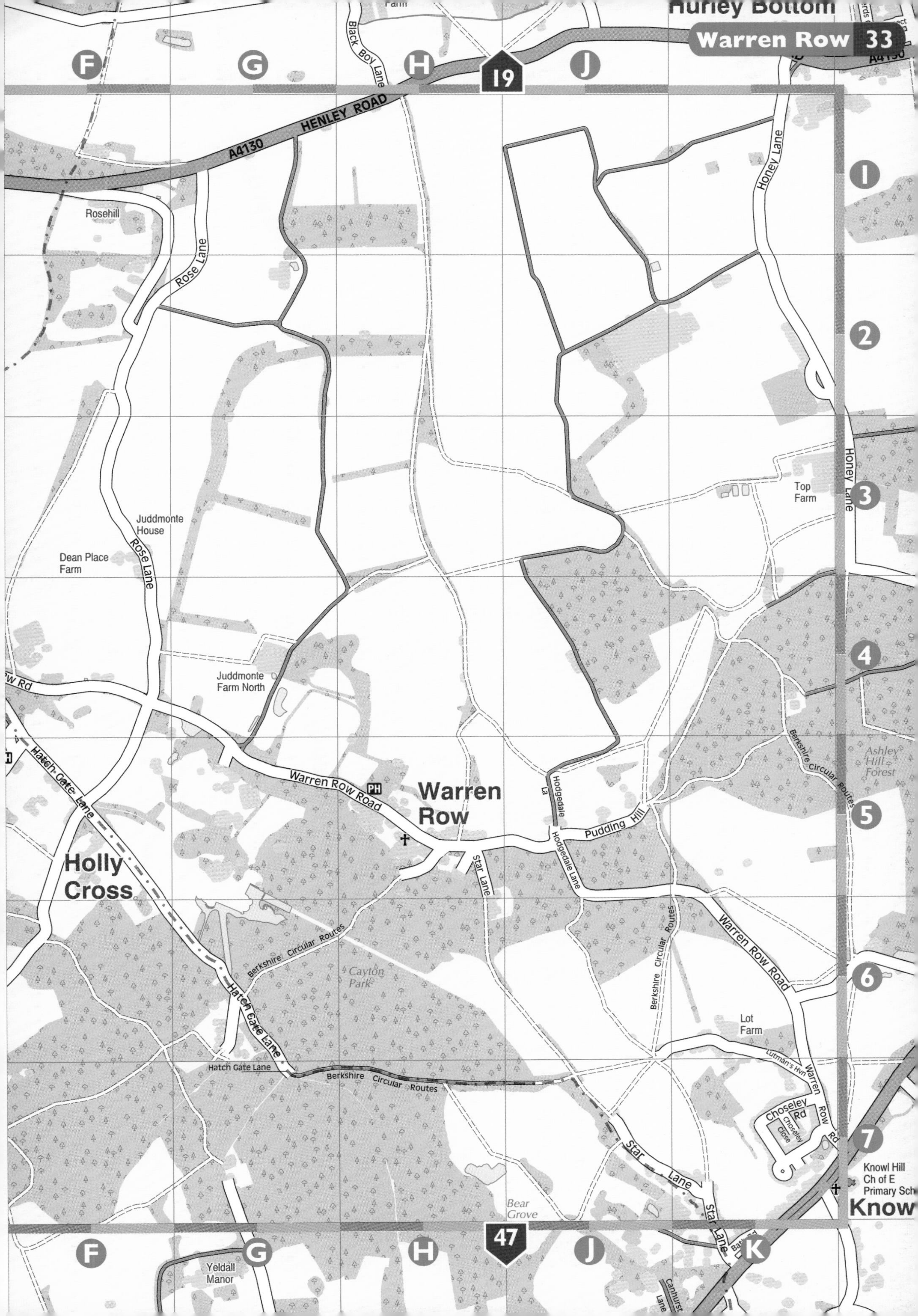

F   G   H   **19**   J

1

2

3

4

5

6

7

HENLEY ROAD

A4130

A4130

Rosehill

Rose Lane

Juddmonte
House

Dean Place
Farm

Rose Lane

Black Boy Lane

Farm

Honey Lane

Honey Lane

Top
Farm

Ashley
Hill
Forest

Juddmonte
Farm North

Warren Row Road

PH

**Warren
Row**

Holly
Cross

Hatch Gate Lane

Hatch Gate Lane

Hatch Gate Lane

Berkshire Circular Routes

Cayton
Park

Star Lane

Hodgedale Lane

Hodgedale Lane

Pudding Hill

La

Berkshire Circular Routes

Berkshire Circular Routes

Warren Row Road

Lot
Farm

Luenan's Hvn

Warren Row Rd

Choseley
Rd

Choseley
Close

Berkshire Circular Routes

Star Lane

Bear
Grove

Star Lane

Canhurst Lane

Knowl Hill
Ch of E
Primary Sch

Know

F   G   **47**   H   J   K

Yeldall
Manor

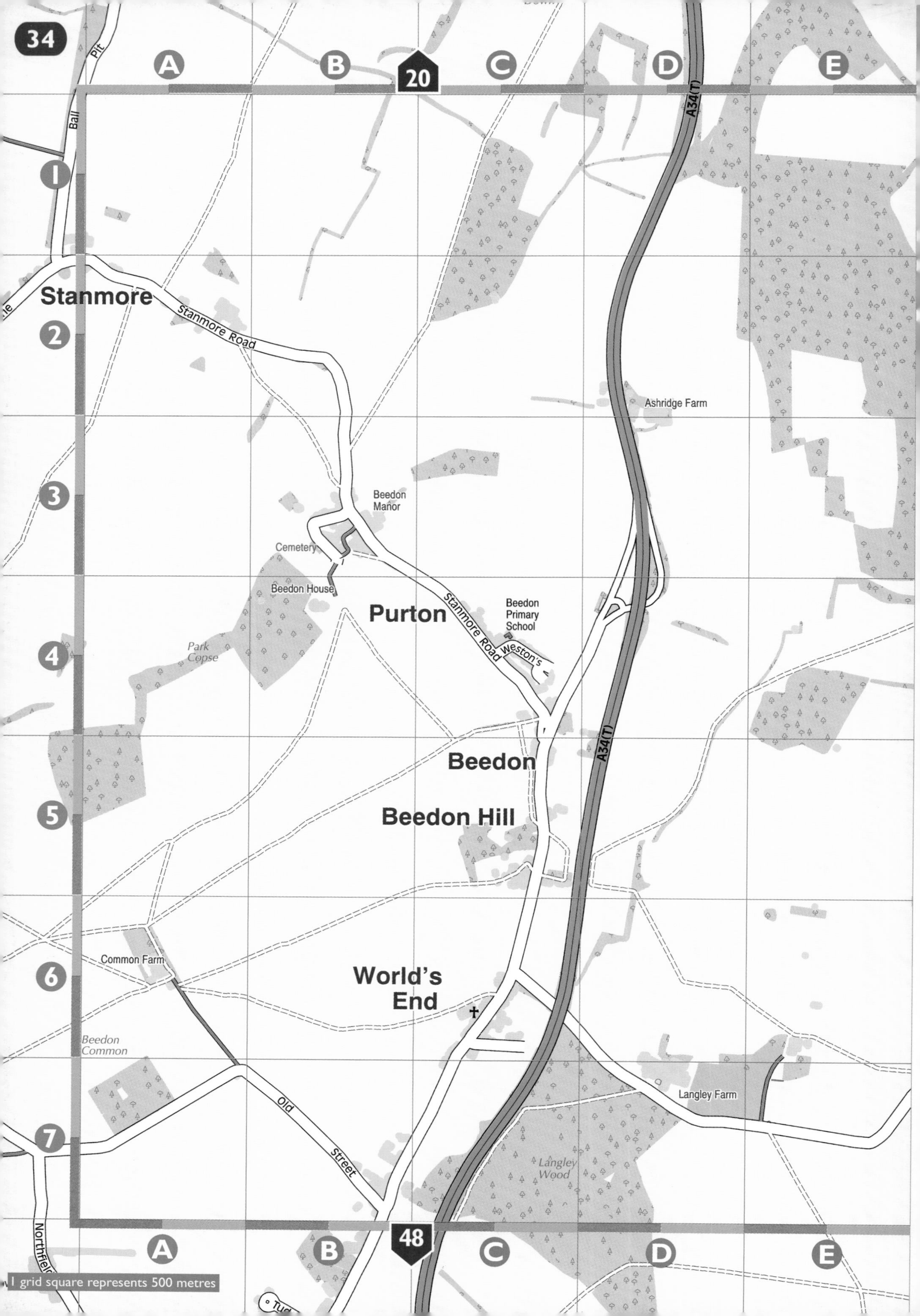

20
A
B
C
D
E
1
2
3
4
5
6
7
Ball
Pit
Stanmore
Stanmore Road
A34(T)
Ashridge Farm
Beedon
Manor
Cemetery
Beedon House
Purton
Stanmore Road
Beedon
Primary
School
Weston's
Park
Copse
Beedon
Beedon Hill
Common Farm
World's
End
Beedon
Common
Old
Street
Langley Farm
Langley
Wood
Northfield
48
1 grid square represents 500 metres

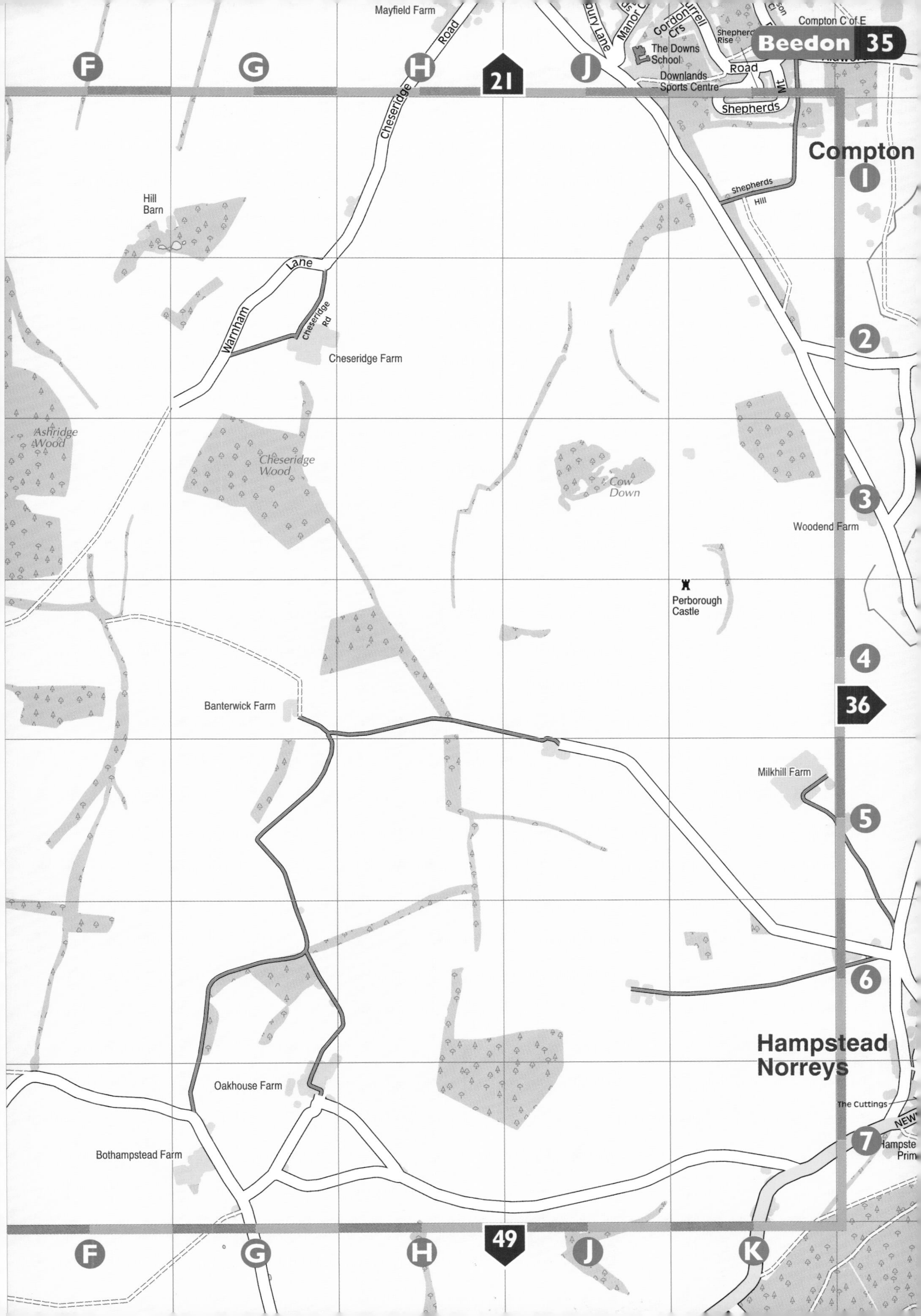

F

G

H

21

J

Mayfield Farm

Cheseridge Road

Gordon Crs

Manor C

Shepherds Rise

The Downs School

Downlands Sports Centre

Road

Shepherds

Compton C of E

Compton

1

Hill Barn

Warnham Lane

Cheseridge Rd

Cheseridge Farm

Shepherds Hill

2

Ashridge Wood

Cheseridge Wood

Cow Down

Woodend Farm

3

Perborough Castle

4

36

Banterwick Farm

Milkhill Farm

5

Oakhouse Farm

Hampstead Norreys

6

The Cuttings

NEW

Bothampstead Farm

Hampste Prim

7

F

G

49

H

J

K

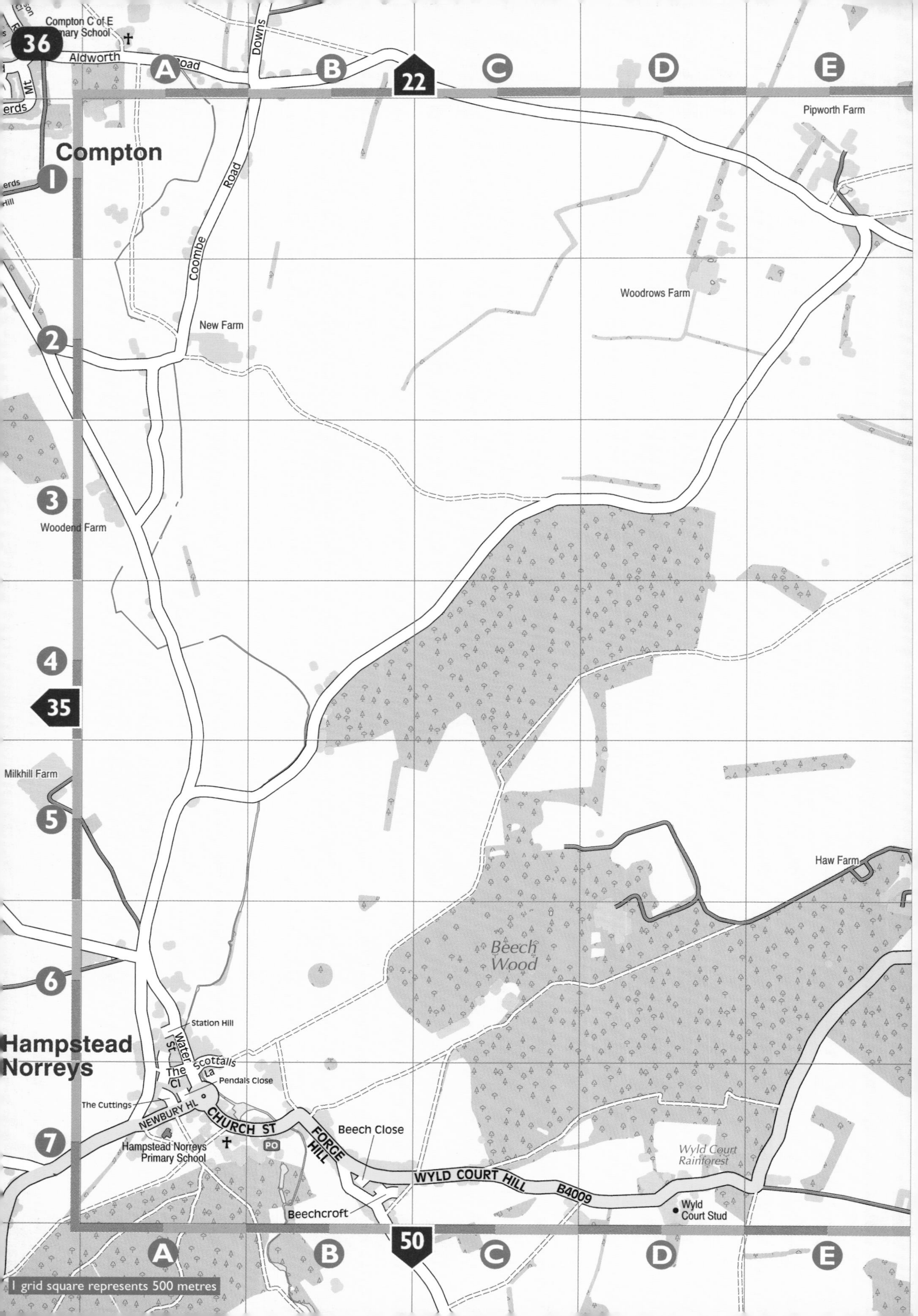
36
Compton C of E Primary School
Aldworth Road
Downs
22
A
B
C
D
E
Pipworth Farm
Compton
Coombe Road
Woodrows Farm
New Farm
1
2
3
4
5
6
7
Woodend Farm
35
Milkhill Farm
Haw Farm
Beech Wood
Station Hill
Water St
Hampstead Norreys
The Cl
Scottalls La
Pendals Close
The Cuttings
NEWBURY HL
CHURCH ST
FORGE HILL
Beech Close
Hampstead Norreys Primary School
PO
WYLD COURT HILL
B4009
Wyld Court Rainforest
Wyld Court Stud
Beechcroft
50
1 grid square represents 500 metres

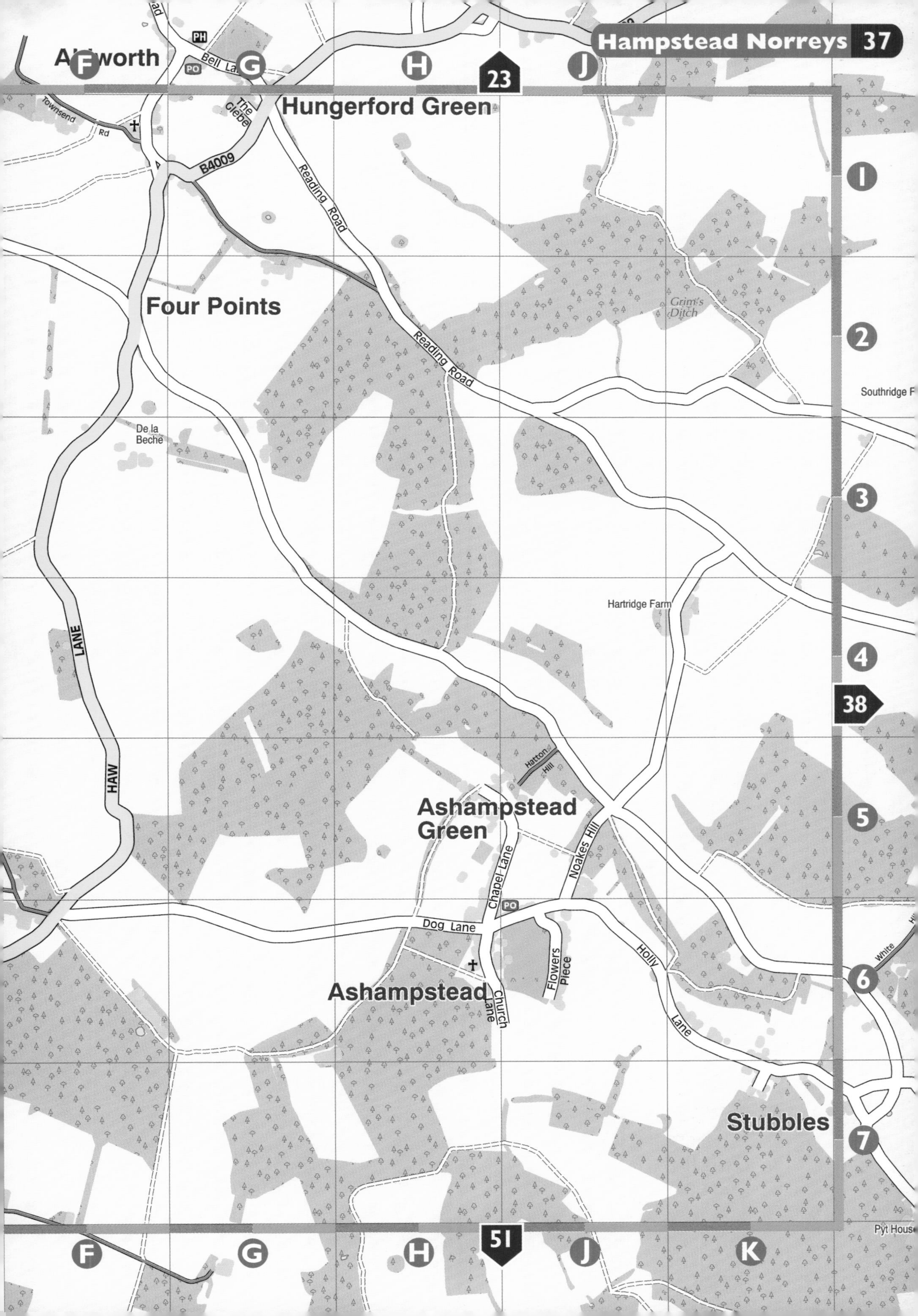

Ashworth

Bell La.

F **G** **H** 23 **J**

Townsend Rd

B4009

The Glebe

Reading Road

Hungerford Green

Four Points

De la Beche

LANE

HAW

Reading Road

Grim's Ditch

Southridge F

I

2

3

Hartridge Farm

4

38

Hatton Hill

Ashampstead Green

Chapel Lane

Noakes Hill

5

Dog Lane

PO

Flowers Piece

Holly Lane

White

6

Ashampstead

Church Lane

Stubbles

7

Pyt House

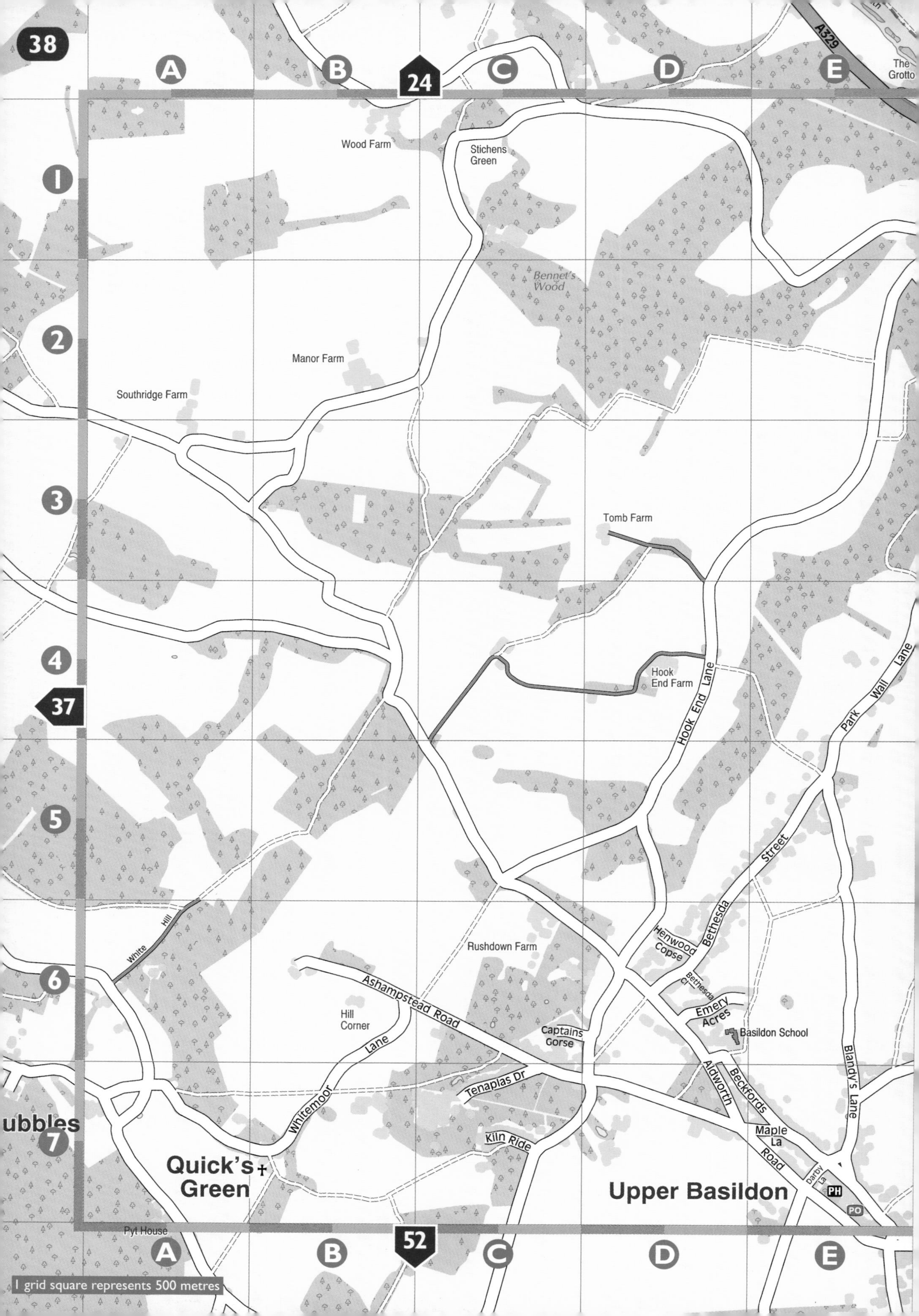
A
B
24
C
D
E
A329
The Grotto
1
2
3
4
37
5
6
7
Wood Farm
Stichens Green
Bennet's Wood
Manor Farm
Southridge Farm
Tomb Farm
Hook End Farm
Hook End Lane
Park Wall Lane
Street
Bethesda
Henwood Copse
Bethesda Cl
Emery Acres
Basildon School
Blandy's Lane
Rushdown Farm
White Hill
Ashampstead Road
Hill Corner
Lane
Whitemoor
Captains Gorse
Tenaplas Dr
Kiln Ride
Aldworth
Beckfords
Maple La
Road
Darby La
PH
PO
ubbles
Quick's Green
Upper Basildon
Pyt House
52
1 grid square represents 500 metres

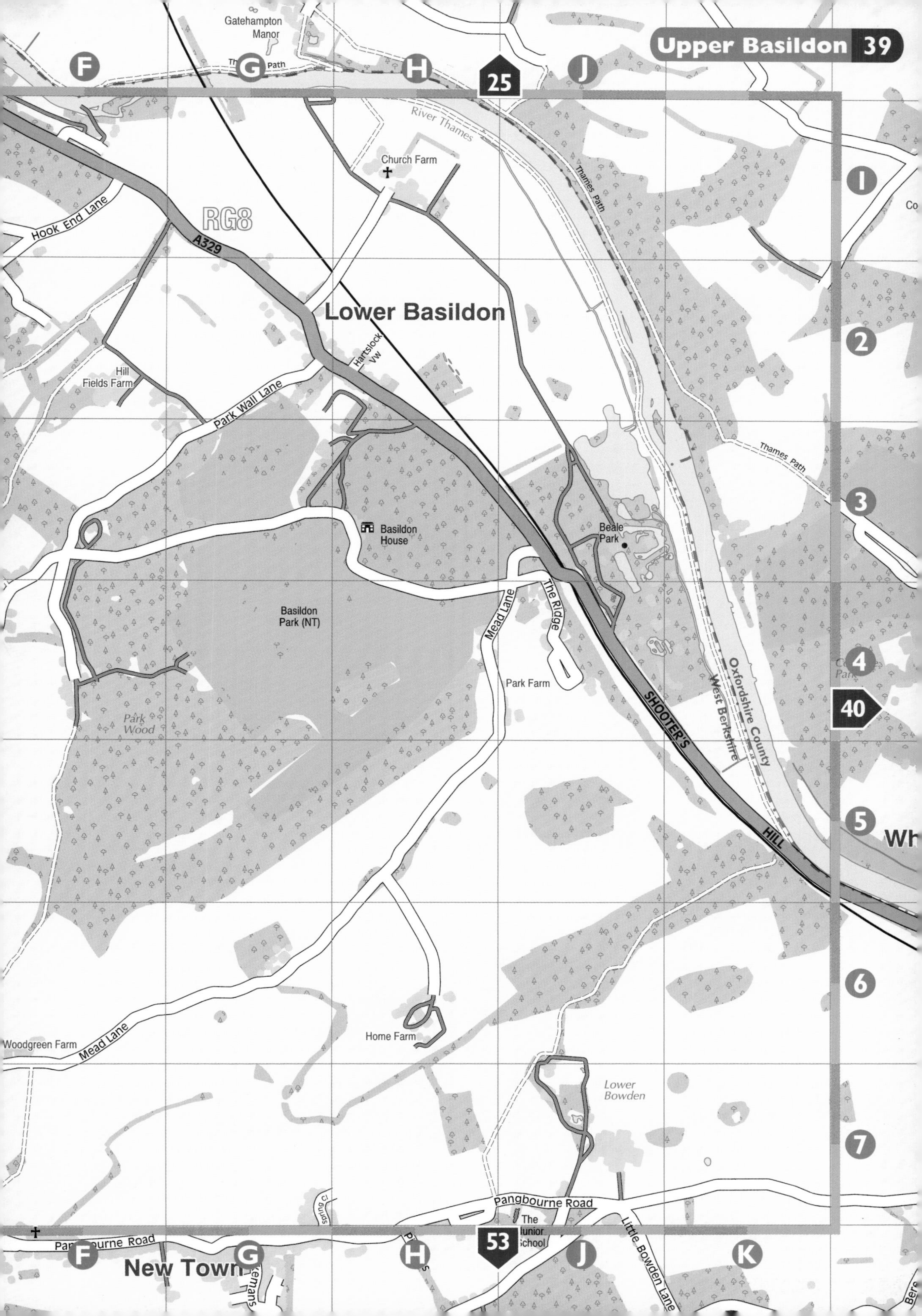

F G H **25** J

River Thames

Gatehampton Manor

The Path

Church Farm

I

Co

RG8

A329

Hook End Lane

Thames Path

Lower Basildon

Hill Fields Farm

Harslock Vw

2

Park Wall Lane

Thames Path

3

Basildon House

Beale Park

Park Wood

Basildon Park (NT)

Mead Lane

The Ridge

Park Farm

Oxfordshire County

West Berkshire

4

40

SHOOTER'S

5 Wh

HILL

Woodgreen Farm

Mead Lane

Home Farm

6

Lower Bowden

7

Pangbourne Road

The Junior School

53

F G H J K

Park Bourne Road

Little Bowden Lane

Bers

New Town

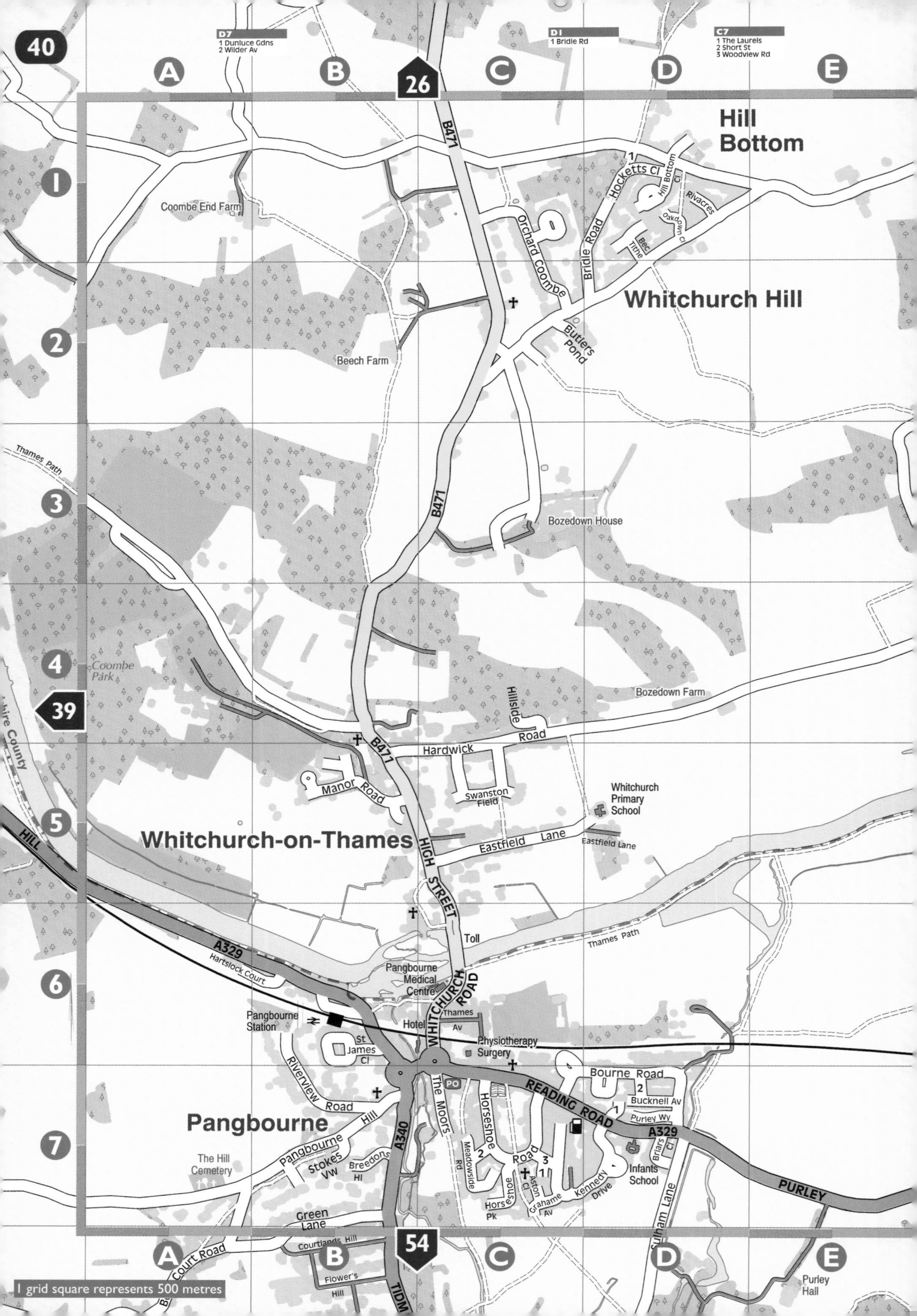

D7
1 Dunluce Gdns
2 Wilder Av

D1
1 Bridle Rd

C7
1 The Laurels
2 Short St
3 Woodview Rd

A   B   26   C   D   E

Hill
Bottom

1

Coombe End Farm

B471

Orchard Coombe

Bridle Road

Hocketts Cl

Hill Bottom Cl

Rivacres

Oakdown Cl

Beic Tithe

Whitchurch Hill

2

Beech Farm

Butler's Pond

Thames Path

3

B471

Bozedown House

4

Coombe Park

39

Bozedown Farm

B471

Hardwick

Hillside   Road

Whitchurch
Primary
School

Manor   Road

Swanston
Field

HILL

5

Whitchurch-on-Thames

Eastfield   Lane

Eastfield Lane

HIGH   STREET

Toll

Thames Path

A329

Hartslock Court

Pangbourne
Medical
Centre

WHITCHURCH   ROAD

6

Pangbourne
Station

Hotel

Thames
Av

Physiotherapy
Surgery

Bourne   Road

2

Bucknell Av

St James Cl

PO

Riverview   Road

The Moors

Horseshoe

Road

READING   ROAD

Purley Wy

Briars Cl

A329

7

Pangbourne

Pangbourne Hill

The Hill
Cemetery

Stokes
Vw

Breedons
Hl

A340

Meadowside   Rd

Horseshoe
Pk

Aston   Cl

Grahame
Av

1   3

Kennedy
Drive

Infants
School

PURLEY

Green
Lane

A   Court Road   B   54   C   D   E

Courtlands Hill

Flower's
Hill

TIDM

Purley
Hall

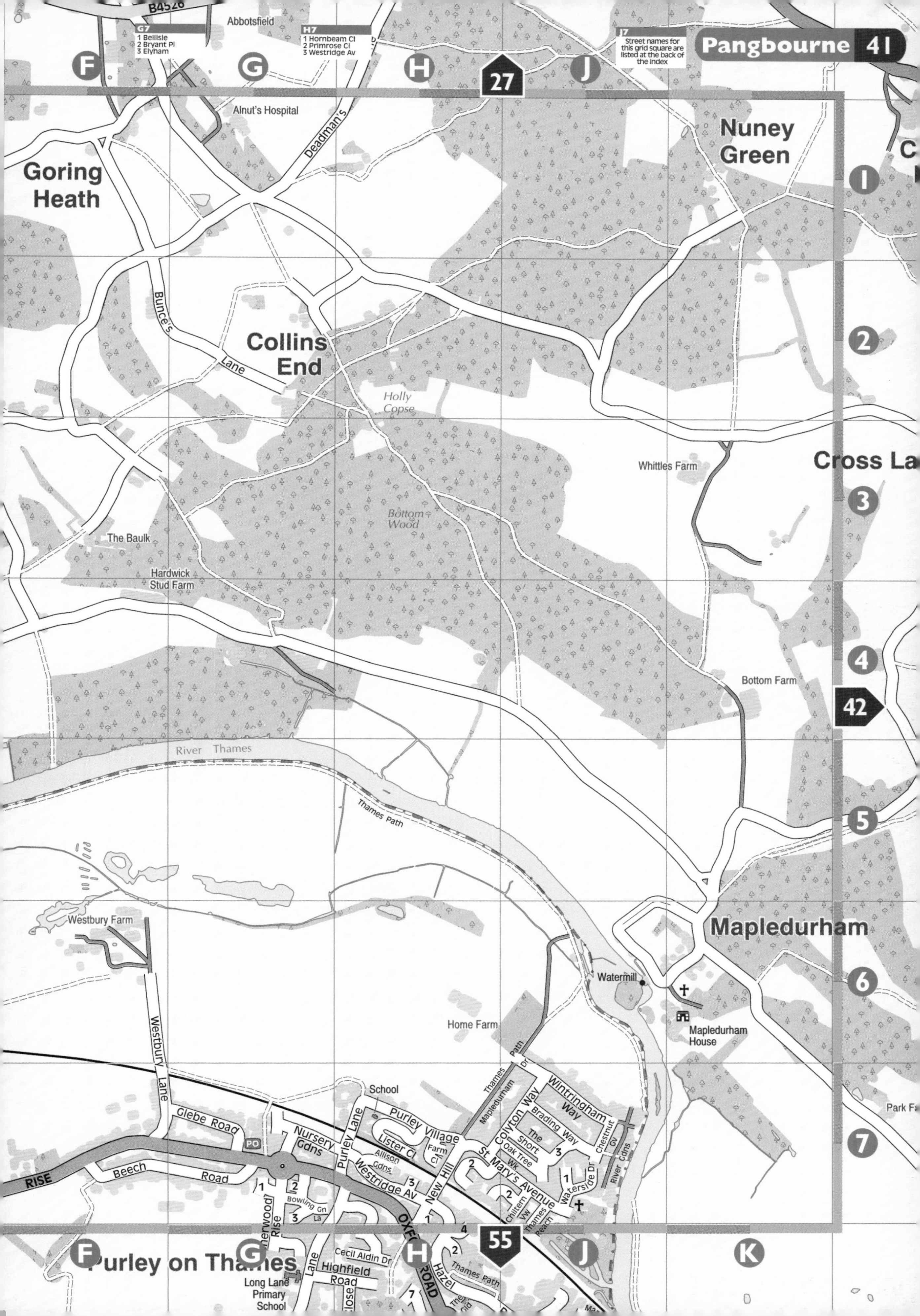

F

G

H

27

J

J7
Street names for
this grid square are
listed at the back of
the index

Nuney
Green

I

Goring
Heath

Alnut's Hospital

Abbotsfield

H7
1 Hornbeam Cl
2 Primrose Cl
3 Westridge Av

B4526

G7
1 Bellisle
2 Bryant Pl
3 Elyham

Cross La

2

Collins
End

Holly
Copse

Whittles Farm

3

Bottom
Wood

The Baulk

Bottom Farm

4

Hardwick
Stud Farm

42

River Thames

5

Thames Path

Westbury Farm

Mapledurham

6

Watermill

Mapledurham
House

Home Farm

School

7

Westbury Lane

Glebe Road

PO

Nursery
Gdns

Purley Lane

Purley Village

Lister Cl

Allison
Gdns

Wintringham Way

Colyton Way

Brading Way

The Short

Oak Tree Wk

Chestnut

River Gdns

Park F

RISE

Beech

Road

Sherwood Rise

Bowling Gn La

Westridge Av

New Hill

St Mary's Avenue

Waterside Dr

Whittern Vw

Thames Reach

Thames Path

OXF ROAD

Hazel

F **Purley on Thames**

G

Cecil Aldin Dr

Highfield
Road

Long Lane
Primary
School

H

55

J

K

55

OXF
ROAD

Thames Path

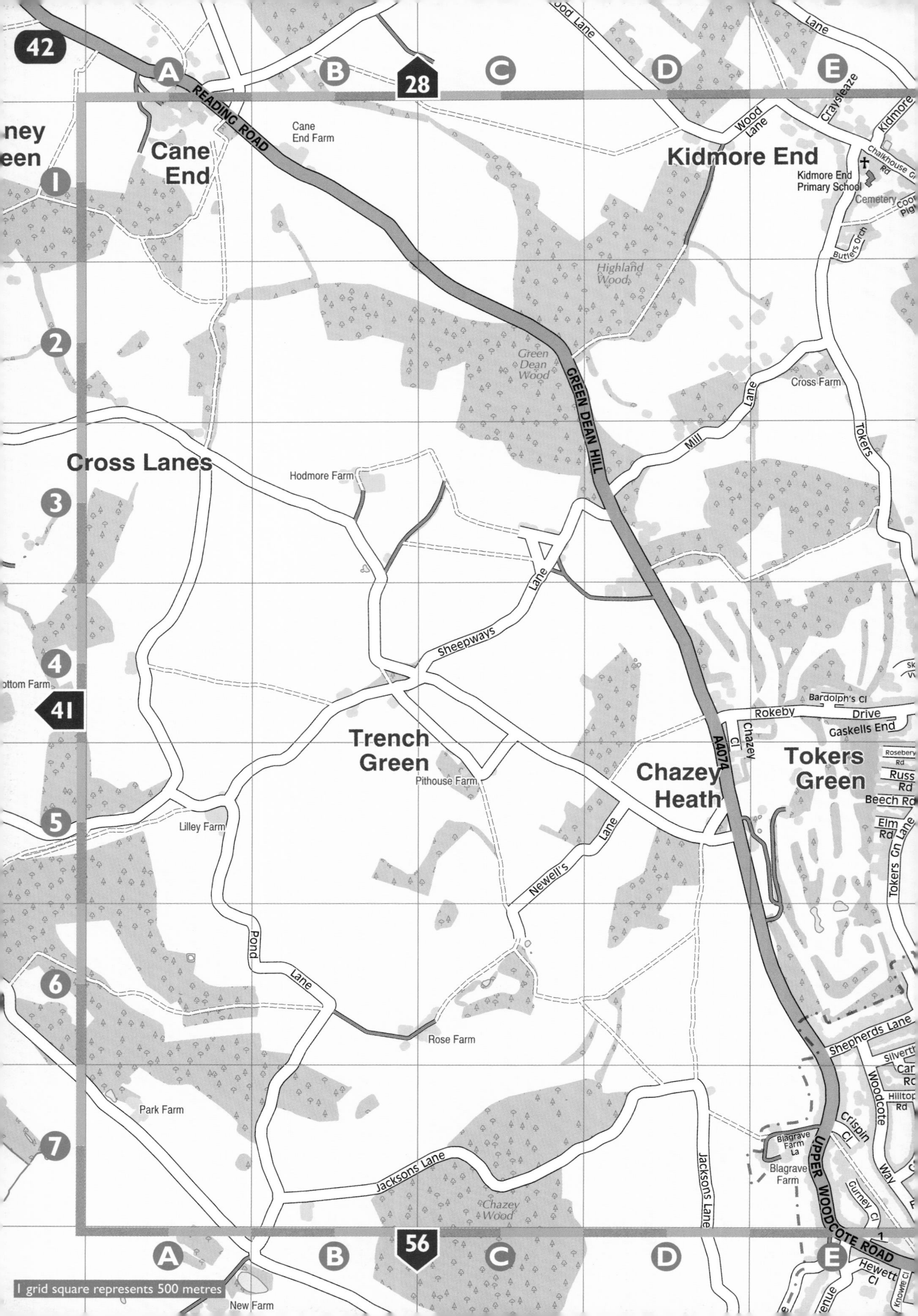
42
28
41
56
A
B
C
D
E
1
2
3
4
5
6
7
READING ROAD
GREEN DEAN HILL
A4074
UPPER WOODCOTE ROAD
Cane End
Cane End Farm
Kidmore End
Kidmore End Primary School
Cemetery
Highland Wood
Green Dean Wood
Cross Farm
Cross Lanes
Hodmore Farm
Mill Lane
Tokers
Sheepways Lane
Trench Green
Pithouse Farm
Chazey Heath
Chazey Cl
Rokeby Drive
Bardolph's Cl
Gaskells End
Tokers Green
Beech Rd
Elm Rd
Tokers Gn Lane
Lilley Farm
Newell's Lane
Pond Lane
Rose Farm
Shepherds Lane
Woodcote Way
Crispin Cl
Blagrave Farm La
Blagrave Farm
Park Farm
Jacksons Lane
Chazey Wood
Gurney Cl
Hewett Cl
Wood Lane
Craysleaze
Kidmore
Chalkhouse Gn Rd
Butlers Orch
Rosebery Rd
Russ Rd
Hilltop Rd
New Farm
1 grid square represents 500 metres

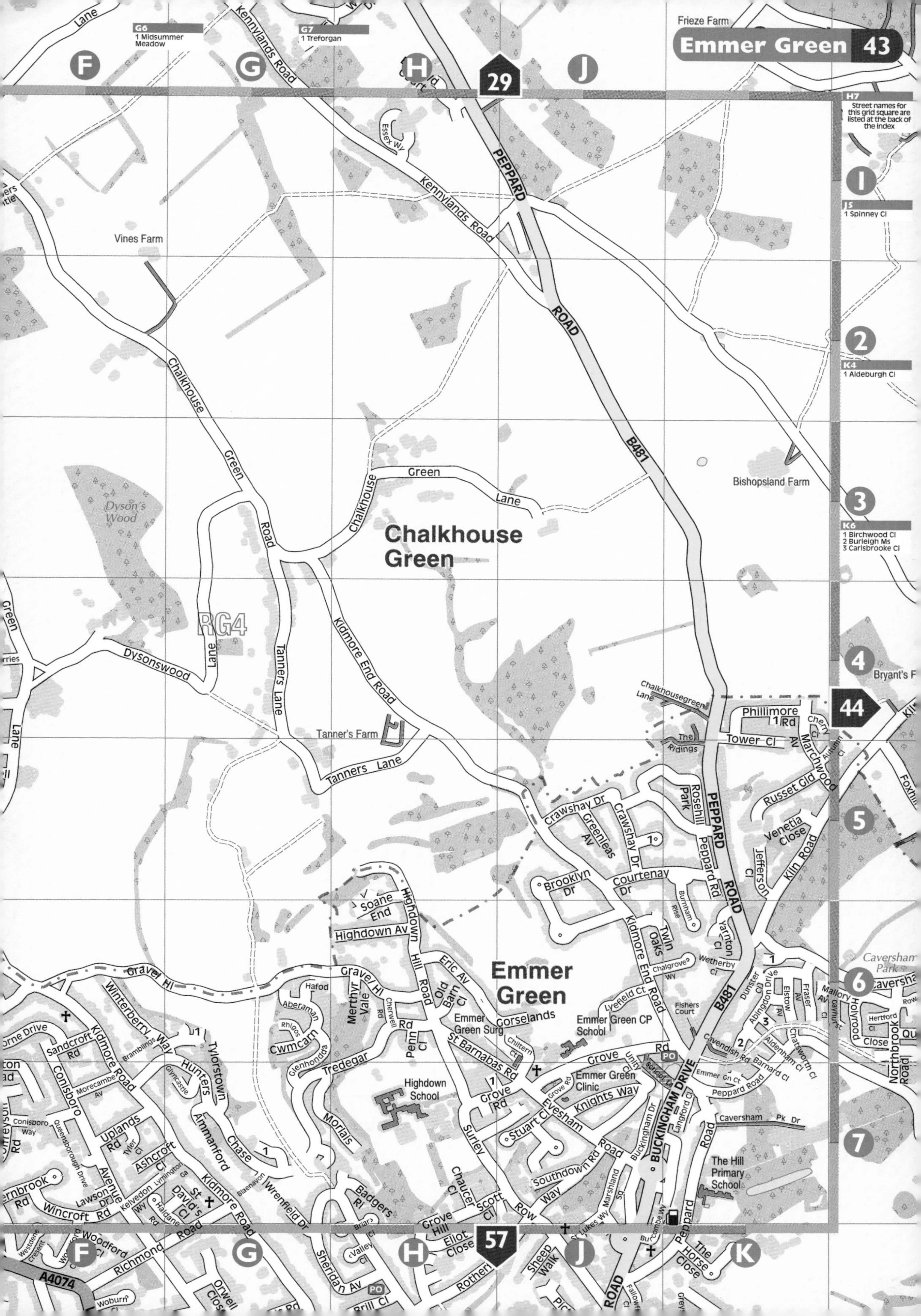

F G H 29 J

Lane

Frieze Farm

I

2

3

Vines Farm

Essex Wy

Kennylands Road

Kennylands Road

PEPPARD

ROAD

B481

Bishopsland Farm

Chalkhouse Green

Green Lane

Chalkhouse Green

Dyson's Wood

RG4

Dysonswood Lane

Chalkhouse Green Road

Tanners Lane

Kidmore End Road

Tanner's Farm

Tanners Lane

4

Bryant's F

Chalkhousegreen Lane

44

Phillimore Rd

The R'dings

Tower Cl

Cherry

Marchwood

Autumn Av

Russet Gld

Peppard Park

Rosehill

Peppard Rd

PEPPARD

ROAD

Venetia Close

Jefferson Cl

Kiln Road

Foxhi

5

Kll

Crawshay Dr

Greenleas Av

Crawshay Dr

Courtenay Dr

Brooklyn Dr

7

Burnham Rise

Highdown

Soane End

Highdown Av

Highdown Hill Road

Gravel Hi

Gravel Hi

Eric Av

Old Barn Cl

Emmer Green

Kidmore End Road

Twin Oaks Cl

Chalgrove Wy

Wetherby Cl

Yarnton Cl

B481

Dunster Cl

Abingdon Drive

Elstow

Fraser Av

Mallory

Caversham Park

Caversha

6

Caversh

Gravel Hi

Winterberry Way

Hafod

Aberaman

Rhigos

Cwmcam

Glenhonddu

Merthyr Vale

Cherwell Rd

Penn Cl

Tredegar

Emmer Green Surg

Gorselands

St Barnabas Rd

Chiltern Cl

Emmer Green CP School

Lyefield Ct Rd

Fishers Court

1

Cavendish Rd

Charnworth Cl

Aldenham Cl

Barnard Cl

2

3

Emmer Gn Ct

Hertford Cl

Holyrood Cl

Northbrook

Qu

Borders La

PO

Orne Drive

Sandcroft Rd

Kidmore Road

Bramblings

Conisboro Av

Morecambe Av

Hunters Chase

Givnestne

Uplands Rd

Ashcroft Cl

St David's Cl

Tyler

Kelvedon

Lymington Ga

Haldane

Tylorstown

Ammanford

Kidmore Road

Blaenavon

Wrenfield Dr

1

Highdown School

Morlais

Grove Rd

Surley

Stuart

Evesham

Knights Way

Grove

Rd

Grove Cl

Emmer Green Clinic

Unity Cl

Langford Cl

Buckingham Dr

BUCKINGHAM DRIVE

Peppard Rd

Caversham Pk Dr

Peppard Road

The Hill Primary School

7

Conisboro Way

Lawson Dr

Queensborough Drive

Wincroft Rd

Woodford Cl

Westdene Crescent

WS

Richmond Road

Woburn

Sheridan Av

Orwell Close

PO

Brill Cl

Badgers Rl

Briar C

Valley

Rother

Chaucer Cl

Grove Hill

Eliot Close

57

Scott Row

Southdown Wy

Marshland

Southdown Rd

Sheep Walk

St Lukes Wy

Burcombe Wy

Fallowfi

Pic

Peppard Road

Greyf

The Horse Close

Grey

F G H J K

A4074

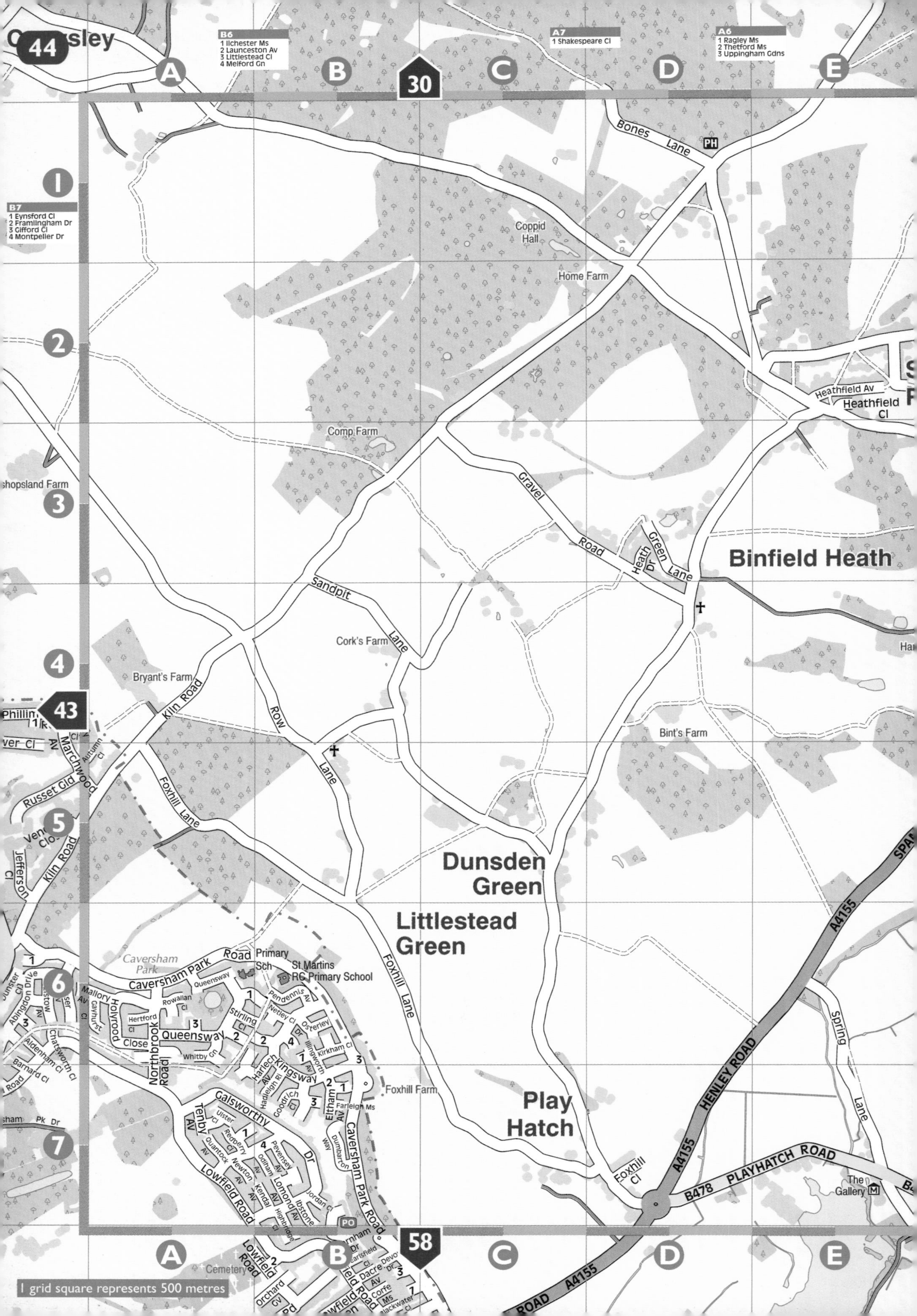

44
30
43
58
B6
1 Ilchester Ms
2 Launceston Av
3 Littlestead Cl
4 Melford Gn
A7
1 Shakespeare Cl
A6
1 Ragley Ms
2 Thetford Ms
3 Uppingham Gdns
B7
1 Eynsford Cl
2 Framlingham Dr
3 Gifford Cl
4 Montpellier Dr
Bones Lane
Coppid Hall
Home Farm
Heathfield Av
Heathfield Cl
Comp Farm
Gravel Road
Heath Dr
Green Lane
Binfield Heath
Sandpit Lane
Cork's Farm
Bryant's Farm
Kiln Road
Row Lane
Bint's Farm
Marchwood
Russet Gld
Foxhill Lane
Jefferson Cl
Kiln Road
Dunsden Green
Littlestead Green
Caversham Park
Caversham Park Road
Primary Sch
St Martins RC Primary School
Queensway
Holyrood Close
Northbrook Road
Kingsway
Galsworthy Dr
Foxhill Farm
Play Hatch
Foxhill Cl
A4155
HENLEY ROAD
Spring Lane
B478 PLAYHATCH ROAD
The Gallery
Lowfield Road
Caversham Park Road
Cemetery
1 grid square represents 500 metres

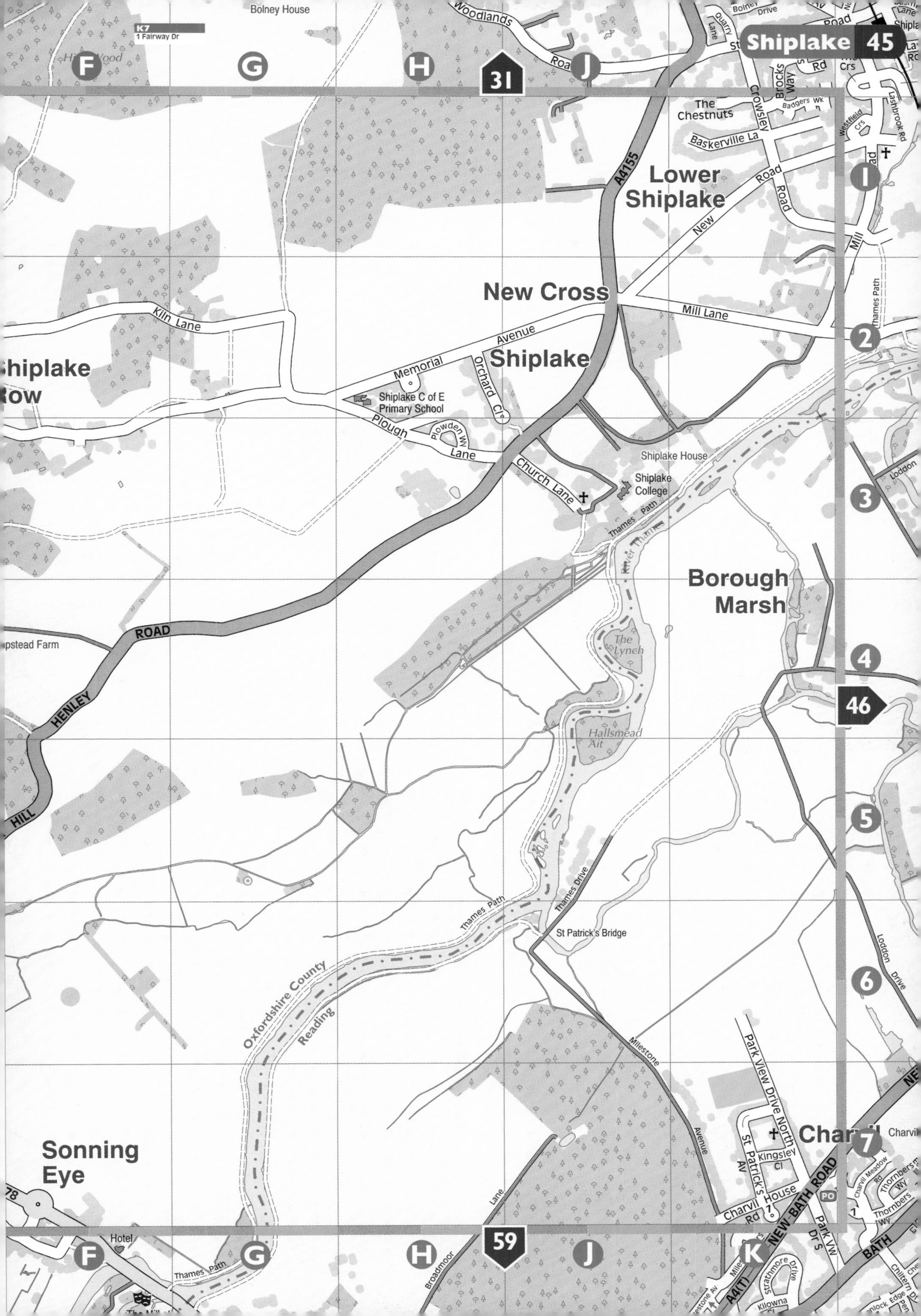

Bolney House

Woodlands Road

K7
1 Fairway Dr

Hi Wood

F

G

H

31

J

The Chestnuts

Crowsley

Badgers Wk

Blocks

Westfield Crs

Lashbrook Rd

I

Baskerville La

Lower Shiplake

A4155

New Road

Road

Mill

Thames Path

New Cross

Mill Lane

2

Kiln Lane

Avenue

Memorial

Shiplake Row

Orchard Cl

Shiplake

Shiplake C of E Primary School

Plough Lane

Plowden Wy

Church Lane

Shiplake House

Shiplake College

Thames Path

3

Loddon

River Thames

Borough Marsh

ROAD

HENLEY HILL

pstead Farm

The Lynch

4

46

Hallsmead Ait

5

Thames Drive

Oxfordshire County

Reading

Thames Path

St Patrick's Bridge

Loddon Drive

6

Milestone

Park View Drive North

Charv

Charvi

Sonning Eye

Avenue

St Patrick's Av

Kingsley Cl

Charvil House

PO

Charvil Meadow Rd

Thornbers Wy

Thornbers

7

78

Hotel

Thames Path

Broadmoor Lane

F

G

H

59

J

Charvil House Rd

strattsmore drive

A4(T)

Kilowna

NEW BATH ROAD

Park VW Dr S

BATH

NE

K

Milestone Av

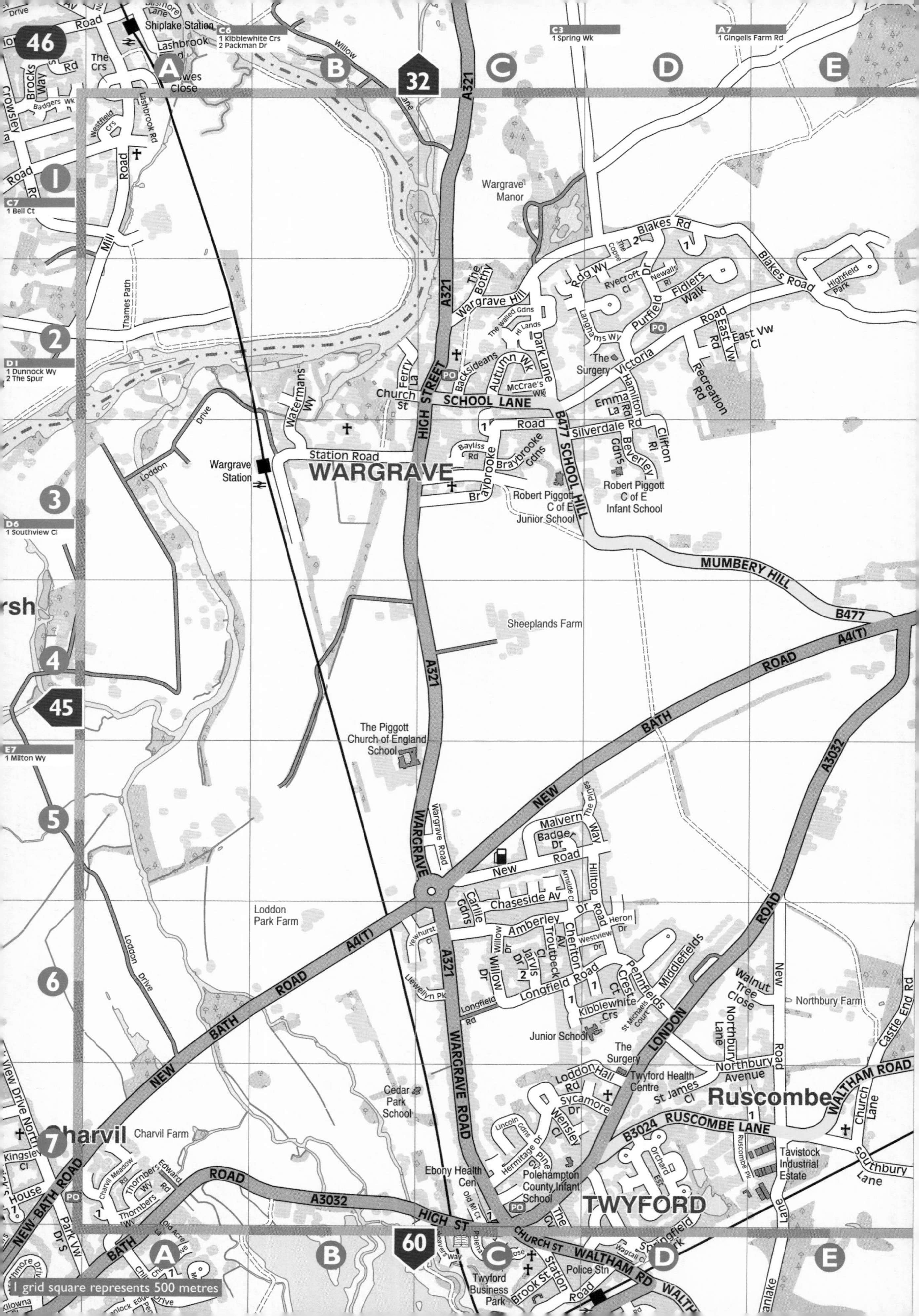

Page content (map):

46

The Crs
Shiplake Station
Lashbrook
Lawes Close

C6
1 Kibblewhite Crs
2 Packman Dr

C3
1 Spring Wk

A7
1 Gingells Farm Rd

32

Wargrave Manor

Blakes Rd

Blakes Road

Highfield Park

The Copse

Rdg Wy
Ryecroft Cl

Newalls
Rl

Fidlers Walk

Purfield Road
East Vw Rd
East Vw Cl

PO

The Bothy

The Walled Gdns
Ht Lands

Wargrave Hill

Dark Lane

Langhams Wy

The Surgery

Victoria

Recreation Rd

Hamilton Rd

Autumn Wk

Ferry La
Church St

PO

Backsideans
McCrae's Wk

SCHOOL LANE

Emma La

Clifton Gdns

Beverley

Silverdale Rd

Road

Bayliss Rd

Braybrooke Gdns

Braybrooke

Robert Piggott C of E Junior School

Robert Piggott C of E Infant School

SCHOOL HILL

B477

Watermans Wy

Station Road
Wargrave Station

WARGRAVE

MUMBERY HILL

B477

Sheeplands Farm

A4(T)

BATH
ROAD

A3032

2

D1
1 Dunnock Wy
2 The Spur

3

D6
1 Southview Cl

4

45

E7
1 Milton Wy

5

The Piggott Church of England School

A321

Wargrave Road

6

Loddon Park Farm

A4(T)
NEW
BATH
ROAD

Loddon Drive

NEW
Malvern
Badger Dr
Road

New

The Gauld Wy

Way

Hilltop Dr

Hilltop Road

Heron Dr

Westview Dr

Pemmberfields

Middlefields

Walnut Tree Close

Northbury Pk

Northbury Farm

New Road

Castle End Rd

Carlile Gdns

Chaseside Av

Amberley Av

Cheriton Troubeck Cl

Crest Cl

St Michaels Court

LONDON ROAD

Northbury Avenue

A3032

Yewhurst

Willow Dr

Jarvis Dr
2

Longfield Road

Kibblewhite Crs

ROAD

Ruscombe

Llewellyn Pk

Longfield Rd

Junior School

The Surgery

Twyford Health Centre

St James Cl

Sycamore Dr

Wensley Dr

Loddon Hall Rd

WALTHAM ROAD

Church Lane

Southbury Lane

7 Charvil

Charvil Farm

Cedar Park School

Lincoln Gdns

Hermitage Dr

Pine Dr

Polehampton County Infant School

B3024 RUSCOMBE LANE

Ruscombe La

Tavistock Industrial Estate

Orchard Est

View Drive North

Kingsley Cl

House

NEW BATH ROAD

PO

Charvil Meadow Rd

Thornbers Wy
Edward Rd
1
Thornbers

Park Vw

A

BATH

B

60

HIGH ST

Old Mill

Ebony Health Cen

polenta

WARGRAVE ROAD

Twyford Business Park

Brook St

Wagtail Cl

CHURCH ST

TWYFORD

C

Police Stn

Station Road

WALTHAM RD

Springfield

D

WALTH

E

A321

HIGH STREET

1 grid square represents 500 metres

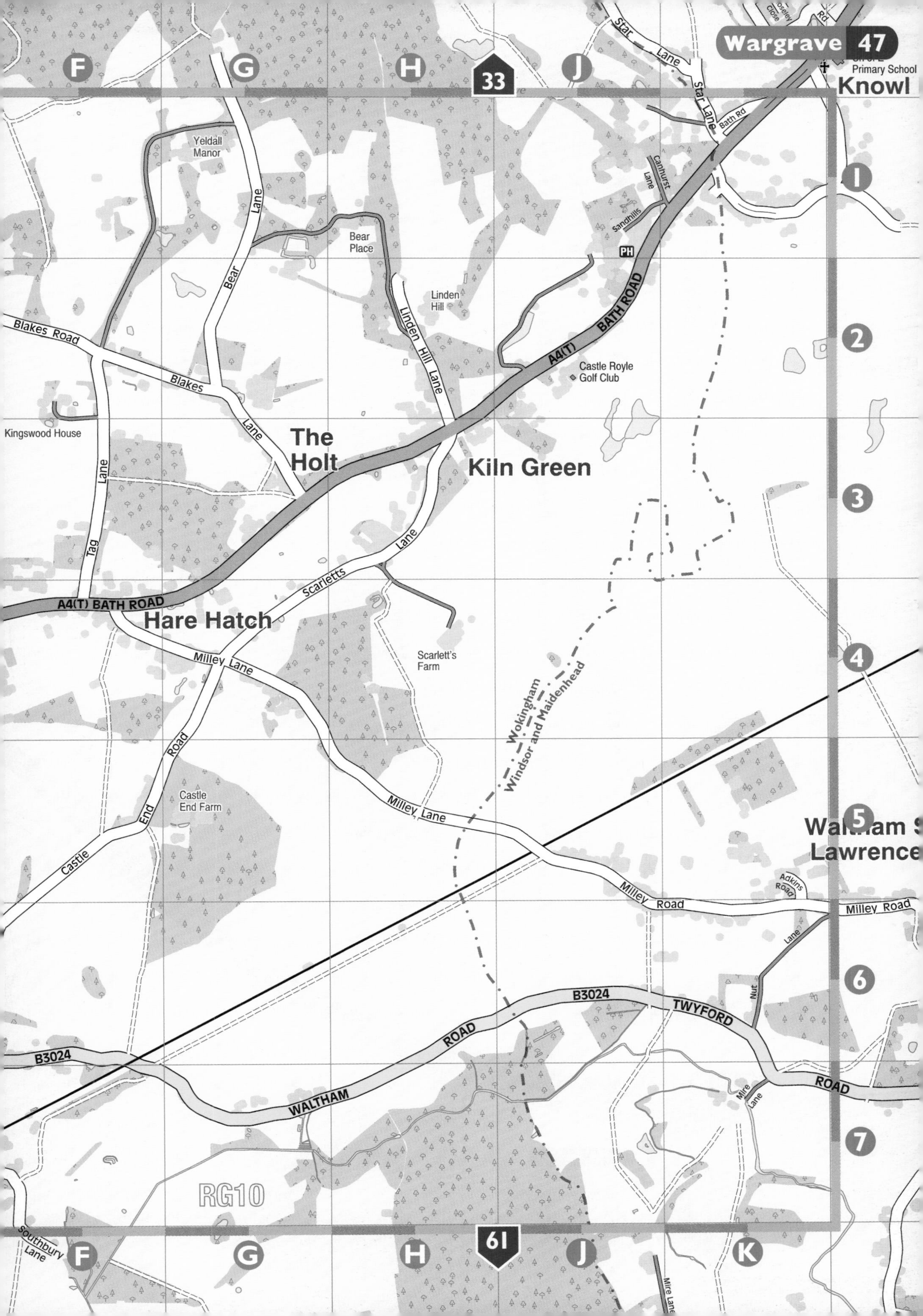

F G H 33 J

Knowl

Star Lane

St. † Primary School

I

Yeldall
Manor

Bear
Place

Bear Lane

Linden
Hill

Canhurst Lane

Sandhills

PH

BATH ROAD

2

Blakes Road

Linden Hill Lane

A4(T)

Castle Royle
◆ Golf Club

Kingswood House

Blakes Lane

**The
Holt**

Kiln Green

3

Tag Lane

Scarletts Lane

Scarlett's
Farm

Wokingham
Windsor and Maidenhead

4

A4(T) BATH ROAD

Hare Hatch

Milley Lane

5

Castle End Road

Castle
End Farm

Milley Lane

Wal\tham St
Lawrence

Adkins Road

Castle

Milley Road

Milley Road

Nut Lane

6

B3024

TWYFORD

B3024

WALTHAM ROAD

ROAD

Mire Lane

7

B3024

RG10

Southbury Lane

F G H 61 J K

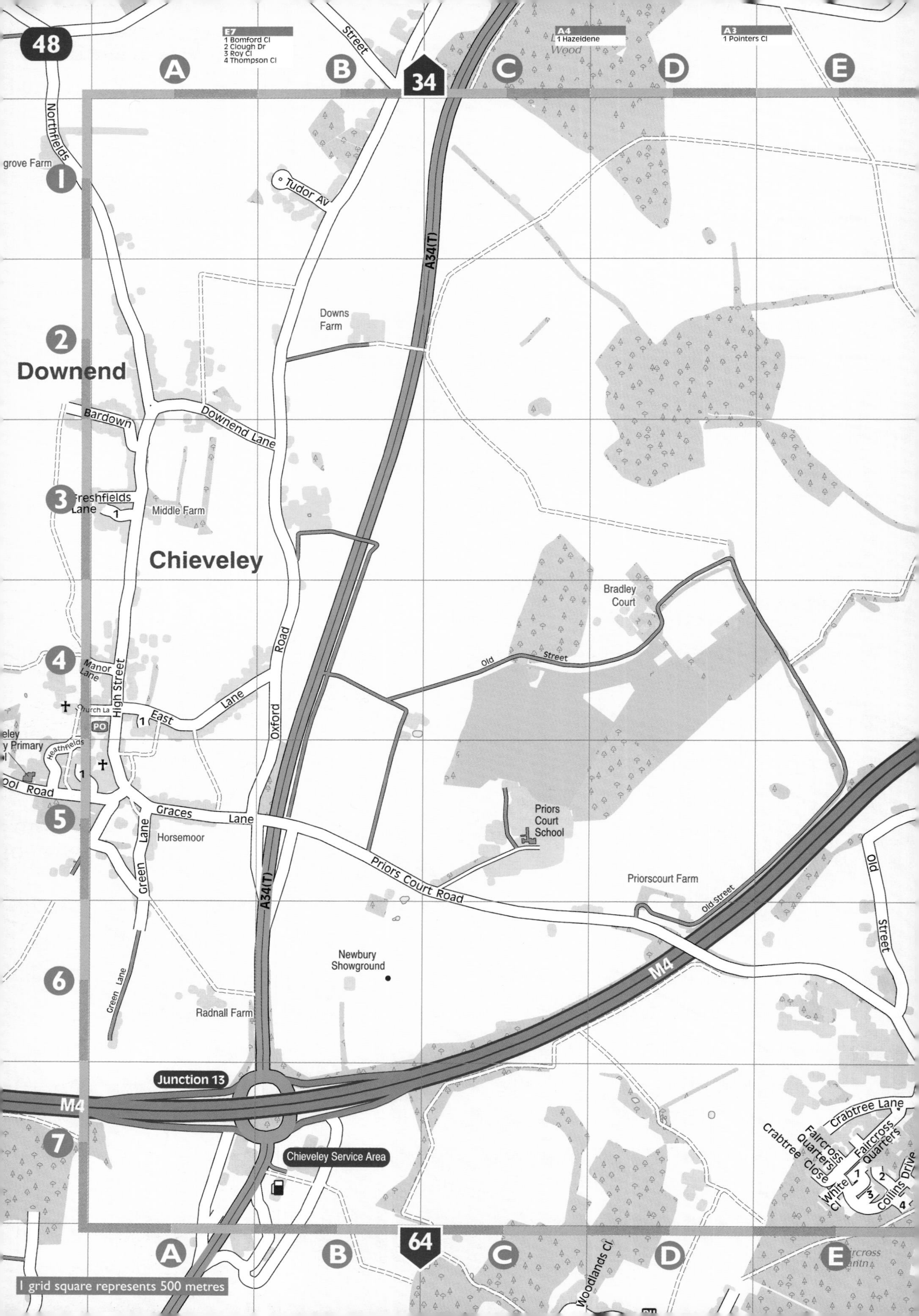
48
E7
1 Bomford Cl
2 Clough Dr
3 Roy Cl
4 Thompson Cl
A4
1 Hazeldene
A3
1 Pointers Cl
34
A
B
C
D
E
Street
Wood
Northfields
grove Farm
1
Tudor Av
A34(T)
Downs
Farm
2
Downend
Bardown
Downend Lane
3
Freshfields
Lane
Middle Farm
Chieveley
Bradley
Court
4
Manor
Lane
High Street
Road
Old
Street
Church La
East
Lane
Oxford
PO
Heathfields
1
Priors
Court
School
Road
Graces
Lane
5
Horsemoor
Green
Lane
A34(T)
Priors Court Road
Priorscourt Farm
Old Street
Old
Street
Newbury
Showground
M4
6
Green Lane
Radnall Farm
Junction 13
M4
Crabtree Lane
Faircross
Quarters
Crabtree Close
7
Chieveley Service Area
White
Cl
Collins Drive
64
Woodlands Cl
1 grid square represents 500 metres

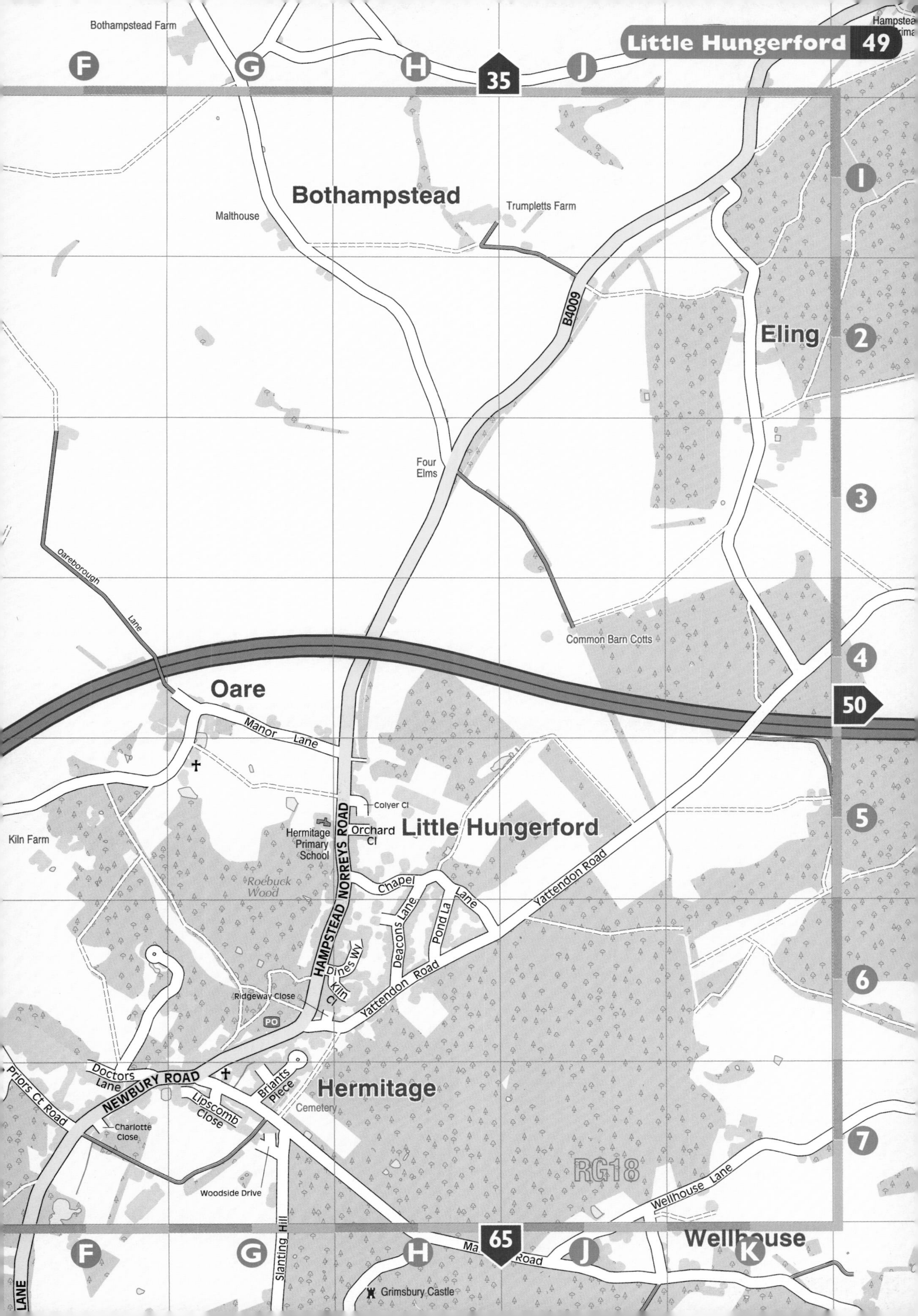

F G H 35 J I

Bothampstead Farm

Hampstead

Bothampstead

Malthouse

Trumpletts Farm

Eling 2

B4009

3

Four
Elms

Common Barn Cotts

4

Oare 50

Manor Lane

5

Colyer Ct

Hermitage
Primary
School

Orchard
Ct

Little Hungerford

Kiln Farm

Roebuck
Wood

Chapel Lane

Yattendon Road

HAMPSTEAD NORREYS ROAD

Deacons Lane

Pond La

6

Dines Wy

Kiln Ct

Yattendon Road

Ridgeway Close

PO

Priors Ct Road

Doctors
Lane

NEWBURY ROAD

Charlotte
Close

Lipscomb
Close

Briants
Piece

Cemetery

Hermitage

7

Woodside Drive

RG18

Wellhouse Lane

LANE

F G H 65 Ma Road J K Wellhouse

Grimsbury Castle

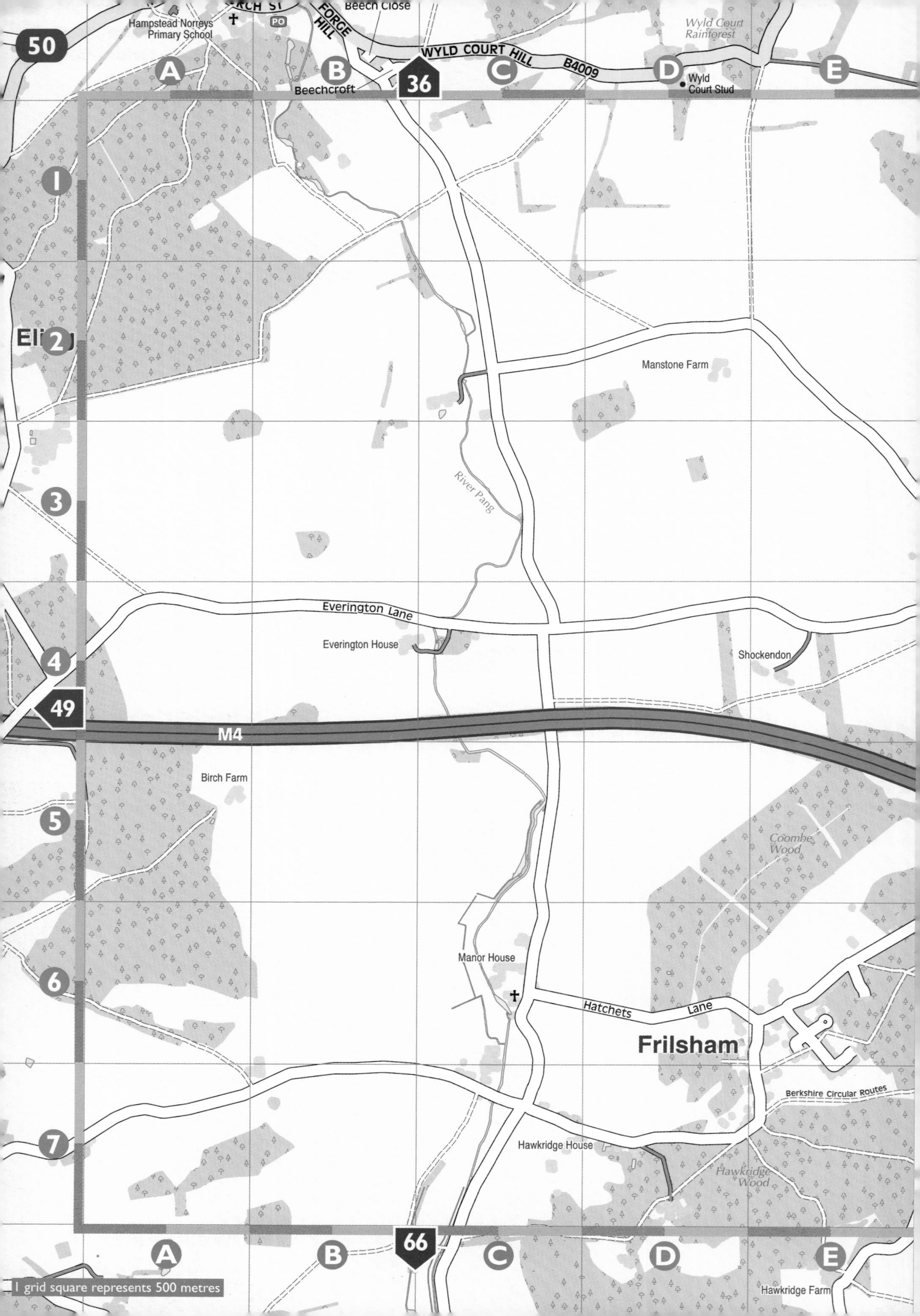

50

A   **B**   **C**   **D**   **E**

Hampstead Norreys Primary School

RCH ST

Beech Close

Beechcroft

FORGE HILL

WYLD COURT HILL   B4009

36

Wyld Court Rainforest

Wyld Court Stud

I

Eli **2**

3

Manstone Farm

River Pang

Everington Lane

Everington House

Shockendon

4

49

M4

Birch Farm

5

Coombe Wood

6

Manor House

Hatchets   Lane

Frilsham

7

Hawkridge House

Berkshire Circular Routes

Hawkridge Wood

Hawkridge Farm

66

A   **B**   **C**   **D**   **E**

I grid square represents 500 metres

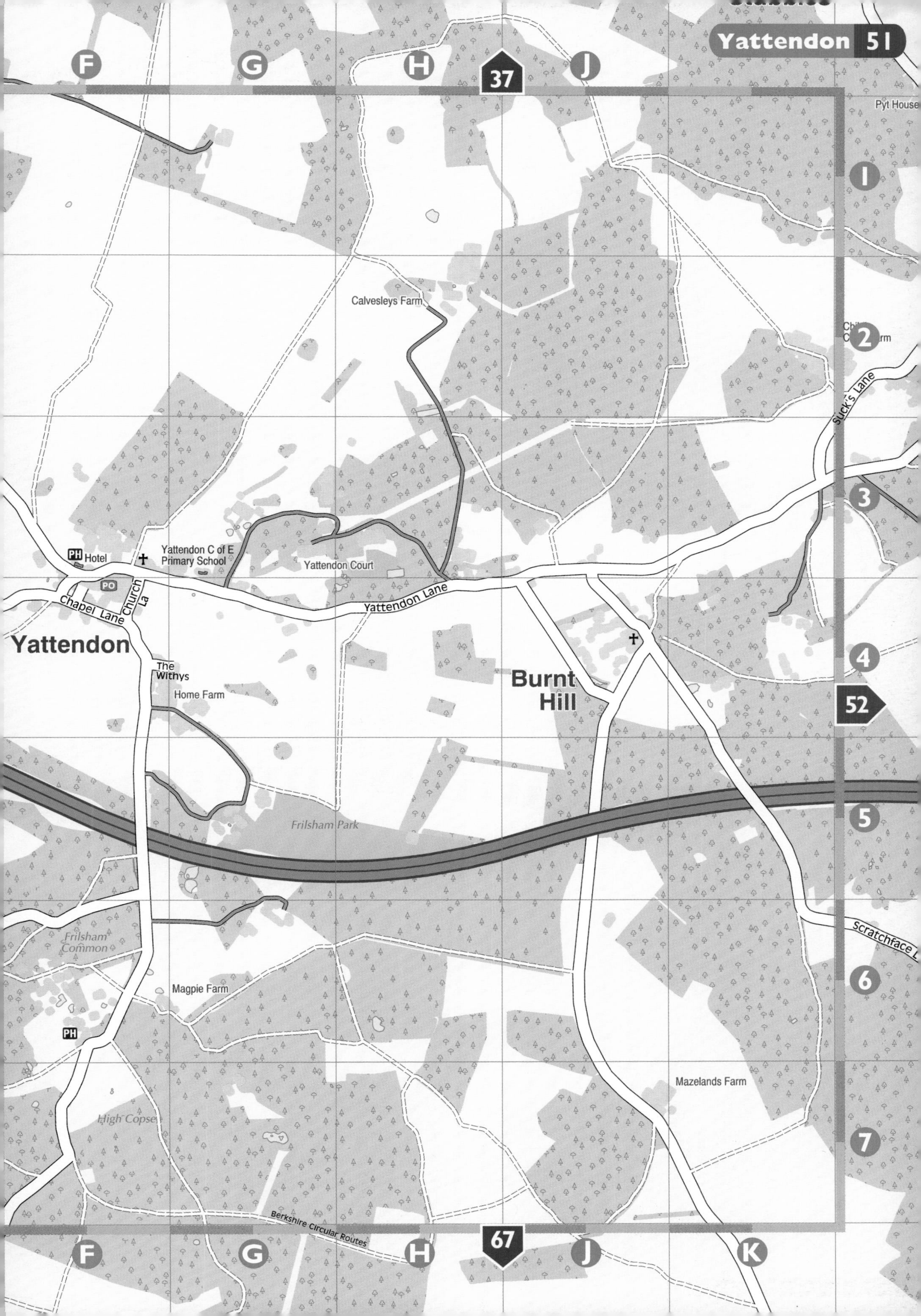
F
G
H
37
J
Pyt House
1
Calvesleys Farm
2
Suck's Lane
3
PH Hotel
Yattendon C of E
Primary School
Yattendon Court
PO
Chapel Lane
Church La
Yattendon Lane
Yattendon
The Withys
Home Farm
Burnt Hill
4
52
Frilsham Park
5
Frilsham Common
Scratchface L
Magpie Farm
6
PH
Mazelands Farm
High Copse
7
Berkshire Circular Routes
F
G
H
67
J
K

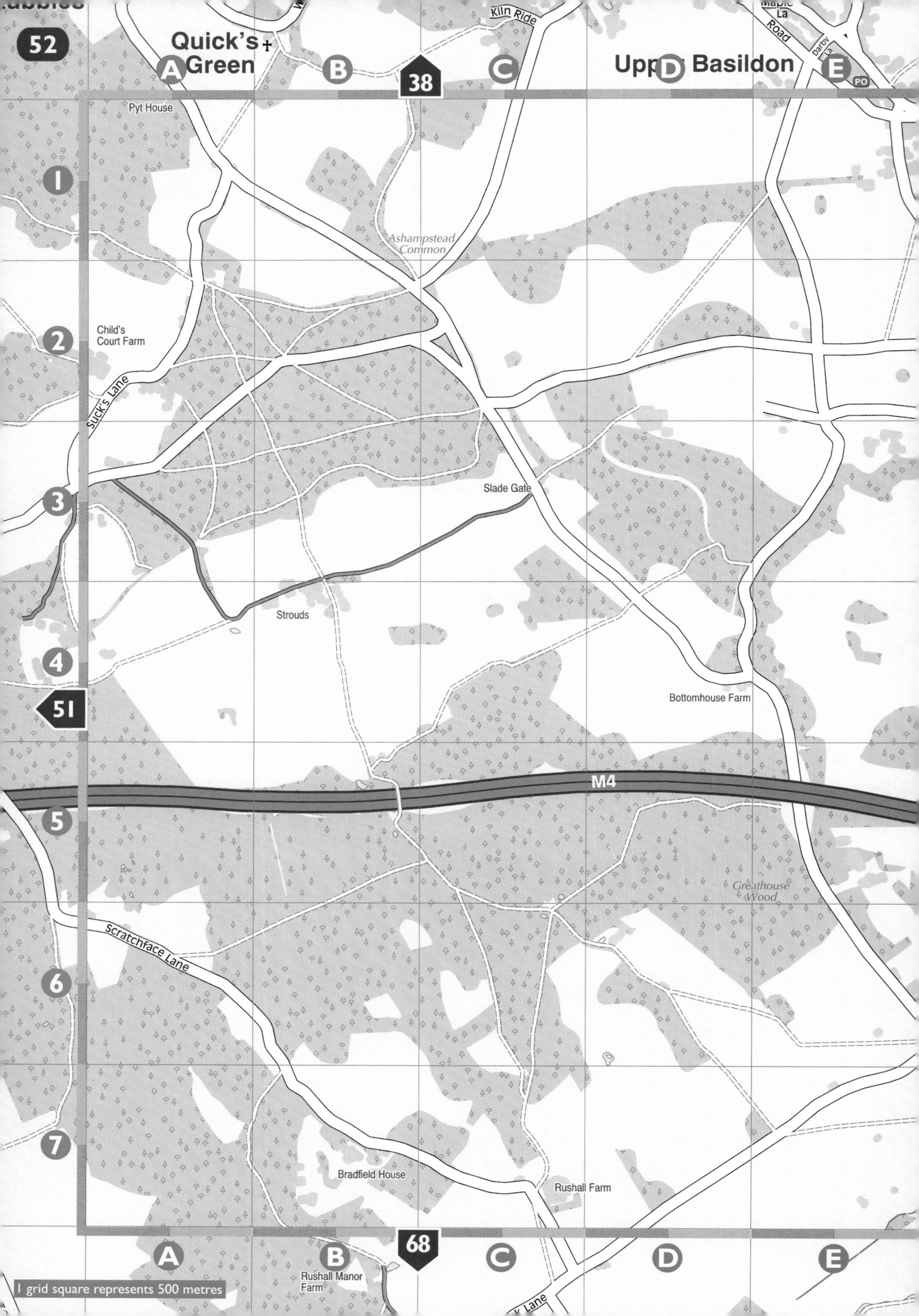

Quick's +
Green

A   **B**   38   **C**   Upp **D** Basildon   **E** PO

Kiln Ride

Maple La

Road

Darby La

Pyt House

1

Ashampstead
Common

Child's
Court Farm

2

Suck's Lane

3

Slade Gate

Strouds

4

51

Bottomhouse Farm

M4

5

Greathouse
Wood

Scratchface Lane

6

7

Bradfield House

Rushall Farm

Rushall Manor
Farm

1 grid square represents 500 metres

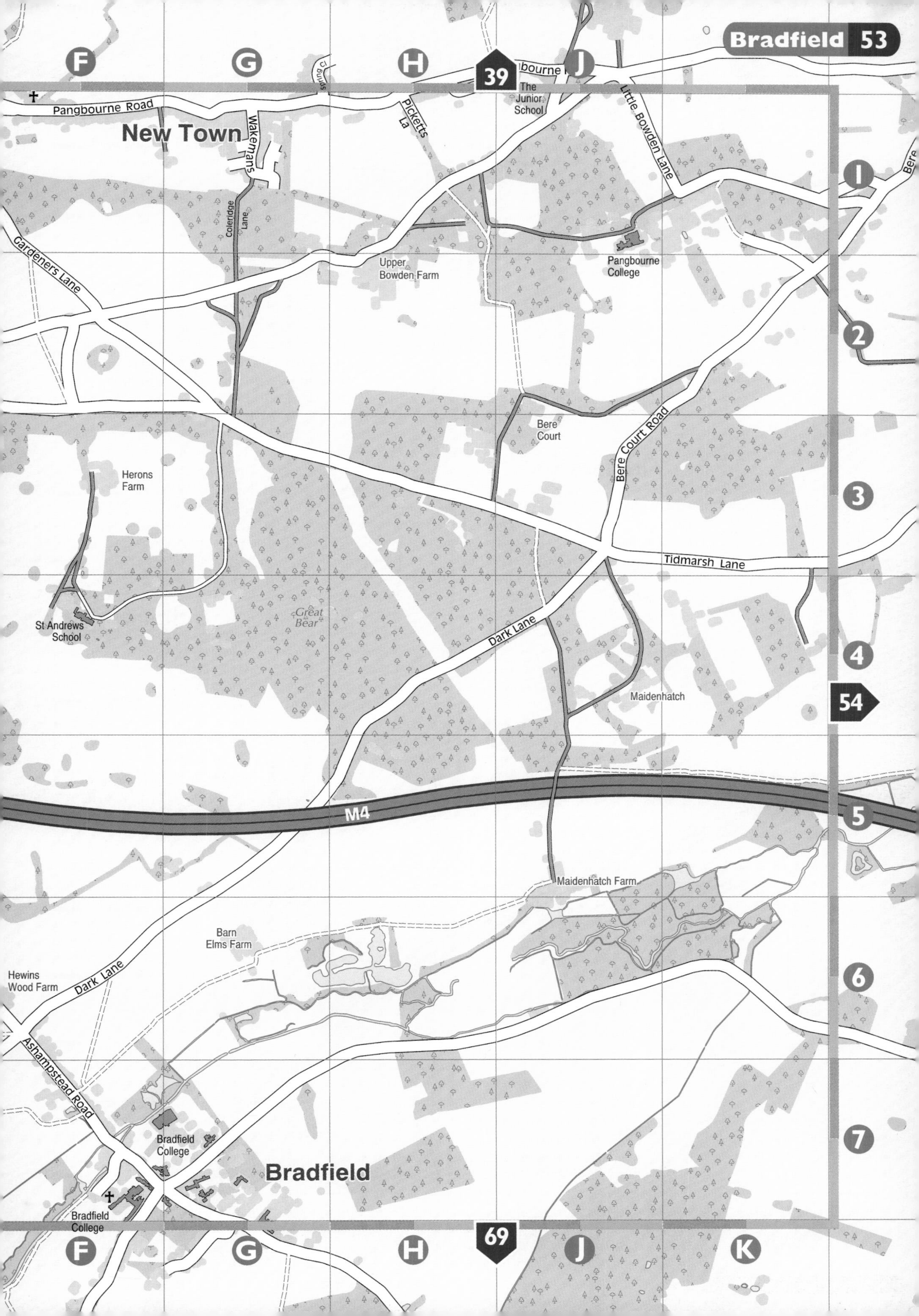

Bradfield 53
F
G
H
39
J
Pangbourne Road
New Town
Wakemans
Picketts La
The Junior School
Little Bowden Lane
Coleridge Lane
Gardeners Lane
Upper Bowden Farm
Pangbourne College
I
2
Bere Court
Bere Court Road
Herons Farm
3
Tidmarsh Lane
St Andrews School
Great Bear
Dark Lane
4
Maidenhatch
54
M4
5
Maidenhatch Farm
Barn Elms Farm
Hewins Wood Farm
Dark Lane
6
Ashampstead Road
Bradfield College
Bradfield
Bradfield College
7
69
K

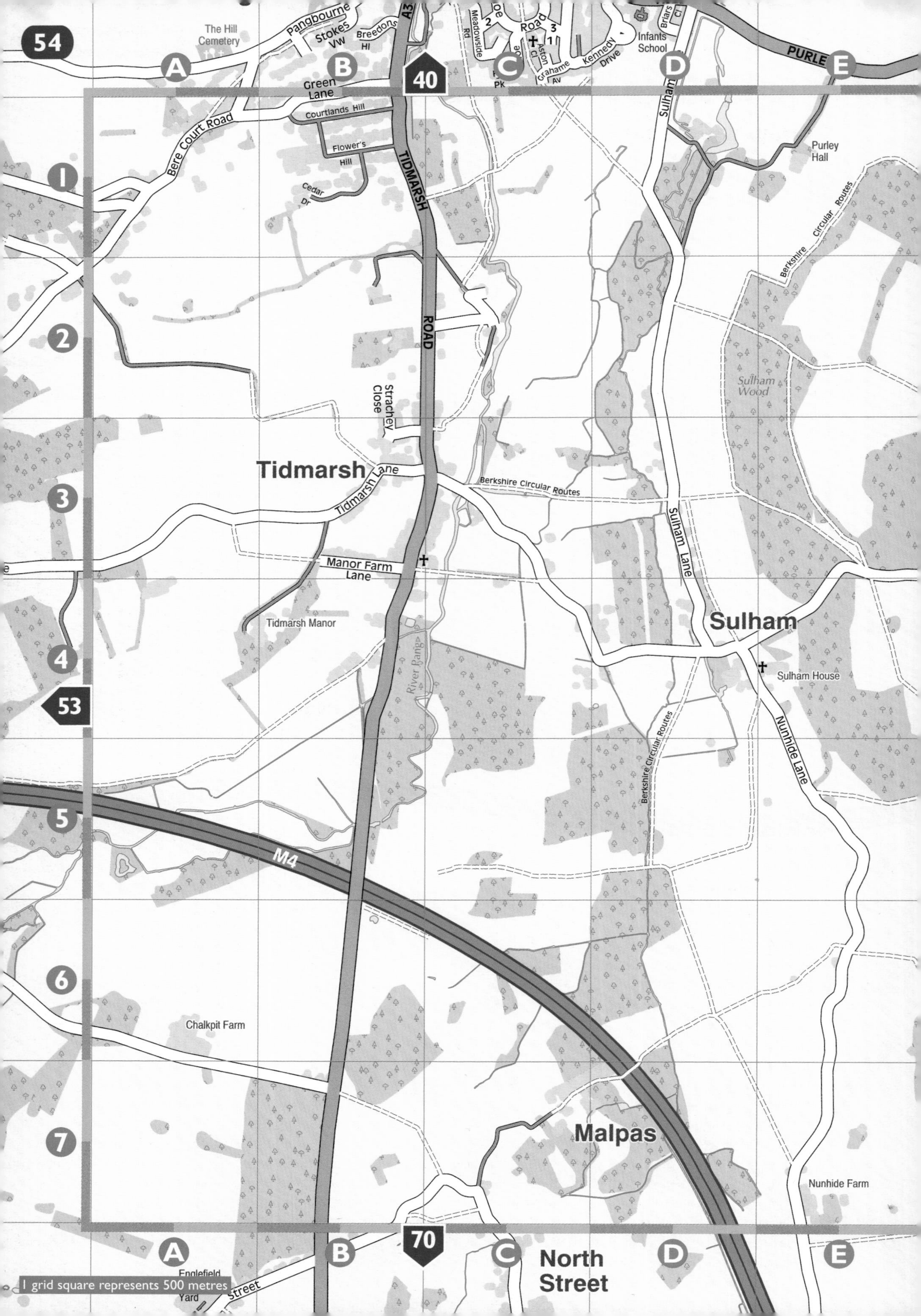
54
The Hill Cemetery
Pangbourne
Stokes Vw
Breedon Hl
Meadowside Rd
Road
Infants School
Briars Cl
PURLEY
Green Lane
Courtlands Hill
Bere Court Road
Flower's Hill
Cedar Dr
TIDMARSH ROAD
Aston Cl
Grahame Av
Kennedy Drive
Sulham Lane
Purley Hall
Berkshire Circular Routes
Sulham Wood
Strachey Close
Tidmarsh
Tidmarsh Lane
Berkshire Circular Routes
Manor Farm Lane
Tidmarsh Manor
Sulham
Sulham House
River Pang
53
Nunhide Lane
M4
Chalkpit Farm
Malpas
Nunhide Farm
North Street
Englefield Yard
Street
40
70
A
B
C
D
E
1
2
3
4
5
6
7
1 grid square represents 500 metres

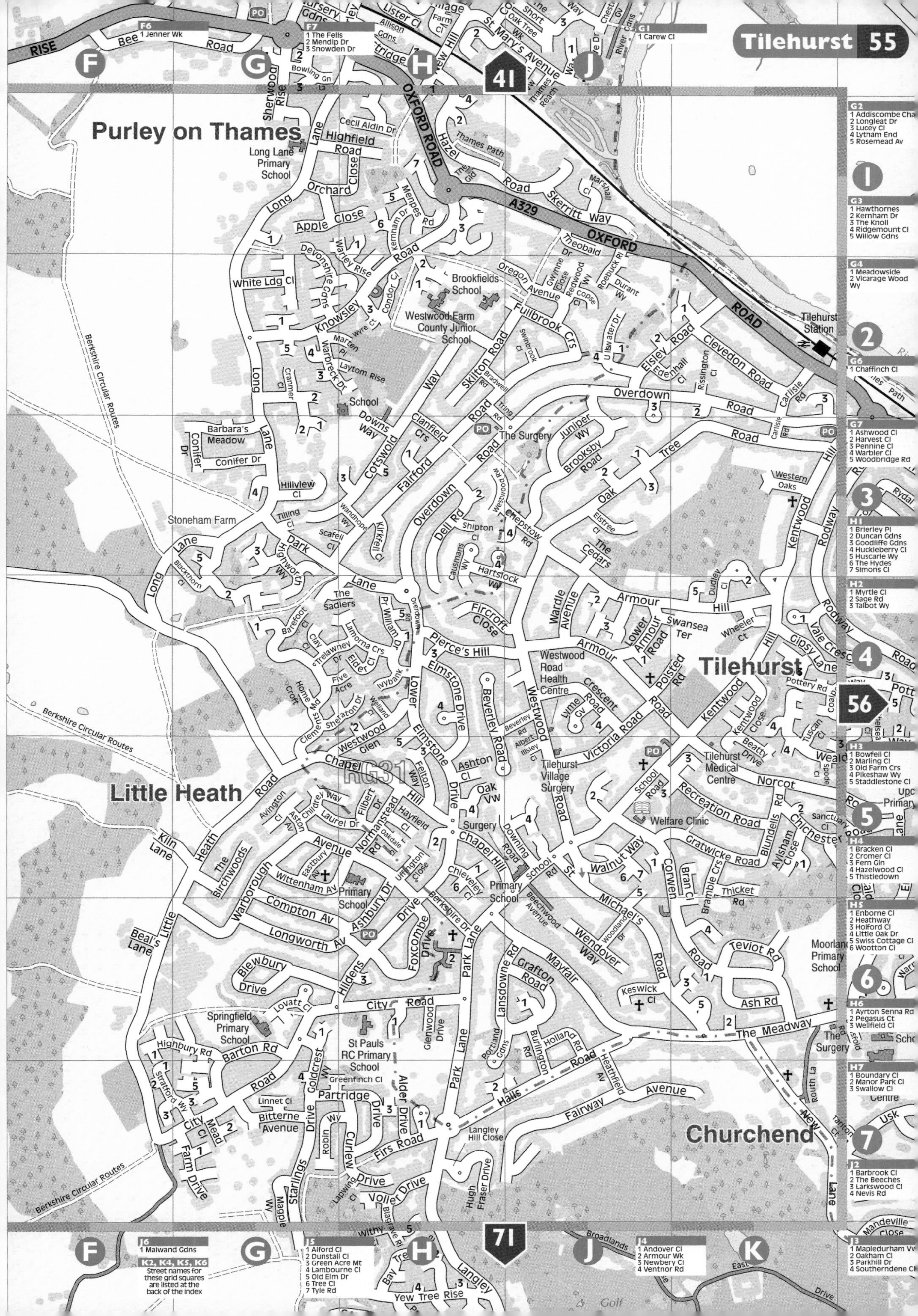
F6
1 Jenner Wk
F7
1 The Fells
2 Mendip Dr
3 Snowden Dr
G1
1 Carew Cl
41
Purley on Thames
Long Lane Primary School
Brookfields School
Westwood Farm County Junior School
OXFORD ROAD
A329
Tilehurst Station
The Surgery
Stoneham Farm
Berkshire Circular Routes
Little Heath
Tilehurst
Westwood Road Health Centre
Tilehurst Village Surgery
Tilehurst Medical Centre
Welfare Clinic
RG31
Primary School
Surgery
Springfield Primary School
St Pauls RC Primary School
Moorlands Primary School
The Surgery
Churchend
56
71
G2
1 Addiscombe Cha
2 Longleat Dr
3 Lucey Cl
4 Lytham End
5 Rosemead Av
G3
1 Hawthornes
2 Kernham Dr
3 The Knoll
4 Ridgemount Cl
5 Willow Gdns
G4
1 Meadowside
2 Vicarage Wood Wy
G6
1 Chaffinch Cl
G7
1 Ashwood Cl
2 Harvest Cl
3 Pennine Cl
4 Warbler Cl
5 Woodbridge Rd
H1
1 Brierley Pl
2 Duncan Gdns
3 Goodliffe Gdns
4 Huckleberry Cl
5 Huscarle Wy
6 The Hydes
7 Simons Cl
H2
1 Myrtle Cl
2 Sage Rd
3 Talbot Wy
H3
1 Bowfell Cl
2 Marling Cl
3 Old Farm Crs
4 Pikeshaw Wy
5 Staddlestone Cl
H4
1 Bracken Cl
2 Cromer Cl
3 Fern Gln
4 Hazelwood Cl
5 Thistledown
H5
1 Enborne Cl
2 Heathway
3 Holford Cl
4 Little Oak Dr
5 Swiss Cottage Cl
6 Wootton Cl
H6
1 Ayrton Senna Rd
2 Pegasus Ct
3 Wellfield Cl
H7
1 Boundary Cl
2 Manor Park Cl
3 Swallow Cl
J2
1 Barbrook Cl
2 The Beeches
3 Larkswood Cl
4 Nevis Rd
J3
1 Mapledurham Vw
2 Oakham Cl
3 Parkhill Dr
4 Southerndene Cl
J6
1 Maiwand Gdns
K2, K4, K5, K6
Street names for these grid squares are listed at the back of the index
J5
1 Alford Cl
2 Dunstall Cl
3 Green Acre Mt
4 Lambourne Cl
5 Old Elm Dr
6 Tree Cl
7 Tyle Rd
J4
1 Andover Cl
2 Armour Wk
3 Newbery Cl
4 Ventnor Rd

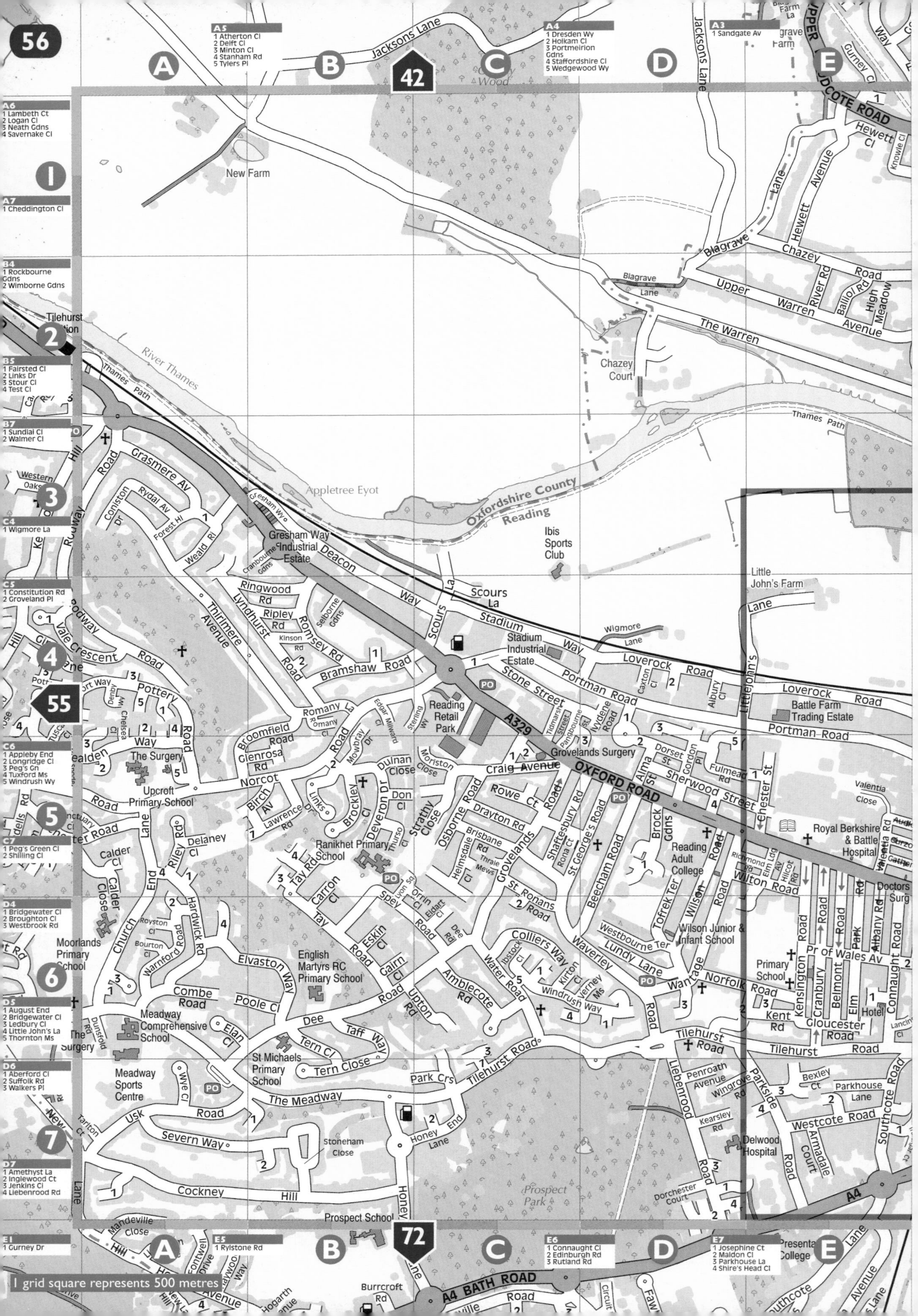
56
A5
1 Atherton Cl
2 Delft Cl
3 Minton Cl
4 Stanham Rd
5 Tylers Pl
A4
1 Dresden Wy
2 Holkam Cl
3 Portmeirion Gdns
4 Staffordshire Cl
5 Wedgewood Wy
A3
1 Sandgate Av
A6
1 Lambeth Ct
2 Logan Cl
3 Neath Gdns
4 Savernake Cl
A7
1 Cheddington Cl
B4
1 Rockbourne Gdns
2 Wimborne Gdns
B5
1 Fairsted Cl
2 Links Dr
3 Stour Cl
4 Test Cl
B7
1 Sundial Cl
2 Walmer Cl
C4
1 Wigmore La
C5
1 Constitution Rd
2 Groveland Pl
C6
1 Appleby End
2 Longridge Cl
3 Peg's Gn
4 Tuxford Ms
5 Windrush Wy
C7
1 Peg's Green Cl
2 Shilling Cl
D4
1 Bridgewater Cl
2 Broughton Cl
3 Westbrook Rd
D5
1 August End
2 Bridgewater Cl
3 Ledbury Cl
4 Little John's La
5 Thornton Ms
D6
1 Aberford Cl
2 Suffolk Rd
3 Walkers Pl
D7
1 Amethyst La
2 Inglewood Ct
3 Jenkins Cl
4 Liebenrood Rd
E1
1 Gurney Dr
E5
1 Rylstone Rd
E6
1 Connaught Cl
2 Edinburgh Rd
3 Rutland Rd
E7
1 Josephine Ct
2 Maldon Cl
3 Parkhouse La
4 Shire's Head Cl
A
B
C
D
E
42
55
72
1
2
3
4
5
6
7
Jacksons Lane
Upper Woodcote Road
Hewett Cl
Knowle Cl
Gurney Cl
Hewett Avenue
Blagrave Lane
Blagrave Farm
New Farm
Chazey Road
Upper Warren Avenue
River Rd
Balliol Rd
High Meadow
The Warren
Chazey Court
Tilehurst Station
River Thames
Thames Path
Appletree Eyot
Oxfordshire County
Reading
Ibis Sports Club
Grasmere Av
Rydal Av
Coniston Dr
Forest Hl
Weald Ri
Gresham Wy
Gresham Way Industrial Estate
Cranbourne Gdns
Deacon Way
Scours La
Stadium Way
Stadium Industrial Estate
Wigmore Lane
Little John's Farm
Little John's Lane
Loverock Road
Portman Road
Battle Farm Trading Estate
Ringwood Rd
Ripley Rd
Kinson Rd
Romsey Rd
Selborne Gdns
Thirlmere Avenue
Lyndhurst Road
Bramshaw Road
Vale Crescent
Pottery Road
Western Oaks
Stone Street
Caxton Cl
Albury Cl
Reading Retail Park
A329
Oxford Road
Tidmarsh Street
Pangbourne St
Wydene Road
Grovelands Surgery
Dorset St
Gordon Pl
Fulmead Rd
Sherwood Street
Chester St
Valentia Close
Royal Berkshire & Battle Hospital
Broomfield Road
Glenrosa Rd
Romany La
Romany Cl
Edgar Milward Cl
Sterling Wy
Mowbray Dr
Dulnan Close
Moriston Close
Craig Avenue
Rowe Ct
Shaftesbury Rd
St George's Road
Alma St
Beecham Road
Brock Gdns
Reading Adult College
Wilton Road
Richmond Rd
Elm Lodge Av
Hilcot Rd
Doctors Surg
The Surgery
Upcroft Primary School
Norcot Road
Birch Av
Lawrence Rd
Links Dr
Brockley Cl
Deveron Dr
Don Cl
Strathy Close
Osborne Road
Drayton Rd
Brisbane Rd
Thrale Mews
Helmsdale Cl
Grovelands Road
Rona Ct
Wilson Road
Toffek Ter
Calder Cl
Calder Close
Delaney Cl
Riley Rd
Church End Lane
Hardwick Rd
Royston Cl
Bourton Cl
Warnford Road
Ranikhet Primary School
Thurso Cl
Tay Rd
Carron Cl
Tay Road
Spey Road
Lyon Sq
Orrin Cl
Eldart Cl
Dee Rd
St Ronans Road
Westbourne Ter
Lundy Lane
Waverley Road
Wilson Junior & Infant School
Moorlands Primary School
Elvaston Way
English Martyrs RC Primary School
Eskin Cl
Gairn Cl
Colliers Way
Ibstock Cl
Kirton Cl
Verney Ms
Water Road
Amblecote Rd
Windrush Way
Wantage Road
Norfolk Road
Kensington Road
Cranbury Road
Belmont Road
Park Road
Elm Rd
Albany Rd
Connaught Road
Pr of Wales Av
Primary School
Kent Rd
Gloucester Road
Hotel
Combe Road
Poole Cl
Meadway Comprehensive School
Dunsfold Rd
The Surgery
Elan Cl
Dee Road
Taff Way
Tern Cl
Tern Close
Upton Rd
St Michaels Primary School
Tilehurst Road
Park Crs
Penroath Avenue
Wingrove Rd
Parkside Road
Bexley Ct
Parkhouse Lane
Southcote Road
Meadway Sports Centre
Wye Cl
The Meadway
Usk Road
Severn Way
Stoneham Close
Honey End Lane
Kearsley Rd
Liebenrood Road
Delwood Hospital
Westcote Road
Armadale Court
Tarlton Ct
Cockney Hill
Prospect Park
Dorchester Court
A4
Prospect School
Mandeville Close
Presentation College
A4 Bath Road
Burrcroft Rd
Hogarth Avenue
1 grid square represents 500 metres

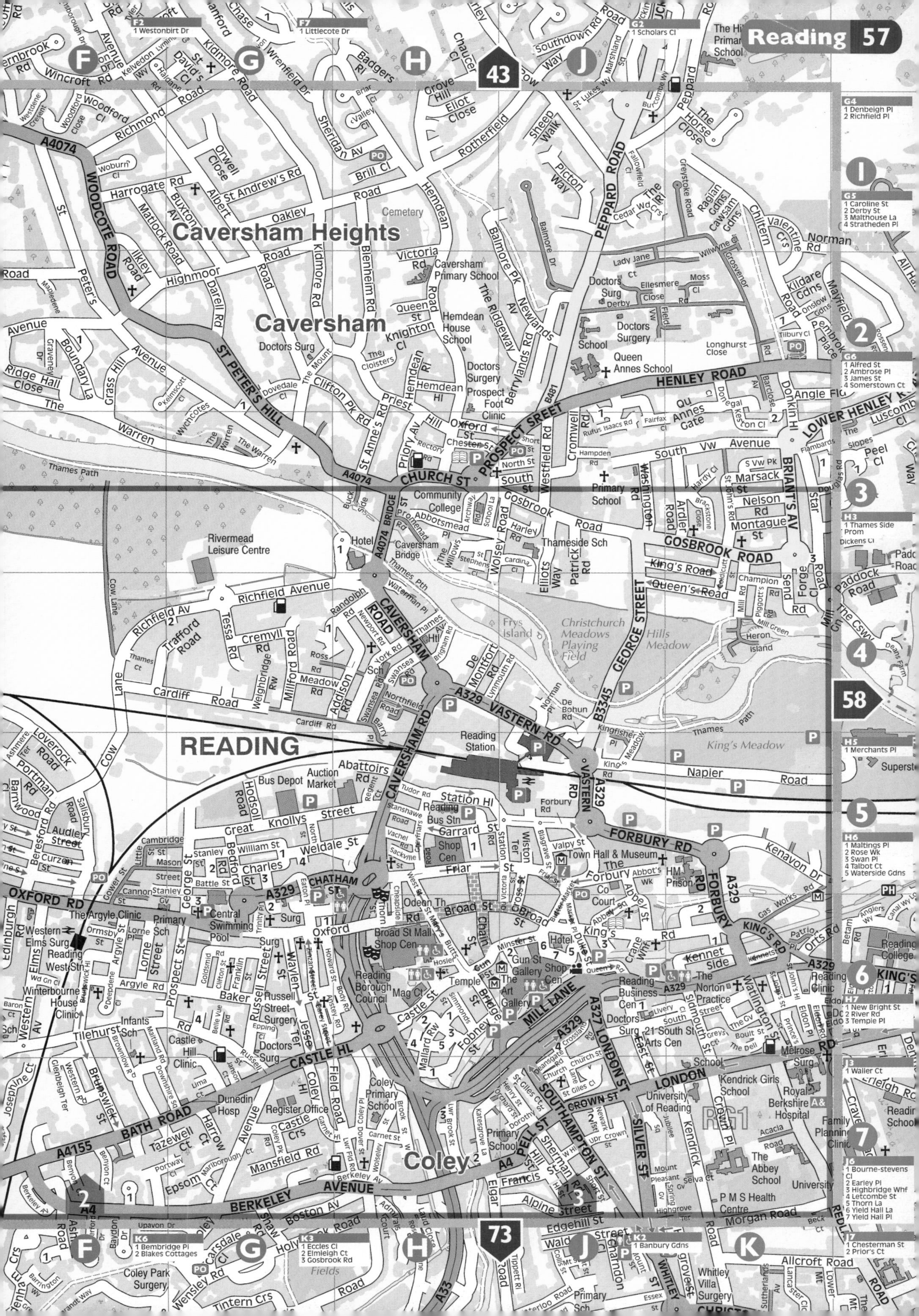

Reading
57
43
58
73
F
G
H
J
K
I
2
3
4
5
6
7
F2
1 Westonbirt Dr
F7
1 Littlecote Dr
G2
1 Scholars Cl
G4
1 Denbeigh Pl
2 Richfield Pl
G5
1 Caroline St
2 Derby St
3 Malthouse La
4 Stratheden Pl
G6
1 Alfred St
2 Ambrose Pl
3 James St
4 Somerstown Ct
H3
1 Thames Side Prom
H5
1 Merchants Pl
H6
1 Maltings Pl
2 Rose Wk
3 Swan Pl
4 Talbot Ct
5 Waterside Gdns
H7
1 New Bright St
2 River Rd
3 Temple Pl
J3
1 Waller Ct
J6
1 Bourne-stevens Cl
2 Earley Pl
3 Highbridge Whf
4 Letcombe St
5 Thorn La
6 Yield Hall La
7 Yield Hall Pl
J7
1 Chesterman St
2 Prior's Ct
K6
1 Bembridge Pl
2 Blakes Cottages
K3
1 Eccles Cl
2 Elmleigh Ct
3 Gosbrook Rd
K2
1 Banbury Gdns
Caversham Heights
Caversham
READING
Coley
RG1
Wincroft Rd
Kidmore Road
Richmond Road
Woodcote Road
A4074
St Peter's Hill
Harrogate Rd
St Andrew's Rd
Oakley Road
Highmoor Road
Darell Rd
Kidmore Rd
Blenheim Rd
Hemdean Road
Priest Hill
Rotherfield
Brill Cl
Cemetery
Victoria Rd
Caversham Primary School
Hemdean House School
Doctors Surg
The Ridgeway
Balmore Pk
Newlands Av
Berrylands Rd
Peppard Road
B481
Queen Annes School
Henley Road
Lower Henley Rd
Prospect Street
Church St
A4074 Bridge
South Vw Avenue
Gosbrook Road
King's Road
Queen's Road
George Street
B3345
Briant's Av
Christchurch Meadows Playing Field
Frys Island
Hills Meadow
Heron Island
King's Meadow
Thames Path
Rivermead Leisure Centre
Richfield Avenue
Cow Lane
Caversham Road
A329 Vastern Rd
Vastern Rd
Reading Station
Napier Road
Forbury Rd
A329
Kenavon Dr
HM Prison
Town Hall & Museum
The Forbury
Kings Rd
Abattoirs Rd
Bus Depot
Auction Market
Station Hl
Reading Bus Stn
Shop Cen
Friar St
Broad St
Broad St Mall Shop Cen
Chatham St
Oxford Rd
Oxford Road
Central Swimming Pool
Russell Street
Castle Hl
Bath Road
A4155
Berkeley Avenue
A4
Mill Lane
A327 London St
Southampton St
Silver St
London Rd
University of Reading
Royal Berkshire Hospital
Kendrick Girls School
The Abbey School
P M S Health Centre
Morgan Road
Reading Borough Council
The Art Gallery
Gun St Gallery
Coley Primary School
Register Office
Dunedin Hosp
Mansfield Rd
Coley Park Surgery
Whitley Villa Surgery
Allcroft Road
A33
Western Elms Surg
Reading West Stn
Winterbourne House Clinic
Castle Hill Clinic
Russell Street Surgery
Reading College
Reading Clinic
Melrose Surg
Family Planning Clinic

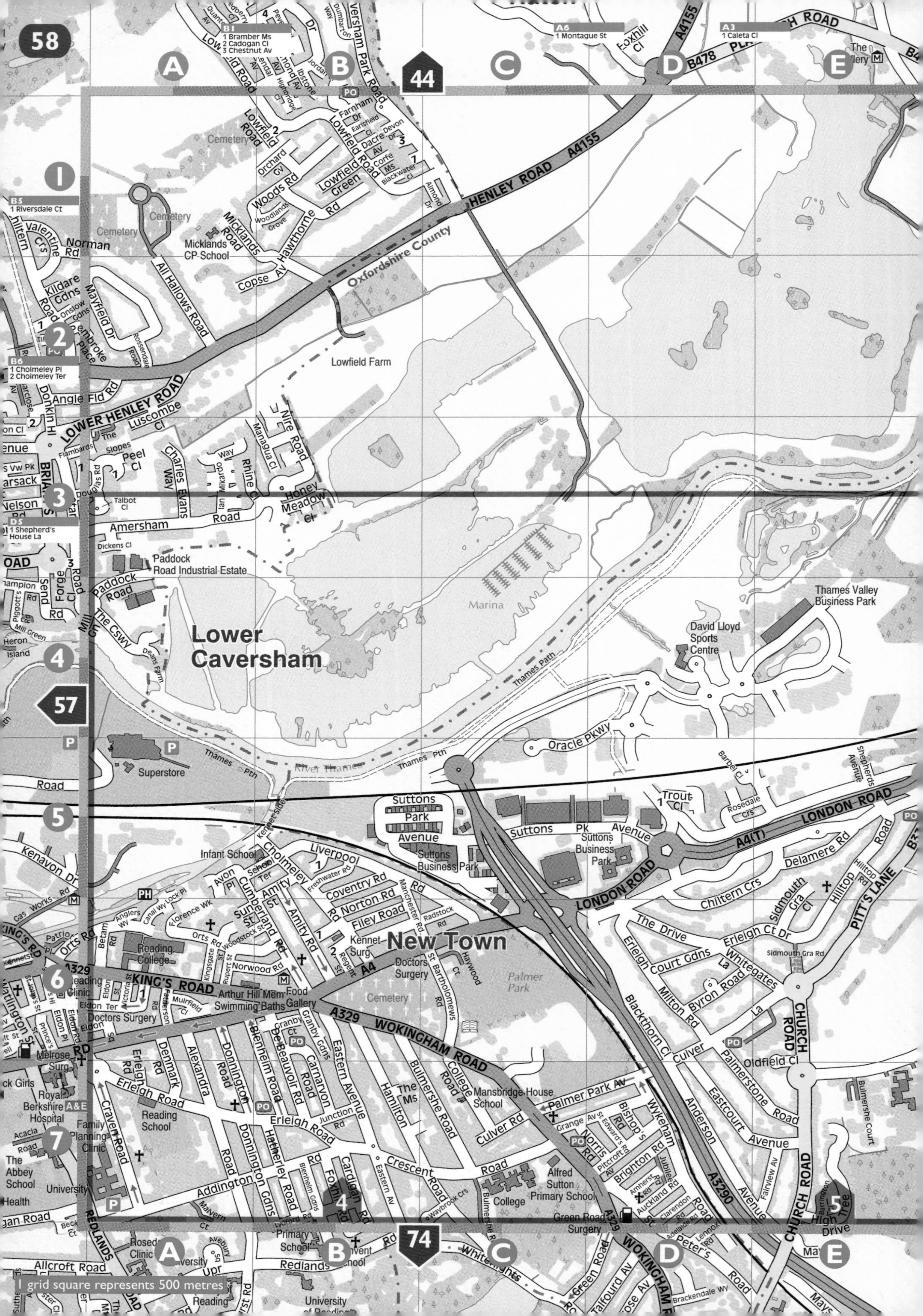

A
B
C
D
E
44
57
74
1
2
3
4
5
6
7
B1
1 Bramber Ms
2 Cadogan Cl
3 Chestnut Av
A6
1 Montague St
A3
1 Caleta Cl
B5
1 Riversdale Ct
B6
1 Cholmeley Pl
2 Cholmeley Ter
D5
1 Shepherd's House La
HENLEY ROAD
A4155
B478
Cemetery
Lowfield Road
Orchard Gv
Woods Rd
Woodlands Grove
Lowfield Green
Farnham Dr
Earlsfield Cl
Dacre Av
Devon Dr
Corfe Ms
Blackwater Cl
Almond Dr
Hawthorne Rd
Micklands Road
Micklands CP School
Copse Av
All Hallows Road
Oxfordshire County
Valentine Crs
Norman Rd
Kildare Gdns
Onslow Gdns
Mayfield Dr
Pembroke Place
Rossendale Road
Lowfield Farm
LOWER HENLEY ROAD
Angle Fld Rd
Donkin Hl
Luscombe Cl
The Slopes
Flambards
Peel Cl
Charles Evans Way
Ian Mikardo Way
Rhine Cl
Managua Cl
Nire Road
Honey Meadow Cl
Talbot Cl
Douglas Rd
Amersham Road
Dickens Cl
Paddock Road Industrial Estate
Paddock Road
Forge Cl
Send Rd
Mill Grn
The Cswy
Deans Farm
Heron Island
Lower Caversham
Marina
Thames Valley Business Park
David Lloyd Sports Centre
Thames Path
Oracle PKWY
Superstore
Thames Pth
River Thames
Kennetside
Road
Suttons Park Avenue
Suttons Business Park
Suttons Pk Avenue
Trout Cl
Rosedale Crs
Barbel Cl
Shepherds Avenue
LONDON ROAD
A4(T)
Delamere Rd
Chiltern Crs
Hilltop Rd
Sidmouth Gra Cl
PITT'S LANE
The Drive
Erleigh Ct Dr
Erleigh Court Gdns
Whitegates La
Sidmouth Gra Rd
Byron Road
Milton Rd
Blackthorn Cl
Culver La
Palmerstone Road
Eastcourt Avenue
Anderson Avenue
CHURCH ROAD
Oldfield Cl
Bulmershe Court
Fairview Av
High Tree Drive
A3290
Kenavon Dr
Gas Works Rd
Infant School
Cholmeley Rd
Liverpool Rd
Freshwater Rd
Coventry Rd
Norton Rd
Filey Road
Radstock Rd
Manchester Rd
Avon Pl
School Ter
Cumberland Rd
Amity Rd
Sun St
Kennet Surg
New Town
Doctors Surgery
St Bartholomews Rd
Haywood Ct
Palmer Park
Cemetery
A329 WOKINGHAM ROAD
Reading College
Orts Rd
Florence Wk
Canal Wy
Anglers Wy
Betam Rd
Kingsgate St
Rupert St
Norwood Rd
KING'S ROAD
Arthur Hill Mem Swimming Baths
Food Gallery
Eldon Ter
Doctors Surgery
Reading Clinic
Melrose Surg
Royal Berkshire Hospital
A&E
Family Planning Clinic
Erleigh Road
Craven Road
Denmark Rd
Alexandra Rd
Donnington Road
Donnington Gdns
Reading School
Blenheim Road
De Beauvoir Rd
Granby Gdns
Carnarvon Road
Eastern Avenue
Junction Rd
Hamilton Rd
The Ms
Bulmershe Road
College Road
Mansbridge House School
Palmer Park Av
Culver Rd
Grange Av
Norris Rd
Bishop's Rd
Wykeham Rd
Brighton Rd
Pitcroft Av
Jubilee Rd
Auckland Rd
Amherst Rd
Clarendon Rd
Alfred Sutton Primary School
College
Crescent Road
Addington Road
Hatherley Road
Foxhill Rd
Cardigan Rd
Green Road Surgery
The Abbey School
University
Health
Acacia Road
Redlands
Malvern Ct
Primary School
Redlands School
Whiteknights
Green Road
WOKINGHAM R
Peter's Road
Lennox Rd
Brackendale Wy
Allcroft Road
University of Reading
PO
PH
P
1 grid square represents 500 metres

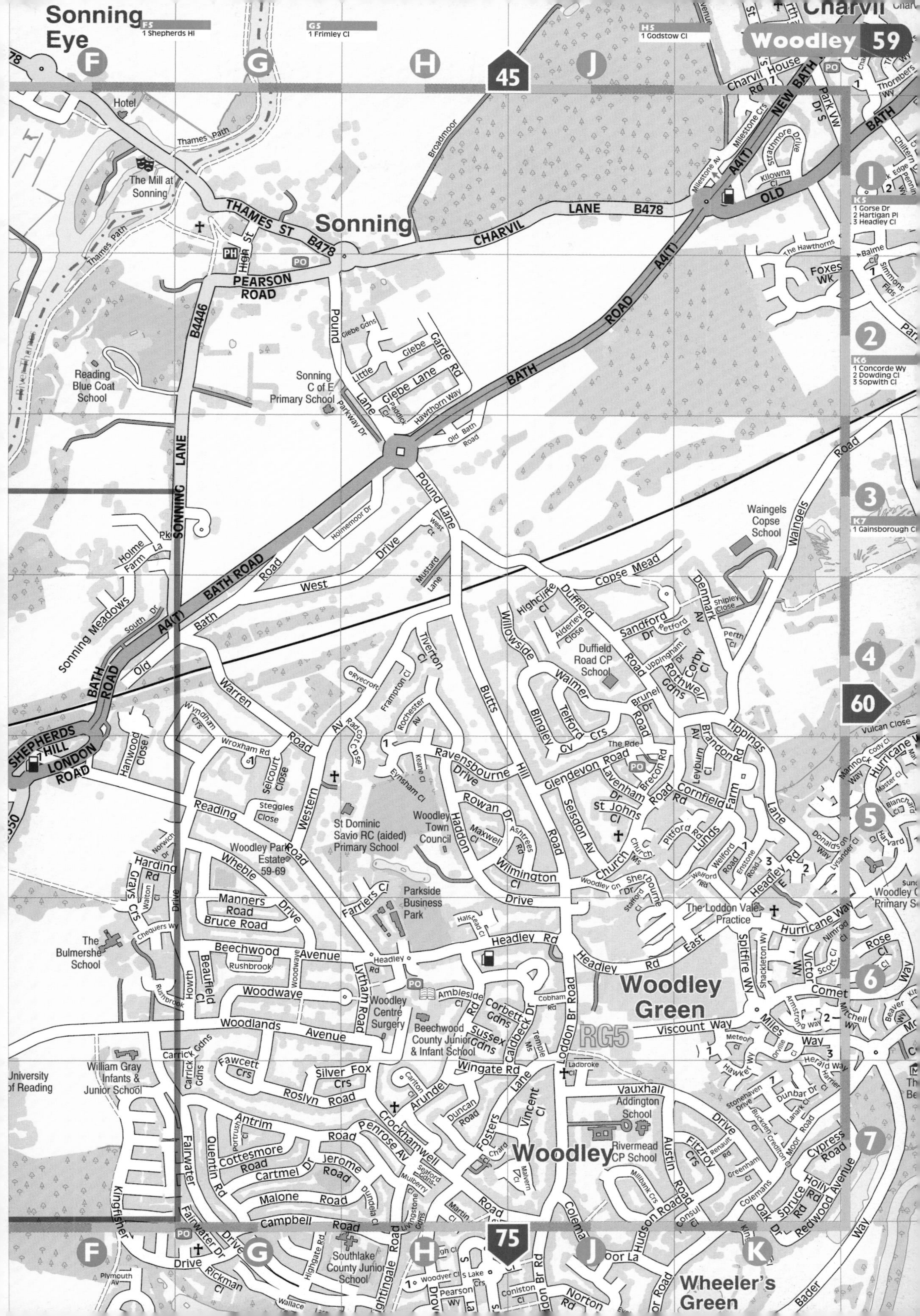
Sonning Eye
F5 1 Shepherds Hl
G5 1 Frimley Cl
H5 1 Godstow Cl
Charvil
45
Hotel
Thames Path
The Mill at Sonning
Thames St
Sonning
B478
Charvil Lane
PH
High St
PO
Pearson Road
B4446
Broadmoor
Charvil House Rd
New Bath Rd
Milestone Crs
Milestone Av
Strathmore Drive
Kilowna Cl
A4(T)
Old Bath Road
Park Vw Dr S
Thornbers Wy
Chiltern Dr
K5 1 Gorse Dr 2 Hartigan Pl 3 Headley Cl
The Hawthorns
Foxes Wk
Balme Cl
Simmons Flds
K6 1 Concorde Wy 2 Dowding Cl 3 Sopwith Cl
K7 1 Gainsborough Cl
Reading Blue Coat School
Pound Lane
Glebe Gdns
Little Glebe
Glebe Lane
Garde Rd
Sonning C of E Primary School
Parkway Dr
Paddick Cl
Hawthorn Way
Old Bath Road
Sonning Lane
Holmemoor Dr
West Drive
West Ct
Mustard Lane
Waingels Copse School
Waingels Road
Copse Mead
Holme Farm La
Holme Pk
Sonning Meadows
South Dr
Bath Road
Old Bath Road
Highcliffe Cl
Duffield Road
Alderley Close
Sandford Dr
Retford Cl
Denmark Av
Shipley Close
Perth Cl
Willowside
Duffield Road CP School
Uppingham Dr
Rothwell Gdns
Corby Cl
Tiverton Cl
Ryecroft Cl
Frampton Cl
Butts Hill
Walmer
Bingley Gv
Telford Crs
Brunel Dr
Warren Road
Shepherds Hill
London Road
Hanwood Close
Wyndham Crs
Wroxham Rd
Selcourt Close
Western Av
Radcot Close
Rochester Av
Ravensbourne Drive
The Ede
Brecon Rd
Glendevon Road
Lavenham Dr
Leyburn Cl
Brandon Av
Tippings Lane
60
Vulcan Close
Cody Cl
Hurricane Way
Mannock Way
Master Cl
Blanchard Cl
Reading Road
Steggles Close
Keane Cl
Eynsham Cl
St Dominic Savio RC (aided) Primary School
Woodley Town Council
Rowan Dr
Haddon Drive
Maxwell Cl
Ashtrees Rd
Seisdon Av
St Johns Cl
Church Road
Cornfield Rd
Farm Rd
Pitford Rd
Lunds Farm Rd
Welford Road
Enstone Road
Headley Rd
Donaldson Way
Lysander Cl
Harvard Cl
Woodley Park Estate 59-69
Norwich Dr
Harding Rd
Grays Crs
Walton Cl
Wheble Drive
Manners Road
Bruce Road
Wilmington Cl
Drive
Woodley Gn
Church Ms
Sherbourne Dr
Stafford Cl
Welford Rd
The Loddon Vale Practice
Woodley Primary School
Chequers Wy
The Bulmershe School
Farriers Cl
Parkside Business Park
Halstead Cl
Headley Rd
Headley Rd East
Spitfire Wy
Shackleton Wy
Victor Wy
Nimrod Cl
Scott Cl
Rose Cl
Comet Way
Beechwood Avenue
Rushbrook
Woodwaye
Beaufield Cl
Howth Drive
Lytham Road
Headley Rd
Woodley Centre Surgery
Ambleside Cl
Corbett Gdns
Cobham Rd
Loddon Br Road
Woodley Green
Armstrong Way
Mitchell Wy
Beaver Wy
Viscount Way
RG5
Woodlands Avenue
Beechwood County Junior & Infant School
Sussex Gdns
Caldbeck Dr
Temple Ms
Meteor Cl
Miles Way
Orville Cl
Herald Way
Harrier Cl
Hawker Wy
Carrick Gdns
University of Reading
William Gray Infants & Junior School
Fawcett Crs
Silver Fox Crs
Roslyn Road
Carlton Cl
Wingate Rd
Ladbroke Cl
Vauxhall Drive
Addington School
Stonehaven Drive
Dunbar Dr
Lanark Cl
Buckden Cl
Crediton Cl
Moor Road
Cypress Road
Arundel Road
Duncan Road
Fosters Lane
Vincent Cl
Rivermead CP School
Woodley
Fitzroy Crs
Renault Rd
Greenham Cl
Austin Road
Antrim Road
Portrush Cl
Cottesmore Road
Quentin Rd
Fairwater Drive
Penrose Av
Crockhamwell Road
Jerome Road
Cartmel Dr
Seaford Gdns
Mulberry Cl
Chard Cl
Malvern Cl
Millbank Crs
Hudson Road
Coleman Dr
Colemans
Oak Dr
Spruce Rd
Holly Rd
Redwood Avenue
Malone Road
Dundela Cl
Campbell Road
Livingstone Gdns
Martin Cl
Consul Cl
Kingfisher Drive
Rickman Cl
Highgate Rd
Southlake County Junior School
Nightingale Road
Woodyer Cl
Pearson Wy
S Lake Crs
Coniston Cl
Norton Rd
Moor La
75
Wheeler's Green
Bader Way
Plymouth Av
Wallace
F G H J K
1 2 3 4 5 6 7

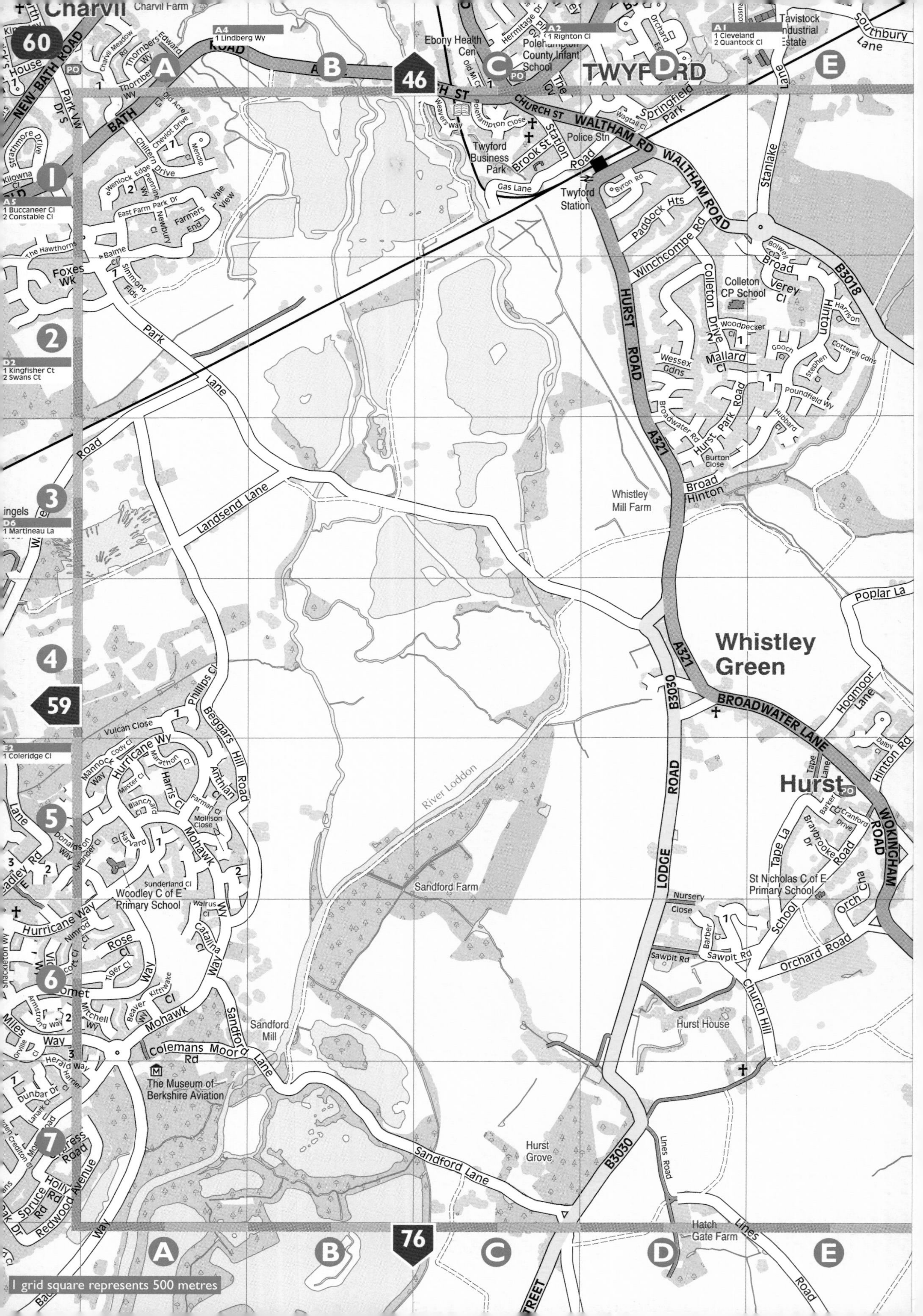

Charvil

Charvil Farm

NEW BATH ROAD

BATH ROAD

A4
1 Lindberg Wy

ROAD

46

H ST

CHURCH ST

WALTHAM RD

Ebony Health Cen

Hermitage Dr
A2

A2
1 Rignton Cl

Polehampton County Infant School

TWYFORD

A1
1 Cleveland Cl
2 Quantock Cl

Tavistock Industrial Estate

Southbury Lane

TWYFORD

PO

Thornbery
Edward Wy

Charvil Meadow

Thornbe

Cheviot Drive

Chiltern Drive

Mendip

7

Wenlock Edge

East Farm Park Dr
Newbury

Jennings

Vale View

Farmers End

Brook Station

Twyford Business Park

Weavers Way

Polehampton Close

Road

Church St

WALTHAM ROAD

Police Stn

Springfield Park

The IGV

Stanlake Lane

House

Strathmore Drive

Park VW Dr S

Kilowna Cl

The Hawthorns

Balme

Simmons

Simmons Flds

Foxes Wk

1

Gas Lane

Twyford Station

Byron Rd

Paddock Hts

Winchcombe Rd

Colleton CP School

Woodpecker

2

Colleton Drive

Bolwel

Broad Verey Cl

Harrison

Hinton

B3018

Park Lane

Wessex Gdns

Mallard Cl

1

Gooch

Cotterell Gdns

Stephen

Poundfield Wy

Hubbard

2

1

Road

Broadwater Rd

Hurst Park Road

Burton Close

Whistley Mill Farm

Broad Hinton

3

ingels

D6
1 Martineau La

W

Landsend Lane

HURST ROAD

A321

Poplar La

4

59

Vulcan Close

Phillips Cl

Cody Cl

Beggar's Hill Road

Whistley Green

A321

B3030 ROAD

BROADWATER LANE

Hogmoor Lane

Mannock Way

Hurricane Wy

Marathon

Master Cl

Farman Cl

Arethian

River Loddon

LODGE ROAD

Hurst

PO

Hinton Rd

Darby

WOKINGHAM ROAD

Lane

Lane

3

Donaldson Way

Lysander Cl

Blancm

Hat Yard

Mollison Close

Mohawk

1

2

Tape

Cranford Drive

Braybrooke Dr

Barker

School

Orch Clo

5

adley Rd

2

Sunderland Cl

Woodley C of E Primary School

Walrus Wy

Catalina Way

2

Sandford Farm

St Nicholas C of E Primary School

1

Orch Clo

Hurricane Way

Nimrod

Rose Cl

Way

Tiger Cl

Kittywke Cl

Nursery Close

Barber

Sawpit Rd

Sawpit Rd

Orchard Road

Shackleton Wy

omet

Cl

Mitchell Wy

Beaver Cl

Mohawk

Sandford Lane

Hurst House

6

Via

Scott Cl

Armstrong Way

Miles Way

2

3

Sandford Mill

Herald Way

Harrier Way

Colemans Moor Rd

Church Hill

7

Dunbar Dr

Lanark Cl

ress Road

M

The Museum of Berkshire Aviation

B3030

Lines Road

Holly Rd

Spruce Dr

Redwood Avenue

Way

Sandford Lane

Hurst Grove

Hatch Gate Farm

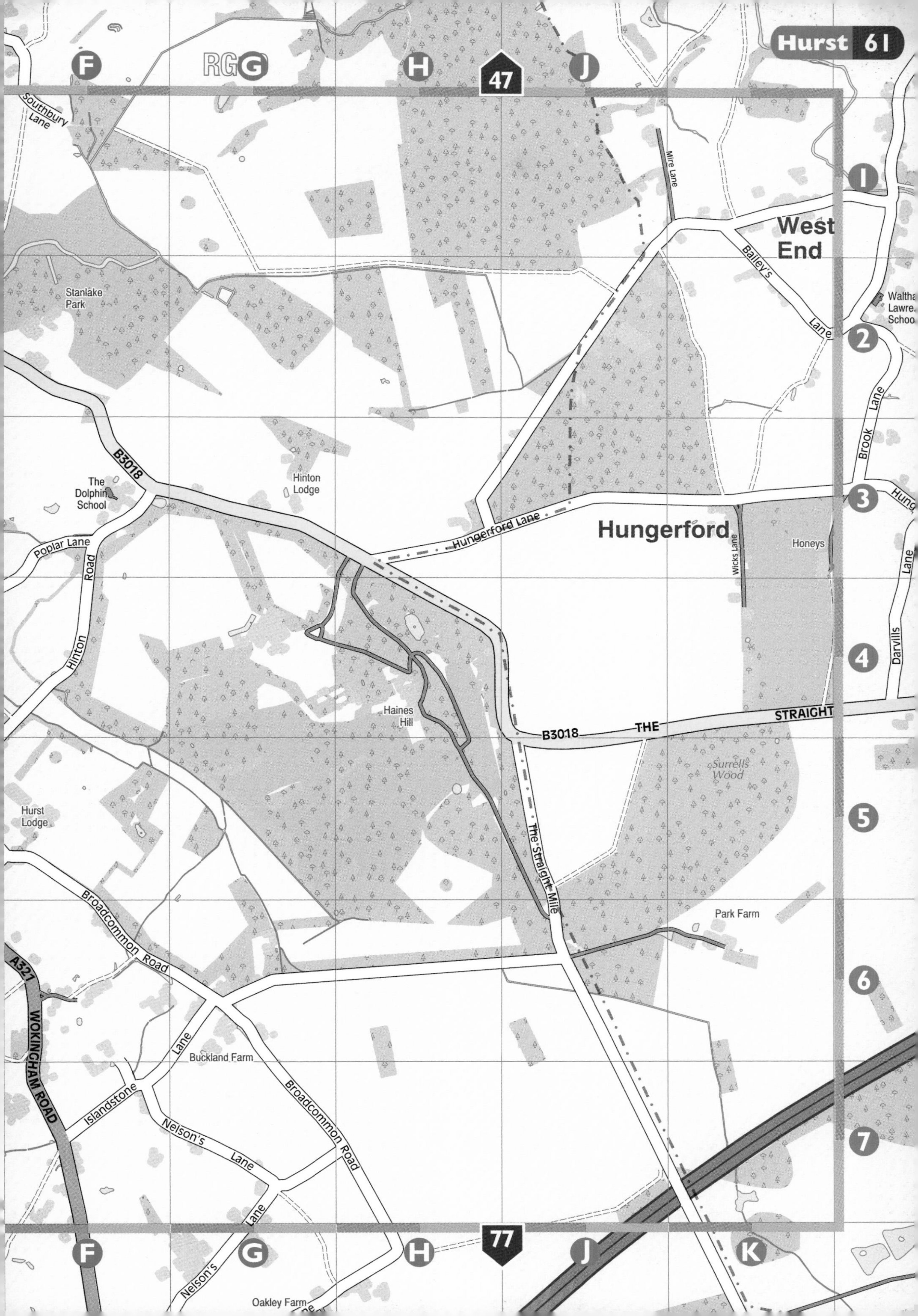

F RG G H 47 J

I

West End

Southbury Lane

Mire Lane

Bailey's Lane

Brook Lane

Waltha Lawre School

2

Stanlake Park

3

Hungerford Lane

Hungerford

Wicks Lane

Honeys

Darvills Lane

B3018

The Dolphin School

Hinton Lodge

4

Poplar Lane

Hinton Road

B3018 THE STRAIGHT

Haines Hill

Surrell's Wood

5

Hurst Lodge

Park Farm

Broadcommon Road

The Straight Mile

6

A321

WOKINGHAM ROAD

Lane

Buckland Farm

Broadcommon Road

7

Islandstone

Nelson's Lane

Nelson's Lane

F G H 77 J K

Oakley Farm

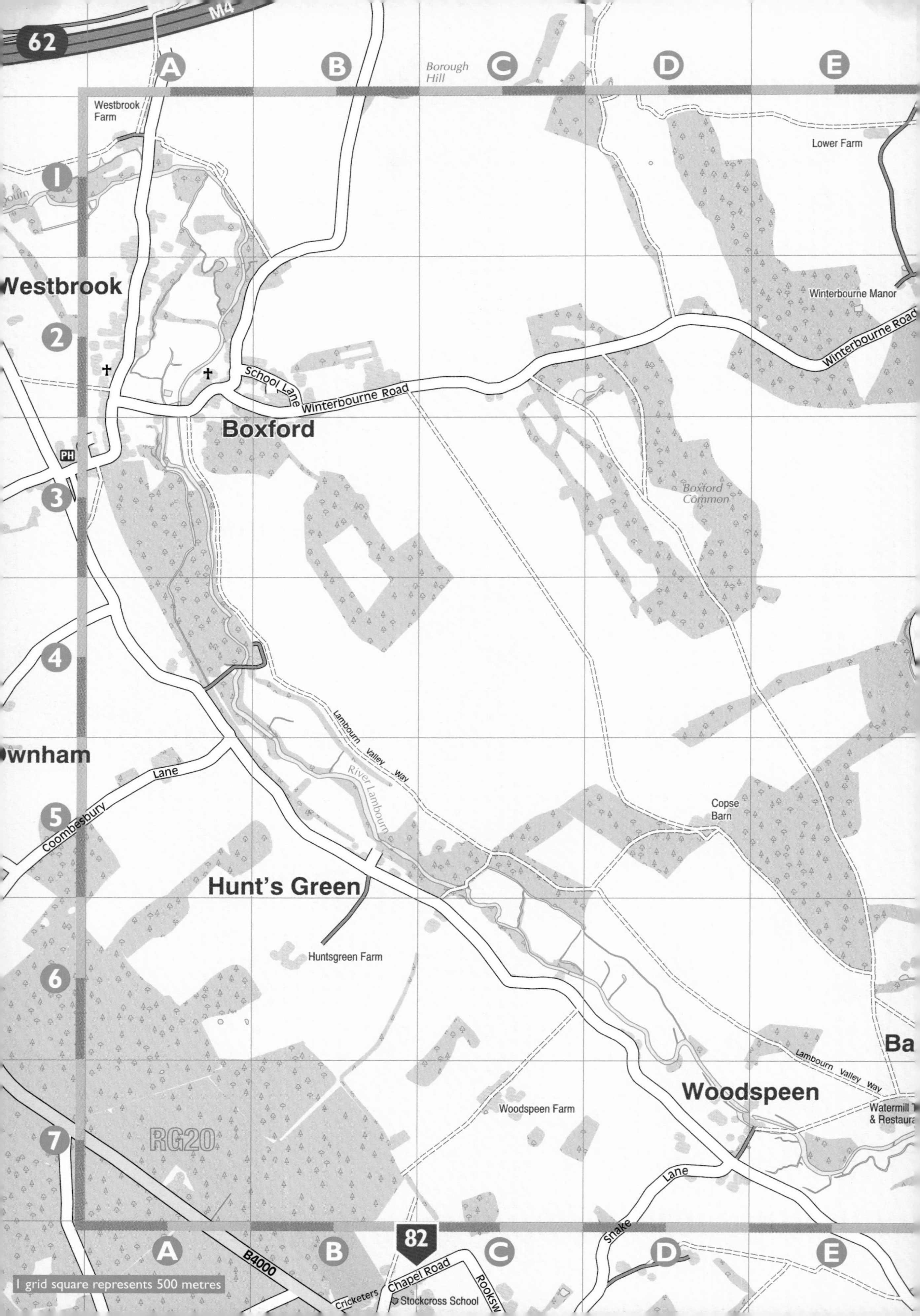
62
M4
A
B
C
D
E
Borough Hill
Westbrook Farm
Lower Farm
1
2
3
4
5
6
7
Westbrook
Winterbourne Manor
Winterbourne Road
School Lane
Winterbourne Road
Boxford
PH
Boxford Common
Lambourn Valley Way
River Lambourn
wnham
Coombesbury Lane
Copse Barn
Hunt's Green
Huntsgreen Farm
Ba
Lambourn Valley Way
Woodspeen
Woodspeen Farm
Watermill
& Restaura
RG20
Snake Lane
82
B4000
Chapel Road
Cricketers
Stockcross School
1 grid square represents 500 metres

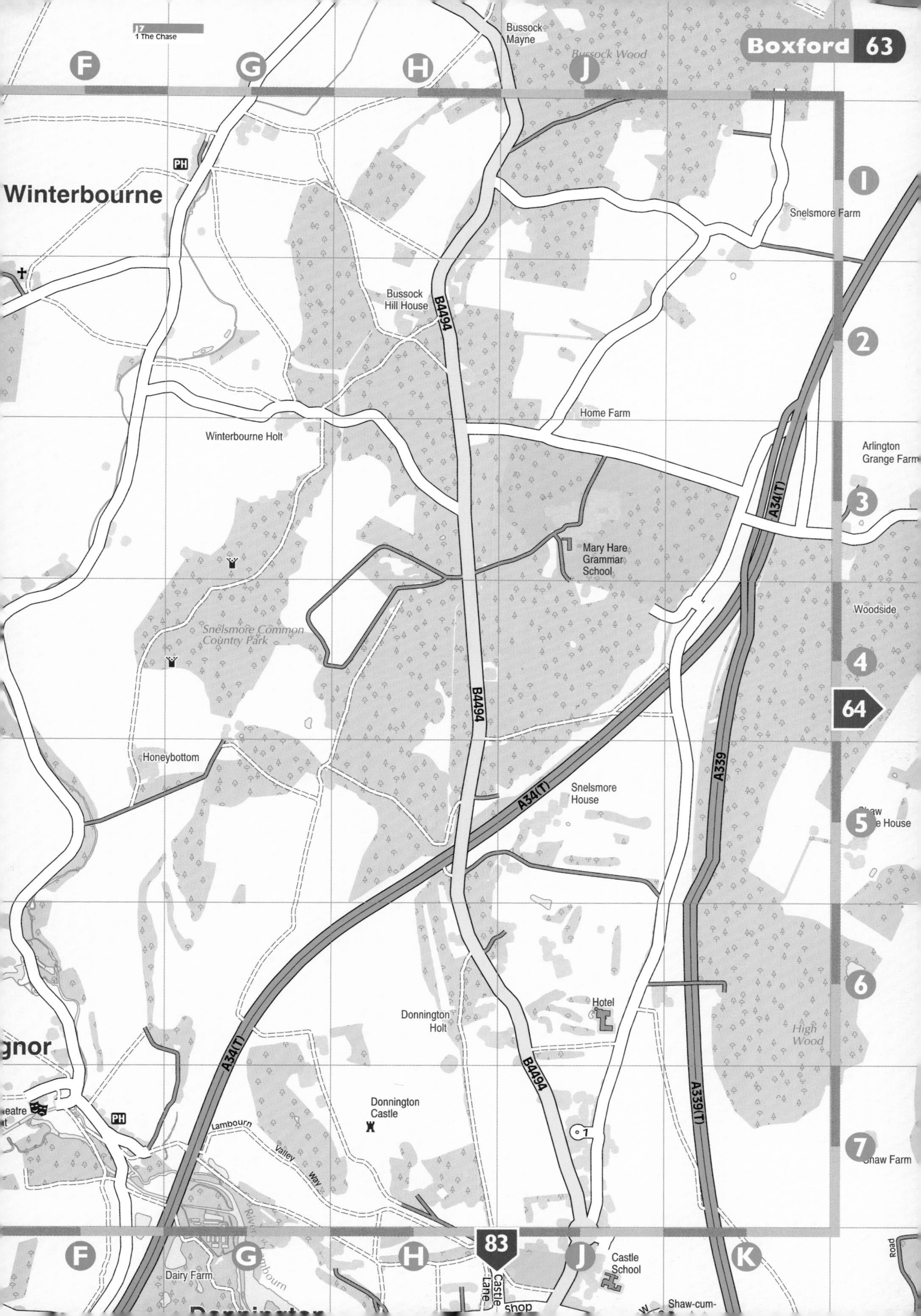

1 The Chase

F

G

H

J

Bussock
Mayne

Bussock Wood

I

Winterbourne

Snelsmore Farm

PH

†

2

B4494

Bussock
Hill House

Arlington
Grange Farm

Home Farm

3

Winterbourne Holt

Mary Hare
Grammar
School

Woodside

4

Snelsmore Common
Country Park

64

B4494

Honeybottom

Snelsmore
House

A34(T)

A339

Shaw
e House

5

gnor

A34(T)

Donnington
Holt

Hotel

High
Wood

6

Lambourn

PH

eatre
t

Donnington
Castle

B4494

A339(T)

7

Valley

Way

River Lambourn

Shaw Farm

F

G

83

H

J

K

Dairy Farm

Castle
Lane

Castle
School

Road

shop

Shaw-cum-

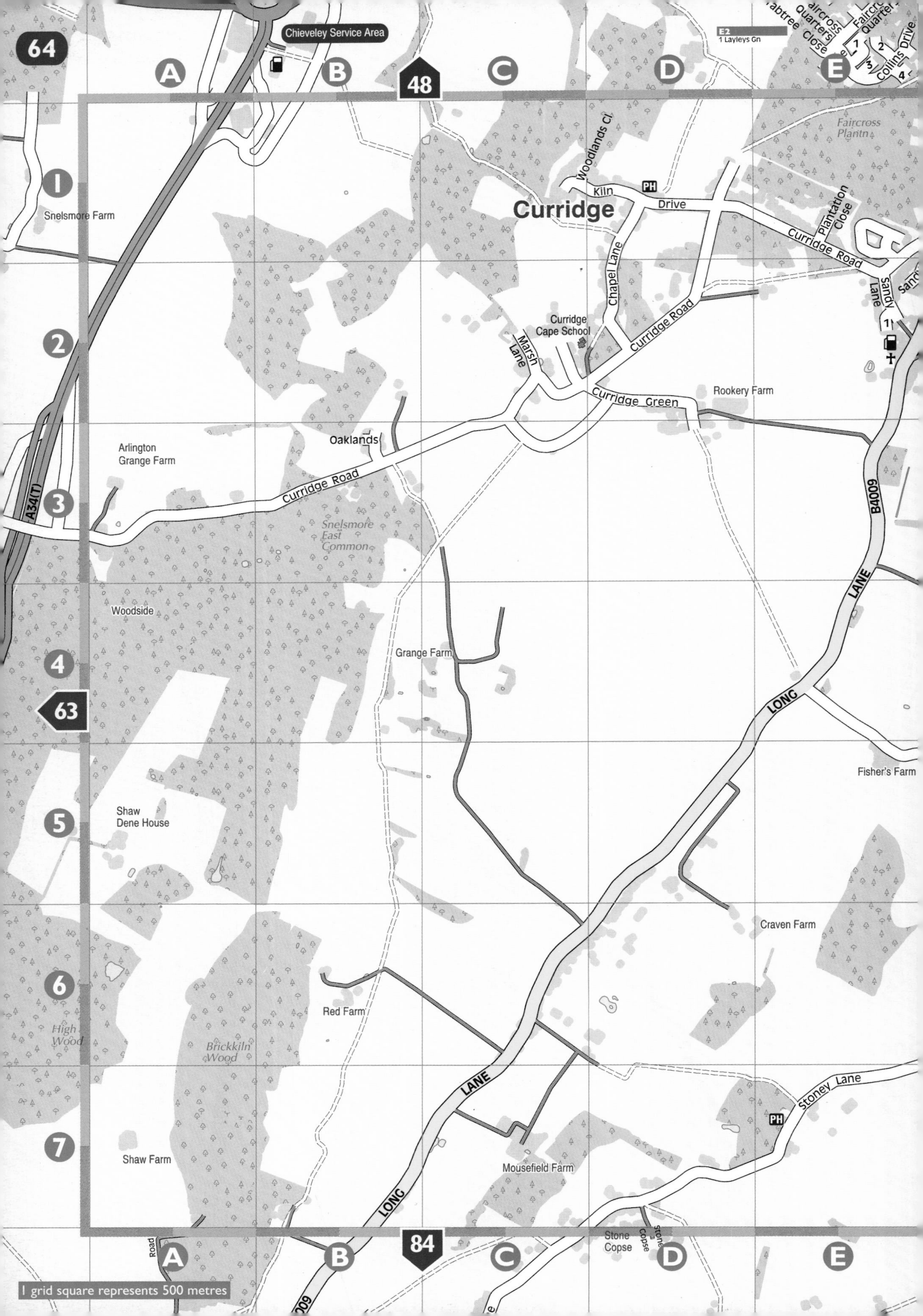

Chieveley Service Area

48

E2
1 Layleys Gn

aircross
Quarters
Faircross
Quarter

7

Collins Drive

2

3

4

Faircross
Plantn

1

Woodlands Cl.

Kiln

PH

Drive

Curridge

Chapel Lane

Curridge Road

Plantation Close

Curridge Road

Sandy

Lane

1

Curridge
Cape School

Marsh
Lane

Curridge Road

Curridge Green

Rookery Farm

Snelsmore Farm

Oaklands

Arlington
Grange Farm

Curridge Road

Snelsmore
East
Common

Woodside

Grange Farm

B4009

LONG

LANE

Fisher's Farm

63

Shaw
Dene House

Craven Farm

High
Wood

Red Farm

Brickkiln
Wood

LANE

Stoney Lane

PH

Shaw Farm

LONG

Mousefield Farm

Stone
Copse

Stone Copse

Road

A

B

84

C

D

E

VENUE NAME	ADDRESS	TOWN	POSTCODE
...CHTON MEMORIAL CHURCH	BANKEND ROAD	DUMFRIES	DG1 4ZZ
...TERBROOK HALL	BANKEND ROAD	DUMFRIES	DG1 4TL
...AT BRAE HOUSE	GEORGE STREET	DUMFRIES	DG1 1EA
...INSTANES, MIDSTEEPLE	HIGH STREET	DUMFRIES	DG1 2BH
...E STOVE	100 HIGH STREET	DUMFRIES	DG1 2BJ
...EATRE ROYAL	66-68 SHAKESPEARE STREET	DUMFRIES	DG1 2JH
...E BRIDGE	GLASGOW ROAD	DUMFRIES	DG2 0LL
...GEND THEATRE	MARKET SQUARE	DUMFRIES	DG2 7AE
...SEBURN CASTLE	CLOSEBURN	THORNHILL	
...NINIANS CHURCH	NORTH STREET	MONIAIVE	DG3 4HR
...HE AIRTS	8-12 HIGH STREET	SANQUHAR	DG4 6BL
...WICK MULTIVERSE	CRAWICK	SANQUHAR	DG4 6ET
...LVEND PUBLIC HALL	COLVEND	DALBEATTIE	DG5 4QD
...OUGHTON HOUSE	12 HIGH STREET	KIRKCUDBRIGHT	DG6 4JX
...STLE DOUGLAS TOWN HALL	5 ST ANDREW STREET	CASTLE DOUGLAS	DG7 1DE
...STRAND	HIGH STREET	NEW GALLOWAY	DG7 3RN
...RY TOWN HALL	MAIN STREET	ST JOHN'S TOWN OF DALRY	DG7 3UW
...WYNE HALL	CARSPHAIRN	CARSPHAIRN	DG7 3TQ
...L ON THE FLEET	65 HIGH STREET	GATEHOUSE	DG7 2HS
...S THREAVE GARDENS VISITOR CENTRE	THREAVE ESTATE	CASTLE DOUGLAS	DG7 1RX
...TIE BOOKS & CAFÉ	6 BANK STREET	WIGTOWN	DG8 9HP
...MILLAN HALL	DASHWOOD SQUARE	NEWTON STEWART	DG8 6EQ
...ALLOW THEATRE	MOSS PARK, RAVENSTONE	WHITHORN	DG8 8DR
...BA BAR	NORTH STRAND STREET	STRANRAER	DG9 7RB
...CHANS COMMUNITY HALL	LOCHANS	STRANRAER	DG9 9BZ
...GAN BOTANIC GARDEN	PORT LOGAN	STRANRAER	DG9 9ND
...AN CENTRE	FAIRHURST ROAD	STRANRAER	DG9 7AP
...FFAT TOWN HALL	HIGH STREET	MOFFAT	DG10 9HF
...D WELL THEATRE	OLD WELL ROAD	MOFFAT	DG10 9AP
...CKERBIE TOWN HALL	HIGH STREET	LOCKERBIE	DG11 2ES
...RNER HOUSE HOTEL	78 HIGH STREET	ANNAN	DG12 6DL
...CCLEUCH CENTRE	BUCCLEUCH SQUARE	LANGHOLM	DG13 0AW
...VINGTON SCHOOLHOUSE	DAVINGTON SCHOOLHOUSE	ESKDALEMUIR	DG13 0QJ
...ETNA GATEWAY OUTLET VILLAGE	GLASGOW ROAD	GRETNA	DG16 5GG

SEASON

er/caper

ventures Of Isabel

TUESDAY 16 APRIL

TUESDAY 28 MAY - ORAN BAGRA

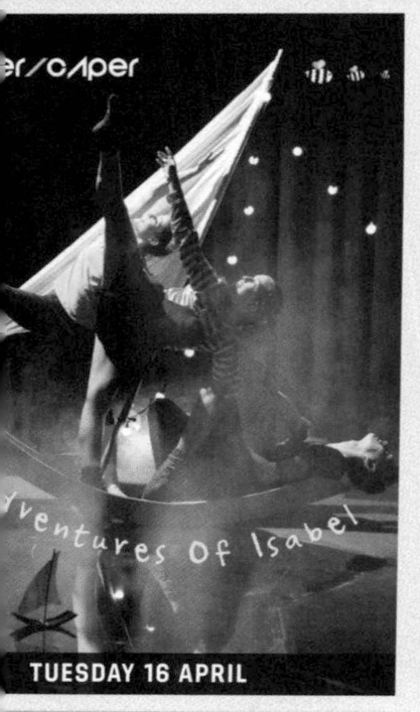

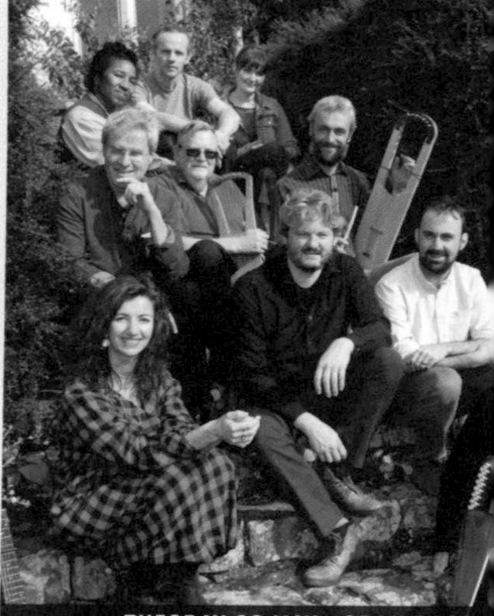

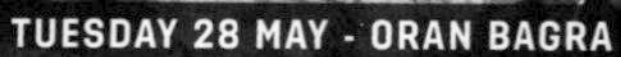

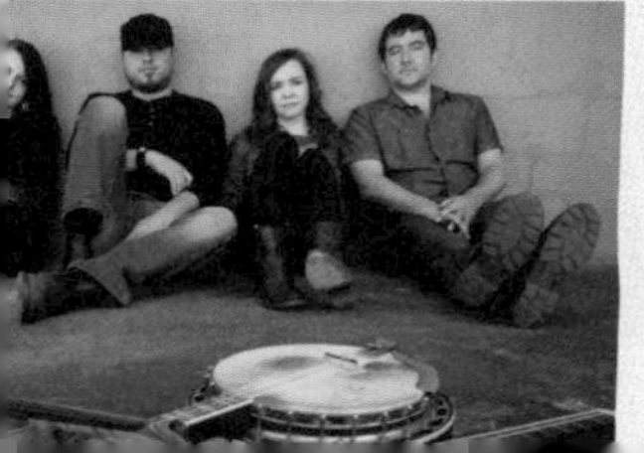

CatStrand
High Street
New Galloway
DG7 3RN

Tickets & In
www.cats
01644 4

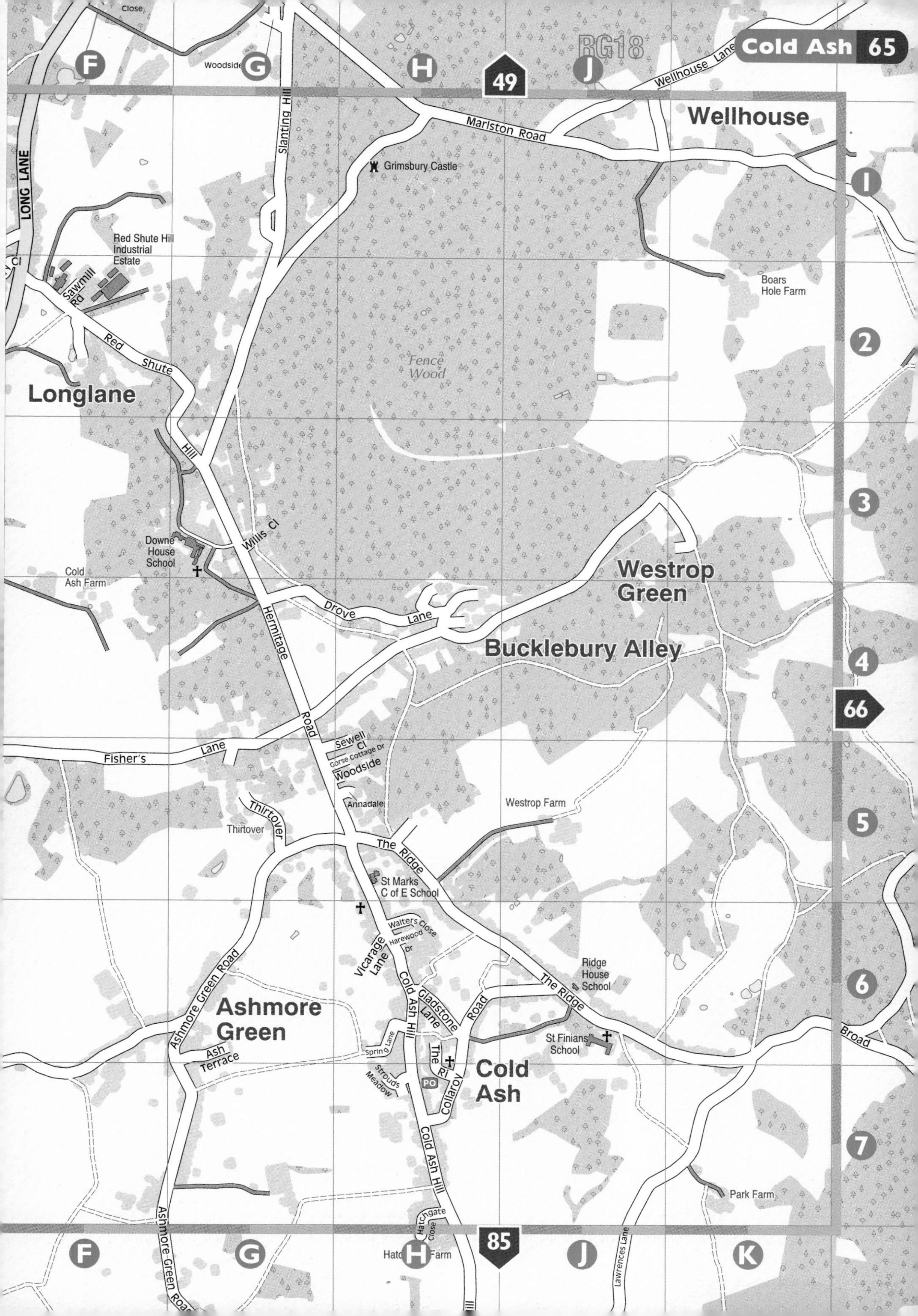

RG18

49

Wellhouse

Wellhouse Lane

Mariston Road

Woodside

Slanting Hill

Grimsbury Castle

Boars
Hole Farm

LONG LANE

Red Shute Hill
Industrial
Estate

Sawmill Rd

Red Shute Hill

Longlane

Fence
Wood

Willis Cl

Downe
House
School

Cold
Ash Farm

Hermitage Road

Drove Lane

**Westrop
Green**

Bucklebury Alley

Fisher's Lane

Sewell Cl

Gorse Cottage Dr

Woodside

Annadale

Westrop Farm

Thirtover

Thirtover

The Ridge

St Marks
C of E School

Walters Close

Harewood Dr

Vicarage Lane

Cold Ash Hill

Gladstone Lane

The Ridge

Ridge
House
School

**Ashmore
Green**

Ash
Terrace

Ashmore Green Road

Sprin Lane

Strouds
Meadow

The RI

PO

Collaroy

Cold Ash Hill

St Finians
School

**Cold
Ash**

Ashmore Green Road

Hatchgate Close

Hatch Farm

85

Lawrences Lane

Park Farm

Broad

66

F **G** **H** **J** **K**

I
2
3
4
5
6
7

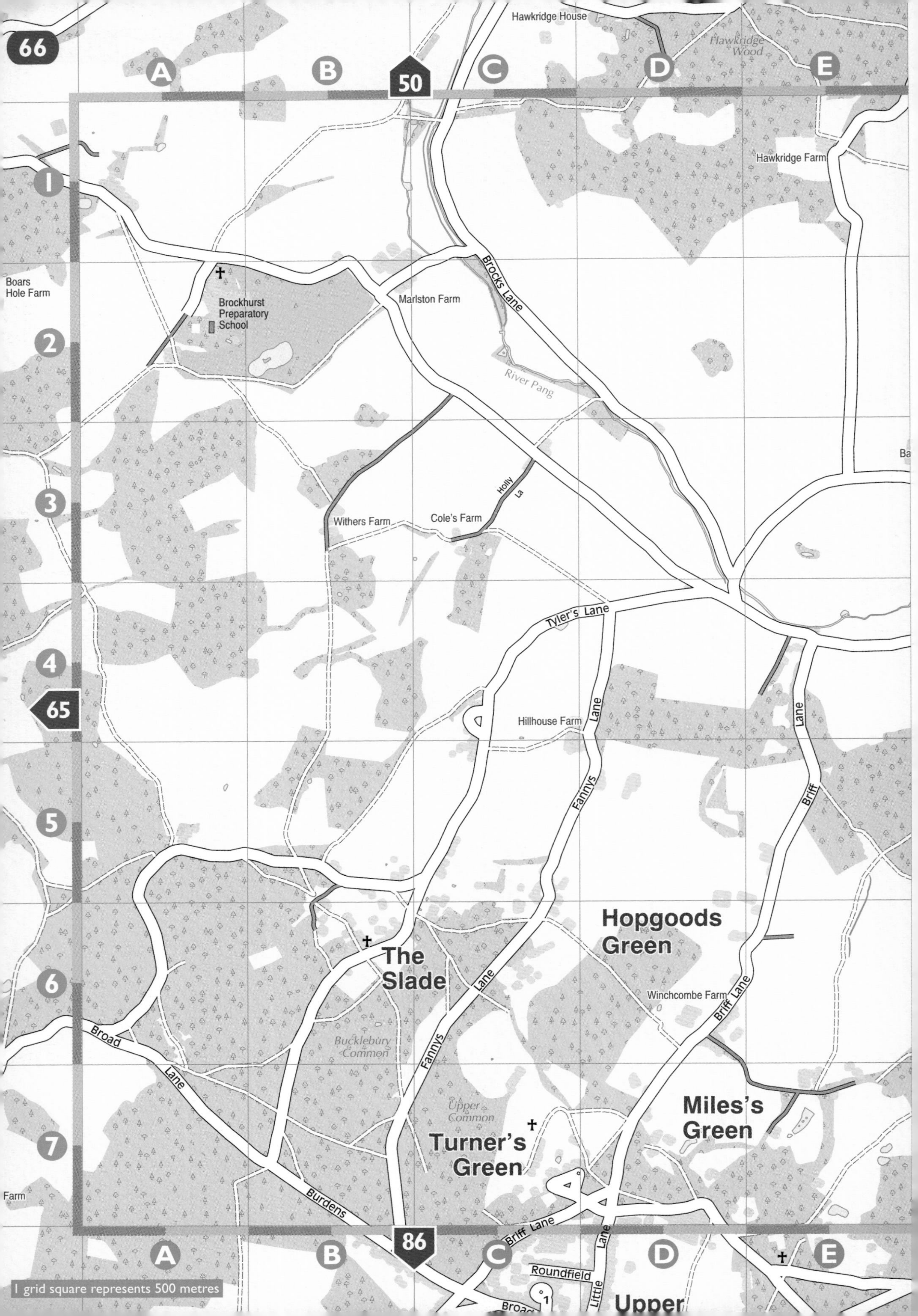

66

A   B   50   C   D   E

1

Boars
Hole Farm

Hawkridge House

Hawkridge
Wood

Hawkridge Farm

† Brockhurst
Preparatory
School

Marlston Farm

Brocks Lane

River Pang

2

Withers Farm   Cole's Farm

Holly La

3

Tyler's Lane

65

4

Hillhouse Farm

Lane

Fannys

Lane

Briff

Lane

Hopgoods
Green

5

6

Broad

Lane

The
Slade

†

Bucklebury
Common

Fannys

Lane

Winchcombe Farm

Briff Lane

Upper
Common

Turner's
Green

†

Miles's
Green

7

Farm

Burdens

86

Broad

Briff Lane

Roundfield

Little
Broad

Lane

1

Upper

A   B   86   C   D   E

1 grid square represents 500 metres

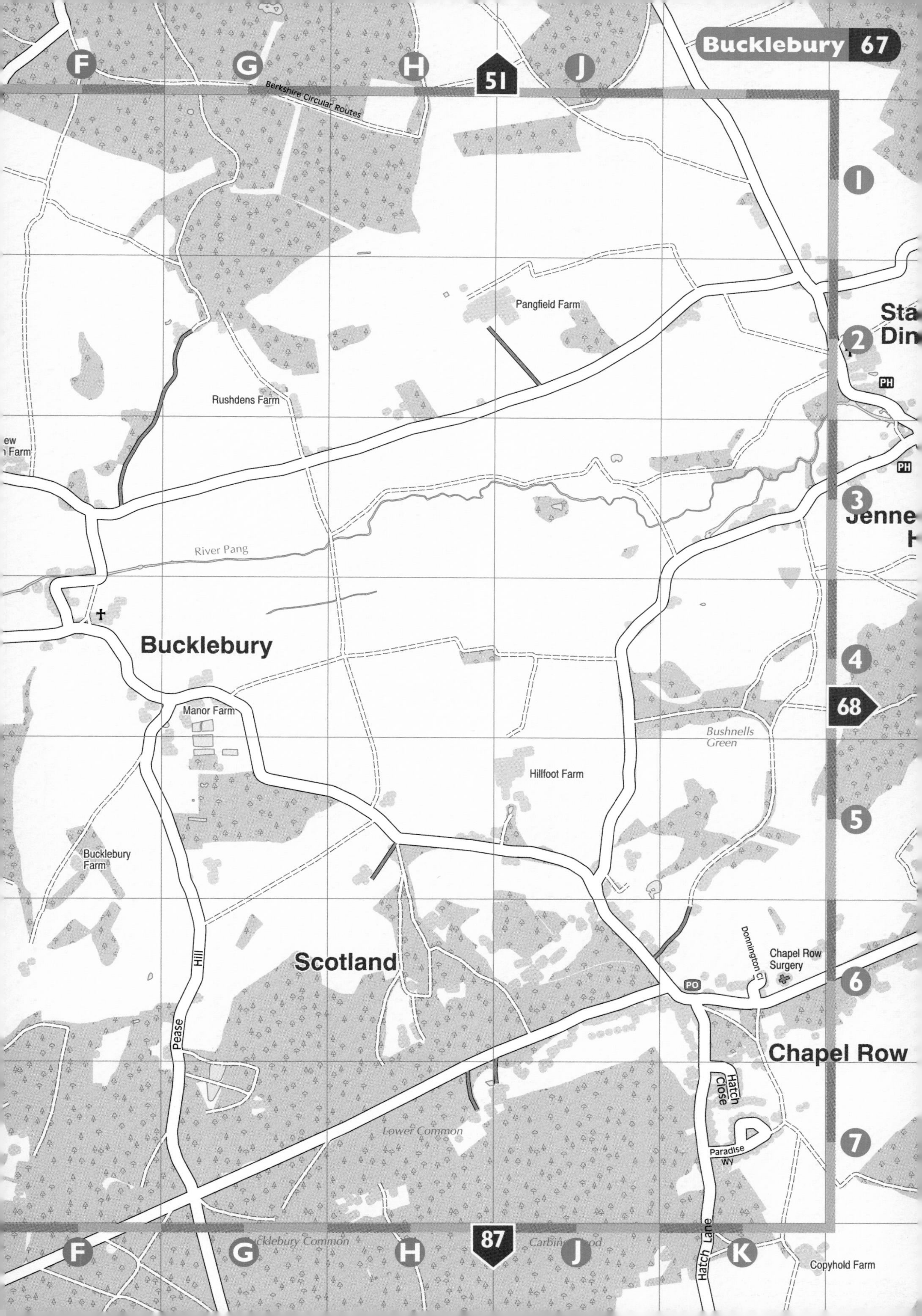

F G H 51 J

I

Berkshire Circular Routes

Pangfield Farm

Sta
Din

2

PH

Rushdens Farm

PH

3

Jenne
H

River Pang

†

Bucklebury

4

68

Manor Farm

Bushnells
Green

Hillfoot Farm

5

Bucklebury
Farm

Hill

Scotland

Donnington Cl

Chapel Row
Surgery

PO

6

Pease

Chapel Row

Hatch
Close

Lower Common

Paradise
Wy

7

F G H 87 J Carbin Wood K

Hatch Lane

Bucklebury Common

Copyhold Farm

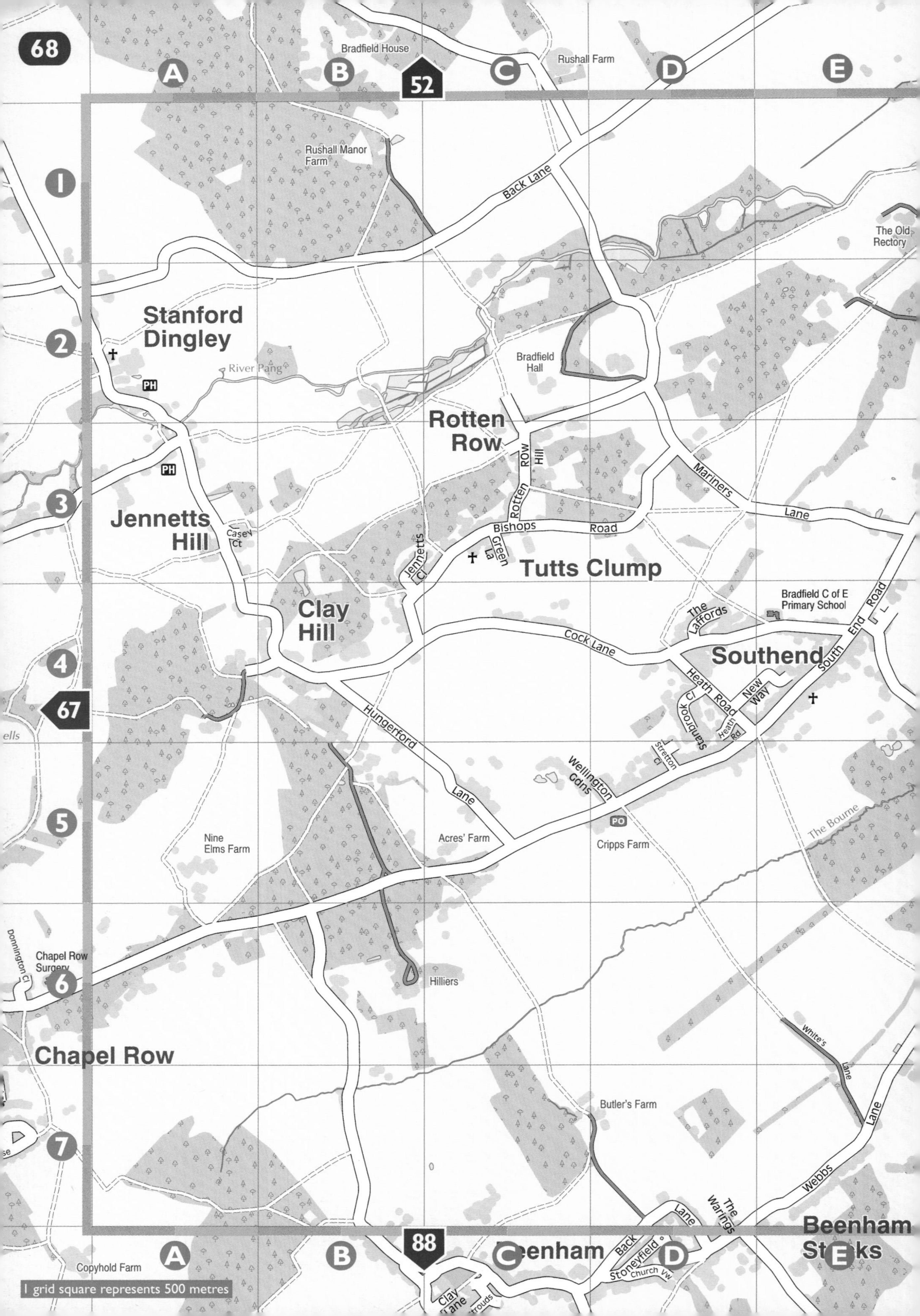

A B 52 C D E

1

Stanford
Dingley

Rushall Manor
Farm

Bradfield House

Rushall Farm

Back Lane

The Old
Rectory

2

PH

River Pang

Bradfield
Hall

Rotten
Row

Rotten Row Hill

Mariners

Lane

3

PH

Jennetts
Hill

Casey
Ct

Bishops

Green La

Jennetts Cl

Road

Tutts Clump

Bradfield C of E
Primary School

South End Road

Clay
Hill

Cock Lane

The Laffords

Southend

4

67

Hungerford

Lane

Heath Road

Stanbrook Cl

New Way

Heath Rd

Nine
Elms Farm

Wellington Gdns

Stretton Cl

The Bourne

5

Acres' Farm

PO

Cripps Farm

Donnington Cl

Chapel Row
Surgery

6

Hilliers

Chapel Row

White's
Lane

Butler's Farm

7

Webbs
Lane

The Warings

Beenham
St eks

A B 88 C eenham D E

Copyhold Farm

Clay Lane

Stoneyfield
Church Vw

Back
Lane

Strouds

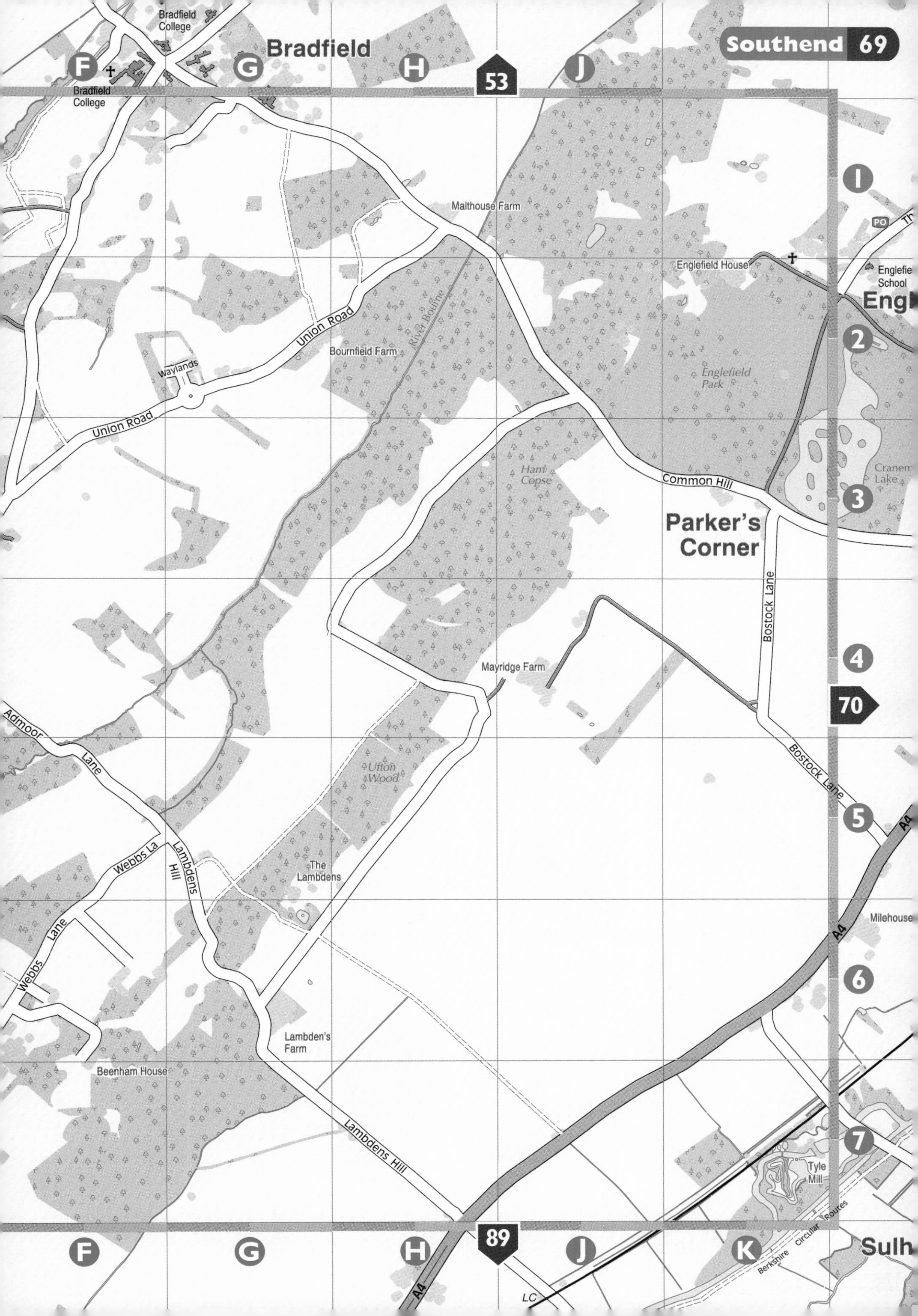
Bradfield College
Bradfield
F
G
H
53
J
Bradfield College
I
Malthouse Farm
Englefield House
Englefield School
Engl
Union Road
River Bourne
Bournfield Farm
2
Englefield Park
Waylands
Union Road
Ham Copse
Cranem Lake
Common Hill
3
Parker's Corner
Bostock Lane
4
Mayridge Farm
70
Admoor Lane
Bostock Lane
Ufton Wood
5
A4
Webbs La
Lambdens Hill
The Lambdens
Webbs Lane
Milehouse
A4
6
Lambden's Farm
Beenham House
7
Lambdens Hill
Tyle Mill
Berkshire Circular Routes
89
F
G
H
J
K
Sulh
A4
LC

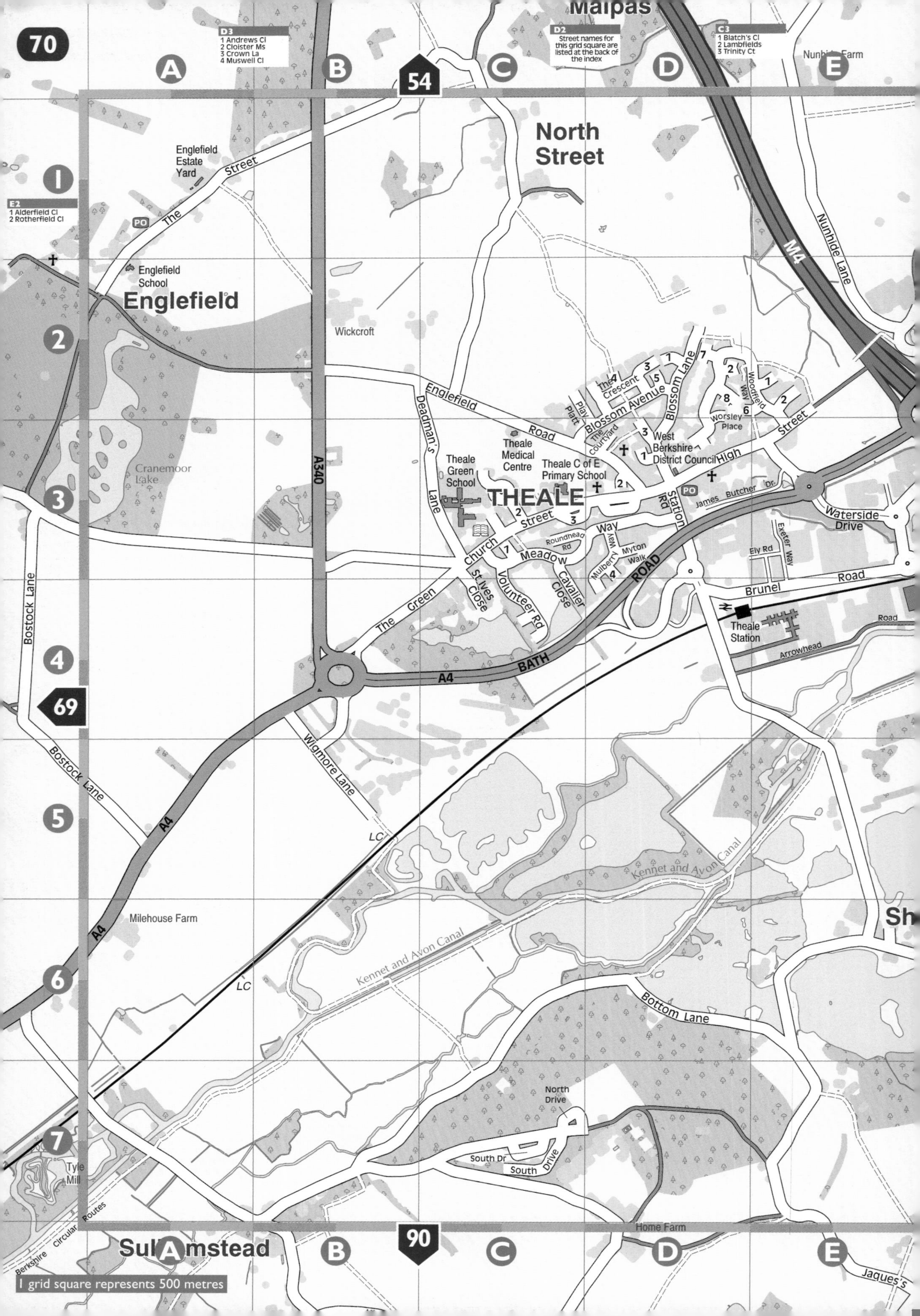

Malpas
D3
1 Andrews Cl
2 Cloister Ms
3 Crown La
4 Muswell Cl
D2
Street names for this grid square are listed at the back of the index
C3
1 Blatch's Cl
2 Lambfields
3 Trinity Ct
E2
1 Alderfield Cl
2 Rotherfield Cl
54
69
90
North Street
Englefield Estate Yard
The Street
Englefield School
Englefield
Wickcroft
Cranemoor Lake
Bostock Lane
A340
Englefield Road
Deadman's Lane
Theale Green School
Theale Medical Centre
Theale C of E Primary School
THEALE
West Berkshire District Council
Blossom Avenue
Blossom Lane
The Crescent
The Courtyard
Play Platt
Woodfield Way
Worsley Place
High Street
Station Rd
James Butcher Dr.
Waterside Drive
Exeter Way
Ely Rd
Brunel Road
Church Street
Meadow Way
Roundhead Rd
Mulberry Way
Mytton Walk
Cavalier Close
Volunteer Rd
St Ives Close
The Green
BATH ROAD
A4
Theale Station
Arrowhead Road
Wigmore Lane
LC
Kennet and Avon Canal
Milehouse Farm
Bottom Lane
North Drive
South Dr
South Drive
Tyle Mill
Home Farm
Sulhamstead
Berkshire Circular Routes
Nunhide Farm
Nunhide Lane
M4
Jaques's
A
B
C
D
E
1
2
3
4
5
6
7

1 grid square represents 500 metres

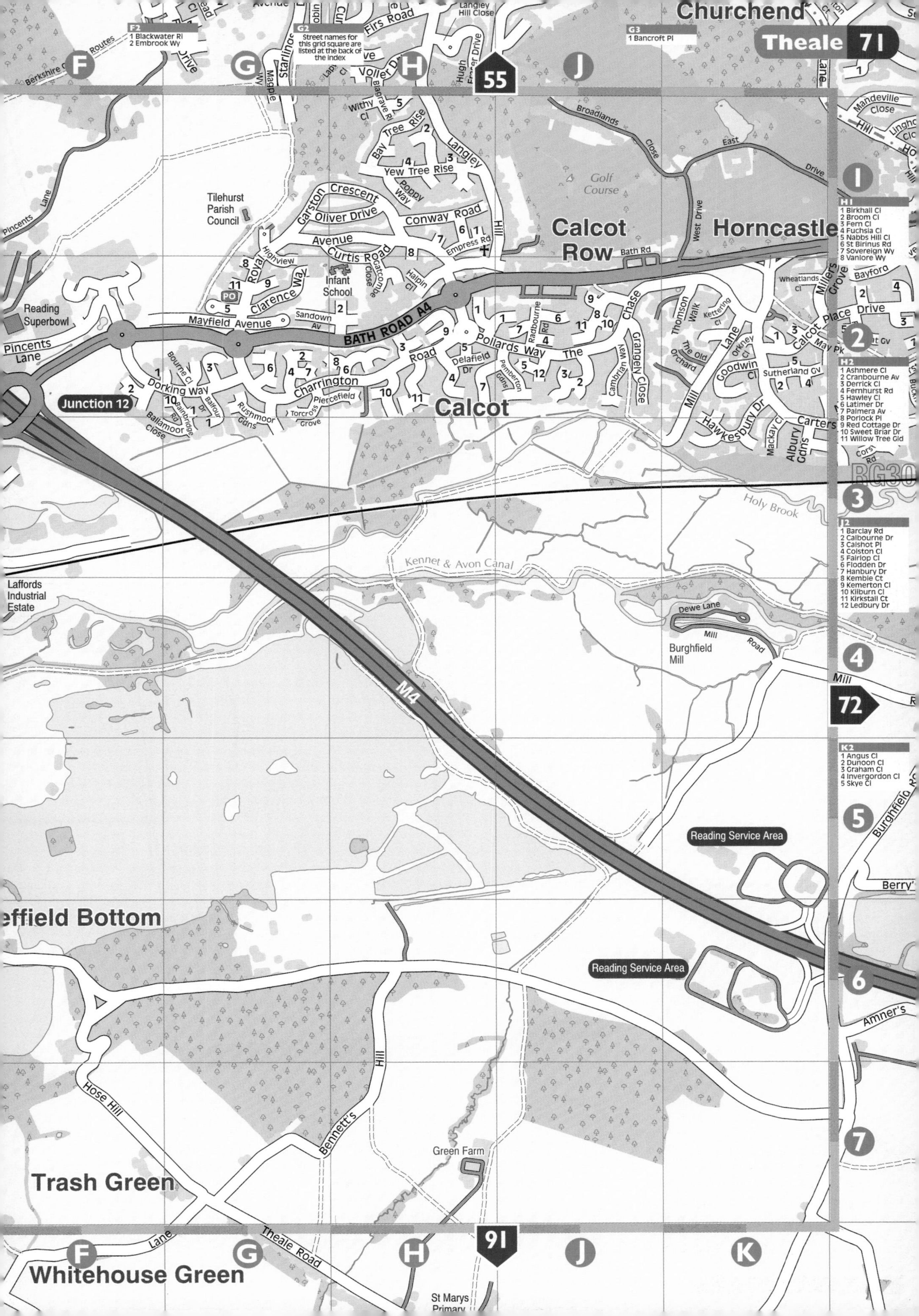
Churchend
F2
1 Blackwater Ri
2 Embrook Wy
G2
Street names for this grid square are listed at the back of the index
G3
1 Bancroft Pl
55
Firs Road
Langley Hill Close
Berkshire Circular Routes
Broadlands Close
East Drive
West Drive
Golf Course
Bay Tree Rise
Yew Tree Rise
Langley Hill
Poppy Way
Withy Cl
Garston Crescent
Oliver Drive
Conway Road
Avenue
Curtis Road
Empress Rd
Tilehurst Parish Council
Calcot Row
Bath Rd
Horncastle
Highview
Royal
Clarence Way
Infant School
Halpin Cl
Gratwicke Close
PO
Reading Superbowl
Mayfield Avenue
Sandown Av
BATH ROAD A4
Pincents Lane
Pollards Way
Delafield Dr
Radbourne Rd
Pemberton Gdns
The Chase
Cambrian Way
Grangely Close
Thomson Walk
Kettering Cl
The Old Orchard
Mill Lane
Orkney Cl
Goodwin Cl
Sutherland Gv
Hawkesbury Dr
Mackay Cl
Albury Gdns
Carters
Wheatlands Cl
Millers Grove
Calcot Place Drive
Bayford
May Pk
Bourne Cl
Dorking Way
Balfour Dr
Bainbridge Rd
Ballamoor Close
Rushmoor Gdns
Charrington Road
Piercefield
Torcross Grove
Junction 12
Calcot
Mandeville Close
Hill
H1
1 Birkhall Cl
2 Broom Cl
3 Fern Cl
4 Fuchsia Cl
5 Nabbs Hill Cl
6 St Birinus Rd
7 Sovereign Wy
8 Vanlore Wy
H2
1 Ashmere Cl
2 Cranbourne Av
3 Derrick Cl
4 Fernhurst Rd
5 Hawley Cl
6 Latimer Dr
7 Palmera Av
8 Porlock Pl
9 Red Cottage Dr
10 Sweet Briar Dr
11 Willow Tree Gld
J2
1 Barclay Rd
2 Calbourne Dr
3 Calshot Pl
4 Colston Cl
5 Fairlop Cl
6 Flodden Dr
7 Hanbury Dr
8 Kemble Ct
9 Kemerton Cl
10 Kilburn Cl
11 Kirkstall Ct
12 Ledbury Dr
K2
1 Angus Cl
2 Dunoon Cl
3 Graham Cl
4 Invergordon Cl
5 Skye Cl
RG30
Holy Brook
Kennet & Avon Canal
Laffords Industrial Estate
Dewe Lane
Mill Road
Burghfield Mill
Mill
72
M4
Reading Service Area
Burghfield Rd
Berry's
Amner's
effield Bottom
Hose Hill
Bennett's Hill
Green Farm
Trash Green
Theale Road
Lane
91
Whitehouse Green
St Marys Primary
F
G
H
J
K
1
2
3
4
5
6
7

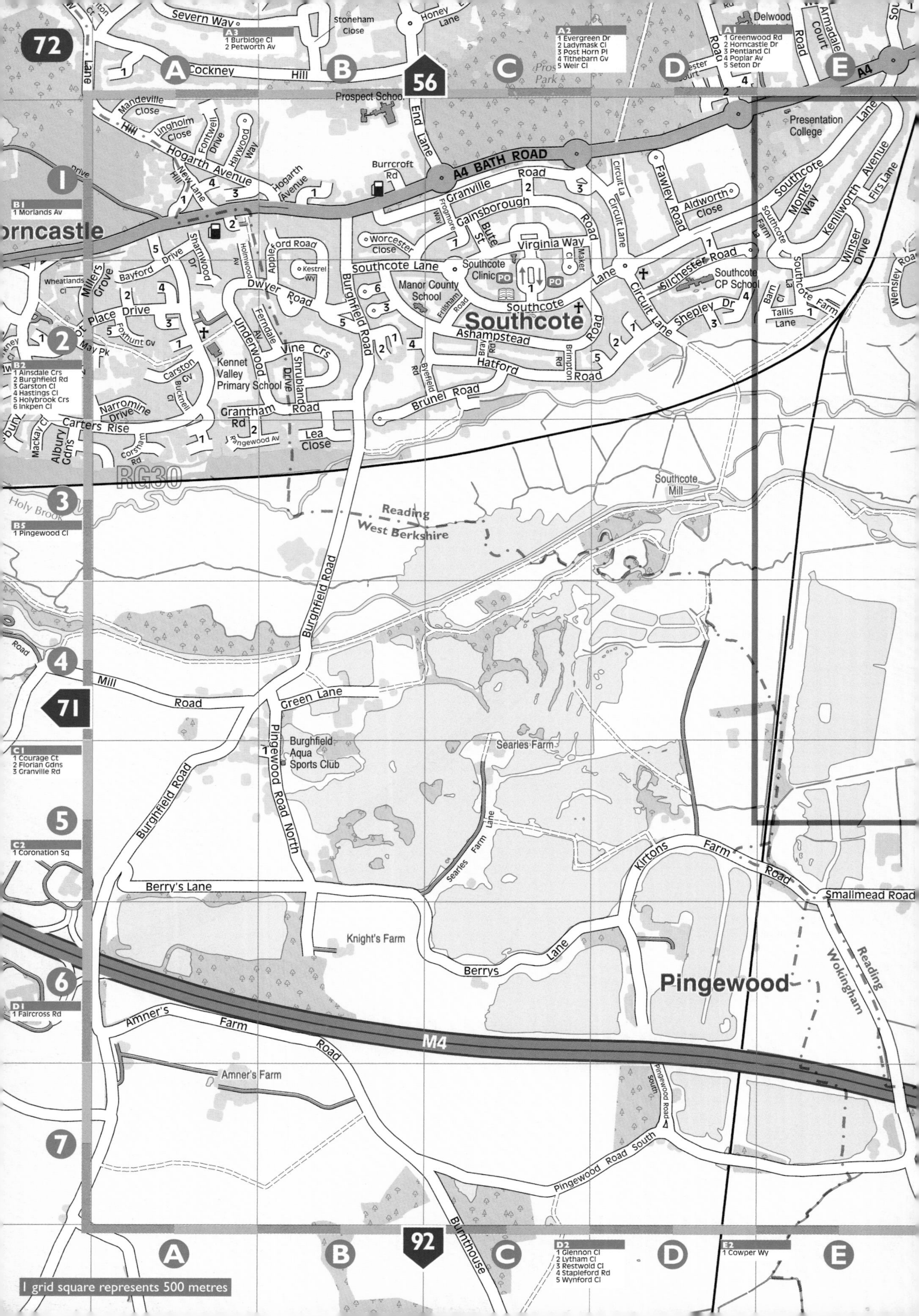

A3
1 Burbidge Cl
2 Petworth Av
A2
1 Evergreen Dr
2 Ladymask Cl
3 Post Horn Pl
4 Tithebarn Gv
5 Weir Cl
A1
1 Greenwood Rd
2 Horncastle Dr
3 Pentland Cl
4 Poplar Av
5 Seton Dr
B1
1 Morlands Av
B2
1 Ainsdale Crs
2 Burghfield Rd
3 Garston Cl
4 Hastings Cl
5 Holybrook Crs
6 Inkpen Cl
B5
1 Pingewood Cl
C1
1 Courage Ct
2 Florian Gdns
3 Granville Rd
C2
1 Coronation Sq
D1
1 Faircross Rd
D2
1 Glennon Cl
2 Lytham Cl
3 Restwold Cl
4 Stapleford Rd
5 Wynford Cl
E2
1 Cowper Wy
56
71
92
Southcote
Pingewood
A4 BATH ROAD
M4
Prospect School
Presentation College
Southcote Clinic
Manor County School
Southcote CP School
Kennet Valley Primary School
Burghfield Aqua Sports Club
Searles Farm
Knight's Farm
Amner's Farm
Southcote Mill
Reading
West Berkshire
RG30
Holy Brook
1 grid square represents 500 metres

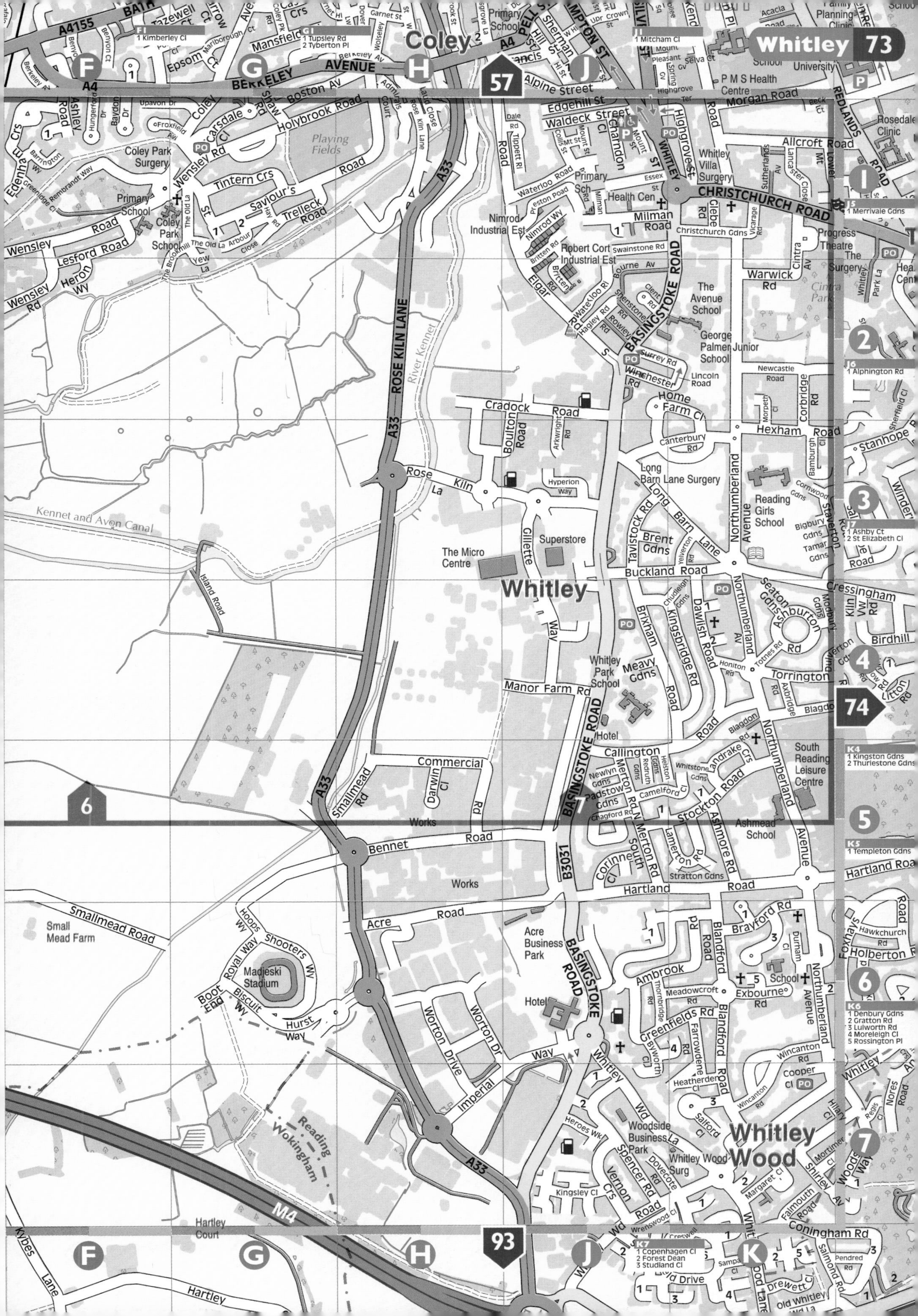
Coley
Whitley
Whitley Wood
57
74
93
6
F
G
H
J
K
I
2
3
4
5
6
7
F1 1 Kimberley Cl
G1 1 Tupsley Rd 2 Tyberton Pl
J1 1 Mitcham Cl
J5 1 Merrivale Gdns
J6 1 Alphington Rd
J7 1 Ashby Ct 2 St Elizabeth Cl
K4 1 Kingston Gdns 2 Thurlestone Gdns
K5 1 Templeton Gdns
K6 1 Denbury Gdns 2 Gratton Rd 3 Lulworth Rd 4 Moreleigh Cl 5 Rossington Pl
K7 1 Copenhagen Cl 2 Forest Dean 3 Studland Cl
A4155
BATH
A4
BERKELEY AVENUE
Boston Av
Holybrook Road
Coley Park Surgery
Primary School
Coley Park School
Wensley Road
Lesford Road
Heron Wy
Tintern Crs
Saviour's Road
Trelleck Road
Playing Fields
ROSE KILN LANE
A33
River Kennet
Kennet and Avon Canal
Island Road
Alpine Street
Edgehill St
Waldeck Street
WHITLEY ST
CHRISTCHURCH ROAD
Christchurch Gdns
Whitley Villa Surgery
Health Cen
Milman Road
Nimrod Industrial Est
Robert Cort Industrial Est
BASINGSTOKE ROAD
The Avenue School
George Palmer Junior School
Progress Theatre
Warwick Rd
Cintra Park
Allcroft Road
Morgan Road
REDLANDS ROAD
University
Rosedale Clinic
Cradock Road
Boulton Road
Home Farm Cl
Hexham Road
Long Barn Lane Surgery
Reading Girls School
Northumberland Avenue
Buckland Road
The Micro Centre
Superstore
Gillette Way
Rose Kiln La
Brent Gdns
Tavistock Rd
Long Barn Lane
Cressingham Road
Ashburton Rd
Torrington Rd
Whitley Park School
Meavy Gdns
Manor Farm Rd
Kingsbridge Road
Dawlish Road
Callington Road
Commercial Rd
Darwin Cl
Smallmead Rd
Works
Stockton Road
South Reading Leisure Centre
Ashmead School
Bennet Road
B3031
Hartland Road
Acre Road
Smallmead Road
Small Mead Farm
Madjeski Stadium
Shooters Wy
Royal Way
Hoops Wy
Boot End
Biscuit Wy
Hurst Way
Acre Business Park
Hotel
Ambrook Rd
Brayford Rd
Blandford Road
Exbourne Rd
Greenfields Rd
Worton Drive
Worton Dr
Imperial Way
Woodside Business Park
Whitley Wood Lane
Whitley Wood Surg
Spencer Rd
Vernon Crs
Kingsley Cl
Heroes Wk
Margaret Cl
Coningham Rd
Cooper Cl
Wincanton Rd
Reading Wokingham
M4
Hartley Court
Kybes Lane
Hartley
Drewett Cl
Old Whitley Wood

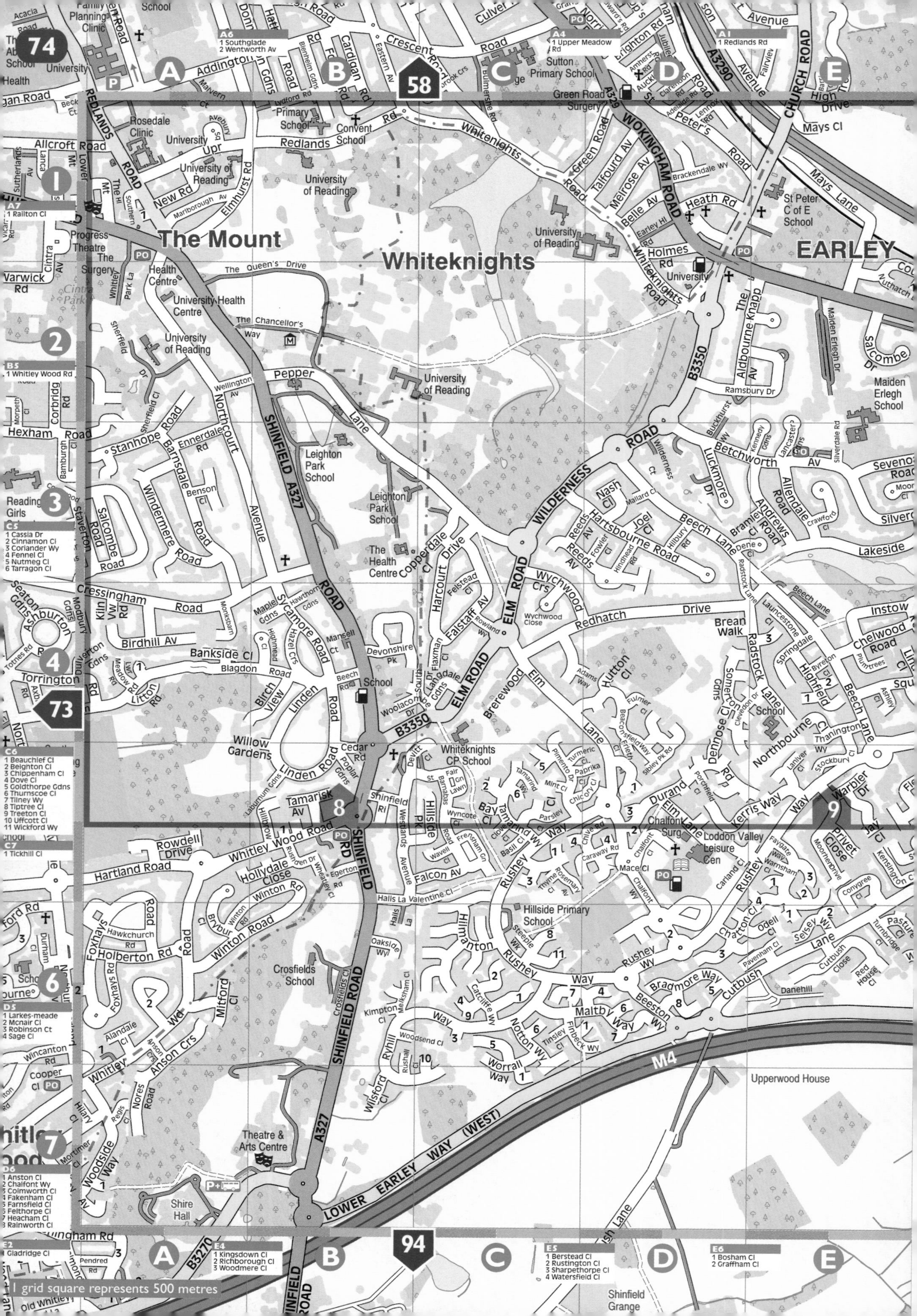
74
58
73
8
9
94
A
B
C
D
E
1
2
3
4
6
7
A6
1 Southglade
2 Wentworth Av
A4
1 Upper Meadow Rd
A1
1 Redlands Rd
A7
1 Railton Cl
B5
1 Whitley Wood Rd
C5
1 Cassia Dr
2 Cinnamon Cl
3 Coriander Wy
4 Fennel Cl
5 Nutmeg Cl
6 Tarragon Cl
C6
1 Beauchief Cl
2 Beighton Cl
3 Chippenham Cl
4 Dove Cl
5 Goldthorpe Gdns
6 Thurnscoe Cl
7 Tilney Wy
8 Tiptree Cl
9 Treeton Cl
10 Uffcott Cl
11 Wickford Wy
C7
1 Ticknill Cl
D5
1 Larkes-meade
2 Mcnair Cl
3 Robinson Ct
4 Sage Cl
D6
1 Anston Cl
2 Chalfont Wy
3 Colmworth Cl
4 Fakenham Cl
5 Farnsfield Cl
6 Felthorpe Cl
7 Heacham Cl
8 Rainworth Cl
E2
1 Gladridge Cl
E4
1 Kingsdown Cl
2 Richborough Cl
3 Woodmere Cl
E5
1 Berstead Cl
2 Rustington Cl
3 Sharpethorpe Cl
4 Watersfield Cl
E6
1 Bosham Cl
2 Graffham Cl
1 grid square represents 500 metres
The Mount
Whiteknights
EARLEY
Planning Clinic
University
Addington Rd
Crescent Road
Sutton Primary School
Green Road Surgery
CHURCH ROAD
A3290
Avenue
High Drive
Mays Cl
Mays Lane
REDLANDS ROAD
Rosedale Clinic
Primary School
Convent School
Redlands Road
Whiteknights Road
WOKINGHAM ROAD
A329
Green Road
Talfourd Av
Melrose Av
Brackendale Wy
Heath Rd
St Peter C of E School
Allcroft Road
Lower Mt
University of Reading
New Rd
Elmhurst Rd
Marlborough Av
Belle Av
Earley Hl
Holmes Rd
University
Progress Theatre
The Surgery
Health Centre
University Health Centre
The Queen's Drive
The Chancellor's Way
Cintra Park
Warwick Rd
Pepper Lane
Wellington Av
Northcourt Avenue
SHINFIELD A327
Leighton Park School
Hexham Road
Stanhope Road
Barnsdale Road
Ennerdale Rd
Benson Cl
Windermere Road
Salcombe Road
Reading Girls
Staverton
Leighton Park School
The Health Centre
Copperdale Cl
Harcourt Drive
WILDERNESS ROAD
B3350
The Knapp
Aldbourne Av
Ramsbury Dr
Maiden Erlegh Dr
Salcombe Dr
Maiden Erlegh School
Betchworth Av
Luckmore Dr
Wilderness Ct
Nash Cl
Mallard Cl
Hartsbourne Road
Joel Cl
Reeds Av
Beech Lane
Andrews Road
Allendale Road
Sevenoaks Road
Silverdale Rd
Lakeside
ELM ROAD
Wychwood Crs
Wychwood Close
Redhatch Drive
Brean Walk
Launcestone
Instow
Chelwood Road
Cressingham Road
Seaton Gdns
Ashburton
Kiln Vw Rd
Birdhill Av
Bankside Cl
Blagdon Road
Torrington
Sycamore Road
Maple Gdns
Hawthorn Gdns
Hazel Crs
Mansell Ct
Devonshire Pk
Falstaff Av
Felstead Cl
Rowland Wy
Flaxman Cl
Langdale Gdns
ELM ROAD
Brerewood
Hutton Cl
Adams Way
Fulmer Cl
Beaconsfield Way
Sibley Pk Rd
Somerton Gdns
Dennose Cl
Radstock Lane
Highfield
School
Northbourne
Thanington Wy
Stockbury Cl
Warbler Dr
Birch View
Linden Road
School
Woolacombe Dr
Willow Gardens
Cedar Rd
Poplar Gdns
Linden Road
Laburnum Gdns
Tamarisk Av
Whiteknights CP School
Shinfield Ri
Hillside Pk
Wyncote
Bay Cl
Tamarind Wy
Parsley
Paprika
Chicory Cl
Mint Cl
Turmeric
Durand Rd
Kerris Way
Elm Lane
Chalfont Surg
Loddon Valley Leisure Cen
Rowdell Drive
Whitley Wood Road
Hartland Road
Hollydale Close
Winton Rd
Winton Road
Egerton Rd
SHINFIELD RD
Westlands Avenue
Falcon Av
Halls La
Valentine Cl
Rushey Way
Mace Cl
Carland Cl
Privet Close
Kensington
Hawkchurch Rd
Holberton Rd
Foxhays Rd
Mitford Cl
Crosfields School
SHINFIELD ROAD
Oakside Wy
Hillside Primary School
Steeple Wk
Himanton
Chatton Cl
Odell Cl
Selsey Wy
Pasture
Cutbush Lane
Cutbush Close
Red House Cl
Danehill
Bradmore Way
Beeston Wy
Maltby Way
Worrall Way
Notton Wy
Catcliffe Wy
Kimpton Cl
Woodsend Cl
Ryhill Cl
Rushall Cl
Wilsford Cl
Whitley
Alandale Cl
Anson Crs
Nores Road
Wincanton
Cooper Cl
Hilary Cl
Regis
Woodside Way
Mortimer
A327
Theatre & Arts Centre
Shire Hall
P+
M4
Upperwood House
LOWER EARLEY WAY (WEST)
Shinfield Grange
B3270
SHINFIELD ROAD
Pendred Rd
Old Whitley

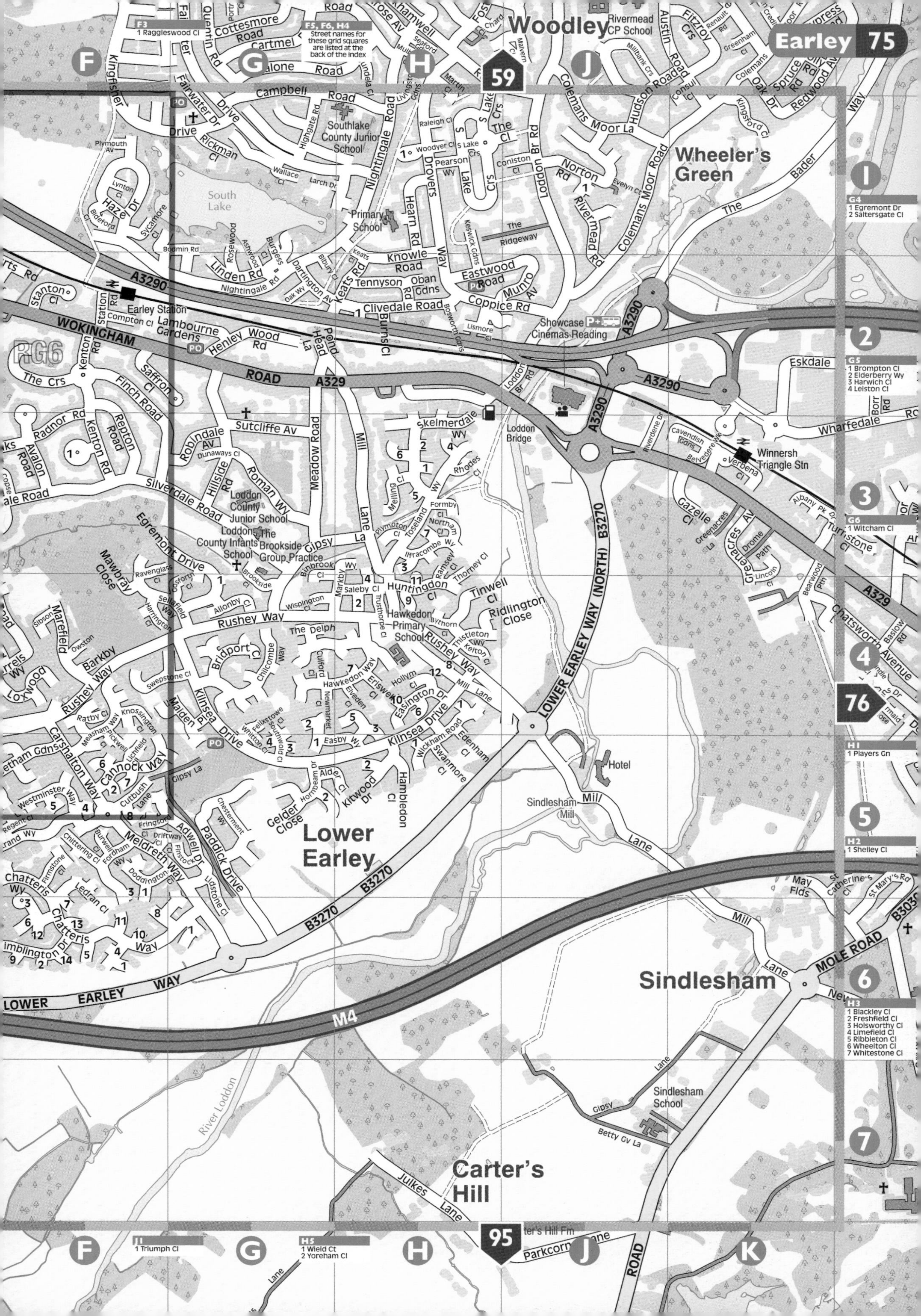
Woodley
Rivermead CP School
F3
1 Raggleswood Cl
F5, F6, H4
Street names for these grid squares are listed at the back of the index
59
Cottesmore Road
Cartmel
Quentin Rd
Kingfisher
Fairwater Dr
Drive
Campbell Road
Southlake County Junior School
Highgate Rd
Nightingale Road
Rickman Cl
Plymouth Av
South Lake
Wallace Cl
Larch Dr
Woodyer Cl
Pearson Wy
Drovers Way
Lake Crs
The Cl
Raleigh Cl
Coniston Cl
Loddon Br Rd
Norton Rd
Rivermead Rd
Colemans Moor Rd
Colemans Moor La
Hudson Road
Austin Road
Fitzroy Crs
Oak Dr
Spruce Rd
Redwood Av
Wheeler's Green
The Bader Way
G4
1 Egremont Dr
2 Saltersgate Cl
Haze Dr
Lynton Cl
Bideford
Sycamore Cl
Bodmin Rd
Rosewood
Ashwood
Burgess Cl
Linden Rd
Primary School
Hearn Rd
Keats Rd
Knowle Road
Tennyson
Oban Gdns
Eastwood Road
Munro Av
The Ridgeway
Keswick Gdns
Nightingale Rd
Dartington Av
Oak Wy
Bibury Cl
Clivedale Road
Coppice Rd
Lismore Cl
Showcase Cinemas Reading
A3290
Stanton Cl
Station Rd
Earley Station
Compton Cl
Lambourne Gardens
Henley Wood Rd
Pond Head La
Burns Cl
Bosworth Gdns
WOKINGHAM ROAD A329
RG6
Kenton Rd
The Crs
Saffron Cl
Finch Road
Repton Road
Radnor Rd
Kenton Rd
Avalon Road
Silverdale Road
Robindale Av
Sutcliffe Av
Dunaways Cl
Hillside Rd
Roman Wy
Meadow Road
Mill Lane
Skelmerdale Wy
Rhodes Cl
Melling Cl
Formby Cl
Northam Cl
Toseland Wy
Plympton Cl
Ilfracombe Wy
Loddon Bridge
Riverdene Dr
Cavendish Gdns
Belvedere Wk
Verbena Cl
Winnersh Triangle Stn
Eskdale
Wharfedale Ro
Borr Rd
G5
1 Brompton Cl
2 Elderberry Wy
3 Harwich Cl
4 Leiston Cl
Loddon County Junior School
Loddon County Infants School
The Brookside Group Practice
Gipsy La
Egremont Drive
Mawbray Close
Ravenglass Cl
Gosforth Cl
Sellafield Way
Harrington Cl
Allonby Cl
Brookside
Binbrook Cl
Markby Wy
Saleby Cl
Huntingdon Cl
Ramsey Cl
Thorney Cl
Tinwell Cl
Ridlington Close
Wispington Cl
Trusthorpe Cl
Hawkedon Primary School
Byrhorn Cl
Thistleton Wy
Kelton Cl
Rushey Way
LOWER EARLEY WAY (NORTH) B3270
Gazelle Cl
Greenacres La
Greenacres Av
Drome Path
Lincoln Cl
Bearwood Pth
Albany Pk Dr
Turnstone Cl
A329
G6
1 Witcham Cl
Chatsworth Avenue
Baslow Rd
76
Marefield
Sibson
Owston
Barkby
Loxwood
The Delph
Bridport Cl
Chilcombe Way
Sweepstone Cl
Culford Cl
Hawkedon Way
Eriswell
Elveden
Newmarket
Hollym Cl
Easington Dr
Mill Lane
Kilnsea Drive
Maiden Pl
Ratby Cl
Knossington
Measham Way
Pickwell Cl
Lichfield Cl
Felixstowe Cl
Southwold Cl
Whitton Cl
Easby Wy
Wickham Road
Swanmore Cl
Edenham Cl
Alder Cl
Hornbeam Dr
Kitwood Dr
Hambledon Cl
Gelder Close
Carshalton Way
Cannock Way
Cutbush Lane
Gipsy La
Lower Gdns
Westminster Way
Chesterment Wy
Paddick Drive
Adwell Dr
Fringsons
Driftway
Finstock
Meldreth Way
Doddington Cl
Lidstone Cl
Hotel
Sindlesham Mill
Mill Lane
H1
1 Players Gn
H2
1 Shelley Cl
Lower Earley
B3270
Chatteris Wy
Ledran Cl
Chatteris Way
Firmstone Cl
Chittering Cl
Bunyan
Fordham Wy
Timblington Dr
Bunwell
LOWER EARLEY WAY
M4
May Flds
St Catherine's Cl
St Mary's Rd
B3030
MOLE ROAD
Mill Lane
Sindlesham
H3
1 Blackley Cl
2 Freshfield Cl
3 Holsworthy Cl
4 Limefield Cl
5 Ribbleton Cl
6 Wheelton Cl
7 Whitestone Cl
River Loddon
Lane
Sindlesham School
Gipsy
Betty Gv La
Carter's Hill
Julkes Lane
95
Carter's Hill Fm
Parkcorner Lane
ROAD
J1
1 Triumph Cl
H5
1 Wield Ct
2 Yoreham Cl
Lane
F
G
H
J
K
1
2
3
4
5
6
7

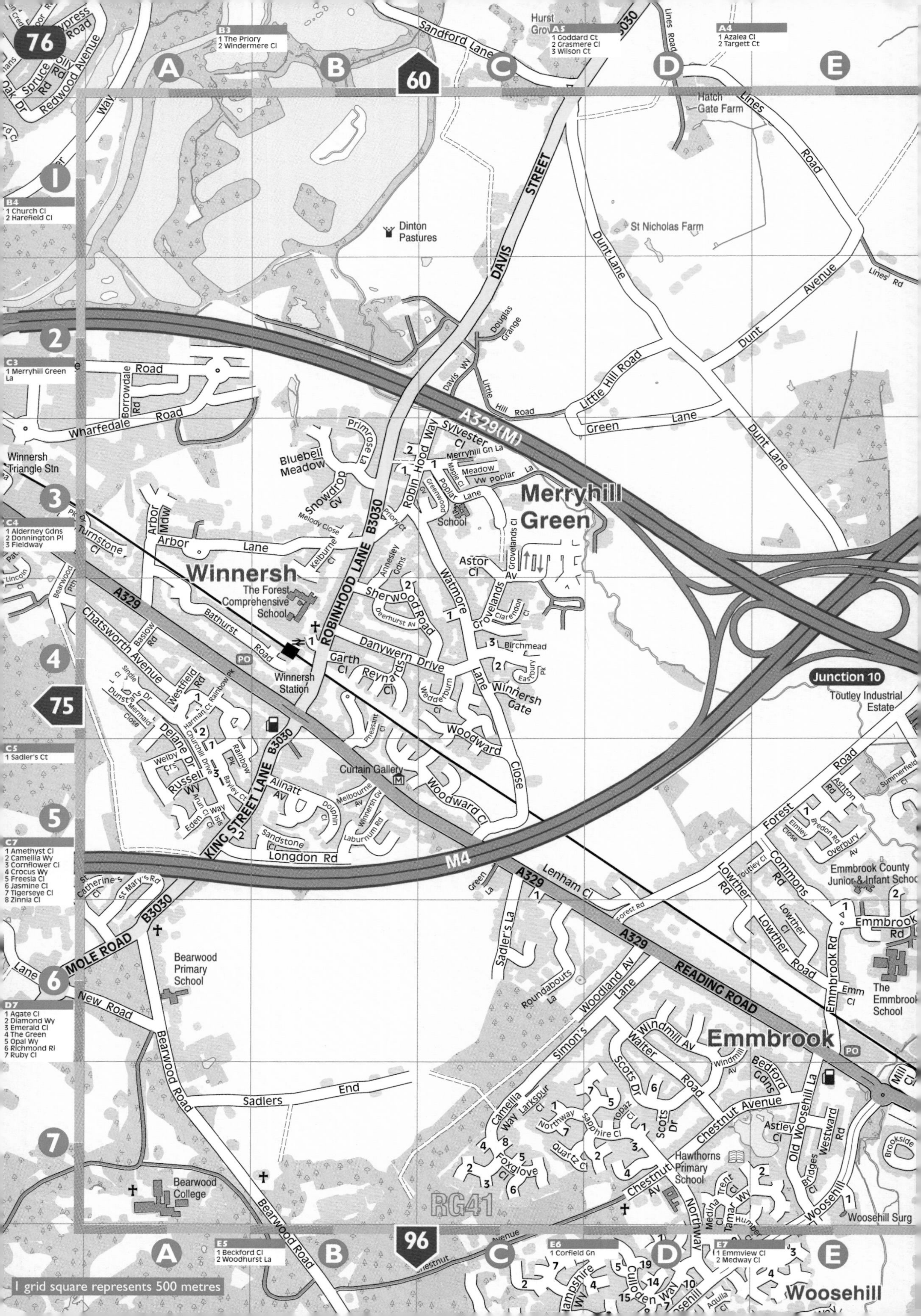

76
60
75
96
A
B
C
D
E
1
2
3
4
5
6
7
B3
1 The Priory
2 Windermere Cl
A5
1 Goddard Ct
2 Grasmere Cl
3 Wilson Ct
A4
1 Azalea Cl
2 Targett Ct
B4
1 Church Cl
2 Harefield Cl
C3
1 Merryhill Green La
C4
1 Alderney Gdns
2 Donnington Pl
3 Fieldway
C5
1 Sadler's Ct
C7
1 Amethyst Cl
2 Camellia Wy
3 Cornflower Cl
4 Crocus Wy
5 Freesia Cl
6 Jasmine Cl
7 Tigerseye Cl
8 Zinnia Cl
D7
1 Agate Cl
2 Diamond Wy
3 Emerald Cl
4 The Green
5 Opal Wy
6 Richmond Ri
7 Ruby Cl
E5
1 Beckford Cl
2 Woodhurst La
E6
1 Corfield Gn
E7
1 Emmview Cl
2 Medway Cl
Winnersh
Merryhill Green
Emmbrook
Woosehill
Dinton Pastures
St Nicholas Farm
Hatch Gate Farm
Winnersh Triangle Stn
Winnersh Station
The Forest Comprehensive School
Curtain Gallery
Bearwood Primary School
Bearwood College
Hawthorns Primary School
Emmbrook County Junior & Infant School
The Emmbrook School
Toutley Industrial Estate
Junction 10
Woosehill Surg
A329(M)
M4
A329
B3030
DAVIS STREET
ROBINHOOD LANE
KING STREET LANE
READING ROAD
MOLE ROAD
Bearwood Road
Sandford Lane
Lines Road
Dunt Lane
Dunt Avenue
Little Hill Road
Green Lane
Hill Road
Wharfedale Road
Borrowdale Rd
Arbor Lane
Arbor Mdw
Chatsworth Avenue
Bathurst Road
Sherwood Road
Danywern Drive
Watmore Lane
Grovelands Av
Woodward Close
Woodward Cl
Winnersh Gate
Alinatt Av
Longdon Rd
Sandstone Cl
Forest Road
Commons Rd
Lowther Rd
Lowther Road
Emmbrook Rd
Woodland Av
Simon's Lane
Windmill Av
Walter Road
Scots Dr
Chestnut Avenue
Old Woosehill La
Westward Rd
Sadlers End
New Road
Delane Dr
Russell Wy
Rainbow Pk
Westfield Rd
Bluebell Meadow
Primrose La
Snowdrop Gv
Sylvester Cl
Astor Cl
Birchmead
Lenham Cl
Sadler's La
Roundabouts La
Foxglove Cl
Northway
Camellia Way
RG41
1 grid square represents 500 metres

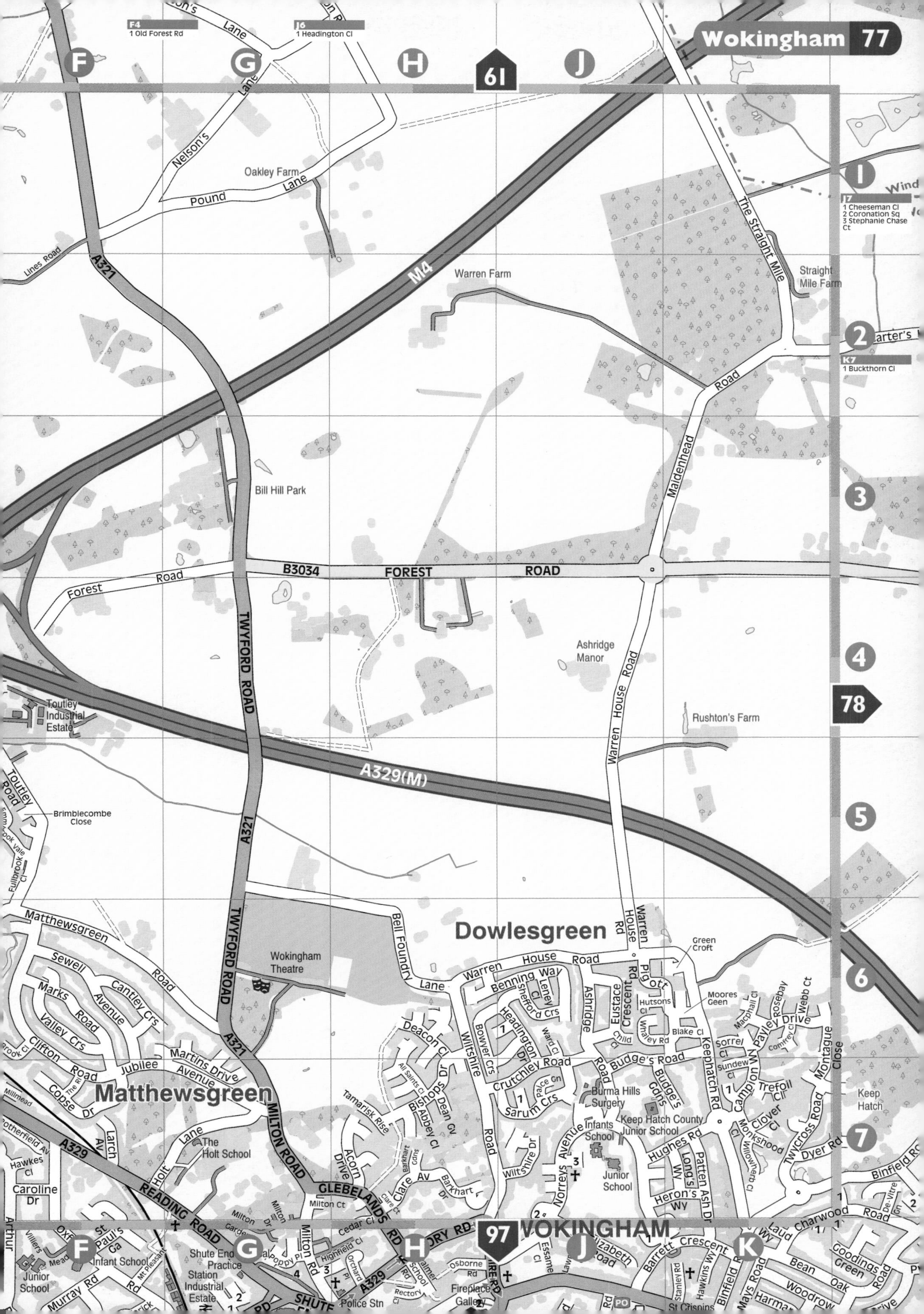
F4
1 Old Forest Rd
J6
1 Headington Cl
J7
1 Cheeseman Cl
2 Coronation Sq
3 Stephanie Chase Ct
K7
1 Buckthorn Cl
61
78
97
M4
A321
A329(M)
B3034
FOREST ROAD
TWYFORD ROAD
MILTON ROAD
Oakley Farm
Warren Farm
Bill Hill Park
Straight Mile Farm
Ashridge Manor
Rushton's Farm
Toutley Industrial Estate
Brimblecombe Close
Dowlesgreen
Matthewsgreen
Wokingham Theatre
The Holt School
Burma Hills Surgery
Keep Hatch County Junior School
Infants School
Junior School
Keep Hatch
WOKINGHAM
Nelson's Lane
Pound Lane
Lines Road
The Straight Mile
Maidenhead Road
Warren House Road
Bell Foundry Lane
Matthewsgreen Road
Reading Road
Glebelands Rd
Wiltshire Road
Budge's Road
Keephatch Rd
Twycross Road
Montague Close
Crutchley Road
Clifton Road
Jubilee Avenue
Martins Drive
Sewell Avenue
Cantley Crs
Marks Road
Valley Crs
Copse Dr
Larch Av
Holt Lane
Hawkes Cl
Caroline Dr
Benning Way
Ashridge Road
Eustace Crescent
Pigott Rd
Hutsons Cl
Blake Cl
Whaley Rd
Payley Drive
Campion Wy
Sorrel Cl
Sundew Cl
Trefoil Cl
Clover Cl
Monkshood Cl
Dyer Rd
Hughes Rd
Long's Wy
Patten Ash Dr
Heron's Wy
Norreys Avenue
Sarum Crs
Headington Dr
Bowyer Crs
Deacon Cl
Bishops Dr
Dean Gv
Abbey Cl
Acorn Drive
Clare Av
Barkhart Dr
Tamarisk Rise
Milton Ct
Barrett Crescent
Binfield Road
Charwood Rd
Goodings Green
Bean Oak Road
Woodrow
St Paul's Ga
Infant School
Junior School
Shute End Practice
Station Industrial Estate
Police Stn
Fireplace Gallery
Osborne Rd
Essame Cl
Elizabeth Road
Stanley Rd
Hawkins Wy
St Crispins
Murray Rd
Toutley Road
Fullbrook Cl
Green Croft
Moores Geen
Leney Cl
Shefford Crs
Ward Cl
Child Cl
Budge's Gdns
Wiltshire Dr
Laud Wy
Mays Road

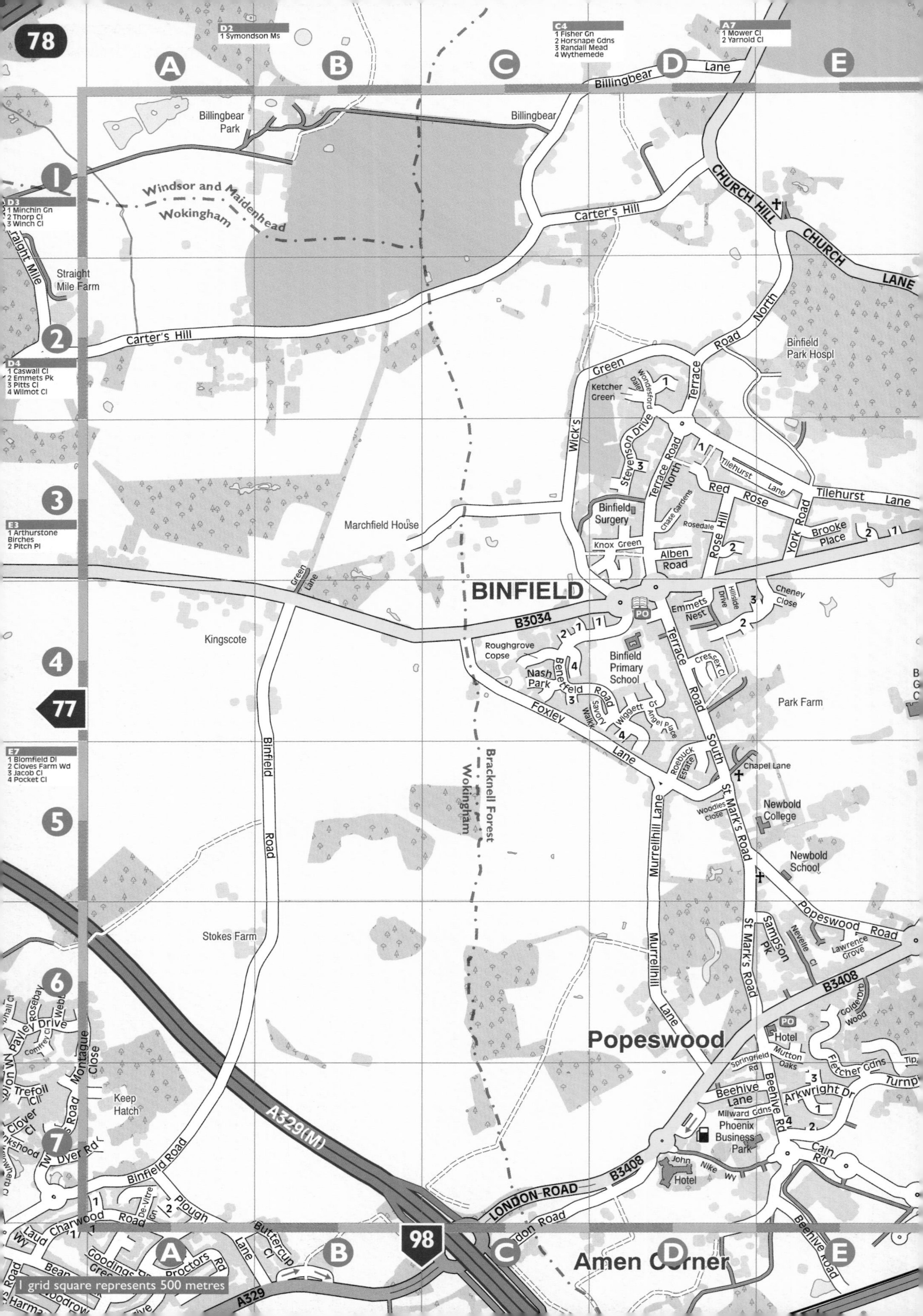
D2
1 Symondson Ms
C4
1 Fisher Gn
2 Horsnape Gdns
3 Randall Mead
4 Wythemede
A7
1 Mower Cl
2 Yarnold Cl
D3
1 Minchin Gn
2 Thorp Cl
3 Winch Cl
D4
1 Caswall Cl
2 Emmets Pk
3 Pitts Cl
4 Wilmot Cl
E3
1 Arthurstone Birches
2 Pitch Pl
E7
1 Blomfield Dl
2 Cloves Farm Wd
3 Jacob Cl
4 Pocket Cl
Billingbear Lane
Billingbear Park
Billingbear
Windsor and Maidenhead
Wokingham
Carter's Hill
Straight Mile
Straight Mile Farm
CHURCH HILL
CHURCH LANE
Terrace Road North
Binfield Park Hospl
Wick's Green
Ketcher Green
Wondesford Dale
Stevenson Drive
Tilehurst Lane
Red Rose
York Road
Binfield Surgery
Chase Gardens
Rosedale
Rose Hill
Brooke Place
Knox Green
Alben Road
Marchfield House
Green Lane
BINFIELD
B3034
Emmets Nest
Hillside Drive
Cheney Close
Kingscote
Roughgrove Copse
Nash Park
Benetfeld Road
Binfield Primary School
Terrace Road South
Cressex Cl
Park Farm
Foxley Lane
Savory Walk
Wiggett Gr
Angel Place
Roebuck Estate
Chapel Lane
Binfield Road
Bracknell Forest
Wokingham
Murrellhill Lane
Woodies Close
St Mark's Road
Newbold College
Newbold School
Popeswood Road
Sampson Pk
Nevelle Cl
Lawrence Grove
Stokes Farm
B3408
Goldcrest Wood
Popeswood
Hotel
Springfield Rd
Mutton Oaks
Fletcher Gdns
Beehive Lane
Beehive Rd
Arkwright Dr
Millward Gdns
Phoenix Business Park
Keep Hatch
A329(M)
Cain Rd
John Nike Wy
Hotel
LONDON ROAD
London Road
Beehive Road
Binfield Road
Plough
De-Vitre Gn
Charwood Road
Rosebay Drive
Payley Drive
Comfrey Cl
Montague Close
Trefoil Cl
Clover Cl
Dyer Rd
Laud Wy
Buttercup Lane
Proctors Rd
Goodings Grn
Amen Corner
A329
Harman
Woodrow
1 grid square represents 500 metres
Turnpike
Tip

77

98

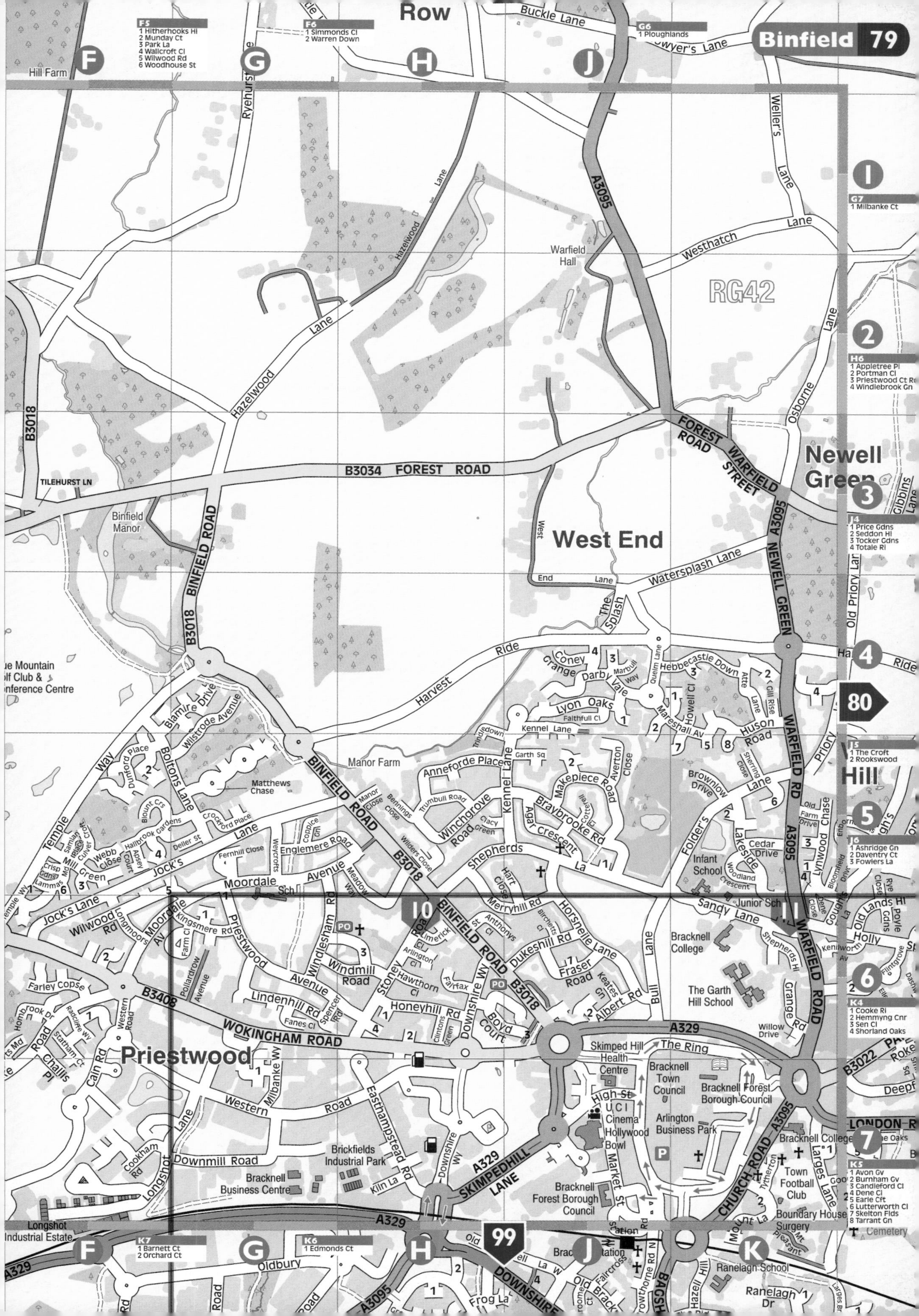
Row
Buckle Lane
F5
1 Hitherhooks Hl
2 Munday Ct
3 Park La
4 Wallcroft Cl
5 Wilwood Rd
6 Woodhouse St
F6
1 Simmonds Cl
2 Warren Down
G6
1 Ploughlands
Bowyer's Lane
Hill Farm
Ryehurst
Weller's Lane
G7
1 Milbanke Ct
Westhatch Lane
Hazelwood Lane
A3095
Warfield Hall
RG42
Osborne Lane
H6
1 Appletree Pl
2 Portman Cl
3 Priestwood Ct Rd
4 Windlebrook Gn
B3018
FOREST ROAD
WARFIELD STREET
Newell Green
Gibbins Lane
TILEHURST LN
B3034 FOREST ROAD
Binfield Manor
BINFIELD ROAD
J4
1 Price Gdns
2 Seddon Hl
3 Tocker Gdns
4 Totale Ri
West End
West End Lane
Watersplash Lane
NEWELL GREEN
Old Priory Lane
The Splash
Harvest Ride
Blue Mountain Golf Club & Conference Centre
Coney Grange
Darby Vale
Marbull Way
Quelm Lane
Hebbecastle Down
Atte Lane
Gill Rise
Lyon Oaks
Faithfull Cl
Howell Cl
Mareshall Av
Huson Road
Blamire Drive
Wilstrode Avenue
Kennel Lane
J5
1 The Croft
2 Rookswood
Hill
Temple Way
Dunford Place
Boltons Lane
Manor Farm
Matthews Chase
Manor Close
Bennings Close
Trumbull Road
Garth Sq
Anneforde Place
Averton Close
Makepiece Road
Brownlow Drive
Sherring Close
Folder's Lane
Old Farm Drive
Lynwood Chase
J6
1 Ashridge Gn
2 Daventry Ct
3 Fowlers La
Samian Place
Culver Croft
Webb Close
Hallbrook Gardens
Blount Crs
Crockford Place
Absey Court
Deller St
Jock's Lane
Fernhill Close
Weycrofts
Englemere Road
Coppice Gn
Wilders Close
Winchgrove Road
Clacy Green
Braybrooke Rd
Agar Crescent
Cotterell
Shepherds La
Lakeside
Cedar Drive
Infant School
Woodland Crescent
Crisp Gdns
Lammas
Mill Green
Moordale Avenue
Meadow Way
B3018
Hart Close
Merryhill Rd
Horsnell Lane
Junior Sch
Sandy Lane
Dene Close
Coughs La
Old Lands Hl
Poyle Gdns
Holly
Jock's Lane
Wilwood Rd
Longmoors
Moordale Av
Kingsmere Rd
Priestwood
Windlesham Rd
Limerick Cl
Stoney Road
St Anthonys Cl
Dukeshill Rd
Bull Lane
Bracknell College
Shepherds Hl
Kenilworth Av
Farm Cl
Arlington Cl
Windmill Road
Hawthorn Cl
Fairfax
Fraser Road
Keates Gn
The Garth Hill School
Grange Rd
Farley Copse
B3408
Pollardrow Avenue
Avenue
Lindenhill Rd
Spencer Rd
Honeyhill Rd
Downshire Wy
Boyd Court
Albert Rd
A329
Willow Drive
K4
1 Cooke Ri
2 Hemmyng Cnr
3 Sen Cl
4 Shorland Oaks
Homebrook Dr
Radcliffe Wy
Statham Ct
Western Road
Fanes Cl
Clintons Green
WOKINGHAM ROAD
Skimped Hill
The Ring
Health Centre
B3022
Priestwood
Challis Pl
Cain Rd
Milbanke Wy
Western Road
Easthampstead Rd
High St
Bracknell Town Council
Bracknell Forest Borough Council
UCI Cinema
Hollywood Bowl
Arlington Business Park
LONDON ROAD
Bracknell College
Cookham Rd
Longshot Lane
Downmill Road
Brickfields Industrial Park
Kiln La
Downshire Wy
A329 SKIMPEDHILL LANE
Market St
CHURCH ROAD
Tyrhenton
Town Football Club
Larges Lane
K5
1 Avon Gv
2 Burnham Gv
3 Candleford Cl
4 Dene Cl
5 Earle Cft
6 Lutterworth Cl
7 Skelton Flds
8 Tarrant Gn
Bracknell Business Centre
Bracknell Forest Borough Council
Boundary House Surgery
Cemetery
Longshot Industrial Estate
A329
Station Rd
Mount La
K7
1 Barnett Ct
2 Orchard Ct
K6
1 Edmonds Ct
Oldbury
Bracknell Station
Ranelagh School
Old Bracknell La W
DOWNSHIRE
Frog La
Crowthorne Rd N
Hazell Hill
Faircross
Ranelagh Dr
80
99
10
11

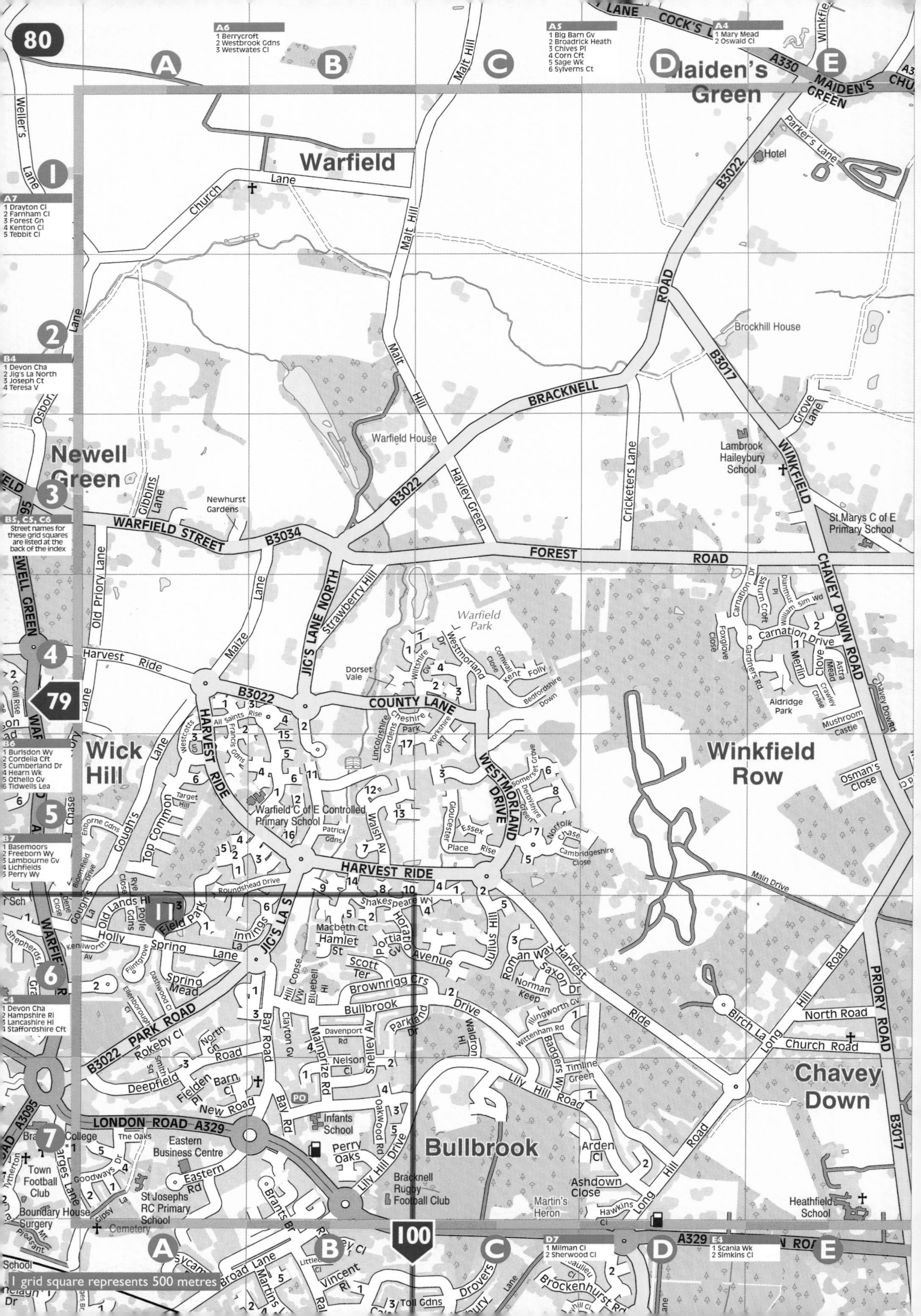

A B C D Maiden's Green E

Warfield

1

2

Church Lane

Malt Hill

BRACKNELL

Warfield House

Brockhill House

Lambrook Haileybury School

Newell Green

3

Gibbins Lane

Newhurst Gardens

WARFIELD STREET

B3034

FOREST ROAD

St Marys C of E Primary School

Old Priory Lane

Hayley Green

Cricketers Lane

Winkfield

Chavey Down Road

Grove Lane

Warfield Park

4

Harvest Ride

Dorset Vale

Carnation Drive

Aldridge Park

Mushroom Castle

79

B3022

COUNTY LANE

Cheshire Park

Winkfield Row

Osman's Close

Wick Hill

5

WESTMORLAND DRIVE

Harvest Ride

HARVEST RIDE

Warfield C of E Controlled Primary School

Gloucester Place

Essex Rise

Cambridgeshire Close

Main Drive

Roundshead Drive

Shakespeare Wy

11

Field Park

Holly Spring Lane

Spring Mead

Hamlet St

Scott Ter

Brownrigg Crs

Bullbrook

Roman Way

Saxon Dr

Norman Keep

Harvest Ride

Birch La

Long Hill Road

North Road

Church Road

6

PARK ROAD

B3022

Rokeby Cl

North Gn Road

Bay Road

Clayton Gv

Davenport Rd

Nelson Cl

Shelley Av

Parkland Dr

Lily Hill Road

Wittenham Rd

Badgers Wy

Timline Green

Chavey Down

B3017

7

LONDON ROAD A329

College

The Oaks

Eastern Business Centre

Eastern Rd

St Josephs RC Primary School

Cemetery

Deepfield

Fielden Pl

Barn Cl

New Road

Bay Rd

PO

Infants School

Perry Oaks

Oakwood Rd

Lily Hill Drive

Bracknell Rugby Football Club

Bullbrook

Arden Cl

Ashdown Close

Martin's Heron

Long Hill Road

Hawkins La

Heathfield School

Town Football Club

Boundary House Surgery

A3095

A **100** B C D A329 E

I grid square represents 500 metres

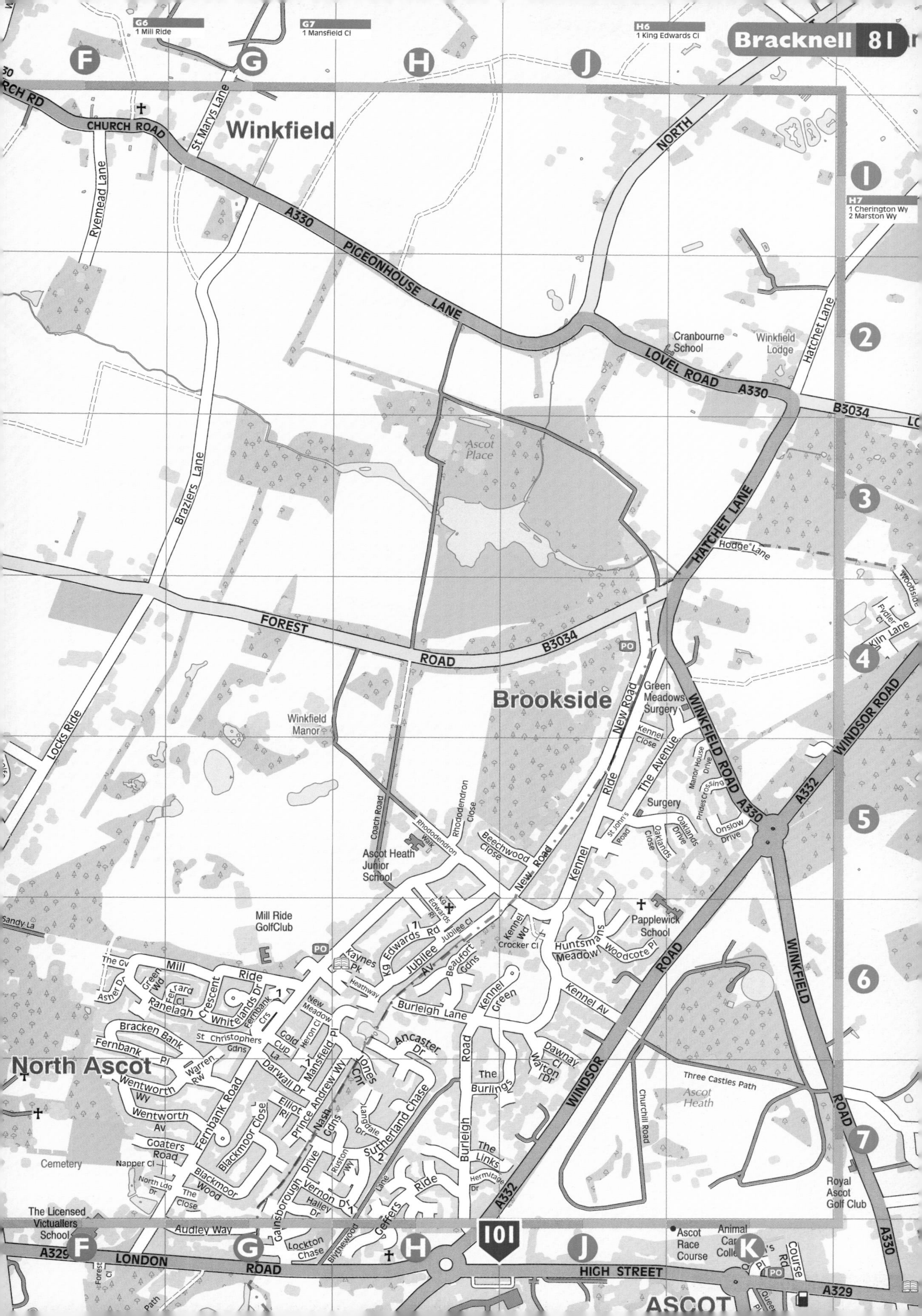

G6
1 Mill Ride

G7
1 Mansfield Cl

H6
1 King Edwards Cl

Winkfield

CHURCH ROAD

RCH RD

Ryemead Lane

St Marys Lane

A330

PIGEONHOUSE LANE

NORTH

LOVEL ROAD   A330

B3034   LO

Cranbourne
School

Winkfield
Lodge

Hatchet Lane

Brazlers Lane

H7
1 Cherington Wy
2 Marston Wy

Ascot
Place

HATCHET LANE

Hodge Lane

Woodside

Fryler Lane

Kiln Lane

FOREST   ROAD   B3034

PO

Brookside

New Road

Green
Meadows
Surgery

Locks Ride

Winkfield
Manor

Coach Road

Rhododendron Walk

Rhododendron Close

Beechwood Close

New Road

Ride

Kennel
Close

The Avenue

Manor House
Drive

Prides Crossing

Onslow
Drive

WINDSOR ROAD

WINDSOR ROAD   A330

A332

Sandy La

Ascot Heath
Junior
School

Edwards Rd

St John's
Road

Surgery

Oaklands
Close

Oaklands
Drive

Mill Ride
GolfClub

PO

Kaynes
Pk

Heathway

Jubilee
Av

Jubilee Cl

Kennel
Wd

Crocker Cl

Beaufort
Gdns

Huntsmans
Meadow

Kennel Av

Woodcote Pl

**Papplewick
School**

The Gv

Asher Dr

Green
Wd

Ferrard
Cl

MILL
RIDE

Ranelagh
Crescent

Whitelands Dr

Fernbank

Crs

New
Meadow

Heron
La

Burleigh Lane

Kennel
Green

Windsor
Road

Kennel Av

Three Castles Path

Ascot
Heath

Bracken Bank

Fernbank

Pl

St Christophers
Gdns

Warren
Rw

Gold
Cup
La

Mansfield Pl

Ancaster
Dr

The
Burlings

Dawnay
Cl

Walton
Dr

Churchill Road

North Ascot

Wentworth
Wy

Wentworth
Av

Goaters
Road

Blackmoor Close

Fernbank Road

Elliot
Rd

Darwall Dr

Prince Andrew Wy

Nash
Gdns

Langdale
Lane

Sutherland Chase

Burleigh
Ride

The
Links

WINDSOR

A332

ROAD

Cemetery

Napper Cl

North Lodge
Dr

Blackmoor
Wood

The
Close

Gainsborough Drive

Vernon Dr

Halley
Dr

Ruston
Wy

Geffers
Ride

Hermitage
Dr

Royal
Ascot
Golf Club

The Licensed
Victuallers
School

The
Forest Cl

Path

A329

LONDON   ROAD

Lockton
Chase

Blythewood

Audley Way

HIGH STREET

101

Ascot
Race
Course

Animal
Care
Coll...

Course
Rd

PO

A330

A329

ASCOT

I 1

2

3

4

5

6

7

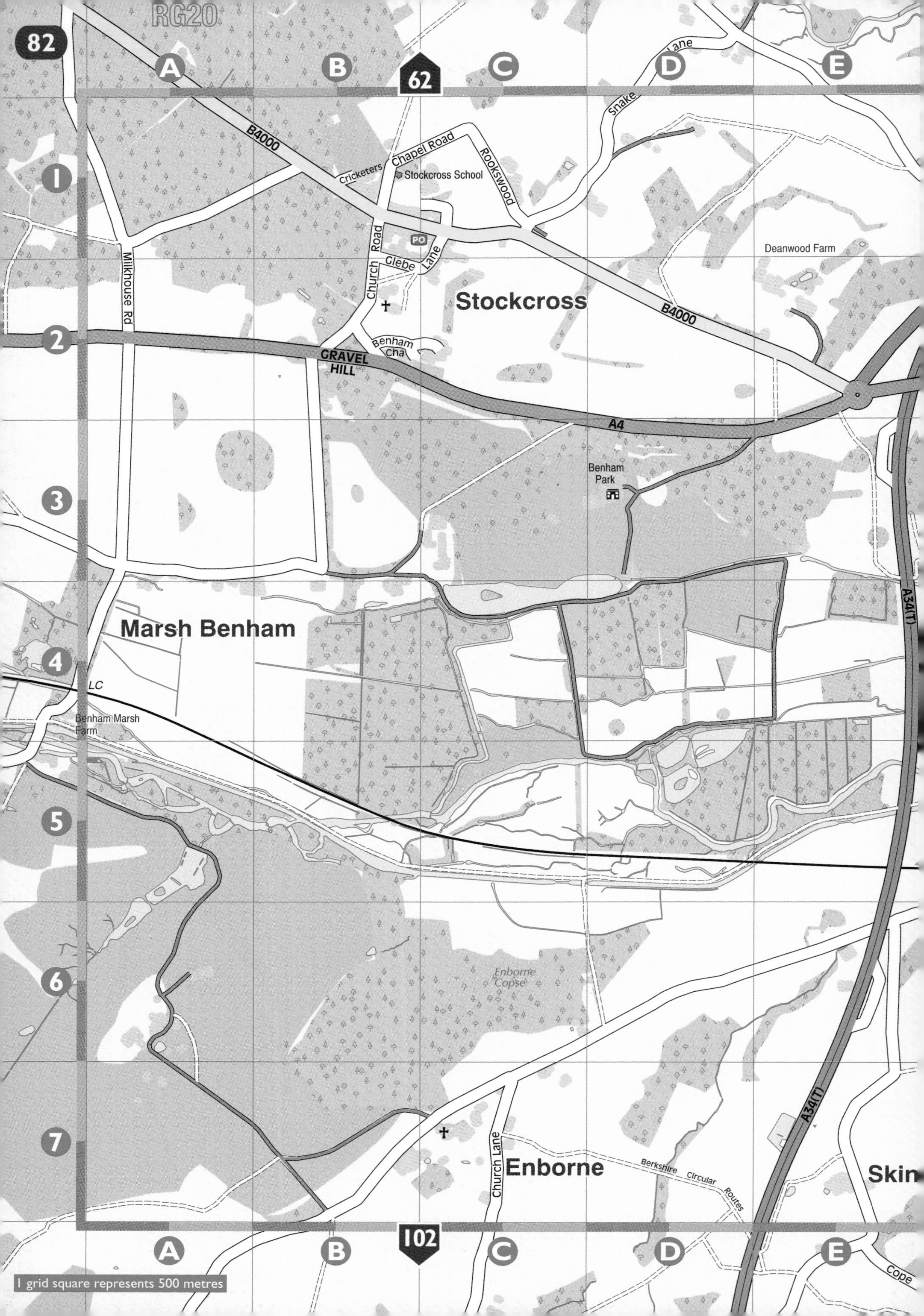
RG20
A
B
62
C
D
E
Snake Lane
B4000
Chapel Road
Rooksword
Cricketers
Stockcross School
PO
Church Road
Glebe
Lane
Milkhouse Rd
Deanwood Farm
Stockcross
B4000
Benham Cha
GRAVEL HILL
A4
Benham Park
1
2
3
4
5
6
7
Marsh Benham
LC
Benham Marsh Farm
A34(T)
Enborne Copse
Church Lane
Enborne
Berkshire Circular Routes
Skin
A34(T)
A
B
102
C
D
E
Cope
1 grid square represents 500 metres

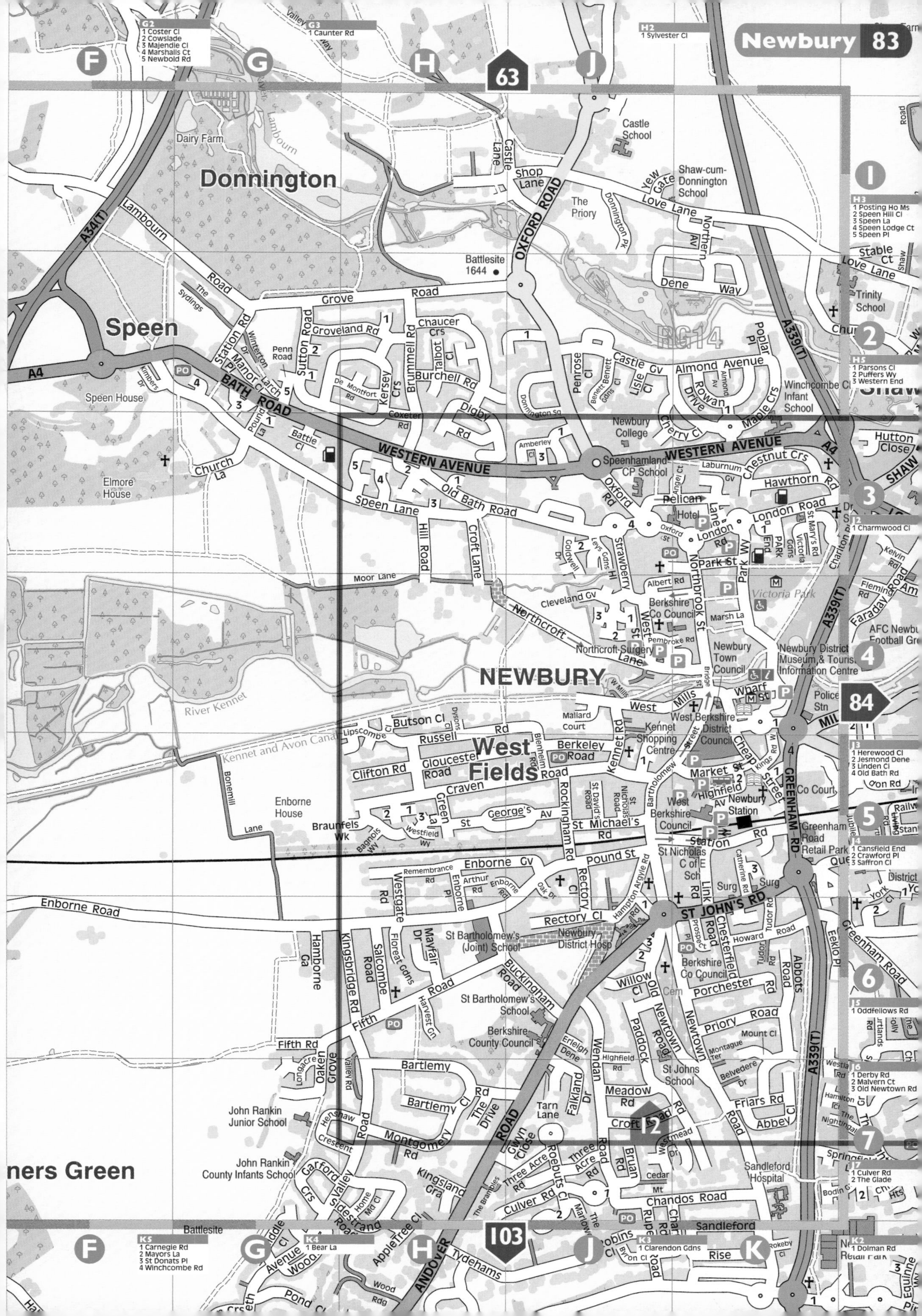
G2
1 Coster Cl
2 Cowslade
3 Majendie Cl
4 Marshalls Ct
5 Newbold Rd
G3
1 Caunter Rd
H2
1 Sylvester Cl
63
Donnington
Dairy Farm
Lambourn
Castle School
Castle Lane
Shop Lane
OXFORD ROAD
Shaw-cum-Donnington School
Yew Gate
Love Lane
The Priory
Donnington Pk
Northern Av
H3
1 Posting Ho Ms
2 Speen Hill Cl
3 Speen La
4 Speen Lodge Ct
5 Speen Pl
Stable Ct
Trinity School
A34(T)
Lambourn Road
The Sydings
Battlesite 1644
Grove Road
Dene Way
Speen
Station Rd
Winterton Dr
Groveland Rd
Sutton Road
Penn Road
Brummell Rd
Chaucer Crs
Talbot Cl
RG14
Poplar Pl
A339(T)
A4
Kimbers Dr
Manor Pl
Larch
Penrose Cl
Castle Gv
Almond Avenue
Rowan Drive
Winchcombe Cl
H5
1 Parsons Cl
2 Puffers Wy
3 Western End
Shaw
BATH ROAD
De Montfort Rd
Kersey Crs
Burchell Rd
Digby Rd
Donnington Sq
Benett Gdns Cl
Lisle Cl
Maple Crs
Winchcombe Infant School
Speen House
Pound La
Battle Cl
Coxeter Rd
Amberley Cl
Newbury College
Cherry Cl
WESTERN AVENUE
Hutton Close
Church La
Elmore House
Speenhamland CP School
Laburnum Gv
Chestnut Crs
Hawthorn Rd
SHAW
Old Bath Road
Speen Lane
Oxford Rd
Pelican Hotel
Angel Ct
Lane
London Road
J2
1 Charmwood Cl
Hill Road
Croft Lane
Coldwell Dr
Leys Gdns
Strawberry Hl
Oxford St
London Rd
Park Wy
End
PARK
Victoria Gdns
St Mary's Rd
Charlton Pl
Kelvin Rd
Park St
Moor Lane
Albert Rd
Northbrook St
Victoria Park
Fleming Rd
Faraday Road
Cleveland Gv
Northcroft
Berkshire Co Council
Marsh La
West St
Pembroke Rd
AFC Newbury Football Gr
Northcroft Surgery
Lane
Newbury Town Council
Newbury District Museum & Tourist Information Centre
NEWBURY
Bridge St
Wharf St
Police Stn
River Kennet
W Mills
West Mills
84
Mallard Court
Kennet Shopping Centre
West Berkshire District Council
Butson Cl
Dysons Cl
Lipscombe Cl
Russell Rd
Kennet and Avon Canal
West Fields
Blenheim Rd
Berkeley Road
Kennet Rd
Bartholomew Street
Cheap Street
Kings Rd
GREENHAM RD
J3
1 Herewood Cl
2 Jesmond Dene
3 Linden Cl
4 Old Bath Rd
Clifton Rd
Gloucester Road
Market St
Co Court
Bonemill Lane
Enborne House
Craven Road
Highfield Av
Newbury Station
St David's Road
St Nicholas Road
Rockingham Rd
West Berkshire Council
Green La
St George's Av
Braunfels Wk
Bagnols Wy
Westfield Wy
St Michael's Rd
Station Rd
Greenham Road Retail Park
Jubilee
J4
1 Cansfield End
2 Crawford Pl
3 Saffron Cl
Enborne Gv
Remembrance Rd
Pound St
St Nicholas C of E Sch
Catherine Rd
Surg
Westgate Rd
Enborne Pl
Arthur Rd
Enborne Rd
Oak Dr
Rectory Cl
Argyle Rd
Hampton Rd
Link Rd
ST JOHN'S RD
Enborne Road
Rectory Cl
Newbury District Hosp
Prospect Pl
Chesterfield Road
Tudor Rd
Howard Road
Abbots Road
Eeklo Pl
Greenham Road
Hamborne Ga
Kingsbridge Rd
Salcombe Road
Floreat Gdns
Mayfair Dr
St Bartholomew's (Joint) School
Buckingham Road
Willow Cl
Old Newtown Road
Berkshire Co Council
Porchester Rd
Cem
Fifth Road
Harvest Gn
St Bartholomew's School
Berkshire County Council
Newtown Road
Priory Road
Mount Cl
J5
1 Oddfellows Rd
Fifth Rd
Oaken Grove
Longacre
Valley Rd
Bartlemy Rd
Erleigh Dene
Wendan Rd
Highfield Rd
Paddock Road
Montague Ter
Belvedere Dr
St Johns School
J6
1 Derby Rd
2 Malvern Ct
3 Old Newtown Rd
Bartlemy Cl
The Drive
Falkland Dr
Meadow Rd
Friars Rd
Abbey Cl
John Rankin Junior School
Henshaw Crescent
Montgomery Rd
ROAD
Tarn Lane
Gwyn Close
Croft Road
12
Westmead Dr
Springfield
ners Green
John Rankin County Infants School
Garford Crs
Valley Road
Kingsland Gra
Three Acre Rd
Roebuts Cl
Three Acre Rd
Brujan Rd
Cedar Mt
Sandleford Hospital
J7
1 Culver Rd
2 The Glade
Home Md Cl
The Brambles
Culver Rd
The Marlowes
Chandos Road
Rupert Rd
Charles Rd
Battlesite
103
Sandleford Rise
K5
1 Carnegie Rd
2 Mayors La
3 St Donats Pl
4 Winchcombe Rd
K4
1 Bear La
Sidestrand Road
AppleTree Cl
ANDOVER
Tydehams
Robins
Byron Cl
K3
1 Clarendon Gdns
Rokeby
K2
1 Dolman Rd
Retail Park
Wood Rdg
Pond Cl

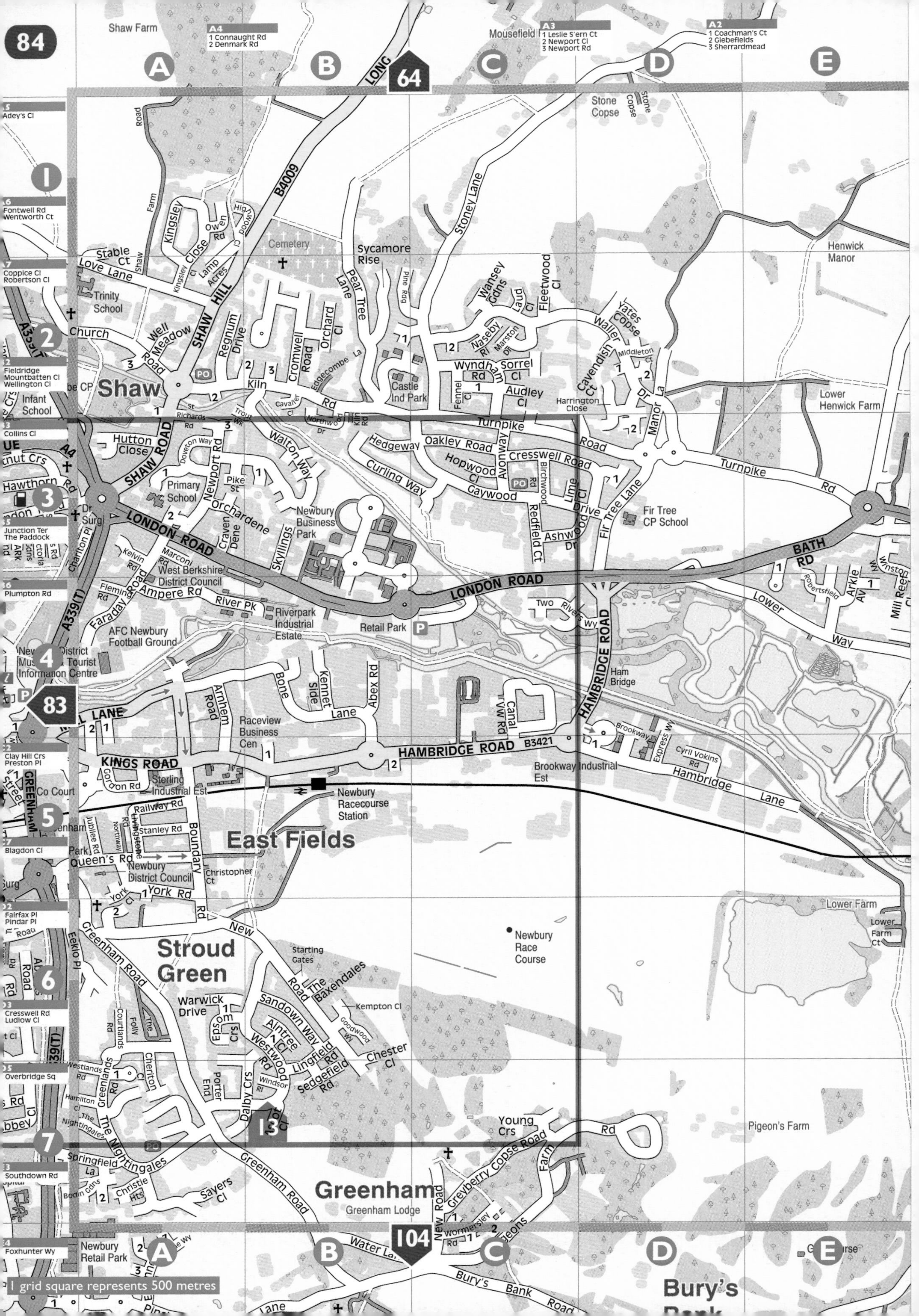

A4
1 Connaught Rd
2 Denmark Rd
A3
1 Leslie S'ern Ct
2 Newport Cl
3 Newport Rd
A2
1 Coachman's Ct
2 Glebefields
3 Sherrardmead
Shaw Farm
Mousefield
64
Stone Copse
Henwick Manor
Lower Henwick Farm
B4009
LONG
Cemetery
Sycamore Rise
Pear Tree Lane
Stoney Lane
Kingsley Close
Owen Rd
Lamp Acres
Stable Ct
Love Lane
Trinity School
Church
Well Meadow Road
SHAW HILL
Regnum Drive
Cromwell Road
Orchard Cl
Edgecombe La
Castle Ind Park
Wyndham Rd
Sorrel Cl
Audley Cl
Naseby Ri
Marston Dr
Wansey Gdns
Laud Cl
Fleetwood Cl
Yates Copse
Waller
Middleton Ct
Cavendish Ct
Harrington Close
Manor La
Shaw
Infant School
Kiln Rd
St Richards Rd
Trout Wk
Walton Way
Hutton Close
SHAW ROAD
Doveton Way
Newport Rd
Pike St
Primary School
Hedgeway
Oakley Road
Hopwood Cl
Avonway
Cresswell Road
Birchwood Rd
Turnpike Road
Turnpike Rd
Curling Way
Gaywood
Redfield Ct
Lime Cl
Ashwood Dr
Fir Tree Lane
Fir Tree CP School
Orchardene
Craven Dene
Skyllings
Newbury Business Park
LONDON ROAD
BATH RD
Robertsfield
Arkle Av
Winston Wy
Mill Reef Cl
Lower Way
Kelvin Rd
Marconi
West Berkshire District Council
Fleming Rd
Faraday Road
Ampere Rd
River Pk
Riverpark Industrial Estate
Retail Park
Two Rivers Wy
HAMBRIDGE ROAD
Ham Bridge
A339(T)
AFC Newbury Football Ground
Newbury District Museum & Tourist Information Centre
83
Bone Lane
Kennet Side
Abex Rd
Canal Vw Rd
Arnhem Road
Raceview Business Cen
HAMBRIDGE ROAD
B3421
Brookway
Express Wy
Cyril Vokins Rd
Brookway Industrial Est
Hambridge Lane
KINGS ROAD
Gordon Rd
Sterling Industrial Est
Newbury Racecourse Station
Railway Rd
Stanley Rd
Boundary Rd
Jubilee Rd
Northway
Livingstone Rd
East Fields
Queen's Rd
Newbury District Council
Christopher Ct
York Rd
York Cl
New Rd
Lower Farm
Lower Farm Ct
Newbury Race Course
Starting Gates
Stroud Green
Greenham Road
Eeklo Pl
The Baxendales
Kempton Cl
Warwick Drive
Sandown Way
Goodwood Wy
Epsom Crs
Aintree Cl
Westwood Rd
Lingfield Rd
Sedgefield Rd
Chester Cl
Courtlands Rd
Folly
Westlands Rd
Greenlands Rd
Cheriton
Porter End
Dalby Crs
Windsor
Hamilton Cl
The Nightingales
13
Young Crs
Pigeon's Farm
Springfield La
Bodin Gdns
Christie Hts
Sayers Cl
Greenham Road
Greenham
Greenham Lodge
Greyberry Copse Road
Farm
New Road
Wormersley Rd
104
Water La
Bury's Bank Road
Newbury Retail Park
Adey's Cl
Fontwell Rd
Wentworth Ct
Coppice Cl
Robertson Cl
Fieldridge
Mountbatten Cl
Wellington Cl
Collins Cl
Hawthorn Rd
Junction Ter
The Paddock
Charlton Pl
Plumpton Rd
Clay Hill Crs
Preston Pl
Co Court
GREENHAM
Blagdon Cl
Fairfax Pl
Pindar Pl
Cresswell Rd
Ludlow Cl
Overbridge Sq
Southdown Rd
Foxhunter Wy
1 grid square represents 500 metres

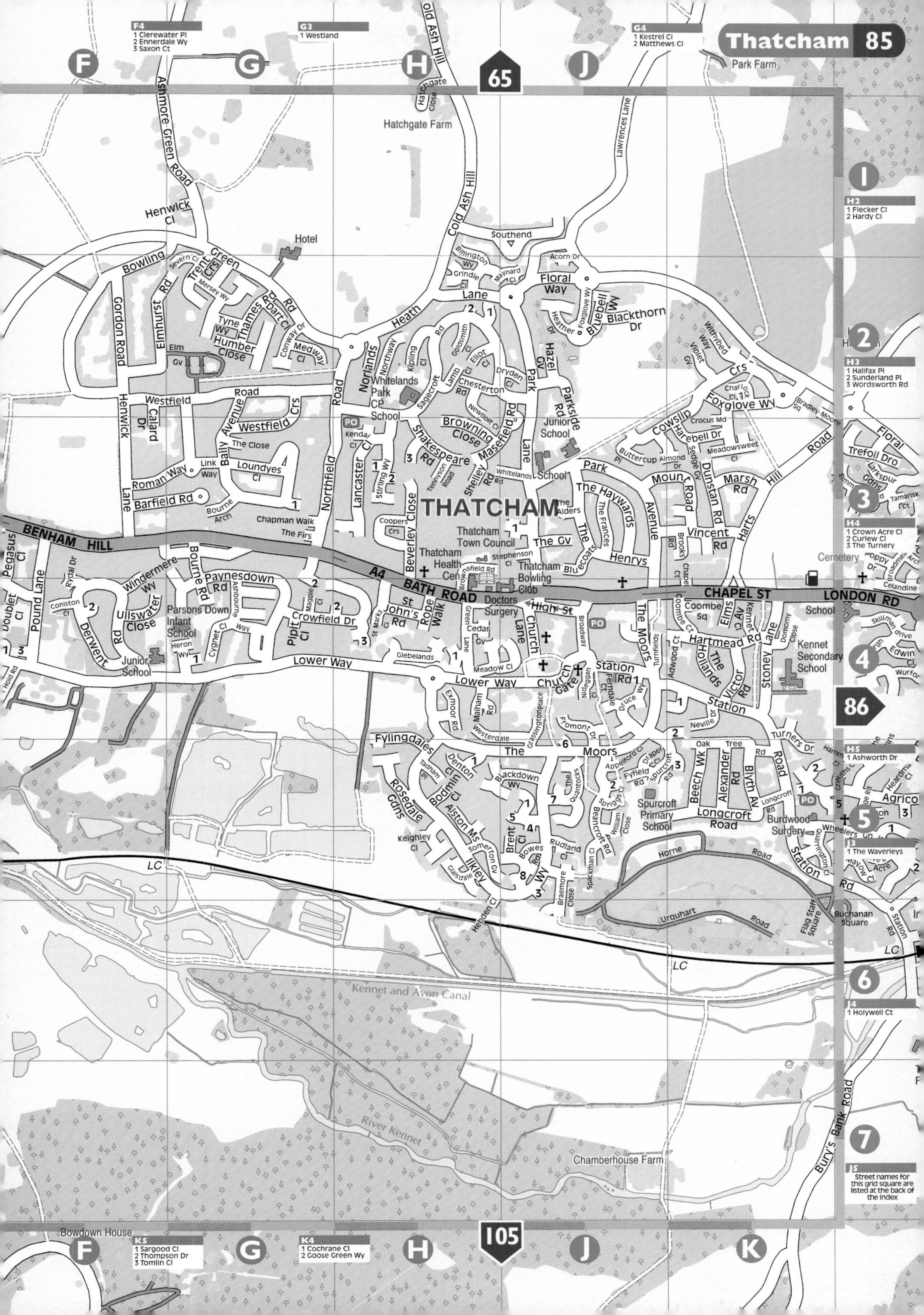

F G H 65 J

I

2

3

4

86

5

6

7

F 105 G H J K

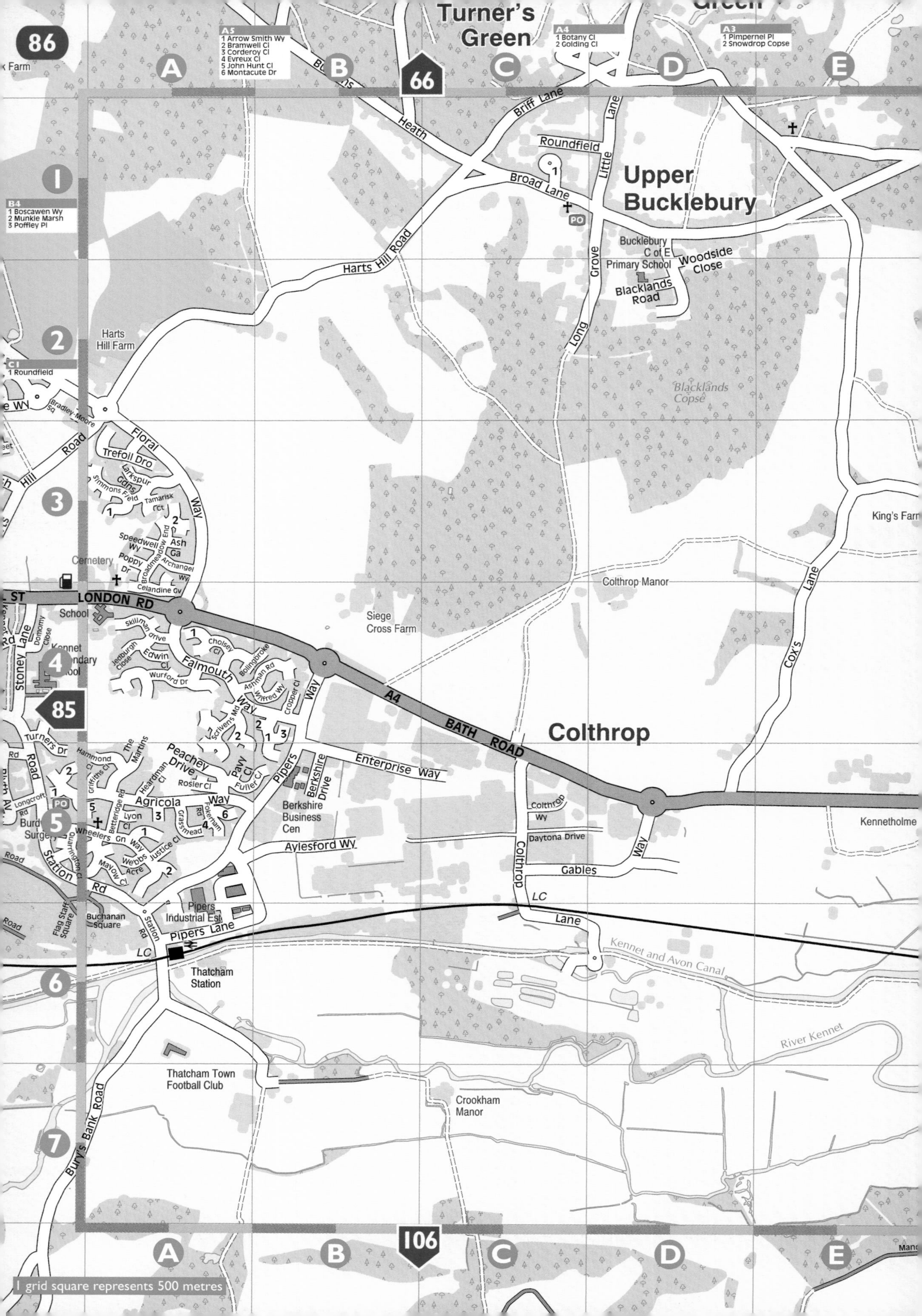

Turner's
Green

Green

Map labels

A5
1 Arrow Smith Wy
2 Bramwell Cl
3 Corderoy Cl
4 Evreux Cl
5 John Hunt Cl
6 Montacute Dr

A4
1 Botany Cl
2 Golding Cl

A3
1 Pimpernel Pl
2 Snowdrop Copse

B4
1 Boscawen Wy
2 Munkle Marsh
3 Poffley Pl

C1
1 Roundfield

66

Upper
Bucklebury

Briff Lane

Roundfield

Broad Lane

Heath

PO

Bucklebury
C of E
Primary School

Woodside
Close

Blacklands
Road

Little Lane

Grove

Long

Harts Hill Road

Harts
Hill Farm

Blacklands
Copse

Floral Way

Trefoil Dro

Larkspur Gdns

Simmons Field

Tamarisk Ct

Ash Ga

Broadmeadow End

Archangel Wy

Speedwell Wy

Poppy Dr

Celandine Gv

Cemetery

King's Farm

Colthrop Manor

Siege
Cross Farm

Cox's Lane

LONDON RD

School

Kennet
Secondary
School

Stoney Lane

Donnovay Close

Skillman drive

Cholsey

Edwin

Jedburgh Close

Wurford Dr

Falmouth Way

Boulingbroke Rd

Ashman Rd

Wniffred Wy

Croppet Rd

Way

A4 BATH ROAD

Colthrop

85

Turners Dr

The Martins

Hammond

Griffiths Cl

Peachey Drive

Heardman

Rosier Cl

Scriveris Md

Paw Cl

Fuller Cl

Pipers

Berkshire Drive

Enterprise Way

Berkshire
Business
Cen

Colthrop
Wy

Kennetholme

PO

Burdwood
Surgery

Longcroft Rd

Wheelers Gn

Lyon Cl

Agricola Way

Betteridge Rd

Grasmead

Foxenham Rd

Aylesford Wy

Colthrop

Daytona Drive

Way

Gables

Justice Cl

Webbs Acre

Maylow Cl

Quarrington Cl

Station Rd

Buchanan
Square

Pipers
Industrial Est

LC

Pipers Lane

LC

Lane

Kennet and Avon Canal

Thatcham
Station

Flag Staff
Square

Bury's Bank Road

Thatcham Town
Football Club

Crookham
Manor

River Kennet

1 grid square represents 500 metres

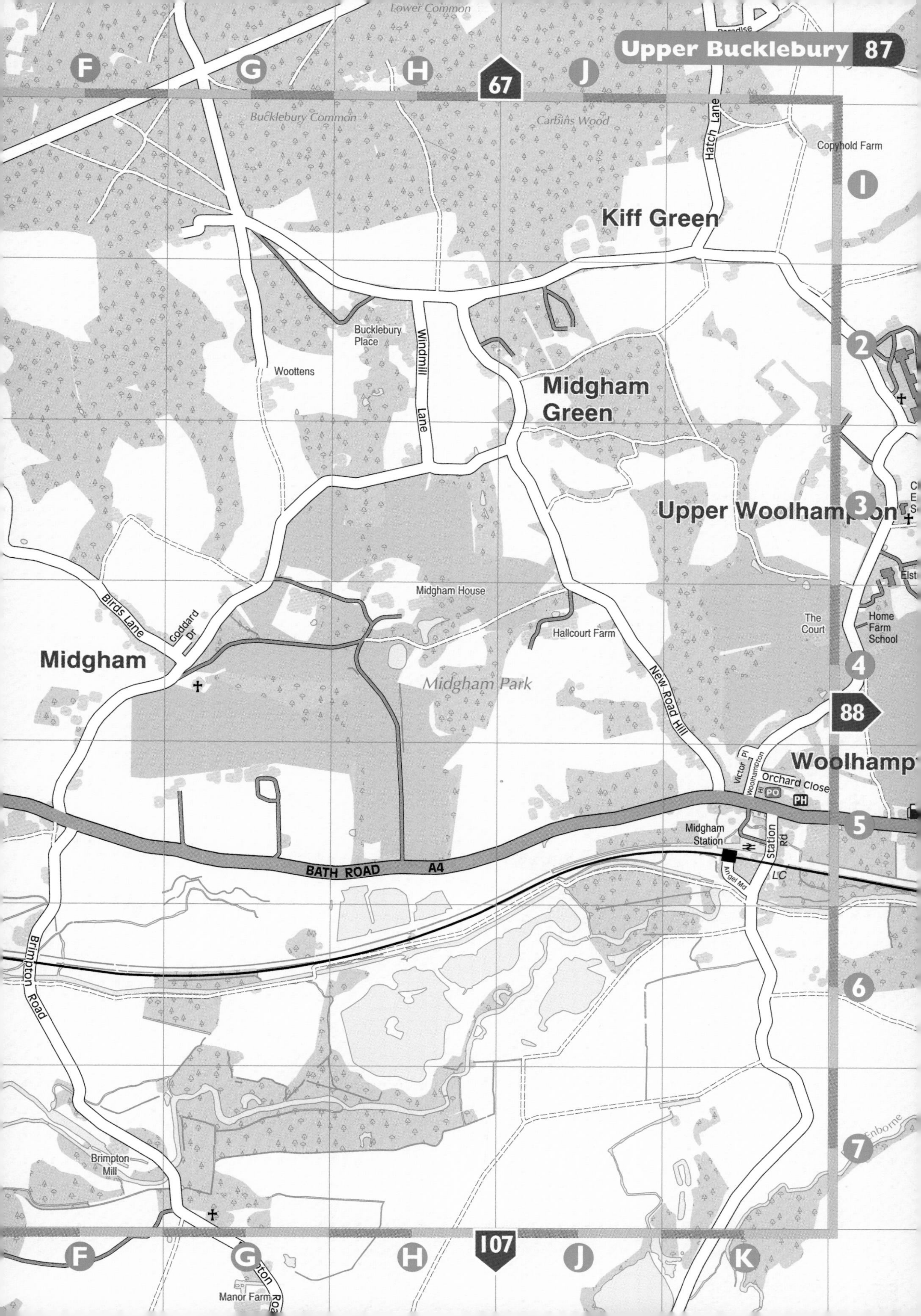

Lower Common
F
G
H
67
J
Bucklebury Common
Carbins Wood
Hatch Lane
Copyhold Farm
Kiff Green
Bucklebury Place
Windmill Lane
Wootens
Midgham Green
Upper Woolhampton
Midgham House
Birds Lane
Coddard Dr
Hallcourt Farm
The Court
Home Farm School
Midgham
Midgham Park
New Road Hill
88
Victor Pl
Woolhampton Hl
Orchard Close
PO
PH
Woolhamp
Midgham Station
Station Rd
Angel Md
LC
BATH ROAD
A4
Brimpton Road
Brimpton Mill
Enborne
Manor Farm
F
G
H
107
J
K
1
2
3
4
5
6
7

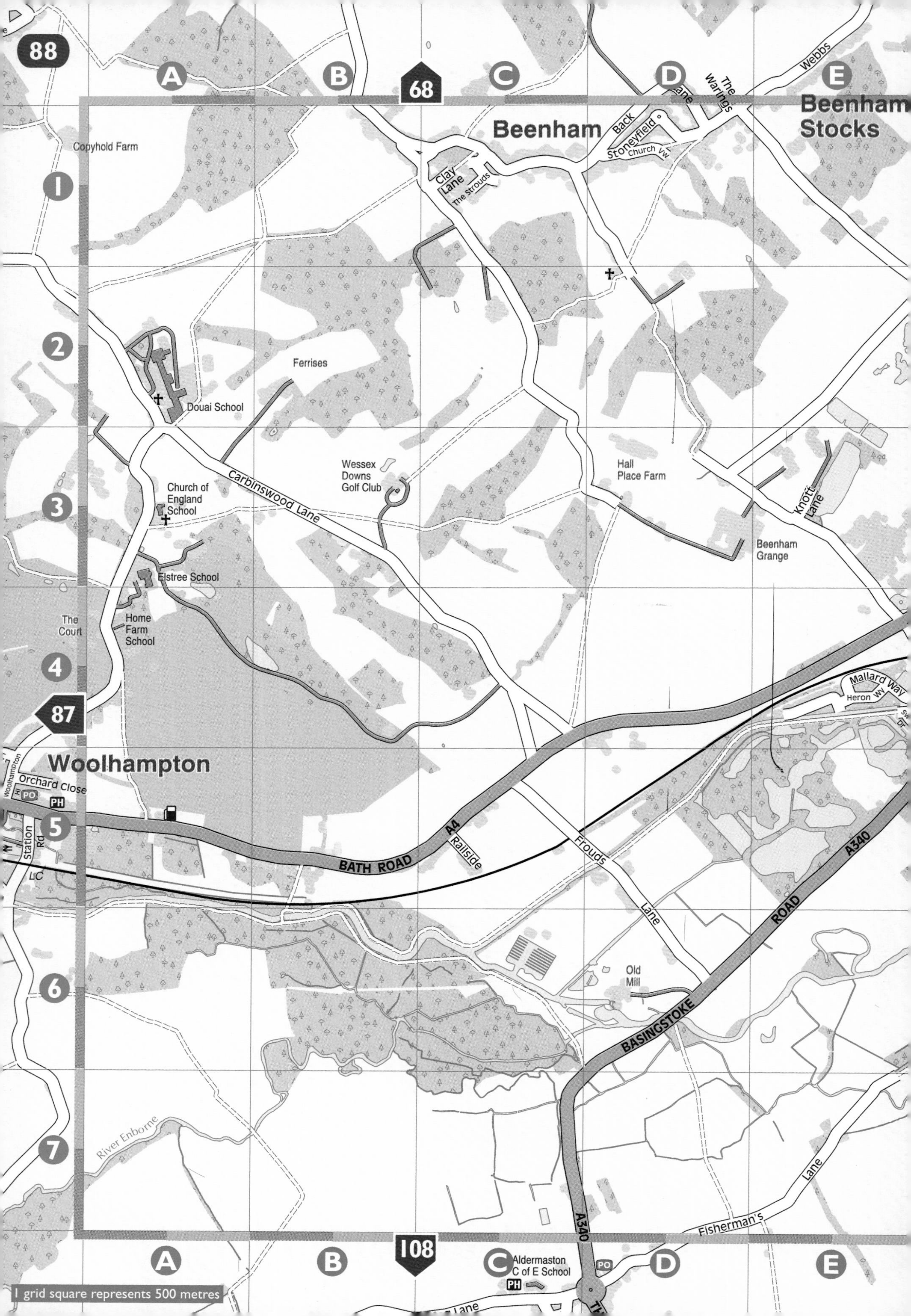

A   B   68   C   D   E

Beenham

Beenham
Stocks

Copyhold Farm

1

Clay
Lane
The Strouds

Back
Stoneyfield
Church Vw
The
Warnigs

Webbs

†

2

Ferrises

†
Douai School

Carbinswood Lane

Wessex
Downs
Golf Club

Hall
Place Farm

3

Church of
England
School
†

Beenham
Grange

Knott
Lane

Elstree School

4

The
Court

Home
Farm
School

87

Mallard Way

Heron Wy

Woolhampton

Orchard Close
PO   PH

A4
Railside

Frouds
Lane

A340

5

Station Rd

N

LC

BATH ROAD

6

Old
Mill

BASINGSTOKE   ROAD

7

River Enborne

A   B   108   C   D   E

Aldermaston
C of E School
PO
PH

Fisherman's
Lane

A340

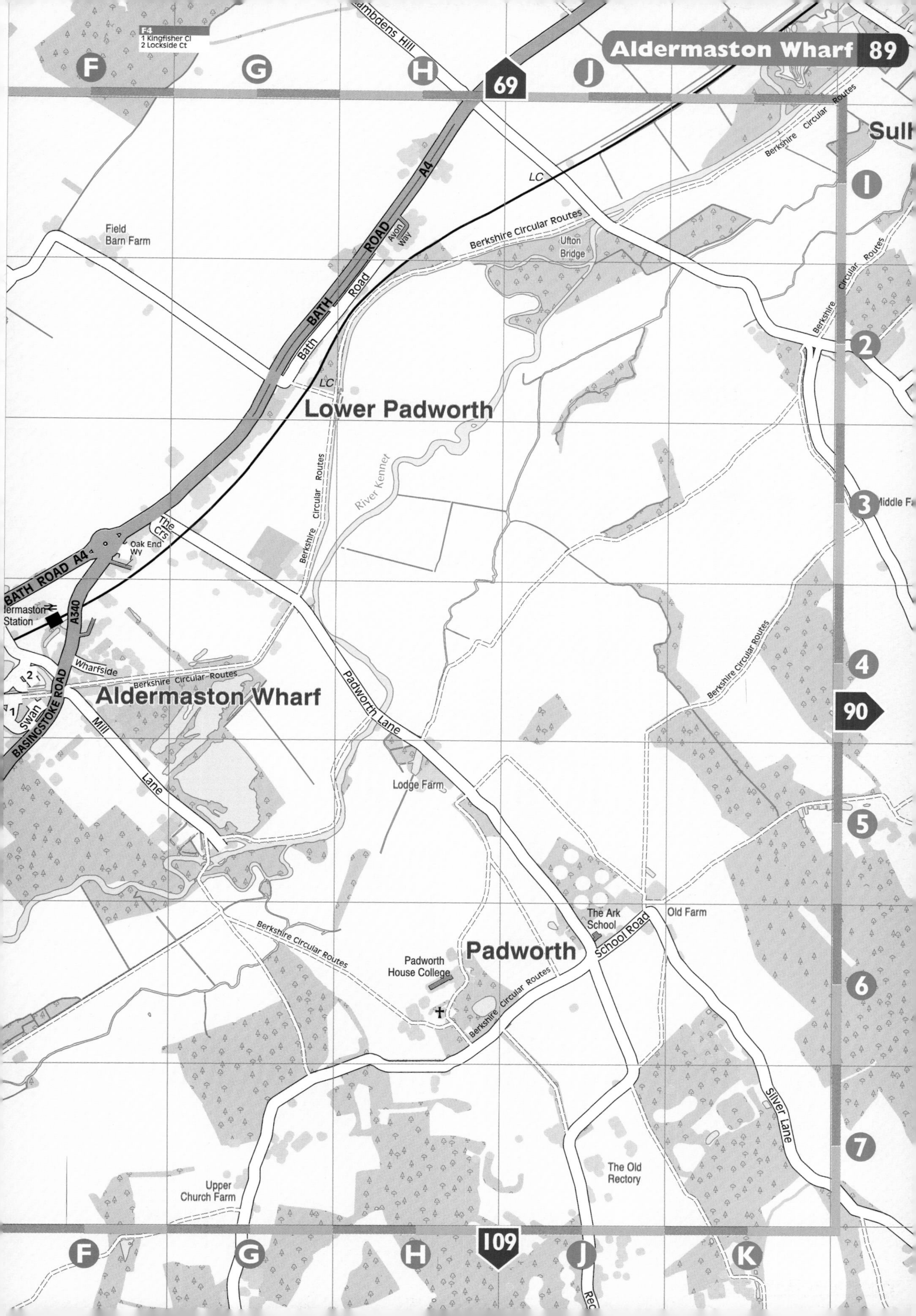

F

G

H

J

F4
1 Kingfisher Cl
2 Lockside Ct

Field
Barn Farm

BATH ROAD A4

Bath Road

Avon Way

LC

LC

Berkshire Circular Routes

Ufton
Bridge

Lower Padworth

River Kennet

Berkshire Circular Routes

The Crs

Oak End
Wy

BATH ROAD A4

A340

Aldermaston
Station

Swan

Wharfside

Berkshire Circular Routes

Aldermaston Wharf

BASINGSTOKE ROAD

Mill Lane

Padworth Lane

Berkshire Circular Routes

Lodge Farm

Berkshire Circular Routes

The Ark
School

School Road

Old Farm

Padworth

Padworth
House College

Berkshire Circular Routes

Upper
Church Farm

The Old
Rectory

Silver Lane

Middle F

1

2

3

4

90

5

6

7

F

G

109

H

J

K

Rec

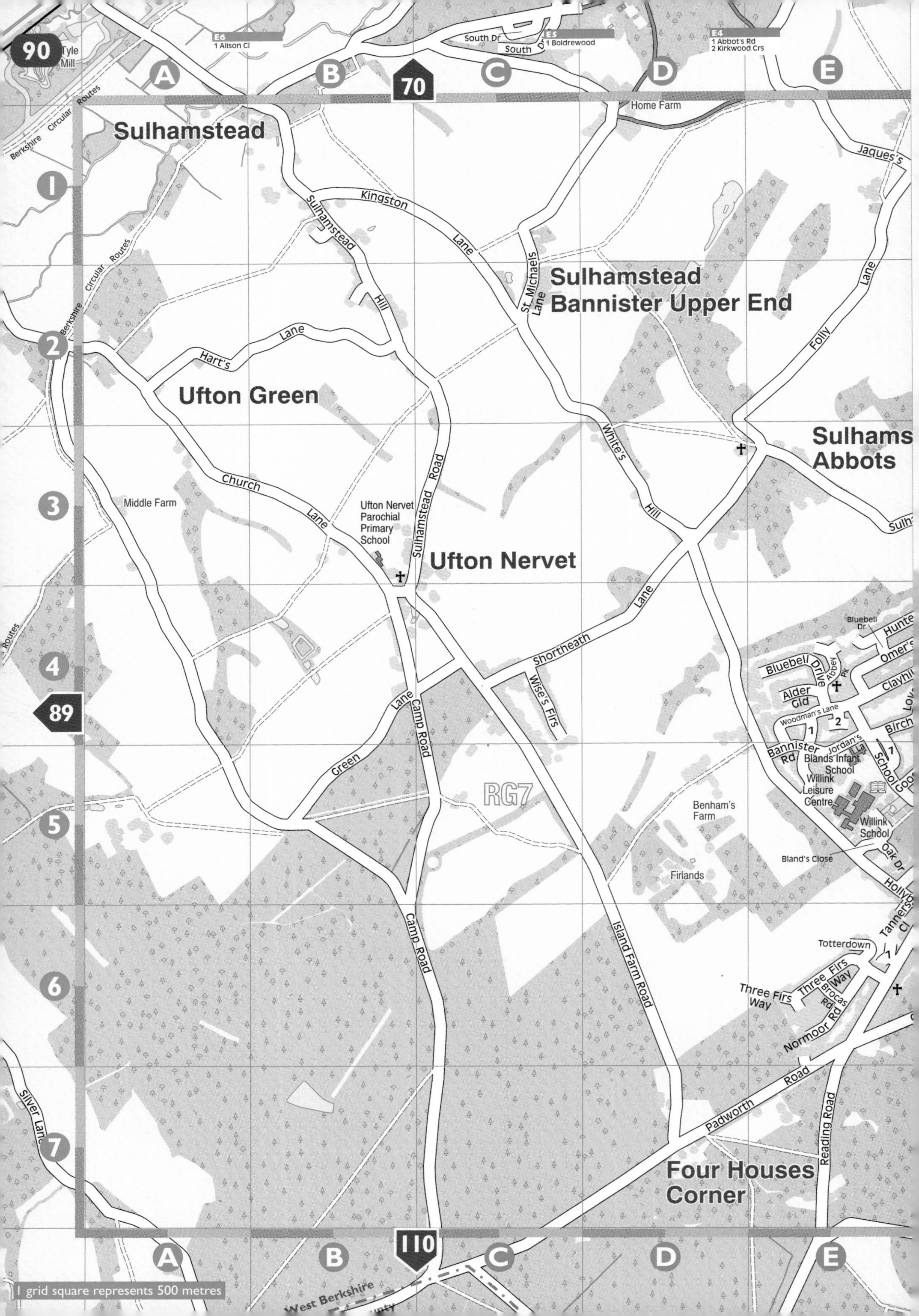

90
Tyle Mill
E6
1 Alison Cl
South Dr
South Dr
E5
1 Boldrewood
E4
1 Abbot's Rd
2 Kirkwood Crs
70
Home Farm
Sulhamstead
Berkshire Circular Routes
Kingston Lane
Sulhamstead Hill
St. Michaels Lane
Sulhamstead Bannister Upper End
Jaques's
Folly Lane
Hart's Lane
Ufton Green
White's Hill
Sulhamstead Abbots
Church Lane
Middle Farm
Sulhamstead Road
Ufton Nervet Parochial Primary School
Ufton Nervet
Shortheath Lane
Wise's Firs
Green Lane
Camp Road
RG7
Bluebell Dr
Bluebell Drive
Abbey Pk
Omer's
Clayhill
Alder Gld
Woodman's Lane
Birch
Bannister Rd
Jordan's La
Blands Infant School
School
Willink Leisure Centre
Willink School
Benham's Farm
Bland's Close
Oak Dr
Firlands
Island Farm Road
Totterdown
Tanners Cl
Three Firs Way
Brocas Rd
Normoor Rd
Padworth Road
Reading Road
Silver Lane
Four Houses Corner
89
110
West Berkshire
1 grid square represents 500 metres

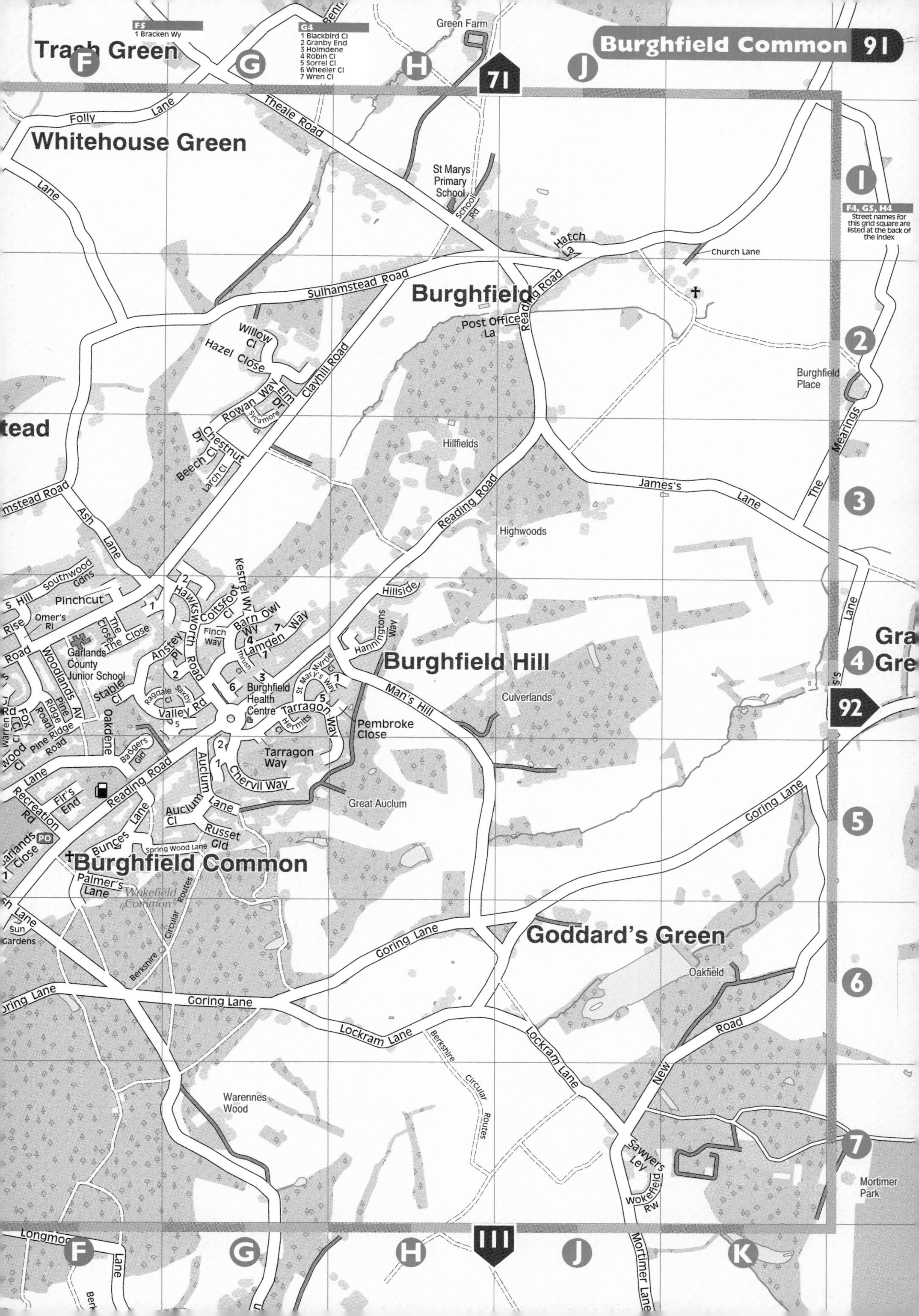

Trach Green

Whitehouse Green

F

G

H

71

J

I

F5
1 Bracken Wy

G4
1 Blackbird Cl
2 Granby End
3 Holmdene
4 Robin Cl
5 Sorrel Cl
6 Wheeler Cl
7 Wren Cl

Green Farm

F4, G5, H4
Street names for this grid square are listed at the back of the index

Folly

Lane

Lane

Theale Road

St Marys Primary School

School Rd

Hatch La

Church Lane

2

Sulhamstead Road

Burghfield

Reading Road

Burghfield Place

Willow Cl

Hazel Close

Post Office La

Rowan Way

Elm

Sycamore Cl

Clayhill Road

The Mearings

3

Chestnut

Beech Cl

Larch Cl

Hillfields

Reading Road

James's

Lane

Lane

stead

Ash

Lane

mstead Road

Highwoods

s Hill

Rise

southwood Gdns

Pinchcut

Omer's Ri

Hawksworth Road

Kestrel Wy

Coltsfoot Cl

Finch Way

Barn Owl Wy

Anstey Road

The Close

The Close

Garlands County Junior School

Woodlands Av

Pine Ridge Road

Stable Cl

Ragdale Cl

Savory

Valley Rd

Lamden Way

Triman

St Mary's Way

Myrtle

Hillside

Hanningtons Way

Burghfield Hill

Gra Gre

4

92

Man's Hill

Culverlands

Burghfield Health Centre

Tarragon

Hermits

Pembroke Close

Fox

Warren Rd

Pine Ridge

Wood

Lane

Oakdene

Badgers Rid

Fir's End

Reading Road

Auclum Lane

Chervil Way

Tarragon Way

Great Auclum

Goring Lane

5

Recreation Rd

PO

Garlands Close

Bunces Lane

Spring Wood Lane

Auclum Cl

Russet Gld

†**Burghfield Common**

Palmer's Lane

Wokefield Common

Berkshire

Circular

Routes

Goring Lane

Goddard's Green

Oakfield

6

Sun Gardens

Goring Lane

Goring Lane

Lockram Lane

New Road

Longmoo

Warennes Wood

Berkshire

Circular

Routes

Lockram Lane

Sawyers Ley

Wokefield Rw

7

Mortimer Park

Longmoo

Lane

Berh

Mortimer Lane

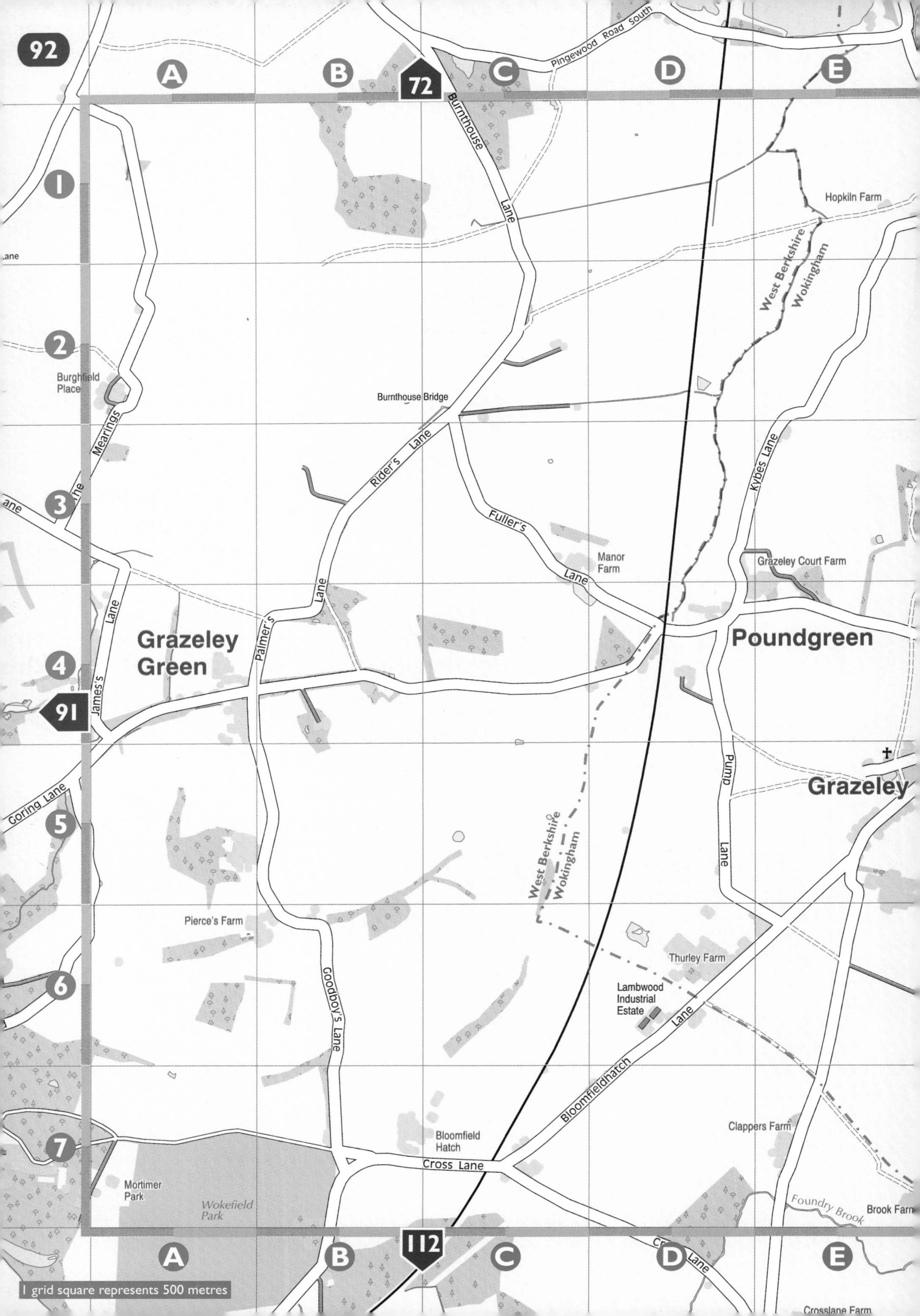

A   B   72   C   D   E

1

2
Burghfield
Place

3

The Mearings

ane

James's Lane

4

91

Goring Lane

5

6

7

Mortimer
Park

Wokefield
Park

Grazeley
Green

Palmer's Lane

Goodboy's Lane

Pierce's Farm

Bloomfield
Hatch

Cross Lane

Burnthouse Lane

Pingewood Road South

Hopkiln Farm

West Bertshire   Wokingham

Burnthouse Bridge

Rider's Lane

Fuller's Lane

Manor
Farm

Kybes Lane

Grazeley Court Farm

Poundgreen

Pump Lane

Grazeley

†

West Bertshire   Wokingham

Thurley Farm

Lambwood
Industrial
Estate

Bloomfieldhatch Lane

Clappers Farm

Foundry Brook

Brook Farm

A   B   112   C   D   Lane   E

Crosslane Farm

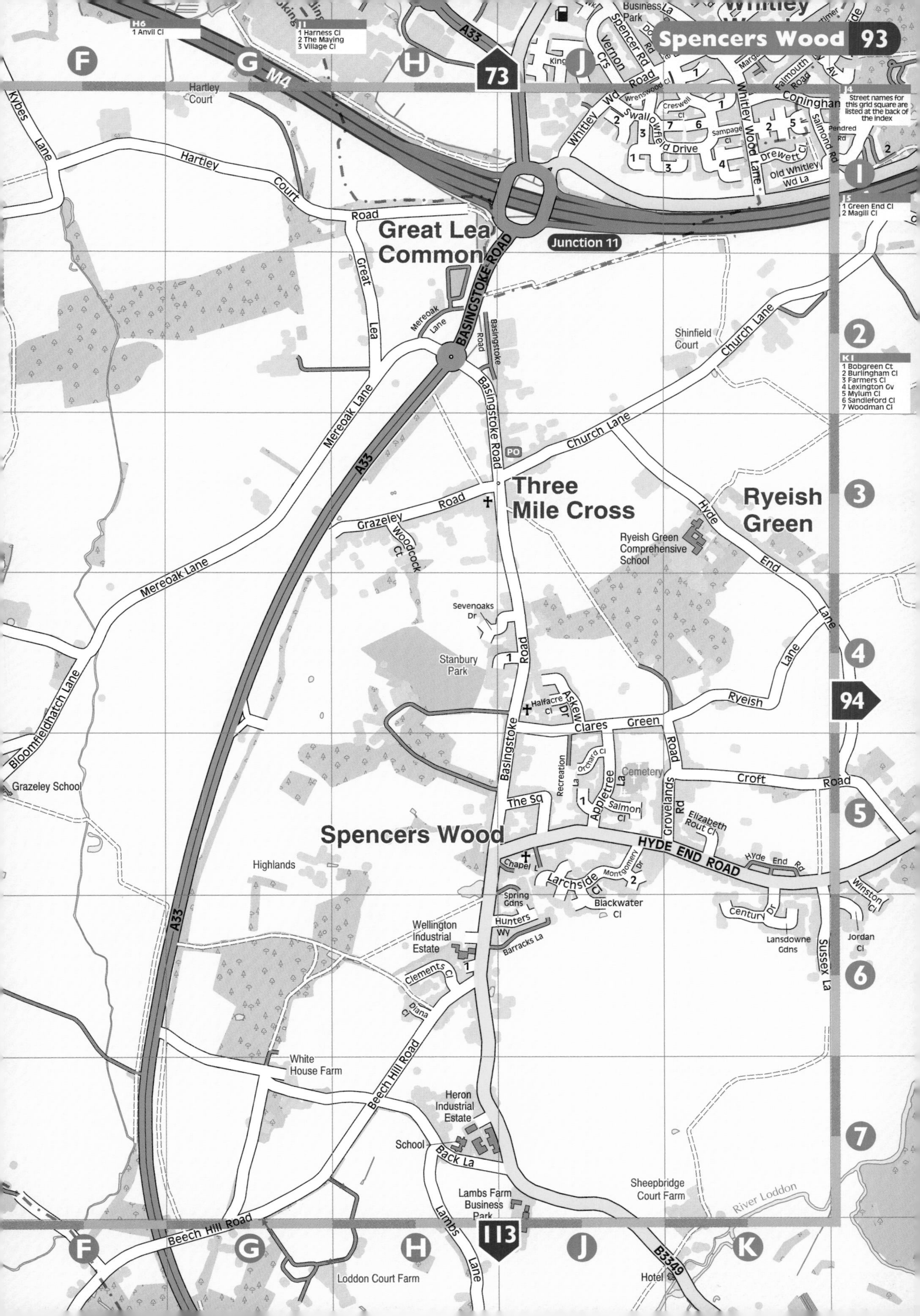

F
H6
1 Anvil Cl

G M4

1 Harness Cl
2 The Maying
3 Village Cl

H

A33

J

73

King

Whitley
Wk

Vernon
Crs

Spencer Rd
Road

Business
Park

Wrensnook Dr

Creswell
Cl

Coningham

Margaret

Falmouth
Road

Pendred
Rd

J4
Street names for
this grid square are
listed at the back of
the index

Whitley Wd
Swallowfield Drive
7
6
Sampage
Cl
3
1
5
2
9
3
Whitley Wood Lane
Drewett
Cl
4
Old Whitley
Wd La

Salmond Rd
1
2

1

J5
1 Green End Cl
2 Magill Cl

Hartley
Court

Hartley

Court
Road

Kybes Lane

Great
Lea

Mereoak
Lane

Great Lea
Common

BASINGSTOKE ROAD

Junction 11

Basingstoke
Road

Shinfield
Court

Church Lane

2

K1
1 Bobgreen Ct
2 Burlingham Cl
3 Farmers Cl
4 Lexington Gv
5 Mylum Cl
6 Sandleford Cl
7 Woodman Cl

Mereoak Lane

A33

Basingstoke Road

PO

Church Lane

Grazeley Road

Three
Mile Cross

Hyde End Lane

Ryeish
Green

3

Bloomfieldhatch Lane

Woodcock
Ct

Sevenoaks
Dr

Stanbury
Park

Ryeish Green
Comprehensive
School

4

94

Grazeley School

Basingstoke Road

1

Halfacre
Cl

Askew Dr

Clares

Green

Ryeish

Lane

Orchard La

Appletree La

Cemetery

Grovelands Rd

Croft

Road

5

Recreation
La

Salmon
Cl

Elizabeth
Rout Cl

Winston

Highlands

The Sq

Spencers Wood

Chapel

Spring
Gdns

Hunters
Wy

Larchside
Cl

Montgomery
Dr

2

Blackwater
Cl

HYDE END ROAD

Hyde End Rd

Century Dr

Lansdowne
Gdns

Jordan
Cl

Sussex La

6

Wellington
Industrial
Estate

Clements Cl

Diana

Barracks La

1

White
House Farm

Beech Hill Road

Heron
Industrial
Estate

7

School

Back La

Lambs Farm
Business
Park

Sheepbridge
Court Farm

River Loddon

F

Beech Hill Road

G

H

Lambs Lane

113

J

B3349

Hotel

K

Loddon Court Farm

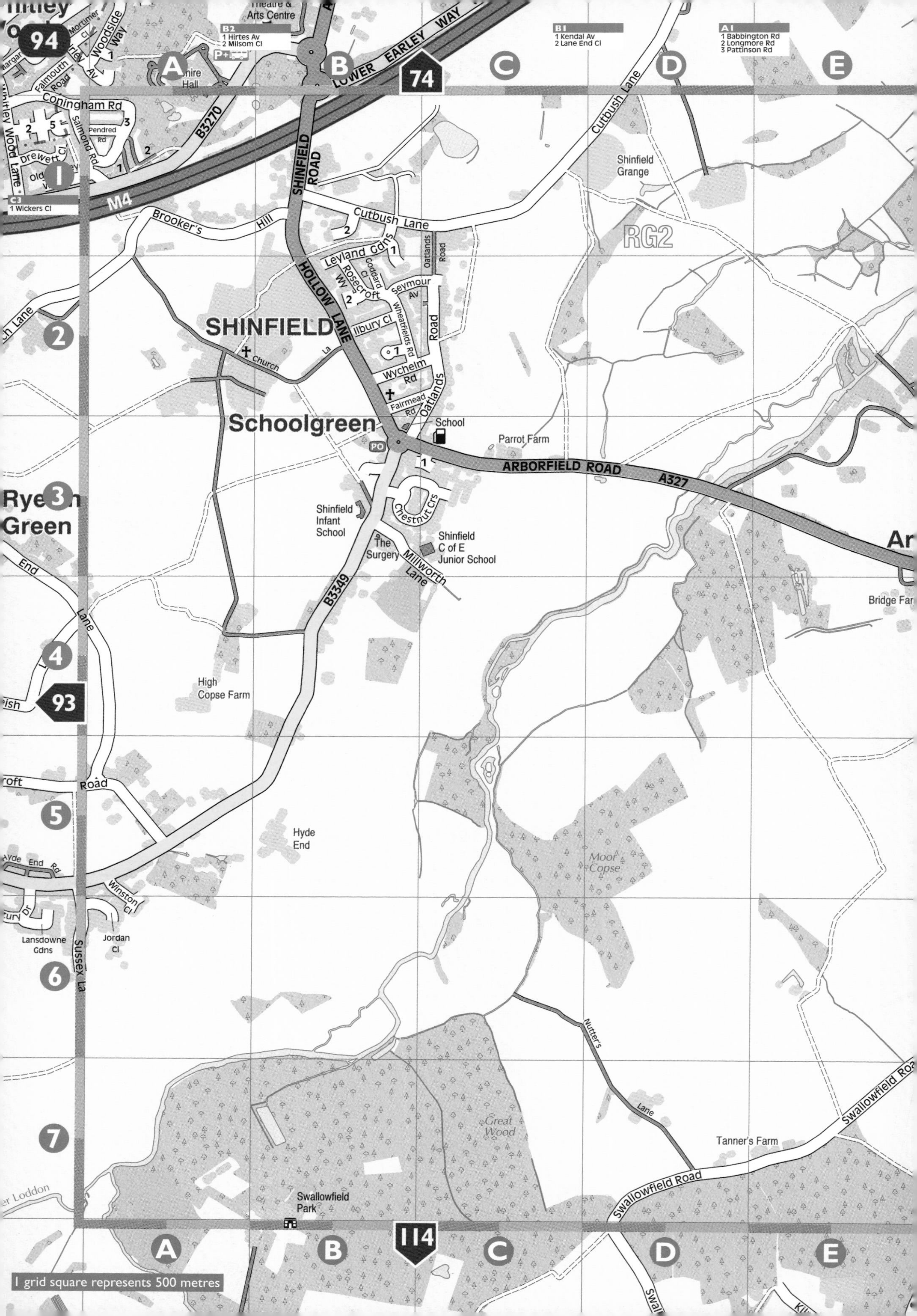

Theatre &
Arts Centre

LOWER EARLEY WAY

A

B

74

C

D

E

Mortimer

Woodside
Way

Margar

Falmouth
Road

Coningham Rd

B3270

anire
Hall

P+

2

5

Salmond Rd

Pendred
Rd

3

Drewett

2

Old

1

C3
1 Wickers Cl

M4

Brooker's

Hill

SHINFIELD ROAD

Cutbush Lane

Shinfield
Grange

Cutbush Lane

2

RG2

Leyland Gdns

1

Oatlands

Goddard
Cl

Rosecroft
Wy

SHINFIELD

HOLLOW LANE

church

La

Ilbury Cl

1

seymour
Av

Wheatfields Rd

Road

Oatlands

Wychelm
Rd

Road

Fairmead Rd

Schoolgreen

PO

School

Parrot Farm

1

ARBORFIELD ROAD

A327

Ar

2

Rye
Green

sh

3

End

Lane

Shinfield
Infant
School

The
Surgery

Chestnut Crs

Millworth Lane

Shinfield
C of E
Junior School

Shinfield

B3349

Bridge Far

4

93

High
Copse Farm

Moor
Copse

croft

Road

5

Hyde
End

Hyde End Rd

Winston
Cl

Jordan
Cl

Lansdowne
Gdns

Sussex La

6

Nutter's

Lane

Swallowfield Rd

7

Great
Wood

Tanner's Farm

r Loddon

Swallowfield
Park

114

Swallowfield Road

Swall

A

B

C

D

E

Kil

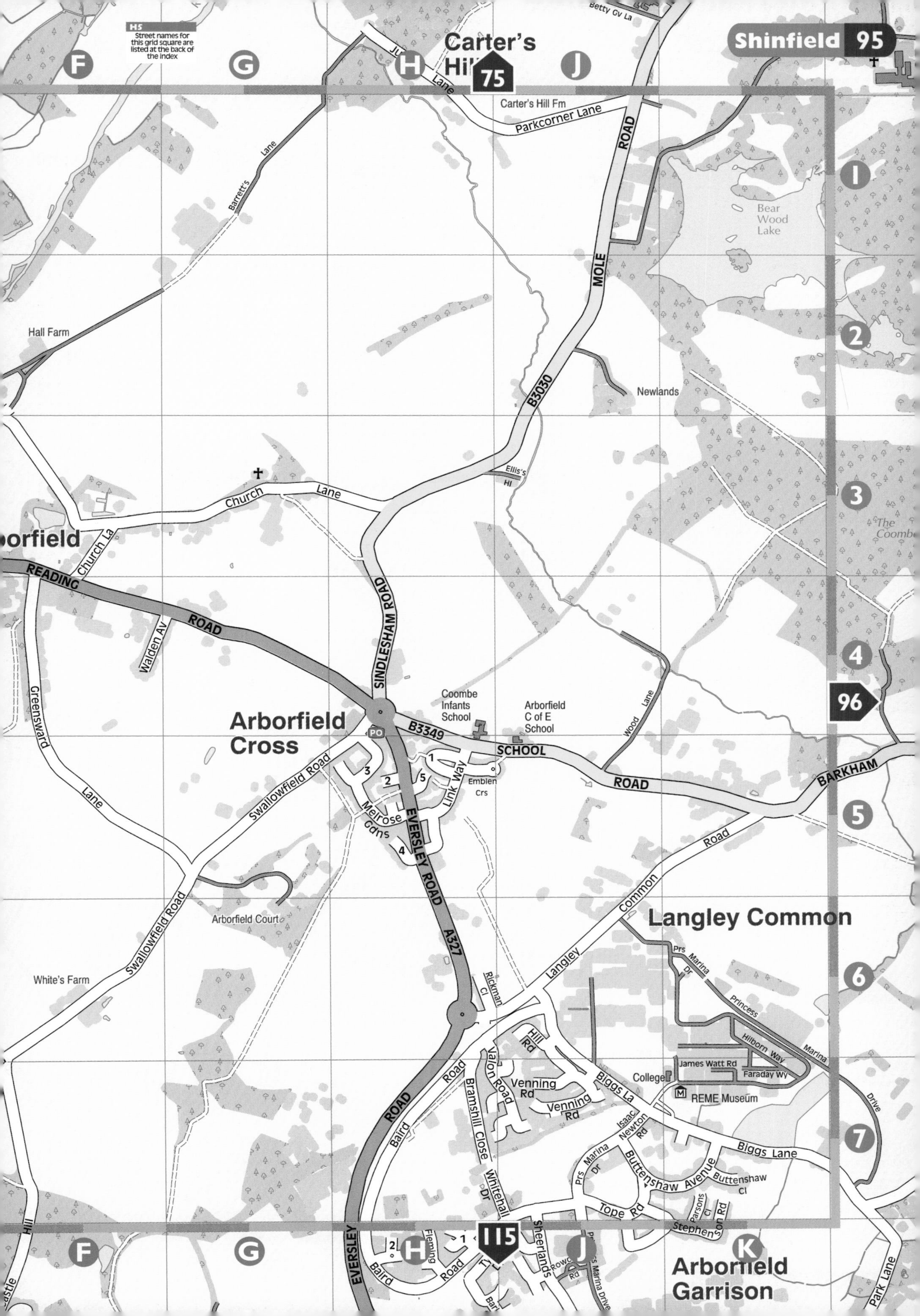
H5
Street names for this grid square are listed at the back of the index
Carter's Hill
75
Shinfield 95
Carter's Hill Fm
Parkcorner Lane
MOLE ROAD
Barrett's Lane
Bear Wood Lake
Hall Farm
B3030
Newlands
Ellis's Hl
Church Lane
The Coombe
Church La
READING ROAD
SINDLESHAM ROAD
Walden Av
Greensward Lane
Coombe Infants School
Arborfield C of E School
Wood Lane
96
Arborfield Cross
B3349
SCHOOL ROAD
BARKHAM
Swallowfield Road
Link Way
Emblen Crs
Melrose Gdns
EVERSLEY ROAD
A327
Road
Common
Langley Common
Langley
Arborfield Court
Swallowfield Road
White's Farm
Rickman Cl
Prs Marina Dr
Princess Marina Drive
Hilborn Way
James Watt Rd
Faraday Wy
College
REME Museum
Hill Rd
Valon Road
Venning Rd
Biggs La
Baird Road
Bramshill Close
Isaac Newton Rd
Biggs Lane
Buttenshaw Avenue
Buttenshaw Cl
Whitehall Dr
Tope Rd
Parsons Cl
Stephenson Rd
Prs Marina Dr
115
Fleming
Sheerlands
Baird Road
EVERSLEY
Hill
Arborfield Garrison
Park Lane
Betty Gv La
F G H J K

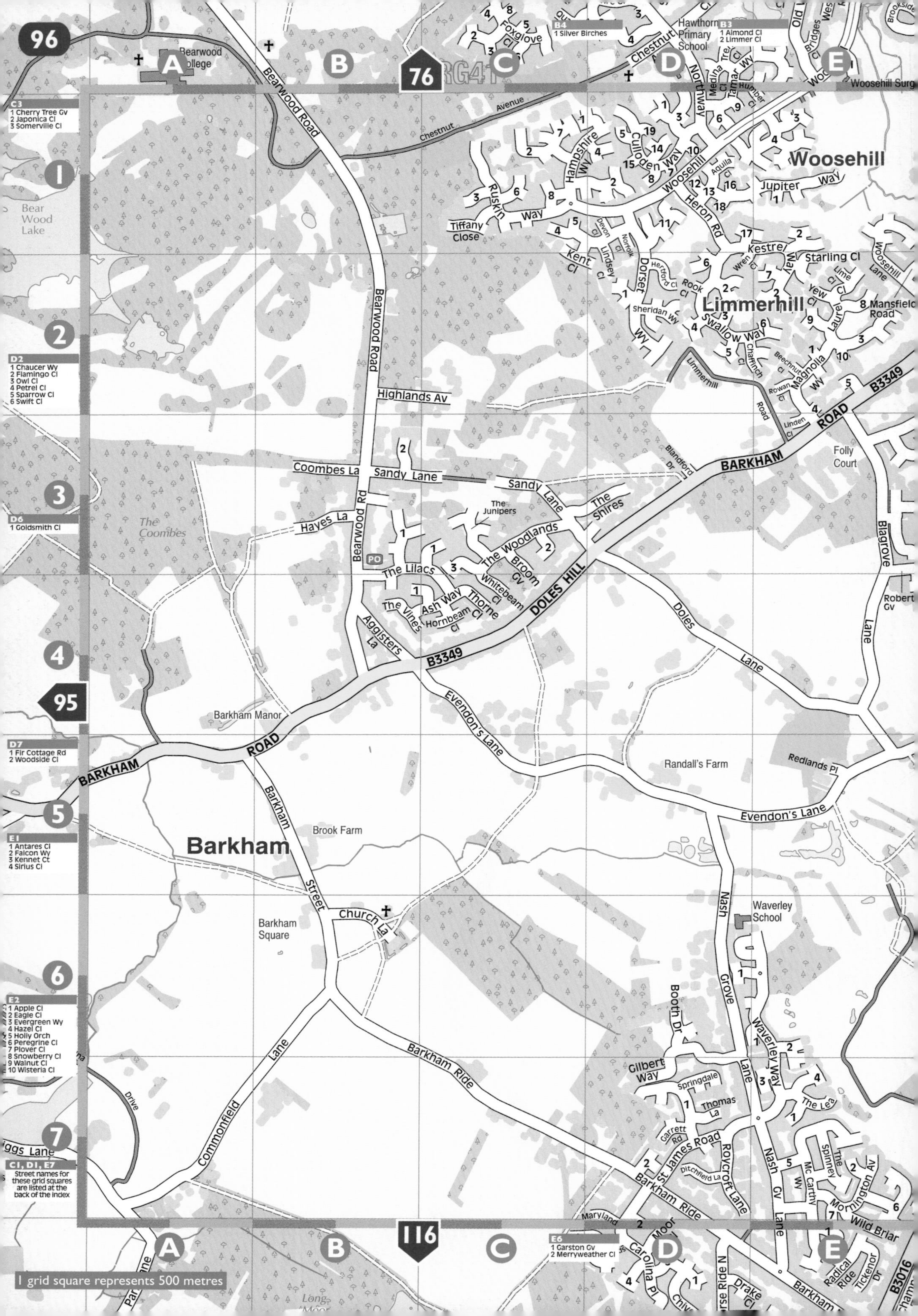

96

A + Bearwood College

B +

76 RG4?

C + Hawthorn Primary School

D + Northway

E Woosehill Surg.

I

Bear Wood Lake

Foxglove

Chestnut Avenue

Chestnut

Hampshire Wy   Culloden Way   Woosehill   Woosehill   Wooseehill

Woosehill

Limmerhill

Tiffany Close   Ruskin Way   Devon   Heron Rd   Aquila   Jupiter Way

Kent Cl   Lindsey   Dorset   Rook   Wren   Kestrel Way   Starling Cl   Lime   Yew Cl   Laurel Cl

2

Sheridan Wy   Swallow Way   Chaffinch   Beechurst   Magnolia   8 Mansfield Road   Wooseehill Lane

Rowan   Wy

Limmerhill   Road   Linden   BARKHAM   ROAD   B3349   Folly Court

Blandford Dr

3

The Coombes

Coombes La   Sandy Lane   Sandy Lane   The Shires   BARKHAM

Hayes La   The Junipers   The Woodlands

Bearwood Rd   The Lilacs   Broom Gv   DOLES HILL

PO   Ash Way   Whitebeam Cl   Thorne Cl

The Vines   Hornbeam Cl   Doles Lane

Highlands Av

4

Aggisters La   B3349

95

Barkham Manor   Evendon's Lane   Randall's Farm   Redlands Pl   Blagrove Lane   Robert Gv

BARKHAM   ROAD

5

Barkham

Brook Farm   Evendon's Lane

Barkham Square   Barkham Street   Church La +

Waverley School

6

Commonfield Lane   Barkham Ride   Gilbert Way   Springdale   Booth Dr   Nash Grove   Thomas La   Waverley Way   The Lea

7

ggs Lane

St James Road   Garrett Rd   Roycroft Lane   Mc Carthy   The Spinney   Mornington Av

Ditchfield La

Barkham Ride   Maryland   Moor   Carolina Pl   Nash Gv   Wild Briar

A   **B**   **116**   **C**   **D**   **E**

Long   Horse Ride N   Drake Cl   Barkham   Radical Ride   Tickenor Dr   B3016

Par   Drive   Par   Long Moor

1 grid square represents 500 metres

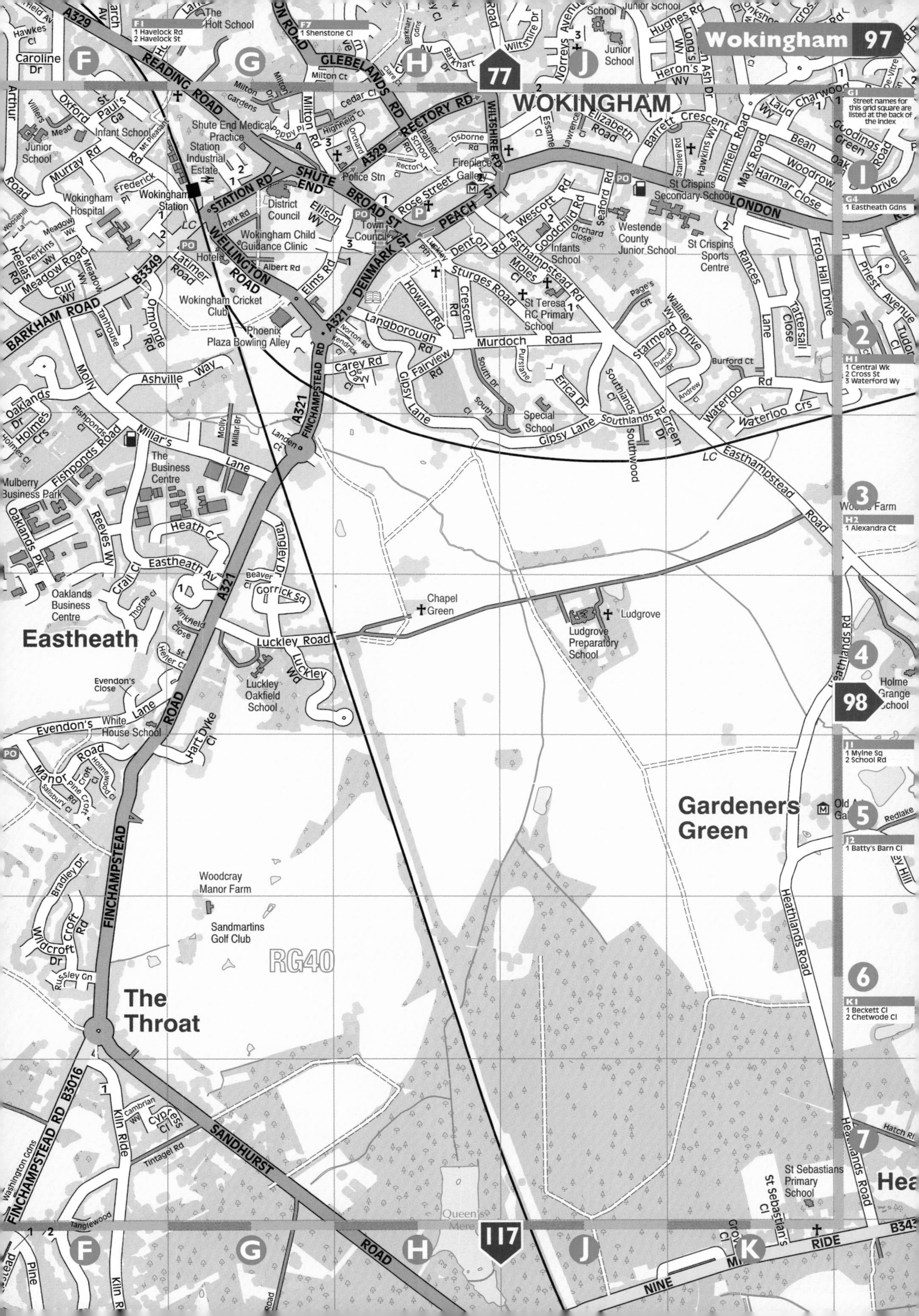
Wokingham 97
WOKINGHAM
Eastheath
Gardeners Green
The Throat
RG40
77
98
117
F1 1 Havelock Rd 2 Havelock St
F7 1 Shenstone Cl
G1 Street names for this grid square are listed at the back of the index
G4 1 Eastheath Gdns
H1 1 Central Wk 2 Cross St 3 Waterford Wy
H2 1 Alexandra Ct
J1 1 Mylne Sq 2 School Rd
J2 1 Batty's Barn Cl
K1 1 Beckett Cl 2 Chetwode Cl
READING ROAD
GLEBELANDS RD
RECTORY RD
WILTSHIRE RD
SHUTE END
STATION RD
BROAD ST
PEACH ST
DENMARK ST
WELLINGTON ROAD
BARKHAM ROAD
B3349
A329
A321
FINCHAMPSTEAD RD
FINCHAMPSTEAD ROAD
FINCHAMPSTEAD RD B3016
SANDHURST ROAD
NINE MILE RIDE
LONDON ROAD
Easthampstead Road
Heathlands Road
Luckley Road
Gipsy Lane
Murdoch Road
Langborough Rd
Ashville Way
Millar's Lane
Eastheath Av
Evendon's Lane
Holt School
Infant School
Junior School
Shute End Medical Practice
Station Industrial Estate
Wokingham Station
Wokingham Hospital
District Council
Town Council
Police Stn
Wokingham Child Guidance Clinic
Wokingham Cricket Club
Phoenix Plaza Bowling Alley
Fireplace Gallery
St Crispins Secondary School
St Crispins Sports Centre
Westende County Junior School
Infants School
St Teresa RC Primary School
Special School
The Business Centre
Mulberry Business Park
Oaklands Business Centre
Chapel Green
Ludgrove
Ludgrove Preparatory School
Luckley Oakfield School
White House School
Woodcray Manor Farm
Sandmartins Golf Club
Queen's Mere
Holme Grange School
St Sebastians Primary School
Woods Farm

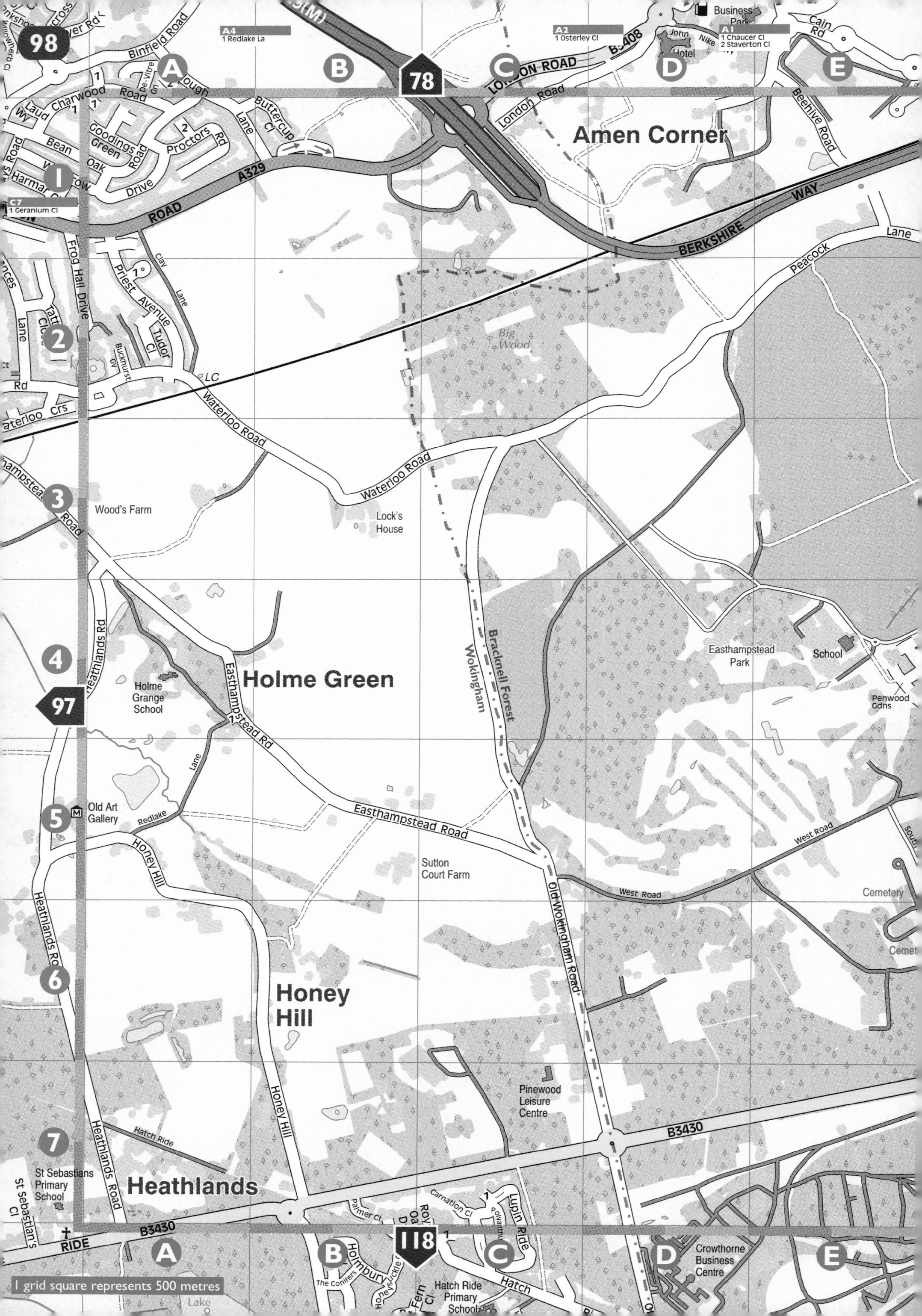

98
78
97
118
A
B
C
D
E
1
2
3
4
5
6
7
Amen Corner
Holme Green
Honey Hill
Heathlands
Big Wood
Wood's Farm
Lock's House
Holme Grange School
Old Art Gallery
Sutton Court Farm
Easthampstead Park
School
Penwood Gdns
Cemetery
Pinewood Leisure Centre
St Sebastians Primary School
Hatch Ride Primary School
Crowthorne Business Centre
Business Park
Hotel
A329
ROAD
BERKSHIRE WAY
LONDON ROAD
London Road
B3408
B3430
RIDE
Waterloo Road
Waterloo Crs
Peacock Lane
Easthampstead Road
Easthampstead Rd
Wokingham Road
Bracknell Forest
Old Wokingham Road
West Road
Honey Hill
Heathlands Road
Heathlands Rd
Hatch Ride
Redlake Lane
Frog Hall Drive
Priest Avenue
Tudor Cl
Clay Lane
Buckhurst Gv
Binfield Road
Charwood Road
Goodings Green
Oak Drive
Proctors Rd
Buttercup Cl
Bean
Laud Wy
Beehive Road
Cain Rd
John Nike Wy
De-Vitre Gn
Lupin Ride
Carnation Cl
Palmer Cl
Holmbury
The Conifers
Honeysuckle
Fern Cl
Royal Oak Dr
Polyanthus
St Sebastian's Cl
LC
A4 1 Redlake La
A2 1 Osterley Cl
A1 1 Chaucer Cl 2 Staverton Cl
C7 1 Geranium Cl
Lake
1 grid square represents 500 metres

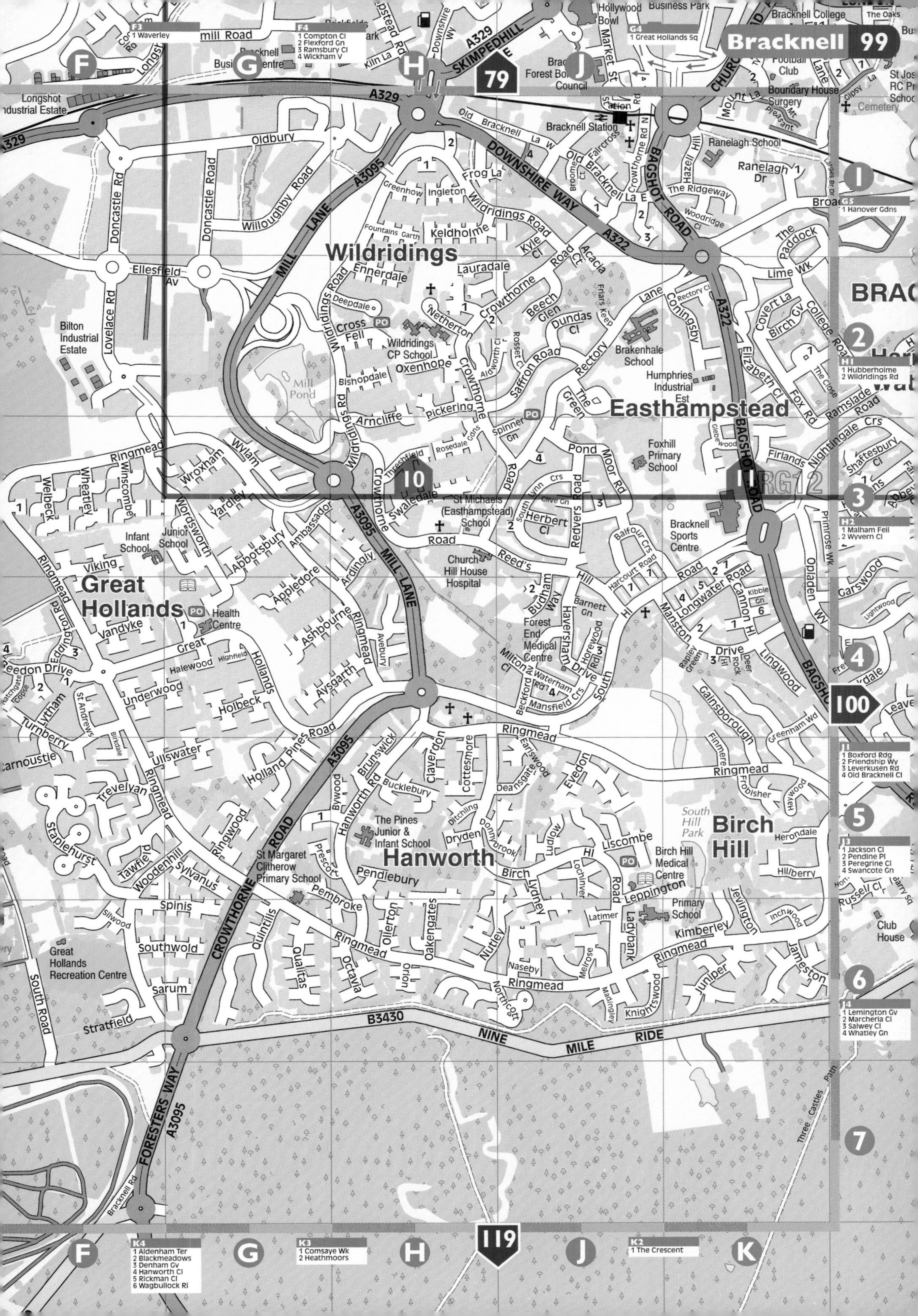
F3
1 Waverley
F4
1 Compton Cl
2 Flexford Gn
3 Ramsbury Cl
4 Wickham V
G4
1 Great Hollands Sq
G5
1 Hanover Gdns
H1
1 Hubberholme
2 Wildridings Rd
H2
1 Malham Fell
2 Wyvern Cl
J1
1 Boxford Rdg
2 Friendship Wy
3 Leverkusen Rd
4 Old Bracknell Cl
J3
1 Jackson Cl
2 Pendine Pl
3 Peregrine Cl
4 Swancote Gn
J4
1 Lemington Gv
2 Marcheria Cl
3 Salwey Cl
4 Whatley Gn
K4
1 Aldenham Ter
2 Blackmeadows
3 Denham Gv
4 Hanworth Cl
5 Rickman Cl
6 Wagbullock Ri
K3
1 Comsaye Wk
2 Heathmoors
K2
1 The Crescent
79
100
119
10
11
RG12
F
G
H
J
K
1
2
3
4
5
6
7
Wildridings
Easthampstead
Great Hollands
Hanworth
Birch Hill
Longshot Industrial Estate
Bilton Industrial Estate
Bracknell College
Bracknell Station
Hollywood Bowl
Business Park
Bracknell Forest Borough Council
Ranelagh School
Football Club
Boundary House Surgery
Cemetery
St Joseph's RC Primary School
Wildridings CP School
Mill Pond
Brakenhale School
Humphries Industrial Est
Foxhill Primary School
St Michaels (Easthampstead) School
Church Hill House Hospital
Bracknell Sports Centre
Forest End Medical Centre
Infant School
Junior School
Health Centre
The Pines Junior & Infant School
St Margaret Clitherow Primary School
Birch Hill Medical Centre
Primary School
South Hill Park
Great Hollands Recreation Centre
Club House
A329
A3095
A322
B3430
SKIMPEDHILL LA
DOWNSHIRE WAY
BAGSHOT ROAD
MILL LANE
CROWTHORNE ROAD
FORESTERS WAY
NINE MILE RIDE
Old Bracknell La W
Old Bracknell La E
Oldbury
Willoughby Road
Doncastle Road
Doncastle Rd
Lovelace Rd
Ellesfield Av
Ringmead
Wildridings Road
Wildridings Rd
Crowthorne Road
Rectory Lane
Reed's Hill
Pond Moor Rd
Holland Pines Road
Great Hollands Road
Eddington Rd
Deedon Drive
Longwater Road
Hanworth Rd
Bracknell Rd
Three Castles Path

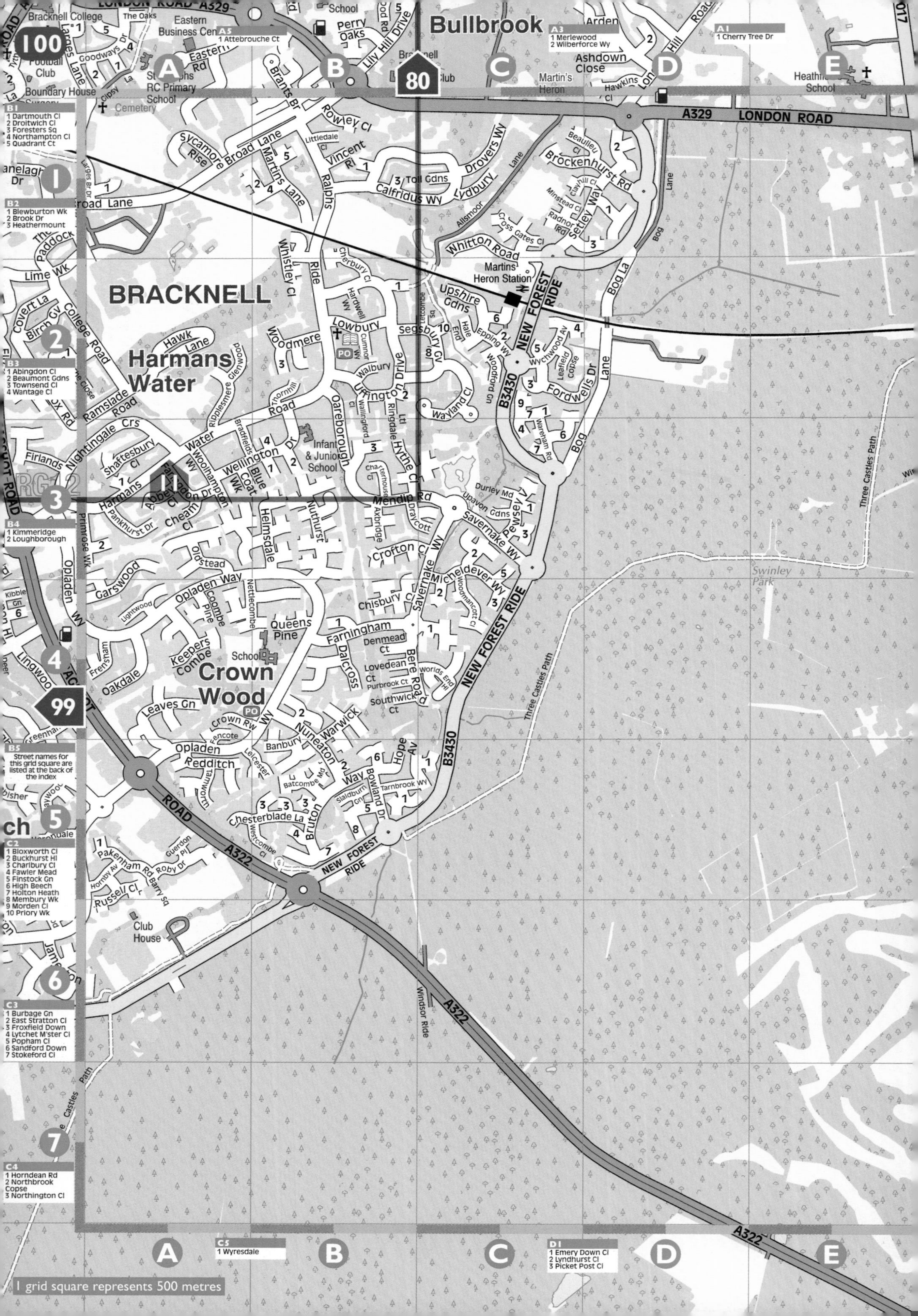

100
80
99
101
Bullbrook
BRACKNELL
Harmans Water
Crown Wood
Martins Heron Station
LONDON ROAD A329
A322
NEW FOREST RIDE
B3430
Swinley Park
Three Castles Path
A5
1 Attebrouche Ct
A3
1 Merlewood
2 Wilberforce Wy
A1
1 Cherry Tree Dr
B1
1 Dartmouth Cl
2 Droitwich Cl
3 Foresters Sq
4 Northampton Cl
5 Quadrant Ct
B2
1 Blewburton Wk
2 Brook Dr
3 Heathermount
B3
1 Abingdon Cl
2 Beaumont Gdns
3 Townsend Cl
4 Wantage Cl
B4
1 Kimmeridge
2 Loughborough
B5
Street names for this grid square are listed at the back of the index
C2
1 Bloxworth Cl
2 Buckhurst Hl
3 Charlbury Cl
4 Fawler Mead
5 Finstock Gn
6 High Beech
7 Holton Heath
8 Membury Wk
9 Morden Cl
10 Priory Wk
C3
1 Burbage Gn
2 East Stratton Cl
3 Froxfield Down
4 Lytchet M'ster Cl
5 Popham Cl
6 Sandford Down
7 Stokeford Cl
C4
1 Horndean Rd
2 Northbrook Copse
3 Northington Cl
C5
1 Wyresdale
D1
1 Emery Down Cl
2 Lyndhurst Cl
3 Picket Post Cl
1 grid square represents 500 metres

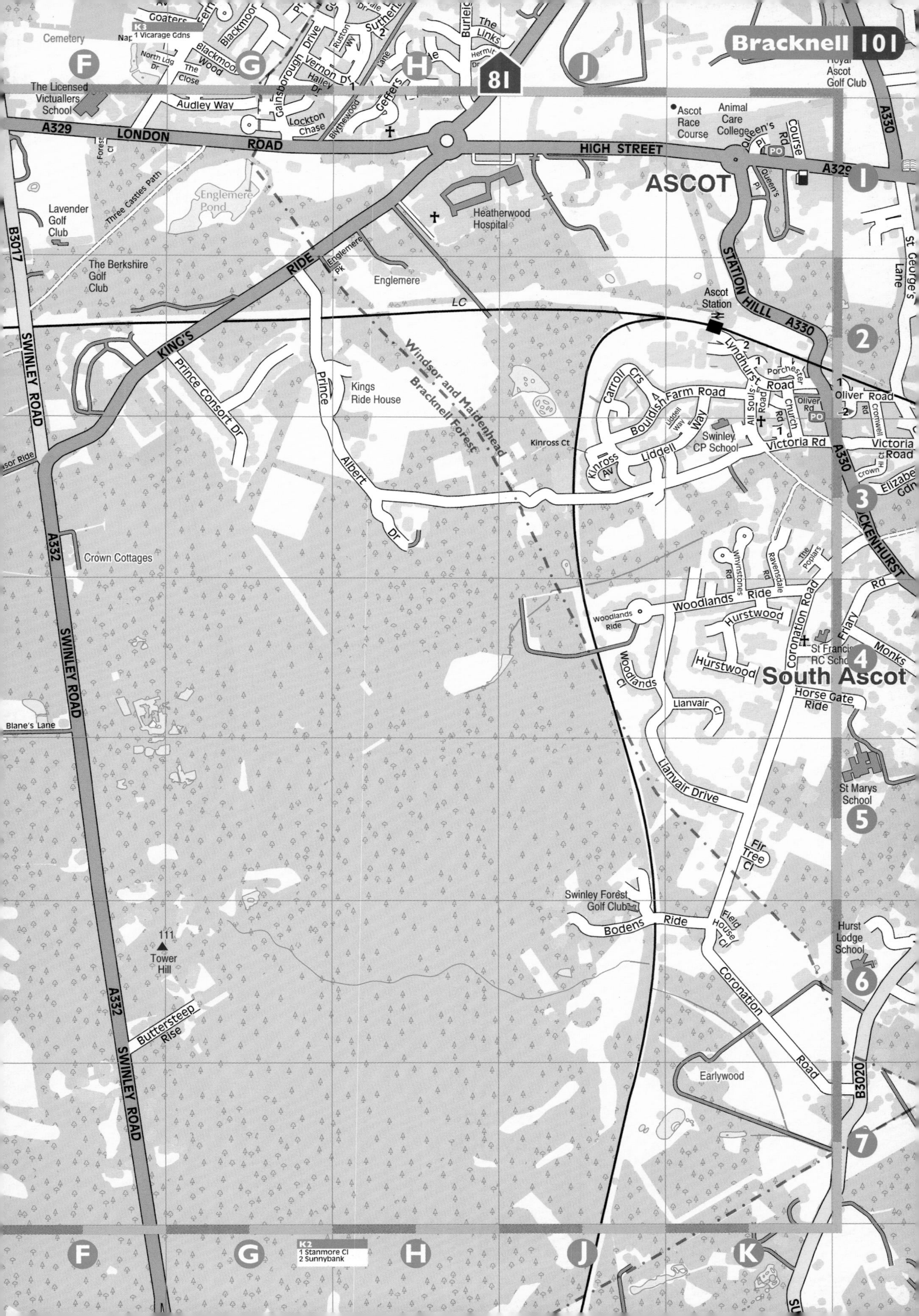

ASCOT

South Ascot

Cemetery

The Licensed Victuallers School

Lavender Golf Club

The Berkshire Golf Club

Crown Cottages

Blane's Lane

111
Tower Hill

Englemere Pond

Heatherwood Hospital

Englemere

Kings Ride House

Kinross Ct

Swinley CP School

Ascot Race Course

Animal Care College

Ascot Station

Royal Ascot Golf Club

St Francis RC School

The Poplars

St Marys School

Hurst Lodge School

Swinley Forest Golf Club

Earlywood

Goaters

Blackmoor Wood

Audley Way

Lockton Chase

The Links

LONDON ROAD A329

HIGH STREET

KING'S RIDE

SWINLEY ROAD A332

SWINLEY ROAD

STATION HILL A330

Windsor and Maidenhead

Bracknell Forest

Prince Consort Dr

Albert Dr

Buttersteep Rise

Three Castles Path

B3017

A330

A329

St George's Lane

Carroll Crs

Bouldish Farm Road

Liddell Way

Lyndhurst Road

Porchester Road

All Souls Rd

Victoria Rd

Oliver Rd

Oliver Road

Cromwell Rd

Victoria Road

Elizabeth Gdns

Woodlands Ride

Hurstwood

Coronation Road

Whynstones Rd

Ravensdale

Friary Rd

Monks

Horse Gate Ride

Llanvair Cl

Llanvair Drive

Fir Tree Cl

Field House Cl

Bodens Ride

Coronation Road

B3020

Kinross Av

Woodlands Ride

Hurstwood

Woodlands

Forest Ct

North Ldg Dr

The Close

1 Vicarage Gdns

Gainsborough Drive

Vernon Dr

Halley Dr

Gefter's

Hermit Dr

Blythewood

Ruston Way

Queen's Pl

Course Rd

PO

Queen's Pl

PO

LC

81

F   G   H   J

I

2

3

4

5

6

7

F   G   H   J   K

K3

K2
1 Stanmore Cl
2 Sunnybank

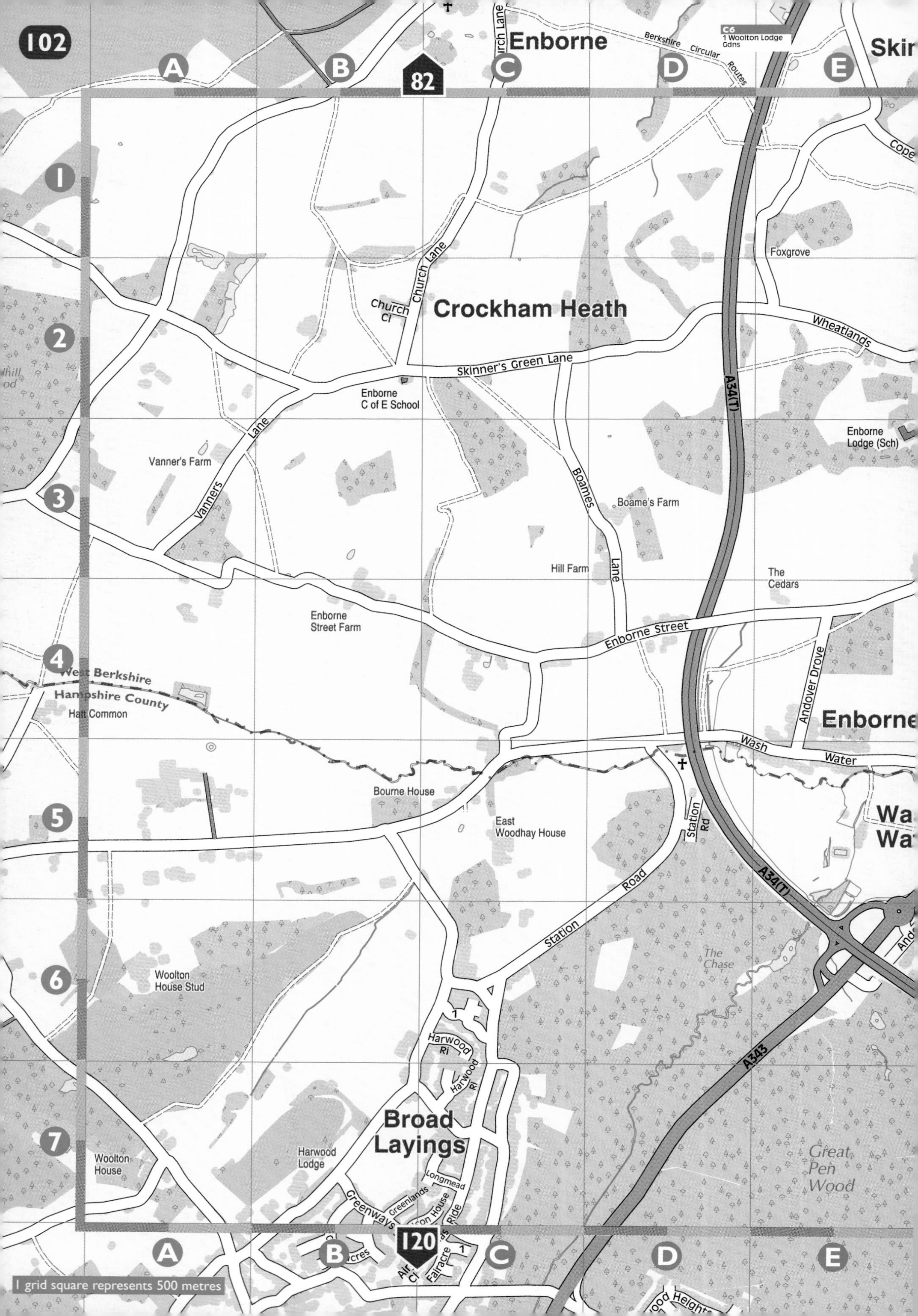

A B 82 C D E

Skir

I

Enborne

Church Lane

Church Cl

Crockham Heath

Foxgrove

2

Skinner's Green Lane

Wheatlands

Berkshire Circular Routes

C6
1 Woolton Lodge
Gdns

A34(T)

Enborne
C of E School

Vanner's Farm

Enborne
Lodge (Sch)

Vanners Lane

3

Boame's Farm

Boames Lane

Hill Farm

The Cedars

Enborne
Street Farm

4 West Berkshire
Hampshire County

Enborne Street

Andover Drove

Enborne

Hatt Common

Wash

Water

Bourne House

Station Rd

Wa
Wa

5

East
Woodhay House

6

Woolton
House Stud

The Chase

A34(T)

Station Road

A343

7

Woolton
House

Harwood
Lodge

Harwood
Ri

1

Harwood Ri

Broad
Layings

Longmead

Great
Pen
Wood

Greenways

Greenlands

House

Ride

Acres

A B 120 C D E

Air Cl

Farracre Cl

1

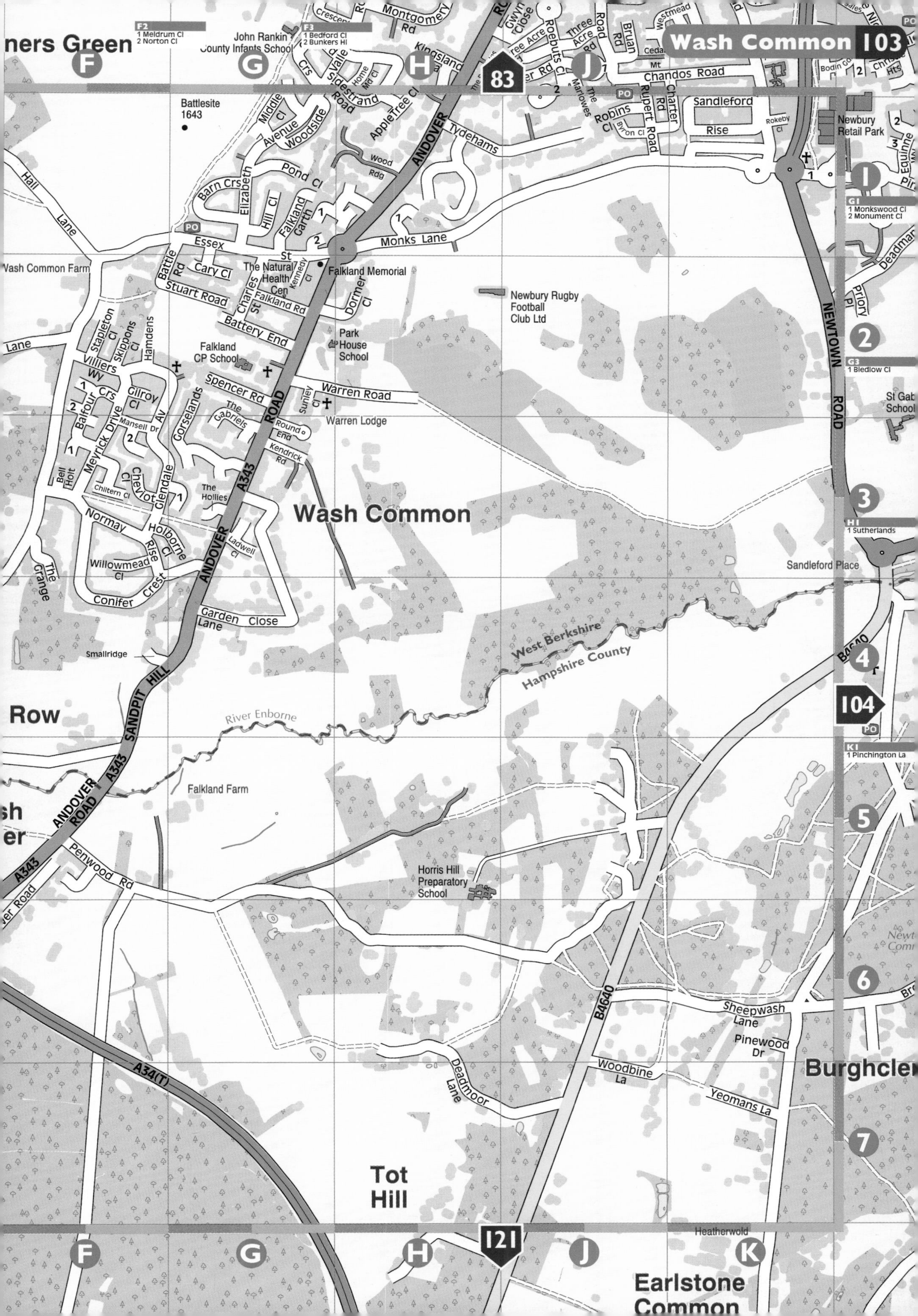

ners Green

F2
1 Meldrum Cl
2 Norton Cl

John Rankin
County Infants School

F3
1 Bedford Cl
2 Bunkers Hi

83

Montgomery Rd

Gwyn Close

Three Acre Rd

Bruan Rd

Chandos Road

Newbury Retail Park

G1
1 Monkswood Cl
2 Monument Cl

G3
1 Bledlow Cl

St Gab School

Battlesite 1643

Hall Lane

Wash Common Farm

Battle Lane

Barn Crsbeth

Elizabeth

Middle Avenue

Woodside

Falkland Garth

Hill Cl

Pond Cl

AppleTree Cl

Wood Rdg

ANDOVER

Tydehams

Monks Lane

Essex

Cary Cl

St Charles St

The Natural Health Cen

Falkland Rd

Battery End

Falkland Memorial

Dormer Cl

Sunley

Kennedy

Stuart Road

Stapleton

Skippons

Hamdens

Villiers Wy

Crs

Gilroy Cl

Mansell Dr

Spencer Rd

Falkland CP School

The Gabriels

ROAD

Corselands

Warren Road

Round End

Warren Lodge

Kendrick Rd

Newbury Rugby Football Club Ltd

Balfour

Meyrick Drive

Chiltern Cl

Cheviot

Glendale

Normay

The Hollies

A343

Bell Holt

Holborne

Rise

Willowmead Cl

Crest

Conifer

ANDOVER

Ladwell Cl

Wash Common

Smallridge

SANDPIT HILL

Garden Close Lane

Row

River Enborne

West Berkshire
Hampshire County

Sandleford Place

BA640

4

104

K1
1 Pinchington La

5

ANDOVER

A343

ROAD

Falkland Farm

Penwood Rd

A34(T)

Horris Hill Preparatory School

Deadmoor Lane

Sheepwash Lane

Pinewood Dr

Woodbine La

Yeomans La

Burghcler

Tot Hill

121

Heatherwold

Earlstone Common

NEWTOWN ROAD

2

3

I

Priory

Sandleford Rise

Robins Cl

Rokeby

6

7

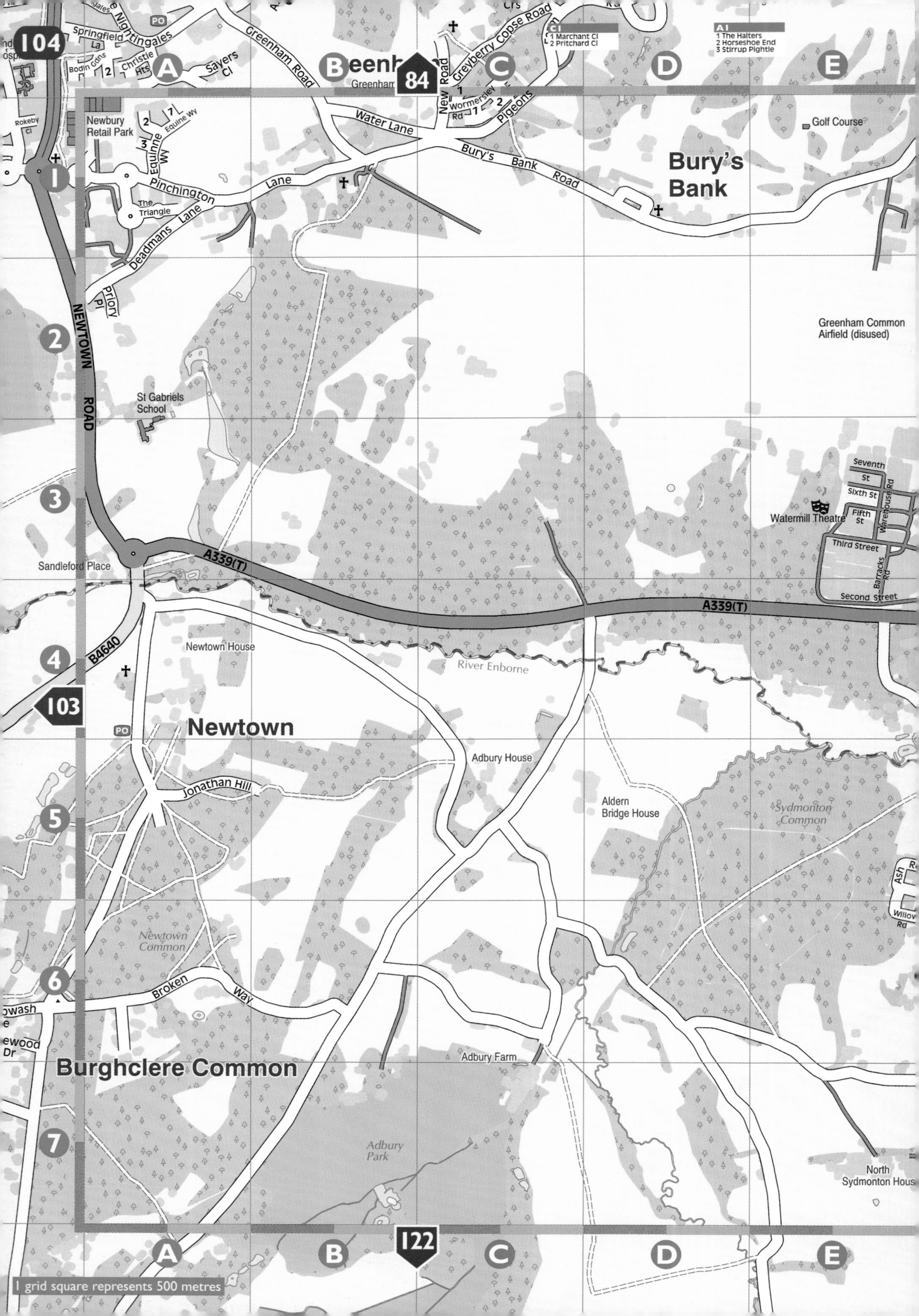

A **B** Beenh **84** **C** **D** **E**

C1
1 Marchant Cl
2 Pritchard Cl

Springfield
Nightingales
La
PO
Greenham Road

Bodin Gdns
2
Christie
Hts
Sayers
Cl
Greenham
New Road
Greyberry Copse Road
Crs
Golf Course

Rokeby
Cl

Newbury
Retail Park
2
7
Equine Wy
Water Lane
Wormersley
Rd
1
2
Pigeons
1

Equine
Wy
3

Pinchington
Lane
Bury's Bank Road
Bury's
Bank

The
Triangle

Deadmans Lane

Priory Pl

NEWTOWN ROAD

Greenham Common
Airfield (disused)

St Gabriels
School

Seventh
St
Sixth St
Warehouse Rd
Watermill Theatre
Fifth
St

A339(T)
Third Street
Barracks Rd

Sandleford Place

A339(T)
Second Street

B4640

Newtown House

River Enborne

Newtown

Adbury House

Aldern
Bridge House

Sydmonton
Common

103

PO

Jonathan Hill

Ash

Willow Rd

Newtown
Common

6

Broken
Way

owash

ewood
Dr

Burghclere Common

Adbury Farm

7

Adbury
Park

North
Sydmonton Hou

A **B** **122** **C** **D** **E**

1 grid square represents 500 metres

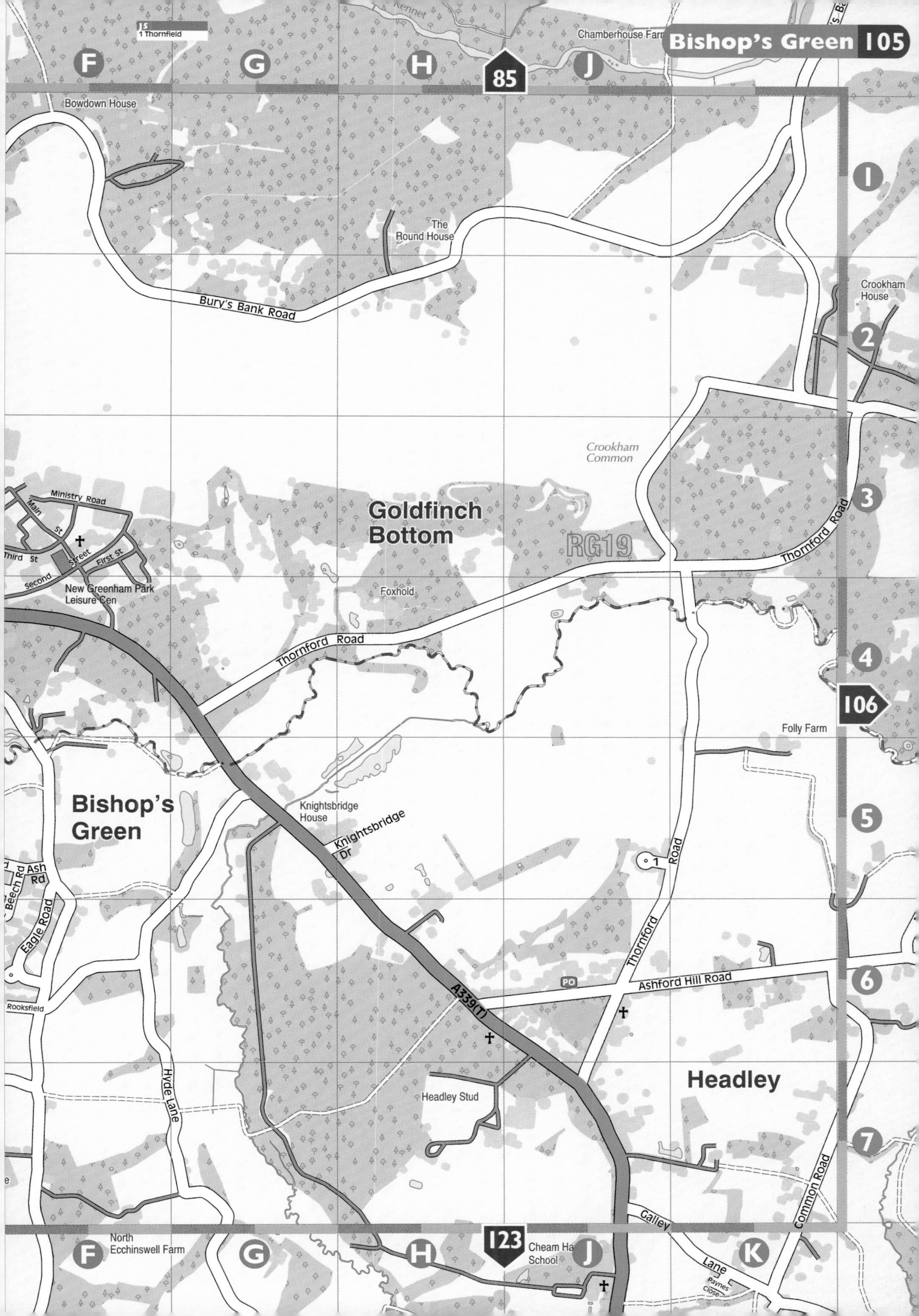

F G H 85 J

I

1 Thornfield

Bowdown House

Crookham House

2

Bury's Bank Road

The Round House

Crookham Common

3

RG19

Thornford Road

Goldfinch Bottom

Foxhold

4

106

Ministry Road

Main St

Third St

Second St First St

New Greenham Park Leisure Cen

Thornford Road

Folly Farm

5

Bishop's Green

Knightsbridge House

Knightsbridge Dr

1

Thornford Road

Ash Rd

Beech Rd

Eagle Road

Rooksfield

PO

Ashford Hill Road

6

A339(T)

Headley

Hyde Lane

Headley Stud

7

North Ecchinswell Farm

Calley Lane

Paynes Close

F G H 123 J K

Cheam Ha School

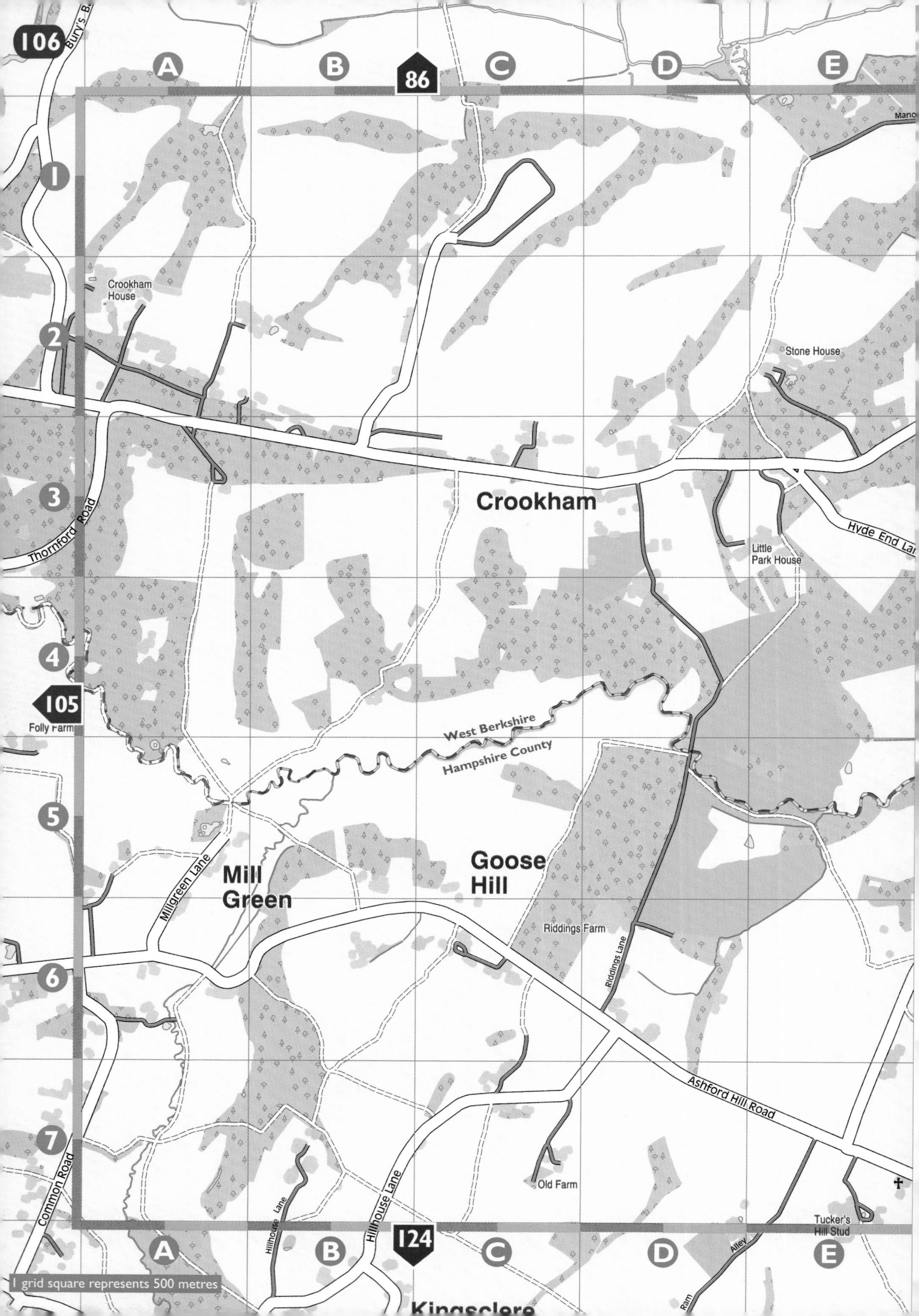
106
Bury's B
A
B
86
C
D
E
Mano
1
Crookham House
2
Stone House
3
Thornford Road
Crookham
Hyde End Lane
Little Park House
4
105
Folly Farm
West Berkshire
Hampshire County
5
Millgreen Lane
Mill Green
Goose Hill
Riddings Farm
6
Riddings Lane
Ashford Hill Road
7
Common Road
Hillhouse Lane
Old Farm
Tucker's Hill Stud
Hillhouse Lane
124
Alley
Ram
A
B
C
D
E
1 grid square represents 500 metres
Kingsclere

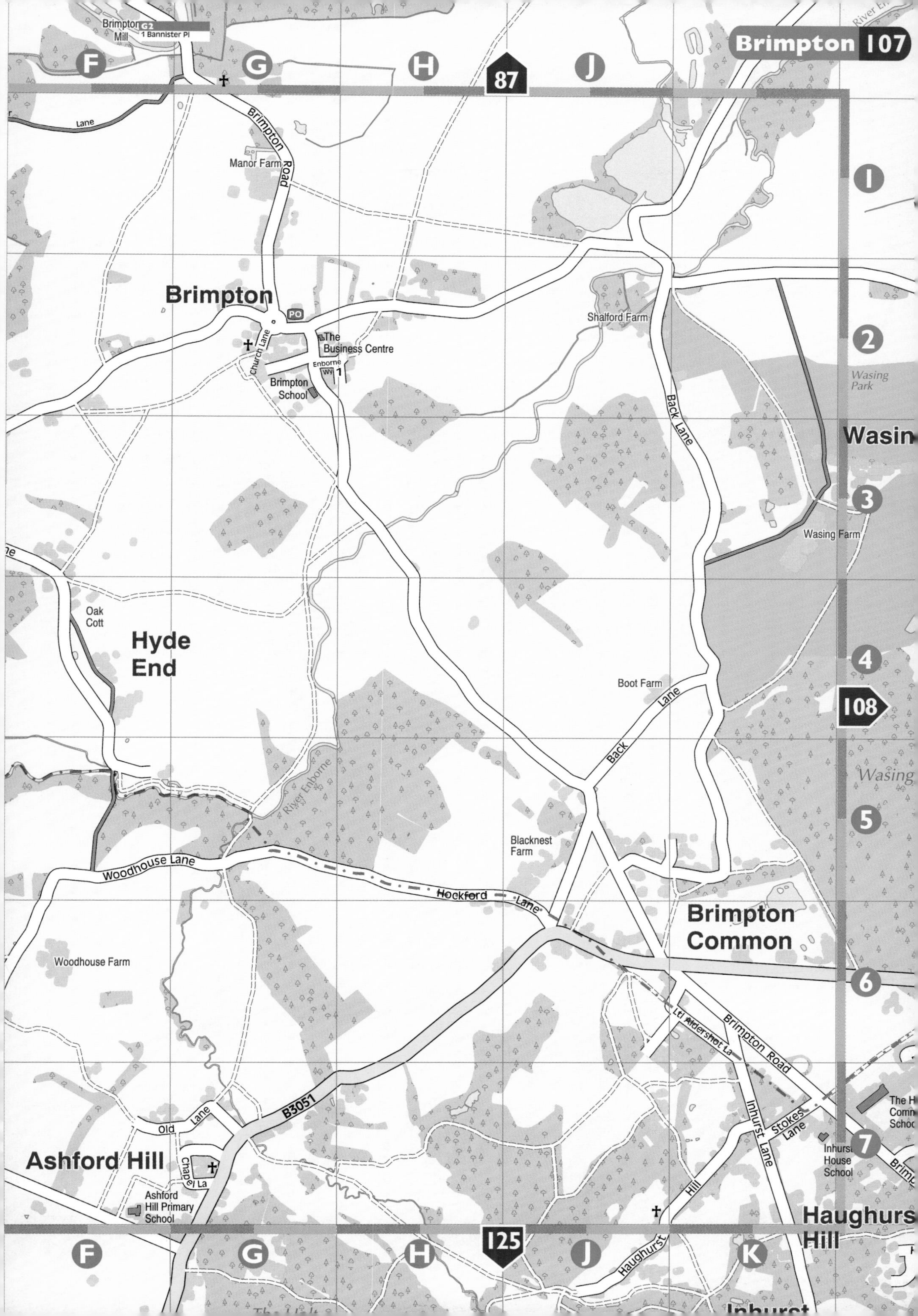

Brimpton Mill G2
1 Bannister Pl

F **G** **H** **87** **J**

Lane

Brimpton Road

Manor Farm

I

Brimpton

PO

2

Shalford Farm

Wasing Park

Church Lane

The Business Centre

Wasin

Enborne Wy 1

Brimpton School

Back Lane

3

Wasing Farm

Oak Cott

Hyde End

Boot Farm

4

108

Back Lane

River Enborne

Wasing

5

Blacknest Farm

Woodhouse Lane

Hockford Lane

Brimpton Common

6

Woodhouse Farm

Brimpton Road

Lt Aldershot La

Old Lane

B3051

Inhurst Lane

Stokes Lane

The H Comn Scho

Ashford Hill

Chapel La

7

Inhurst House School

Brimp

Ashford Hill Primary School

Hill

Haughurst

Haughurs Hill

F **G** **H** **125** **J** **K**

Inhurst

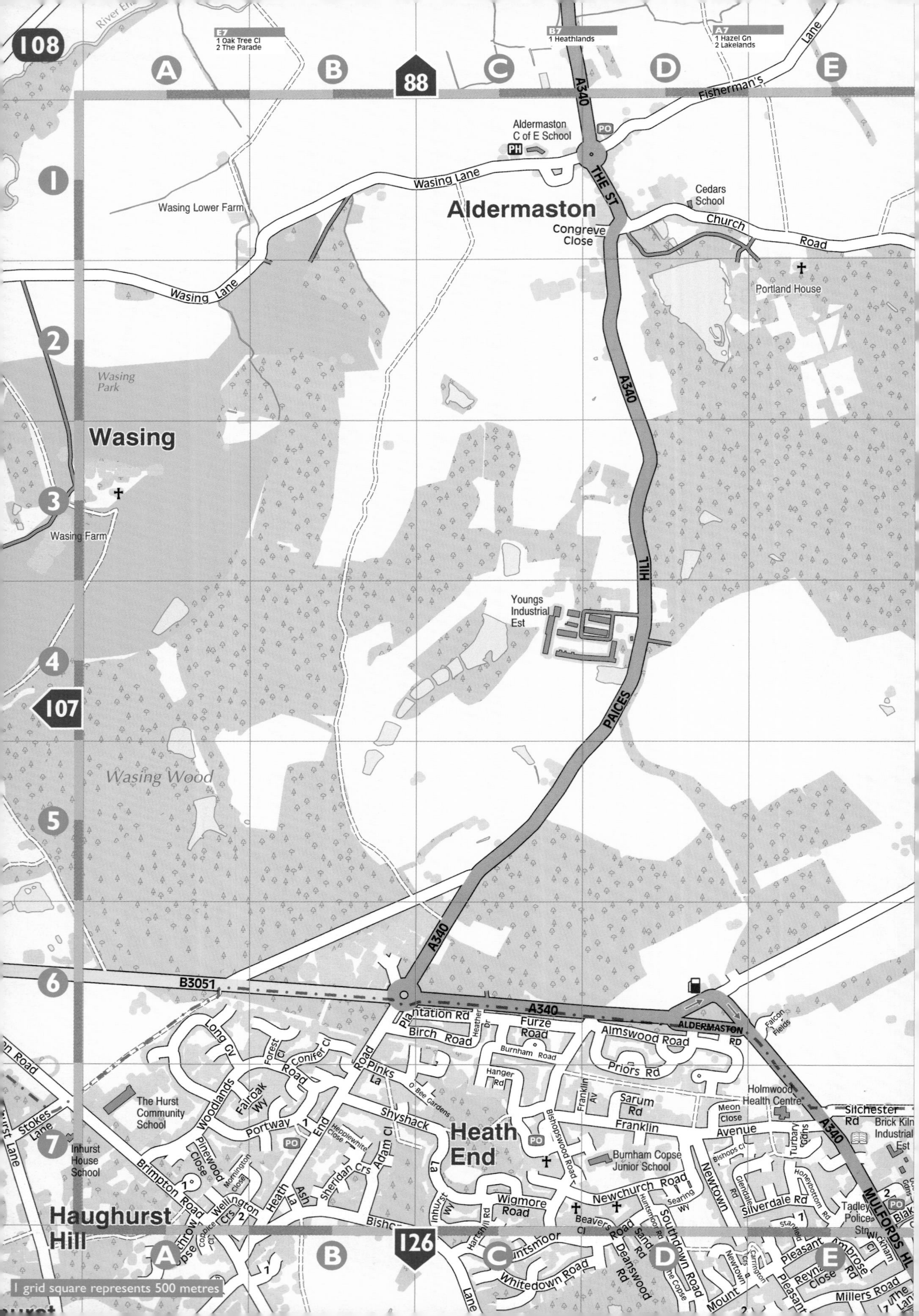
108
88
107
126
A
B
C
D
E
1
2
3
4
5
6
7
E7
1 Oak Tree Cl
2 The Parade
B7
1 Heathlands
A7
1 Hazel Gn
2 Lakelands
Aldermaston
Aldermaston C of E School
Cedars School
Congreve Close
Church Road
Fisherman's Lane
Wasing Lane
Wasing Lower Farm
Portland House
Wasing Park
Wasing
Wasing Farm
Wasing Wood
Youngs Industrial Est
PAICES HILL
THE ST
A340
B3051
Plantation Rd
Birch Road
Furze Road
Almswood Road
ALDERMASTON RD
Burnham Road
Priors Rd
Sarum Rd
Franklin Av
Franklin Avenue
Holmwood Health Centre
Meon Close
Silchester Rd
Brick Kiln Industrial Est
Heath End
Burnham Copse Junior School
Newchurch Road
Newtown
Silverdale Rd
MULFORDS HL
The Hurst Community School
Inhurst House School
Haughurst Hill
Woodlands
Fairoak Wy
Portway
Conifer Cl
Forest Cl
Long Gv
Pinks La
Shyshack
Sheridan Crs
Adam Cl
Wigmore Road
Whitedown Road
Deanswood Rd
Southdown Road
Pleasant
Millers Road
Tadley Police Stn
1 grid square represents 500 metres

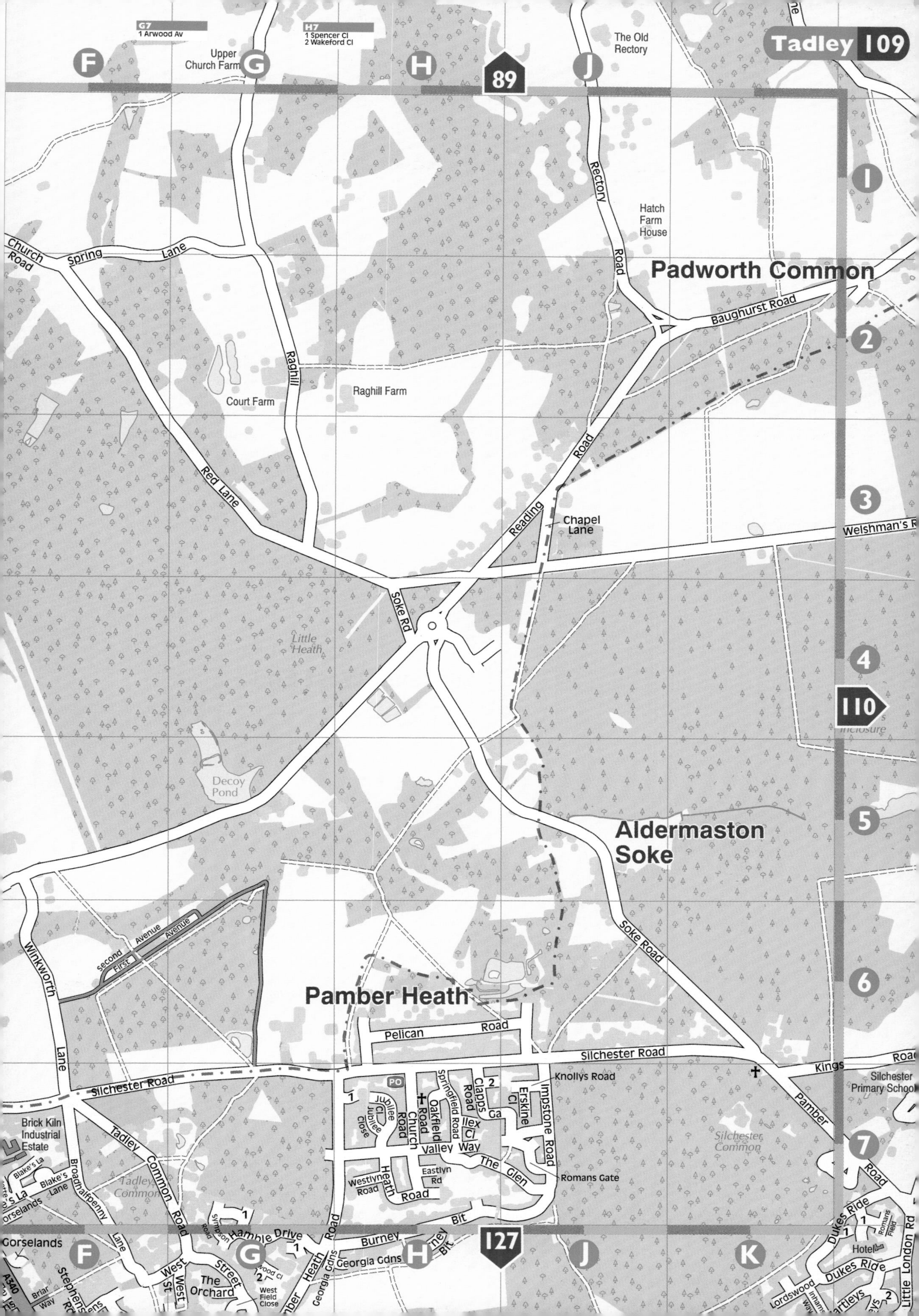

G7
1 Arwood Av

H7
1 Spencer Cl
2 Wakeford Cl

F

Upper
Church Farm

G

H

89

J

The Old
Rectory

I

Rectory Road

Hatch
Farm
House

Church Road

Spring Lane

Padworth Common

Baughurst Road

2

Raghill

Court Farm

Raghill Farm

Red Lane

Reading Road

Chapel
Lane

Welshman's R

3

Little
Heath

Soke Rd

4

110

Inclosure

Decoy
Pond

5

**Aldermaston
Soke**

Soke Road

Winkworth Lane

Second Avenue
First Avenue

6

Pamber Heath

Pelican Road

Silchester Road

Knollys Road

Kings Road

Silchester
Primary School

7

Brick Kiln
Industrial
Estate

Silchester Road

PO

Tadley Common Road

Broadhalfpenny

Blake's La
Blake's Lane

Tadley
Common

1

Jubilee Close
Jubilee Close

Springfield Road
Church Road
Oakfield Road

Clapps Road
Ilex Cl
Ga

Erskine Cl
Impstone Road

†

Silchester
Common

Gorselands Road

Gorselands

Westlyne Road
Heath Road

Valley Way
Eastlyn Rd

The Glen

Romans Gate

Pamber Road

Dukes Ride

Hotel

Little London Rd

F

West La
West St
Stephens Rd
Briar Way
A340

The
Orchard

Pamber Heath Road

G

Hamble Drive
Simpson Rd
1
Arwood Cl
Georgia Gdns
West Field Close

1
2

Burney
Honey Bit

Georgia Gdns

H

127

J

K

Dukes Ride
Lordswood
Inhams
Bartleys Rd
Romans Field

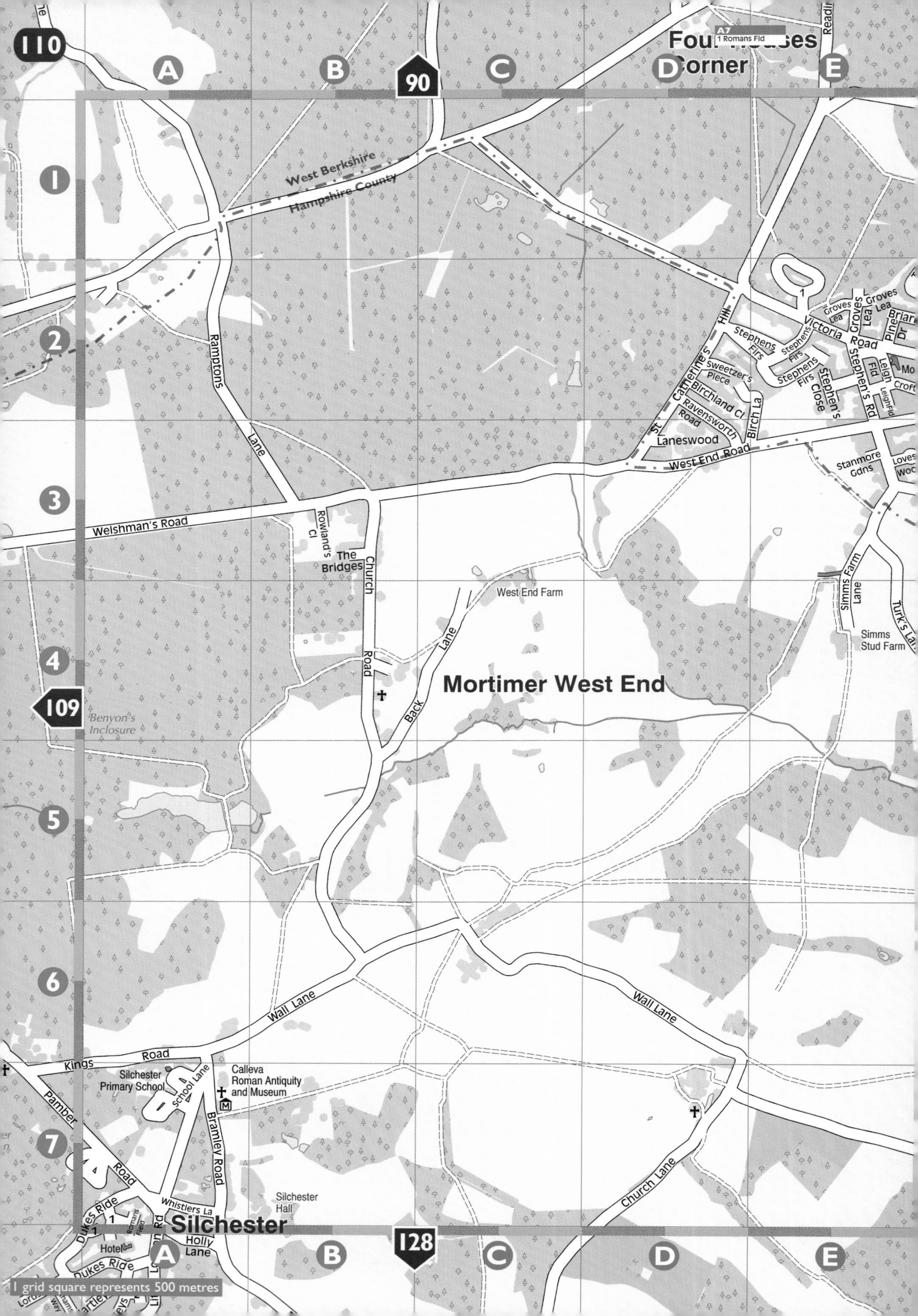

A B 90 C D E

Four Houses
Corner

A7
1 Romans Fld

Readin

1

West Berkshire
Hampshire County

2

Ramptons
Lane

Victoria

Groves
Lea

Groves
Lea

Groves
Road

Briar
Pine
Dr

St. Catherine's

Stephens Firs

Stephens
Firs

Leigh
Fld

Leighfiel

Mo

Mc
Croft

Sweetzer's
Piece

Birchland Cl

Stephens
Firs

Stephen's
Close

Stephen's
Rd

3

Welshman's Road

Rowland's
Cl

Ravensworth
Road

Birch La

Laneswood

West End Road

Stanmore
Gdns

Loves
Woo

The
Bridges

Church
Road

West End Farm

Simms Farm
Lane

Turk's La

4

109

'Benyon's
Inclosure'

Back
Lane

Mortimer West End

Simms
Stud Farm

5

6

Wall Lane

Wall Lane

Kings

Road

Silchester
Primary School

School Lane

Calleva
Roman Antiquity
and Museum

7

Pamber

Road

Bramley Road

Silchester
Hall

Church Lane

Dukes Ride

Lor   Rd

Whistlers La

Silchester

Holly
Lane

Hotel

Dukes Ride

A B 128 C D E

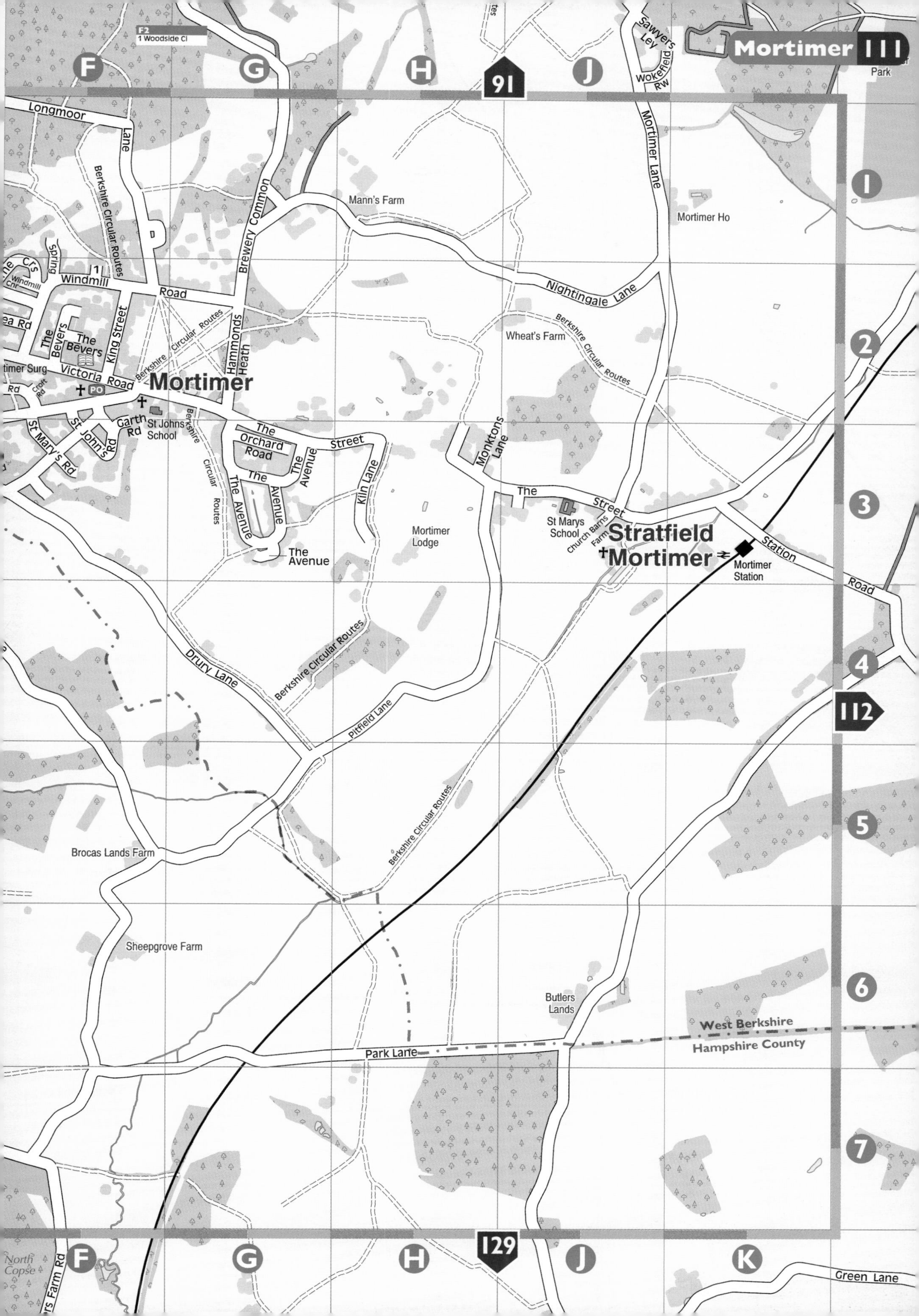

F2
1 Woodside Cl

F G H 91 J

Park

I

Longmoor Lane

Berkshire Circular Routes

Mann's Farm

Mortimer Ho

Nightingale Lane

2

Windmill

The Bevers

The Bevers

Wheat's Farm

Berkshire Circular Routes

King Street

Hammonds Heath

Brewery Common

Road

Berkshire Circular Routes

Mortimer

Victoria Road

PO

Garth Rd

St Johns School

Monktons Lane

3

St Mary's Rd

St John's Rd

The Orchard Road

The Avenue

Street

Kiln Lane

Berkshire Circular Routes

Mortimer Lodge

Monktons Lane

St Marys School

Church Barns Farm

The

Street

Stratfield
Mortimer

Mortimer Station

Station

Road

The Avenue

The Avenue

Berkshire Circular Routes

Drury Lane

Pitfield Lane

4

112

5

Brocas Lands Farm

Berkshire Circular Routes

Sheepgrove Farm

6

Butlers Lands

West Berkshire
Hampshire County

Park Lane

7

North Copse

's Farm Rd

F G H 129 J K

Green Lane

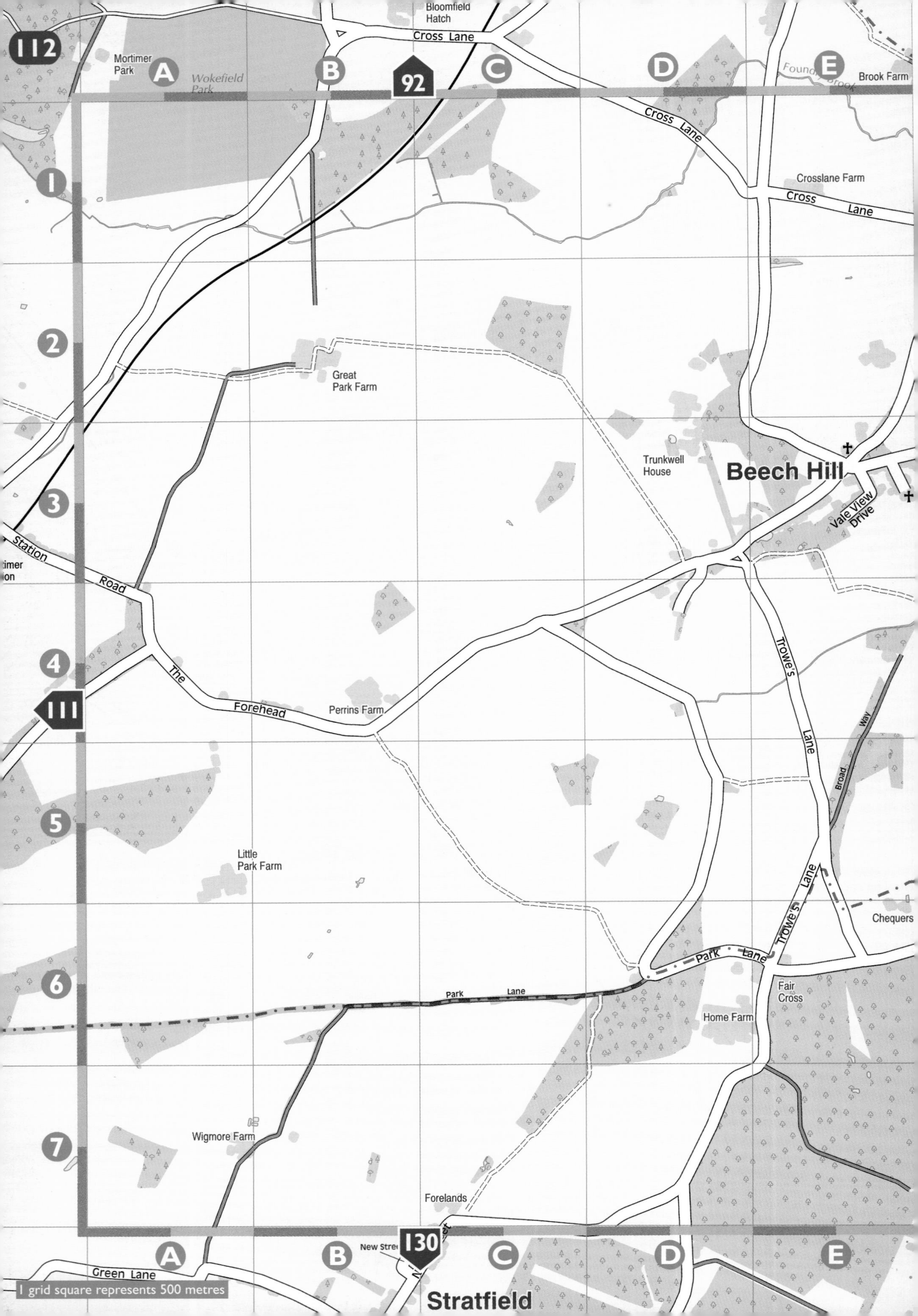

112

A Mortimer Park
Wokefield Park
B
92
C
D
E Foundry Brook
Brook Farm

Cross Lane
Bloomfield Hatch

Cross Lane

Crosslane Farm

Cross Lane

1

2

Great Park Farm

Trunkwell House

Beech Hill

Vale View Drive

3
Station Road

4
The Forehead
Perrins Farm

111

Trowe's Lane

Broad Way

Chequers

5
Little Park Farm

Trowe's Lane

6
Park Lane

Park Lane
Fair Cross
Home Farm

7
Wigmore Farm

Forelands

A Green Lane
B New Street
130
C
D
E

Stratfield

1 grid square represents 500 metres

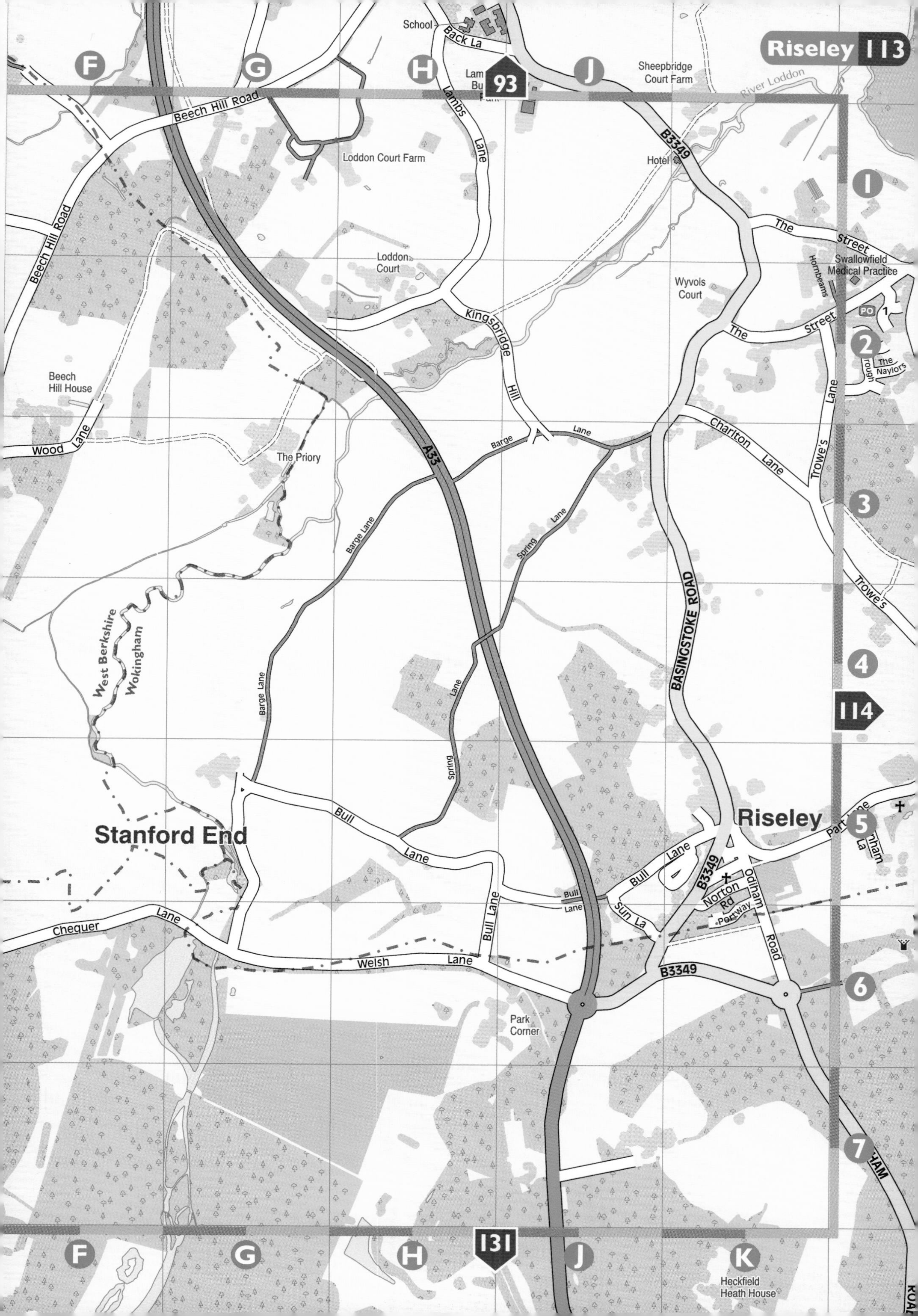

F
G
H
J
93
131
114
School
Back La
Lambs Lane
Sheepbridge Court Farm
River Loddon
Beech Hill Road
Loddon Court Farm
B3349
Hotel
Loddon Court
The Street
Swallowfield Medical Practice
Hornbeams
Wyvols Court
Kingsbridge Hill
PO
The Naylors
Beech Hill House
Wood Lane
Barge Lane
Charlton Lane
Trowe's Lane
The Priory
A33
Spring Lane
BASINGSTOKE ROAD
West Berkshire
Wokingham
Bull Lane
Riseley
Stanford End
Norton Rd
Odiham Road
Portway
Sun La
Chequer Lane
Welsh Lane
Park Lane
Park Corner
Heckfield Heath House
I
2
3
4
5
6
7
K

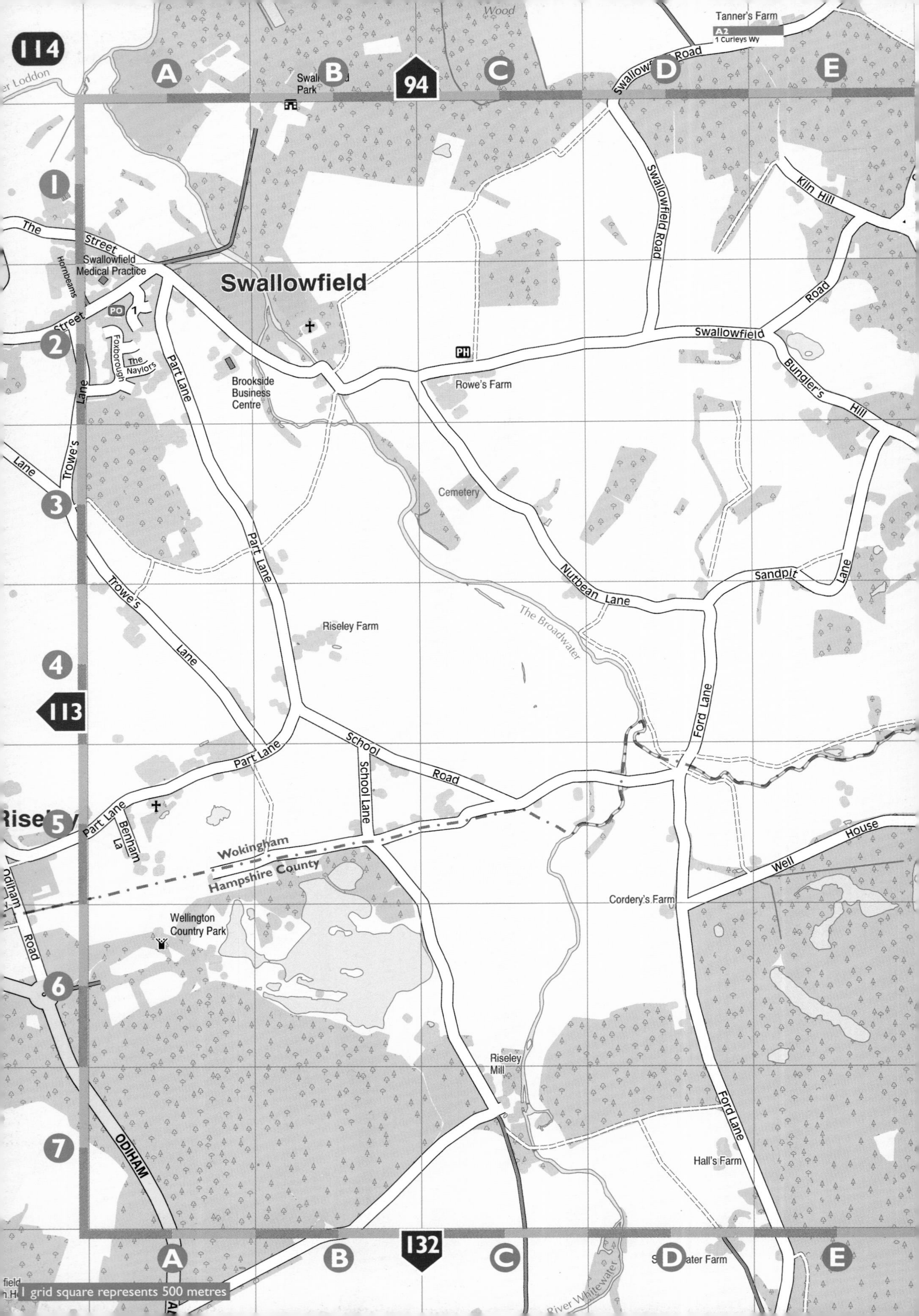

94

A   B   C   D   E

1

The
Street

Hornbeams

Swallowfield
Medical Practice

Street

PO 1

Foxborough

The Naylors

Trowe's
Lane

Part Lane

Swallowfield

Swall___
Park

Brookside
Business
Centre

PH

Rowe's Farm

Swallowfield
Road

Swallowfield

Tanner's Farm
A2
1 Curleys Wy

Swallowfield Road

Kiln Hill

Road

Bungler's Hill

2

Lane

Lane

3

Part Lane

Trowe's
Lane

Cemetery

Nutbean Lane

Sandpit   Lane

4

113

Riseley Farm

The Broadwater

Ford Lane

5

Rise___

Part Lane

Part Lane

Benham La

School Lane

School   Road

Wokingham
Hampshire County

Cordery's Farm

Well   House

6

Road

Wellington
Country Park

Riseley
Mill

7

ODIHAM

Hall's Farm

A   B   C   D   E

132

S___ater Farm

River Whitewater

1 grid square represents 500 metres

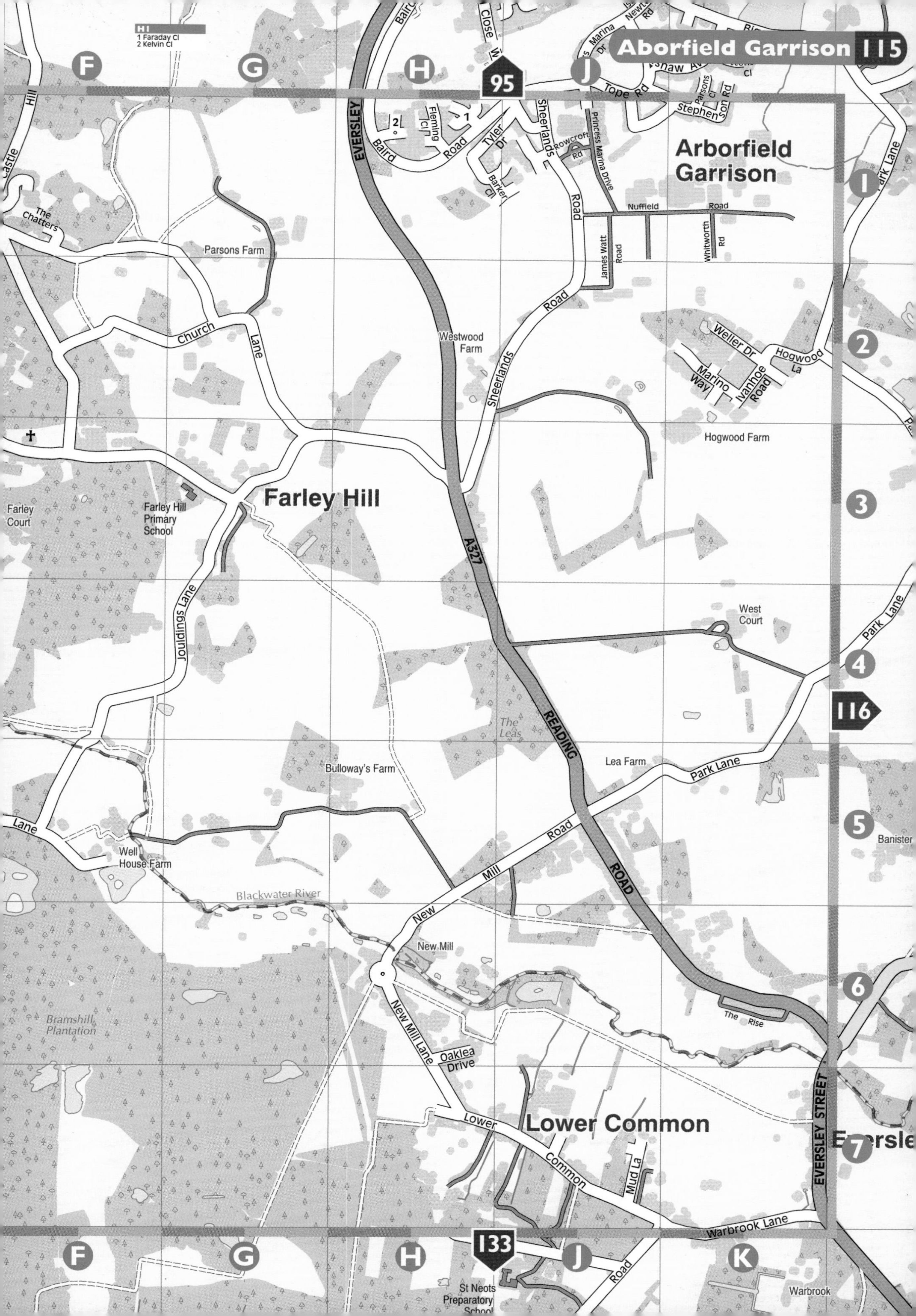

Arborfield
Garrison

H1
1 Faraday Cl
2 Kelvin Cl

F   G   H   95   J

Castle Hill

The Chatters

Parsons Farm

Church Lane

EVERSLEY

Baird

Fleming Cl

Tyler Dr

Barker Cl

Westwood Farm

Sheerlands Road

Sheerlands Road

Rowcroft Rd

Princess Marina Drive

Nuffield Road

James Watt Road

Whitworth Rd

Weller Dr

Marino Way

Ivanhoe Road

Hogwood La

Hogwood Farm

S Marina Dr

Shaw Av

Tope Rd

Parsons Rd

Stephens

Farley Court

✝

Farley Hill Primary School

Farley Hill

Jouldings Lane

A327

West Court

Park Lane

116

Lea Farm

Park Lane

Banister

The Leas

Bulloway's Farm

Lane

Well House Farm

Blackwater River

New Mill Road

New Mill Road

READING

ROAD

READING

The Rise

Bramshill Plantation

New Mill Lane

New Mill

Oaklea Drive

Lower Common

Lower Common

Mud La

EVERSLEY STREET

E ersle

Warbrook Lane

Warbrook

133

St Neots Preparatory School

F   G   H   133   J   K

1   2   3   4   5   6   7

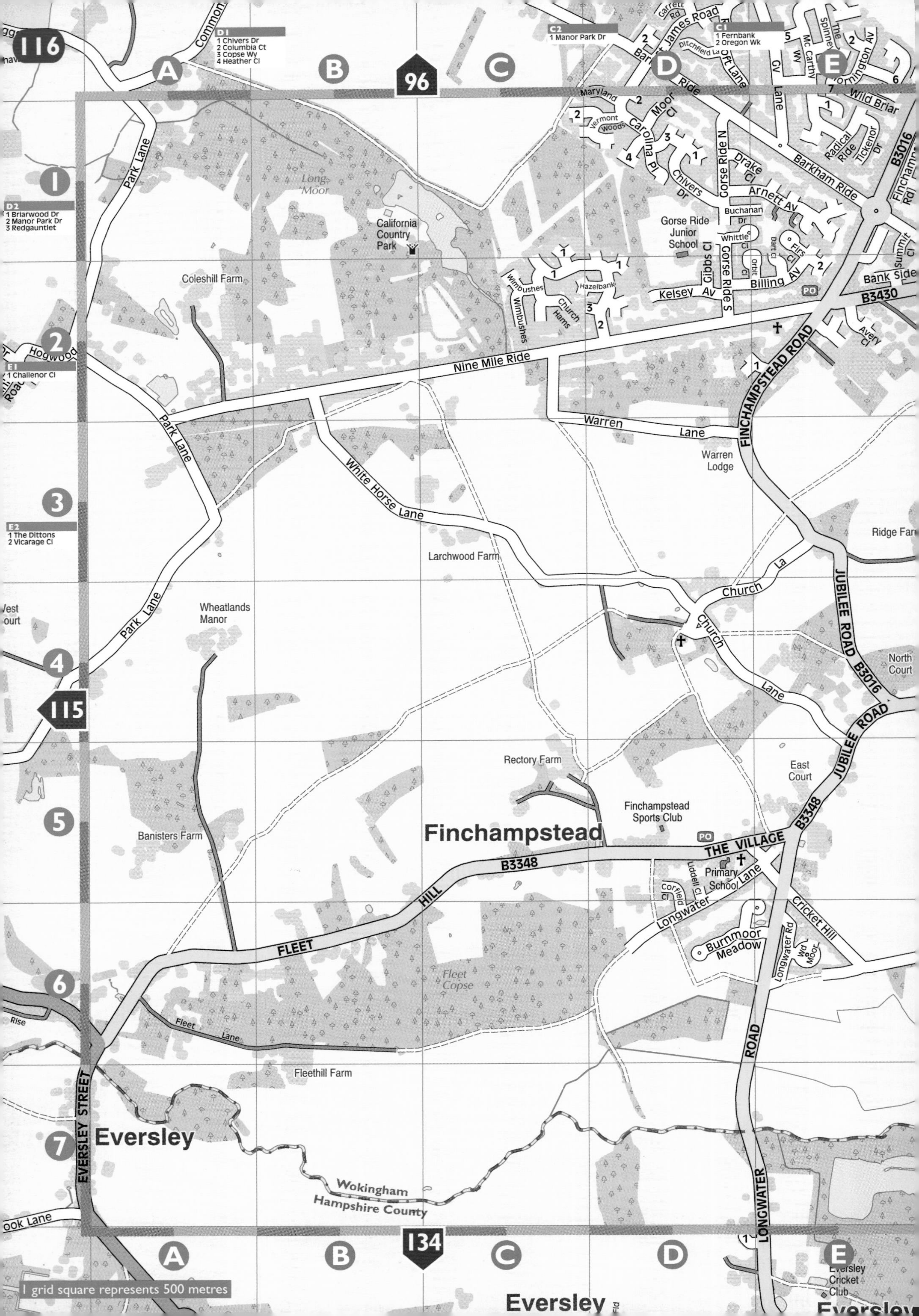

96

D1
1 Chivers Dr
2 Columbia Ct
3 Copse Wy
4 Heather Cl

C2
1 Manor Park Dr

C1
1 Fernbank
2 Oregon Wk

Common

D2
1 Briarwood Dr
2 Manor Park Dr
3 Redgauntlet

Maryland

Barry James Road

Ditchfield La

Moor Ct

Barkham Ride

The Spinne

Mc Carthy

Thornington Av

Wild Briar

B3016

Finchamp

Long Moor

California
Country
Park

Vermont
Woods

Carolina Pl

Drake Cl

Gorse Ride N

Arnett Av

Buchanan
Dr

Radical
Ride

Tickenor
Dr

Summit
Av

Park Lane

Coleshill Farm

Gorse Ride
Junior
School

Chivers
Dr

Gibbs Cl

Whittle

Gorse Ride S

Orbit

Fir

Dart Cl

Billing Av

Bank Side

B3430

E1
1 Challenor Cl

Hogwood

Wimbushes

Wimbushes

Church
Hams

Hazelbank

Kelsey
Av

PO

Avery
Cl

Nine Mile Ride

Warren   Lane

FINCHAMPSTEAD ROAD

+

E2
1 The Dittons
2 Vicarage Cl

Park Lane

White Horse Lane

Warren
Lodge

Ridge La

Larchwood Farm

Church

JUBILEE ROAD B3016

West
Court

Park Lane

Wheatlands
Manor

Church
Lane

North
Court

+

115

B3348

JUBILEE ROAD

Rectory Farm

East
Court

Banisters Farm

Finchampstead

Finchampstead
Sports Club

PO

THE VILLAGE

Corfield
Cl

Liddell Cl

Longwater

Primary
School Lane

+

B3348

Cricket Hill

Longwater Rd

FLEET   HILL

B3348

Fleet
Copse

Burnmoor
Meadow

Wd
Moor

6

Rise

Fleet   Lane

Fleethill Farm

ROAD

EVERSLEY STREET

Eversley

Wokingham
Hampshire County

LONGWATER

ook Lane

1 grid square represents 500 metres

134

Eversley

Eversley
Cricket
Club

Eversley

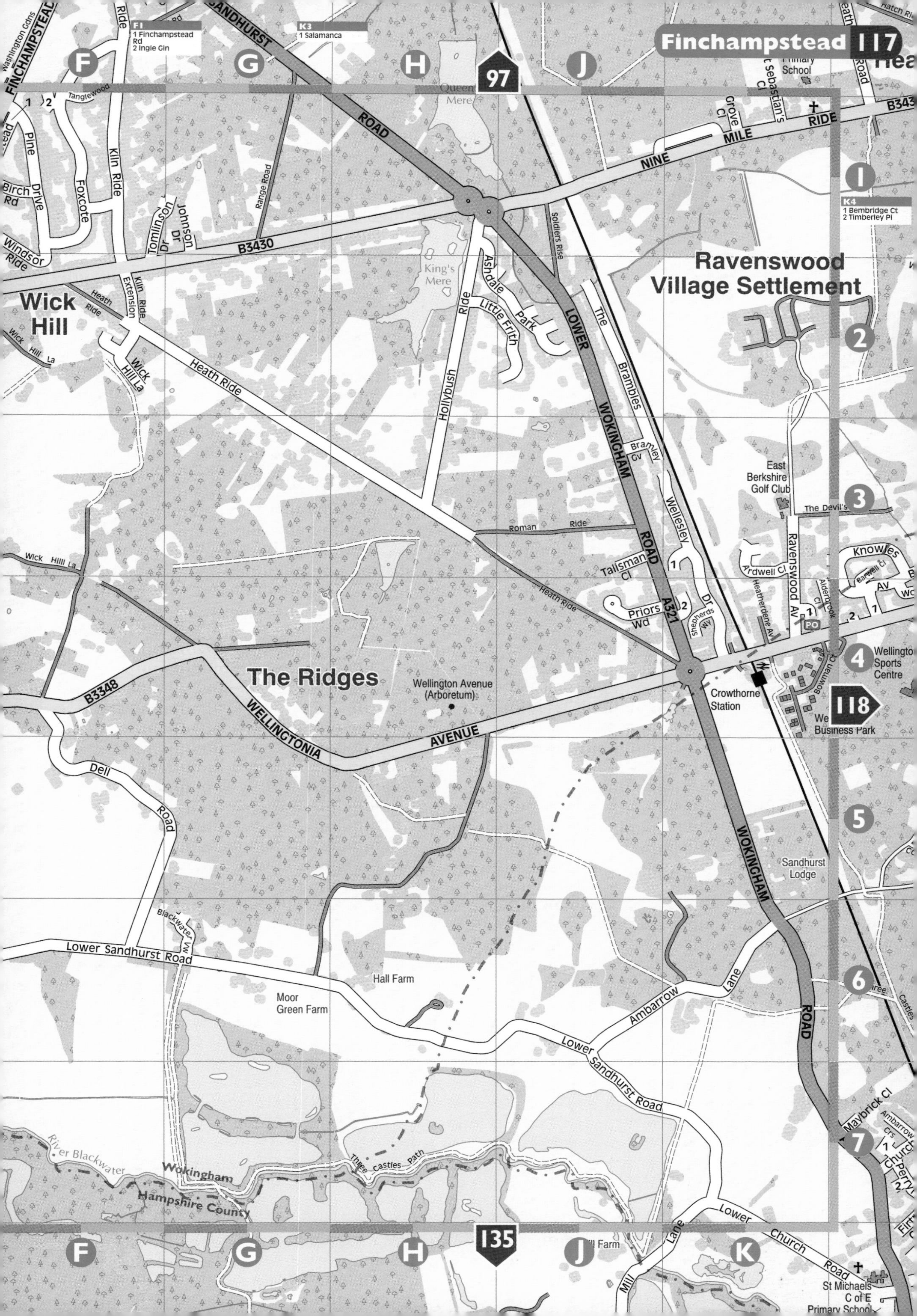

Hea

F
G
H
J
97
I
K3
1 Salamanca

F1
1 Finchampstead Rd
2 Ingle Gln

K4
1 Bembridge Ct
2 Timberley Pl

SANDHURST
ROAD
NINE
MILE
RIDE
B343

Queen
Mere

Tanglewood
Pine
Foxcote
Kiln Ride
Tomlinson Dr
Johnson Dr
Range Road
B3430

Birch Rd
Drive
Windsor Ride

Wellington Gdns
FINCHAMPSTEAD

St Sebastian's
Primary School
Grove Cl

I

**Ravenswood
Village Settlement**

2

King's Mere

Ashdale Park
Little Frith
Hollybush Ride
Ride

Heath Ride Extension
Kiln Ride

**Wick
Hill**

Wick Hill La
Heath Ride

Wick Hill La

Roman Ride

Heath Ride

The Brambles
LOWER
WOKINGHAM
ROAD
Bramley Gv
Wellesley

East Berkshire
Golf Club

3

The Devil's

Ravenswood Av

Knowles
Barwell Cl
Av

The Ridges

Wellington Avenue
(Arboretum)

WELLINGTONIA
AVENUE

Talisman Cl
Priors Wd
A321
1
2
Shepherds Ln
Dr
Heatherdene Av
Ardwell Cl
Alderbrook
PO

Bowman Ct

4
Wellington
Sports
Centre

Crowthorne
Station

118
We
Business Park

B3348

Dell Road

5

Sandhurst
Lodge

WOKINGHAM
ROAD

Lower Sandhurst Road

Blackwater Vw

Hall Farm

Moor
Green Farm

Ambarrow
Lane

6

Lower Sandhurst Road

Maybrick Cl
Ambarrow Crs
Church
Perry
7

River Blackwater
Wokingham
Hampshire County

Three Castles Path

Mill Lane
ill Farm
Lower
Church Road

St Michaels
C of E
Primary School

F
G
135
H
J
K

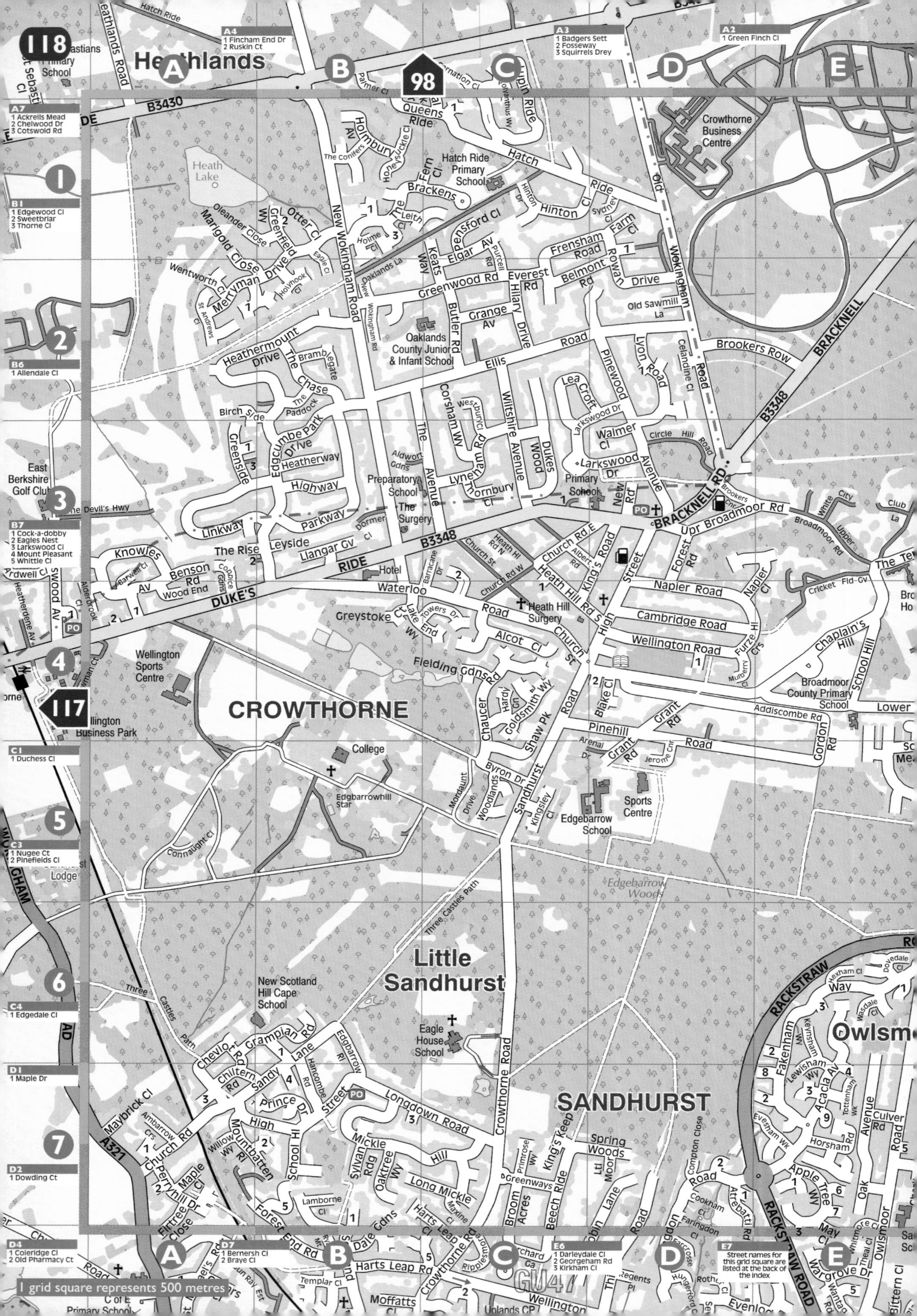

118
Heathlands
Heathlands Road
Hatch Ride
A4
1 Fincham End Dr
2 Ruskin Ct
98
A3
1 Badgers Sett
2 Fosseway
3 Squirrels Drey
A2
1 Green Finch Cl
A7
1 Ackrells Mead
2 Chelwood Dr
3 Cotswold Rd
B1
1 Edgewood Cl
2 Sweetbriar
3 Thorne Cl
B6
1 Allendale Cl
B7
1 Cock-a-dobby
2 Eagles Nest
3 Larkswood Cl
4 Mount Pleasant
5 Whittle Cl
C1
1 Duchess Cl
C3
1 Nugee Ct
2 Pinefields Cl
C4
1 Edgedale Cl
D1
1 Maple Dr
D2
1 Dowding Ct
D4
1 Coleridge Cl
2 Old Pharmacy Ct
D7
1 Bernersh Cl
2 Braye Cl
E6
1 Darleydale Cl
2 Georgeham Rd
3 Kirkham Cl
E7
Street names for this grid square are listed at the back of the index
B3430
Heath Lake
Crowthorne Business Centre
Hatch Ride Primary School
Queens Ride
Holmbury Av
The Conifers
Fern Cl
The Brackens
New Wokingham Road
Oaklands La
Marigold Close
Oleander Close
Greenfield Wy
Otter Cl
Merryman Drive
Wentworth Cl
Hinton Cl
Hinton Dr
Sydney Cl
Farm Cl
Frensham Road
Pensford Cl
Elgar Av
Purcell Rd
Keats Way
Everest Rd
Belmont Rd
Rowan Drive
Greenwood Rd
Hilary Drive
Grange Av
Butler Rd
Old Sawmill La
Old Wokingham Road
Oaklands County Junior & Infant School
Ellis Road
Pinewood
Lyon Road
Celandine Cl
Brookers Row
BRACKNELL
B3348
Heathermount Drive
The Chase
Bramblegate
The Paddock
Birch Side
Edgcumbe Park Drive
Heatherway
Highway
Greenside
Lea Croft
Larkswood Dr
Walmer Cl
Circle Hill Road
Corsham Wy
Westbury Cl
Lyneham Rd
Wiltshire Avenue
Dukes Wood
Tornbury Cl
Aldworth Gdns
Preparatory School
The Surgery
The Avenue
Primary School
Larkswood Dr
New Rd
Avenue
BRACKNELL RD.
Brookers Cnr
Upr Broadmoor Rd
White City
Club La
Broadmoor Rd
Upper Broadmoor Rd
East Berkshire Golf Club
The Devil's Hwy
Linkway
Parkway
Leyside
The Rise
Dormer Cl
Llangar Gv
DUKE'S RIDE
Hotel
Knowles Av
Benson Rd
Wood End
Coppice Gdns
Barwell Cl
Heatherdene Av
Alderbrook
Heath Hl Rd N
Church St
Church Rd E
Church Rd W
Albert Rd
King's Road
High Street
Forest Rd
Napier Road
Napier Cl
Cricket Fld Gv
Heath Hill Rd S
Heath Hill Surgery
Cambridge Road
Wellington Road
Furze Hl Crs
Mulberry Cl
Chaplain's Hill
School Hill
Broadmoor County Primary School
Lower
Waterloo Road
Barracane Dr
Greystoke Ct
Lake End Wy
Towers Dr
Alcot Cl
Fielding Gdns
Wellington Sports Centre
Wellington Business Park
CROWTHORNE
Goldsmith Wy
Hardy Cl
Chaucer Rd
Shaw Pk
Blake Cl
Grant Rd
Pinehill Road
Arenal Dr
Jerome Cnr
Addiscombe Rd
Gordon Rd
College
Edgbarrowhill Star
Byron Dr
Mordaunt Drive
Woodlands
Sandhurst Road
Kingsley Cl
Edgebarrow School
Sports Centre
Connaught Cl
Edgebarrow Woods
Three Castles Path
117
Lodge
WOKINGHAM ROAD
Little Sandhurst
New Scotland Hill Cape School
Eagle House School
Crowthorne Road
Cheviot Rd
Grampian Rd
Chiltern Rd
Sandy Lane
Hancombe Rd
Edgbarrow Rl
Prince Dr
High Street
School Hl
Mountbatten Rl
Willow Wy
Maybrick Cl
Ambarrow Crs
Church Rd
Perryhill Dr
Maple Cl
Firtree Close
A321
Longdown Road
Mickle Hill
Sylvan Rdg
Oaktree Wy
Long Mickle
Lamborne Cl
Harts Leap Cl
Dale Gdns
Forest End Rd
Harts Leap Rd
Ripplesmere
Templar Cl
Moffatts Cl
Wellington
Uplands CP
Greenways
Primrose Wy
Broom Acres
Beech Ride
King's Keep
Spring Woods
Ltl Moor
Robin Lane
SANDHURST
Compton Close
Cookham Rd
Atrebatti Rd
Faringdon Cl
Regents Pl
Evenlode
RACKSTRAW ROAD
Hexham Cl
Dovedale Cl
Way
Wasdale Cl
Owlsmoor
Fakenham
Keynsham Wy
Lewisham Wy
Acacia Av
Tottenham Wk
Evesham Wk
Horsham Rd
Avenue
Culver Rd
Apple Tree Wy
Oak Avenue
Owlsmoor Road
May Cl
Whitmore Cl
Theal Cl
Wargrove Dr
Bittern Cl
Crowthorne Business Centre
GU47
C of E Primary School
1 grid square represents 500 metres

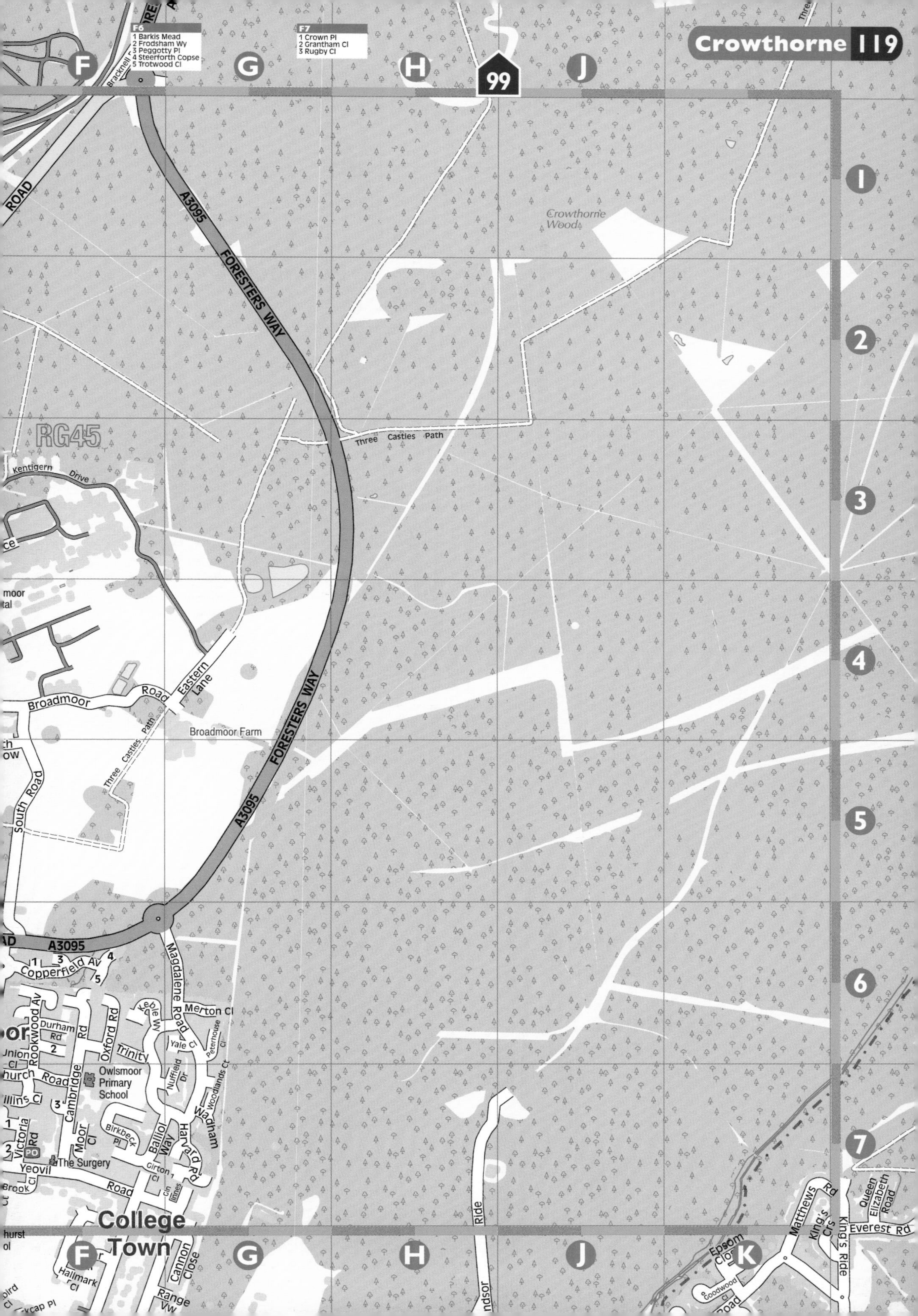

F6
1 Barkis Mead
2 Frodsham Wy
3 Peggotty Pl
4 Steerforth Copse
5 Trotwood Cl

F7
1 Crown Pl
2 Grantham Cl
3 Rugby Cl

F   G   H   99   J

I
2
3
4
5
6
7

RG45

A3095 FORESTERS WAY

Crowthorne Wood

Three Casties Path

Kentigern Drive

moor

Broadmoor Road

Eastern Lane

Three Casties Path

Broadmoor Farm

A3095 FORESTERS WAY

South Road

A3095
Copperfield Av
Magdalene Road
Merton Cl
Durham Rd
Rookwood Av
Oxford Rd
Lele Wy
Yale Cl
Peterhouse Cl
Woodlands Ct
Trinity
Cambridge Road
Nuffield Dr
Wadham
Union Cl
Church Road
Owlsmoor Primary School
illins Cl
Victoria Rd
PO
Moor Cl
Birkbeck Pl
Baliol Way
Harvard Rd
Girton
Cln
The Surgery
Yeovil
Brook
Road

College Town

hurst

Hallmark Cl
Cannon Close
Range Vw
cap Pl

Windsor Ride

Epsom Cl
Goodwood Cl
Goodwood Road
Matthews Rd
King's Crs
Queen Elizabeth Road
Everest Rd
King's Ride

F   G   H   J   K

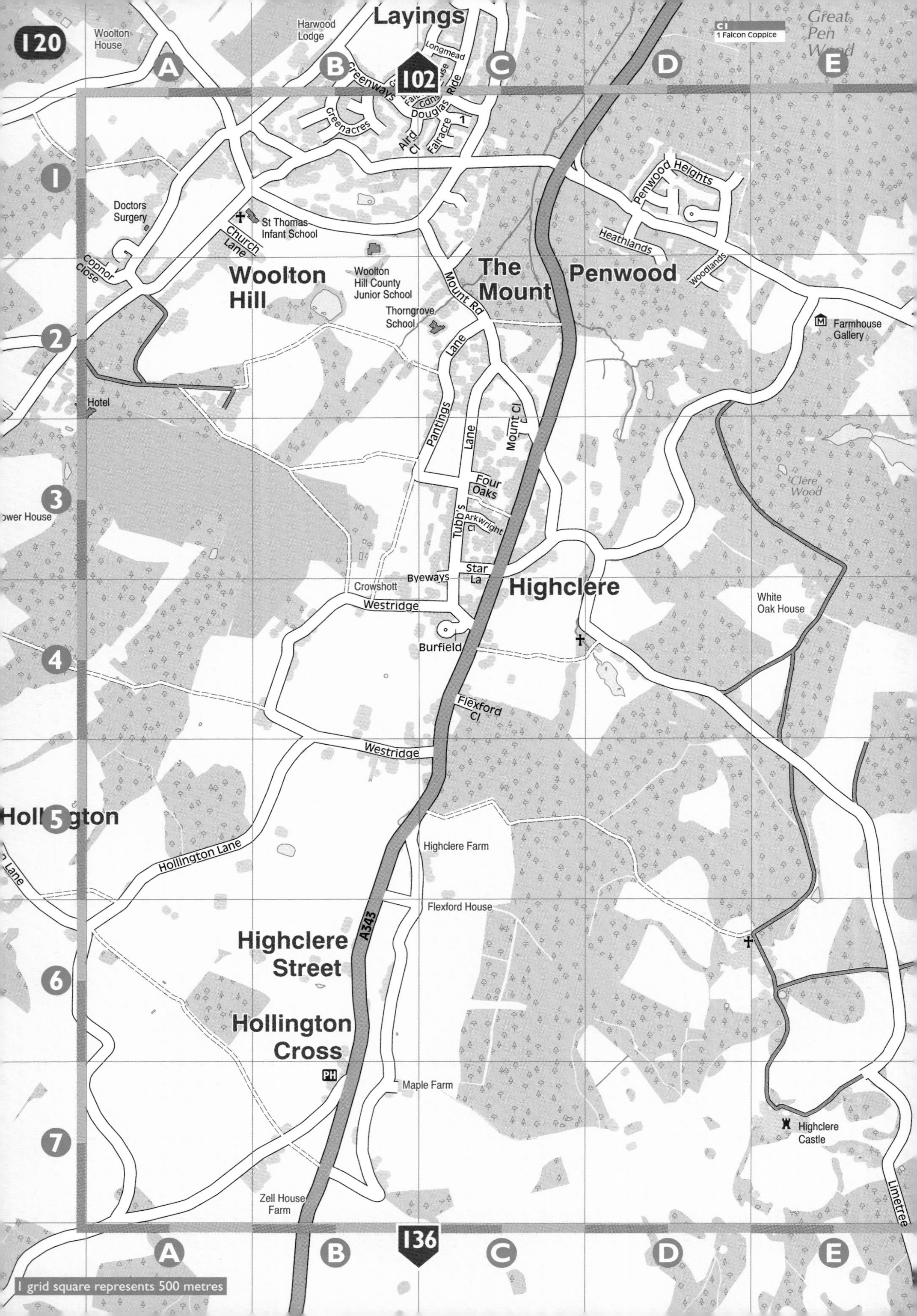

Great
Pen
Wood

C1
1 Falcon Coppice

A

Woolton
House

Harwood
Lodge

Layings

B

Greenways

Longmead

102

C

Greenacres

Douglas
Gdns

Aird Cl

Falcon
Ride

Falacre Ride

1

D

E

1

Doctors
Surgery

St Thomas
Infant School

Church Lane

Penwood Heights

Heathlands

Woodlands

Woolton
Hill

Woolton
Hill County
Junior School

Thorngrove
School

Mount Rd

The
Mount

Penwood

M Farmhouse
Gallery

2

Copnor Close

Hotel

3

ower House

Pantings

Lane

Mount Cl

Clere
Wood

Four
Oaks

Tubbs

ArkWright
Cl

Star
La

Highclere

White
Oak House

4

Crowshott

Westridge

Byeways

Burfield

†

Flexford
Cl

5

Holl gton

Westridge

Hollington Lane

Highclere Farm

6

Highclere
Street

A343

Flexford House

†

Hollington
Cross

PH

Maple Farm

7

Highclere
Castle

Zell House
Farm

A

136

B

C

D

E

Limetree

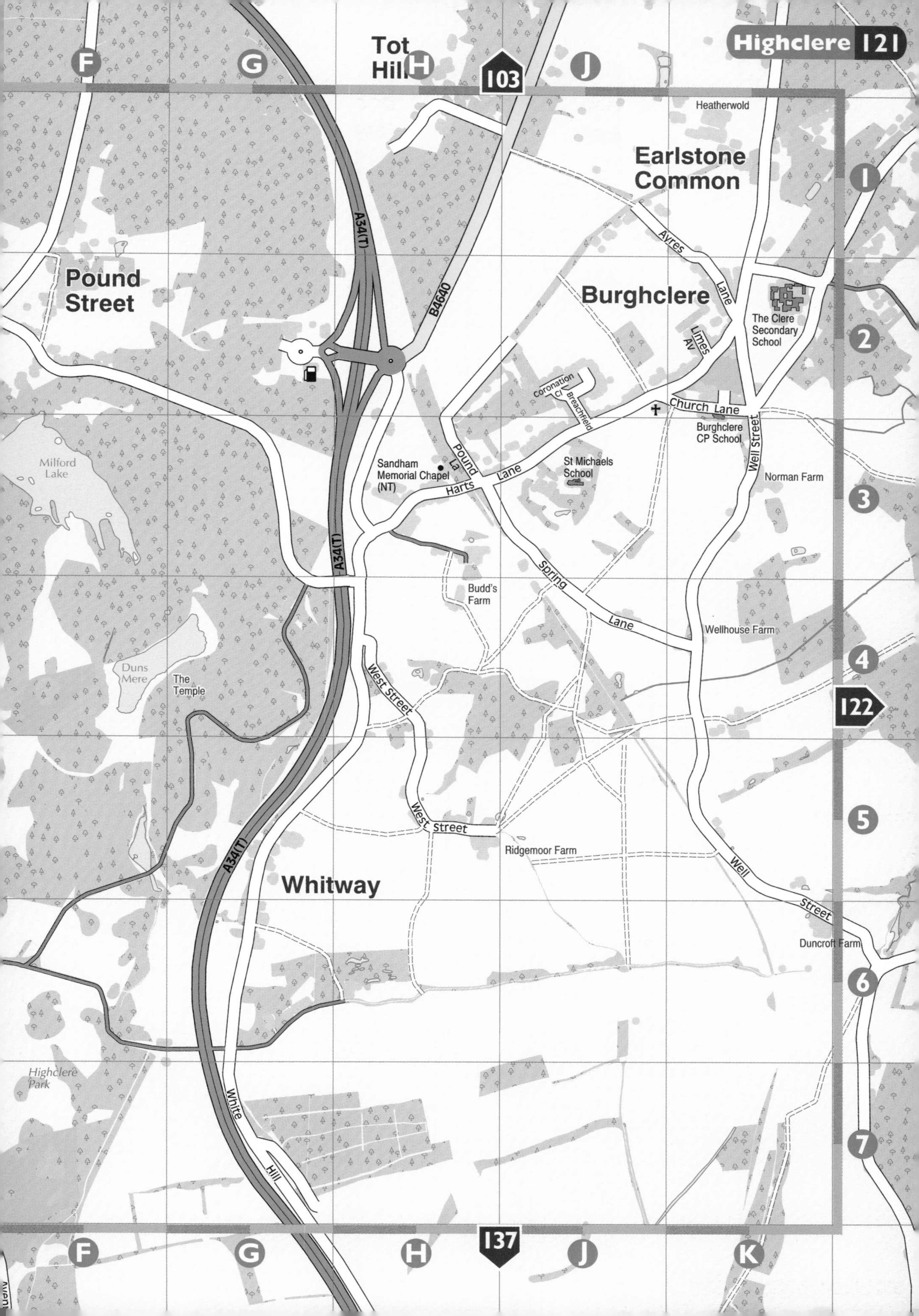

F
G
Tot Hill **H**
103
J

Heatherwold

Earlstone Common

I

Pound Street

Ayres Lane

Burghclere

The Clere Secondary School

2

Limes Av

Coronation Cl

Breachfield

Church Lane

Burghclere CP School

Well Street

Norman Farm

3

Milford Lake

A34(T)

B4640

Pound La

Harts

Lane

St Michaels School

Sandham Memorial Chapel (NT)

Duns Mere

Budd's Farm

Spring

Lane

Wellhouse Farm

4

122

The Temple

West Street

5

Well

Street

Whitway

West Street

Ridgemoor Farm

Duncroft Farm

6

Highclere Park

White

Hill

7

A34(T)

F
G
H
137
J
K

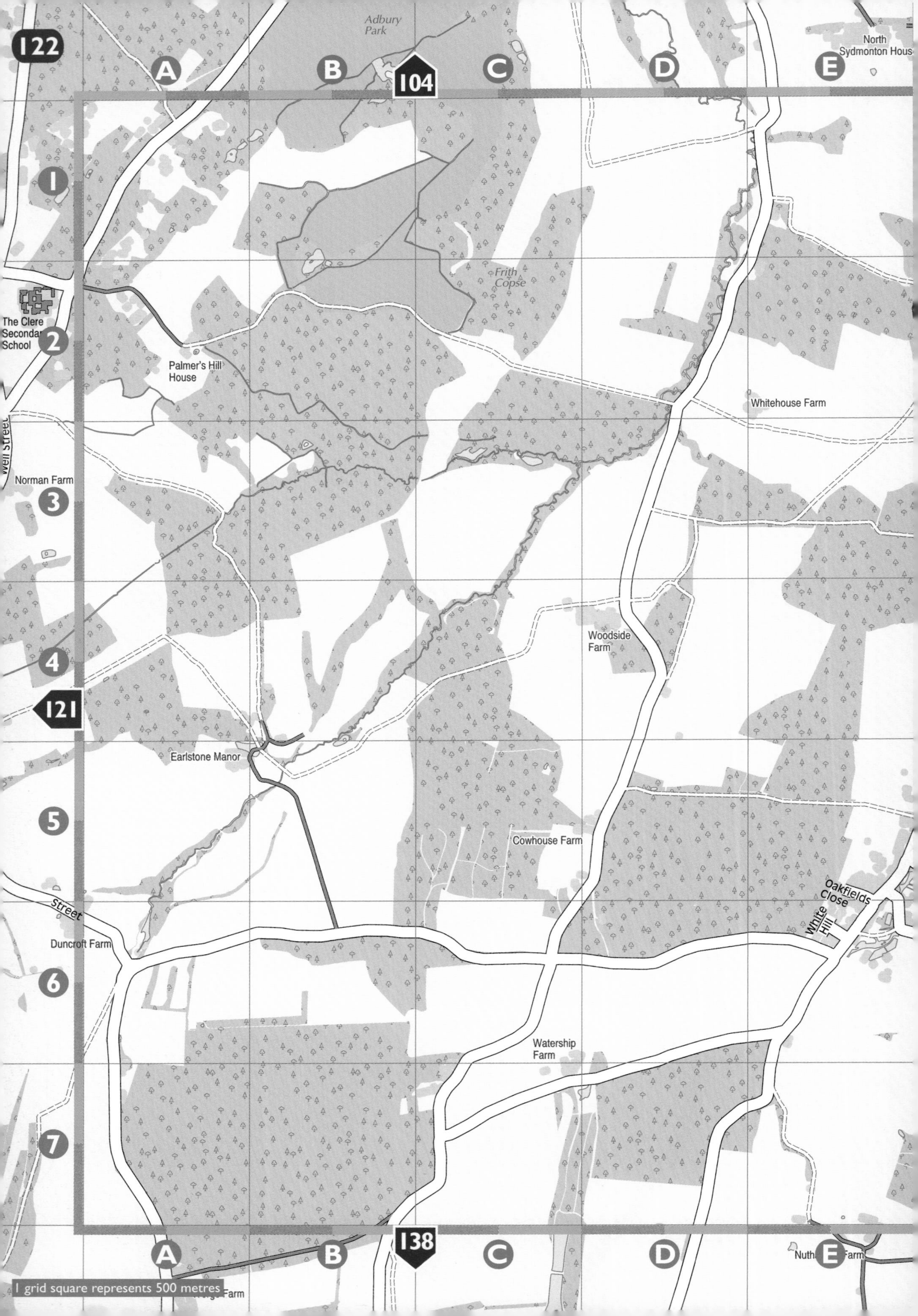
122
Adbury Park
104
A
B
C
D
E
North Sydmonton Hous
1
The Clere Secondar School
2
Palmer's Hill House
Frith Copse
Whitehouse Farm
Norman Farm
3
4
121
Woodside Farm
Earlstone Manor
5
Cowhouse Farm
Oakfields Close
White Hill
Street
Duncroft Farm
6
Watership Farm
7
138
1 grid square represents 500 metres

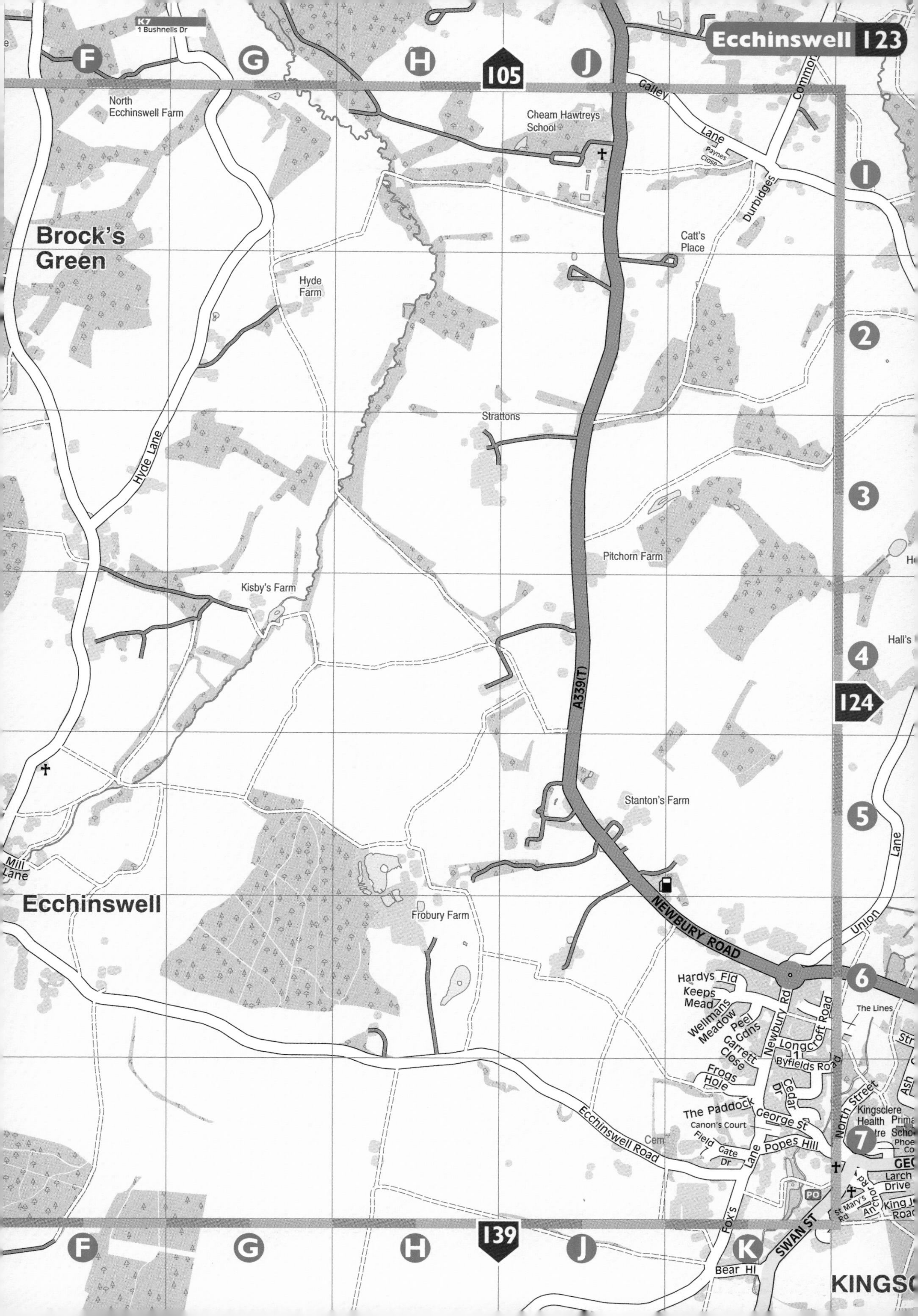

F G H J

105

I

2

3

4

124

5

6

7

Brock's
Green

North
Ecchinswell Farm

K7
1 Bushnells Dr

Cheam Hawtreys
School

Galley

Lane

Common

Paynes
close

Durbidges

Catt's
Place

Hyde
Farm

Hyde Lane

Strattons

Pitchorn Farm

Hall's

Kisby's Farm

Stanton's Farm

Mill
Lane

Ecchinswell

Frobury Farm

NEWBURY ROAD

A339(T)

Union
Lane

Hardys Fld
Keeps
Mead

Newbury Rd

The Lines

Wellmans
Meadow

Peel
Gdns

Garrett
Close

Longcroft Road

Byfields Road

Frogs
Hole

Cedar
Dr

Kingsclere
Health

Prima
Schoo

North Street

The Paddock

Canon's Court

George St

Field Gate
Dr

Ecchinswell Road

Cem

Lane

Popes Hill

St Mary's
Rd

Larch
Drive

PO

Fox's

Bear Hi

SWAN ST

K

KINGSC

F G H J

139

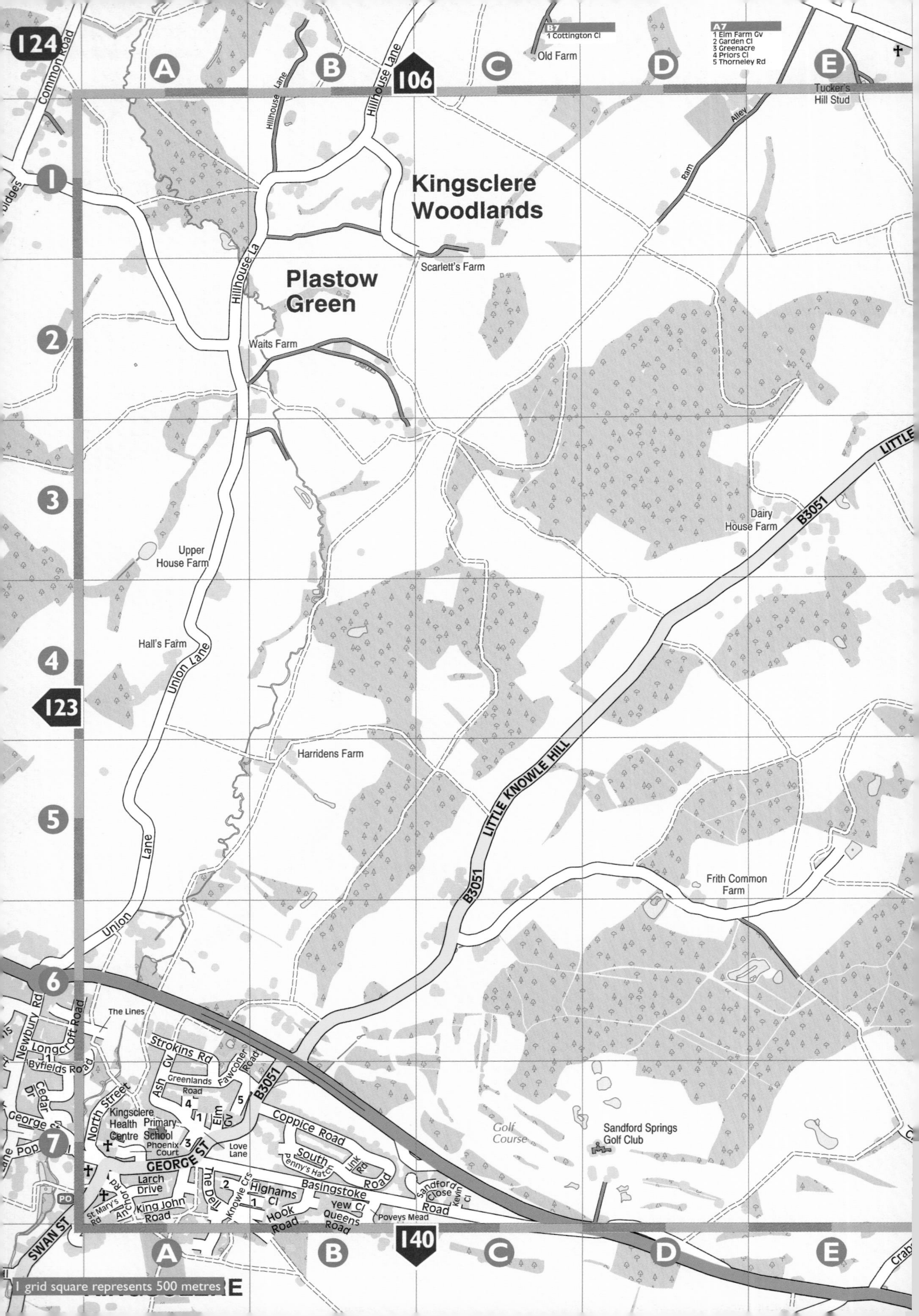
124
106
123
140
A
B
C
D
E
1
2
3
4
5
6
7
B7
1 Cottington Cl
A7
1 Elm Farm Gv
2 Garden Cl
3 Greenacre
4 Priors Cl
5 Thorneley Rd
Common Road
Old Farm
Tucker's Hill Stud
Hillhouse Lane
Alley
Ram
Kingsclere Woodlands
Scarlett's Farm
Plastow Green
Hillhouse La
Waits Farm
Dairy House Farm
B3051
LITTLE
Upper House Farm
Hall's Farm
Union Lane
LITTLE KNOWLE HILL
Harridens Farm
Frith Common Farm
Union
Lane
Golf Course
Sandford Springs Golf Club
The Lines
Newbury Rd
Longcroft Road
Longcroft
Byfields Road
Cedar Dr
George St
Strokins Rd
Ash Gv
Greenlands Road
Fawconer Road
North Street
Kingsclere Health Centre
Primary School
Phoenix Court
Elm Gv
Coppice Road
Love Lane
GEORGE ST
South Road
Penny's Hatch
Link Rd
Larch Drive
The Dell
Knowle Crs
Highams Cl
Basingstoke Road
Sandford Close
Kevin Cl
Yew Cl
St Mary's Rd
Anchor Rd
King John Road
Hook Road
Queens Road
Poveys Mead
PO
SWAN ST
Crab
1 grid square represents 500 metres

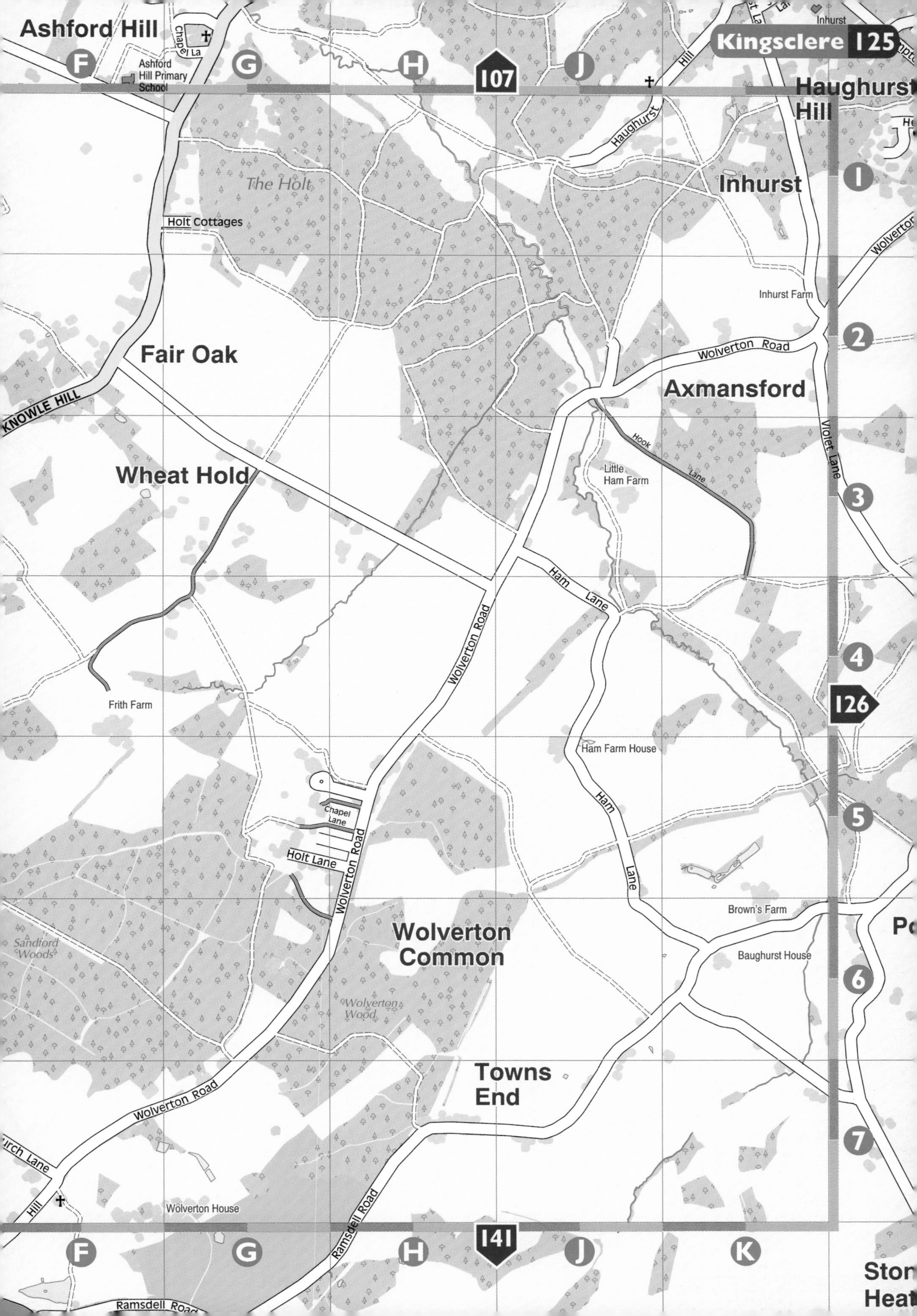

Ashford Hill

F

Ashford
Hill Primary
School

Chapel La

G

The Holt

Holt Cottages

H

107

J

Haughurst Hill

Inhurst

Inhurst

Haughurst
Hill

I

Wolverton

Inhurst Farm

2

Fair Oak

KNOWLE HILL

Wheat Hold

Wolverton Road

Axmansford

Little
Ham Farm

Hook Lane

Violet Lane

3

Ham Lane

Frith Farm

Wolverton Road

4

126

Ham Farm House

Ham Lane

5

Chapel
Lane

Holt Lane

Wolverton Road

Brown's Farm

Baughurst House

Po

Sandford
Woods

Wolverton
Common

Wolverton
Wood

6

Towns
End

7

Wolverton Road

Ramsdell Road

rch Lane

Hill

Wolverton House

F

G

H

141

J

K

Ston
Heat

Ramsdell Road

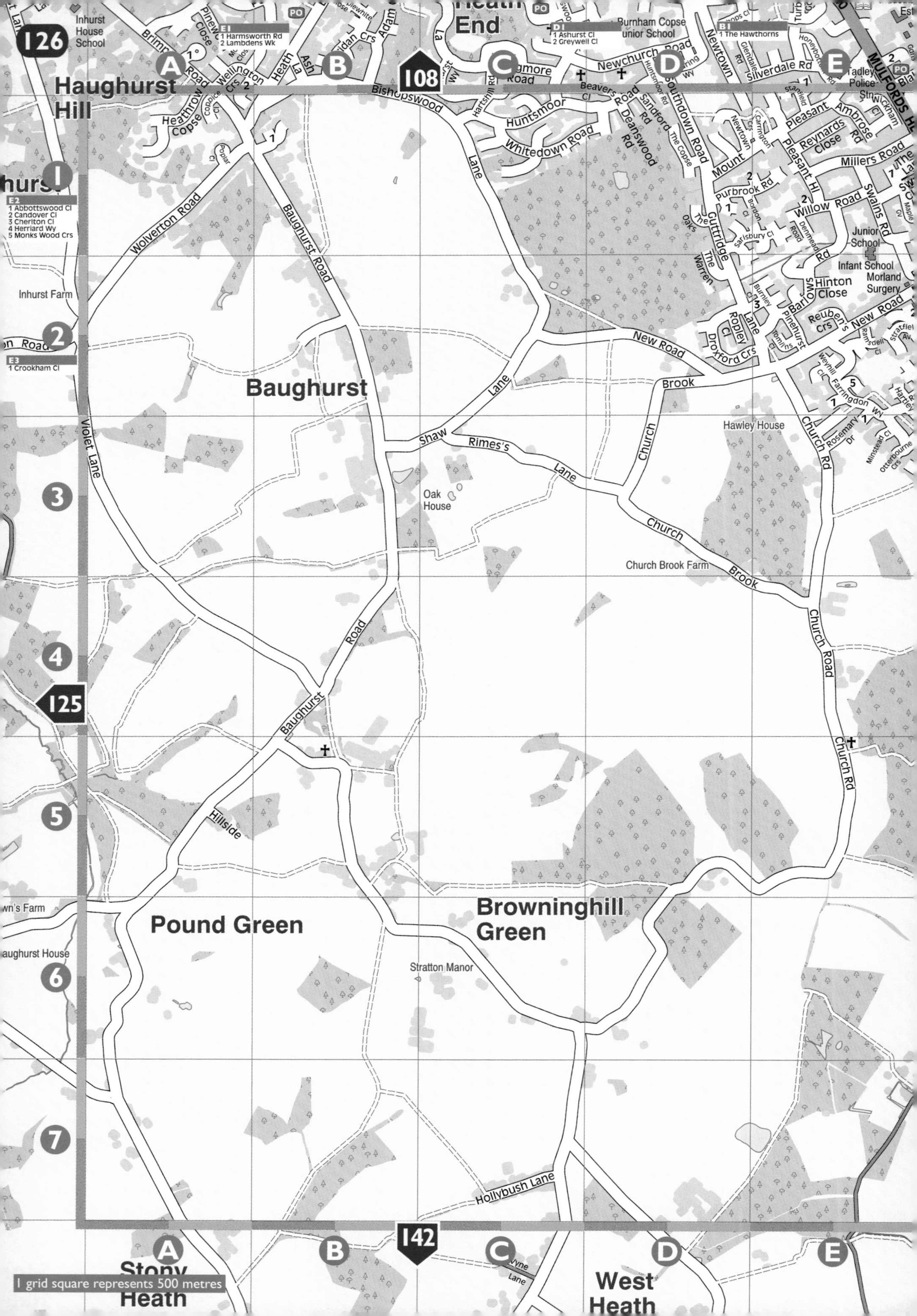

126
Inhurst House School
Haughurst Hill
Heath End
108
Burnham Copse Junior School
E1
1 Harmsworth Rd
2 Lambdens Wk
D1
1 Ashurst Cl
2 Greywell Cl
B1
1 The Hawthorns
E2
1 Abbottswood Cl
2 Candover Cl
3 Cheriton Cl
4 Herriard Wy
5 Monks Wood Crs
E3
1 Crookham Cl
Inhurst Farm
Tadley Police Stn
MULFORDS HILL
Bishopswood Road
Wolverton Road
Baughurst Road
Whitedown Road
Huntsmoor
Deanswood Rd
Southdown Road
Newchurch Road
Silverdale Rd
Pleasant Hl
Reynards Close
Millers Road
Willow Road
Purbrook Rd
Cuttridge
The Warren
Junior School
Infant School
Morland Surgery
Hinton Close
Reuben's Crs
New Road
Droxford Crs
Ropley Cl
Hawley House
Baughurst
Violet Lane
Shaw Lane
Rimes's Lane
Church Brook
Church Rd
Oak House
Church Brook Farm
Church Road
125
Hillside
Baughurst Road
Pound Green
Browninghill Green
Stratton Manor
Baughurst House
Hollybush Lane
142
Vyne Lane
Stony Heath
West Heath
1 grid square represents 500 metres

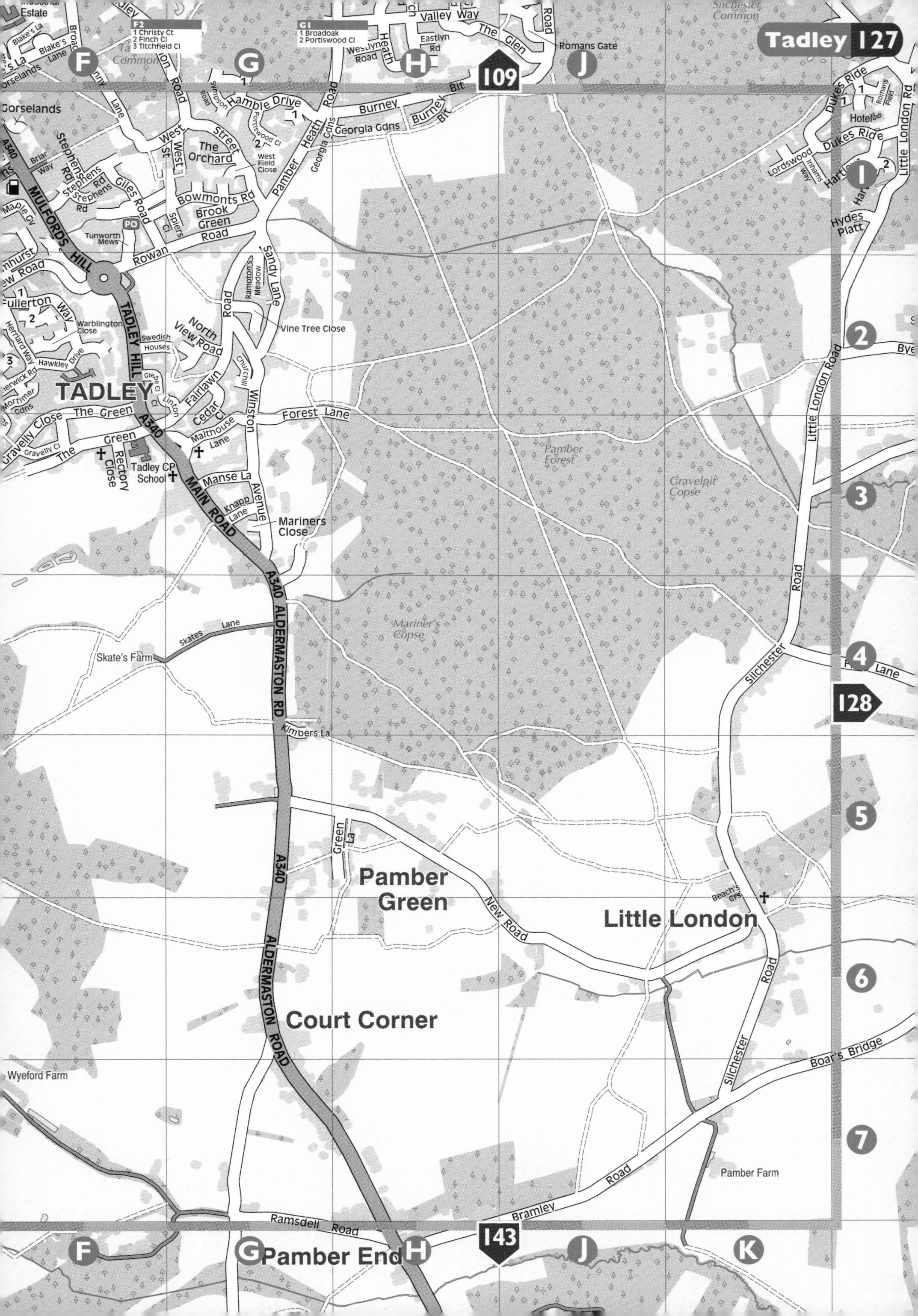

TADLEY

Pamber Green

Court Corner

Little London

Pamber End

A340 MAIN ROAD

A340 ALDERMASTON RD

ALDERMASTON ROAD

MULFORDS HILL

TADLEY HILL

Little London Road

Silchester Road

Dukes Ride

New Road

Bramley Road

Ramsdell Road

Boar's Bridge

Forest Lane

Sandy Lane

Skates Lane

Kimbers La

Green La

Manse La

Knapp La

Avenue

Winston

North View Road

Street Parade

Pamber Heath Road

Georgia Gdns

Burney Bit

Burney

The Glen

Valley Way

Westlynheath Road

Hamble Drive

Rowan

Giles Road

West St

Stephens Rd

West St

Bowmonts Rd

Brook Green Road

The Orchard

West Field Close

Vine Tree Close

Mariners Close

Mariner's Copse

Pamber Forest

Gravelpit Copse

Skate's Farm

Wyeford Farm

Pamber Farm

Romans Gate

Romans Way

Hartleys

Lordswood

Inhams Way

Hydes Platt

Hotel

Fullerton Way

Hawkley Drive

Warblington Close

Swedish Houses

Gravelly Close

Gravelly Cl

The Green

The Green

Rectory Close

Tadley CP School

Cedar Cl

Malthouse Lane

Fairlawn

Linton

Glen Cl

Church Hill

Ramtons Rd

Mopeds Rd

Spoilers

Gorselands

Gorselands

Gorselands Estate

Blake's La

Broad La

Blake's Lane

Common

Elm Lane

Swynson Road

Portswood Cl

Maple Gv

Briar Way

Stephens Rd

Stephens Rd

Tunworth Mews

PO

Mariner's Close

Beach's Cres

Eastlyn Rd

Georgia Gdns

Industrial Estate

Hurst Rd

New Road

Maybotha

Cheeswell

Mortimer Gdns

109

128

143

F G H J

I

1 2 3 4 5 6 7

F G H J K

F2
1 Christy Ct
2 Finch Cl
3 Titchfield Cl

G1
1 Broadoak
2 Portiswood Cl

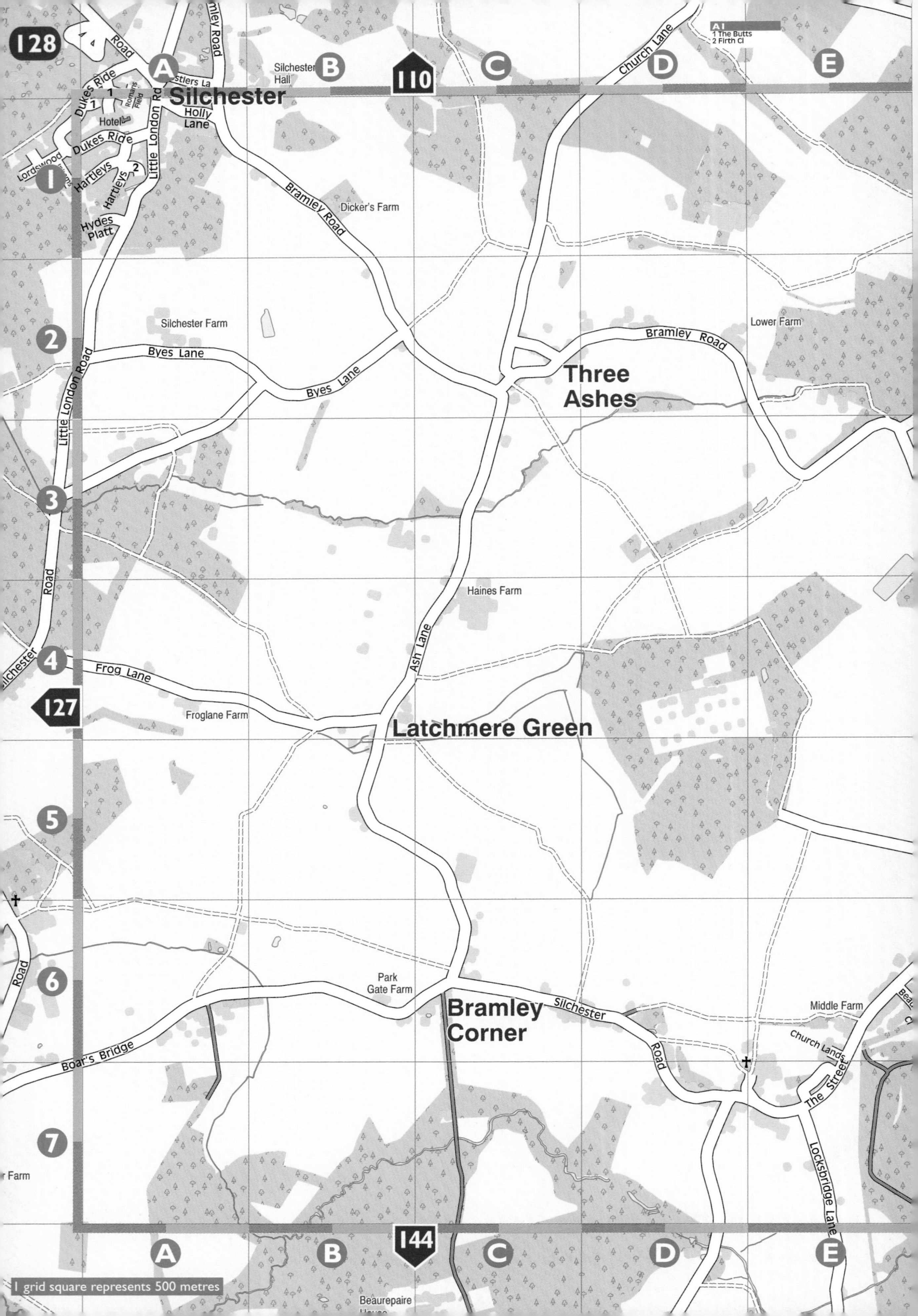

128

A Silchester
Dukes Ride
Lordswood
Hartleys
Hydes Platt
Dukes Ride
Hotel
Holly Lane
Little London Rd
Romans Field
estiers La

B Silchester Hall

110

C

Church Lane **D**

A1
1 The Butts
2 Firth Cl

E

Bramley Road
Dicker's Farm

2 Silchester Farm
Byes Lane
Little London Road
Byes Lane

Bramley Road
Lower Farm

Three Ashes

3 Road

Haines Farm

4 Frog Lane
Ash Lane
Silchester Road

127
Froglane Farm

Latchmere Green

5 †

6 Road
Park Gate Farm
Boar's Bridge
Silchester Road

Bramley Corner
Middle Farm
Church Lands
†
The Street

7 Farm
Locksbridge Lane

A **B** **144** **C** **D** **E**

I grid square represents 500 metres

Beaurepaire House

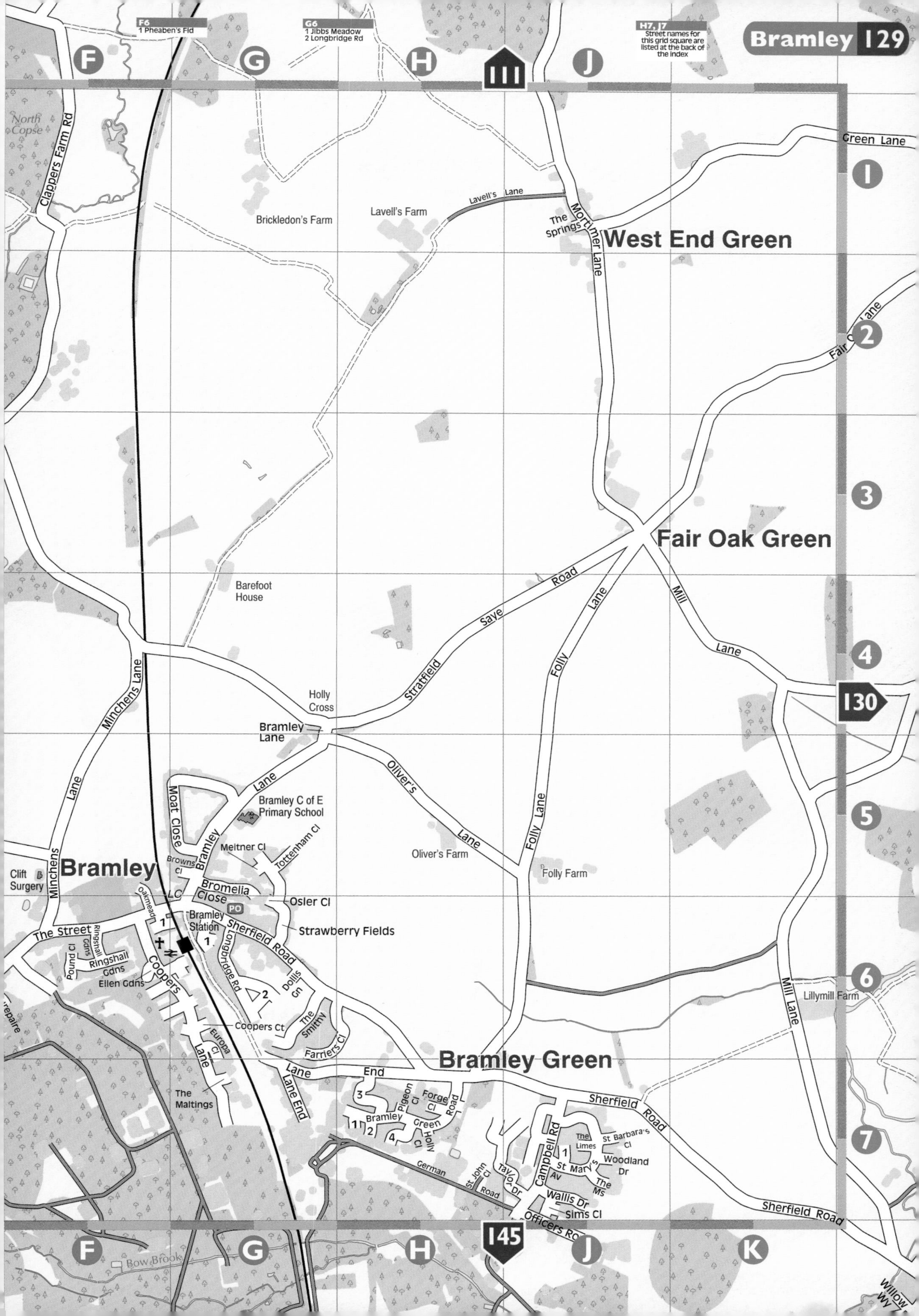

F6
1 Pheaben's Fld

G6
1 Jibbs Meadow
2 Longbridge Rd

H7, I7
Street names for
this grid square are
listed at the back of
the index

F

G

H

J

I

Green Lane

North
Copse

Clappers Farm Rd

Brickledon's Farm

Lavell's Farm

Lavell's Lane

The
springs

Mortimer Lane

West End Green

Fair Oak Lane

2

3

Fair Oak Green

Save

Stratfield

Road

Folly

Lane

Mill

Lane

4

130

Barefoot
House

Holly
Cross

Bramley
Lane

Lane

Bramley
Lane

Oliver's

Lane

Folly Lane

5

Minchens Lane

Moat Close

Bramley C of E
Primary School

Meitner Cl

Tottenham Cl

Oliver's Farm

Folly Farm

Browns Cl

Bromelia
Close

PO

Osler Cl

Strawberry Fields

Clift
Surgery

Bramley

Minchens Lane

LC

Sherfield Road

Longbridge Rd

Dollis Gn

Lillymill Farm

Mill Lane

6

The Street

Ringshall Gdns

Pound Cl

Ringshall Gdns

Ellen Gdns

Coopers

Oakmead

1

1

2

The Smithy

Coopers Ct

Farriers Cl

The
Maltings

Europa Cl

Lane End

Lane

End

3

1 Bramley 2

4

Pigeon Cl

Green Cl

Holly Cl

Forge Cl

Road

Bramley Green

Sherfield Road

Campbell Rd

The
Limes

St Mary's

St Barbara's
Cl

Woodland
Dr

The
Ms

7

German

St John
Road

Taylor Dr

Wallis Dr

Sims Cl

Officers Rd

Sherfield Road

Willow Wy

F

G

H

J

K

145

Bow Brook

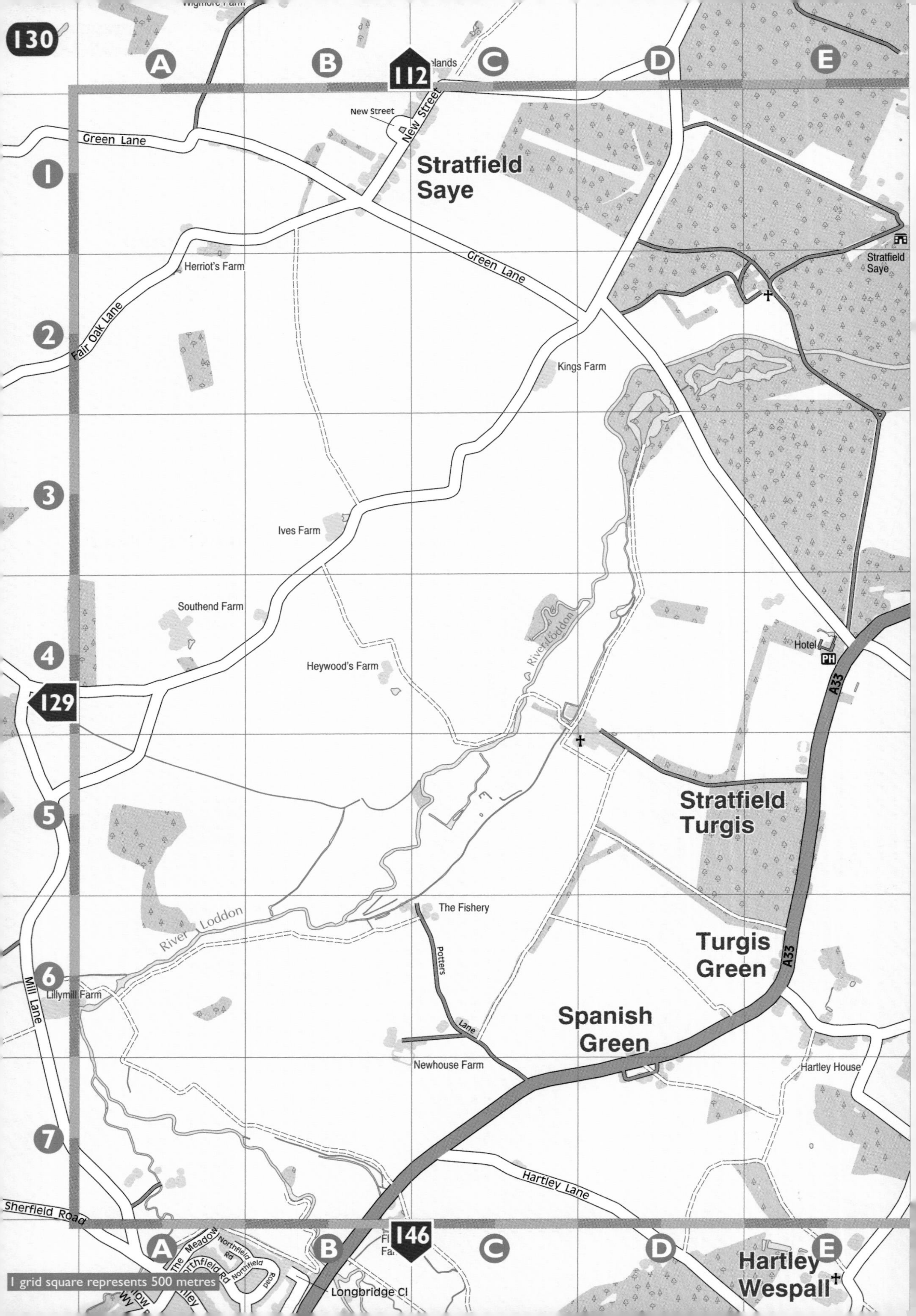

A
B
C
D
E
112
New Street
Green Lane
Stratfield Saye
Herriot's Farm
Green Lane
Fair Oak Lane
Kings Farm
Stratfield Saye
Ives Farm
Southend Farm
Heywood's Farm
River Loddon
Hotel
PH
A33
129
Stratfield Turgis
The Fishery
River Loddon
Turgis Green
Potters Lane
Lillymill Farm
Mill Lane
Spanish Green
Newhouse Farm
Hartley House
Hartley Lane
Sherfield Road
146
The Meadow
Northfield Rd
Northfield Road
Longbridge Cl
Hartley Wespall
1 grid square represents 500 metres
1
2
3
4
5
6
7

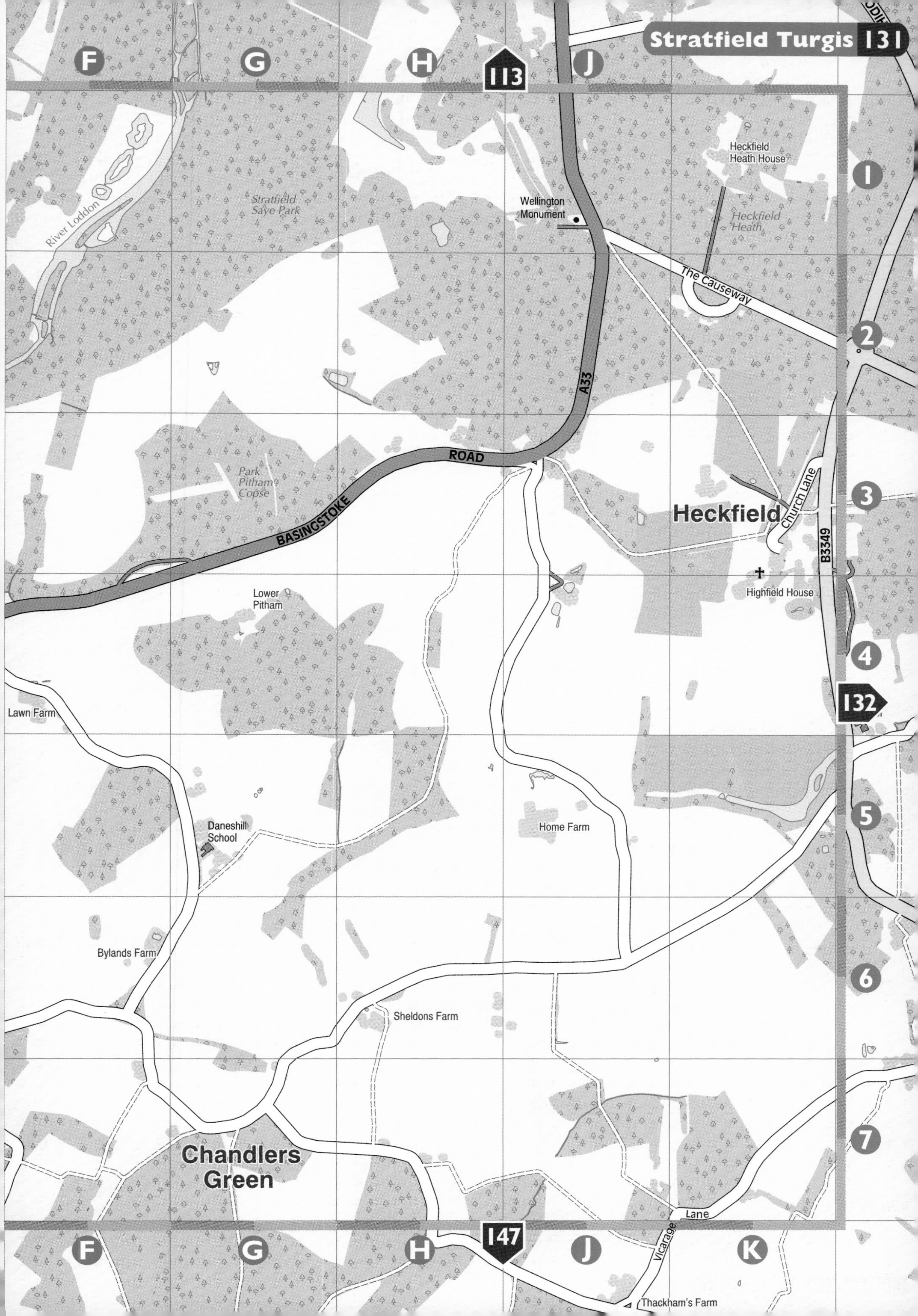

F G H `113` J

I

2

3

4

`132`

5

6

7

F G H `147` J K

Heckfield
Heath House

Heckfield
Heath

Wellington
Monument

The Causeway

Stratfield
Saye Park

River Loddon

A33

ROAD

BASINGSTOKE

Park
Pitham
Copse

Lower
Pitham

Heckfield

Church Lane

B3349

Highfield House

Lawn Farm

Daneshill
School

Home Farm

Bylands Farm

Sheldons Farm

Chandlers
Green

Vicarage Lane

Thackham's Farm

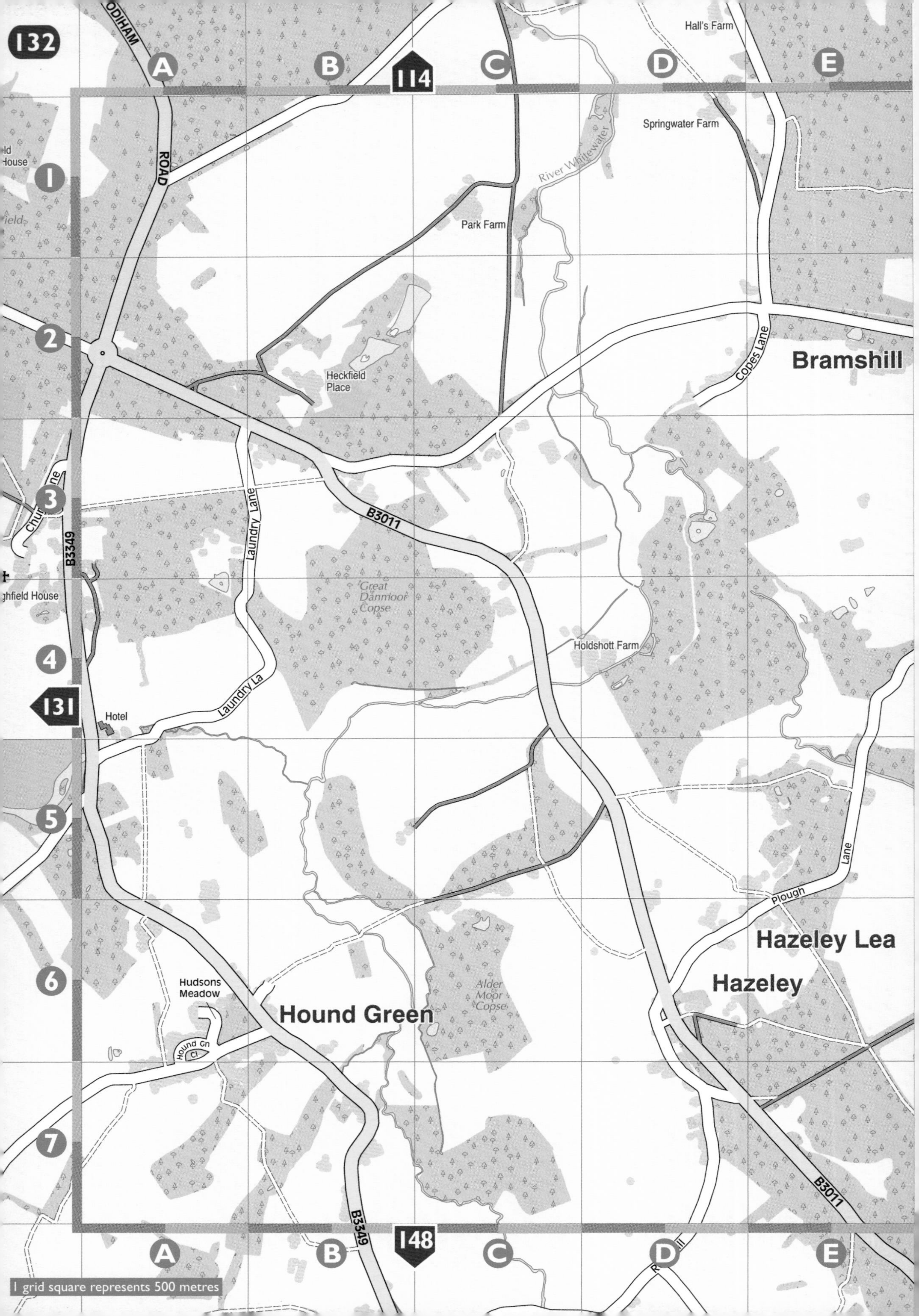
ODIHAM
ROAD
A
B
114
C
D
E
Hall's Farm
Springwater Farm
River Whitewater
Park Farm
1
2
3
4
5
6
7
Heckfield Place
Bramshill
Copes Lane
B3011
B3349
Laundry Lane
Laundry La
Great Danmoor Copse
Holdshott Farm
131
Hotel
Plough Lane
Hazeley Lea
Hazeley
Hudsons Meadow
Hound Green
Alder Moor Copse
Hound Gn Cl
148
1 grid square represents 500 metres

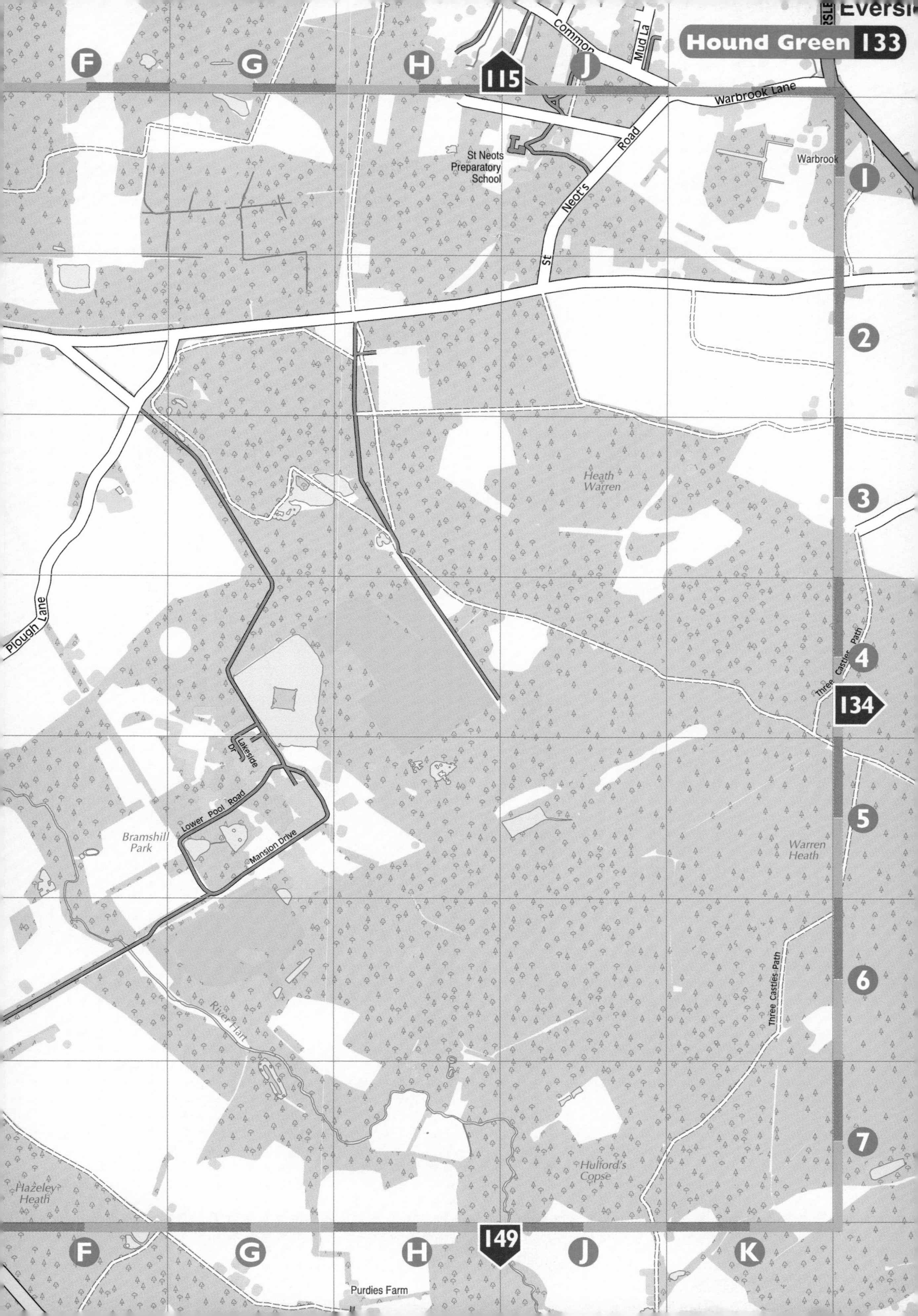

F   G   H   `115`   J

`I`

St Neots
Preparatory
School

Warbrook Lane

Warbrook

Mud La

Common

St Neot's Road

`2`

`3`

Heath
Warren

Plough Lane

`4`

`134`

Three Castles Path

Lakeside Dr

Bramshill
Park

Lower Pool Road

Mansion Drive

`5`

Warren
Heath

`6`

River Hart

Three Castles Path

`7`

Hazeley
Heath

Hulford's
Copse

Purdies Farm

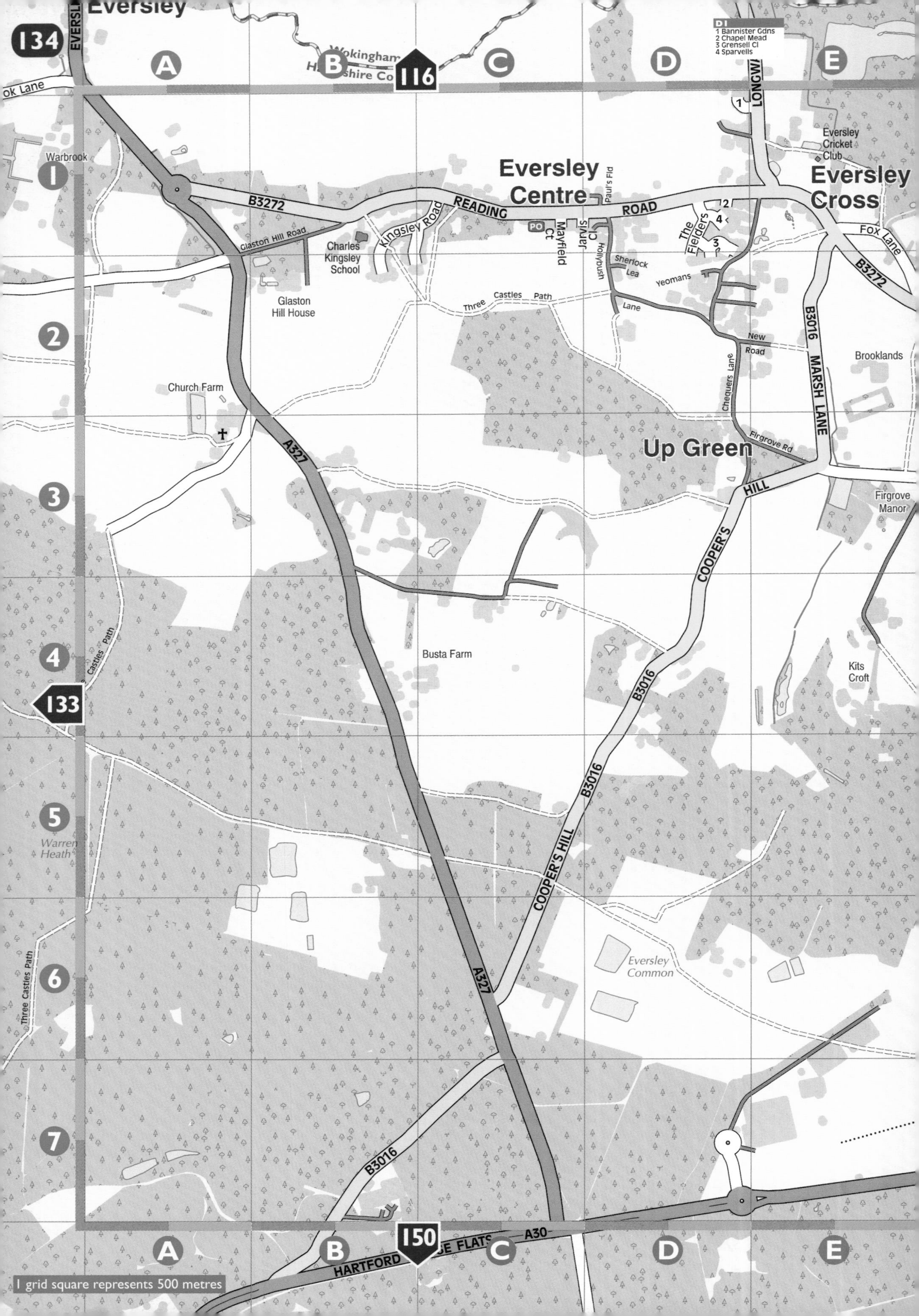

Eversley

A **B** Wokingham **C** **D** **E**
Hampshire Co

116

D1
1 Bannister Gdns
2 Chapel Mead
3 Grensell Cl
4 Sparvells

Warbrook

1

LONGW

Eversley
Cricket
Club

**Eversley
Cross**

B3272

Glaston Hill Road

Kingsley Road

READING

**Eversley
Centre**

Paul's Fld

ROAD

PO

Mayfield
Ct

Silver
Cl

Hollybush

The
Fielders

2

4

3

Fox Lane

B3272

Charles
Kingsley
School

Sherlock
Lea

Yeomans

B3016

MARSH LANE

2

Glaston
Hill House

Three Castles Path

Lane

New
Road

Chequers Lane

Brooklands

Church Farm

✝

Firgrove Rd

Up Green

Firgrove
Manor

3

A327

Castles Path

COOPER'S HILL

Kits
Croft

4

133

Busta Farm

B3016

B3016

COOPER'S HILL

5

Warren
Heath

Three Castles Path

Eversley
Common

6

A327

7

B3016

A **B** HARTFORD **C** A30 **D** **E**
E FLATS

150

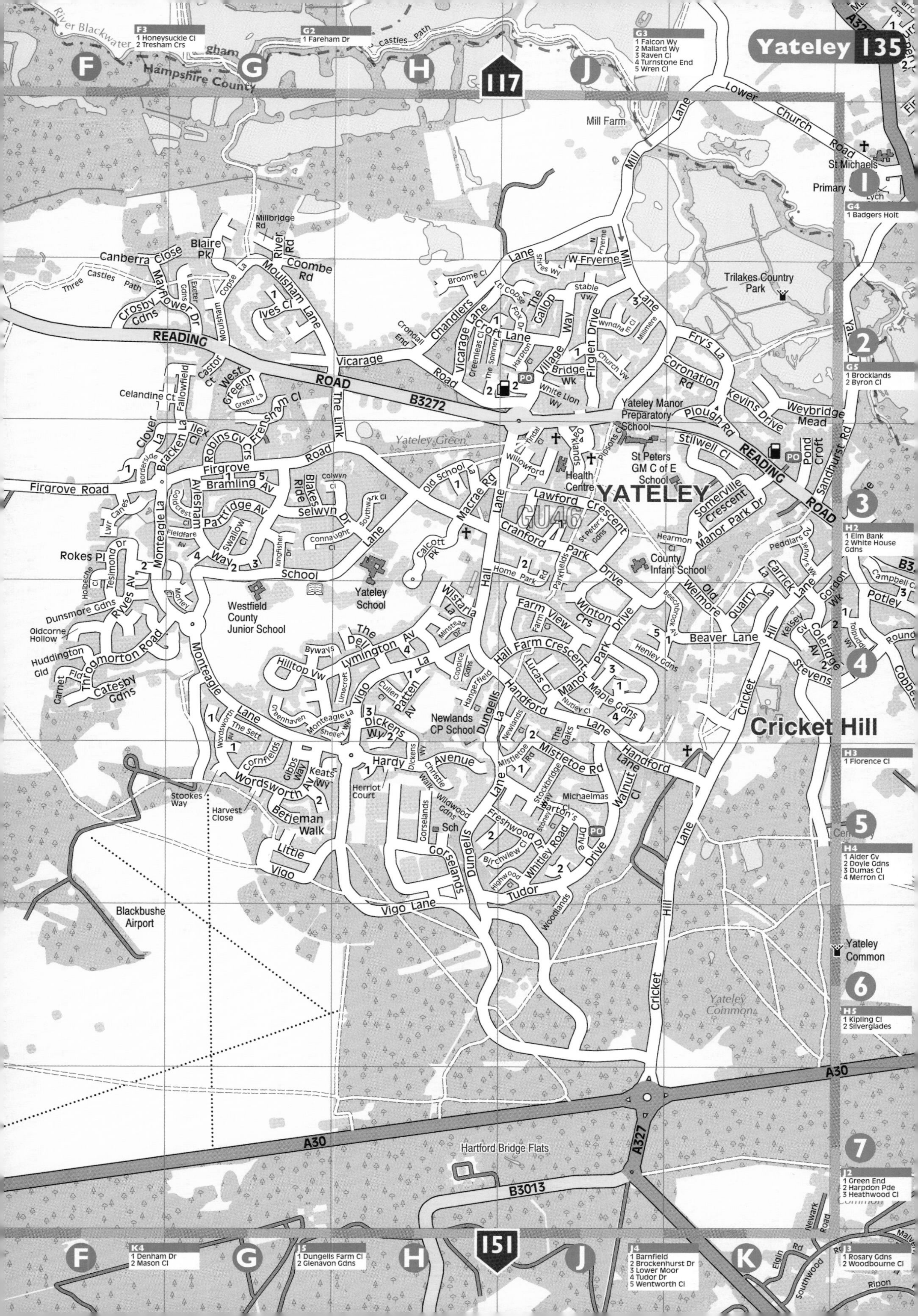

Yateley 135
117
151
F
G
H
J
K
2
3
4
5
6
7
F3
1 Honeysuckle Cl
2 Tresham Crs
G2
1 Fareham Dr
G3
1 Falcon Wy
2 Mallard Wy
3 Raven Cl
4 Turnstone End
5 Wren Cl
G4
1 Badgers Holt
G5
1 Brocklands
2 Byron Cl
H2
1 Elm Bank
2 White House Gdns
H3
1 Florence Cl
H4
1 Alder Gv
2 Doyle Gdns
3 Dumas Cl
4 Merron Cl
H5
1 Kipling Cl
2 Silverglades
J2
1 Green End
2 Harpdon Pde
3 Heathwood Cl
K4
1 Denham Dr
2 Mason Cl
J5
1 Dungells Farm Cl
2 Glenavon Gdns
J4
1 Barnfield
2 Brockenhurst Dr
3 Lower Moor
4 Tudor Dr
5 Wentworth Cl
J3
1 Rosary Gdns
2 Woodbourne Cl
River Blackwater
Hampshire County
Castles Path
Three Castles Path
Mill Farm
Lower Church Road
St Michaels Primary School
Trilakes Country Park
YATELEY
GU46
Cricket Hill
Yateley Green
Yateley Manor Preparatory School
St Peters GM C of E School
Health Centre
County Infant School
Yateley School
Westfield County Junior School
Newlands CP School
Blackbushe Airport
Yateley Common
Hartford Bridge Flats
READING ROAD
B3272
A30
A327
B3013
Firgrove Road
Vicarage Road
The Link
School Lane
Monteagle Lane
Vigo Lane
Little Vigo
Dungells Lane
Hall Lane
Cricket Hill Lane
Handford Lane
Mill Lane
Coronation Rd
Plough Rd
Kevins Drive
Weybridge Mead
Sandhurst Rd
Pond Croft
Stilwell Cl
Lawford Crescent
Cranford Park Drive
Somerville Crescent
Manor Park Dr
Winton Crs
Farm View
Hall Farm Crescent
Manor Park Drive
Maple Gdns
Lucas Cl
Mistletoe Rd
Walnut Cl
Beaver Lane
Welmore
Quarry La
Carrick Lane
Coleridge Av
Stevens
Potley
Gordon Wk
Canberra Close
Blaire Pk
Mayflower Dr
Crosby Gdns
Moulsham Lane
Coombe Rd
River Rd
Ives Cl
Millbridge Rd
West Green
Castor Ct
Frensham Cl
Celandine Ct
Fallowfield
Clover La
Bracken La
Ilex Cl
Robins Gv Crs
Bramling Av
Aylesham Way
Partridge Av
Swallow Cl
Blakes Ride
Selwyn Dr
Kingfisher Dr
Connaught Cl
Rokes Pl
Tesimond Dr
Dunsmore Gdns
Ryves Av
Throgmorton Road
Catesby Gdns
Oldcorne Hollow
Huddington Gld
Garnet Fld
Macrae Rd
Calcott Pk
Old School La
Wistaria La
Lymington Av
The Dell
Hilltop Vw
Byways
Patten Av
Cullen Cl
Dickens Wy
Hardy Avenue
Wordsworth Av
Betjeman Walk
Cornfields
Gibbs Way
Keats Wy
The Sett
Stookes Way
Harvest Close
Herriot Court
Corselands
Gorselands
Wildwood Gdns
Freshwood Dr
Birchview Cl
Whitley Road
Tudor Drive
Barton's Drive
Michaelmas Cl
Woodlands
Chandlers Lane
Vicarage Lane
Croft Lane
The Gallop
Village Way
Bridge Wk
Firgien Drive
White Lion Wy
W Fryerne
Stable Vw
Fry's La
Church Vw
Broome Cl
Crondall End
Yateley Common
Newark Road
Elgin Rd
Southwood Rd
Ripon

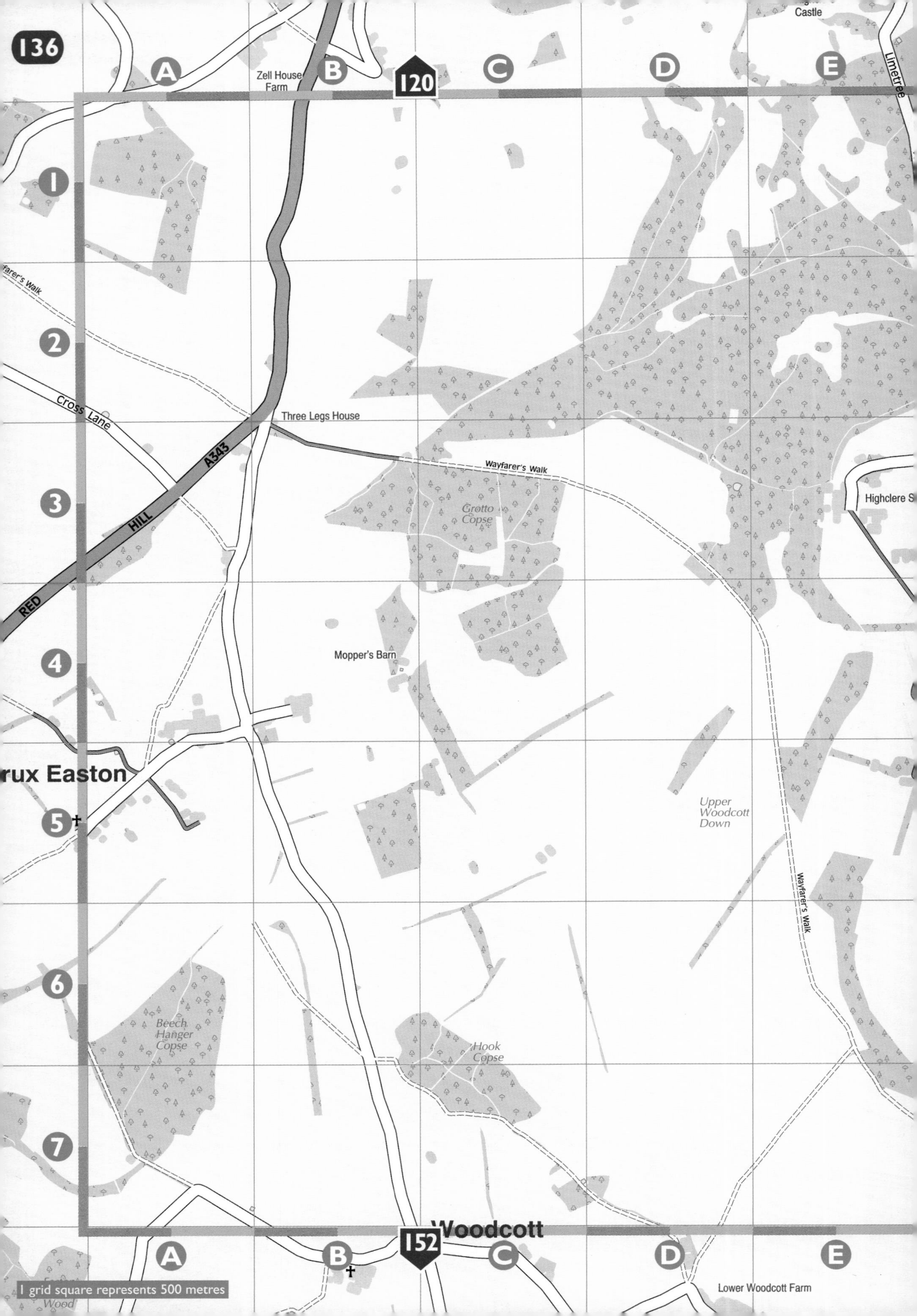

Castle
Limetree
Zell House Farm
A
B
120
C
D
E
1
2
3
4
5
6
7
Wayfarer's Walk
Cross Lane
Three Legs House
RED HILL A343
Wayfarer's Walk
Highclere S
Grotto Copse
Mopper's Barn
rux Easton
Upper Woodcott Down
Wayfarer's Walk
Beech Hanger Copse
Hook Copse
Woodcott
152
Lower Woodcott Farm
Wood

1 grid square represents 500 metres

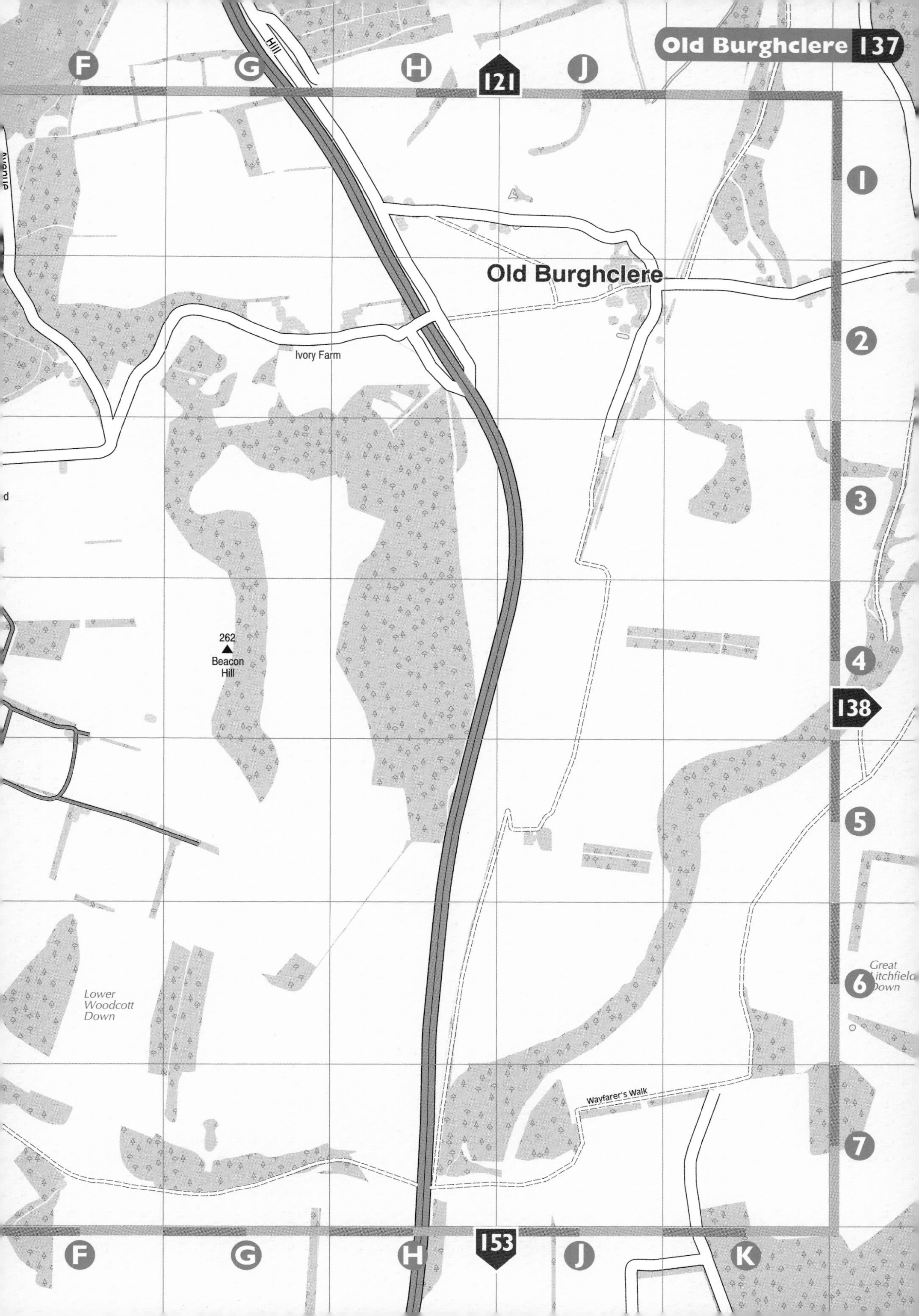

F G HILL H **121** J

1

Old Burghclere

2

Ivory Farm

3

262
▲
Beacon
Hill

4

138

5

Lower
Woodcott
Down

Great
itchfiel
Down
6

Wayfarer's Walk

7

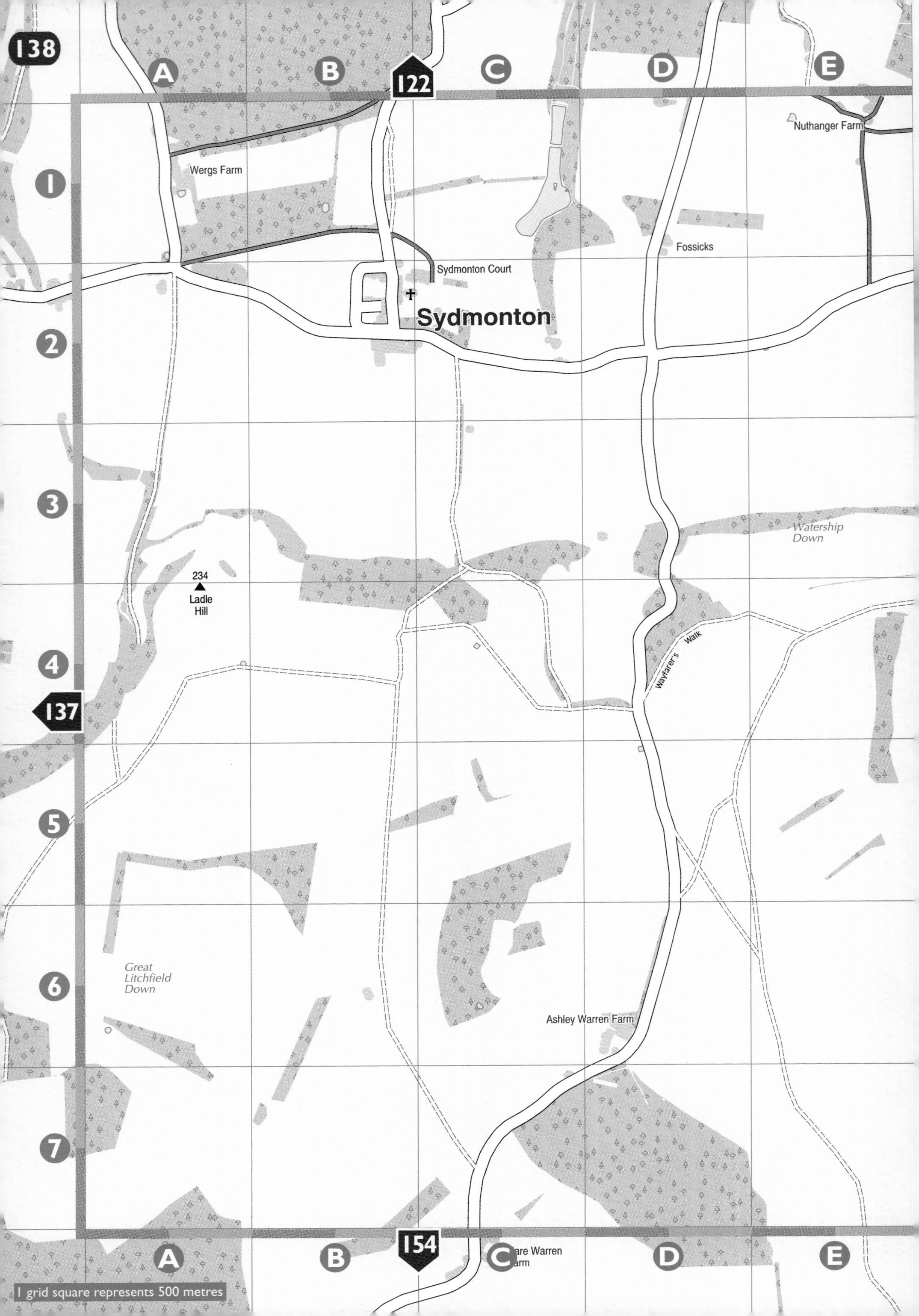

A   B   122   C   D   E

1

Nuthanger Farm

Wergs Farm

Fossicks

Sydmonton Court

† Sydmonton

2

3

Watership Down

234
▲
Ladle
Hill

4

Warfarer's Walk

5

Great
Litchfield
Down

6

Ashley Warren Farm

7

A   B   154   C   are Warren
arm   D   E

1 grid square represents 500 metres

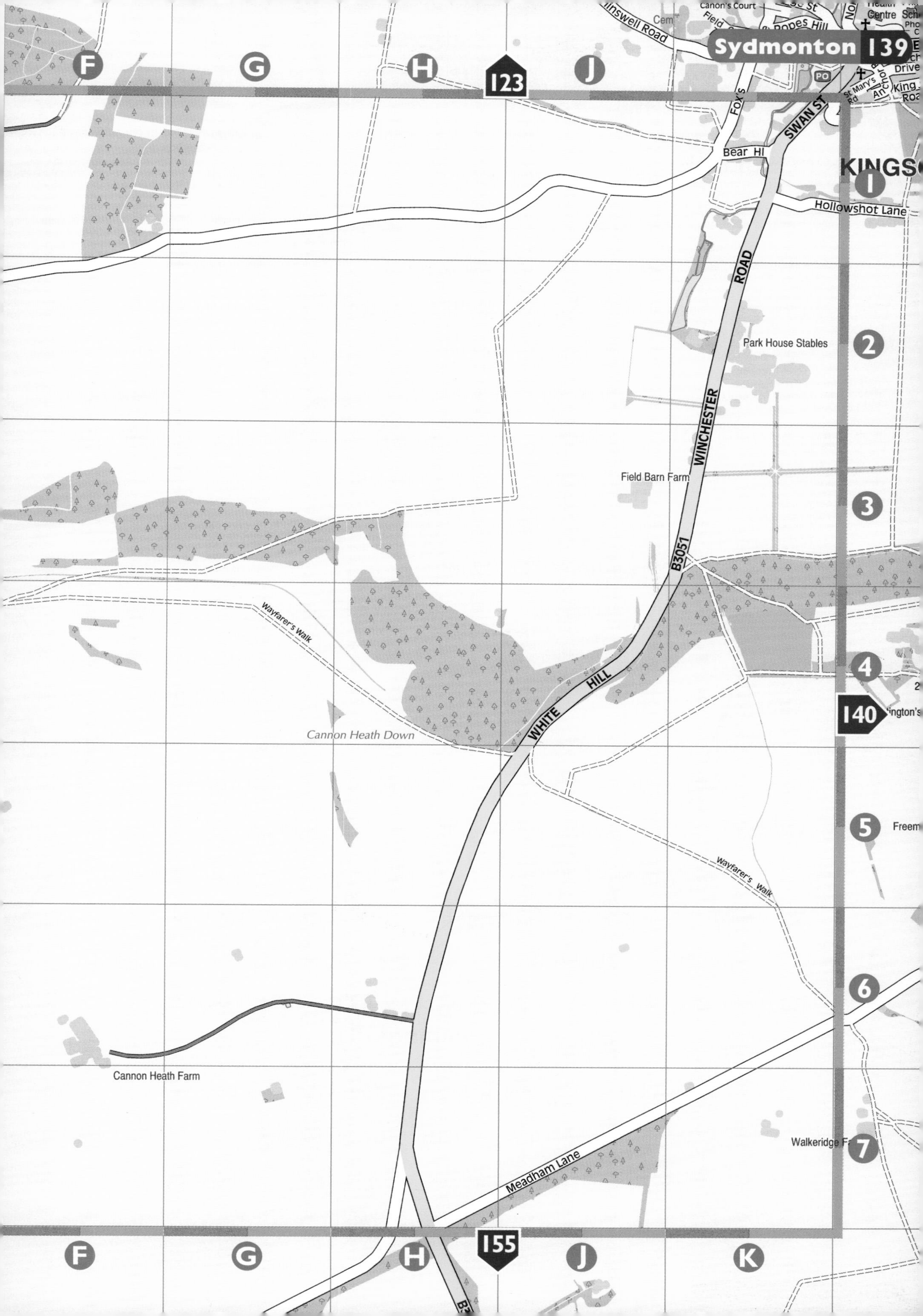

Sydmonton 139
123
140
155
F
G
H
J
K
1
2
3
4
5
6
7
KINGS
Canon's Court
Popes Hill
PO
Fox's
Swan St
Bear Hl
Hollowshot Lane
Winchester Road
B3051
White Hill
Park House Stables
Field Barn Farm
Wayfarer's Walk
Cannon Heath Down
Cannon Heath Farm
Meadham Lane
Walkeridge F

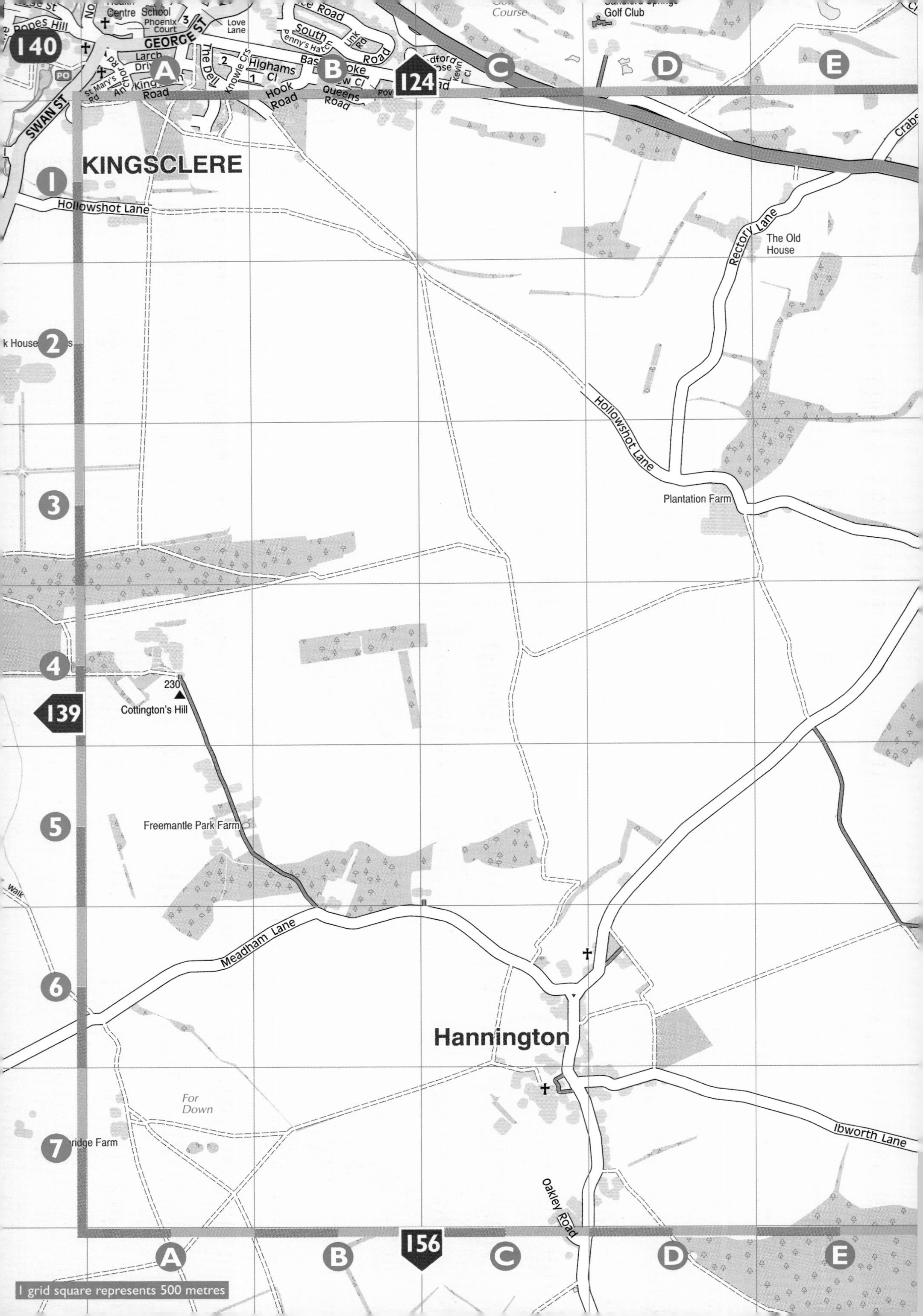

140
124
139
156
KINGSCLERE
Hannington
GEORGE ST
SWAN ST
Centre
School
Phoenix Court
Love Lane
The Dell
Knowle Crs
Highams Cl
Hook Road
Queens Road
Penny's Hatch
South
Link Rd
St Mary's Rd
Anchor Rd
PO
Golf Club
Course
Hollowshot Lane
Rectory Lane
The Old House
Plantation Farm
230
Cottington's Hill
Freemantle Park Farm
Meadham Lane
For Down
Ibworth Lane
Oakley Road
A
B
C
D
E
1
2
3
4
5
6
7
1 grid square represents 500 metres

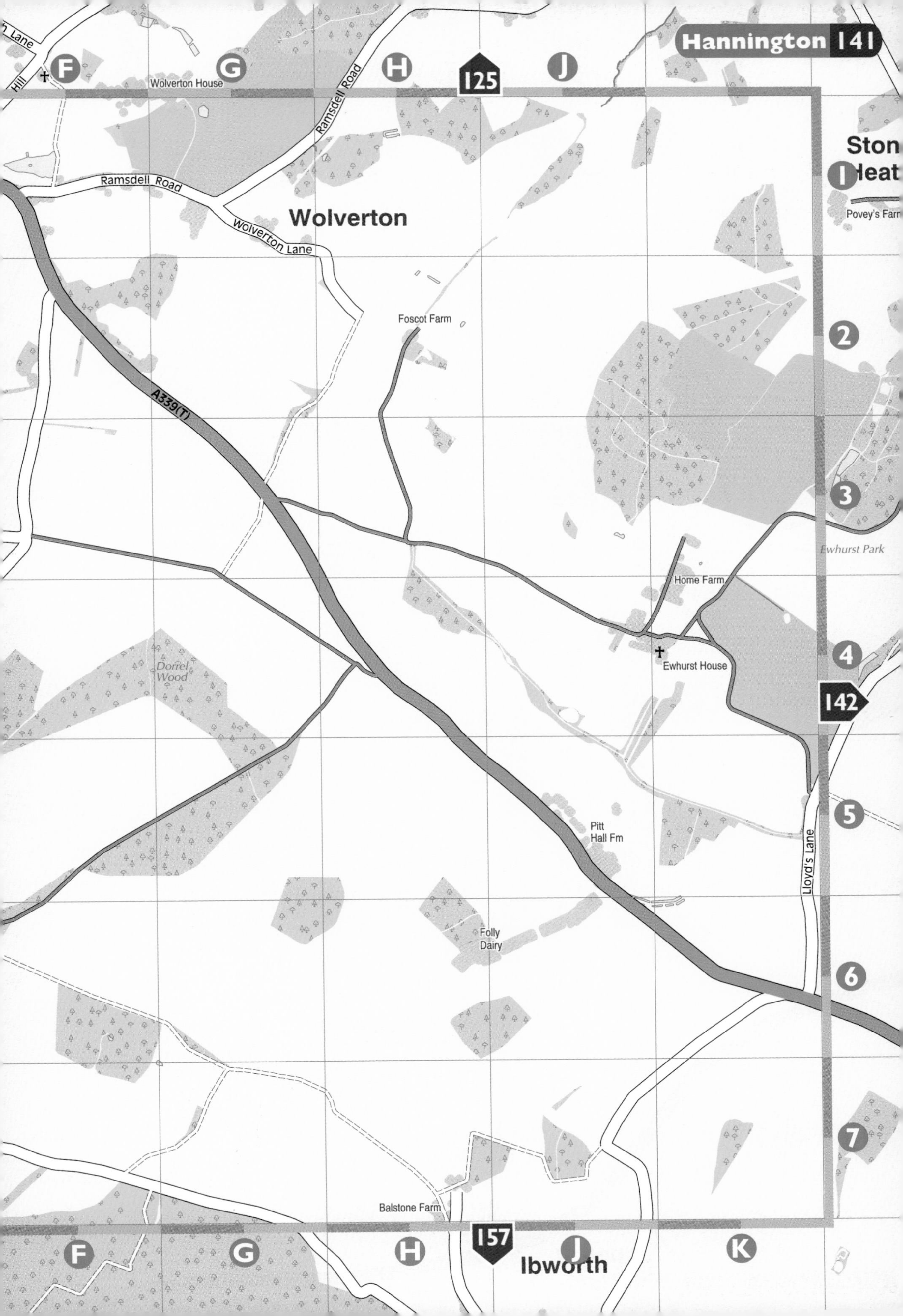

F

✝ Wolverton House

G

Ramsdell Road

H

125

J

Ston
Heat

Povey's Farm

Ramsdell Road

Wolverton Lane

Wolverton

Foscot Farm

A339(T)

2

3

Ewhurst Park

Home Farm

*Dorrel
Wood*

✝ Ewhurst House

4

142

5

Lloyd's Lane

Pitt
Hall Fm

6

Folly
Dairy

7

Balstone Farm

F

G

H

157

J

Ibworth

K

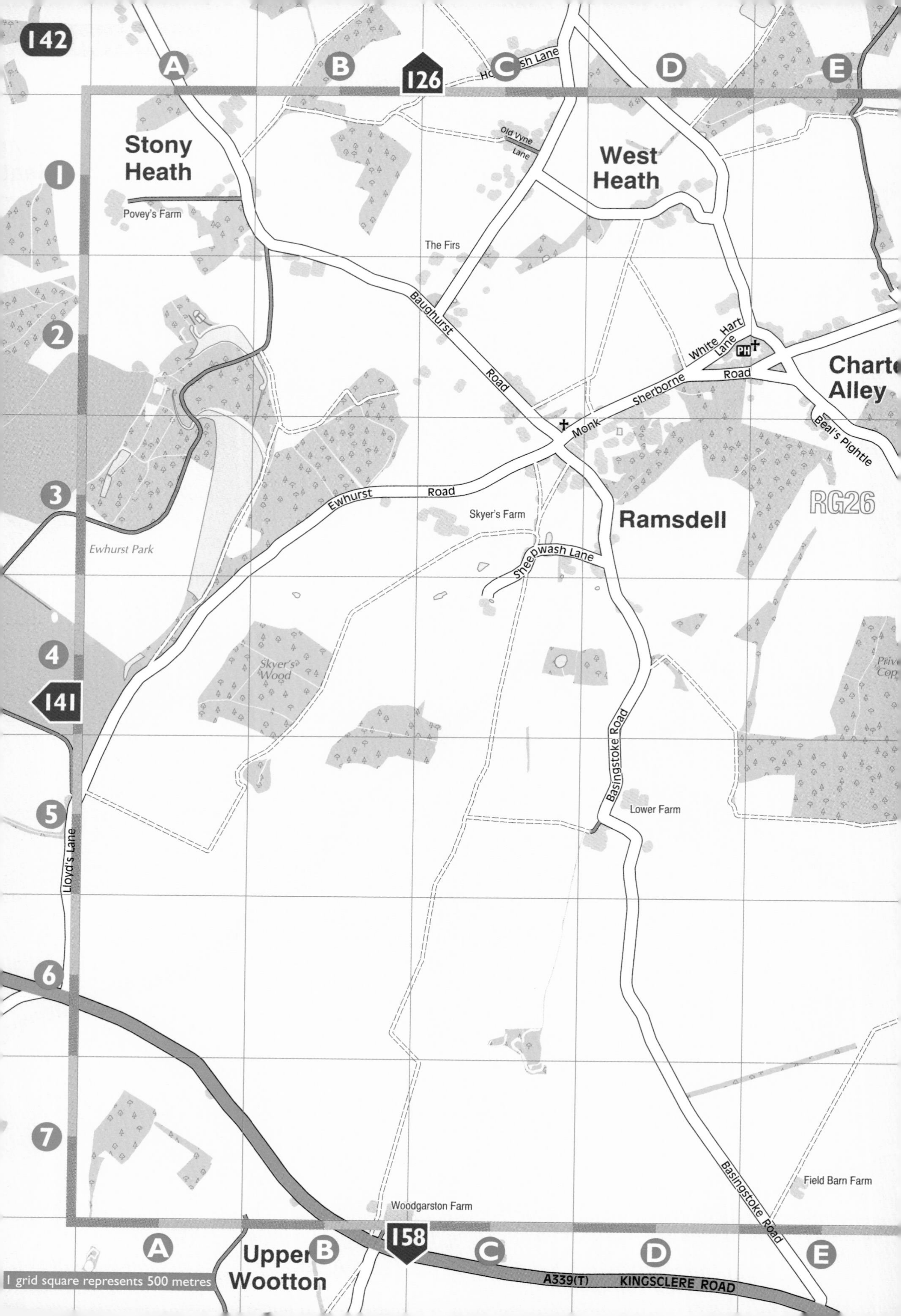
A
B
126
C
D
E
Ho sh Lane
Stony Heath
Old Vyne Lane
West Heath
Povey's Farm
The Firs
Baughurst Road
White Hart Lane
PH
Charte Alley
Sherborne Road
Monk
Beal's Pightle
Ewhurst Road
Skyer's Farm
Ramsdell
RG26
Ewhurst Park
Sheepwash Lane
Skyer's Wood
Priv Cop
141
Basingstoke Road
Lower Farm
Lloyd's Lane
Woodgarston Farm
Field Barn Farm
Basingstoke Road
158
Upper Wootton
1 grid square represents 500 metres
A339(T)
KINGSCLERE ROAD
1
2
3
4
5
6
7

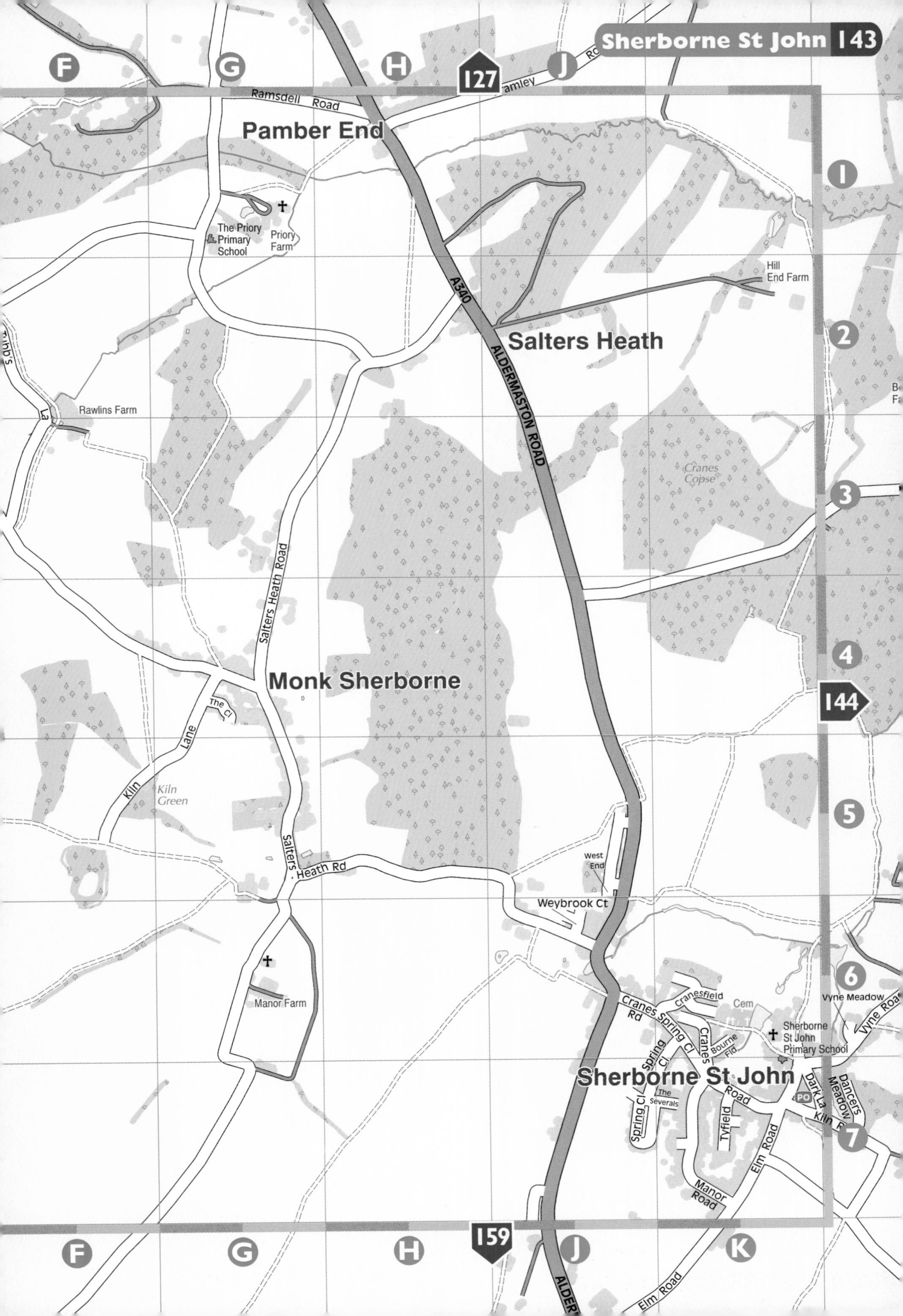

F G H **127** J

I

Ramsdell Road

Pamber End

The Priory Primary School

Priory Farm

A340

Salters Heath

ALDERMASTON ROAD

Hill End Farm

2

Cranes Copse

3

Rawlins Farm

Salters Heath Road

Monk Sherborne

4

144

The Cl

Lane

Kiln

Kiln Green

Salters Heath Rd

West End

5

Weybrook Ct

Manor Farm

Cranes Rd

Cranesfield

Spring Cl

Cranes

Bourne Fld

Cem

Vyne Meadow

6

Sherborne St John Primary School

Vyne Road

Spring Cl

The Severals

Cranes Road

PO

Dancers Meadow

Sherborne St John

Tyfield

Elm Road

Dark La

Kiln R

7

Manor Road

F G H **159** J ALDER K

Elm Road

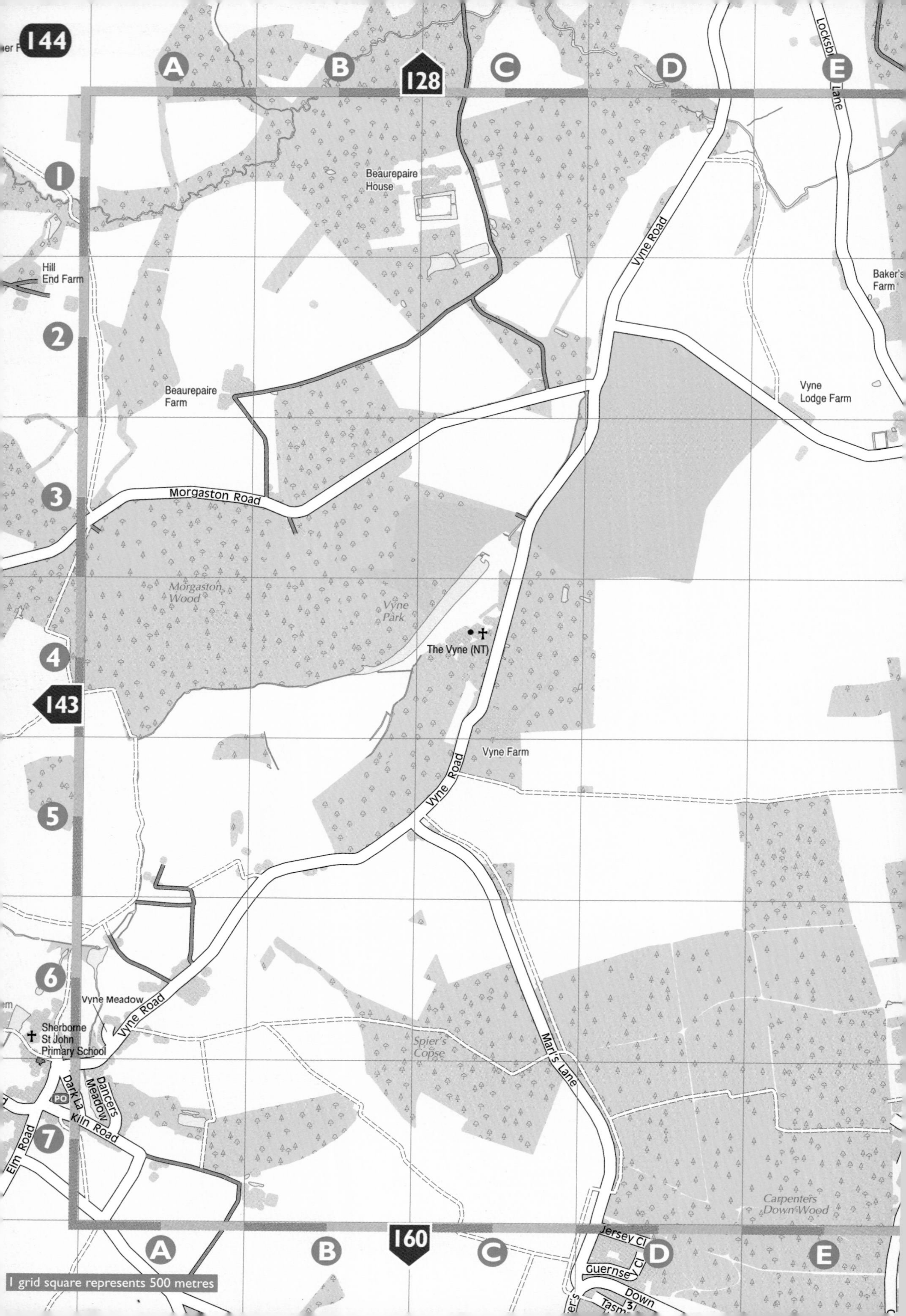

A   B   **128**   C   D   E

1

Hill
End Farm

Beaurepaire
House

Vyne Road

Baker's
Farm

2

Beaurepaire
Farm

Vyne
Lodge Farm

3

Morgaston Road

4

Morgaston
Wood

Vyne
Park

The Vyne (NT) •†

143

Vyne Farm

5

Vyne Road

6

Vyne Meadow

Vyne Road

Sherborne
St John
Primary School

Spier's
Copse

Marl's Lane

Dancers
Meadow

Dark La

PO

7

Elm Road

Kiln Road

Jersey Cl

Carpenters
Down Wood

A   B   **160**   C   D   Guernse   E

Down

Tasm

Locksb
Lane

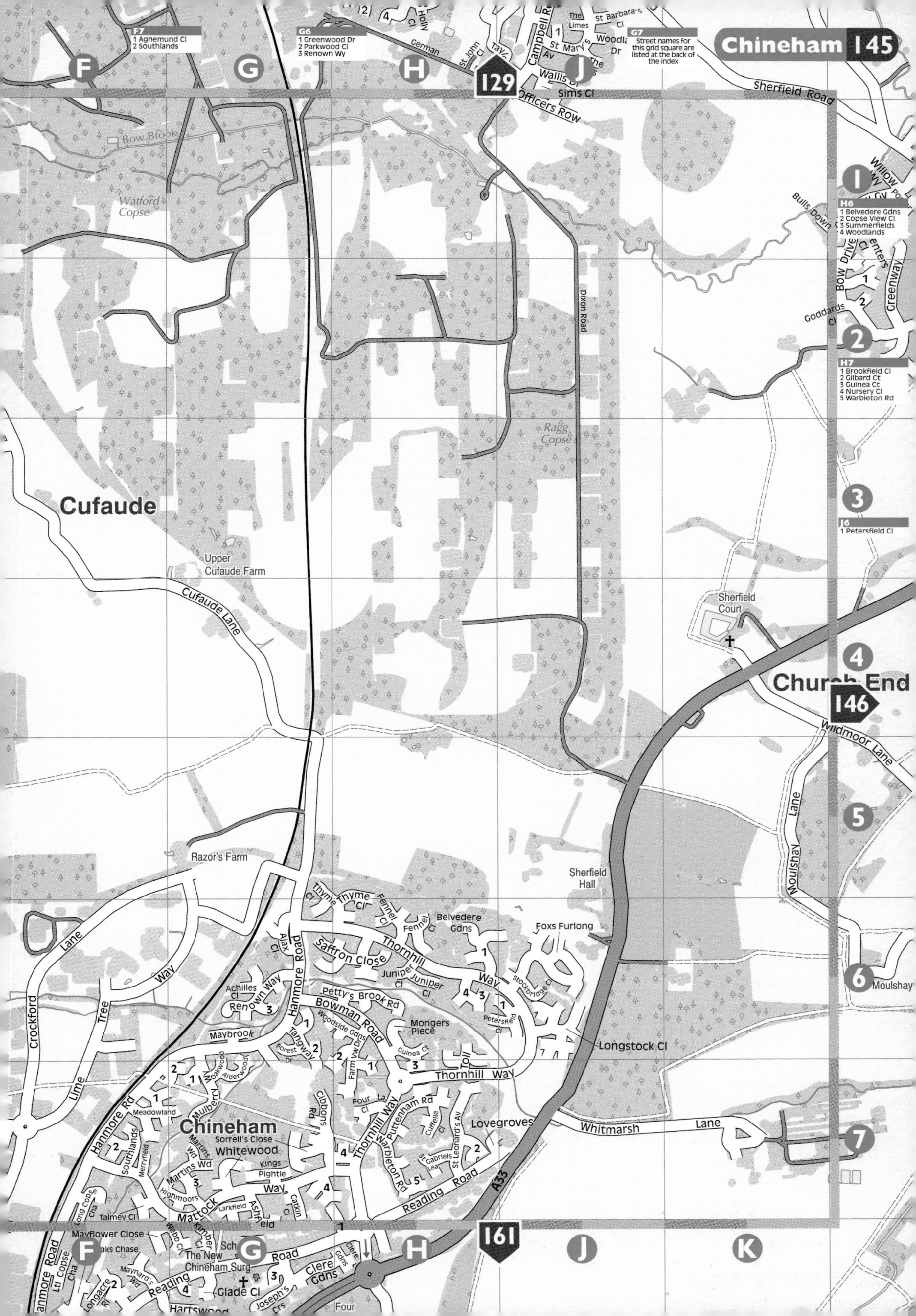

F7
1 Aghemund Cl
2 Southlands

G6
1 Greenwood Dr
2 Parkwood Cl
3 Renown Wy

G7
Street names for
this grid square are
listed at the back of
the index

129

Bow Brook

Watford Copse

Cufaude

Upper
Cufaude Farm

Cufaude Lane

Razor's Farm

Chineham

Whitewood

Ragg Copse

Dixon Road

St John St

Tave

Campbell Rd

The Limes

St Barbara's Cl

St Mar

Woodla
Dr

Wallis Dr

Sims Cl

Officers Row

Sherfield Road

I

H6
1 Belvedere Gdns
2 Copse View Cl
3 Summerfields
4 Woodlands

WILLOW
WY
GV

Bulls Down

Bow Drive

enter's

Greenway

Goddards
Cl

2

H7
1 Brookfield Cl
2 Gilbard Ct
3 Guinea Ct
4 Nursery Cl
5 Warbleton Rd

3

J6
1 Petersfield Cl

Sherfield
Court

4
Church End
146

Widmoor Lane

Moulshay Lane

5

Sherfield
Hall

Foxs Furlong

6 Moulshay

Thyme Thyme
Cl

Fennel Rd

Belvedere
Gdns

Fennel

Thornhill

Alax
Cl

Saffron Close

Juniper
Cl Juniper
Cl

Way

Stockbridge Cl

Achilles
Cl

Renown Way

Hanmore Road

Petty's Brook Rd

Bowman Road

Mongers
Piece

Petershe

Longstock Cl

Maybrook

Woodside Gdns

Forest
Dr

Farm Vw

Guinea Ct

Toll

Thornhill Way

Tree

Way

Crockford Lane

Lime

Tangway

Oakwood

Alderwood

Meadowland

Mulberry

Martins Wd

Meryfield

Clibbons
Rd

Thornhill Way

Warbleton Rd

Four La

Puttenham Rd

Curfelle

St Gabriels
Lea

St Leonard's Av

Lovegroves

Whitmarsh Lane

7

Southlands

Highmoors

Mattock

Larkfield

Ashfield

Catkin
Cl

Glebe
Gdns

Reading Road

A33

Kings
Pightle

Way

Talmey Cl

Mayflower Close

Long Copse
Cha

aks Chase

Webb Cl

Kimber
Cl

The New
Chineham Surg

Sch

Clere Gdns

Maynard's

Longacre
Wd

Reading

Road

Glade Cl

Joseph's
Crs

Hartswood

Four

F **G** **H** **161** **J** **K**

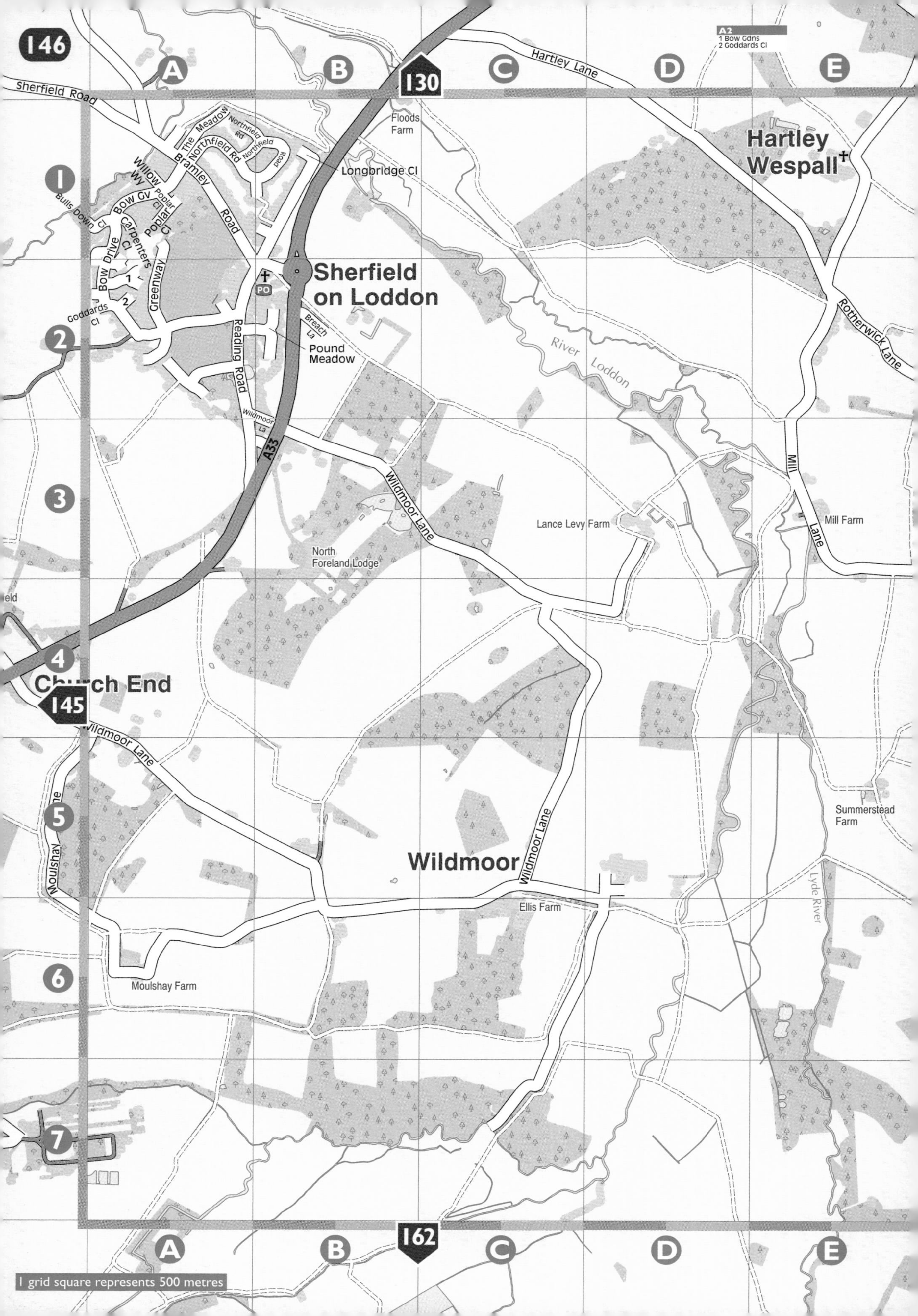

Sherfield Road

A2
1 Bow Gdns
2 Goddards Cl

A　　　**B**　　　**130**　　　**C**　Hartley Lane　**D**　　　**E**

Floods
Farm

**Hartley
Wespall**†

The Meadow

Northfield Rd

Northfield Road

Willow Wy

Bramley

Poplar Cl

Longbridge Cl

I

Bulls Down Cl

Bow Gv

Carpenters Cl

Bow Drive

Poplar

Greenway

1

Reading Road

✝

**Sherfield
on Loddon**

PO

2

Goddards Cl

2

Breach La

**Pound
Meadow**

River Loddon

Rotherwick Lane

3

Wildmoor La

A33

North
Foreland Lodge

Wildmoor Lane

Lance Levy Farm

Mill Lane

Mill Farm

field

4
Church End

145

Wildmoor Lane

Moulshay

5

Wildmoor

Wildmoor Lane

Wildmoor

Ellis Farm

Summerstead
Farm

Lyde River

6

Moulshay Farm

7

A　　　**B**　**162**　　　**C**　　　**D**　　　**E**

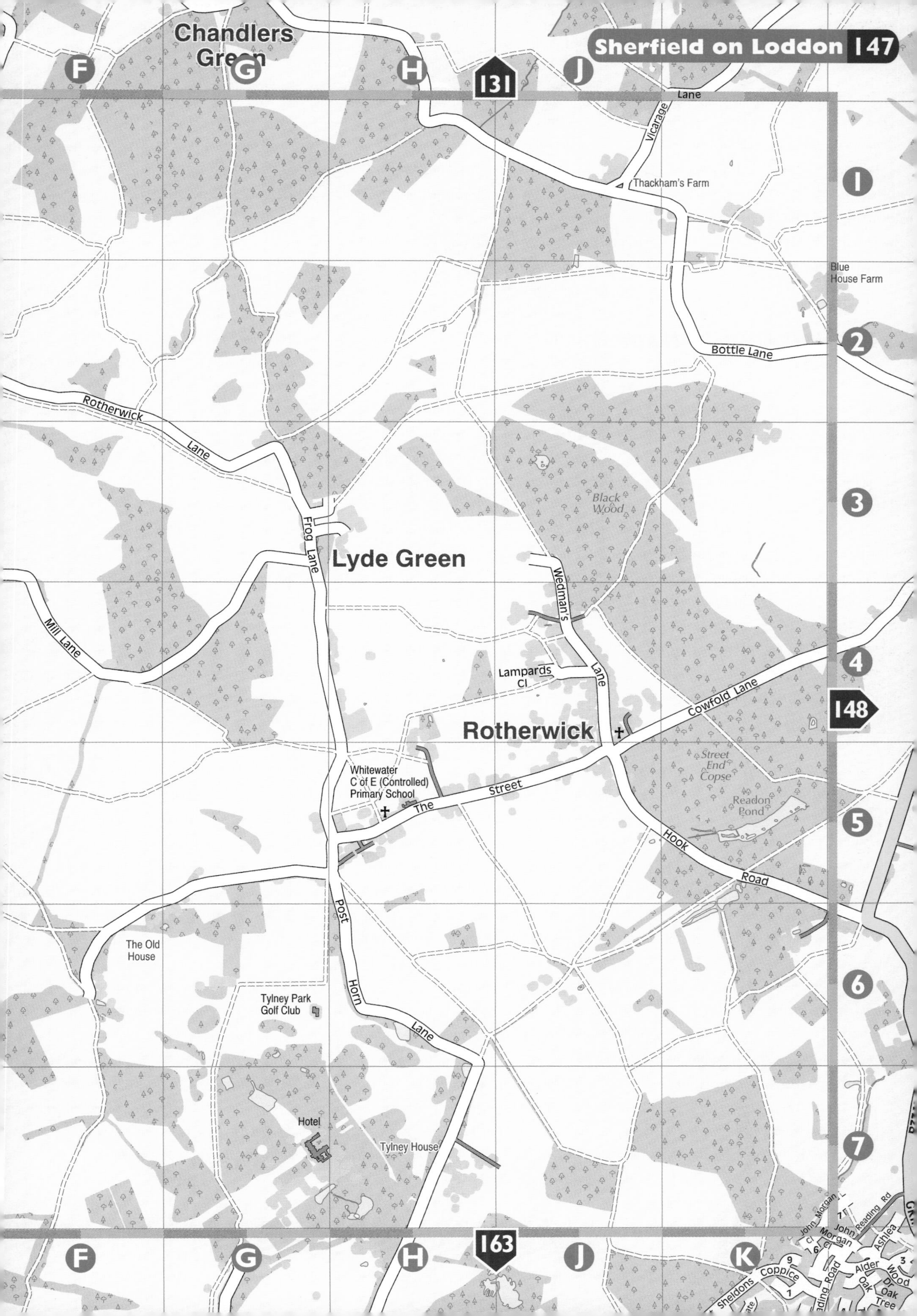

Chandlers Green

131

Vicarage Lane

Thackham's Farm

Blue House Farm

Bottle Lane

Rotherwick Lane

Frog Lane

Black Wood

Lyde Green

Mill Lane

Wedman's Lane

Lampards Cl

Rotherwick

Cowfold Lane

148

Street End Copse

Whitewater C of E (Controlled) Primary School

The Street

Readon Pond

Hook Road

The Old House

Post Horn Lane

Tylney Park Golf Club

Hotel

Tylney House

163

John Morgan

John Morgan Cl

John Reading Rd

Ashlea

Coppice

Sheldons

Reading Road

Oak Tree Wood

Oak

Alder

F   G   H   J

1 2 3 4 5 6 7

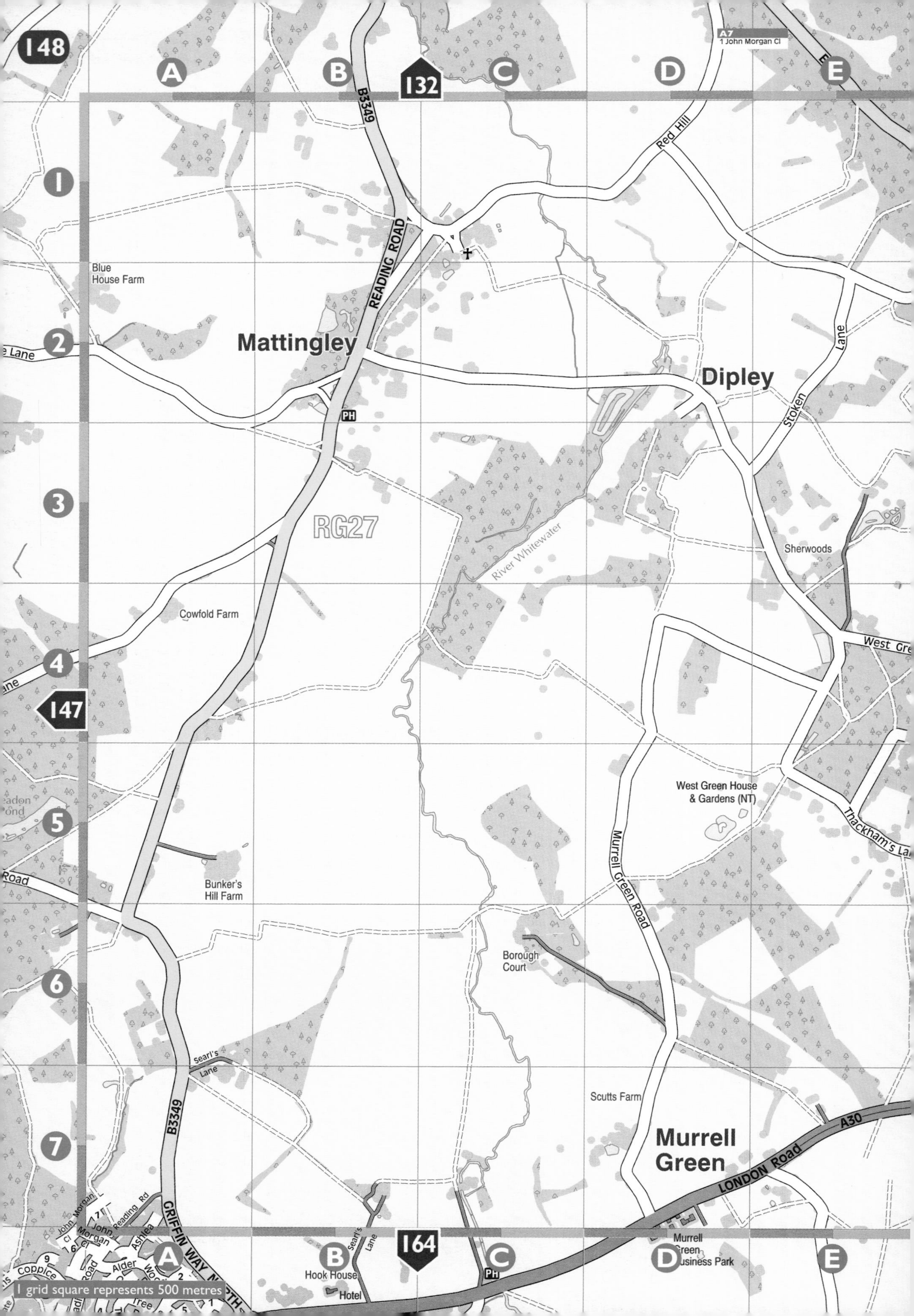

A   B   C   D   E

132

A7
1 John Morgan Cl

I

Red Hill

Blue
House Farm

Stoken Lane

2

Mattingley

Dipley

RG27

PH

River Whitewater

Sherwoods

West Gre

3

Cowfold Farm

4

147

West Green House
& Gardens (NT)

Thackham's La

5

eadon
ond

Bunker's
Hill Farm

Murrell Green Road

6

Borough
Court

Searl's
Lane

B3349

7

Scutts Farm

Murrell
Green

A30

LONDON ROAD

John Morgan
Reading Rd
Coppice
Alder
Tree
GRIFFIN WAY NORTH

A   B   C   D   E

164

Hook House
Hotel

PH

Murrell
Green
Business Park

1 grid square represents 500 metres

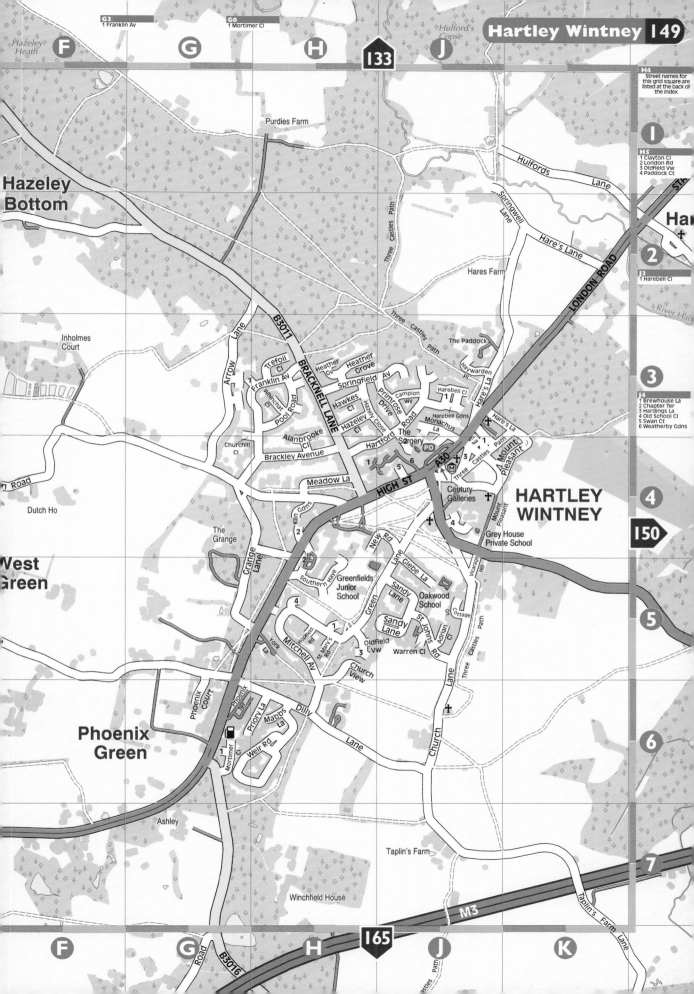

Hazeley
Bottom

Hazeley
Heath

G3
1 Franklin Av

G6
1 Mortimer Cl

Purdies Farm

Hulford's
Copse

H4
Street names for
this grid square are
listed at the back of
the index

I

H5
1 Clayton Cl
2 London Rd
3 Oldfield Vw
4 Paddock Ct

Har

Hulfords   Lane

Springwell   Lane

LONDON ROAD

2

J3
1 Harebell Cl

Hare's Lane

Hares Farm

River Har

Inholmes
Court

Three   Castles   Path

The Paddock

3

J4
1 Brewhouse La
2 Chapter Ter
3 Hardings La
4 Old School Cl
5 Swan Ct
6 Weatherby Gdns

Arrow   Lane

B3011   BRACKNELL LANE

Trefoil
Cl

Heather
Gv

Heather
Grove

Franklin Av

Whinchat

Pool Road

Hawkes
Cl

Springfield   Av

Primrose
Drive

Campion
Wy

Hazeley   Road

Hazeley Close

Harebell Cl

Haywarden
Pl

Harebell Gdns

Monachus
La

Hare's La

Hare's La

Alanbrooke
Cl

Churchill
Cl

Hartford   Road

The
Surgery

Mount
Pleasant

Brackley Avenue

PO

Three   Castles   Path

Dutch Ho

Meadow La

HIGH ST

A30

M

Century
Galleries

**HARTLEY
WINTNEY**

4

Road

The
Grange

Kiln Gdns

Mount
Pleasant

150

West
Green

Grange   Lane

New Rd

Glebe La

Grey House
Private School

Southern Haye

Greenfields
Junior
School

Green   Lane

Sandy
Lane

Oakwood
School

Vicarage   Hill

5

Mitchell Av

Hopfield
Rd

St Mary's Rd

Sandy
Lane

St Johns   Rd

Adrian

Cottage

Three   Castles   Path

York
La

Oldfield
Vw

Warren Cl

Church
View

Church   Lane

Phoenix
Court

Phoenix
Ter

Priory La

Mabbs
La

Dilly

6

Phoenix
Green

Mortimer
Ct

Weir Rd

Lane

Ashley

Taplin's Farm

7

Winchfield House

M3

Taplin's Farm Lane

Road

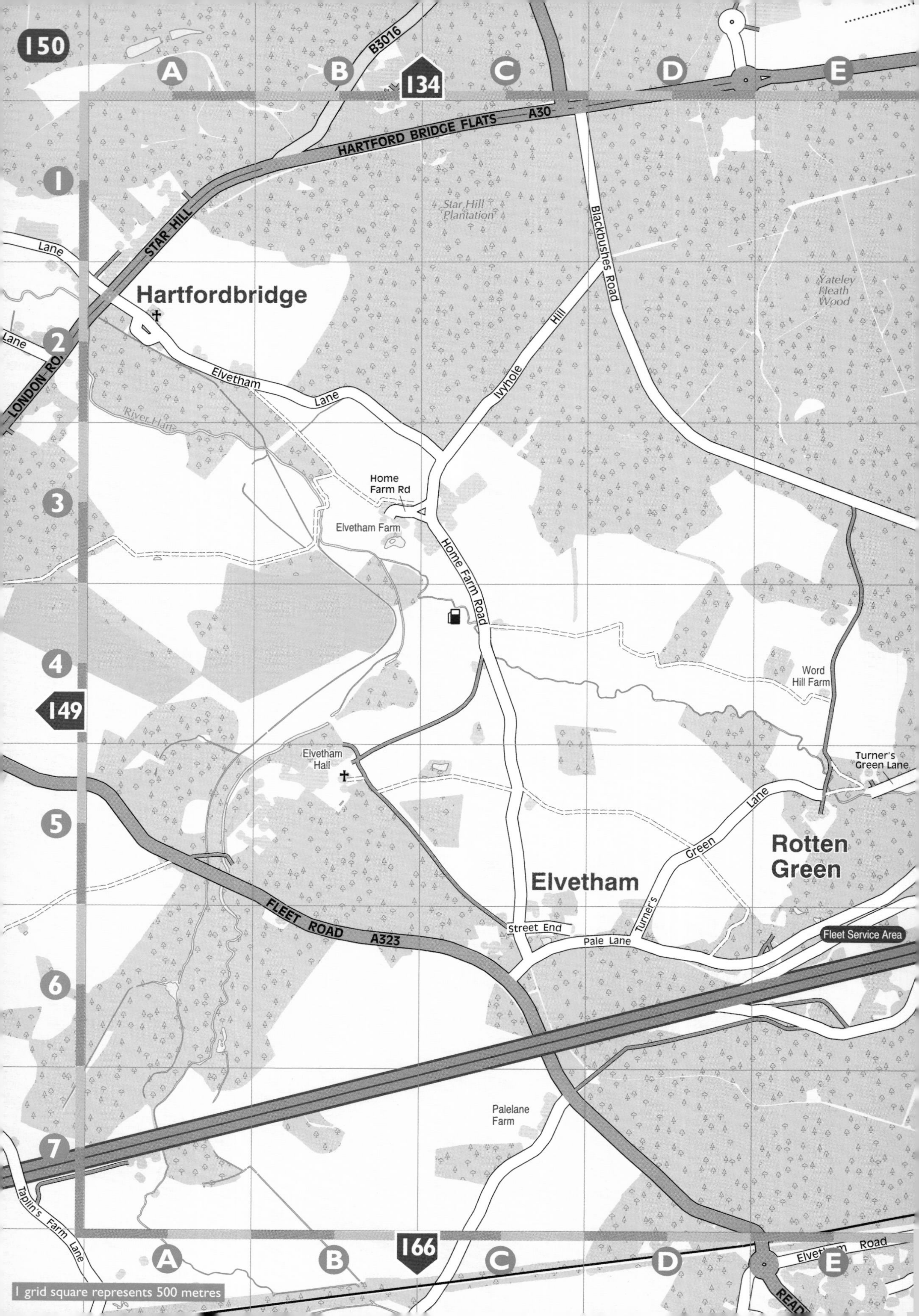

150

A B 134 C D E

B3016

HARTFORD BRIDGE FLATS A30

Star Hill
Plantation

Yateley
Heath
Wood

1

Lane

STAR HILL

Blackbushes Road

Hartfordbridge

2

Lane

LONDON RD

Elvetham
Lane

Ivynole Hill

River Hart

3

Home
Farm Rd

Elvetham Farm

Home Farm Road

4

149

Word
Hill Farm

Elvetham
Hall

Turner's
Green Lane

5

Rotten
Green

FLEET ROAD A323

Elvetham

Green Lane

Turner's Lane

Street End

Pale Lane

Fleet Service Area

6

Palelane
Farm

7

Taplin's Farm Lane

A B 166 C D E

Elvetham Road

READ

1 grid square represents 500 metres

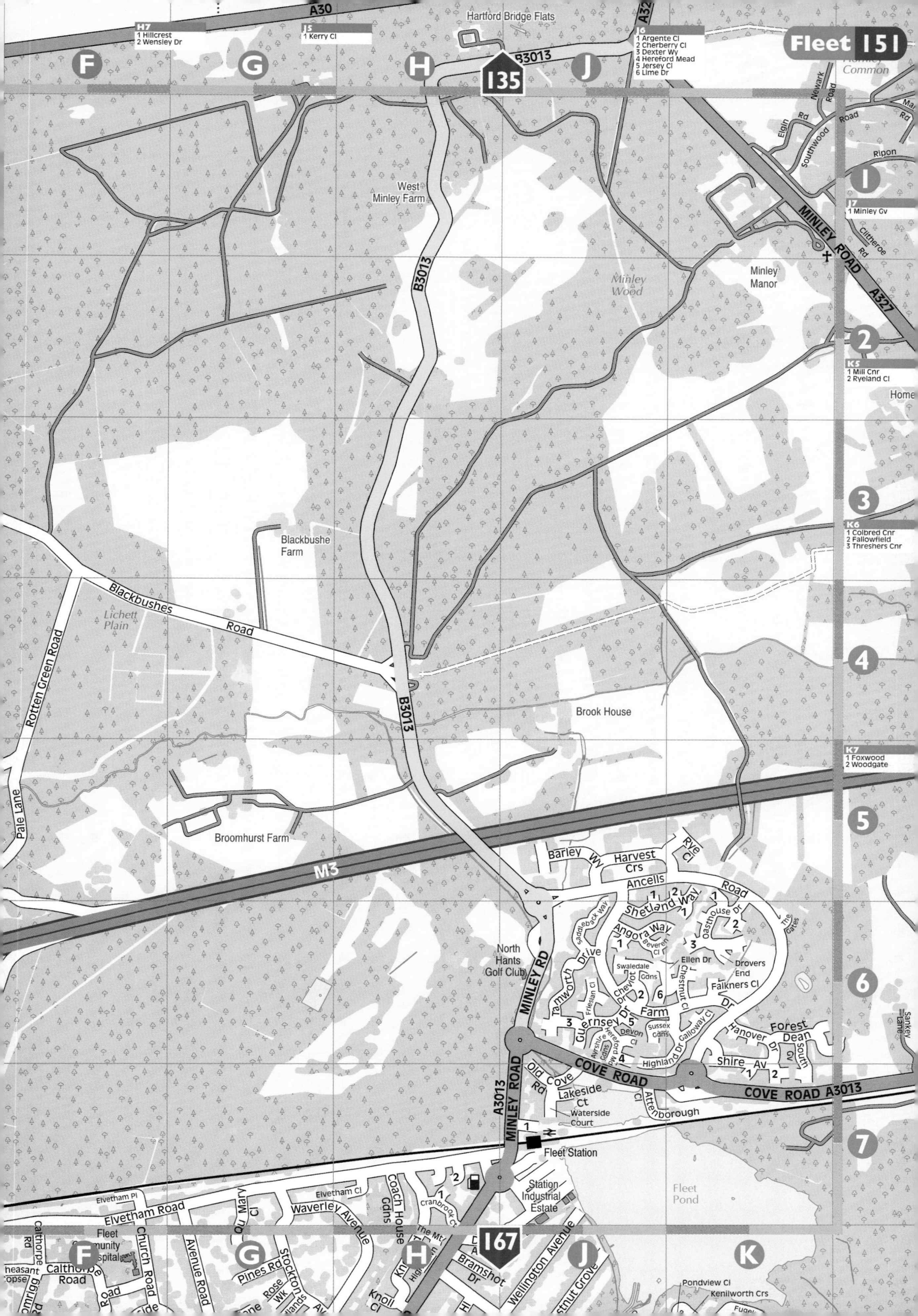
H7
1 Hillcrest
2 Wensley Dr
J5
1 Kerry Cl
J6
1 Argente Cl
2 Cherberry Cl
3 Dexter Wy
4 Hereford Mead
5 Jersey Cl
6 Lime Dr
J7
1 Minley Gv
K5
1 Mill Cnr
2 Ryeland Cl
K6
1 Colbred Cnr
2 Fallowfield
3 Threshers Cnr
K7
1 Foxwood
2 Woodgate
A30
A327
Hartford Bridge Flats
B3013
135
167
West Minley Farm
Minley Wood
Minley Manor
MINLEY ROAD
Blackbushe Farm
Blackbushes Road
Lichett Plain
Rotten Green Road
Pale Lane
Brook House
Broomhurst Farm
M3
North Hants Golf Club
MINLEY RD
A3013
Barley Wy
Harvest Crs
Rye Cl
Ancells Road
Shetland Way
Angora Way
Tamworth Drive
Swaledale Gdns
Cheviot Dr
Chestnut Cl
Ellen Dr
Drovers End
Falkners Cl
Farm Dr
Guernsey Dr
Friesian Cl
Sussex Gdns
Devon Cl
Highland Dr
Calloway Cl
Hanover Dr
Forest Dean
Shire Av
COVE ROAD
COVE ROAD A3013
Old Cove Rd
Lakeside Ct
Waterside Court
Attenborough Cl
Fleet Station
Station Industrial Estate
Fleet Pond
Elvetham Pl
Elvetham Road
Elvetham Cl
Waverley Avenue
Coach House Gdns
Cranbrook Ct
Church Road
Avenue Road
Calthorpe Road
Pines Rd
Stockton Av
Wellington Avenue
Bramshot Dr
Pondview Cl
Kenilworth Crs
Newark Road
Elgin Rd
Southwood Road
Ripon
Clitheroe Rd
Sankey Lane
F
G
H
J
K
1
2
3
4
5
6
7

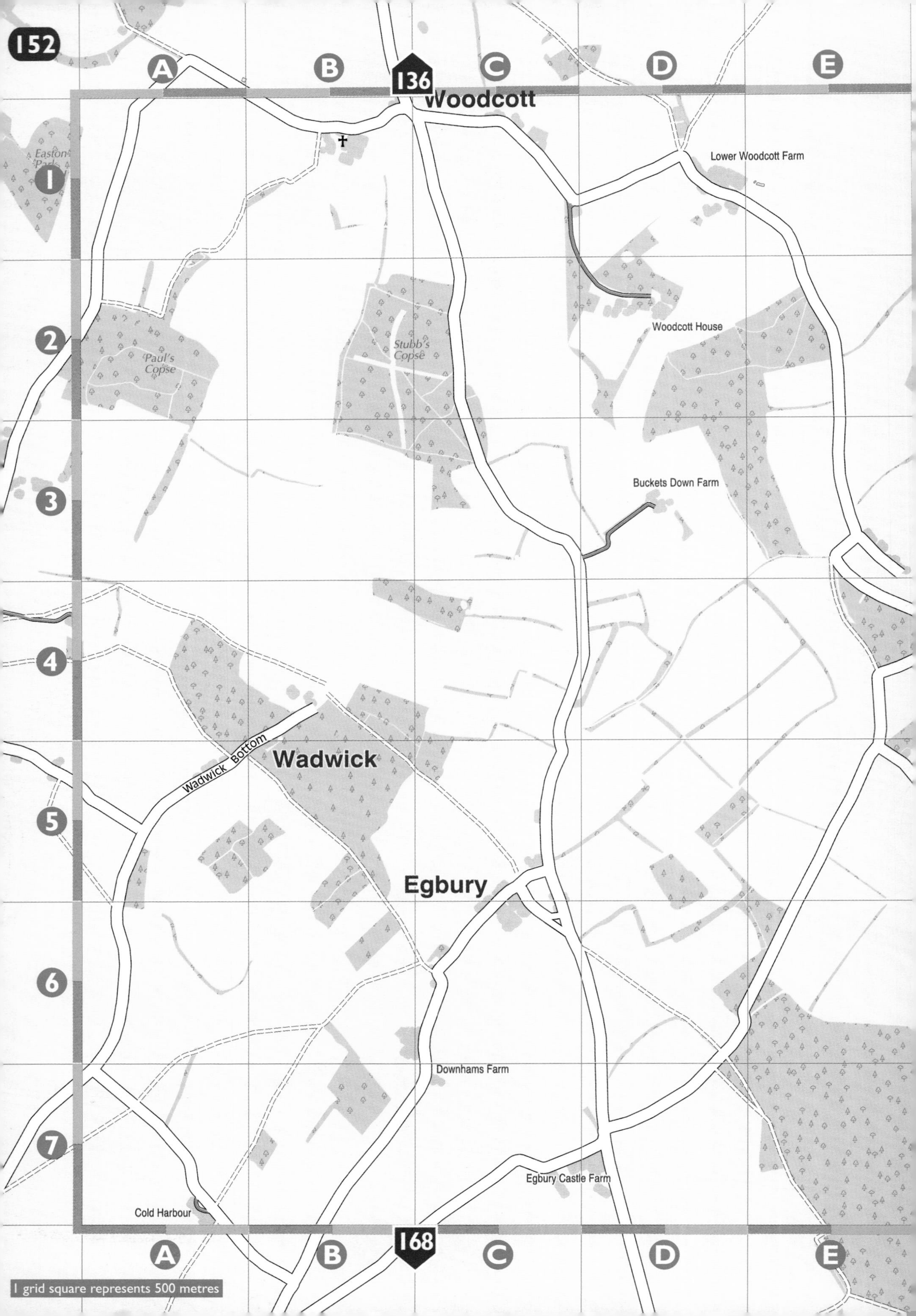

152

A B 136 Woodcott C D E

1 Easton Park

Lower Woodcott Farm

2 Paul's Copse Stubb's Copse Woodcott House

3 Buckets Down Farm

4

Wadwick Bottom **Wadwick**

5

Egbury

6 Downhams Farm

7 Egbury Castle Farm

Cold Harbour

A B 168 C D E

1 grid square represents 500 metres

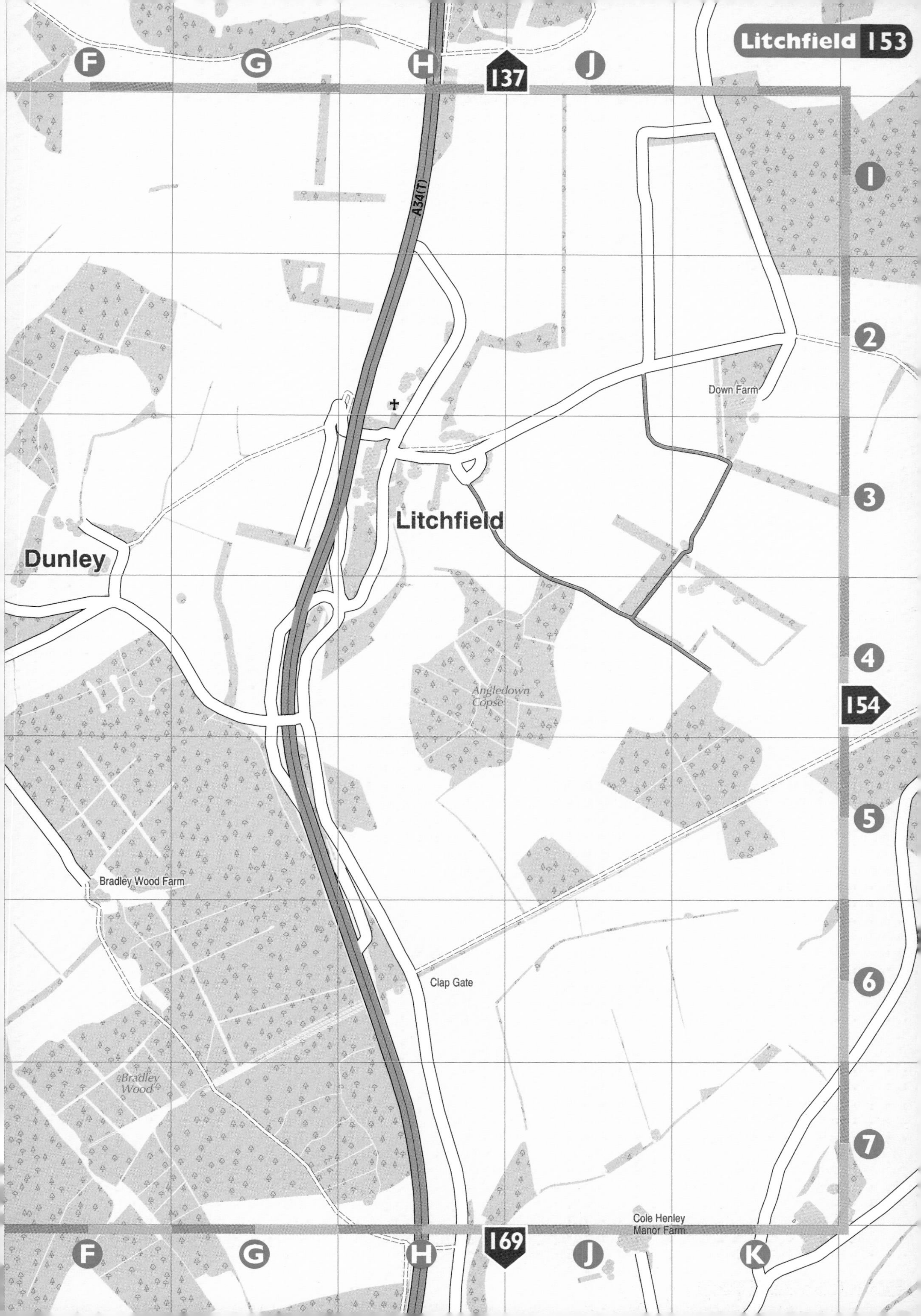

F
G
H
137
J

1

2

Down Farm

3

Litchfield

Dunley

4

Angledown
Copse

154

5

Bradley Wood Farm

6

Clap Gate

Bradley
Wood

7

Cole Henley
Manor Farm

A34(T)

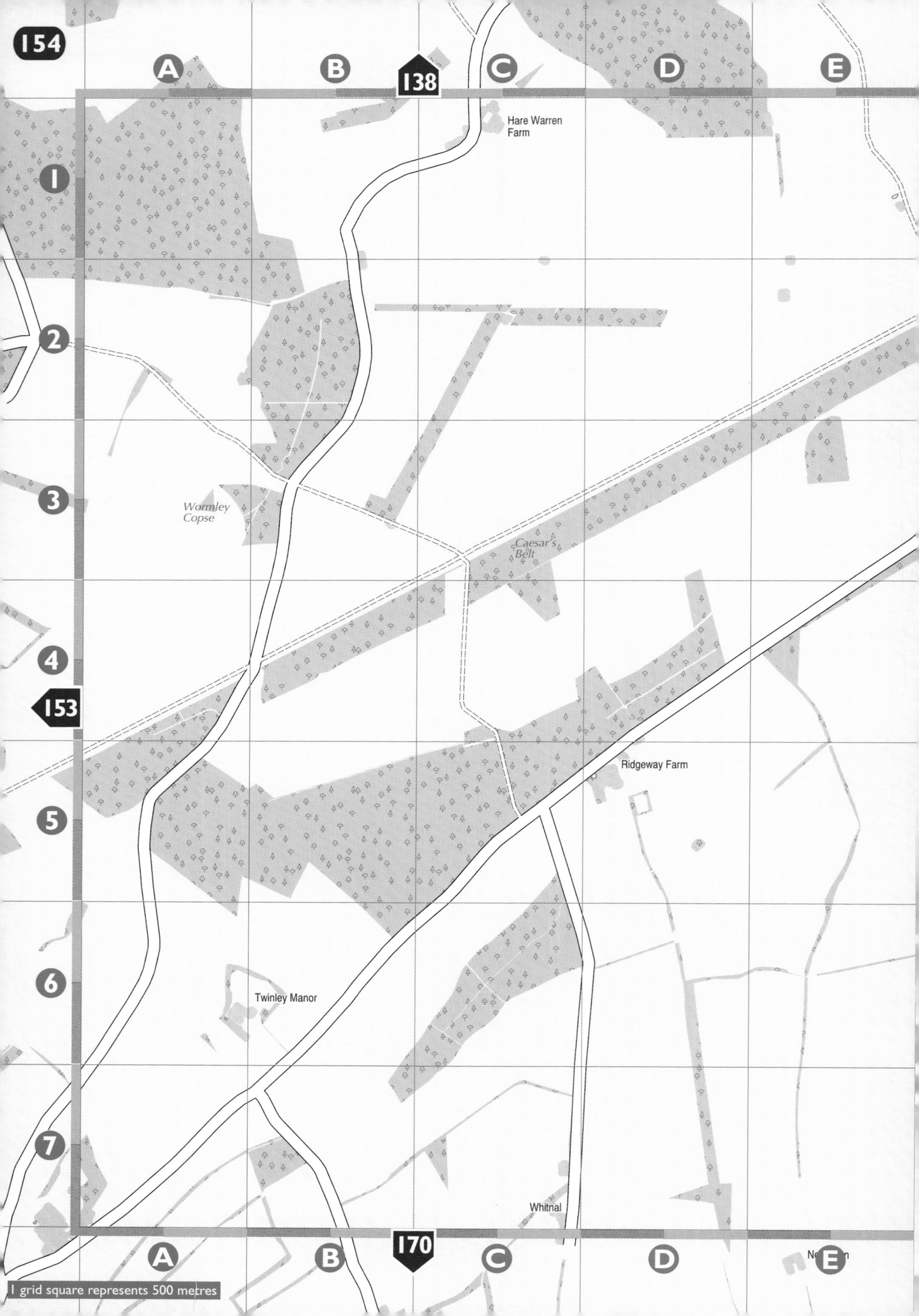

A   B   138   C   D   E

Hare Warren
Farm

1

2

3

Wormley
Copse

Caesar's
Belt

4

153

Ridgeway Farm

5

6

Twinley Manor

7

Whitnal

A   B   170   C   D   E

1 grid square represents 500 metres

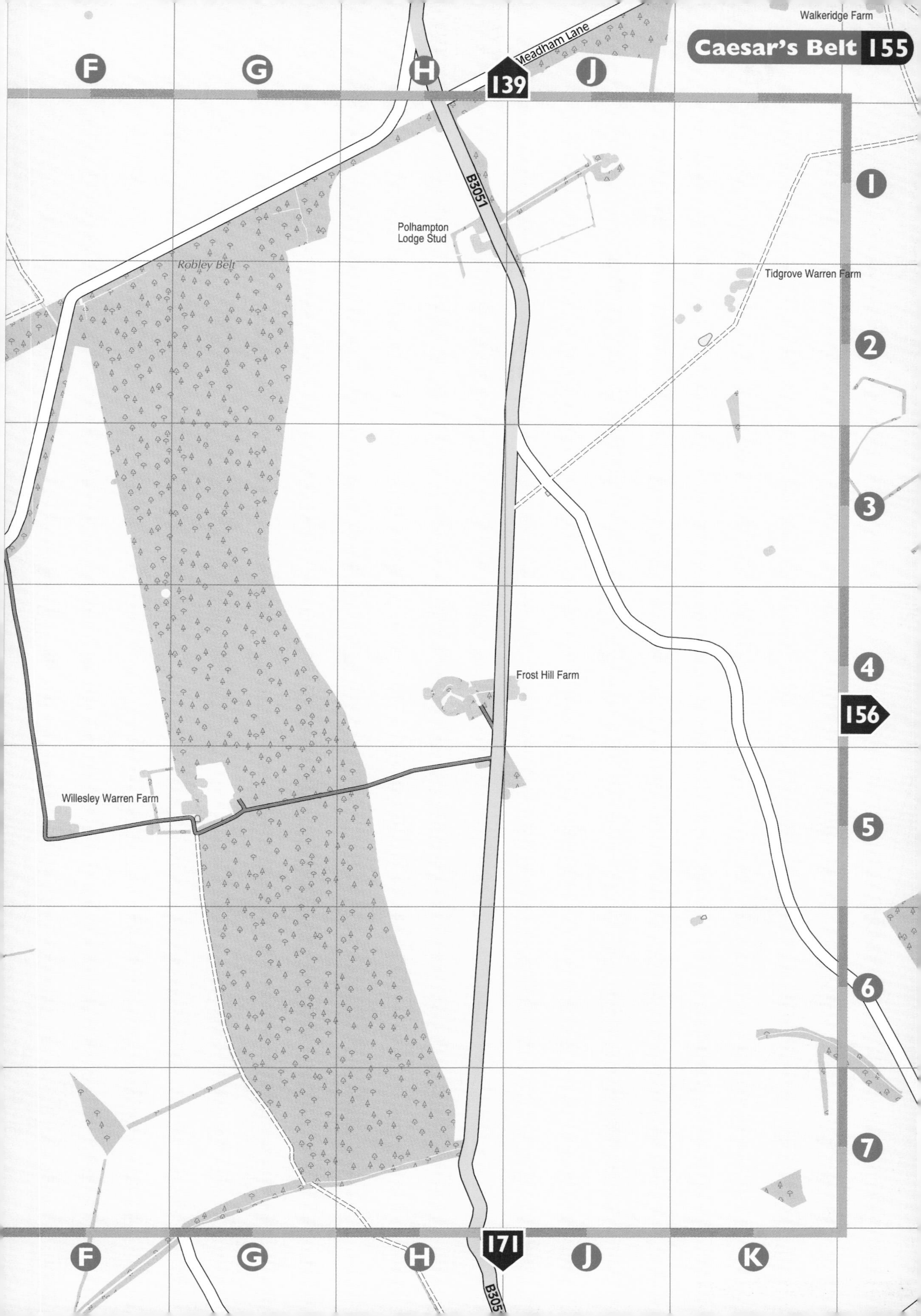

Walkeridge Farm

F **G** **H** **139** Meadham Lane **J**

B3051

Polhampton
Lodge Stud

Robley Belt

Tidgrove Warren Farm

1

2

3

Frost Hill Farm

4

156

Willesley Warren Farm

5

6

7

F **G** **H** **171** **J** **K**

B305

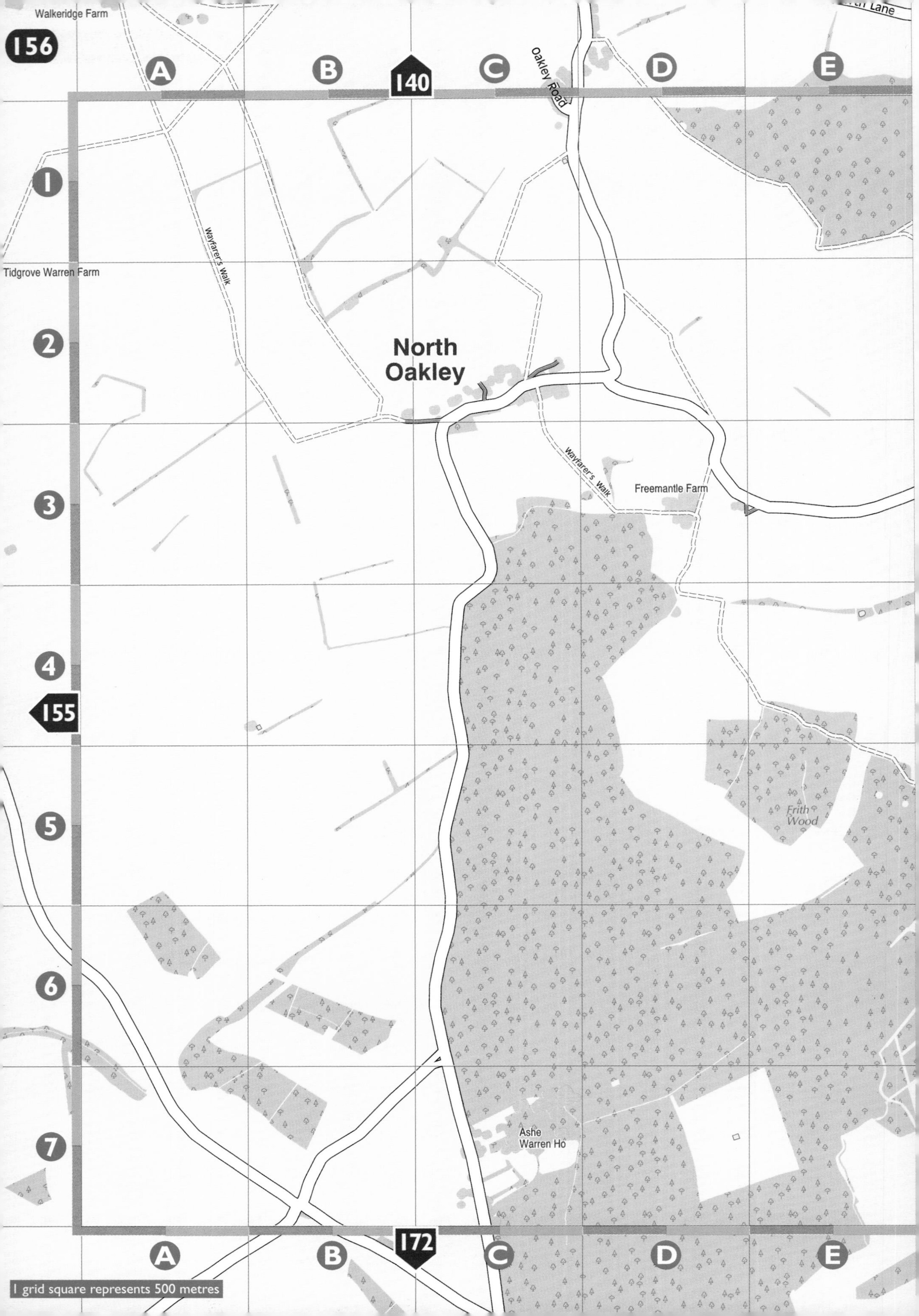

156

A   B   140   C   Oakley Road   D   E

1

Walkeridge Farm

Tidgrove Warren Farm

Wayfarer's Walk

2

North
Oakley

3

Wayfarer's Walk

Freemantle Farm

4

155

5

Frith
Wood

6

7

Ashe
Warren Ho

A   B   172   C   D   E

1 grid square represents 500 metres

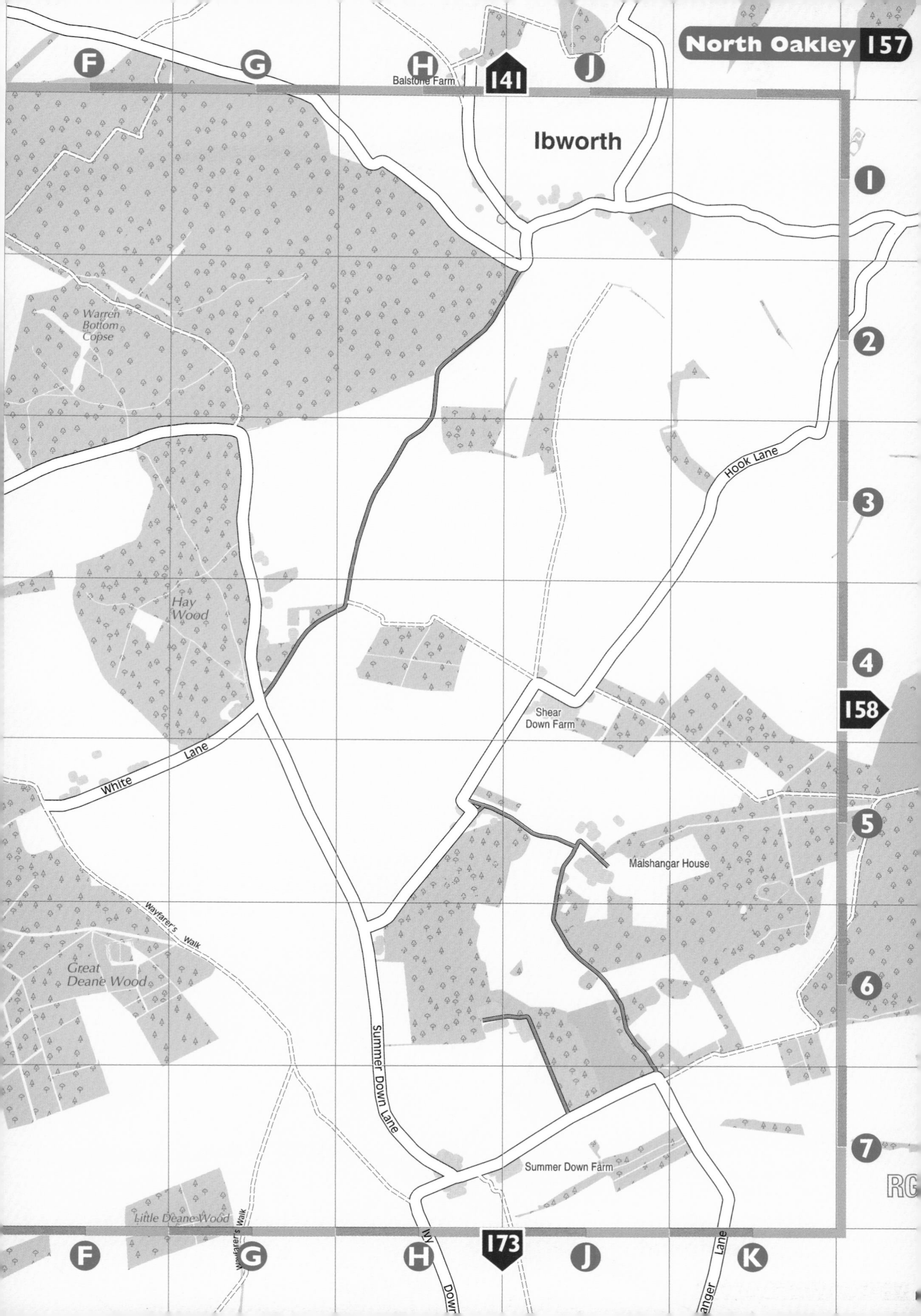

F G H J

141

Balstone Farm

Ibworth

I

2

Warren
Bottom
Copse

Hook Lane

3

Hay
Wood

4

158

Shear
Down Farm

White Lane

5

Malshangar House

Wayfarer's Walk

6

Great
Deane Wood

Summer Down Lane

7

RG

Little Deane Wood

Wayfarer's Walk

Summer Down Farm

F G H **173** J K

Ivy Down

anger Lane

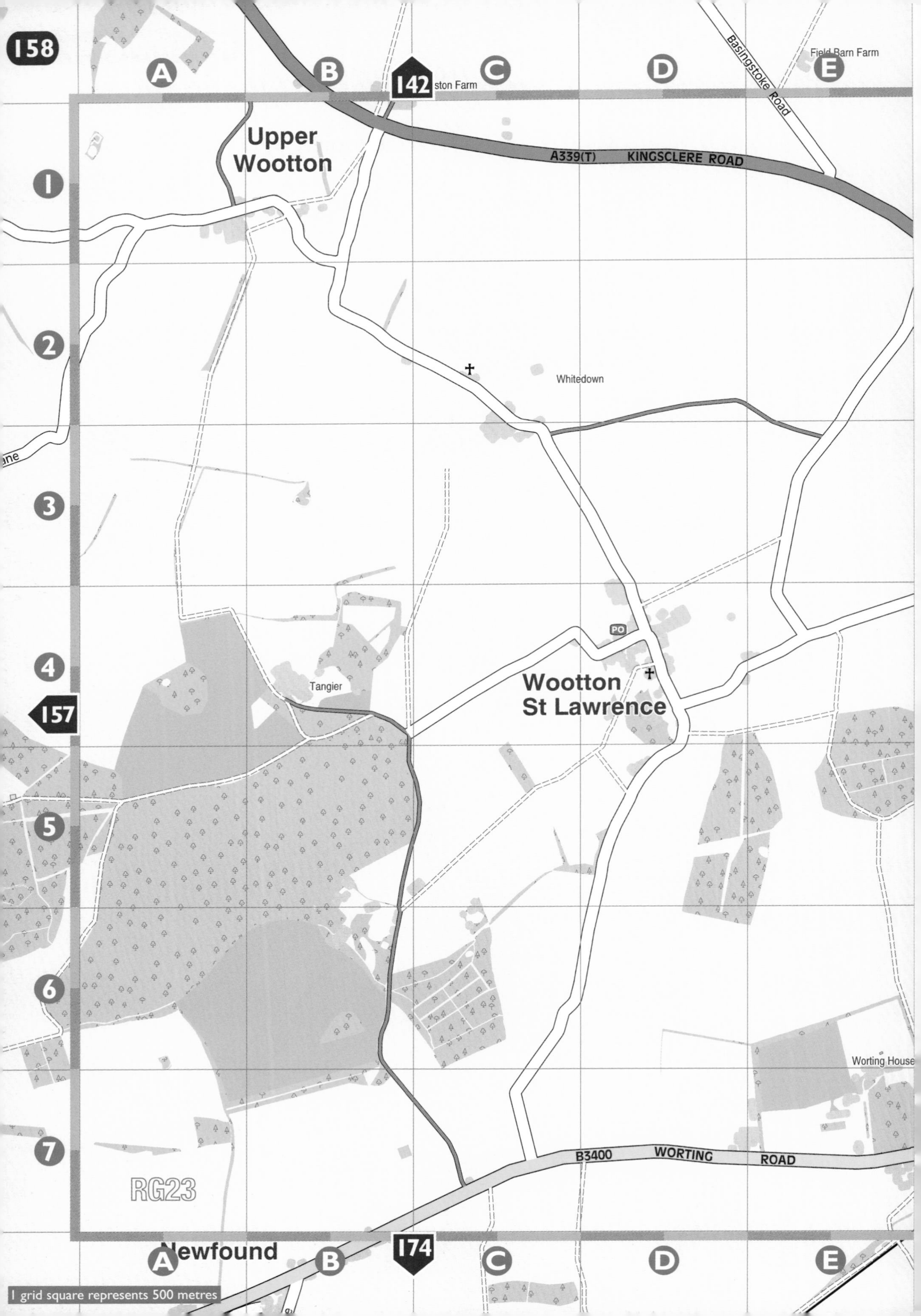
A
B
C
D
E
142
ston Farm
Field Barn Farm
Basingstoke Road
Upper
Wootton
A339(T)
KINGSCLERE ROAD
1
2
3
4
5
6
7
Whitedown
PO
Tangier
Wootton
St Lawrence
157
Worting House
B3400
WORTING
ROAD
RG23
174
Newfound
1 grid square represents 500 metres

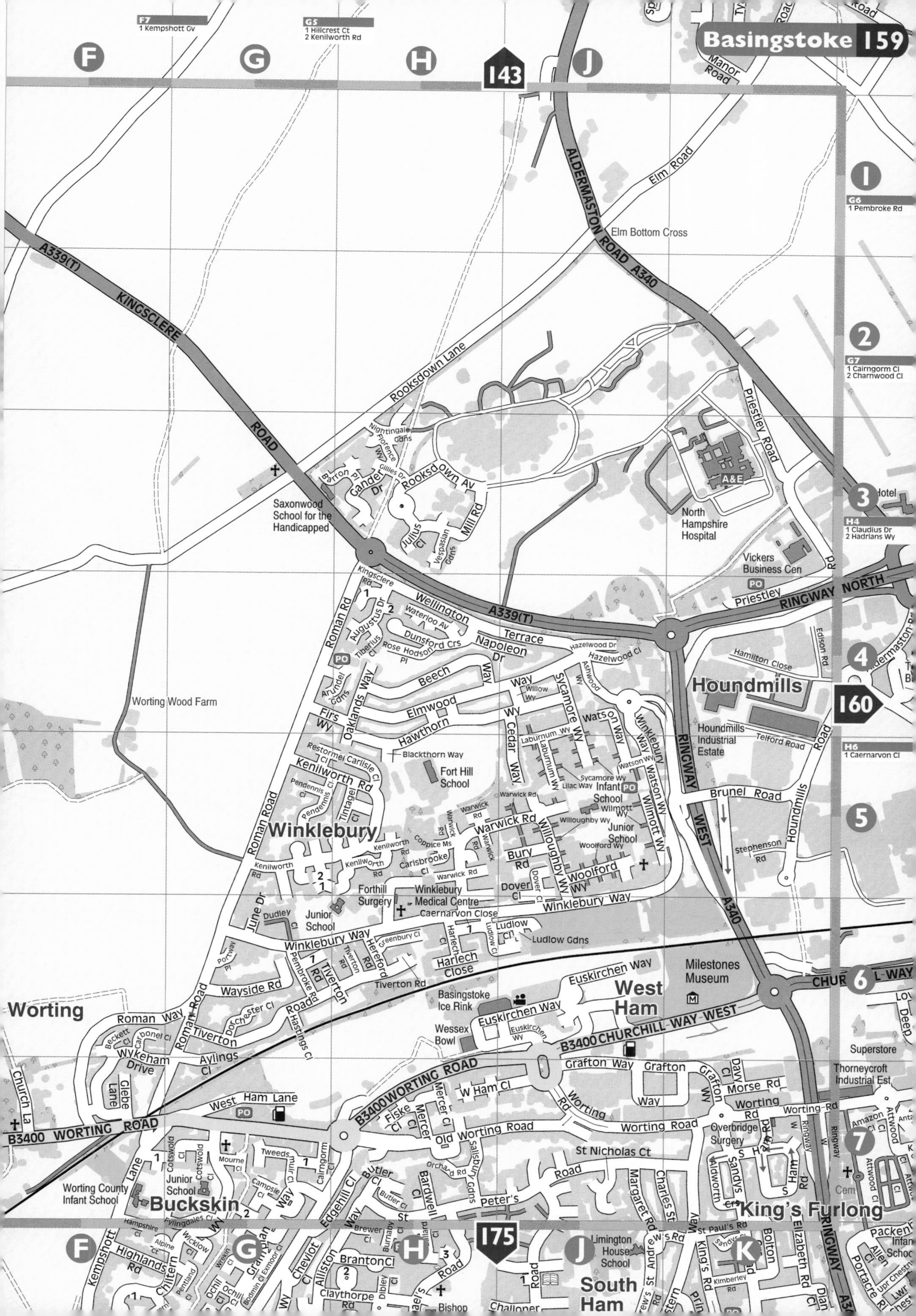
Basingstoke 159
F7
1 Kempshott Gv
G5
1 Hillcrest Ct
2 Kenilworth Rd
F
G
H
143
J
I
G6
1 Pembroke Rd
2
G7
1 Cairngorm Cl
2 Charnwood Cl
3
H4
1 Claudius Dr
2 Hadrians Wy
4
160
H6
1 Caernarvon Cl
5
6
7
A339(T) KINGSCLERE ROAD
ALDERMASTON ROAD A340
Elm Road
Elm Bottom Cross
Rooksdown Lane
Manor Road
Priestley Road
A&E
North Hampshire Hospital
Hotel
Vickers Business Cen
PO
Priestley
RINGWAY NORTH
Saxonwood School for the Handicapped
Nightingale Gdns
Florence Wy
Barron Pl
Gillies Dr
Gander Dr
Rooksdown Av
Mill Rd
Julius Cl
Vespasian Gdns
Kingsclere
Roman Rd
Augustus Dr
Wellington
Waterloo Av
A339(T)
Terrace
Napoleon Dr
Dunsford Crs
Rose Hodson Pl
Tiberius Cl
Hazelwood Dr
Hazelwood Cl
Ashwood Wy
Hamilton Close
Edison Rd
Houndmills
Houndmills Industrial Estate
Telford Road
Road
Arundel Gdns
Beech Way
Oaklands Way
Willow Wy
Sycamore Wy
Watson Way
Winklebury Way
Firs Wy
Elmwood Wy
Hawthorn
Cedar Way
Laburnum Wy
Worting Wood Farm
Blackthorn Way
Fort Hill School
Restormel Cl
Carlisle Cl
Kenilworth Rd
Pendennis Cl
Tintagel Cl
Watson Wy
Sycamore Wy
Lilac Way
Infant School
Wilmott Wy
Junior School
Wilmott Wy
RINGWAY WEST
Brunel Road
Houndmills
Warwick Rd
Willoughby Wy
Woolford Wy
Stephenson Rd
Roman Road
Winklebury
Kenilworth
Coppice Ms
Carisbrooke Cl
Bury Rd
Dover Cl
Woolford Wy
Kenilworth Rd
Forthill Surgery
Winklebury Medical Centre
Caernarvon Close
Winklebury Way
June Dr
Dudley Cl
Junior School
Ludlow Cl
Ludlow Gdns
Harlech Cl
A340
Winklebury Way
Greenbury Cl
Hereford Rd
Tiverton Rd
Portway Pl
Pembroke Rd
Harlech Close
Milestones Museum
Euskirchen Way
West Ham
CHURCHILL WAY
Wayside Rd
Tiverton Rd
Basingstoke Ice Rink
Euskirchen Way
Worting
Roman Way
Roman Road
Dorchester Cl
Hastings Cl
Wessex Bowl
B3400 CHURCHILL WAY WEST
Beckett Cl
Carbonel Cl
Tiverton
Aylings Cl
Wykeham Drive
Superstore
Thorneycroft Industrial Est
Church La
Glebe Lane
B3400 WORTING ROAD
Grafton Way
Grafton Way
Davy Cl
Morse Rd
West Ham Lane
W Ham Cl
Mercer Cl
Fiske Cl
Worting Rd
B3400 WORTING ROAD
Old Worting Road
Worting Road
Overbridge Surgery
Amazon Cl
Attwood Cl
B3400 WORTING ROAD
Cotswold Cl
Tweeds
Cairngorm Cl
Mourne Cl
Campsie Cl
St Nicholas Ct
Road
Orchard Rd
Salisbury Gdns
Aldworth Cres
Sandys Rd
Ham Rd
Junior School
Worting County Infant School
Buckskin
Butler Cl
Bardwell Cl
Peter's
Margaret Rd
Charles St
King's Furlong
Cem
Hampshire
Fylingdales Cl
Edgehill Cl
Way
Brewer Cl
175
Limington House School
St Paul's Rd
Packenham
Kempshott
Highlands Rd
Chiltern
Wicklow
Alpine
Bodmin Cl
Exmoor Cl
Ochil Cl
Chevlot
Alliston Way
BrantonCl
Claythorpe Rd
Dibley Cl
Road
Bishop
Challoner
South Ham
King's Rd
Kimberley Rd
Bolton
Elizabeth Rd
Portacre Rise

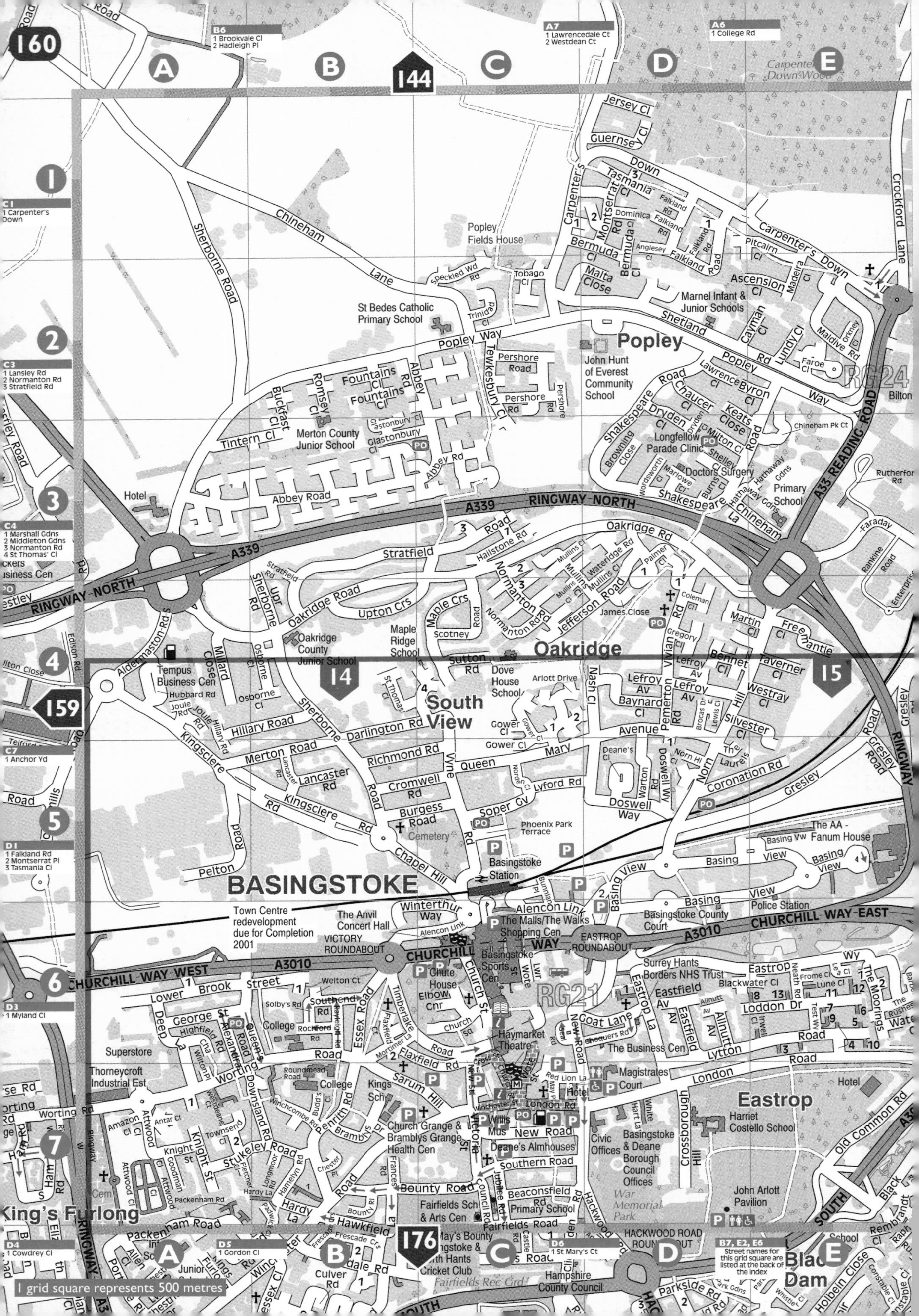

160
144
159
176
14
15
A
B
C
D
E
1
2
3
4
5
6
7
B6
1 Brookvale Cl
2 Hadleigh Pl
A7
1 Lawrencedale Ct
2 Westdean Ct
A6
1 College Rd
C1
1 Carpenter's Down
C3
1 Lansley Rd
2 Normanton Rd
3 Stratfield Rd
C4
1 Marshall Gdns
2 Middleton Gdns
3 Normanton Rd
4 St Thomas' Cl
C7
1 Anchor Yd
D1
1 Falkland Rd
2 Montserrat Pl
3 Tasmania Cl
D3
1 Myland Cl
D4
1 Cowdrey Cl
D5
1 Gordon Cl
D6
1 St Mary's Ct
B7, E2, E6
Street names for this grid square are listed at the back of the index
Carpenters Down Wood
Jersey Cl
Guernsey Cl
Tasmania Cl
Down
Falkland Rd
Dominica
Montserrat Rd
Bermuda Cl
Bermuda
Malta Close
Anglesey Cl
Falkland Road
Pitcairn Cl
Carpenter's Down
Crockford Lane
Ascension Cl
Madeira Cl
Marnel Infant & Junior Schools
Shetland
Cayman Cl
Lundy Cl
Maldive Rd
Orkney Cl
Faroe Cl
RG24
Bilton
Popley Fields House
Chineham Lane
Sherborne Road
Speckled Wd Rd
Tobago Cl
Trinidad Cl
St Bedes Catholic Primary School
Popley Way
Popley
Popley Rd
John Hunt of Everest Community School
Tewkesbury Cl
Pershore Road
Pershore Rd
Fountains Cl
Romsey Cl
Buckfast Cl
Abbey Rd
Glastonbury Cl
Merton County Junior School
Tintern Cl
Abbey Road
Hotel
Lawrence Cl
Byron Cl
Chaucer Cl
Keats Close
Shakespeare Road
Dryden Cl
Milton Cl
Longfellow Parade Clinic
Browning Close
Shelley Cl
Wordsworth Cl
Marlowe Cl
Doctors Surgery
Burns Cl
Hathaway Gdns
Primary School
Chineham Pk Ct
A33 READING ROAD
Rutherford Rd
Shakespeare
Chineham La
Faraday
Rankine Road
Enterprise
A339 RINGWAY NORTH
RINGWAY NORTH
A339
Oakridge Rd
Hailstone Rd
Stratfield Road
Stratfield Rd
Mullins Cl
Wateridge Rd
Palmer Cl
Normanton Rd
Jefferson Road
Coleman Cl
James Close
Martin Cl
Freemantle Cl
Upr Sherborne Rd
Oakridge Road
Upton Crs
Maple Crs
Scotney Road
Oakridge County Junior School
Maple Ridge School
Oakridge
Sutton Rd
Dove House School
Arlott Drive
Nash Cl
Vivian Rd
Gregory Cl
Lefroy Av
Bennet Cl
Taverner Cl
Westray Cl
Aldermaston Rd
Edison Rd
Tempus Business Cen
Millard Close
Osborne Cl
Hubbard Rd
Joule Rd
Hillary Rd
Hillary Road
Kingsclere
Merton Road
Sherborne Road
Darlington Rd
St Thomas' Cl
South View
Gower Cl
Baynard Cl
Pemberton Rd
Brocas Dr
Lewis Cl
Silvester Cl
Avenue
Mary
Deane's Cl
Doswell Way
Norn Hill
The Laurels
Coronation Rd
Gresley Road
Gresley
RINGWAY
Richmond Rd
Lancaster Rd
Queen
Norden Cl
Lyford Rd
Warton Rd
Cromwell Rd
Vyne Road
Kingsclere Rd
Burgess Road
Soper Gv
Phoenix Park Terrace
Cemetery
Chapel Hill
Pelton Road
Basingstoke Station
BASINGSTOKE
Bunnian Pl
Basing View
The AA - Fanum House
Police Station
Town Centre redevelopment due for Completion 2001
The Anvil Concert Hall
Winterthur Way
Alencon Link
VICTORY ROUNDABOUT
The Malls/The Walks Shopping Cen
EASTROP ROUNDABOUT
Basingstoke County Court
A3010 CHURCHILL WAY EAST
CHURCHILL WAY
CHURCHILL WAY WEST
A3010
Basingstoke Sports Cen
Chute House
Elbow Cnr
Church St
Wote St
Surrey Hants Borders NHS Trust
Eastrop Wy
Neath Rd
Frome Cl
Lea Cl
Lune Cl
Blackwater Cl
The Moorings
RG21
Lower Brook Street
Welton Ct
Solby's Rd
Southend Rd
Deep La
George St
Highfield Rd
College Rd
Rochford Rd
Essex Road
Timberlake Rd
Eastfield Av
Eastrop La
Allnutt Av
Loddon Dr
Coat Lane
New Road
Chequers Rd
Haymarket Theatre
Mortimer La
Flaxfield Rd
Cross St
Superstore
Thorneycroft Industrial Est
Worting Road
Downsland Rd
Roundmead Road
College
Kings Sch
Sarum Hill
Winchcombe Rd
Penrith Rd
Red Lion La
May Pl
Hotel
Magistrates Court
London Road
The Business Cen
Lytton Road
Eastrop
Harriet Costello School
Old Common Rd
Worting Rd
Antar Cl
Amazon Cl
Attwood Cl
Westdeane Ct
Townsend Cl
Knight St
Stukeley Road
Brambys Dr
Church Grange & Bramblys Grange Health Cen
Winchester St
Willis Mus
London Rd
New Road
Victoria St
Deane's Almshouses
Southern Road
Civic Offices
Basingstoke & Deane Borough Council Offices
Crossborough Hill
Goodman Cl
Packenham Rd
Hardy La
Chester Pl
Frances Rd
Bounty Road
Fairfields Sch & Arts Cen
Beaconsfield Rd
Primary School
Hackwood Rd
War Memorial Park
John Arlott Pavilion
SOUTH
Black Dam
King's Furlong
Cem
Packenham Road
Hawkfield
Frescade Crs
Council Rd
Fairfields Road
HACKWOOD ROAD ROUNDABOUT
Rembrandt Cl
Holbein Close
Constable Cl
Junior School
Culver Rd
Fairfields Rec Grd
Hampshire County Council
Parkside Rd
1 grid square represents 500 metres

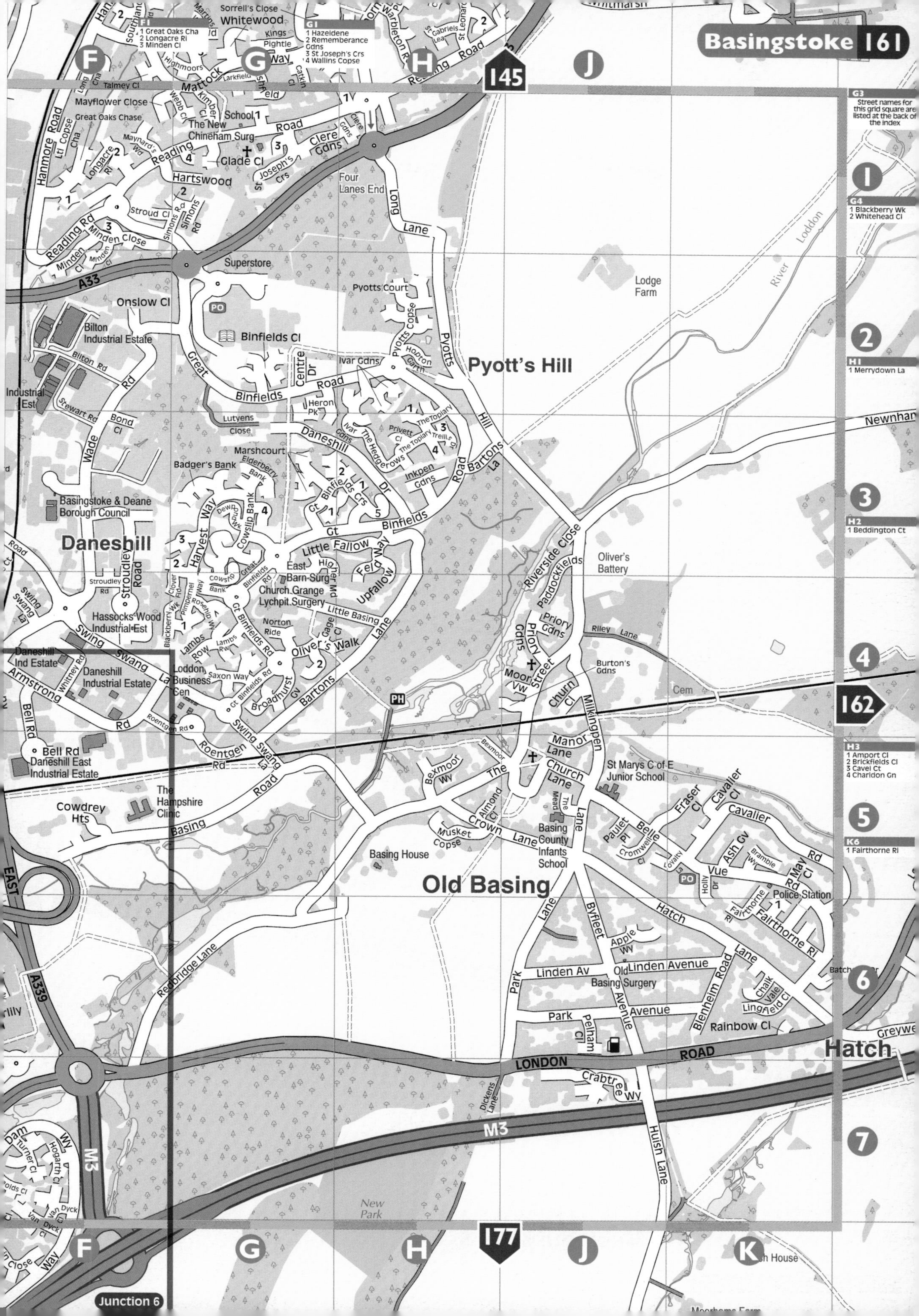

Whitewood

F | G | H | J

145

1 Great Oaks Cha
2 Longacre Ri
3 Minden Cl

G1
1 Hazeledene
2 Remembrance Gdns
3 St Joseph's Crs
4 Wallins Copse

Sorrell's Close

kings Pightle

Mayflower Close

Great Oaks Chase

Highmoors

Maynard's

The New Chineham Surg

School

Glade Cl

Joseph's Crs

Clere Gdns

Hartswood

Stroud Cl

Simons

Minden Close

Reading Rd

Minden Cl

Longace Ri

Four Lanes End

Long Lane

G4
1 Blackberry Wk
2 Whitehead Cl

River Loddon

Onslow Cl

Bilton Industrial Estate

Superstore

PO

Binfields Cl

Pyotts Court

Pyotts Copse

Lodge Farm

Pyott's Hill

H1
1 Merrydown La

Bilton Rd

Stewart Rd

Great Binfields Road

Centre Dr

Lutyens Close

Ivar Gdns

Privett Cl

The Topiary

Heron Pk

Hodson Gdns

Newnham

Bond Cl

Wade Rd

Daneshill Dr

Marshcourt

Badger's Bank

Elderberry Bank

The Hedgerows

Inkpen Gdns

Bartons Rd

Bartons La

H2
1 Beddington Ct

Basingstoke & Deane Borough Council

Danesbill

Harvest Way

Cowslip Bank

Binfields Crs

Binfields Rd

Gt Binfields Rd

Little Fallow

East Barn Surg

Church.Grange Lychpit.Surgery

Little Basing

Upfallow Lane

Hill Road

Riverside Close

Paddockfields

Oliver's Battery

Stroudley Road

Hassocks Wood Industrial Est

Lambs Row

Blackberry Wk

Saxon Way

Norton Ride

Oliver's Walk

Priory Gdns

Priory Gdns

Moors Vw

Riley Lane

Burton's Gdns

Cem

162

Daneshill Ind Estate

Daneshill Industrial Estate

Armstrong Rd

Loddon Business Cen

Broadhurst Gv

Bartons

Roentgen Rd

Swing Swang La

PH

Bexmoor

Church Cl

Milkingpen Lane

Manor Lane

St Marys C of E Junior School

Fraser Cl

Cavalier Cl

Cavalier

H3
1 Amport Cl
2 Brickfields Cl
3 Cavel Ct
4 Charldon Gn

Bell Rd

Daneshill East Industrial Estate

Cowdrey Hts

The Hampshire Clinic

Roentgen Rd

Basing Rd

Bexmoor Wy

The Almond Cl

Church Lane

The Mead

Basing County Infants School

Paulet Pl

Belle Vue

Cromwell

Ash Gv

Bramble Wy

May Rd

Fairthorne Ri

Police Station

K6
1 Fairthorne Ri

Musket Copse

Crown Lane

PO

Holly Dr

Fairthorne Ri

EAST

A339

Bell Rd

Basing House

Old Basing

Park Lane

Byfleet Lane

Linden Av

Old Linden Avenue

Basing Surgery

Hatch Lane

Chalk Vale

Lingfield Cl

6

M3

Reedbridge Lane

Park Avenue

Pelham

Blenheim Road

Avenue

Rainbow Cl

Hatch

Greywell

LONDON ROAD

Dickens Lane

Crabtree Wy

Hulsh Lane

Batchelor

Dam

Turner Cl

Hogarth Cl

Van Dyck

M3

New Park

177

Moorhams Farm

Junction 6

F | G | H | J | K

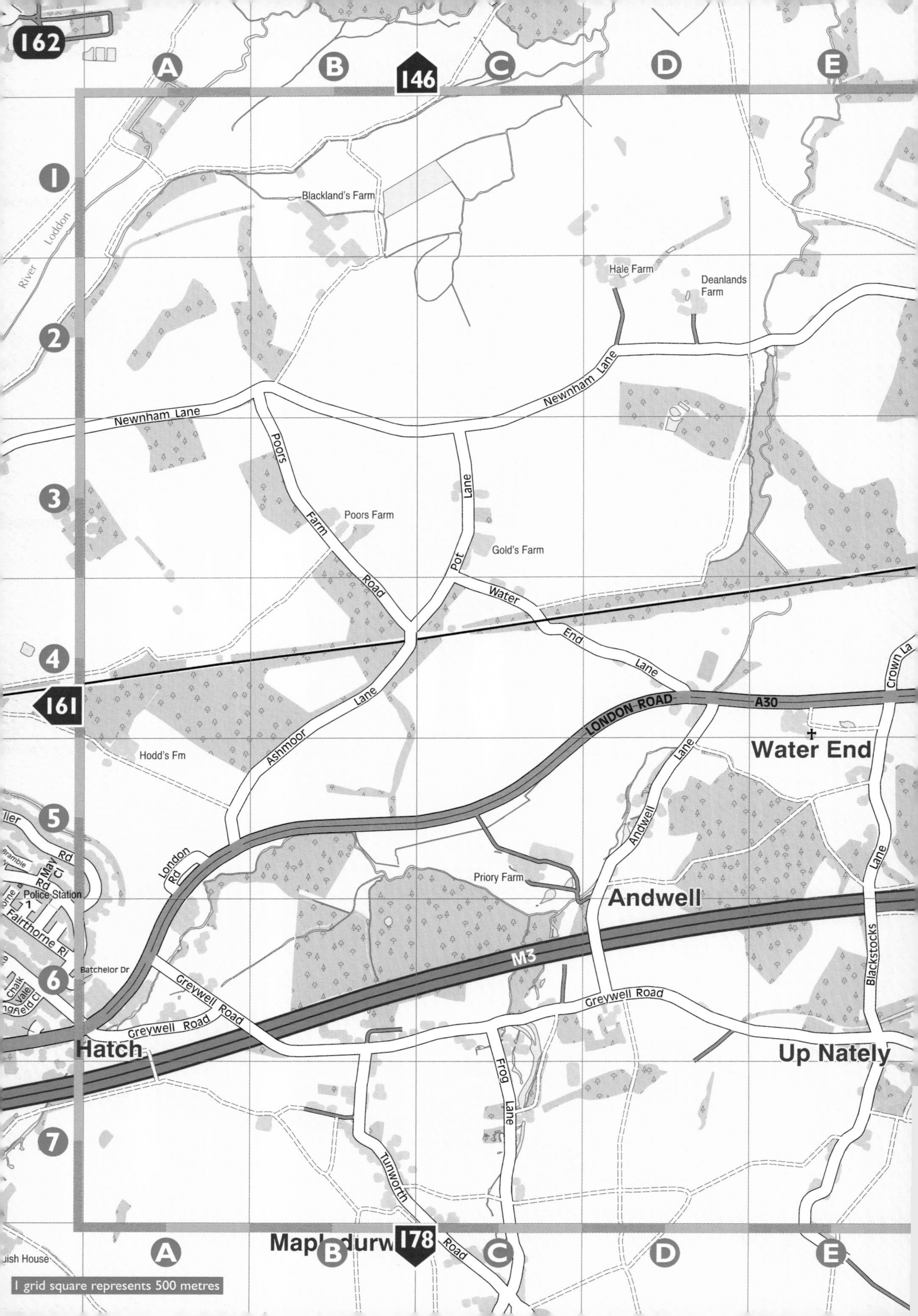

A   B   146   C   D   E

1

River Loddon

Blackland's Farm

2

Hale Farm

Deanlands Farm

Newnham Lane

Newnham Lane

3

Poors Lane

Poors Farm

Farm Road

Pot Lane

Gold's Farm

Water

4

End

Lane

Ashmoor Lane

LONDON ROAD   A30   Crown La

161

Hodd's Fm

Water End

5

London Rd

May Rd
Police Station
Fairthorne Rl
Batchelor Dr

Priory Farm

Andwell Lane

Andwell

Blackstocks Lane

6

Greywell Road

M3

Greywell Road

Greywell Road

Hatch

Frog Lane

Up Nately

7

Tunworth Road

A   B   Mapledurw 178   C   D   E

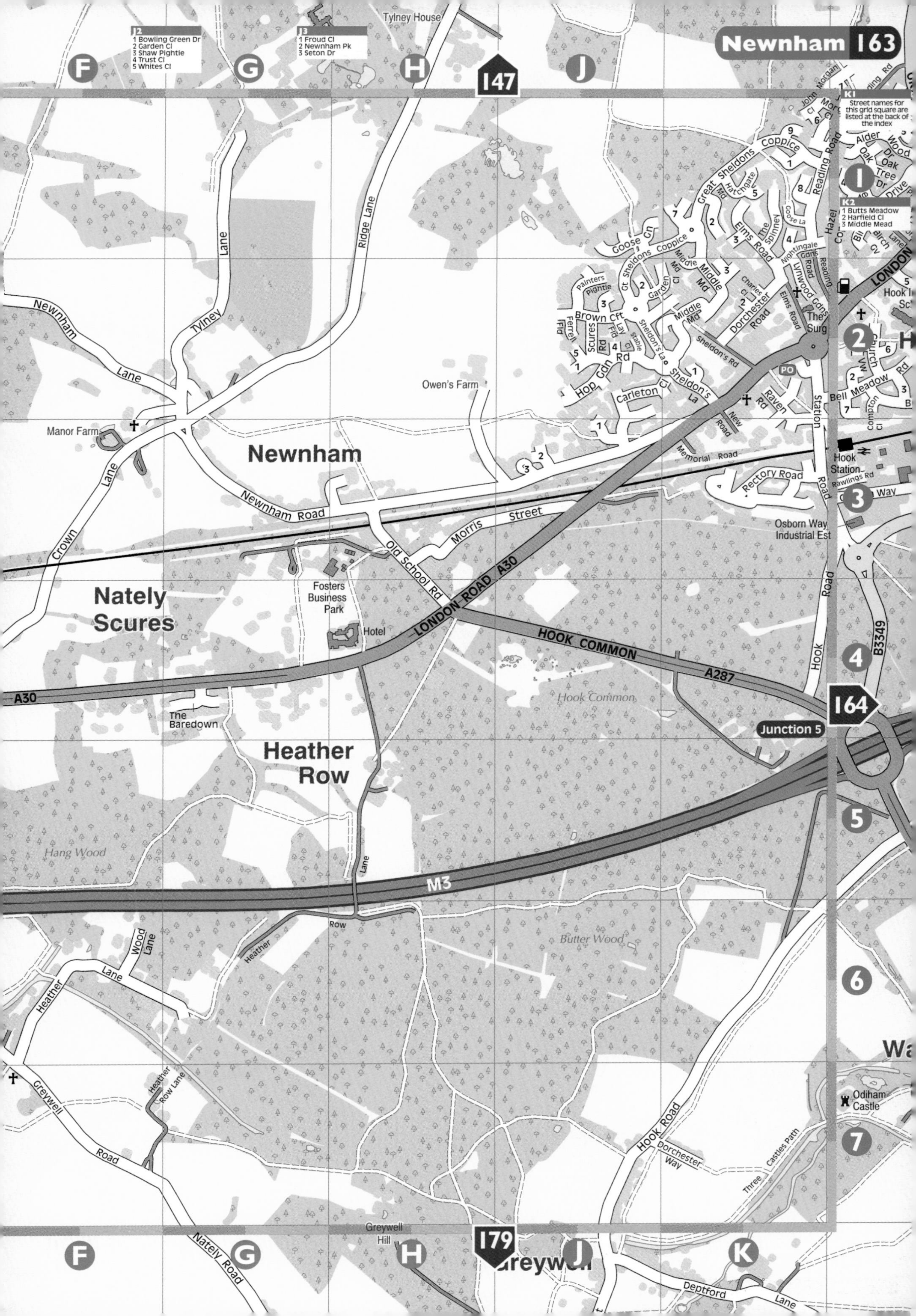
J2
1 Bowling Green Dr
2 Garden Cl
3 Shaw Pightle
4 Trust Cl
5 Whites Cl
J3
1 Froud Cl
2 Newnham Pk
3 Seton Dr
K1
Street names for this grid square are listed at the back of the index
K2
1 Butts Meadow
2 Harfield Cl
3 Middle Mead
147
164
179
F
G
H
J
K
1
2
3
4
5
6
7
Tylney House
Tylney Lane
Ridge Lane
Newnham Lane
Crown Lane
Manor Farm
Newnham
Newnham Road
Owen's Farm
Great Sheldons Coppice
Gt Sheldons Coppice
Goose Gn
Painters Pightle
Brown Cft
Ferrell Fld
Scures Rd
Hop Gdn Rd
Carleton Cl
Sheldon's La
Sheldon's Rd
Elms Road
Dorchester Road
Lynwood Gdns
Reading Road
Station Road
Raven Rd
New Road
Memorial Road
Rectory Road
Hook Station
Rawlings Rd
Bell Meadow Rd
Alder
Oak Tree Dr
Osborn Way Industrial Est
Morris Street
Old School Rd
LONDON ROAD A30
Fosters Business Park
Hotel
Nately Scures
A30
HOOK COMMON
A287
Hook Common
Hook Road
B3349
Junction 5
The Baredown
Heather Row
Hang Wood
M3
Row Lane
Heather Row
Wood Lane
Heather Lane
Butter Wood
Heather Row Lane
Greywell Road
Nately Road
Greywell Hill
Hook Road
Dorchester Way
Three Castles Path
Odiham Castle
Deptford Lane

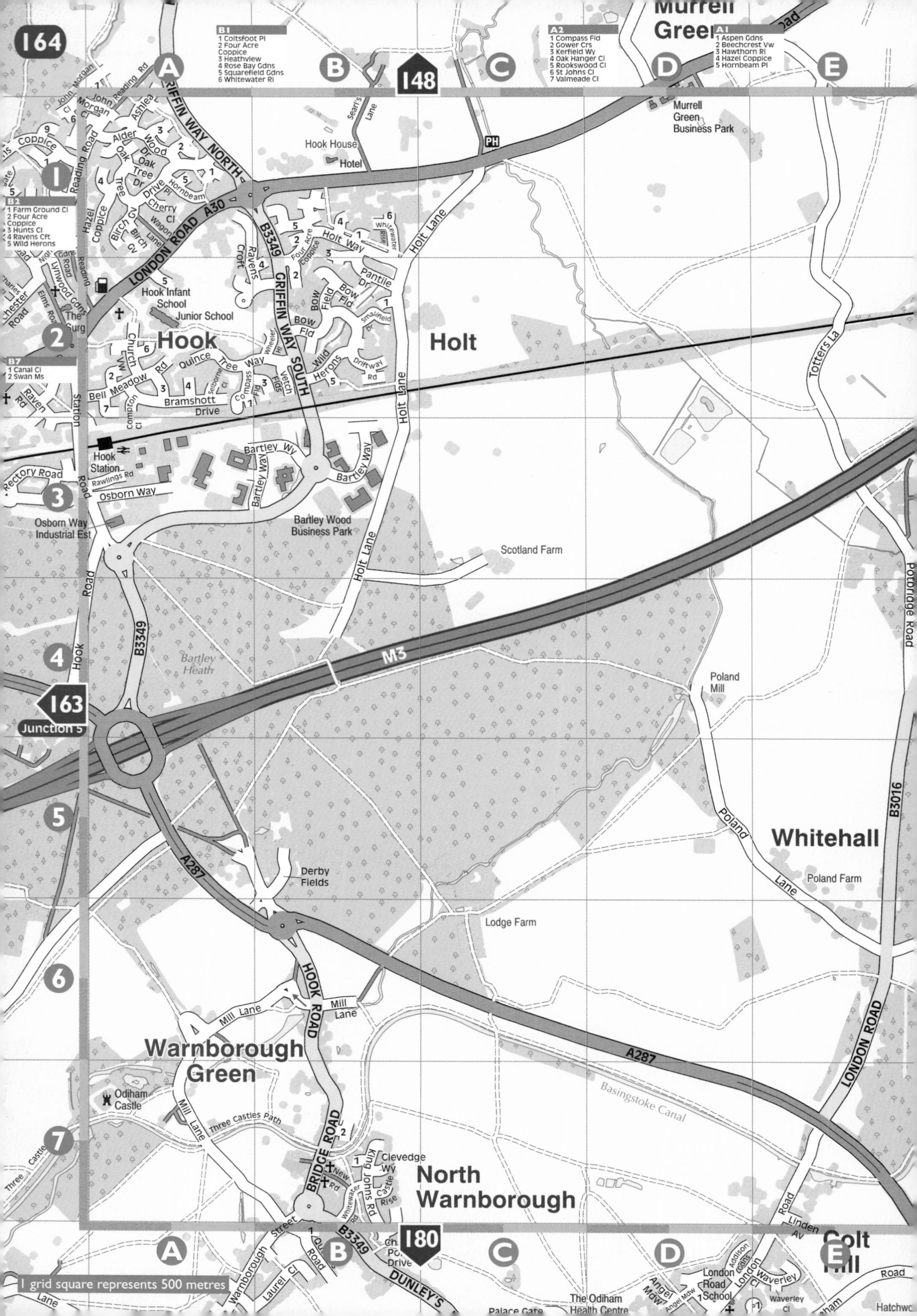
164
A
B
C
D
E
148
B1
1 Coltsfoot Pl
2 Four Acre Coppice
3 Heathview
4 Rose Bay Gdns
5 Squarefield Gdns
6 Whitewater Ri
A2
1 Compass Fld
2 Gower Crs
3 Kerfield Wy
4 Oak Hanger Cl
5 Rookswood Cl
6 St Johns Cl
7 Valmeade Cl
A1
1 Aspen Gdns
2 Beechcrest Vw
3 Hawthorn Ri
4 Hazel Coppice
5 Hornbeam Pl
B2
1 Farm Ground Cl
2 Four Acre Coppice
3 Hunts Cl
4 Ravens Cft
5 Wild Herons
B7
1 Canal Cl
2 Swan Ms
Murrell Green
Murrell Green Business Park
Hook House Hotel
Sear's Lane
PH
GRIFFIN WAY NORTH
GRIFFIN WAY SOUTH
LONDON ROAD A30
B3349
Holt Lane
Holt Way
Pantile Dr
Bow Field
Bow Fld
Smallfield Dr
Driftway Rd
Wild Herons
Vetch Flds
Wheeler Hl
Hook
Holt
Hook Infant School
Junior School
John Morgan Cl
John Reading Rd
Reading Road
Alder Wood Dr
Ashlea
Oak Tree Dr
Tree Drive
Hornbeam Pl
Cherry Cl
Wagon Lane
Hazel Coppice
Birch Gv
Ravens Croft
Four Acre Coppice
Lynwood Gdns
Elms Road
The Surg
Church Vw
Quince Tree Way
Bell Meadow Rd
Bramshott Drive
Compass Fld
Compton Cl
Selborne Cl
Station Road
Raven Rd
Rectory Road
Hook Station
Rawlings Rd
Osborn Way
Osborn Way Industrial Est
Bartley Wy
Bartley Way
Bartley Wood Business Park
Scotland Farm
Totters La
Potbridge Road
Hook Road
Bartley Heath
M3
163
Junction 5
Poland Mill
Poland Lane
Whitehall
Poland Farm
B3016
A287
Derby Fields
Lodge Farm
HOOK ROAD
Mill Lane
Warnborough Green
Odiham Castle
Mill Lane
Three Castles Path
Basingstoke Canal
LONDON ROAD
BRIDGE ROAD
Clevedge Wy
King Johns Rd
Castle Rise
New Rd
Whitewater Rd
North Warnborough
180
Colt Hill
Linden Av
Warnborough Street
Laurel Cl
B3349
DUNLEY'S
Angel Mdw
London Road School
Waverley Cl
The Odiham Health Centre
Palace Gate
Hatchwo
1 grid square represents 500 metres
1
2
3
4
5
6
7

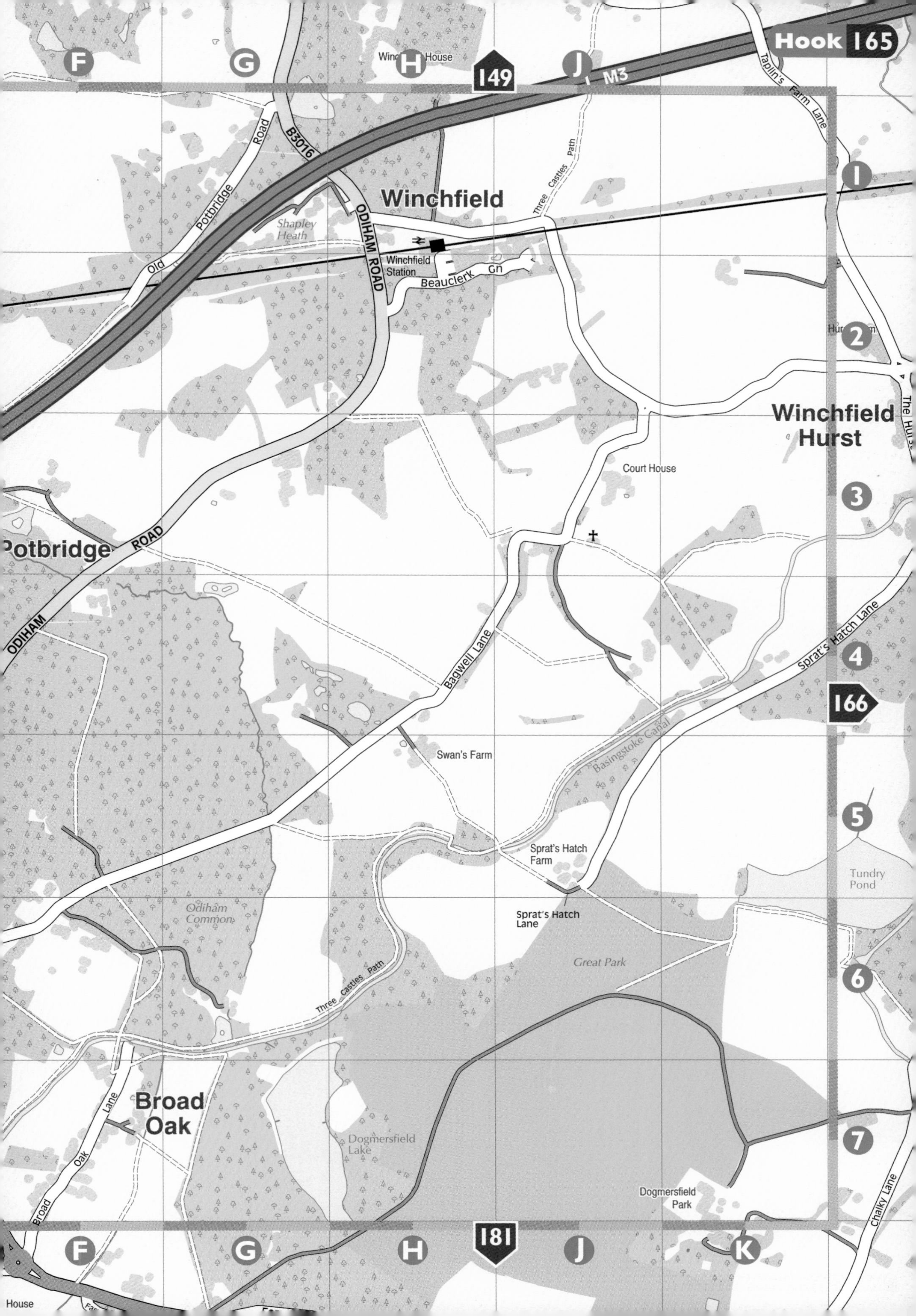

Hook 165
149
166
181
F
G
H
J
K
I
2
3
4
5
6
7
M3
Winchfield
Winchfield Station
Beauclerk Gn
Shapley Heath
Old Potbridge Road
B3016
ODIHAM ROAD
Three Castles Path
Taplin's Farm Lane
Winchfield Hurst
The Hurst
Court House
Potbridge
ODIHAM ROAD
Bagwell Lane
Sprat's Hatch Lane
Basingstoke Canal
Swan's Farm
Sprat's Hatch Farm
Tundry Pond
Odiham Common
Great Park
Three Castles Path
Broad Oak
Broad Oak Lane
Dogmersfield Lake
Dogmersfield Park
Chalky Lane
House

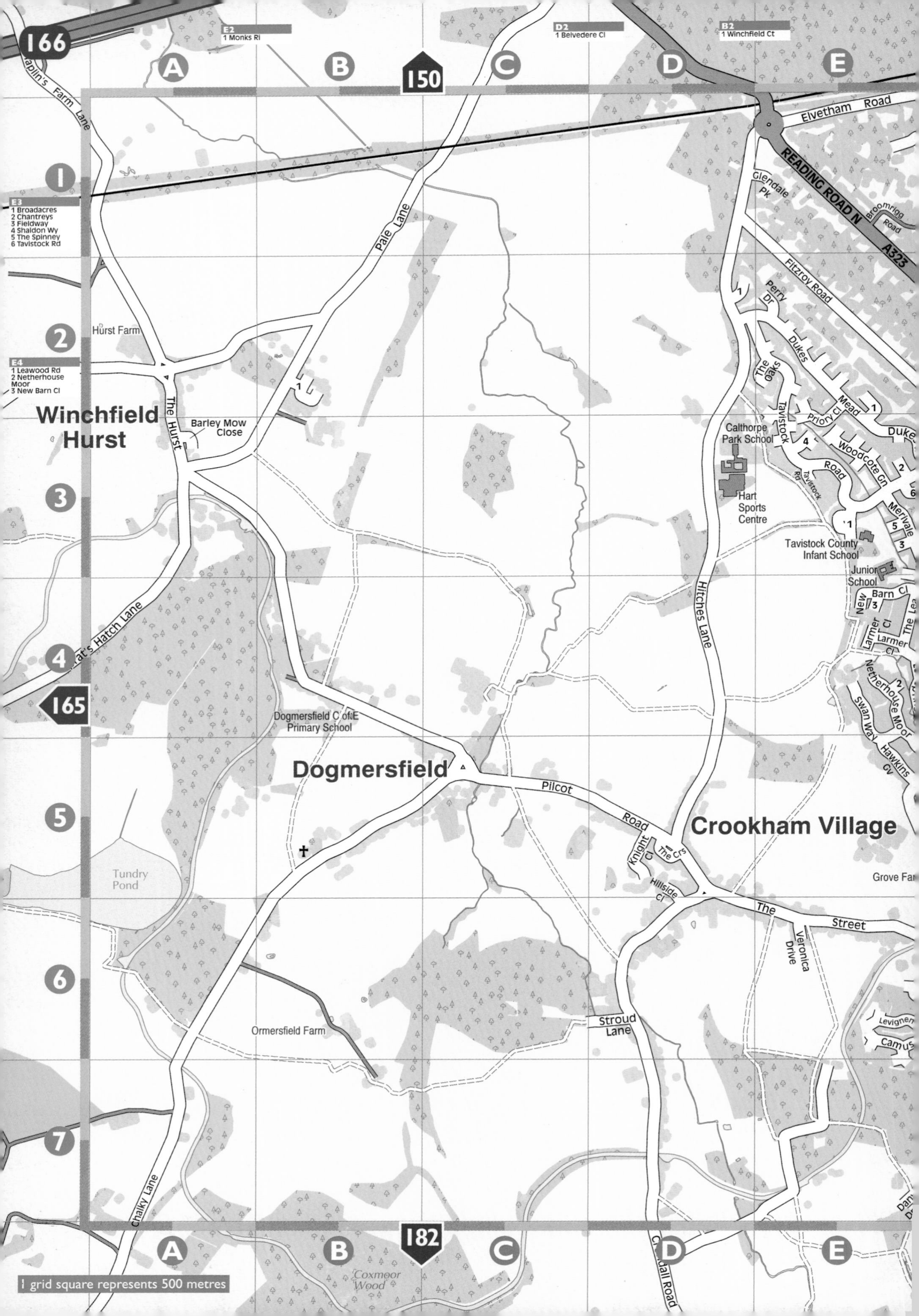

A B 150 C D E

Elvetham Road

READING ROAD N

A323

Broomrigg Road

1

I

E3
1 Broadacres
2 Chantreys
3 Fieldway
4 Shaldon Wy
5 The Spinney
6 Tavistock Rd

Pale Lane

Glendale Pk

Fitzroy Road

Perry Dr

The Oaks

Dukes Mead

2

Hurst Farm

1

Calthorpe Park School

Tavistock Rd

Priory Cl

Woodcote Gn

Duke

Winchfield Hurst

The Hurst

Barley Mow Close

Hart Sports Centre

4

5

Merivale

3

3

Hat's Hatch Lane

Tavistock County Infant School

Junior School

New Barn Cl

3

The Lea

4

165

Dogmersfield C of E Primary School

Dogmersfield

Hitches Lane

Larmer Cl

Netherhouse Moor

Swan Way

Hawkins Gv

5

Tundry Pond

†

Pilcot Road

Crookham Village

Knight Cl

The Crs

Hillside Cl

Grove Farm

The Street

Veronica Drive

Levignen

Camus

6

Ormersfield Farm

Stroud Lane

7

Chalky Lane

A B 182 C Crondall Road D E

Coxmoor Wood

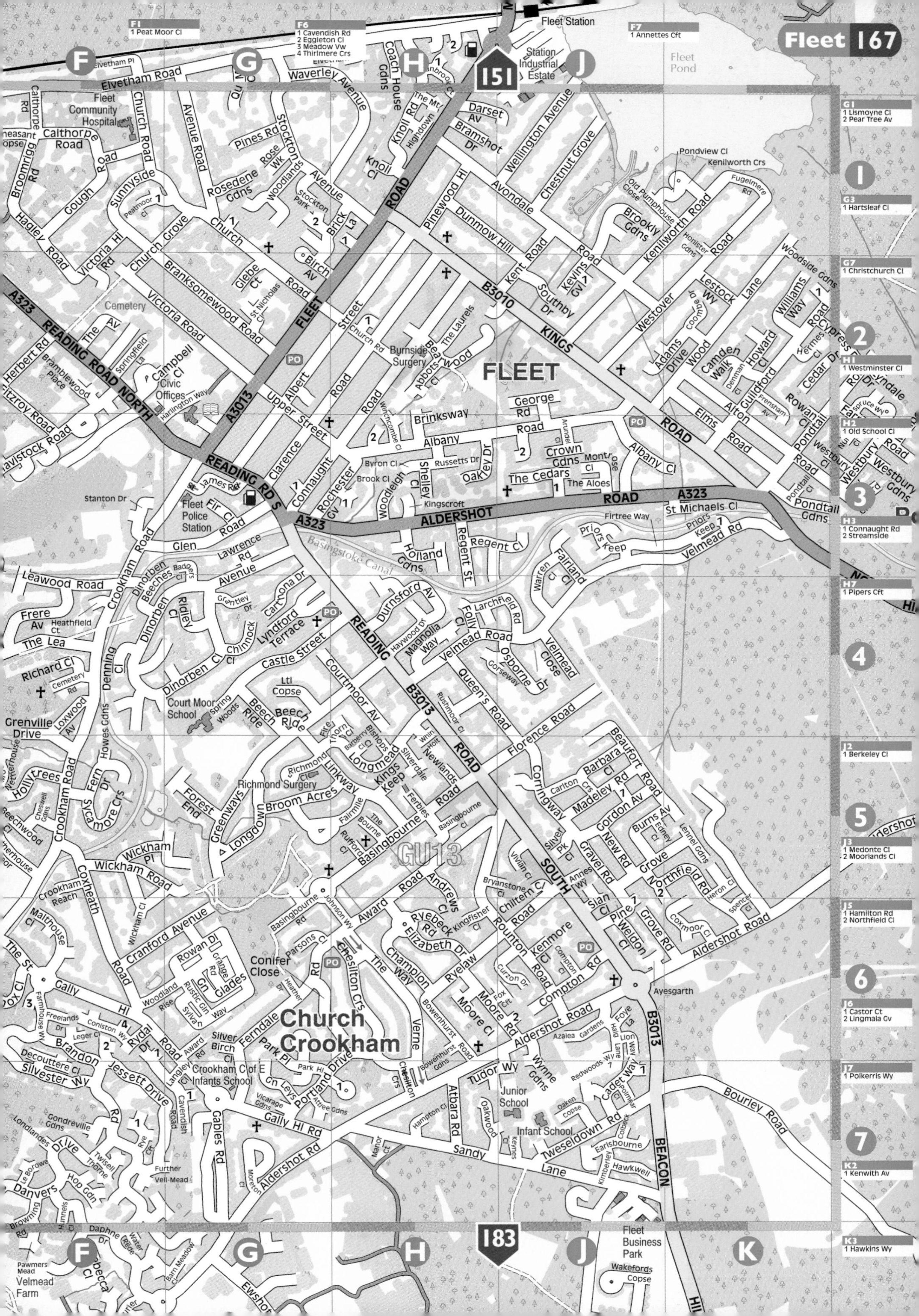

F1 1 Peat Moor Cl
F6 1 Cavendish Rd 2 Eggleton Cl 3 Meadow Vw 4 Thirlmere Crs
F7 1 Annettes Cft
Fleet Station
Station Industrial Estate
Fleet Pond
151
F
G
H
J
Elvetham Pl
Elvetham Road
Waverley Avenue
Coach House Gdns
Fleet Community Hospital
Calthorpe Rd
Calthorpe Road
Church Road
Avenue Road
Stockton Avenue
Pines Rd
Rose Wk
Woodlands
Rosedene Gdns
Knoll Rd
Highdown
The Mt
Darset Av
Bramshot Dr
Knoll Cl
Wellington Avenue
Chestnut Grove
Pondview Cl
Kenilworth Crs
Fugelmere Rd
Old Pumphouse Close
Broomrigg Rd
Gough Road
Sunnyside
Peatmoor Cl
Hagley Road
Victoria Hl Rd
Church Grove
Church Road
Stockton Park
Brick La
Birch Av
Fleet Road
Pinewood Hl
Dunmow Hill
Avondale
Brookly Gdns
Kenilworth Road
Honister Gdns
Woodside Gdns
Branksomewood Road
Glebe Ct
St Nicholas Cl
Kent Road
Kevins Gv
Southby Dr
Lestock Wy
Westover
Coombe Dr
Lane
Williams Way
A323
Reading Road North
Cemetery
Victoria Road
The Av
Springfield La
Church Rd
Street
Burnside Surgery
Beaumont Wood
The Laurels
B3010 Kings Road
Adams Drive
Wood
Camden Walk
Denman Cl
Howard Cl
Hermes Cl
Cypress
Cedar Dr
Herbert Rd
Bramblewood Place
Campbell Cl
Civic Offices
Harlington Way
A3013
Albert
Upper Street
Road
Abbots Cl
FLEET
George Rd
Road
Elms
Alton
Guildford
Frensham Av
Rowan Cl
Pondtail
Fitzroy Road
Tavistock Road
Clarence
Winchcombe Cl
Brinksway
Albany
Arundel Cl
Albany Cl
Road
Westbury
Reading Rd S
St James Rd
Connaught
Rochester Gv
Byron Cl
Brook Cl
Russetts Dr
Oakley Dr
Crown Gdns
Montrose Cl
The Cedars
The Aloes
Shelley Cl
Woodleigh
Kingscroft
Road
Pondtail Gdns
Stanton Dr
Fleet Police Station
Fir Cl
Road
A323 Aldershot
Firtree Way
St Michaels Cl
Priors Keep
Velmead Rd
Glen
Lawrence Rd
Avenue
Holland Gdns
Regent St
Regent Cl
Basingstoke Canal
Warren Cl
Fairland Cl
Leawood Road
Crookham Road
Dinorben Beeches
Badgers Cl
Dinorben Cl
Ridley Cl
Grantley Dr
Carmona Dr
Durnsford Av
Larchfield Rd
Folly Cl
Frere Av
Heathfield Ct
The Lea
Lyndford Terrace
Chinnock Cl
Reading
Haywood Dr
Magnolia Way
Velmead Road
Osborne Dr
Velmead Close
Richard Cl
Cemetery Rd
Denning Cl
Dinorben Cl
Castle Street
Courtmoor Av
B3013
Queen's Road
Gorseway
Ltl Copse
Rushmoor Cl
Court Moor School
Spring Woods
Beech Ride
Grenville Drive
Loxwood Av
Howes Gdns
Fike Cl
Thorn Cl
Barberry Cl
Bishops Cl
Winn Holt
Newlands
Florence Road
Beaufort Road
Hollytrees
Fern Dr
Sycamore Crs
Crookham Road
Cheswell Gdns
Richmond Cl
Longmead
Silverdale
Kings Keep
Linkway
Road
Corringway
Barbara Cl
Carlton Crs
Madeley Rd
Richmond Surgery
Forest End
Broom Acres
Greenways
Longdown
Fairmile
The Bourne
Ferbies
Basingbourne Cl
Gordon Av
Burns Av
Edney Cl
Lennel Gdns
Beechwood Cl
Wickham Pl
Wickham Road
Rufford Cl
Basingbourne Road
GU13
Silver Pk Cl
Vivian Cl
Gravel Rd
New Rd
Grove
Northfield Rd
Heron Cl
South
Crookham Reach
Coxheath
Wickham Cl
Malthouse Cl
Road
Andrews Cl
Bryanstone Cl
Chiltern Cl
Annes Wy
Slan Cl
Pine Cl
Weldon Cl
Grove Rd
Coxmoor Cl
Spencer Cl
Aldershot Road
Cranford Avenue
Rowan Dl
Grange Rd
Gn Glades
Basingbourne Cl
Johnson Wy
Award Road
Ryebeck Rd
Elizabeth Dr
Kingfisher Cl
Rounton Road
Kenmore Cl
Compton Cl
Parsons Cl
Conifer Close
Chesilton Crs
The Way
Champion Way
Ryelaw
Curzon Dr
Compton Rd
Ayesgarth
The St
Gally Hl
Farmhouse Wy
Woodland Rise
Rustic Gln
Sylvan Way
Heather Dr
Road
Rd
Fox Cft
Moore Cl
Moore Rd
Aldershot Road
B3013
Freelands Dr
Coniston Wy
Leger Cl
Rydal Dr
Brandon Rd
Decouttere Cl
Silvester Wy
Jessett Drive
Award Rd
Silver Birch Cl
Ferndale
Church Crookham
Park Pl
Park Hl
Portland Drive
Verne
Bowenhurst Road
Bowenhurst Gdns
Azalea Gardens
Foye La
Hag Lane
Lion Way
Redwoods Wy
Cadet Way
Polmear Cl
Langley Cl
Crookham C of E Infants School
Gn Leys
Vicarage Gdns
Attree Gdns
Chesilton Crs
Tudor Wy
Wynne Gdns
Junior School
Oakwood
Infant School
Oaken Copse
Tweseldown Rd
Colbeck
Earlsbourne
Hawkwell
Kimberley
Bourley Road
Beacon
Gondreville Gdns
Londlandes Drive
Twisell Thorne
Rye Cft
Cavendish Rd
Gables Rd
Gally Hl Rd
Hampton Cl
Atbara Rd
Sandy Lane
Keynes Cl
Manor Ct
Aldershot Rd
Moreton Cl
Le Borowe
Danvers
Hop Gdn
Further Vell-Mead
Browning Rd
Hunnels Cl
Daphne Dr
Water Rede
Barn Meadow
Ewshot
Pawmers Mead
Velmead Farm
183
Fleet Business Park
Wakefords Copse
K
G1 1 Lismoyne Cl 2 Pear Tree Av
G3 1 Hartsleaf Cl
G7 1 Christchurch Cl
H1 1 Westminster Cl
H2 1 Old School Cl
H3 1 Connaught Rd 2 Streamside
H7 1 Pipers Cft
J2 1 Berkeley Cl
J3 1 Medonte Cl 2 Moorlands Cl
J5 1 Hamilton Rd 2 Northfield Cl
J6 1 Castor Ct 2 Lingmala Gv
J7 1 Polkerris Wy
K2 1 Kenwith Av
K3 1 Hawkins Wy
I
2
3
4
5
6
7

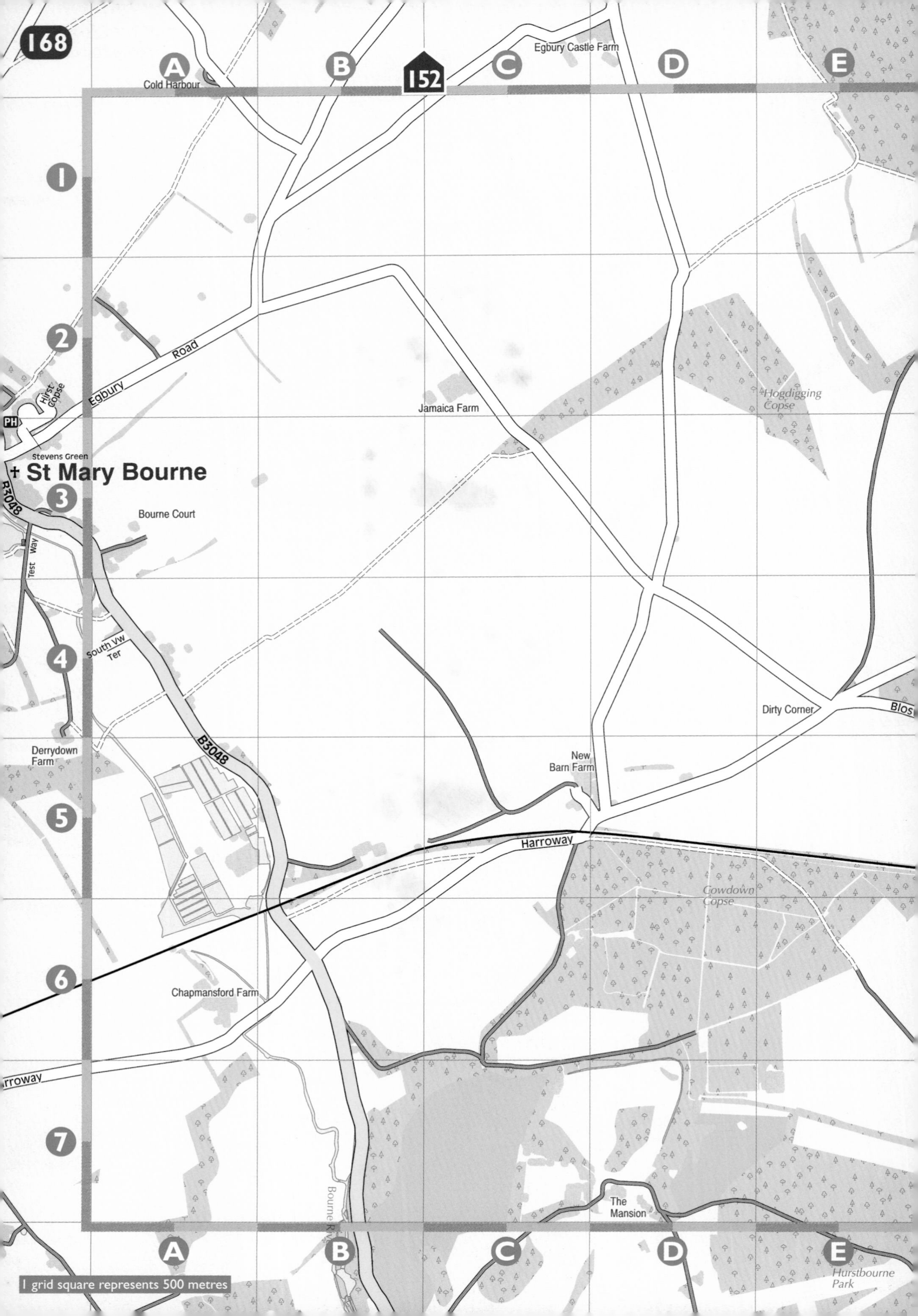

168

A — Cold Harbour
B
152
C — Egbury Castle Farm
D
E

1

2 — Hirst Copse — Egbury Road

PH

Stevens Green
✝ **St Mary Bourne**

3 — Bourne Court — B3048

Jamaica Farm

Hogdigging Copse

4 — South Vw Ter — Test Way

Dirty Corner — Blos

Derrydown Farm

New Barn Farm

5 — B3048

6 — Chapmansford Farm — Harroway — Cowdown Copse

rroway

7 — Bourne River — The Mansion — Hurstbourne Park

A
B
C
D
E

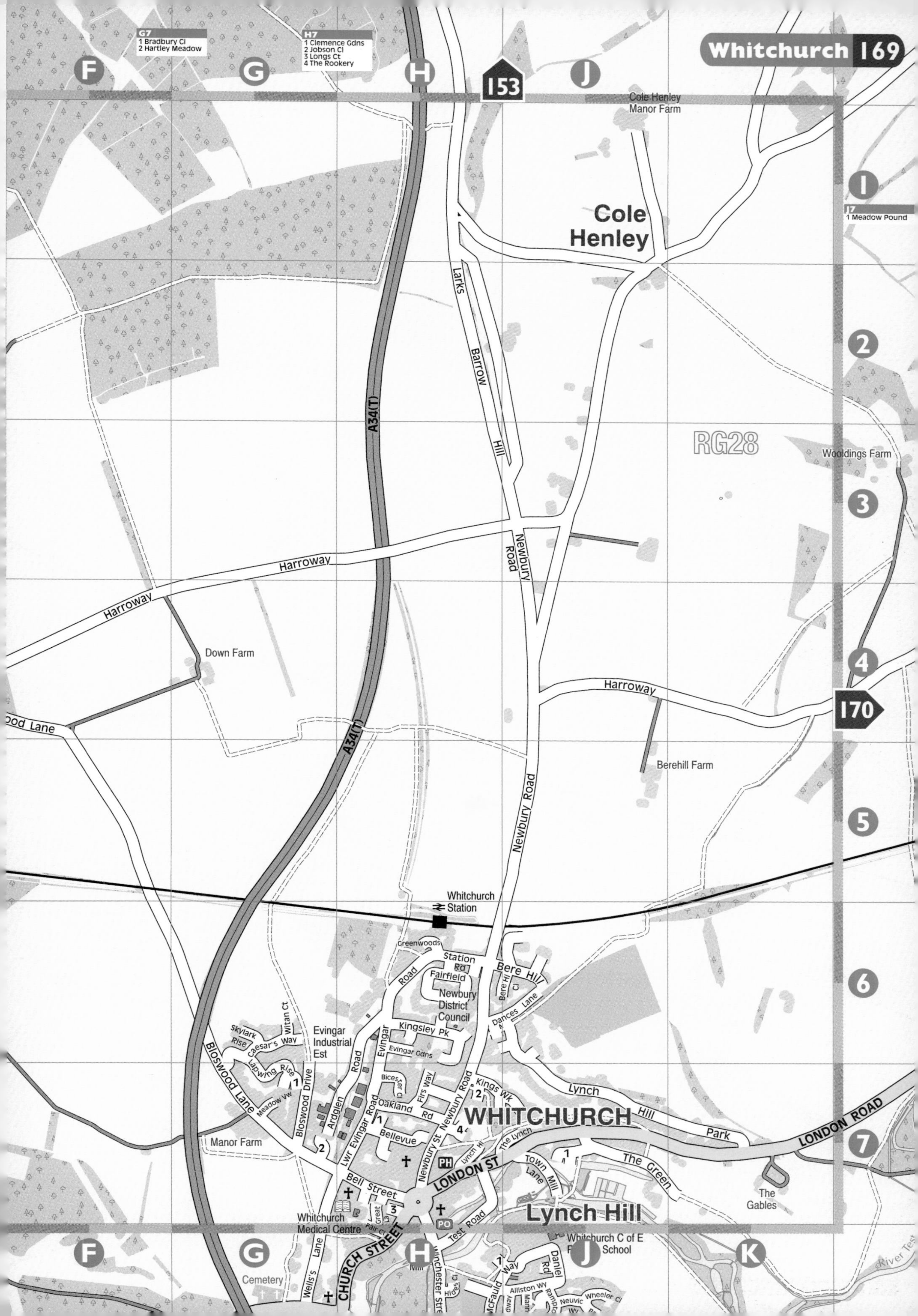

G7
1 Bradbury Cl
2 Hartley Meadow

H7
1 Clemence Gdns
2 Jobson Cl
3 Longs Ct
4 The Rookery

F G H **153** J

I

I7
1 Meadow Pound

2

Cole Henley
Manor Farm

Cole
Henley

RG28

3

Wooldings Farm

Larks Barrow Hill

Newbury Road

Harroway

Harroway

4

170

Down Farm

Harroway

Berehill Farm

Wood Lane

A34(T)

A34(T)

5

Whitchurch
Station

6

Greenwoods

Station Rd

Fairfield

Newbury
District
Council

Bere Hill

Bere Hill Cl

Dances Lane

Witan Ct

Skylark Rise

Caesar's Way

Lapwing Rise

Evingar Road

Evingar
Industrial
Est

Kingsley Pk

Evingar Gdns

Bices

Firs Way

Newbury Road

Kings Wk

Lynch Hill Park

London Road

7

Bloswood Drive

Bloswood Lane

Meadow Vw

Ardglen

Oakland

Lwr Evingar Road

Bellevue

Newbury St

Oakland Rd

WHITCHURCH

Kings Wk

Lynch Hill

Manor Farm

Bell Street

Great

PH
LONDON ST

Lynch Hl

The Lynch

Town Mill

The Green

The Gables

Whitchurch
Medical Centre

CHURCH STREET

Fair Cl

PO

Test Road

Lynch Hill

F Cemetery G Wells's Lane Winchester Street H Mill McFauld Way Daniel Rd Alliston Wy Neuvic Wheeler Cl Whitchurch C of E
Primary
School J K

River Test

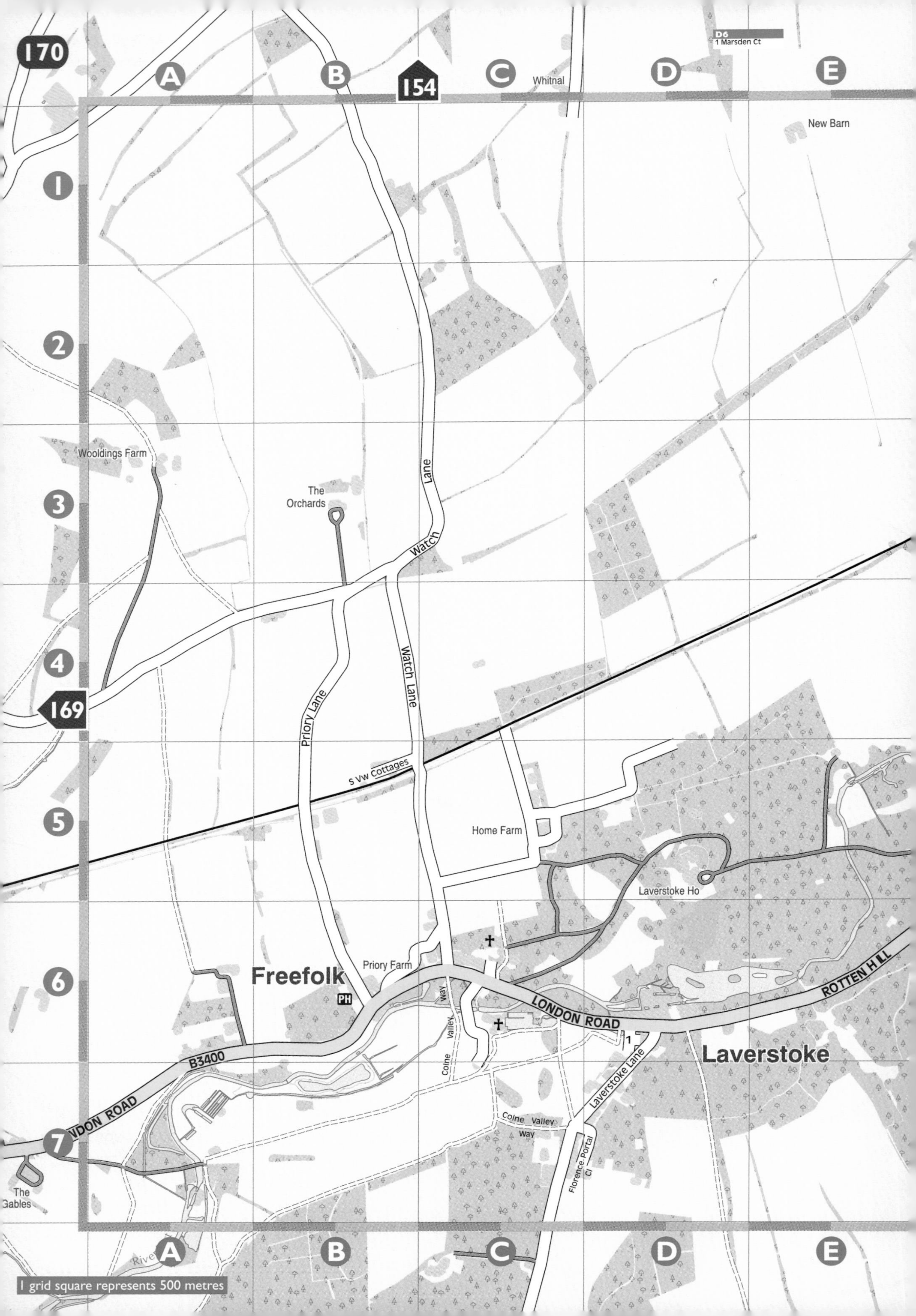

170
154
169
A
B
C
D
E
1
2
3
4
5
6
7
D6
1 Marsden Ct
Whitnal
New Barn
Wooldings Farm
The
Orchards
Watch
Lane
Watch Lane
Priory Lane
S Vw Cottages
Home Farm
Laverstoke Ho
Priory Farm
Freefolk
PH
Way
Valley
Colne
LONDON ROAD
ROTTEN HILL
B3400
LONDON ROAD
Laverstoke
Laverstoke Lane
Colne Valley
Way
Florence Portal
Cl
The
Gables
River
1 grid square represents 500 metres

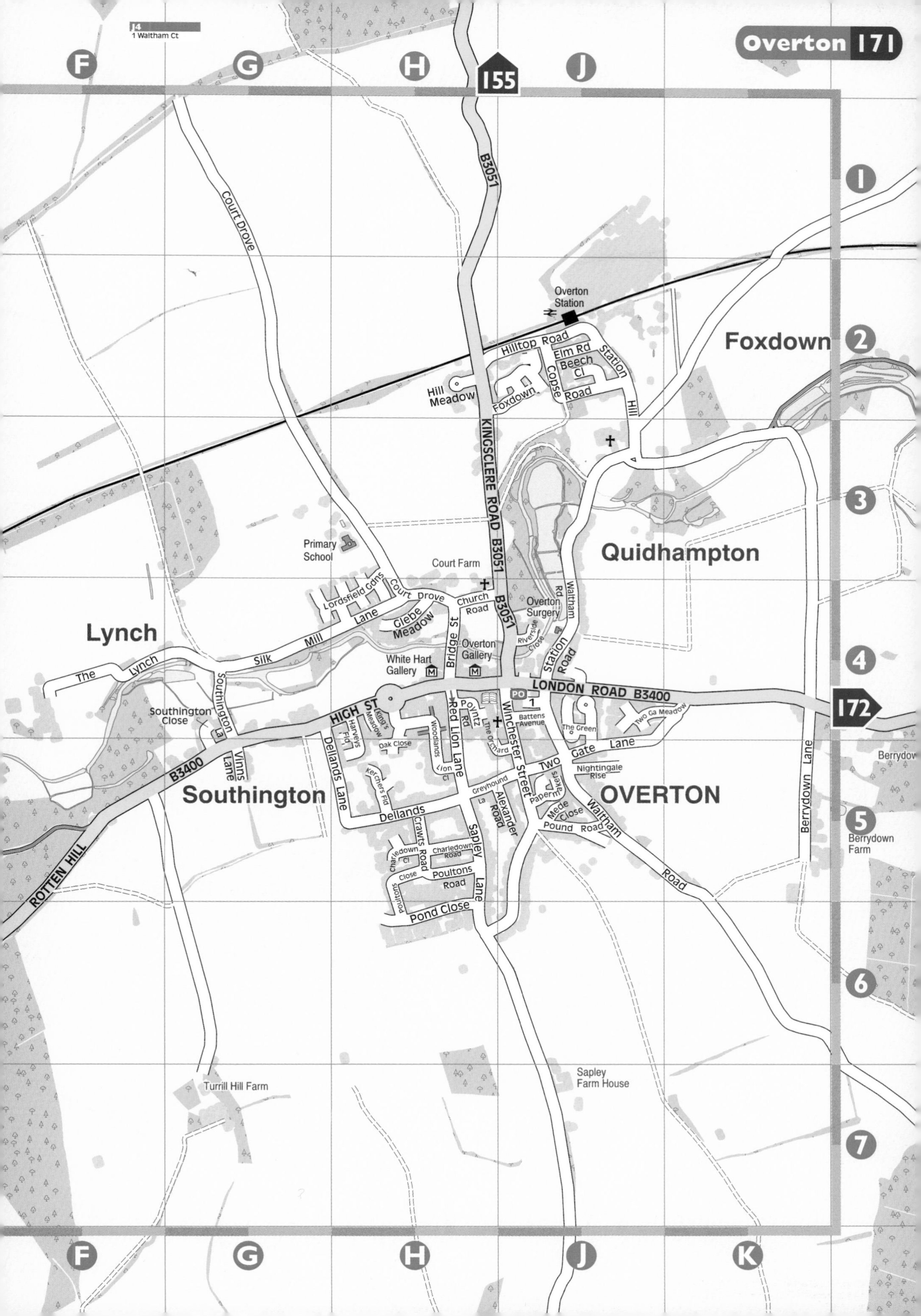
J4
1 Waltham Ct
F
G
H
J
K
155
172
1
2
3
4
5
6
7
Overton Station
Foxdown
Quidhampton
Lynch
Southington
OVERTON
Berrydown Farm
Court Drove
B3051
KINGSCLERE ROAD B3051
Hilltop Road
Elm Rd
Beech Cl
Copse Road
Station Hill
Hill Meadow
Foxdown
Primary School
Court Farm
Lordsfield Gdns
Church Road
Glebe Meadow
Silk Mill Lane
Overton Surgery
Riverside Close
Waltham Rd
Station Road
Overton Gallery
White Hart Gallery
Bridge St
The Lynch
Southington La
Southington Close
HIGH ST
LONDON ROAD B3400
Red Lion Lane
Poyntz Rd
Winchester Street
Battens Avenue
The Green
Two Ga Meadow
Two Gate Lane
Nightingale Rise
Harveys Fld
King's Meadow
Oak Close
Woodlands
Lion Cl
The Orchard
Dellands Lane
Vinns Lane
B3400
Kerchers Fld
Greyhound La
Alexander Road
Papermakers
Mede Close
Pound Road
Waltham Road
Dellands
Crawts Road
Sapley Lane
Charledown Cl
Charledown Road
Poultons Close
Poultons Road
Pond Close
ROTTEN HILL
Berrydown Lane
Berrydow
Turrill Hill Farm
Sapley Farm House

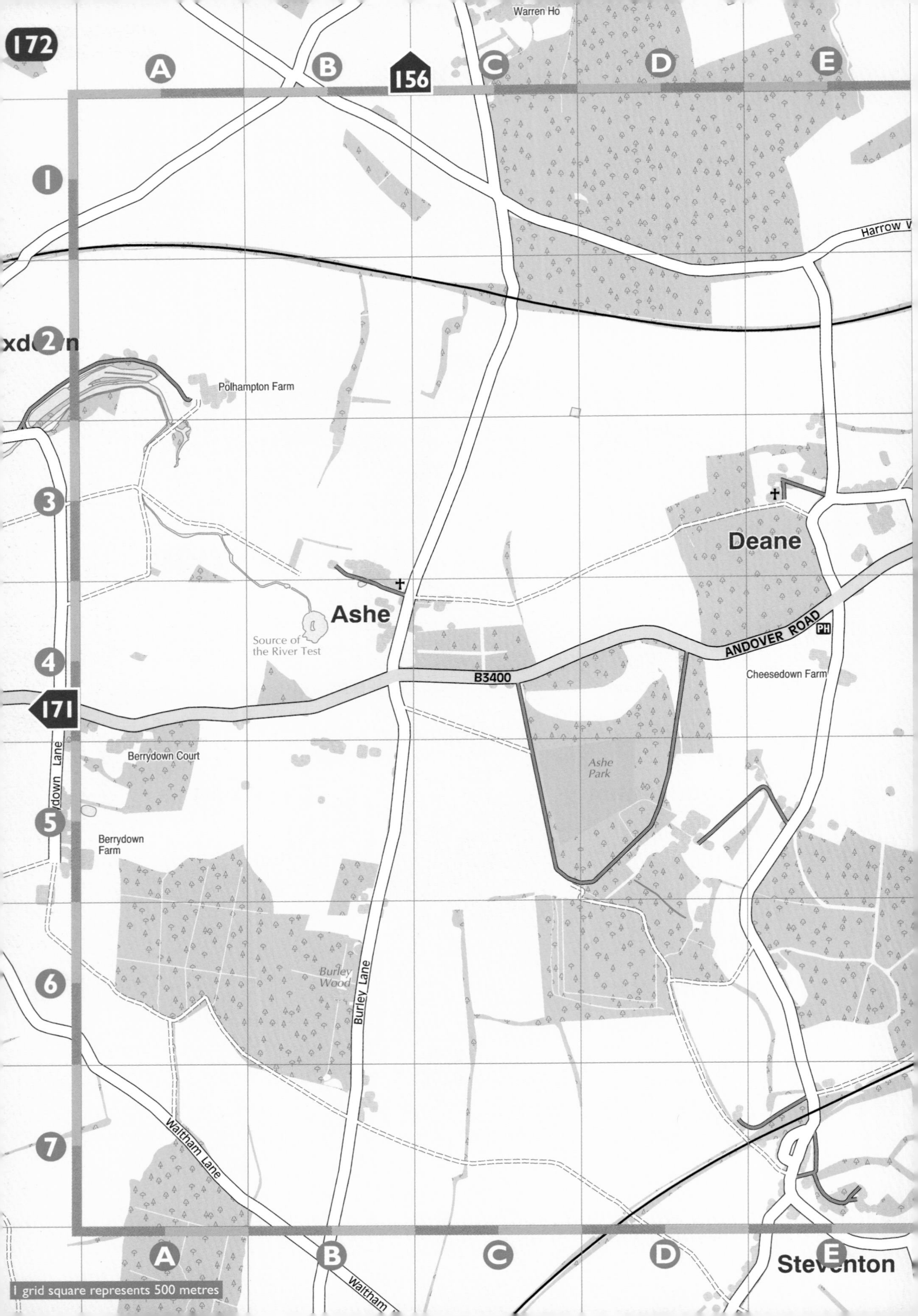

A   B   C   D   E

156

I

xd 2 n

Polhampton Farm

Harrow V

3

Deane

†

†

4

Source of
the River Test

Ashe

B3400

ANDOVER ROAD

PH

Cheesedown Farm

171

Berrydown Court

Ashe
Park

down Lane

5

Berrydown
Farm

6

Burley
Wood

Burley Lane

7

Waltham Lane

A   B   C   D   E

Steventon

Waltham

Warren Ho

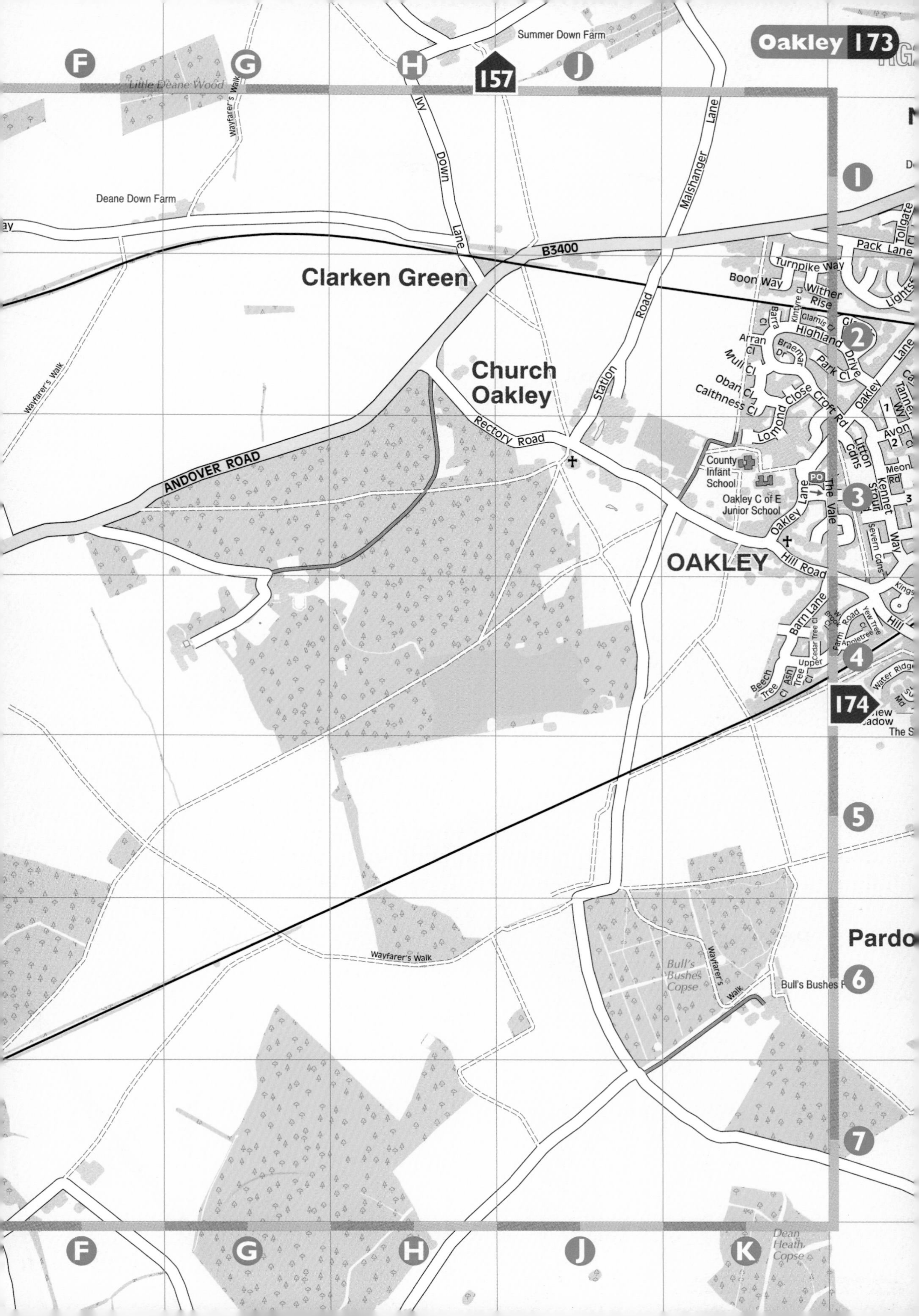

157

F
G
H
J

Summer Down Farm

Little Deane Wood

Wayfarer's Walk

Ivy Down Lane

Malshanger Lane

Deane Down Farm

B3400

Pack Lane

Tollgate

Turnpike Way

Wither Rise

Boon Way

Clarken Green

Barta Cl

Kintyre Cl

Highland Drive

Arran Cl

Mull Cl

Braemar Dr

Park Cl

Glamis Cl

Oakley Lane

Tanne

Church Oakley

Oban Cl

Caithness Cl

Lomond Close

Croft Rd

Avon

7

Litton Gdns

Meon

Kennet

Meon Rd

ANDOVER ROAD

Rectory Road

Station Road

County Infant School

PO

The Vale

Strud

Severn Gdns

Oakley C of E Junior School

Oakley Lane

OAKLEY

Hill Road

Kings

Barn Lane

Yew Tree

Farm Road

Appletree

Hill

174

Beech Tree Cl

Ash Tree Cl

Cedar Tree Cl

Upper

Water Ridge

New adow

The S

Pardo

Wayfarer's Walk

Bull's Bushes Copse

Wayfarer's Walk

Bull's Bushes F

Dean Heath Copse

F
G
H
J
K

I
2
3
4
5
6
7

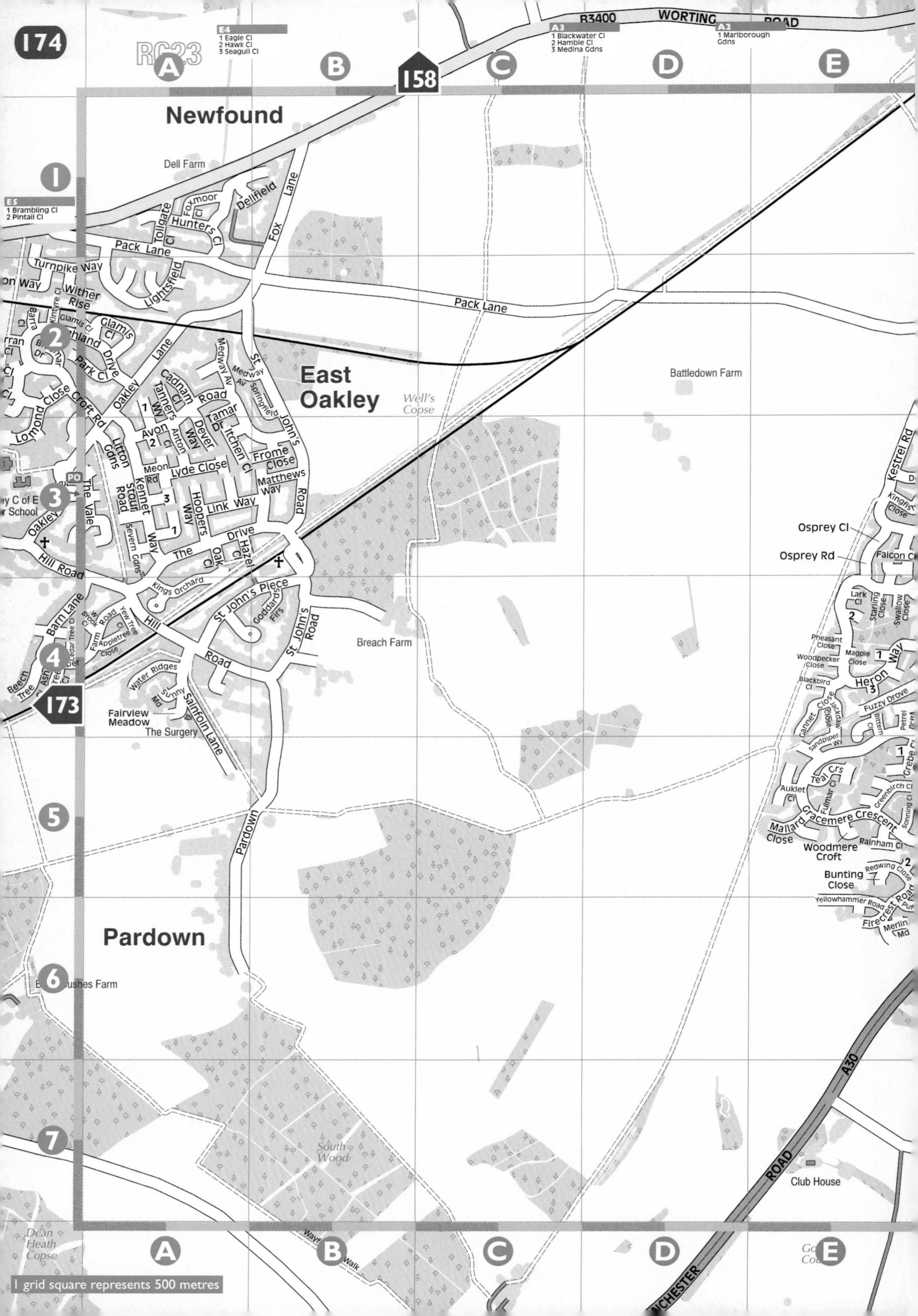

B3400 WORTING ROAD
E4
1 Eagle Cl
2 Hawk Cl
3 Seagull Cl
A3
1 Blackwater Cl
2 Hamble Cl
3 Medina Gdns
A2
1 Marlborough Gdns
RG23
158
Newfound
Dell Farm
E5
1 Brambling Cl
2 Pintail Cl
Pack Lane
Fox Lane
Dellfield
Hunters Cl
Tollgate Cl
Foxmoor Cl
Lightsfield
Turnpike Way
Wither Rise
Glamis Cl
Park Cl
Oakley Lane
Lomond Close
Croft Rd
East Oakley
Well's Copse
Battledown Farm
Medway Av
Springfield
St John's Road
Cadnam Cl
Tanners Way
Road
Tamar Dr
Dever Way
Avon Cl
Anton
Itchen Cl
Frome Close
Matthews Way
Litton Gdns
Lyde Close
Meon Rd
Kennet Road
Stour Road
Link Way
Hoopers Way
The Vale
Oakley
Hill Road
Severn Gdns
The Drive
Oak Cl
Hazel Cl
Kings Orchard
St John's Piece
Goddards Firs
Breach Farm
Barn Lane
Farm Road
Yew Tree Cl
Appletree Close
Cedar Tree Cl
Beech Tree Cl
Water Ridges
Saintfoin Lane
Fairview Meadow
The Surgery
173
Pardown
Pardown
Rushes Farm
South Wood
Dean Heath Copse
Wayfarers Walk
Kestrel Rd
Kingfisher Close
Osprey Cl
Osprey Rd
Falcon Cl
Lark Cl
Starling Close
Swallow Close
Pheasant Close
Woodpecker Close
Magpie Close
Heron Way
Blackbird Cl
Fuzzy Drove
Gannet Close
Jackdaw Close
Bittern Cl
Petrel
Sandpiper Way
Grebe Cl
Teal Crs
Fulmar Cl
Auklet Cl
Greenbirch Cl
Gracemere Crescent
Sonning Cl
Mallard Close
Woodmere Croft
Rainham Cl
Bunting Close
Redwing Close
Yellowhammer Road
Firecrest Road
Merlin Md
A30
WINCHESTER ROAD
Club House
A B C D E
1 2 3 4 5 6 7
PO
1 grid square represents 500 metres

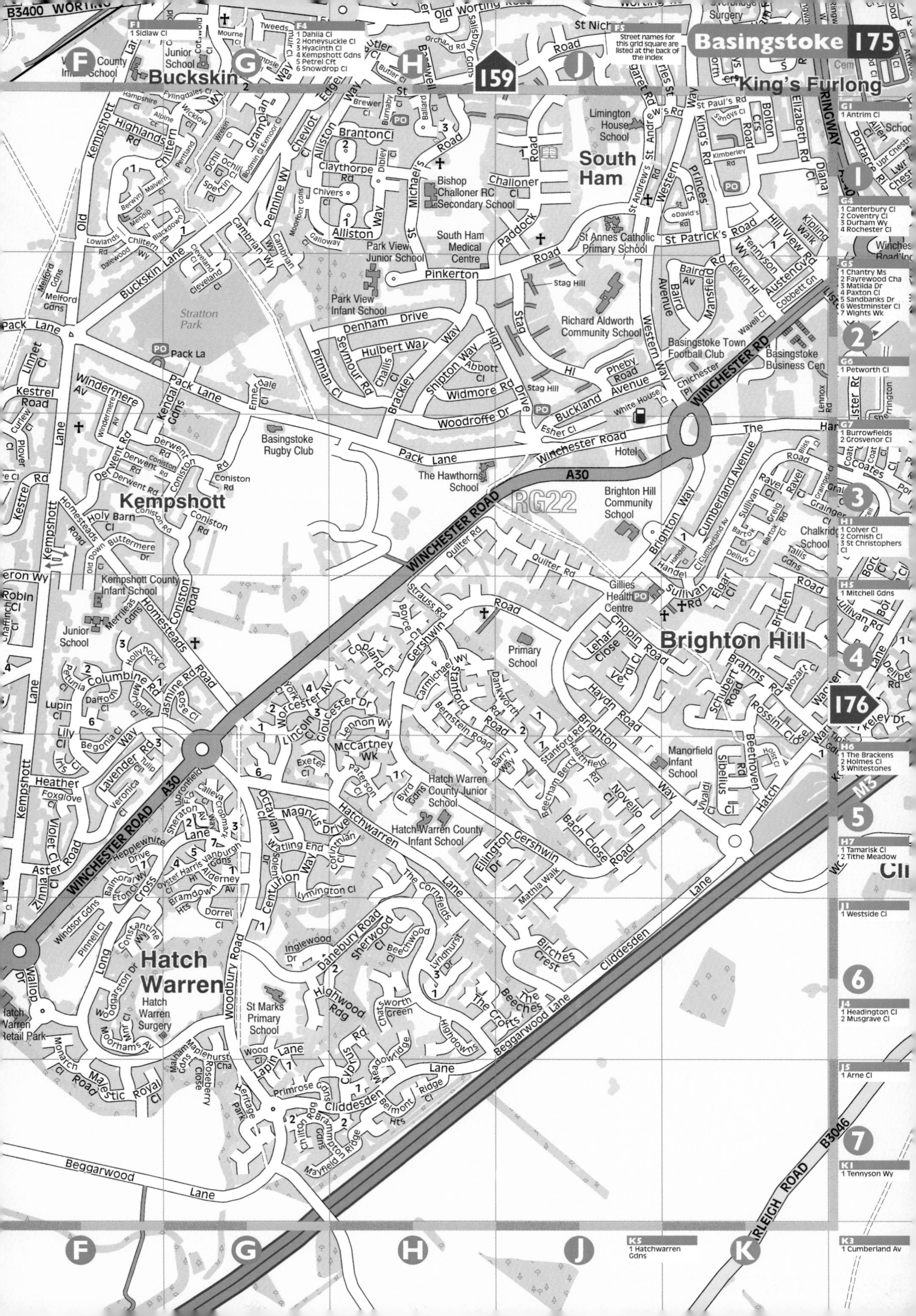
Basingstoke 175
F1 1 Sidlaw Cl
F4 1 Dahlia Cl 2 Honeysuckle Cl 3 Hyacinth Cl 4 Kempshott Gdns 5 Petrel Cft 6 Snowdrop Cl
F5 Street names for this grid square are listed at the back of the index
159
176
King's Furlong
Buckskin
South Ham
Kempshott
Brighton Hill
Hatch Warren
G1 1 Antrim Cl
G4 1 Canterbury Cl 2 Coventry Cl 3 Durham Wy 4 Rochester Cl
G5 1 Chantry Ms 2 Fayrewood Cha 3 Matilda Dr 4 Paxton Cl 5 Sandbanks Dr 6 Westminster Cl 7 Wights Wk
G6 1 Petworth Cl
G7 1 Burrowfields 2 Grosvenor Cl
H1 1 Colyer Cl 2 Cornish Cl 3 St Christophers Cl
H5 1 Mitchell Gdns
H6 1 The Brackens 2 Holmes Cl 3 Whitestones
H7 1 Tamarisk Cl 2 Tithe Meadow
J1 1 Westside Cl
J4 1 Headington Cl 2 Musgrave Cl
J5 1 Arne Cl
K1 1 Tennyson Wy
K3 1 Cumberland Av
K5 1 Hatchwarren Gdns
B3400 WORTING
RINGWAY
WINCHESTER RD
WINCHESTER ROAD
A30
RG22
M3
B3046
Limington House School
Bishop Challoner RC Secondary School
South Ham Medical Centre
Park View Junior School
Park View Infant School
St Annes Catholic Primary School
Richard Aldworth Community School
Basingstoke Town Football Club
Basingstoke Business Cen
Stratton Park
Basingstoke Rugby Club
The Hawthorns School
Brighton Hill Community School
Gillies Health Centre
Kempshott County Infant School
Junior School
Primary School
Manorfield Infant School
Hatch Warren County Junior School
Hatch Warren County Infant School
St Marks Primary School
Hatch Warren Surgery
Hatch Warren Retail Park
Pack Lane
Winchester Road
Kempshott Lane
Buckskin Lane
Pinkerton Road
Western Way
Brighton Way
Cumberland Avenue
Homesteads Road
Coniston Road
Hatchwarren Lane
Woodbury Road
Cliddesden Lane
Beggarwood Lane
Gershwin Road
Chopin Road
Haydn Road
Sullivan Rd
Buckland Avenue
Stag Hill
High Drive
Woodroffe Dr
Denham Drive
Hulbert Way
Brackley Way
Pitman Cl
Old Kempshott Lane
Highlands Rd
Chiltern Wy
Windermere Av
Kestrel Road
Linnet Cl
Columbine Rd
Lavender Rd
Heather Way
Magnus Drive
Octavian Cl
Centurion Way
Worcester Av
Gloucester Dr
Lincoln Cl
McCartney Wk
Stanford Road
Dankworth Rd
Bach Close
Novello Cl
Ellington Dr
Beethoven Rd
Schubert Road
Brahms Rd
Rossini Close
Quilter Rd
Elgar Cl
Lapin Lane
Highwood Rdg
The Cornfields
Birches Crest
The Beeches
The Crofts
Majestic Road
Royal Cl
Heritage Park
Long Cross Lane
Wallop Dr
Moorhams Av
Woodgarston Dr
St Patrick's Road
Hill View Rd
Western Rd
St Andrew's Rd
Princes Crs
Elizabeth Rd
Bolton Crs
Kimberley Rd

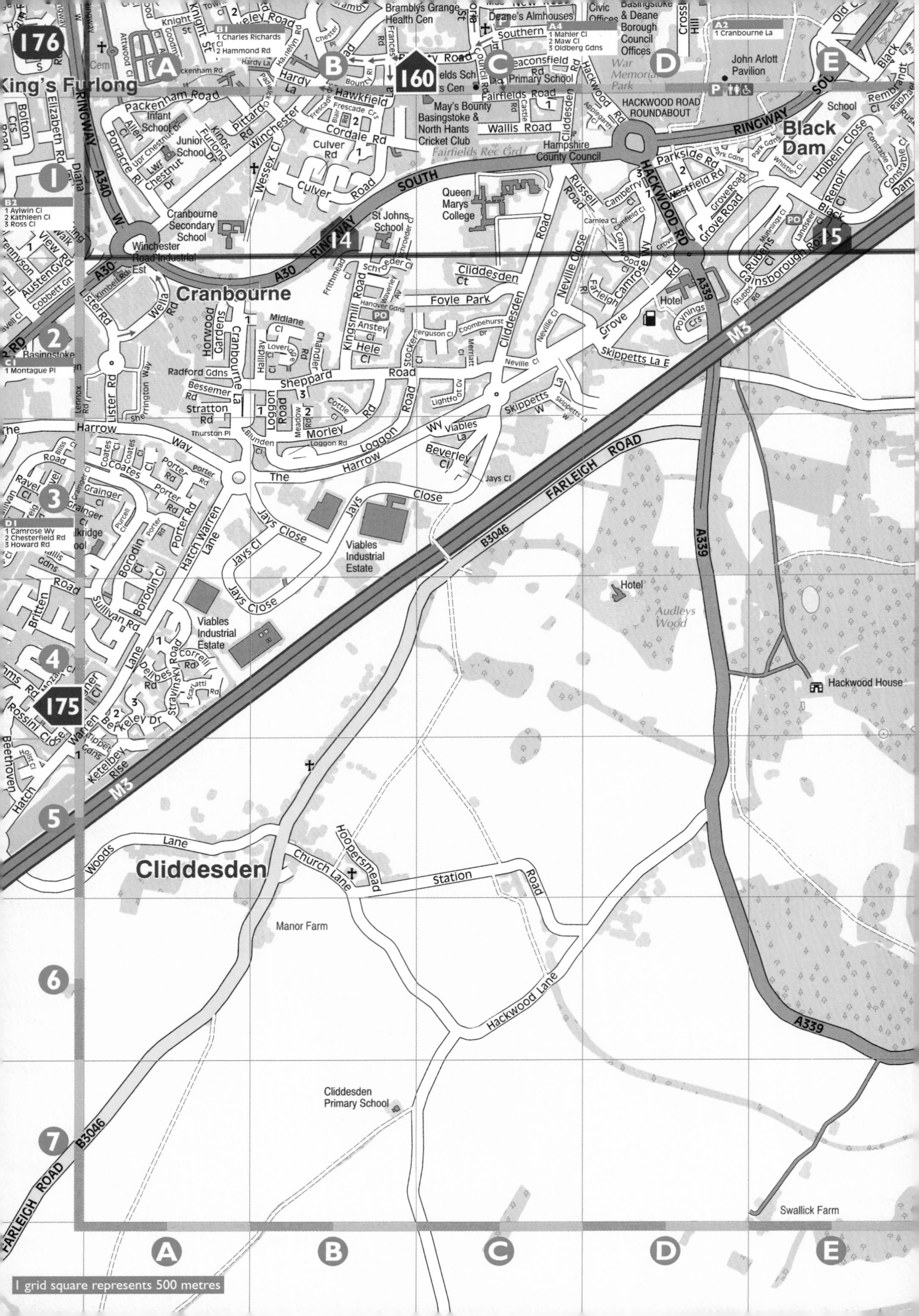

176
160
175
14
15
King's Furlong
Cranbourne
Black Dam
Cliddesden
B1
1 Charles Richards Cl
2 Hammond Rd
A4
1 Mahler Cl
2 Maw Cl
3 Oldberg Gdns
A2
1 Cranbourne La
B2
1 Aylwin Cl
2 Kathleen Cl
3 Ross Cl
C1
1 Montague Pl
D1
1 Camrose Wy
2 Chesterfield Rd
3 Howard Rd
Bramblys Grange Health Cen
Deane's Almhouses
Civic Offices
Basingstoke & Deane Borough Council Offices
John Arlott Pavilion
War Memorial Park
HACKWOOD ROAD ROUNDABOUT
Infant School
Junior School
May's Bounty Basingstoke & North Hants Cricket Club
Fairfields Rec Grd
Hampshire County Council
Cranbourne Secondary School
Queen Marys College
St Johns School
Winchester Road Industrial Est
Viables Industrial Estate
Hotel
Audleys Wood
Hackwood House
Manor Farm
Cliddesden Primary School
Swallick Farm
RINGWAY
RINGWAY SOUTH
A30
A340
A339
M3
B3046
FARLEIGH ROAD
HACKWOOD RD
Harrow Way
The Harrow Wy
Cranbourne La
Sheppard Road
Cliddesden Road
Grove Rd
Skippetts La E
Jays Close
Woods Lane
Church Lane
Hoopersmead
Station Road
Hackwood Lane
Packenham Road
Winchester Rd
Cordale Rd
Culver Road
Wallis Road
Fairfields Road
Beaconsfield Rd
Hawkfield La
Foyle Park
Neville Close
Russell Road
Camrose Wy
Morley Rd
Loggon Road
Kingsmill Road
Porter Rd
Borodin Cl
Sullivan Rd
Hatch Warren Lane
Berkeley Dr
Ketelbey Rise
Rossini Close
Beethoven
Britten Road
Stravinsky Road
Lister Rd
Wella Rd
Horwood Gardens
Holbein Close
Gainsborough Rd
Grove Road
Westfield Rd
Parkside Rd
A B C D E
1 2 3 4 5 6 7
1 grid square represents 500 metres

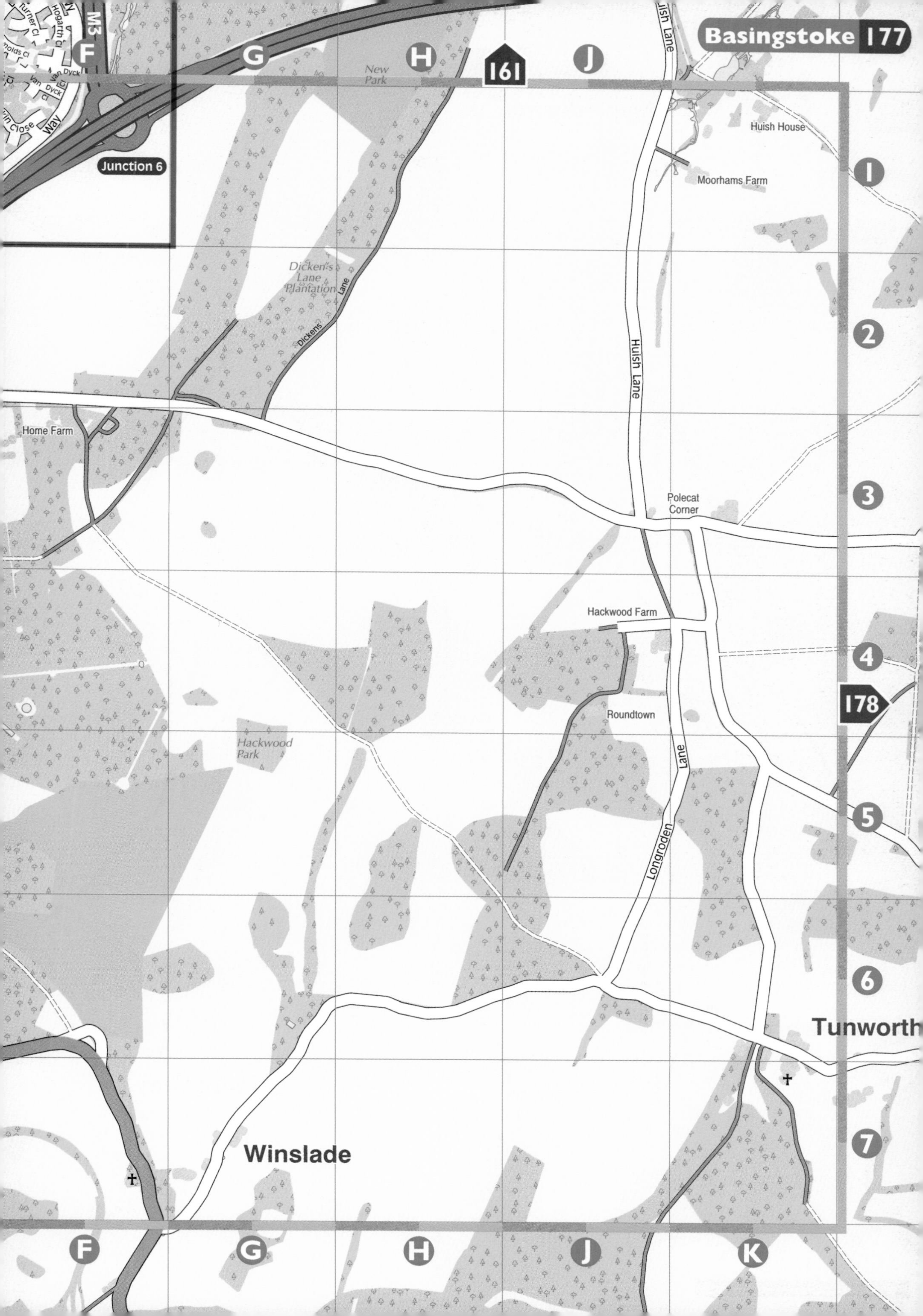

F
G
H
J

New Park

161

ish Lane

Junction 6

Huish House

Moorhams Farm

I

Dicken's
Lane
Plantation

2

Dickens
Lane

Huish Lane

Home Farm

Polecat
Corner

3

Hackwood Farm

4

178

Roundtown

Hackwood
Park

Longroden Lane

5

6

Tunworth

7

Winslade

F
G
H
J
K

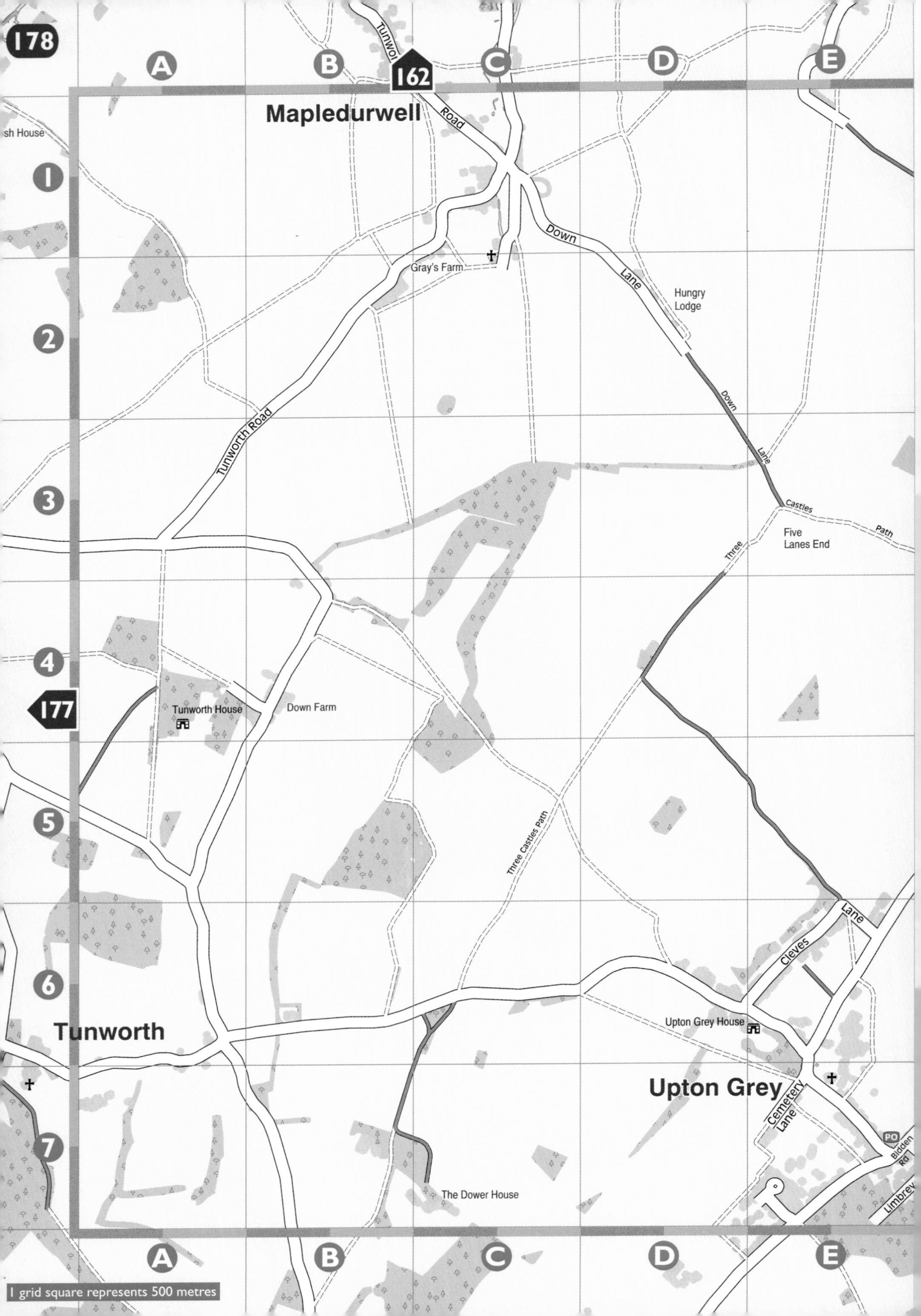
178
162
177
A
B
C
D
E
1
2
3
4
5
6
7
Mapledurwell
Tunworth Road
Road
Gray's Farm
Down Lane
Hungry Lodge
Down Lane
Castles Path
Five Lanes End
Three
Tunworth House
Down Farm
Three Castles Path
Cleves Lane
Lane
Tunworth
Upton Grey House
Upton Grey
Cemetery Lane
PO
Bidden Rd
Limbrey
The Dower House
1 grid square represents 500 metres

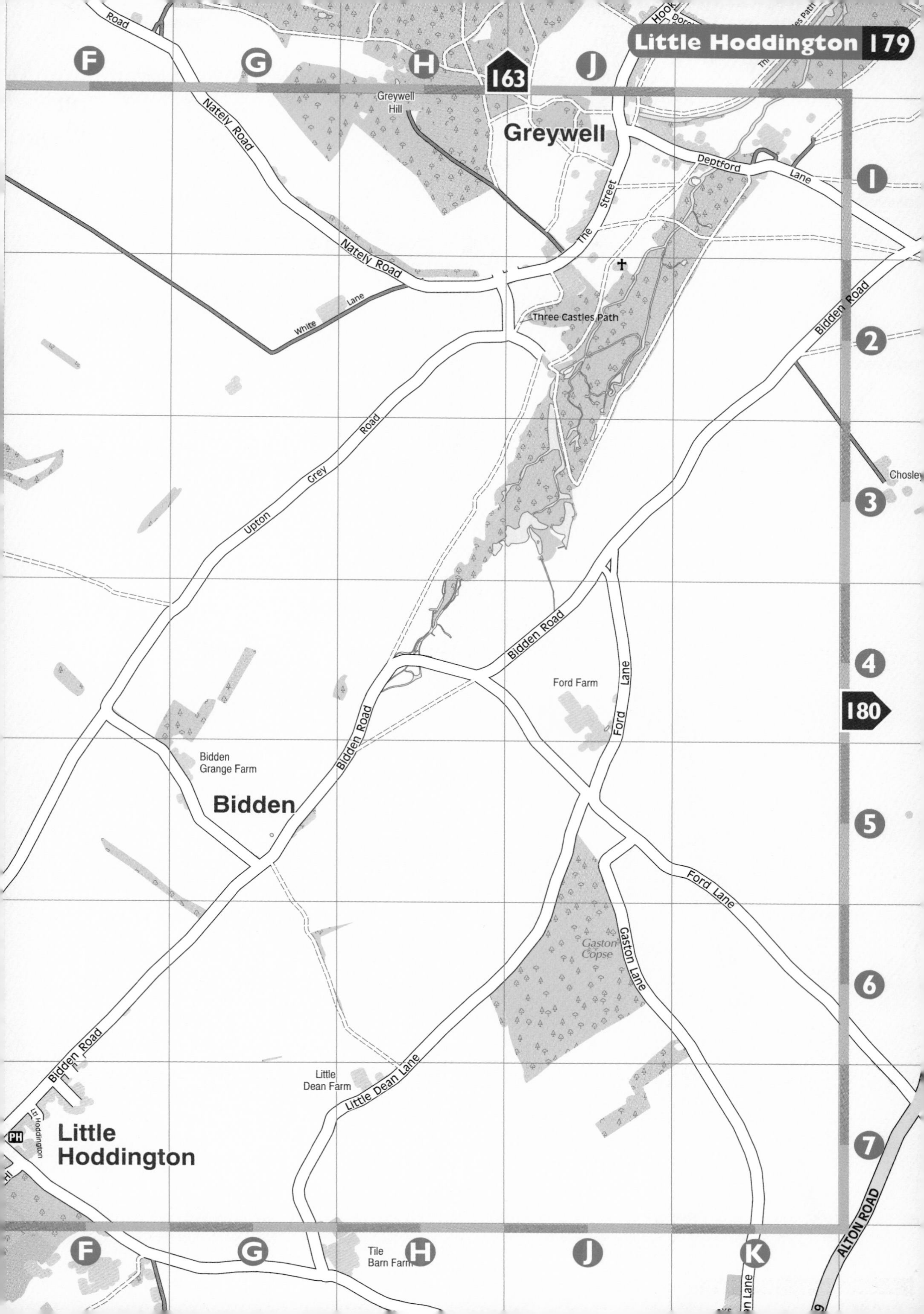

F G H J

163

Greywell Hill

Greywell

Deptford Lane

Nately Road

Nately Road

White Lane

Bidden Road

I

2

Chosley

3

Three Castles Path

Upton Grey Road

Bidden Road

Ford Farm

Ford Lane

4

180

Bidden
Grange Farm

Bidden

Bidden Road

5

Ford Lane

Gaston
Copse

Gaston Lane

6

Bidden Road

Little
Dean Farm

Little Dean Lane

PH

**Little
Hoddington**

7

ALTON ROAD

F G H J K

Tile
Barn Farm

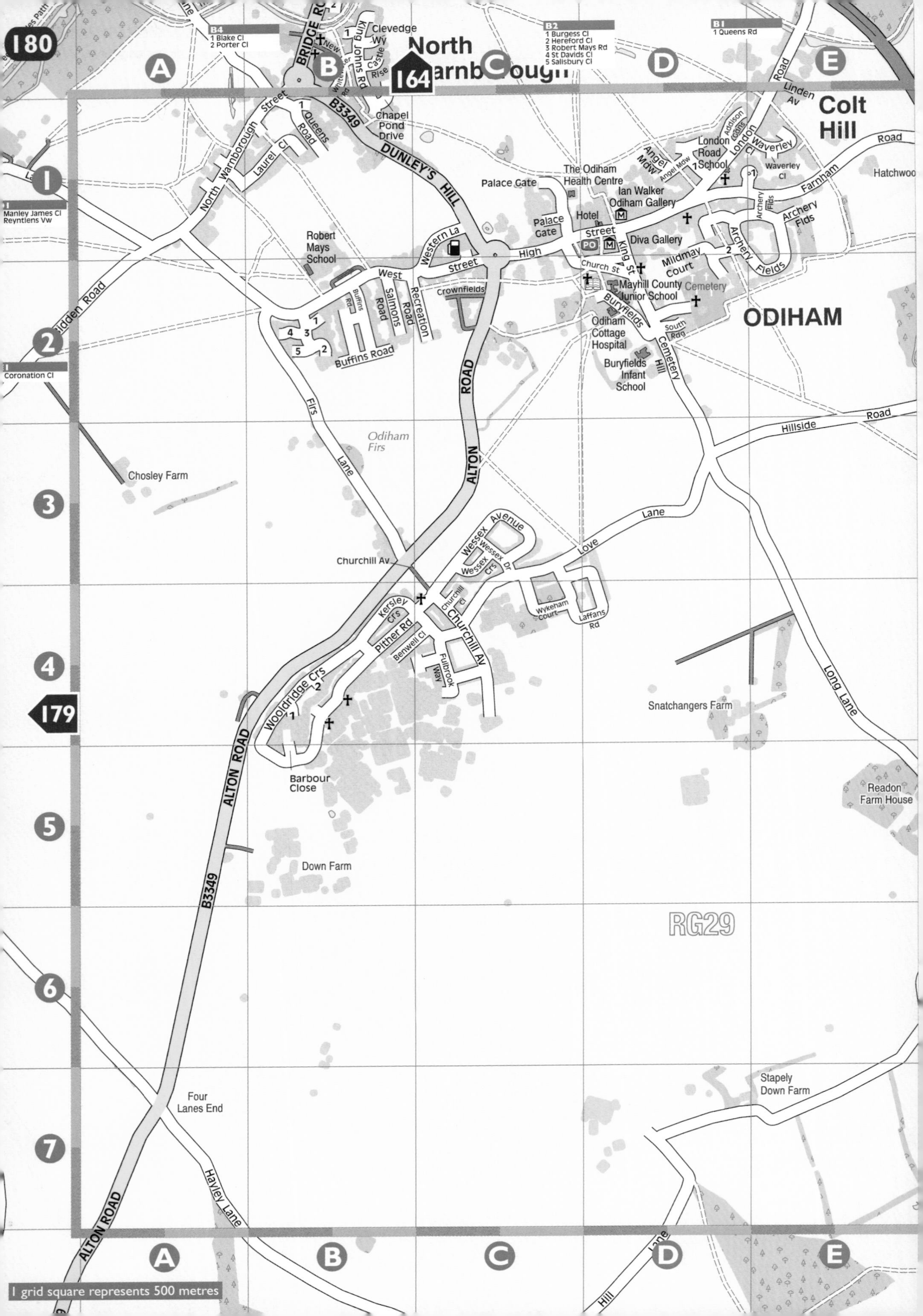

A

B

Clevedge

North

164

Warnborough

D

E

Colt
Hill

BRIDGE RD

New

White

Johns Rd

Bury

Castle

Rise

Wy

Linden
Av

1

North Warnborough Street

Laurel Cl

Queens
Road

B3349

DUNLEY'S HILL

Chapel
Pond
Drive

Palace Gate

The Odiham
Health Centre

Ian Walker
Odiham Gallery

Odiham

Angel
Mdw

Angel Mdw

7

London
Road School

London

Waverley
Cl

Waverley

Road

Hatchwoo

Ridden Road

Robert
Mays
School

Western La

Palace
Gate

Hotel
Street

High

Street

PO

King St

Church St

Diva Gallery

Mildmay
Court

Cemetery

Addison Gdns

Archery
Flds

Archery

Archery Flds

Fields

ODIHAM

Farnham

2

West
Salmons
Road

Buffins
Rd

Recreation
Road

Crownfields

Church St

Mayhill County
Junior School

Odiham
Cottage
Hospital

Buryfields

South Rdg

Cemetery Hill

4 3 1
5 2

Buffins Road

ALTON ROAD

Odiham
Firs

Buryfields
Infant
School

Hillside

Road

3

Chosley Farm

Firs

Lane

Lane

Love

Lane

4

179

Wooldridge Crs

2
1

Churchill Av

Kersley Crs

Pither Rd

Benwell Cl

Wessex Avenue

Wessex Dr

Wessex

Wessex Crs

Churchill Cl

Churchill Av

Fulbrook Way

Wykeham
Court

Laffans
Rd

Snatchangers Farm

Long Lane

Readon
Farm House

5

Barbour
Close

Down Farm

RG29

6

7

Four
Lanes End

Stapely
Down Farm

B3349

Havley Lane

ALTON ROAD

Lane

Hill

A

B

C

D

E

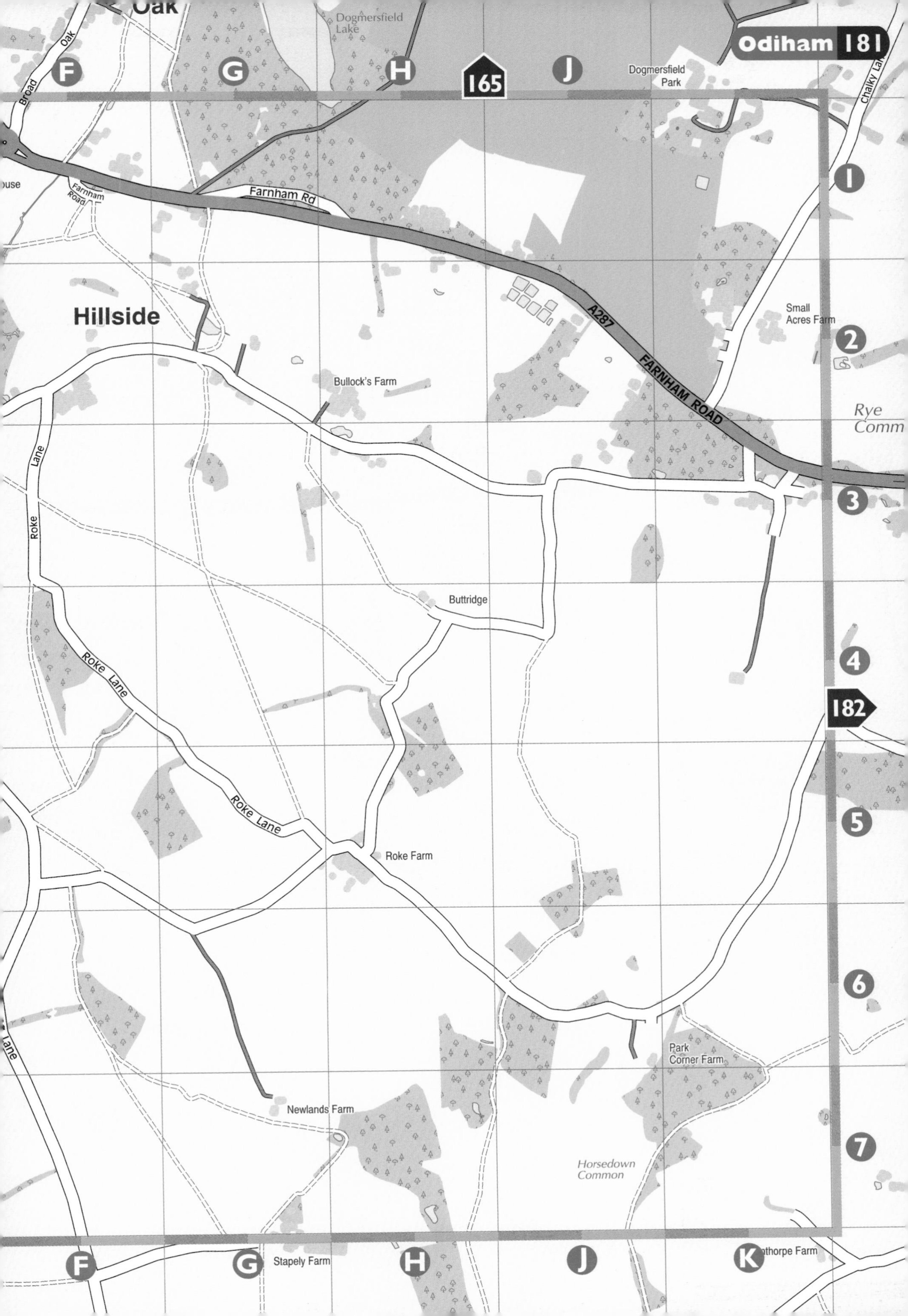

Oak
Dogmersfield Lake
F
G
H
165
J
Dogmersfield Park
Chalky Lane
Broad Oak
Farnham Road
Farnham Rd
1
Hillside
A287
FARNHAM ROAD
Small Acres Farm
2
Bullock's Farm
Rye Comm
Lane
Roke
3
Buttridge
4
Roke Lane
182
Roke Lane
Roke Farm
5
6
Lane
Park Corner Farm
Newlands Farm
7
Horsedown Common
F
G
Stapely Farm
H
J
K
thorpe Farm

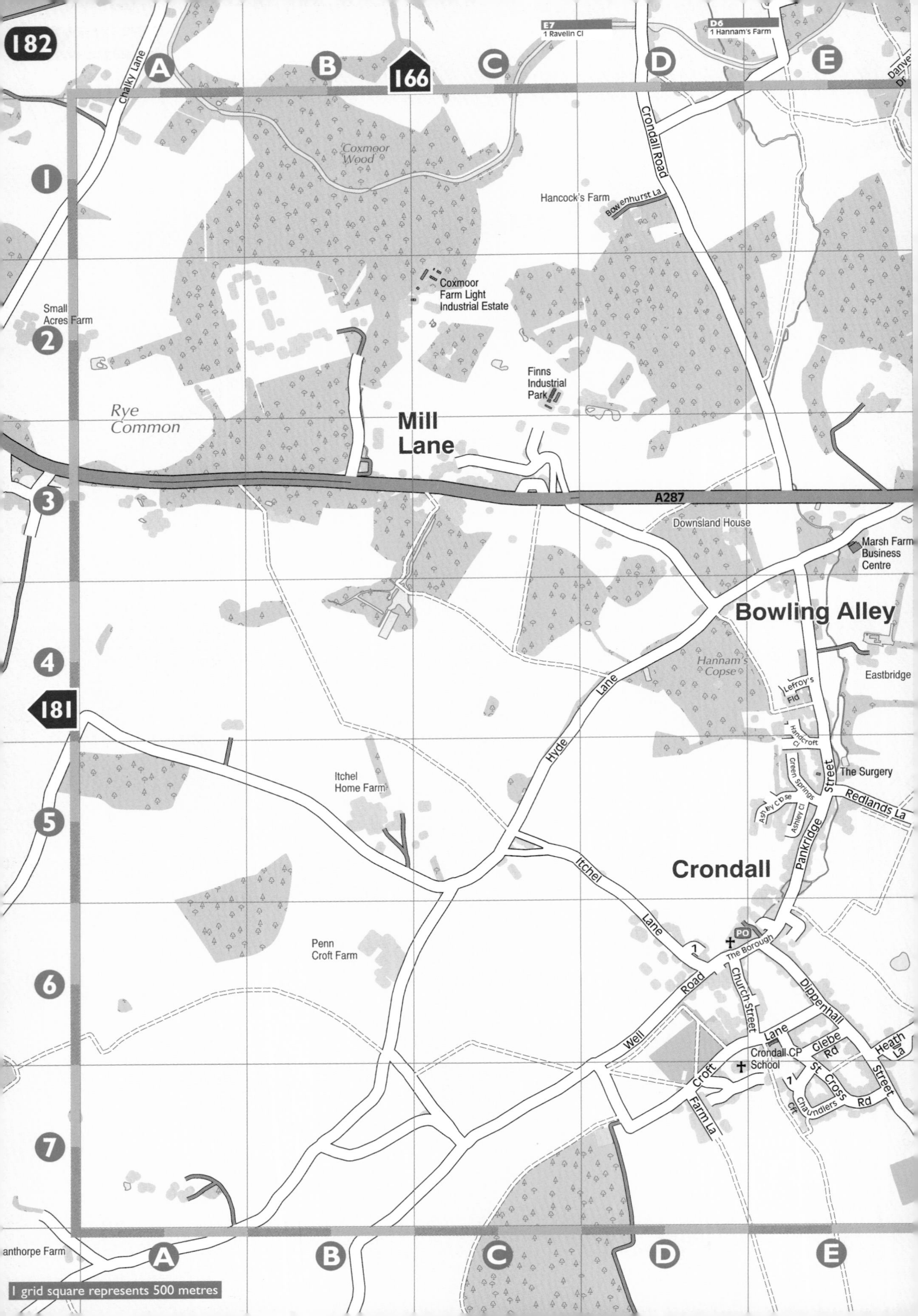

A B 166 C D E

E7
1 Ravelin Cl

D6
1 Hannam's Farm

Danver Dr

1

Crondall Road

Coxmoor
Wood

Hancock's Farm

Bowenhurst La

2

Small
Acres Farm

Coxmoor
Farm Light
Industrial Estate

Rye
Common

Finns
Industrial
Park

Mill
Lane

3

A287

Downsland House

Marsh Farm
Business
Centre

Bowling Alley

4

Hannam's
Copse

Eastbridge

Lefroy's
Fld

Lane

Hyde

Handcroft Cl

The Surgery

5

Itchel
Home Farm

Green Springs

Ashley Cl Cse

Ashley Cl

Pankridge

Street

Redlands La

Crondall

Itchel

Lane

PO

The Borough

6

Penn
Croft Farm

Well

Road

Church Street

Lane

Dippenhall

Glebe
Rd

Heath
La

Crondall CP
School

St Cross Rd

Street

Croft

Chandlers
Cl

Farm La

7

anthorpe Farm

A B C D E

1 grid square represents 500 metres

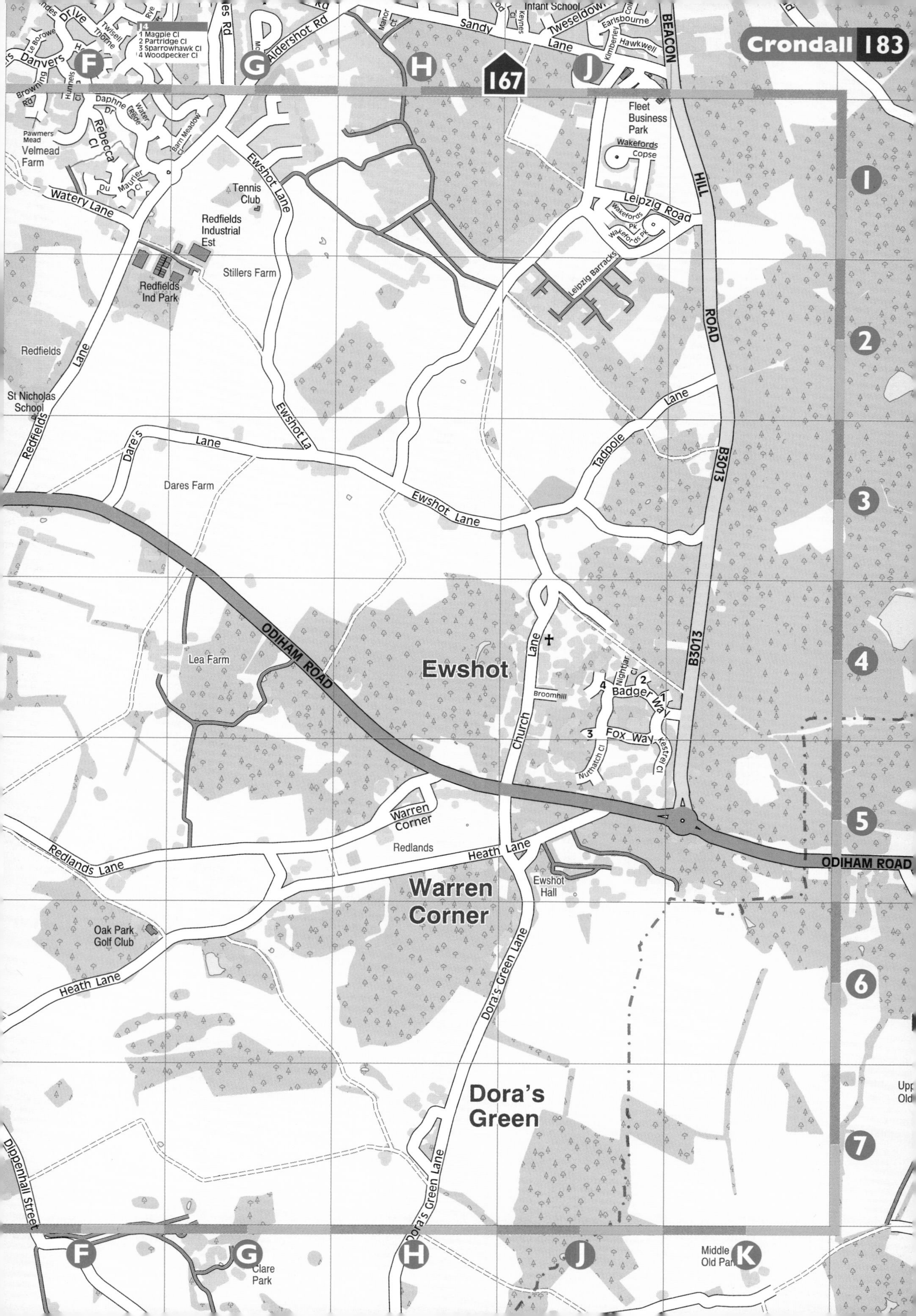
167
1 Magpie Cl
2 Partridge Cl
3 Sparrowhawk Cl
4 Woodpecker Cl
Danvers Drive
Aldershot Rd
Sandy Lane
Tweseldown
Infant School
Earlsbourne
Hawkwell
Kimberley
BEACON HILL ROAD
B3013
Fleet Business Park
Wakefords Copse
Leipzig Road
Wakefords Pk
Leipzig Barracks
Browning Rd
Daphne Dr
Rebecca Cl
Pawmers Mead
Velmead Farm
Watery Lane
Barn Meadow Cl
Ewshot Lane
Tennis Club
Redfields Industrial Est
Redfields Ind Park
Stillers Farm
Redfields
Redfields Lane
St Nicholas School
Dare's Lane
Ewshot La
Tadpole Lane
Dares Farm
Lea Farm
ODIHAM ROAD
Ewshot
Church Lane
Broomhill
Badger Way
Fox Way
Nightjar Cl
Nuthatch Cl
Kestrel Cl
Warren Corner
Redlands
Redlands Lane
Heath Lane
Ewshot Hall
Oak Park Golf Club
Dora's Green Lane
Dora's Green
Dippenhall Street
Clare Park
Middle Old Park
F G H J K
1 2 3 4 5 6 7

Aldermaston 108 C1
Aldermaston Soke 109 J5
Aldermaston Wharf 89 F4
Aldworth 23 F7
Amen Corner 98 C1
Andwell 162 D6
Arborfield 94 E3
Arborfield Cross 95 G4
Arborfield Garrison 115 K1
Ascot 101 J1
Ashampstead 37 G6
Ashampstead Green 37 H5
Ashe 172 B4
Ashford Hill 107 F7
Ashmore Green 65 G6
Aston 18 B5
Axmansford 125 K2
Bagnor 62 E6
Barkham 96 A5
Basingstoke 14 C3
Baughurst 126 A2
Beech Hill 112 D3
Beedon 34 C5
Beedon Hill 34 B5
Beenham 88 C1
Beenham Stocks 88 E1
Bidden 179 G5
Binfield 78 C4
Binfield Heath 44 D3
Birch Hill 99 K5
Bishop's Green 105 F5
Bix 16 A3
Black Dam 15 J8
Bockmer End 19 H1
Borough Marsh 45 K4
Bothampstead 49 G1
Bowling Alley 182 D4
Boxford 62 A3
Bracknell 10 F4
Bradfield 53 G7
Bramley 129 F5
Bramley Corner 128 C6
Bramley Green 129 H7
Bramshill 132 E2
Brighton Hill 175 J4
Brimpton 107 F2
Brimpton Common 107 K6
Broad Layings 102 B7
Broad Oak 165 F7
Broadplat 16 B6
Brock's Green 123 F1
Brookside 81 H4
Browninghill Green 126 C6
Bucklebury 67 F4
Bucklebury Alley 65 H4
Buckskin 159 F7
Bullbrook 80 C7
Burghclere 121 J2
Burghclere Common 103 K7
Burghfield 91 H2
Burghfield Common 91 F5
Burghfield Hill 91 H4
Burnt Hill 51 J4
Bury's Bank 104 D1
Calcot 71 H2
Calcot Row 71 J1
Cane End 42 A1
Carter's Hill 75 H7
Caversham 57 G2
Caversham Heights 57 G1
Chalkhouse Green 43 H3
Chandlers Green 131 G7
Chapel Row 67 K6
Charter Alley 142 E2
Charvil 45 K7
Chavey Down 80 E7
Chazey Heath 42 D5
Chieveley 48 A3
Chineham 145 G7
Church Crookham 167 G6
Churchend 55 K7
Church End 145 K4
Church Oakley 173 H2
Clarken Green 173 G2
Clay Hill 68 B4
Cleeve 25 F3
Cliddesden 176 A5
Cockpole Green 32 E3
Cold Ash 65 H7
Cold Harbour 26 A7
Cole Henley 169 J1
Coley 3 G9
Collins End 41 G2
Colt Hill 180 E1
Colthrop 86 C4
Compton 21 J6
Compton 35 K1
Court Corner 127 G6
Cranbourne 176 A2
Cray's Pond 26 C5
Crazies Hill 32 D5
Cricket Hill 135 K4
Crockham Heath 102 C2
Crondall 182 D5
Crookham 106 C3
Crookham Village 166 D5
Cross Lanes 41 K3
Crown Wood 100 A4
Crowsley 29 K7
Crowthorne 118 A4
Cufaude 145 F3
Curridge 64 C1
Danesfield 19 J4
Daneshill 161 F3
Deane 172 D3
Dipley 148 D2
Dogmersfield 166 B5
Donnington 83 G1
Dora's Green 183 H7
Dowlesgreen 77 H6
Dunley 153 F3
Dunsden Green 44 C5
Earley 9 K2
Earlstone Common 121 J1
East Fields 13 G6
Easthampstead 10 F8
Eastheath 97 F4
East Ilsley 20 E5
East Oakley 174 B2
Eastrop 15 J6
Ecchinswell 123 F6
Egbury 152 B5
Eling 49 K2
Elvetham 150 C5
Emmbrook 76 D6
Emmer Green 43 H6
Enborne 82 C7
Enborne Row 102 E4
Englefield 70 A2
Eversley 116 A7
Eversley Centre 134 C1
Eversley Cross 134 E1
Ewshot 183 H4
Exlade Street 27 G3
Fair Oak 125 F2
Fair Oak Green 129 J3
Farley Hill 115 G3
Finchampstead 116 C5
Fleet 167 H2
Four Houses Corner 90 D7
Four Points 37 F2
Foxdown 171 K2
Freefolk 170 A6
Frilsham 50 D6
Gallowstree Common 28 C6
Gardeners Green 97 K5
Goddard's Green 91 J6
Goldfinch Bottom 105 H3
Goose Hill 106 C5
Goring 25 F5
Goring Heath 41 F1
Grazeley 92 E5
Grazeley Green 92 A4
Great Hollands 99 F4
Great Lea Common 93 H1
Greenham 84 B7
Greenlands 17 K2
Greys Green 30 A1
Greywell 179 H1
Hambleden 18 A1
Hampstead Norreys 35 K6
Hannington 140 C6
Hanworth 99 H5
Hare Hatch 47 F4
Harmans Water 11 J8
Harpsden 31 H5
Harpsden Bottom 31 F5
Hartfordbridge 150 A2
Hartley Wespall 146 D1
Hartley Wintney 149 K4
Hatch 161 K6
Hatch Warren 175 F6
Haughurst Hill 107 K7
Hazeley 132 D6
Hazeley Bottom 149 F1
Hazeley Lea 132 E6
Headley 105 K7
Heath End 108 C7
Heather Row 163 G5
Heathlands 98 A7
Heckfield 131 K3
Henley-on-Thames 31 G2
Hermitage 49 G7
Highclere 120 C4
Highclere Street 120 A6
Hill Bottom 40 D1
Hillside 181 F2
Hollington Cross 120 A6
Holly Cross 33 F5
Holme Green 98 A4
Holt 164 C2
The Holt 47 G3
Honey Hill 98 B6
Hook 164 A2
Hook End 27 J3
Hopgoods Green 66 D6
Horncastle 71 K1
Hound Green 132 B6
Houndmills 159 K4
Hungerford 61 J3
Hungerford Green 37 G1
Hunt's Green 62 A5
Hurley 19 K6
Hurley Bottom 19 J7
Hurst 60 E5
Hyde End 107 F4
Ibworth 157 J1
Inhurst 125 K1
Jennetts Hill 68 A3
Kempshott 175 F3
Kidmore End 42 D1
Kiff Green 87 J1
Kiln Green 47 H3
Kingsclere 139 K1
Kingsclere Woodlands 124 B1
King's Furlong 14 A7
Langley Common 95 J6
Latchmere Green 128 B4
Laverstoke 170 D7
Limmerhill 96 D2
Litchfield 153 H3
Little Heath 55 F5
Little Hoddington 179 F7
Little Hungerford 49 H5
Little London 127 J6
Little Sandhurst 118 B6
Littlestead Green 44 B6
Longlane 65 F2
Lower Assendon 16 C4
Lower Basildon 39 G2
Lower Caversham 4 B2
Lower Common 115 J7
Lower Earley 75 G5
Lower Padworth 89 G2
Lower Shiplake 45 J1
Lyde Green 147 H3
Lynch 171 F4
Lynch Hill 169 J7
Malpas 54 C7
Mapledurham 41 K6
Mapledurwell 178 B1
Marsh Benham 82 A4
Matthewsgreen 77 F7
Mattingley 148 A2
Mays Green 30 E6
Medmenham 19 G5
Merryhill Green 76 C3
Middle Assendon 16 C2
Midgham 87 F4
Midgham Green 87 J2
Miles's Green 66 D7
Mill End 18 B3
Mill Green 106 A5
Mill Lane 182 B3
Monk Sherborne 143 G4
Mortimer 111 F2
Mortimer West End 110 C4
The Mount 8 A2
The Mount 120 C2
Murrell Green 148 D7
Nately Scures 163 F4
Newbury 12 C4
New Cross 45 H2
Newell Green 79 K3
Newfound 174 A1
Newnham 163 G3
New Town 4 D6
New Town 53 F1
Newtown 31 H3
Newtown 104 A4
North Ascot 81 F7
North Oakley 156 B2
North Street 70 C1
North Warnborough 164 B7
Nuney Green 41 K1
Oakley 173 K3
Oakridge 160 C4
Oare 49 G4
Odiham 180 D2
Old Basing 161 H5
Old Burghclere 137 H2
Overton 171 J5
Owlsmoor 118 E6
Padworth 89 H6
Padworth Common 109 J2
Pamber End 143 G1
Pamber Green 127 H5
Pamber Heath 109 G6
Pangbourne 40 A7
Pardown 174 A6
Parker's Corner 69 K3
Penwood 120 C2
Pheonix Green 149 F6
Pingewood 72 D6
Plastow Green 124 B2
Play Hatch 44 C7
Popeswood 78 C6
Popley 160 D2
Potbridge 165 F3
Poundgreen 92 D4
Pound Green 126 A6
Pound Street 121 F2
Priestwood 10 B1
Purley on Thames 55 F1
Purton 34 B4
Pyott's Hill 161 H2
Quick's Green 38 A7
Quidhampton 171 J3
Ramsdell 142 D3
Ravenswood
Village Settlement 117 K2
Reading 3 H6
Remenham 17 K5
Remenham Hill 32 B1
The Ridges 117 G4
Riseley 113 K5
Rotherfield Greys 29 K2
Rotherfield Peppard 29 G4
Rotherwick 147 H4
Rotten Green 150 E5
Rotten Row 68 C3
Ruscombe 46 D7
Ryeish Green 93 K3
Salters Heath 143 J2
Sandhurst 118 C7
Schoolgreen 94 A3
Scotland 67 G6
Shaw 84 A2
Sheffield Bottom 70 E6
Sherborne St John 143 J7
Sherfield on Loddon 146 B2
Shinfield 94 A2
Shiplake 45 H2
Shiplake Bottom 29 F5
Shiplake Row 44 E2
Silchester 128 A1
Sindlesham 75 J6
Skinners Green 82 E7
The Slade 66 B6
Sonning 59 G1
Sonning Common 29 F5
Sonning Eye 45 F7
South Ascot 101 K4
Southcote 72 C2
Southend 68 D4
South Ham 175 J1
Southington 171 G5
South View 14 E1
Spanish Green 130 C6
Speen 83 F2
Spencers Wood 93 G5
Stanford Dingley 68 A2
Stanford End 113 F5
Stockcross 82 C2
Stony Heath 142 A1
Stratfield Mortimer 111 J3
Stratfield Saye 130 C1
Stratfield Turgis 130 D5
Streatley 24 D4
Stroud Green 13 G7
Stubbles 37 K7
Sulham 54 D4
Sulhampstead Abbots 90 E3
Sulhampstead
Bannister Upper End 90 C2
Sulhamstead 90 A1
Swallowfield 114 A2
Sydmonton 138 C2
Tadley 127 F2
Thatcham 85 H3
Theale 70 C3
Three Ashes 128 C2
Three Mile Cross 93 J3
The Throat 97 F6
Tidmarsh 54 A3
Tilehurst 55 K4
Tokers Green 42 E5
Tot Hill 103 H7
Towns End 125 H7
Trash Green 71 F7
Trench Green 42 B5
Tunworth 177 K6
Turgis Green 130 D6
Turner's Green 66 C7
Tutts Clump 68 C3
Twyford 46 D7
Ufton Green 90 A2
Ufton Nervet 90 C3
Up Green 134 D3
Up Nately 162 E7
Upper Basildon 38 D7
Upper Bucklebury 86 D1
Upper Woolhampton 87 J3
Upper Wootton 158 B1
Upton Grey 178 D7
Wadwick 152 B5
Waltham St Lawrence 47 K5
Warfield 80 B1
Wargrave 46 B3
Warnborough Green 164 A6
Warren Corner 183 H5
Warren Row 33 H5
Wash Common 103 G3
Wash Water 102 E5
Wasing 108 A3
Water End 162 E5
Wellhouse 65 K1
West End 61 K1
West End Green 129 J1
West Fields 12 B5
West Green 148 E5
West Ham 159 J6
West Heath 142 D1
Westridge Green 23 H7
Westrop Green 65 J3
Wheat Hold 125 F3
Wheeler's Green 75 K1
Whistley Green 60 D4
Whitchurch 169 H7
Whitchurch Hill 40 D2
Whitchurch-on-Thames 40 A5
Whitehall 164 E5
Whitehouse Green 91 F1
Whiteknights 8 E3
Whitley 7 J7
Whitley Wood 73 K7
Whitway 121 G5
Wick Hill 80 A5
Wick Hill 117 F2
Wildmoor 146 B5
Wildridings 10 C7
Winchfield 165 H1
Winchfield Hurst 165 K3
Winkfield 81 G1
Winkfield Row 80 D5
Winklebury 159 G5
Winnersh 76 A4
Winslade 177 G7
Winterbourne 63 F1
Wokingham 97 J1
Wolverton 141 G1
Wolverton Common 125 H6
Woodcote 26 D3
Woodcott 152 C1
Woodlands 31 H1
Woodley 59 J7
Woodley Green 59 J6
Woodspeen 62 D7
Woolhampton 87 K5
Woolton Hill 120 A2
Woose Hill 96 E1
Wootton St Lawrence 158 C4
World's End 34 B6
Worting 159 F6
Yateley 135 J3
Yattendon 51 F4

USING THE STREET INDEX

Street names are listed alphabetically. Each street name is followed by its postal town or area locality, the Postcode District, the page number, and the reference to the square in which the name is found.

Example: **Abbots Cl** *GOR/PANG* RG8 **26** E3 1

Some entries are followed by a number in a blue box. This number indicates the location of the street within the referenced grid square. The full street name is listed at the side of the map page.

GENERAL ABBREVIATIONS

Abbreviation	Meaning
ACC	ACCESS
ALY	ALLEY
AP	APPROACH
AR	ARCADE
ASS	ASSOCIATION
AV	AVENUE
BCH	BEACH
BLDS	BUILDINGS
BND	BEND
BNK	BANK
BR	BRIDGE
BRK	BROOK
BTM	BOTTOM
BUS	BUSINESS
BVD	BOULEVARD
BY	BYPASS
CATH	CATHEDRAL
CEM	CEMETERY
CEN	CENTRE
CFT	CROFT
CH	CHURCH
CHA	CHASE
CHYD	CHURCHYARD
CIR	CIRCLE
CIRC	CIRCUS
CL	CLOSE
CLFS	CLIFFS
CMP	CAMP
CNR	CORNER
CO	COUNTY
COLL	COLLEGE
COM	COMMON
COMM	COMMISSION
CON	CONVENT
COT	COTTAGE
COTS	COTTAGES
CP	CAPE
CPS	COPSE
CR	CREEK
CREM	CREMATORIUM
CRS	CRESCENT
CSWY	CAUSEWAY
CT	COURT
CTRL	CENTRAL
CTS	COURTS
CTYD	COURTYARD
CUTT	CUTTINGS
CV	COVE
CYN	CANYON
DEPT	DEPARTMENT
DL	DALE
DM	DAM
DR	DRIVE
DRO	DROVE
DRY	DRIVEWAY
DWGS	DWELLINGS
E	EAST
EMB	EMBANKMENT
EMBY	EMBASSY
ESP	ESPLANADE
EST	ESTATE
EX	EXCHANGE
EXPY	EXPRESSWAY
EXT	EXTENSION
F/O	FLYOVER
FC	FOOTBALL CLUB
FK	FORK
FLD	FIELD
FLDS	FIELDS
FLS	FALLS
FLS	FLATS
FM	FARM
FT	FORT
FWY	FREEWAY
FY	FERRY
GA	GATE
GAL	GALLERY
GDN	GARDEN
GDNS	GARDENS
GLD	GLADE
GLN	GLEN
GN	GREEN
GND	GROUND
GRA	GRANGE
GRG	GARAGE
GT	GREAT
GTWY	GATEWAY
GV	GROVE
HGR	HIGHER
HL	HILL
HLS	HILLS
HO	HOUSE
HOL	HOLLOW
HOSP	HOSPITAL
HRB	HARBOUR
HTH	HEATH
HTS	HEIGHTS
HVN	HAVEN
HWY	HIGHWAY
IMP	IMPERIAL
IN	INLET
IND EST	INDUSTRIAL ESTATE
INF	INFIRMARY
INFO	INFORMATION
INT	INTERCHANGE
IS	ISLAND
JCT	JUNCTION
JTY	JETTY
KG	KING
KNL	KNOLL

L ... LAKE
LA ... LANE
LDG ... LODGE
LGT ... LIGHT
LK ... LOCK
LKS ... LAKES
LNDG ... LANDING
LTL ... LITTLE
LWR ... LOWER
MAG ... MAGISTRATE
MAN ... MANSIONS
MD ... MEAD
MDW ... MEADOWS
MEM ... MEMORIAL
MKT ... MARKET
MKTS ... MARKETS
ML ... MALL
ML ... MILL
MNR ... MANOR
MS ... MEWS
MSN ... MISSION
MT ... MOUNT
MTN ... MOUNTAIN
MTS ... MOUNTAINS
MUS ... MUSEUM
MWY ... MOTORWAY
N ... NORTH
NE ... NORTH EAST
NW ... NORTH WEST
O/P ... OVERPASS
OFF ... OFFICE
ORCH ... ORCHARD
OV ... OVAL
PAL ... PALACE
PAS ... PASSAGE
PAV ... PAVILION
PDE ... PARADE
PH ... PUBLIC HOUSE
PK ... PARK
PKWY ... PARKWAY
PL ... PLACE
PLN ... PLAIN
PLNS ... PLAINS
PLZ ... PLAZA
POL ... POLICE STATION
PR ... PRINCE
PREC ... PRECINCT
PREP ... PREPARATORY
PRIM ... PRIMARY
PROM ... PROMENADE
PRS ... PRINCESS
PRT ... PORT
PT ... POINT
PTH ... PATH
PZ ... PIAZZA
QD ... QUADRANT
QU ... QUEEN
QY ... QUAY
R ... RIVER
RBT ... ROUNDABOUT
RD ... ROAD
RDG ... RIDGE
REP ... REPUBLIC
RES ... RESERVOIR
RFC ... RUGBY FOOTBALL CLUB
RI ... RISE
RP ... RAMP
RW ... ROW
S ... SOUTH
SCH ... SCHOOL
SE ... SOUTH EAST
SER ... SERVICE AREA
SH ... SHORE
SHOP ... SHOPPING
SKWY ... SKYWAY
SMT ... SUMMIT
SOC ... SOCIETY
SP ... SPUR
SPR ... SPRING
SQ ... SQUARE
ST ... STREET
STN ... STATION
STR ... STREAM
STRD ... STRAND
SW ... SOUTH WEST
TDG ... TRADING
TER ... TERRACE
THWY ... THROUGHWAY
TNL ... TUNNEL
TOLL ... TOLLWAY
TPK ... TURNPIKE
TR ... TRACK
TRL ... TRAIL
TWR ... TOWER
U/P ... UNDERPASS
UNI ... UNIVERSITY
UPR ... UPPER
V ... VALE
VA ... VALLEY
VIAD ... VIADUCT
VIL ... VILLA
VIS ... VISTA
VLG ... VILLAGE
VLS ... VILLAS
VW ... VIEW
W ... WEST
WD ... WOOD
WHF ... WHARF
WK ... WALK
WKS ... WALKS
WLS ... WELLS
WY ... WAY
YD ... YARD
YHA ... YOUTH HOSTEL

POSTCODE TOWNS AND AREA ABBREVIATIONS

ASC ... Ascot
BFOR ... Bracknell Forest/Windlesham
BLKW ... Blackwater
BNFD ... Binfield
BRAK ... Bracknell
BSTK ... Basingstoke
CAV/SC ... Caversham/Sonning Common
CBLY ... Camberley
CHIN ... Chineham
CWTH ... Crowthorne
DEAN ... Deane/Oakley
DID ... Didcot
EARL ... Earley
EWKG ... Wokingham east
FARN ... Farnborough
FLET ... Fleet
GOR/PANG ... Goring/Pangbourne
HEN ... Henley-on-Thames
HTWY ... Hartley Wintney
KEMP ... Kempshott
KSCL ... Kingsclere/Rural Newbury
MDHD ... Maidenhead
MLW ... Marlow
NTHA ... Thatcham north
NWBY ... Newbury
ODIM ... Odiham
OVTN ... Overton/Rural Basingstoke
RAND ... Rural Andover
RDGW ... Reading west
READ ... Reading
RFNM ... Rural Farnham
SHST ... Sandhurst
STHA ... Thatcham south
TADY ... Tadley
THLE ... Theale/Rural Reading
TLHT ... Tilehurst
WAR/TWY ... Wargrave/Twyford
WDSR ... Windsor
WGFD ... Wallingford
WHCH ... Whitchurch
WHIT ... Whitley/Arborfield
WODY ... Woodley
WWKG ... Wokingham west
YTLY ... Yateley

Index - streets

A

Abattoirs Rd READ RG1 ... 3 G4
Abbey Cl BRAK RG12 ... 100 A3
EWKG RG40 ... 77 H7
NWBY RG14 ... 12 F9
Abbey Pk THLE RG7 ... 90 E4
Abbey Rd CHAM RG24 ... 160 B2
Abbey Sq READ RG1 ... 3 K6
Abbey St READ RG1 ... 3 K6
Abbotsbury BRAK RG12 ... 99 G3
Abbots Cl FLET GU13 ... 167 H2
GOR/PANG RG8 ... 26 E3
Abbotsmead Pl READ RG1 ... 3 G1
Abbots Rd NWBY RG14 ... 12 F7
THLE RG7 ... 90 E4
Abbot's Wk READ RG1 ... 3 K5
Abbott Cl KEMP RG22 ... 175 H2
Abbottswood Cl TADY RG26 ... 126 E2
Aberaman CAV/SC RG4 ... 43 G6
Aberford Cl TLHT RG30 ... 56 D6
Abex Rd NWBY RG14 ... 13 K4
Abingdon Cl BRAK RG12 ... 11 L9
Abingdon Dr CAV/SC RG4 ... 43 K6
Abingdon Rd KSCL RG20 ... 20 D4
Abrahams Rd HEN RG9 ... 17 F7
Acacia Av SHST GU47 ... 118 E7
Acacia Ct BRAK RG12 ... 10 E6
Acacia Rd READ RG1 ... 3 M9
Achilles Cl CHAM RG24 ... 145 G6
Ackrells Md SHST GU47 ... 118 A7
Acorn Dr EWKG RG40 ... 77 H7
NTHA RG18 ... 85 J2
Acre Rd WHIT RG2 ... 73 H6
Adam Cl TADY RG26 ... 108 B7
Adam Ct HEN RG9 ... 31 G1
Adams Dr FLET GU13 ... 167 J2
Adams Wy EARL RG6 ... 8 F7
Addington Rd READ RG1 ... 4 A9
Addiscombe Cha CALC RG31 ... 55 G2
Addiscombe Rd CWTH RG45 ... 118 D4
Addison Gdns ODIM RG29 ... 180 D1
Addison Rd READ RG1 ... 3 G3
Adelaide Rd EARL RG6 ... 9 H1
Adey's Cl NWBY RG14 ... 13 G7
Adkins Rd WAR/TWY RG10 ... 47 K5
Admirals Ct WHIT RG2 ... 3 G9
WHIT RG2 ... 7 G1
Admoor La THLE RG7 ... 69 F4
Adrian Cl HTWY RG27 ... 149 J5
Adwell Dr EARL RG6 ... 9 M9
EARL RG6 ... 75 G5
Adwell Sq HEN RG9 ... 31 G1
Adwood Ct STHA RG19 ... 85 K4
Agar Crs BNFD RG42 ... 79 J5
Agate Cl WWKG RG41 ... 76 D7
Aggisters La WWKG RG41 ... 96 B4
Aghemund Cl CHAM RG24 ... 145 F7
Agincourt Cl WWKG RG41 ... 96 D1
Agricola Wy STHA RG19 ... 86 A5
Ainsdale Crs TLHT RG30 ... 72 B2
Aintree Cl NWBY RG14 ... 13 J8
Aird Cl KSCL RG20 ... 120 B1
Ajax Cl CHAM RG24 ... 145 G6
Alanbrooke Cl HTWY RG27 ... 149 H4
Alandale Cl WHIT RG2 ... 74 A6
Albany Cl FLET GU13 ... 167 J3
Albany Park Dr WWKG RG41 ... 75 K3
Albany Rd FLET GU13 ... 167 H3
TLHT RG30 ... 2 B6
Alben Rd BNFD RG42 ... 78 D3
Albert Illsley Cl CALC RG31 ... 55 J5
Albert Rd BNFD RG42 ... 10 F2
CAV/SC RG4 ... 57 G1
CWTH RG45 ... 118 C3
EWKG RG40 ... 97 G2
HEN RG9 ... 31 H2
NWBY RG14 ... 12 D3
Albert St FLET GU13 ... 167 G2
Albury Cl TLHT RG30 ... 56 D4
Albury Gdns CALC RG31 ... 71 K3
Alcot Cl CWTH RG45 ... 118 C4
Aldbourne Av EARL RG6 ... 9 H4
Aldeburgh Cl CAV/SC RG4 ... 43 K4
Aldenham Cl CAV/SC RG4 ... 43 K6
Aldenham Ter BRAK RG12 ... 99 K4
Alderbrook Cl CWTH RG45 ... 117 K4
Alder Cl EARL RG6 ... 75 G5
Alder Dr CALC RG31 ... 55 H7
Alderfield Cl THLE RG7 ... 70 E2
Alder Gld THLE RG7 ... 90 E4
Alder Gv YTLY GU46 ... 135 H4
Alderley Cl WODY RG5 ... 59 J4
Alderman Willey Cl
EWKG RG40 ... 97 G1
Aldermaston Rd TADY RG26 ... 108 D6
TADY RG26 ... 127 G4
Aldermaston Rd South
BSTK RG21 ... 14 A1
Alderney Av KEMP RG22 ... 175 G5
Alderney Gdns WWKG RG41 ... 76 C4
Aldershot Rd FLET GU13 ... 167 K6
The Alders NTHA RG18 ... 85 J3
Alderwood CHAM RG24 ... 145 G7
Alder Wood Dr HTWY RG27 ... 164 A1
Aldridge Pk BNFD RG42 ... 80 E4
Aldworth Cl BRAK RG12 ... 10 D8
TLHT RG30 ... 72 D1
Aldworth Crs KEMP RG22 ... 159 K7
Aldworth Gdns CWTH RG45 ... 118 B3
Aldworth Rd GOR/PANG RG8 ... 38 D6
KSCL RG20 ... 21 K7
Alencon Link BSTK RG21 ... 14 D4
Alexander Rd OVTN RG25 ... 171 H5
STHA RG19 ... 85 K5
Alexandra Ct EWKG RG40 ... 97 H2
Alexandra Rd BSTK RG21 ... 14 B5
READ RG1 ... 4 B8
Alford Cl TLHT RG30 ... 55 J5
Alfred St READ RG1 ... 2 F6
Alison Cl THLE RG7 ... 90 E6
Allcroft Rd READ RG1 ... 7 M1
Allen Cl BSTK RG21 ... 14 A8
Allendale Cl SHST GU47 ... 118 B6
Allendale Rd EARL RG6 ... 9 J5
All Hallows Rd CAV/SC RG4 ... 58 A2
Allison Gdns GOR/PANG RG8 ... 41 H7
Alliston Wy KEMP RG22 ... 175 H1
Allnatt Av WWKG RG41 ... 76 B5
Allnutt Av BSTK RG21 ... 15 H5
Allonby Cl EARL RG6 ... 75 G4
All Saints Cl EWKG RG40 ... 77 H7
All Saints Ri BNFD RG42 ... 80 B5
Allsmoor La BRAK RG12 ... 100 C1
All Souls' Rd ASC SL5 ... 101 K3
Alma St TLHT RG30 ... 56 D5
Almond Av NWBY RG14 ... 83 K2
Almond Cl CHAM RG24 ... 161 H5
WWKG RG41 ... 96 B3
Almond Dr CAV/SC RG4 ... 58 C1
NTHA RG18 ... 85 J3
Almswood Rd TADY RG26 ... 108 D6
The Aloes FLET GU13 ... 167 J3
Alphington Rd WHIT RG2 ... 73 J6
Alpine Ct KEMP RG22 ... 175 F1
Alpine St READ RG1 ... 4 C3
Alston Ms STHA RG19 ... 85 H5
Alton Rd FLET GU13 ... 167 K2
ODIM RG29 ... 180 C3
Amazon Cl BSTK RG21 ... 14 A6
Ambarrow Crs SHST GU47 ... 118 A7
Ambarrow La CWTH RG45 ... 117 J6
Ambassador BRAK RG12 ... 99 G3
Amberley Cl NWBY RG14 ... 12 C1
Amberley Dr WAR/TWY RG10 ... 46 C6
Amblecote Rd TLHT RG30 ... 56 C6
Ambleside Cl WODY RG5 ... 59 H6
Ambrook Rd WHIT RG2 ... 73 J6
Ambrose Pl READ RG1 ... 2 F6
Ambrose Rd TADY RG26 ... 126 E1
Ambury Rd GOR/PANG RG8 ... 23 F6
Amersham Rd CAV/SC RG4 ... 4 A1
Amethyst Cl WWKG RG41 ... 76 C7
Amethyst La TLHT RG30 ... 56 D7
Amherst Rd EARL RG6 ... 5 G9
Amity Rd READ RG1 ... 4 C6
Amity St READ RG1 ... 4 C5
Ammanford CAV/SC RG4 ... 43 G7
Amners Farm Rd TLHT RG30 ... 72 A6
Ampere Rd NWBY RG14 ... 13 G3
Amport Cl CHAM RG24 ... 161 H3
Ancaster Dr ASC SL5 ... 81 H6
Ancastle Gn HEN RG9 ... 31 F2
Ancells Rd FARN GU14 ... 151 J5
Anchor Rd KSCL RG20 ... 124 A7
Anchor Yd BSTK RG21 ... 14 F6
Anderson Av EARL RG6 ... 5 H8
Anderson Crs WHIT RG2 ... 95 H5
Andover Cl CALC RG31 ... 55 J4
Andover Dro KSCL RG20 ... 102 E4
Andover Rd DEAN RG23 ... 173 G3
KSCL RG20 ... 102 E6
NWBY RG14 ... 103 H1
OVTN RG25 ... 172 D4
Andrew Cl EWKG RG40 ... 97 K2
Andrews Cl FLET GU13 ... 167 H5
THLE RG7 ... 70 D3
Andrews Rd EARL RG6 ... 9 J5
Andwell La HTWY RG27 ... 162 D5
Angel Ct NWBY RG14 ... 12 E2
Angel Md THLE RG7 ... 87 K5
Angel Mdw ODIM RG29 ... 180 D1
Angel Pl BNFD RG42 ... 78 D4
Angle Field Rd CAV/SC RG4 ... 57 K2
Anglers Wy READ RG1 ... 4 A6
Anglesey Cl CHAM RG24 ... 160 D1
Angora Wy FARN GU14 ... 151 J6
Angus Cl CALC RG31 ... 71 K2
Annadale NTHA RG18 ... 65 H5
Anneforde Pl BNFD RG42 ... 79 H5
Annesley Gdns WWKG RG41 ... 76 B3
Annes Wy FLET GU13 ... 167 J5
Annettes Cft FLET GU13 ... 167 F7
Anson Crs WHIT RG2 ... 74 A7
Anstey Cl BSTK RG21 ... 176 B2
Anstey Pl THLE RG7 ... 91 F4
Anstey Rd READ RG1 ... 3 G7
Anston Cl EARL RG6 ... 74 D6
Antar Cl BSTK RG21 ... 14 A6
Antares Cl WWKG RG41 ... 96 E1
Anthian Cl WODY RG5 ... 60 A5
Anton Cl DEAN RG23 ... 174 A3
Antrim Cl KEMP RG22 ... 175 G1
Antrim Rd WODY RG5 ... 59 G7
Anvil Cl THLE RG7 ... 93 H6
Appelford Cl STHA RG19 ... 85 J5
Appleby End TLHT RG30 ... 56 C6
Apple Cl CALC RG31 ... 55 G1
WWKG RG41 ... 96 E2
Appledore BRAK RG12 ... 99 G4
Appleford Rd TLHT RG30 ... 72 B2
Applegarth Cl BSTK RG21 ... 15 G8
Apple Tree Cl NWBY RG14 ... 103 H1
Appletree Cl CAV/SC RG4 ... 29 F5
DEAN RG23 ... 174 A4
Appletree La THLE RG7 ... 93 J5
Appletree Pl BNFD RG42 ... 10 C2
Apple Tree Wy SHST GU47 ... 118 E7
Apple Wy CHAM RG24 ... 161 J6
Apsey Ct BNFD RG42 ... 79 F5
Aquila Cl WWKG RG41 ... 96 D1
Arborfield Rd WHIT RG2 ... 94 C3
Arbor La WWKG RG41 ... 76 A3
Arbor Mdw WWKG RG41 ... 76 A3
Arbour Cl READ RG1 ... 6 E2
Archangel Wy NTHA RG18 ... 86 A3
Archery Flds ODIM RG29 ... 180 E1
Archway Rd READ RG1 ... 3 H1
Arden Cl BRAK RG12 ... 80 D7
Ardglen Rd WHCH RG28 ... 169 G7
Ardingly BRAK RG12 ... 99 H4
Ardwell Cl CWTH RG45 ... 117 K3
Arenal Dr CWTH RG45 ... 118 C5
Argente Cl FARN GU14 ... 151 J6
Argyle Rd NWBY RG14 ... 12 D6
READ RG1 ... 2 D7
Argyle St READ RG1 ... 2 D6
Arkle Av STHA RG19 ... 84 E4
Arkwright Cl KSCL RG20 ... 120 C3
Arkwright Dr BNFD RG42 ... 78 E7
Arkwright Rd WHIT RG2 ... 7 J5
Arlington Cl BNFD RG42 ... 10 C1
Arlott Dr BSTK RG21 ... 14 F1
Armadale Ct TLHT RG30 ... 2 A9
Armour Hl CALC RG31 ... 55 J4
Armour Rd CALC RG31 ... 55 J4
Armour Wk CALC RG31 ... 55 J4
Armstrong Rd CHAM RG24 ... 15 L1
Armstrong Wy WODY RG5 ... 59 K6
Arncliffe BRAK RG12 ... 10 C8
Arne Cl KEMP RG22 ... 175 J5
Arnett Av EWKG RG40 ... 116 D1
Arnhem Rd NWBY RG14 ... 13 H4
Arnside Cl WAR/TWY RG10 ... 46 C5
Arran Cl DEAN RG23 ... 173 K2
Arrowhead Rd THLE RG7 ... 70 E4
Arrow La HTWY RG27 ... 149 G3
Arrow Smith Wy STHA RG19 ... 86 A5
Arthur Rd NWBY RG14 ... 12 B6
WWKG RG41 ... 77 F7
Arthurstone Birches
BNFD RG42 ... 78 E3
Arun Cl WWKG RG41 ... 76 A5
Arundel Cl FLET GU13 ... 167 J3
Arundel Gdns DEAN RG23 ... 159 G4
Arundel Rd WODY RG5 ... 59 H7
Arwood Av TADY RG26 ... 109 G7
Ascension Cl CHAM RG24 ... 160 D2
Ascot Cl NWBY RG14 ... 13 J9
Ashampstead Rd
GOR/PANG RG8 ... 38 B6
THLE RG7 ... 53 F6
TLHT RG30 ... 72 C2
Ashbourne BRAK RG12 ... 99 G4
Ashbourne Wy STHA RG19 ... 85 G4
Ashburton Rd WHIT RG2 ... 7 M7
Ashbury Dr CALC RG31 ... 55 H6
Ashby Ct WHIT RG2 ... 73 J7
Ashcroft Cl CAV/SC RG4 ... 43 F7
Ashdale Pk EWKG RG40 ... 117 H1
Ashdown Cl BRAK RG12 ... 80 C7
Asher Dr ASC SL5 ... 81 F6
Ashfield CHAM RG24 ... 145 G7
Ashford Av CAV/SC RG4 ... 29 F6
Ashford Hill Rd STHA RG19 ... 105 J6
Ash Ga NTHA RG18 ... 86 A3
Ash Gv CHAM RG24 ... 161 K5
KSCL RG20 ... 124 A7
Ash La TADY RG26 ... 108 B7
TADY RG26 ... 128 C4
THLE RG7 ... 91 F3
Ashlea HTWY RG27 ... 164 A1
Ashlee Wk GOR/PANG RG8 ... 26 E3
Ashley Cl EARL RG6 ... 9 K8
NFNM GU10 ... 182 E5
Ashley Rd READ RG1 ... 6 C1
Ashman Rd STHA RG19 ... 86 A4
Ashmere Cl CALC RG31 ... 71 H2
Ashmere Ter TLHT RG30 ... 2 C4
Ashmoor La CHAM RG24 ... 162 B5
Ashmore Green Rd NTHA RG18 ... 65 F7
Ashmore Rd WHIT RG2 ... 7 L9
Ashridge Gn BNFD RG42 ... 10 E1
Ashridge Rd EWKG RG40 ... 77 J6
Ash Rd KSCL RG20 ... 104 E5
TLHT RG30 ... 55 K6
Ash Ter NTHA RG18 ... 65 G6
Ashton Cl CALC RG31 ... 55 H5
Ashton Rd WWKG RG41 ... 76 E5
Ash Tree Cl DEAN RG23 ... 173 K4
Ashtrees Rd WODY RG5 ... 59 J5
Ashurst Cl TADY RG26 ... 126 D1
Ashville Wy WWKG RG41 ... 96 E2
Ash Wy WWKG RG41 ... 96 C4
Ashwood WODY RG5 ... 75 G1
Ashwood Cl CALC RG31 ... 55 G7
Ashwood Dr NWBY RG14 ... 13 M2
Ashwood Wy DEAN RG23 ... 159 J4
Ashworth Dr STHA RG19 ... 85 H5
Askew Dr THLE RG7 ... 93 J4
Aspen Gdns HTWY RG27 ... 164 A1
Aster Rd KEMP RG22 ... 175 F5
Astley Cl WWKG RG41 ... 76 E7
Aston Av CALC RG31 ... 55 G5
Aston Cl GOR/PANG RG8 ... 40 C7
Aston Ferry La HEN RG9 ... 18 B5
Aston La HEN RG9 ... 18 B7
Astor Cl WWKG RG41 ... 76 C3
Astra Md BNFD RG42 ... 80 E4
Atbara Rd FLET GU13 ... 167 H7
Atherton Cl TLHT RG30 ... 56 A5
Atrebatti Rd SHST GU47 ... 118 D7
Attebrouche Ct BRAK RG12 ... 100 A5
Atte La BNFD RG42 ... 79 K4
Attenborough Cl FARN GU14 ... 151 J7
Attlee Gdns FLET GU13 ... 167 G7
Attwood Cl BSTK RG21 ... 14 A7
Auckland Rd EARL RG6 ... 5 G9
Auclum Cl THLE RG7 ... 91 G5
Auclum La THLE RG7 ... 91 G5
Audley Cl NWBY RG14 ... 84 C2
Audley St TLHT RG30 ... 2 B5
Audley Wy ASC SL5 ... 101 G1
August End TLHT RG30 ... 56 D5
Augustine Wk BNFD RG42 ... 80 B5
Augustus Dr DEAN RG23 ... 159 H4
Auklet Cl KEMP RG22 ... 174 E5
Austen Gv KEMP RG22 ... 175 K2
Austin Rd WODY RG5 ... 59 J7
Auton Pl HEN RG9 ... 31 G3
Autumn Cl CAV/SC RG4 ... 43 K5
Autumn Wk WAR/TWY RG10 ... 46 C2
Avalon Rd EARL RG6 ... 9 L5
Avebury BRAK RG12 ... 99 H4
Avebury Sq READ RG1 ... 8 B1
Avenue Rd FLET GU13 ... 167 G1
The Avenue ASC SL5 ... 81 J5
CWTH RG45 ... 118 B3
FLET GU13 ... 167 F2
THLE RG7 ... 111 G3
Averton Cl BNFD RG42 ... 79 J5
Avery Cl EWKG RG40 ... 116 E2
Avington Cl CALC RG31 ... 55 G5
Avondale Rd FLET GU13 ... 167 H1
Avon Gv BRAK RG12 ... 79 K5
Avon Pl READ RG1 ... 4 B5
Avon Rd DEAN RG23 ... 174 A3
Avonway NWBY RG14 ... 13 M1
Avon Wy THLE RG7 ... 89 H1
Award Rd FLET GU13 ... 167 G6
Axbridge BRAK RG12 ... 100 B3
Axbridge Rd WHIT RG2 ... 7 M8
Ayesgarth FLET GU13 ... 167 J6
Aylesford Wy STHA RG19 ... 86 B5
Aylesham Wy YTLY GU46 ... 135 G3
Aylings Cl DEAN RG23 ... 159 G7
Aylsham Cl TLHT RG30 ... 55 K5
Aylwin Cl BSTK RG21 ... 176 B2
Ayres La KSCL RG20 ... 121 J1
Ayrshire Gdns FARN GU14 ... 151 J6
Ayrton Senna Rd CALC RG31 ... 55 H6
Aysgarth BRAK RG12 ... 99 G4
Azalea Cl WWKG RG41 ... 76 A4
Azalea Gdns FLET GU13 ... 167 J6

B

Babbington Rd WHIT RG2 ... 94 A1
Bach Cl KEMP RG22 ... 175 J5
Back La THLE RG7 ... 68 C1
THLE RG7 ... 88 D1
THLE RG7 ... 93 H7
THLE RG7 ... 107 J5
THLE RG7 ... 110 B4
Backsideans WAR/TWY RG10 ... 46 C2
The Bader Wy WODY RG5 ... 75 K1
Badgemore La HEN RG9 ... 17 G7
Badger Dr WAR/TWY RG10 ... 46 C5
Badger's Bank CHAM RG24 ... 161 G3
Badgers Cl FLET GU13 ... 167 G3
Badgers Gld THLE RG7 ... 91 F5
Badgers Holt YTLY GU46 ... 135 G4
Badgers Ri CAV/SC RG4 ... 43 H7
Badgers Sett CWTH RG45 ... 118 A3
Badgers Wk HEN RG9 ... 45 K1
Badgers Wy BRAK RG12 ... 80 C6
Badger Wy NFNM GU10 ... 183 J4
Bagnols Wy NWBY RG14 ... 12 A6
Bagshot Rd BRAK RG12 ... 10 F6
BRAK RG12 ... 99 K4
Bagwell La ODIM RG29 ... 165 H4
Bailey's La WAR/TWY RG10 ... 61 K1
Baily Av NTHA RG18 ... 85 G3
Bainbridge Rd CALC RG31 ... 71 G2
Baird Av KEMP RG22 ... 175 K2
Baird Rd WHIT RG2 ... 95 H7

Baker St READ RG1 2 E7
Baldons Cl GOR/PANG RG8 26 E3 2
Balfour Crs BRAK RG12 99 J3
NWBY RG14 103 F3
Balfour Dr CALC RG31 71 G2
Ballamoor Cl CALC RG31 71 F2
Ballard Cl KEMP RG22 175 H1
Balliol Rd CAV/SC RG4 56 E2
Balliol Wy SHST GU47 119 F7
Ball Pit Rd KSCL RG20 20 B5
Balme Cl WAR/TWY RG10 60 A2
Balmoral Wy KEMP RG22 175 F5
Balmore Dr CAV/SC RG4 57 J1
Balmore Pk CAV/SC RG4 57 H1
Bamburgh Cl WHIT RG2 7 M5
Bamford Pl CALC RG31 71 G2 1
Banbury BRAK RG12 100 B5
Banbury Gdns CAV/SC RG4 57 K2 1
Bancroft Pl CALC RG31 71 G3 1
Bank Side EWKG RG40 116 E2
Bankside Cl WHIT RG2 8 B7
Bannister Gdns HTWY RG27 134 D1 1
Bannister Pl THLE RG7 107 G2 1
Bannister Rd THLE RG7 90 E5
Barbara Cl FLET GU13 167 J5
Barbara's Meadow CALC RG31 55 G3
Barbel Av BSTK RG21 15 K4
Barbel Cl EARL RG6 5 H4
Barber Cl WAR/TWY RG10 60 D6
Barberry Cl FLET GU13 167 H5
Barbour Cl ODIM RG29 180 B5
Barbrook Cl CALC RG31 55 J2 1
Barclay Rd CALC RG31 71 J2 1
Barclose Av CAV/SC RG4 57 K2
Bardolph's Cl CAV/SC RG4 42 E4
Bardwell Cl KEMP RG22 159 H7
The Baredown HTWY RG27 163 G4
Barefoot Cl CALC RG31 55 G4
Barfield Rd NTHA RG18 85 F3
Barge La THLE RG7 113 H3
Barholm Cl EARL RG6 75 H4 1
Barkby EARL RG6 9 M8
Barker Cl WHIT RG2 115 H1
Barker Ct WAR/TWY RG10 60 E5
Barkham Ride EWKG RG40 96 B6
EWKG RG40 116 E1
Barkham Rd WHIT RG2 95 H4
WWKG RG41 95 K5
Barkham St EWKG RG40 96 B5
Barkhart Dr EWKG RG40 77 H7
Barkhart Gdns EWKG RG40 77 H7
Barkis Md SHST GU47 119 F6 1
Barkwith Cl EARL RG6 75 H4 2
Barley Md BNFD RG42 80 B5 3
Barley Mow Cl HTWY RG27 166 A3
Barley Wy FARN GU14 151 J5
Barlows Rd TADY RG26 126 E2
Barnard Cl CAV/SC RG4 43 K6
Barn Cl BRAK RG12 11 K3
TLHT RG30 6 A3
Barn Crs NWBY RG14 103 G1
Barnett Ct BRAK RG12 11 H3
Barnett Gn BRAK RG12 99 J4
Barnfield YTLY GU46 135 J4 1
Barn La DEAN RG23 173 K4
HEN RG9 17 F6
Barn Meadow Cl FLET GU13 183 G1
Barn Owl Wy THLE RG7 91 G4
Barnsdale Rd WHIT RG2 8 B5
Barnwood Cl TLHT RG30 2 C4
Baron Ct TLHT RG30 2 C7
Baronsmead HEN RG9 31 G1 2
Barracane Dr CWTH RG45 118 C4
Barracks La THLE RG7 93 J6
Barracks Rd STHA RG19 104 E4
Barra Cl DEAN RG23 173 K2
Barrett Crs EWKG RG40 97 J1
Barrett's La WHIT RG2 95 G1
Barrington Cl EARL RG6 5 J9
Barrington Wy READ RG1 6 C1
Barron Pl CHAM RG24 159 G3
Barry Pl READ RG1 3 G3
Barry Sq BRAK RG12 100 A5
Barry Wy KEMP RG22 175 J5
Bartholomew Pl BNFD RG42 80 B5 4
Bartholomew St NWBY RG14 12 D6
Bartlemy Cl NWBY RG14 12 A9
Bartlemy Rd NWBY RG14 12 A9
Bartley Wy HTWY RG27 164 B3
Bartok Cl KEMP RG22 175 K3
Barton Rd CALC RG31 55 G7
Barton's Dr YTLY GU46 135 J5
Bartons La CHAM RG24 161 H3
Barwell Cl CWTH RG45 118 A4
Basemoors BRAK RG12 11 L3
Basil Cl EARL RG6 74 C5
Basingbourne Cl FLET GU13 167 H5
Basingbourne Rd FLET GU13 167 G6
Basing Rd CHAM RG24 15 M3
CHAM RG24 161 G5
Basingstoke Rd HTWY RG27 131 G3
KSCL RG20 124 B7
TADY RG26 142 D5
THLE RG7 88 D6
THLE RG7 93 H2
THLE RG7 113 J1
WHIT RG2 7 K5
WHIT RG2 73 J5
Basing Vw BSTK RG21 15 H3
Baskerville La HEN RG9 45 K1
Baskerville Rd CAV/SC RG4 29 F6
Baslow Rd WWKG RG41 76 A4
Basmore La HEN RG9 32 A4
Bassett Cl EARL RG6 75 F6 1
Batchelor Dr CHAM RG24 161 K6
Batcombe Md BRAK RG12 100 B5
Bath Rd CALC RG31 71 J1
CAV/SC RG4 59 G4
EARL RG6 5 M3
NTHA RG18 84 E3
NWBY RG14 83 G2
READ RG1 2 D9
THLE RG7 70 C4
THLE RG7 87 G5
THLE RG7 89 G2
TLHT RG30 6 A1
WAR/TWY RG10 47 K1
Bathurst Rd WWKG RG41 76 A4
Battens Av OVTN RG25 171 J4
Battery End NWBY RG14 103 G2
Battle Cl NWBY RG14 83 G3
Battle Rd GOR/PANG RG8 25 J4
NWBY RG14 103 F2
Battle St READ RG1 2 E5
Batty's Barn Cl EWKG RG40 97 J2 1
Baughurst Rd TADY RG26 126 B4
TADY RG26 142 B2
THLE RG7 109 K2
The Baxendales NWBY RG14 13 J8
Bay Cl EARL RG6 8 E9
Baydon Dr READ RG1 6 D1
Bayford Dr CALC RG31 72 A2
Bayley Ct WWKG RG41 76 A5
Bayliss Rd WAR/TWY RG10 46 C3
Baynard Cl BSTK RG21 15 G1
Bay Rd BRAK RG12 11 L3
Bay Tree Ri CALC RG31 71 H1
Beach's Crs TADY RG26 127 K6
Beacon Hill Rd FLET GU13 167 J7
Beaconsfield Rd BSTK RG21 14 F7
Beaconsfield Wy EARL RG6 9 G8
Beal's La CALC RG31 55 F6
Beal's Pightle TADY RG26 142 E3
Beancroft Rd STHA RG19 85 J5
Bean Oak Rd EWKG RG40 97 K1
Bear Hl KSCL RG20 139 K1
Bear La NWBY RG14 12 E4
WAR/TWY RG10 47 G2
Bearwood FLET GU13 167 H2
Bearwood Pth WWKG RG41 75 K4
Bearwood Rd WWKG RG41 76 A6
Beatty Dr TLHT RG30 55 K5
Beauchief Cl EARL RG6 74 C6 1
Beauclerk Gn HTWY RG27 165 H2
Beaufield Cl WODY RG5 59 G6
Beaufort Gdns ASC SL5 81 H6
Beaufort Rd FLET GU13 167 J4
Beaulieu Cl BRAK RG12 100 C1
Beaumont Gdns BRAK RG12 11 L9
Beaurepaire Cl TADY RG26 128 E6
Beaver Cl WWKG RG41 97 G4
Beaver La YTLY GU46 135 K4
Beavers Cl TADY RG26 108 C7
Beaver Wy WODY RG5 60 A6
Beck Ct READ RG1 3 M9
Beckett Cl DEAN RG23 159 F6
EWKG RG40 97 K1 1
Beckford Av BRAK RG12 99 J4
Beckford Cl WWKG RG41 76 E5 1
Beckfords GOR/PANG RG8 38 D7
Beckley Cl GOR/PANG RG8 26 E3 3
Bec Tithe GOR/PANG RG8 40 D1
Beddington Ct CHAM RG24 161 H2 1
Bedford Cl NWBY RG14 103 F3 1
Bedford Gdns WWKG RG41 76 E6
Bedford Rd READ RG1 2 E5
Bedfordshire Down BNFD RG42 80 C4
Bedfordshire Wy WWKG RG41 96 D1 2
Beecham Berry KEMP RG22 175 J5
Beecham Rd TLHT RG30 56 D6
Beechbrook Av YTLY GU46 135 J4
Beech Cl NTHA RG18 36 B7
OVTN RG25 171 J2
TADY RG26 129 H7 1
TLHT RG30 91 G3
Beechcrest Vw HTWY RG27 164 A1 2
Beechcroft NTHA RG18 36 B7
The Beeches CALC RG31 55 J2 2
GOR/PANG RG8 24 E6
KEMP RG22 175 J6
Beech Gln BRAK RG12 10 E7
Beech Hill Rd THLE RG7 113 F2
Beech La EARL RG6 9 J7
GOR/PANG RG8 25 J2
Beechnut Cl WWKG RG41 96 E2
Beech Ride FLET GU13 167 G4
Beech Ri CAV/SC RG4 29 F5
Beech Rd CAV/SC RG4 42 E5
GOR/PANG RG8 41 F7
KSCL RG20 105 F6
WHIT RG2 8 D8
Beech Tree Cl DEAN RG23 173 K4
Beech Wk STHA RG19 85 K5
Beech Wy DEAN RG23 159 H4
Beechwood Av CALC RG31 55 J5
WODY RG5 59 G6
Beechwood Cl ASC SL5 81 H5
FLET GU13 167 F5
GOR/PANG RG8 26 C5 1
KEMP RG22 175 H6
Beedon Dr BRAK RG12 98 E4
Beehive La BRAK RG12 78 D7
Beehive Rd BRAK RG12 78 E7
Beeson Cl GOR/PANG RG8 26 E3 4
Beeston Wy EARL RG6 74 D6
Beethoven Rd KEMP RG22 175 K4
Beggars Hill Rd WODY RG5 60 A4
Beggarwood La DEAN RG23 175 F7
KEMP RG22 175 J6
Begonia Cl KEMP RG22 175 F5
Behoes La GOR/PANG RG8 26 C2
Beighton Cl EARL RG6 74 C6 2
Bell Ct WAR/TWY RG10 46 C7 1
Belle Av EARL RG6 9 G2
Bellevue WHCH RG28 169 H7
Belle Vue Rd CHAM RG24 161 J5
HEN RG9 31 G3
READ RG1 2 E7
Bell Foundry La EWKG RG40 77 H6
Bell Holt NWBY RG14 103 F3
Bell House Gdns EWKG RG40 97 G1 2
Bellisle GOR/PANG RG8 41 G7 1
Bell La GOR/PANG RG8 23 G7
HEN RG9 17 H7
Bell Meadow Rd HTWY RG27 164 A2
Bell Rd CHAM RG24 15 L2
Bell St HEN RG9 31 H1
WHCH RG28 169 H7
Belmont Hts KEMP RG22 175 H7
Belmont Rd CWTH RG45 118 C2
TLHT RG30 2 B7
Belvedere Cl FLET GU13 166 D2 1
Belvedere Dr NWBY RG14 12 E9
Belvedere Gdns CHAM RG24 145 H6 1
Belvedere Wk WWKG RG41 75 K3
Bembridge Ct CWTH RG45 117 K4 1
Bembridge Pl READ RG1 3 L6 1
Benedict Gn BNFD RG42 80 B5 1
Benetfeld Rd BNFD RG42 78 C4
Benett Cl NWBY RG14 83 J2
Benett Gdns NWBY RG14 83 J2
Benham Cha KSCL RG20 82 B2
Benham Hl NTHA RG18 85 F3
Benham La THLE RG7 114 A5
Bennet Cl BSTK RG21 15 H1
BSTK RG21 160 D4
Bennet Rd WHIT RG2 73 H5
Bennett's Hl TLHT RG30 71 G7
Bennings Cl BNFD RG42 79 H5
Benning Wy EWKG RG40 77 H6
Bensgrove Cl GOR/PANG RG8 26 E3 5
Benson Cl WHIT RG2 8 B5
Benson Rd CWTH RG45 118 A3
Benwell Cl ODIM RG29 180 B4
Benyon Ct READ RG1 2 D9
Bere Court Rd GOR/PANG RG8 53 J3
Bere Hl WHCH RG28 169 H6
Bere Hill Cl WHCH RG28 169 J6
Bere Rd BRAK RG12 100 B4
Beresford Rd TLHT RG30 2 C5
Berewyk Cl KEMP RG22 175 F5 1
Berkeley Av READ RG1 2 C9
WHIT RG2 3 H9
Berkeley Cl FLET GU13 167 J2 1
Berkeley Dr KEMP RG22 176 A4
Berkeley Rd NWBY RG14 12 C5
Berkshire Circular Route
KSCL RG20 20 A3
KSCL RG20 21 F3
Berkshire Circular Routes
GOR/PANG RG8 54 C3
KSCL RG20 82 D7
THLE RG7 51 G7
THLE RG7 89 H1
THLE RG7 111 G2
WAR/TWY RG10 33 G6
Berkshire Dr CALC RG31 55 H5
STHA RG19 86 B5
Berkshire Rd HEN RG9 31 G3
Berkshire Wy BRAK RG12 10 A5
EWKG RG40 98 D1
Bermuda Cl CHAM RG24 160 D2
Bernadine Cl BNFD RG42 80 B5 6
Bernersh Cl SHST GU47 118 D7 1
Bernstein Rd KEMP RG22 175 H4
Berrycroft BNFD RG42 11 K1
Berrydown La OVTN RG25 171 K5
Berrylands Rd CAV/SC RG4 57 J2
TLHT RG30 72 A5
Berrys La TLHT RG30 72 C6
Berstead Cl EARL RG6 74 E5 1
Berwyn Cl KEMP RG22 175 F1
Bessemer Rd BSTK RG21 176 A2
Beswick Gdns BRAK RG12 80 C6 1
Betam Rd READ RG1 4 A6
Betchworth Av EARL RG6 9 H5
Bethesda Cl GOR/PANG RG8 38 D6
Bethesda St GOR/PANG RG8 38 D6
Betjeman Wk YTLY GU46 135 G5
Betteridge Rd STHA RG19 86 A5
Betty Grove La WWKG RG41 75 J7
Beveren Cl FARN GU14 151 J6
Beverley Cl BSTK RG21 176 C3
NTHA RG18 85 H3
Beverley Gdns WAR/TWY RG10 46 D3
Beverley Rd CALC RG31 55 J4
The Bevers THLE RG7 111 F2
Bexley Ct TLHT RG30 2 A8
Bexmoor CHAM RG24 161 H5
Bexmoor Wy CHAM RG24 161 H5
Bibury Cl WODY RG5 75 G2
Bicester Cl WHCH RG28 169 H7
Bidden Rd ODIM RG29 179 K2
OVTN RG25 178 E7
Bideford Cl WODY RG5 9 M2
Big Barn Gv BNFD RG42 80 A5 1
Bigbury Gdns WHIT RG2 7 M6
Biggs La EWKG RG40 95 J7
Billing Av EWKG RG40 116 D2
Billington Wy NTHA RG18 85 H1
Binbrook Cl EARL RG6 75 G4
Binfield Rd BNFD RG42 79 G5
EWKG RG40 78 A7
EWKG RG40 97 K1
Binfields Cl CHAM RG24 161 G2
Bingley Gv WODY RG5 59 J4
Birch Av FLET GU13 167 G2
TLHT RG30 56 B5
Birch Cl CAV/SC RG4 29 G7
Birchen Cl GOR/PANG RG8 26 E3 6
Birches Crest KEMP RG22 175 J6
Birchetts Cl BNFD RG42 10 E1
Birch Gv BRAK RG12 11 H7
HTWY RG27 164 A1
Birch Hill Rd BRAK RG12 99 J5
Birchland Cl THLE RG7 110 D2
Birch La ASC SL5 80 D6
THLE RG7 110 E3
Birchmead WWKG RG41 76 C4
Birch Rd EWKG RG40 117 F1
TADY RG26 108 B6
THLE RG7 91 F4
Birch Side CWTH RG45 118 A2
Birch Vw WHIT RG2 8 C8
Birchview Cl YTLY GU46 135 H5
Birchwood CHAM RG24 145 G7 1
Birchwood Cl CAV/SC RG4 43 K6 1
Birchwood Rd NWBY RG14 13 M1
The Birchwoods CALC RG31 55 G5
Birdhill Av WHIT RG2 8 A7
Bird Ms EWKG RG40 97 G1 3
Birds La THLE RG7 87 F4
Bird Wood Ct CAV/SC RG4 29 H7
Birkbeck Pl SHST GU47 119 F7
Birkdale BRAK RG12 99 F4
Birkhall Cl CALC RG31 71 H1 1
Biscuit Wy WHIT RG2 73 G6
Bishopdale BRAK RG12 10 C8
Bishops Cl FLET GU13 167 H4
TADY RG26 108 D7
Bishops Dr EWKG RG40 77 H7
Bishop's Rd EARL RG6 5 G8
THLE RG7 68 C3
Bishopswood La TADY RG26 108 B7
Bishopswood Rd TADY RG26 108 C7
Bittern Cl KEMP RG22 174 E4
Bitterne Av CALC RG31 55 G7
Bix Hl HEN RG9 16 B3
Blackberry Wk CHAM RG24 15 M1
CHAM RG24 161 G4 1
Blackbird Cl KEMP RG22 174 E4
THLE RG7 91 G4 1
Black Boy La WAR/TWY RG10 19 H7
Blackbushes Rd HTWY RG27 150 D1
Black Dam Wy BSTK RG21 15 K7
Blackdown Cl KEMP RG22 175 F1
Blackdown Wy STHA RG19 85 H5
Blacklands Rd THLE RG7 86 D2
Blackley Cl EARL RG6 75 H3 1
Blackmeadows BRAK RG12 99 K4 2
Blackmoor Cl ASC SL5 81 G7
Blackmoor Wd ASC SL5 81 G7
Blackmore La CAV/SC RG4 29 H6
Blackstocks La HTWY RG27 162 E6
Blackthorn Cl CALC RG31 55 G3
EARL RG6 5 G7
Blackthorn Dr NTHA RG18 85 J2
Blackthorn Wy DEAN RG23 159 H5
Blackwater Cl BSTK RG21 15 H5
CAV/SC RG4 58 B1
DEAN RG23 174 A3 1
THLE RG7 93 J6
Blackwater Ri CALC RG31 71 F2 1
Blackwater Vw EWKG RG40 117 F6
Blaenavon CAV/SC RG4 43 G7
Blagdon Cl STHA RG19 84 C7 1
Blagdon Rd WHIT RG2 7 L8
Blagrave Farm La CAV/SC RG4 42 E7
Blagrave La CAV/SC RG4 56 D2
Blagrave Ri CALC RG31 55 H7
Blagrave St READ RG1 3 J5
Blagrove La WWKG RG41 96 E3
Blaire Pk YTLY GU46 135 G1
Blair Rd BSTK RG21 14 D8
Blake Cl CWTH RG45 118 D4
EWKG RG40 77 K6
ODIM RG29 180 B4 1
Blakes Cottages READ RG1 3 L6
Blake's La TADY RG26 108 E7
WAR/TWY RG10 47 G2
Blakes Ride YTLY GU46 135 G3
Blakes Rd WAR/TWY RG10 46 D1
Blamire Dr BNFD RG42 79 F4
Blanchard Cl WODY RG5 60 A5
Blandford Dr WWKG RG41 96 D3
Blandford Rd WHIT RG2 73 K6
Bland's Cl THLE RG7 90 E5
Blandy Rd HEN RG9 31 G3
Blandy's La GOR/PANG RG8 38 E6
Blane's La ASC SL5 101 F4
Blatch's Cl THLE RG7 70 C3 1
Bledlow Cl NWBY RG14 103 G3 1
Blenheim Cl WWKG RG41 96 D1 3
Blenheim Gdns READ RG1 4 C9
Blenheim Rd CAV/SC RG4 57 H1
CHAM RG24 161 K6
NWBY RG14 12 C4
READ RG1 4 B7
Blewburton Wk BRAK RG12 11 M7
Blewbury Dr CALC RG31 55 G6
Bliss Cl KEMP RG22 175 K3
Blomfield Dl BNFD RG42 78 E7 1
Bloomfield Dr BRAK RG12 79 K5
Bloomfieldhatch La THLE RG7 92 C7
Blossom Av THLE RG7 70 D3
Blossom La THLE RG7 70 D3
Bloswood Dr WHCH RG28 169 G7
Bloswood La WHCH RG28 168 E4
Blount Crs BNFD RG42 79 F5
Blounts Court Rd CAV/SC RG4 29 H5
Bloxworth Cl BRAK RG12 100 C2 1
Bluebell Dr THLE RG7 90 E4
Bluebell Hl BRAK RG12 11 L2
Bluebell Meadow WWKG RG41 76 B3
Bluebell Wy NTHA RG18 85 J2
Bluecoats NTHA RG18 85 J3
Blue Coat Wk BRAK RG12 11 K9
Blundells Rd TLHT RG30 55 K5
Blunden Cl BSTK RG21 176 A3
Blyth Av STHA RG19 85 K5
Blythewood La ASC SL5 101 G1
Boames La KSCL RG20 102 C3
Boar's Br TADY RG26 127 K7
Bobgreen Ct WHIT RG2 93 K1 1
Bockmer La MLW SL7 19 G4
Bodens Ride ASC SL5 101 J6
Bodin Gdns NWBY RG14 83 K7
Bodmin Cl KEMP RG22 175 G1
STHA RG19 85 H5
Bodmin Rd WODY RG5 9 M3
Body Rd READ RG1 3 G7
Bog La ASC SL5 100 D1
BRAK RG12 100 C3
Boldrewood THLE RG7 90 E5 1
Bolingbroke Wy STHA RG19 86 A4
Bolney La HEN RG9 31 K6
Bolney Rd HEN RG9 32 A6
Bolney Trevor Dr HEN RG9 31 K7
Bolton Crs KEMP RG22 175 K1
Boltons La BNFD RG42 79 F5
Bolwell Cl WAR/TWY RG10 60 E1
Bomford Cl NTHA RG18 48 E7 1
Bond Cl CHAM RG24 161 F3
Bone La NWBY RG14 13 H4
Bonemill La KSCL RG20 83 G7
Bones La HEN RG9 44 D1
Boon Wy DEAN RG23 173 K2
Boot End WHIT RG2 73 G6
Booth Dr EWKG RG40 96 D6
Borderside YTLY GU46 135 F3
Bordon Cl TADY RG26 126 D1
Borodin Cl KEMP RG22 176 A4
The Borough NFNM GU10 182 D6
Borrowdale Rd WWKG RG41 76 A2
Boscawen Wy STHA RG19 86 B4 1
Bosham Cl EARL RG6 74 E6 1
Bostock La THLE RG7 69 K4
Boston Av READ RG1 2 F9
Boston Rd HEN RG9 31 H3
Bosworth Gdns WODY RG5 75 H2
Botany Cl STHA RG19 86 A4 1
The Bothy WAR/TWY RG10 46 C2
Bottisham Cl EARL RG6 75 F6 2
Bottle La HTWY RG27 147 K2
Bottom La THLE RG7 70 D6
Bouldish Farm Rd ASC SL5 101 J3
Boulton Rd WHIT RG2 7 H5
Boult St READ RG1 3 L7
Boundary Cl CALC RG31 55 H7 1
Boundary La CAV/SC RG4 57 F2
Boundary Rd NWBY RG14 13 H5
Bounty Ri BSTK RG21 14 D7
Bounty Rd BSTK RG21 14 D7
Bourley Rd FLET GU13 167 K7
Bourn Cl EARL RG6 75 F5 1
Bourne Arch NTHA RG18 85 G3
Bourne Av WHIT RG2 7 K3
Bourne Cl CALC RG31 71 G2
Bourne Fld CHAM RG24 143 K6
Bourne Rd GOR/PANG RG8 40 D7
STHA RG19 85 G3
Bourne-stevens Cl READ RG1 3 K7
The Bourne FLET GU13 167 H5
Bourton Cl TLHT RG30 56 A6
Bow Dr HTWY RG27 146 A2
Bowenhurst Gdns FLET GU13 167 H7
Bowenhurst Rd FLET GU13 167 H6
bowenhust La NFNM GU10 182 D1
Bowes Rd STHA RG19 85 J5
Bowfell Cl CALC RG31 55 H3 1
Bow Fld HTWY RG27 164 B2
Bow Gdns HTWY RG27 146 A2 1
Bow Gv HTWY RG27 146 A1
Bowland Dr BRAK RG12 100 B5
Bowling Ct HEN RG9 17 F7
Bowling Green Dr
HTWY RG27 163 J2 1
Bowling Green La
GOR/PANG RG8 41 G7
Bowling Green Rd NTHA RG18 85 F2
Bowman Ct CWTH RG45 117 K4
Bowman Rd CHAM RG24 145 G6
Bowmonts Rd TADY RG26 127 G1
Bowyer Crs EWKG RG40 77 H6
Boxford Rdg BRAK RG12 10 F6
Boyce Cl KEMP RG22 175 H4
Boyd Ct BNFD RG42 10 D2
Bracken Bank ASC SL5 81 F6
CHAM RG24 161 G3 1
Bracken Cl CALC RG31 55 H4 1
Brackendale Wy EARL RG6 9 G1
Bracken La YTLY GU46 135 F3
The Brackens CWTH RG45 118 B1
KEMP RG22 175 H6 1
Bracken Wy THLE RG7 91 F5 1
Brackley Av HTWY RG27 149 H4
Brackley Wy KEMP RG22 175 H3
Bracknell La HTWY RG27 149 H3
Bracknell Rd BNFD RG42 80 C2
CWTH RG45 99 F7
CWTH RG45 118 E2
Brackstone Cl CAV/SC RG4 3 L1
Bradbury Cl WHCH RG28 169 G7 1
Bradfields BRAK RG12 11 K9
Brading Wy GOR/PANG RG8 41 J7
Bradley Dr EWKG RG40 97 F6
Bradley-moore Sq NTHA RG18 85 K2
Bradmore Wy EARL RG6 74 D6
Bradwell Rd CALC RG31 55 H2
Braemar Dr DEAN RG23 173 K2
Braemore Cl STHA RG19 85 J6
Brahms Rd KEMP RG22 175 K4
Bramber Ms CAV/SC RG4 58 B1 1
Bramble Crs TLHT RG30 55 K6
Bramblegate CWTH RG45 118 B2
The Brambles CWTH RG45 117 J2
NWBY RG14 83 H7
Bramble Wy CHAM RG24 161 K5
Bramblewood Pl FLET GU13 167 F2
Brambling Cl KEMP RG22 174 E5 1
Bramblings CAV/SC RG4 43 F6
Bramblys Cl BSTK RG21 14 D6
Bramblys Dr BSTK RG21 14 C6
Bramdown Hts KEMP RG22 175 G6
Bramley Cl EARL RG6 9 H6
Bramley Crs CAV/SC RG4 29 F6 1
Bramley Green Rd TADY RG26 129 H7
Bramley Gv CWTH RG45 117 J3
Bramley La TADY RG26 129 G4
Bramley Rd HTWY RG27 146 A1
TADY RG26 143 J1
THLE RG7 110 A7
Bramling Av YTLY GU46 135 G3
Brammpton Gdns KEMP RG22 175 G7
Brampton Cha HEN RG9 31 K7
Bramshaw Rd TLHT RG30 56 B4
Bramshill Cl WHIT RG2 95 H7
Bramshot Dr FLET GU13 167 H1
Bramshott Dr HTWY RG27 164 A2
Bramwell Cl STHA RG19 86 A5 2
Bran Cl TLHT RG30 55 K5
Brandon Av WODY RG5 59 K4
Brandon Rd FLET GU13 167 F6
Branksomewood Rd
FLET GU13 167 F2
Branton Cl KEMP RG22 175 H1
Brants Br BRAK RG12 11 L4
Brants Cl WHIT RG2 95 H5 2
Braunfels Wk KSCL RG20 12 A6
KSCL RG20 83 G5
NWBY RG14 12 A5
Braybrooke Dr WAR/TWY RG10 60 E5
Braybrooke Gdns
WAR/TWY RG10 46 C3
Braybrooke Rd BNFD RG42 79 J5
WAR/TWY RG10 46 C3
Braye Cl SHST GU47 118 D7 2
Brayford Rd WHIT RG2 73 K6
Bray Rd TLHT RG30 72 C2
Braziers La ASC SL5 81 G3
Breachfield KSCL RG20 121 J2
Breach La HTWY RG27 146 B2
Brean Wk EARL RG6 9 H7
Brecon Rd WODY RG5 59 J5
Bredon Rd WWKG RG41 76 E5
Breedons Hl GOR/PANG RG8 40 B7
Brendon Cl TLHT RG30 55 K4 1
Brent Cl STHA RG19 85 J5
Brent Gdns WHIT RG2 7 K6
Brerewood EARL RG6 8 F8

Brewer Cl KEMP RG22 175 H1
Brewery Common THLE RG7 111 G2
Brewhouse La HTWY RG27 149 J4 1
Briant's Av CAV/SC RG4 57 K3
Briants Piece NTHA RG18 49 G7
Briar Cl CAV/SC RG4 57 H1
Briarlea Rd THLE RG7 110 E2
Briars Cl GOR/PANG RG8 40 D7
Briar Wy TADY RG26 127 F1
Briarwood Dr EWKG RG40 116 D2 1
Brickfields Cl CHAM RG24 161 H3 2
Brick La FLET GU13 167 H1
Bridge Rd ODIM RG29 164 B7
Bridges Cl WWKG RG41 76 E7
The Bridges THLE RG7 110 B3
Bridge St NWBY RG14 12 E4
OVTN RG25 171 H4
READ RG1 3 G1
READ RG1 3 H7
Bridge Wk YTLY GU46 135 J2
TLHT RG30 56 D4 1
Bridgewater Cl TLHT RG30 56 D5 2
Bridle Pth GOR/PANG RG8 26 D3
Bridle Rd GOR/PANG RG8 40 D1 1
Bridport Cl EARL RG6 75 G4
Brierley Pl CALC RG31 55 H1 1
Briff La THLE RG7 66 E5
THLE RG7 86 C1
Brigham Rd READ RG1 3 H3
Brighton Rd EARL RG6 5 G9
Brighton Wy KEMP RG22 175 J3
Brill Cl CAV/SC RG4 57 H1
Brimblecombe Cl WWKG RG41 77 F5
Brimpton Rd THLE RG7 87 F6
THLE RG7 107 G1
THLE RG7 107 K6
TLHT RG30 72 C2
Brinds Cl CAV/SC RG4 29 G6
Brinksway FLET GU13 167 H3
Brisbane Rd TLHT RG30 56 C5
Britten Rd WHIT RG2 7 J3
Brixham Rd WHIT RG2 7 K7
Broadacres FLET GU13 166 E3 1
Broadcommon Rd
WAR/TWY RG10 61 G7
Broadhalfpenny La TADY RG26 109 F7
Broad Hinton WAR/TWY RG10 60 D3
Broadhurst Gv CHAM RG24 161 G4
Broadlands Cl CALC RG31 71 J1
Broad La BRAK RG12 11 H6
NTHA RG18 66 A6
THLE RG7 86 C1
Broad Leaze HTWY RG27 163 K1 1
Broadmeadow End NTHA RG18 86 A4
Broadmoor La CAV/SC RG4 59 H1
Broadoak TADY RG26 127 G1 1
Broad Oak La ODIM RG29 181 F1
Broadrick Heath BNFD RG42 80 A5 2
Broad St EWKG RG40 97 H1
KSCL RG20 20 D4
READ RG1 3 H6
Broadwater La WAR/TWY RG10 60 D4
Broadwater Rd WAR/TWY RG10 60 D2
Broad Wy THLE RG7 112 E5
Broadway STHA RG19 85 J4
Brocas Dr BSTK RG21 15 H1
Brocas Rd THLE RG7 90 E6
Brockenhurst Dr YTLY GU46 135 J4 2
Brockenhurst Rd BRAK RG12 100 C1
Brock Gdns TLHT RG30 56 D5
Brocklands YTLY GU46 135 G5 1
Brockley Cl TLHT RG30 56 B5
Brocks La NTHA RG18 66 C1
Brocks Wy HEN RG9 45 K1
Broken Wy KSCL RG20 104 A6
Bromelia Cl TADY RG26 129 G5
Brompton Cl EARL RG6 75 G5 1
Brook Cl FLET GU13 167 H3
SHST GU47 119 F7
WWKG RG41 77 F6
Brook Dr BRAK RG12 11 M8
Brooke Pl BNFD RG42 78 E3
Brookers Cnr CWTH RG45 118 D3
Brooker's Hl WHIT RG2 94 A1
Brookers Rw CWTH RG45 118 D2
Brookfield Cl CHAM RG24 145 H7 1
Brook Gn TADY RG26 127 G1
Brookly Gdns FLET GU13 167 J1
Brooklyn Dr CAV/SC RG4 43 J5
The Brookmill READ RG1 6 D3
Brooksby Rd CALC RG31 55 J3
Brookside WWKG RG41 76 E7
Brookside Cl EARL RG6 75 G3
Brooks Rd NTHA RG18 85 K3
Brook St WAR/TWY RG10 60 C1
Brook St West READ RG1 3 G8
Brookvale Cl BSTK RG21 14 C5
Brookway NWBY RG14 84 D4
Broom Acres FLET GU13 167 G5
Broom Cl CALC RG31 71 H1 2
Broome Cl YTLY GU46 135 H2
Broome Ct BRAK RG12 10 E6
Broomfield Rd TLHT RG30 56 A5
Broom Gv WWKG RG41 96 C3
Broomhill NFNM GU10 183 J4
Broomrigg Rd FLET GU13 166 E1
Broughton Cl TLHT RG30 56 D4 2
Brown Cft HTWY RG27 163 J2
Browning Cl CHAM RG24 160 D3
NTHA RG18 85 H3
Browning Rd FLET GU13 183 F1
Brownlow Dr BNFD RG42 79 K5
Brownlow Rd READ RG1 2 D7
Brownrigg Crs BRAK RG12 11 M2
Browns Cl TADY RG26 129 F5
Brownsfield Rd NTHA RG18 85 H4
Brtten Rd KEMP RG22 175 K4
Bruan Rd NWBY RG14 83 J7
Bruce Rd WODY RG5 59 G6
Brummell Rd NWBY RG14 12 A1
NWBY RG14 83 H2
Brunel Dr WODY RG5 59 J4
Brunel Rd BSTK RG21 159 K5
THLE RG7 70 D4
TLHT RG30 72 B2
Brunswick BRAK RG12 99 H5
Brunswick Hl READ RG1 2 C7
Brunswick St READ RG1 2 D8
Bruton Wy BRAK RG12 100 B5
Bryanstone Cl FLET GU13 167 H5
Bryant Pl GOR/PANG RG8 41 G7 2
Brybur Cl WHIT RG2 74 A6
Buccaneer Cl WODY RG5 60 A5 1
Buchanan Dr EWKG RG40 116 D1
Buchanan Sq STHA RG19 85 K6
Buckby La BSTK RG21 15 K4
Buckden Cl WODY RG5 59 K7
Buckfast Cl CHAM RG24 160 B2
Buckhurst Gv EWKG RG40 98 A2
Buckhurst Hl BRAK RG12 100 C2 2
Buckhurst Wy EARL RG6 9 H5
Buckingham Dr CAV/SC RG4 43 J7
Buckingham Ga MLW SL7 19 J3
Buckingham Rd NWBY RG14 12 B7
Buckland Av KEMP RG22 175 J3
Buckland Rd WHIT RG2 7 K6
Bucklebury BRAK RG12 99 H5
Bucknell Av GOR/PANG RG8 40 D7
Bucknell Cl CALC RG31 72 A2
Buck Side READ RG1 3 G1
Buckskin La KEMP RG22 175 F2
Buckthorn Cl EWKG RG40 77 K7 1
Budd's Cl BSTK RG21 14 C6
Budge's Gdns EWKG RG40 77 J7
Budge's Rd EWKG RG40 77 J7
Budham Wy BRAK RG12 99 J4
Buffins Rd ODIM RG29 180 B2
Bullbrook Dr BRAK RG12 11 L2
Bull La BRAK RG12 10 F2
THLE RG7 113 J5
The Bull Meadow
GOR/PANG RG8 24 D5
Bulls Down Cl HTWY RG27 145 K1
Bulmershe Ct EARL RG6 5 K8
Bulmershe Rd READ RG1 4 E9
Bunce's La GOR/PANG RG8 41 F2
THLE RG7 91 F5
Bungler's Hl THLE RG7 114 E2
Bunkers Hl NWBY RG14 103 F3 2
Bunnian Pl BSTK RG21 14 F3
Bunting Cl KEMP RG22 174 E5
Bunting Ms KEMP RG22 175 F5 2
Burbage Gn BRAK RG12 100 C3 1
Burbidge Cl CALC RG31 72 A3 1
Burchell Rd NWBY RG14 83 H2
Burchett Coppice EWKG RG40 96 E7 1
Burcombe Wy CAV/SC RG4 57 J1
Burdens Heath NTHA RG18 66 B7
Burdock Cl THLE RG7 91 G5
Burfield KSCL RG20 120 B4
Burford Ct EWKG RG40 97 K2
Burgess Cl ODIM RG29 180 B2 1
WODY RG5 75 G1
Burgess Rd BSTK RG21 14 D2
Burghfield Rd TLHT RG30 72 B2 2
Burleigh La ASC SL5 81 H6
Burleigh Ms CAV/SC RG4 43 K6 2
Burleigh Rd ASC SL5 81 H7
Burlingham Cl WHIT RG2 93 K1 1
The Burlings ASC SL5 81 H7
Burlington Rd TLHT RG30 55 J6
Burlsdon Wy BRAK RG12 11 L2
Burnaby Cl KEMP RG22 175 H1
Burney Bit TADY RG26 127 H1
Burnham Gv BNFD RG42 79 K5 2
Burnham Ri CAV/SC RG4 43 K5
Burnham Rd TADY RG26 108 C6
Burniston Cl EARL RG6 75 H4 3
Burnley Cl TADY RG26 126 E2
Burn Moor Cha BRAK RG12 100 B5 1
Burnmoor Meadow
EWKG RG40 116 D6
Burns Av FLET GU13 167 J5
Burns Cl CHAM RG24 160 D3
WODY RG5 75 H2
Burnthouse Br TLHT RG30 92 B2
Burnthouse Gdns BNFD RG42 80 B5 2
Burnthouse La TLHT RG30 72 C7
Burnt Oak EWKG RG40 96 E7 2
Burrcroft Rd TLHT RG30 72 B1
Burrell Rd KSCL RG20 21 K7
Burrowfields KEMP RG22 175 G7 1
Burton Cl WAR/TWY RG10 60 D3
Burton's Gdns CHAM RG24 161 J4
Burwell Cl EARL RG6 75 F5
Buryfields ODIM RG29 180 D2
Bury Rd DEAN RG23 159 J5
Bury's Bank Rd STHA RG19 85 K7
STHA RG19 104 C1
Bushnells Dr KSCL RG20 123 K7 1
Bute St TLHT RG30 72 C1
Butler Cl KEMP RG22 159 H7
Butler Rd CWTH RG45 118 C2
Butlers Orch CAV/SC RG4 42 E1
Butlers Pond GOR/PANG RG8 40 C2
Butson Cl NWBY RG14 12 A4
Buttenshaw Av WHIT RG2 95 J7
Buttenshaw Cl WHIT RG2 95 K7
Buttercup Cl EWKG RG40 98 A1
Buttercup Pl NTHA RG18 85 J3
Butter Market READ RG1 3 J6
Buttermere Dr KEMP RG22 175 F3
Buttermere Gdns BRAK RG12 11 H5
Buttersteep Ri ASC SL5 101 F6
Butts Hill Rd WODY RG5 59 H4
Butts Meadow HTWY RG27 163 K2 1
The Butts THLE RG7 128 A1 1
The Butty BSTK RG21 15 K4
Buxton Av CAV/SC RG4 57 G1
Byefield Rd TLHT RG30 72 B2
Byes La THLE RG7 128 A2
Byeways KSCL RG20 120 B4
Byfields Rd KSCL RG20 123 K7
Byfleet Av CHAM RG24 161 J6
Byrd Gdns KEMP RG22 175 H5
Byreton Cl EARL RG6 9 J8
Byron Cl CHAM RG24 160 D2
FLET GU13 167 H3
NWBY RG14 103 J1
YTLY GU46 135 G5 2
Byron Dr CWTH RG45 118 C5
Byron Rd EARL RG6 5 H7
WAR/TWY RG10 60 D1
Bythorn Cl EARL RG6 75 H4
Byways YTLY GU46 135 G4
Bywood BRAK RG12 99 H5
Byworth Cl WHIT RG2 73 J6

C

Cabin Moss BRAK RG12 100 B5 2
Cadet Wy FLET GU13 167 J7
Cadnam Cl DEAN RG23 174 A2
Cadogan Cl CAV/SC RG4 58 B1 2
TLHT RG30 55 K6 1
Caernarvon Cl DEAN RG23 159 H6 1
Caesars Ga BNFD RG42 80 B5 3
Caesar's Wy WHCH RG28 169 G6
Cain Rd BNFD RG42 78 E7
BRAK RG12 79 F7
Cairngorm Cl KEMP RG22 159 G7 1
Cairngorm Rd STHA RG19 85 J5 1
Caistor Cl CALC RG31 71 G2 2
Caithness Cl DEAN RG23 173 K2
Calard Dr NTHA RG18 85 F2
Calbourne Dr CALC RG31 71 J2 2
Calcot Place Dr CALC RG31 71 K2
Calcott Pk YTLY GU46 135 H3
Caldbeck Dr WODY RG5 59 J7
Calder Cl TLHT RG30 56 A5
Caleta Cl CAV/SC RG4 58 A3 1
Calfridus Wy BRAK RG12 11 L6
Calleva Cl KEMP RG22 175 G5
Callington Rd WHIT RG2 7 K9
Calshot Pl CALC RG31 71 J2 3
Calthorpe Rd FLET GU13 167 F1
HTWY RG27 151 F7
Camberry Cl BSTK RG21 15 G9
Cambrian Wy CALC RG31 71 J2
EWKG RG40 97 F7
KEMP RG22 175 G1
Cambridge Rd CWTH RG45 118 D4
SHST GU47 119 F7
Cambridgeshire Cl BNFD RG42 80 C5
WWKG RG41 96 D1 4
Cambridge St READ RG1 2 D5
Camden Pl CALC RG31 71 G2 3
Camden Wk FLET GU13 167 K2
Camelford Cl WHIT RG2 7 K9
Camellia Wy WWKG RG41 76 C7 2
Camfield Cl BSTK RG21 15 G9
Campbell Cl FLET GU13 167 F2
Campbell Rd TADY RG26 129 J7
WODY RG5 75 G1
Campion Wy EWKG RG40 77 K7
HTWY RG27 149 J3
Camp Rd THLE RG7 90 B4
Campsie Cl KEMP RG22 159 G7
Camrose Wy BSTK RG21 15 G9
BSTK RG21 176 D2
Camus Cl FLET GU13 166 E6
Camwood Cl BSTK RG21 15 G9
Canal Cl ODIM RG29 164 B7 1
Canal View Rd NWBY RG14 13 M4
Canal Wy READ RG1 4 A6
Canberra Cl HTWY RG27 135 F2
Candleford Cl BRAK RG12 79 K5 3
Candover Cl TADY RG26 126 E2 2
Canhurst La WAR/TWY RG10 47 J1
Cannock Wy EARL RG6 9 M9
Cannon Hl BRAK RG12 99 K4
Cannon St READ RG1 2 D5
Canon's Ct KSCL RG20 123 K7
Cansfield End NWBY RG14 12 D3
Canterbury Cl KEMP RG22 175 G4 1
Canterbury Rd WHIT RG2 7 K5
Cantley Crs WWKG RG41 77 F6
Captains Gorse GOR/PANG RG8 38 C6
Caraway Rd EARL RG6 74 D5
Carbinswood La THLE RG7 88 A3
Carbonel Cl DEAN RG23 159 F6
Cardiff Rd READ RG1 2 F3
Cardigan Gdns READ RG1 8 D1
Cardigan Rd READ RG1 4 D9
Cardinal Cl READ RG1 3 J1
Carew Cl CALC RG31 55 G1 1
Carey Rd EWKG RG40 97 H2
Carey St READ RG1 2 F7
Carisbrooke Cl CAV/SC RG4 43 K6 3
DEAN RG23 159 H5
Carland Cl EARL RG6 74 D5
Carleton Cl HTWY RG27 163 J2
Carlile Gdns WAR/TWY RG10 46 C5
Carling Rd CAV/SC RG4 29 F5
Carlisle Cl DEAN RG23 159 H5
Carlisle Rd CALC RG31 55 K2
Carlton Cl WODY RG5 59 H7
Carlton Crs FLET GU13 167 J5
Carlton Rd CAV/SC RG4 42 E7
Carmichael Wy KEMP RG22 175 H4
Carnarvon Rd READ RG1 4 C7
Carnation Cl EWKG RG40 98 C7
Carnation Dr BNFD RG42 80 D4
Carnegie Rd NWBY RG14 12 F5
Carnoustie BRAK RG12 99 F5
Carolina Pl EWKG RG40 116 D1
Caroline Dr WWKG RG41 77 F7
Caroline St READ RG1 2 F5
Carpenters Cl HTWY RG27 146 A1
CHAM RG24 160 C1
Carpenter's Down
CHAM RG24 160 C1 1
Carrick Gdns WODY RG5 5 M7
WODY RG5 59 G7
Carrick La YTLY GU46 135 K3
Carrington Crs TADY RG26 126 E1
Carroll Crs ASC SL5 101 J2
Carron Cl TLHT RG30 56 B6
Carsdale Cl READ RG1 6 E1
Carshalton Wy EARL RG6 9 L9
Carston Gv CALC RG31 72 A2
Carter's Hl EWKG RG40 78 A2
Carters Ri CALC RG31 71 K3
Carthona Dr FLET GU13 167 G4
Cartmel Dr WODY RG5 59 G7
Cary Cl NWBY RG14 103 G2
Casey Ct THLE RG7 68 A3
Cassia Dr EARL RG6 74 C5 1
Castle Crs READ RG1 2 F8
Castle End Rd WAR/TWY RG10 46 E6
Castle Gv NWBY RG14 83 J2
Castle Hl READ RG1 2 F8
THLE RG7 115 F1
Castle La NWBY RG14 83 H1
Castle Ri ODIM RG29 164 B7
Castle Rd BSTK RG21 14 F8
Castle St FLET GU13 167 G4
READ RG1 3 G7
Castor Ct FLET GU13 167 J6 1
YTLY GU46 135 G2
Caswall Cl BNFD RG42 78 D4 1
Catalina Cl WODY RG5 60 A6
Catcliffe Wy EARL RG6 74 C6
Catesby Gdns YTLY GU46 135 F4
Catherine Rd NWBY RG14 12 E6
Catherine St TLHT RG30 2 B5
Catkin Cl CHAM RG24 145 G7
Caunter Rd NWBY RG14 83 G3 1
The Causeway CAV/SC RG4 4 A2
HTWY RG27 131 K2
Causmans Wy CALC RG31 55 H4
Cavalier Cl CHAM RG24 161 K5
NWBY RG14 84 B2
THLE RG7 70 C3
Cavalier Rd CHAM RG24 161 K5
Cavel Ct CHAM RG24 161 H3 3
Cavendish Ct NWBY RG14 84 D2
Cavendish Gdns WWKG RG41 75 K3
Cavendish Rd CAV/SC RG4 43 K6
FLET GU13 167 F6 1
Caversham Br READ RG1 2 F1
Caversham Park Dr CAV/SC RG4 43 K7
Caversham Park Rd CAV/SC RG4 44 A6
Caversham Rd READ RG1 3 G2
Cawsam Gdns CAV/SC RG4 57 K1
Caxton Cl TLHT RG30 56 D4
Cayman Cl CHAM RG24 160 D2
Cecil Aldin Dr CALC RG31 55 G1
Cedar Cl EWKG RG40 97 H1
TADY RG26 127 G3
Cedar Dr BNFD RG42 79 K5
FLET GU13 167 K2
GOR/PANG RG8 54 B1
KSCL RG20 123 K7
Cedar Gv STHA RG19 85 H4
Cedar Mt NWBY RG14 83 J7
Cedar Rd WHIT RG2 8 D9
The Cedars CALC RG31 55 J3
FLET GU13 167 J3
Cedar Tree Cl DEAN RG23 173 K4
Cedar Wy DEAN RG23 159 J4
Cedar Wood Crs CAV/SC RG4 57 J1
Celandine Cl CWTH RG45 118 D2
Celandine Ct YTLY GU46 135 F2
Celandine Gv NTHA RG18 86 A4
Cemetery Hl ODIM RG29 180 D2
Cemetery La OVTN RG25 178 E7
Cemetery Rd FLET GU13 167 F4
Central Wk EWKG RG40 97 H1 1
Centre Dr CHAM RG24 161 G2
Centurion Wy KEMP RG22 175 G6
Century Dr THLE RG7 93 K6
Chaffinch Cl CALC RG31 55 G6 1
KEMP RG22 175 F4
WWKG RG41 96 D2
Chagford Rd WHIT RG2 73 J5
Chain St READ RG1 3 H6
Chalcraft Cl HEN RG9 31 F3
Chalfont Cl EARL RG6 74 D5
Chalfont Wy EARL RG6 9 G9
EARL RG6 74 D6 2
Chalford Rd NWBY RG14 12 A5
Chalgrove Wy CAV/SC RG4 43 J6
Chalk Hl HEN RG9 31 F6
Chalkhouse Green La
CAV/SC RG4 43 H3
Chalkhousegreen La
CAV/SC RG4 43 J4
Chalkhouse Green Rd
CAV/SC RG4 42 E1
Chalk V CHAM RG24 161 K6
Chalky Copse HTWY RG27 163 K1 1
Chalky La HTWY RG27 182 A1
Challenor Cl EWKG RG40 116 E1 1
Challis Cl KEMP RG22 175 H2
Challis Pl BNFD RG42 79 F6
Challoner Cl KEMP RG22 175 H1
Chamberlain's Gdns
WHIT RG2 95 H5 3
Champion Rd CAV/SC RG4 3 L2
Champion Wy FLET GU13 167 H6
The Chancellor's Wy EARL RG6 8 C3
Chandler Rd BSTK RG21 176 B2
Chandlers La YTLY GU46 135 H2
Chandos Rd NWBY RG14 83 J7
Chantreys FLET GU13 166 E3 2
Chantry Ms KEMP RG22 175 G5 1
Chapel Ct NTHA RG18 85 K3
Chapel Hl BSTK RG21 14 D3
CALC RG31 55 G5
Chapel La BNFD RG42 78 D5
GOR/PANG RG8 37 H6
NTHA RG18 49 H5
NTHA RG18 51 F4
NTHA RG18 64 D2
STHA RG19 107 G7
TADY RG26 125 G5
THLE RG7 93 J5
THLE RG7 109 J3
Chapel Md HTWY RG27 134 D1 2
Chapel Pond Dr ODIM RG29 180 B1
Chapel Rd KSCL RG20 82 B1
Chapel St NTHA RG18 85 K4
Chaplain's Hl CWTH RG45 118 E4
Chapman Wk NTHA RG18 85 G3
Chapter Ter HTWY RG27 149 J4 2
Chard Cl WODY RG5 59 H7
Charlbury Cl BRAK RG12 100 C2 3
Charldon Gn CHAM RG24 161 H3 4
Charledown Cl OVTN RG25 171 H5
Charledown Rd OVTN RG25 171 H5
Charles Cl HTWY RG27 163 K2
Charles Evans Wy CAV/SC RG4 58 A3
Charles Richards Cl BSTK RG21 14 D8
Charles St KEMP RG22 159 J7
NWBY RG14 103 G2
READ RG1 2 E5
Charlock Cl NTHA RG18 85 K2
Charlotte Cl NTHA RG18 49 F7
Charlton Cl EWKG RG40 96 E7 3
Charlton Ct SHST GU47 118 E7
Charlton La THLE RG7 113 K3
Charlton Pl NWBY RG14 12 F2
Charlville Dr CALC RG31 71 G2 2
Charmwood Cl NWBY RG14 83 J2 1
Charndon Cl WHIT RG2 7 K1
Charnwood Cl KEMP RG22 159 G7 2
Charrington Rd CALC RG31 71 G2
Charterhouse Cl BRAK RG12 11 M9
Charter Rd NWBY RG14 83 J7
Charvil House Rd
WAR/TWY RG10 45 K7
Charvil La CAV/SC RG4 59 H1
Charvil Meadow Rd
WAR/TWY RG10 46 A7
Charwood Rd EWKG RG40 97 K1
Chase Gdns BNFD RG42 78 D3
Chaseside Av WAR/TWY RG10 46 C6
The Chase CALC RG31 71 J2
CWTH RG45 118 B2
NWBY RG14 63 J7 1
Chatham St READ RG1 2 F5
Chatsworth Av WWKG RG41 75 K4
Chatsworth Cl CAV/SC RG4 43 K6
Chatsworth Gn KEMP RG22 175 H6
Chatteris Wy EARL RG6 75 F5
The Chatters THLE RG7 115 F1
Chatton Cl EARL RG6 74 D6
Chaucer Cl CAV/SC RG4 43 H7
CHAM RG24 160 D2
EWKG RG40 98 A1 1
Chaucer Crs NWBY RG14 83 H2
Chaucer Rd CWTH RG45 118 C4
Chaucer Wy WWKG RG41 96 D2 1
Chaundlers Cft NFNM GU10 182 E7
Chavey Down Rd BNFD RG42 80 E4
Chazey Cl CAV/SC RG4 42 D4
Chazey Rd CAV/SC RG4 56 E1
Cheam Cl BRAK RG12 100 A3
Cheapside READ RG1 3 G5
Cheap St KSCL RG20 21 K6
NWBY RG14 12 E4
Cheddington Cl TLHT RG30 56 A7 1
Cheeseman Cl EWKG RG40 77 J7 1
Chelsea Cl TLHT RG30 56 A4
Chelwood Dr SHST GU47 118 A7 2
Chelwood Rd EARL RG6 9 K7
Cheney Cl BNFD RG42 78 E4
Chepstow Rd CALC RG31 55 H3
Chequer La THLE RG7 113 F6
Chequers La HTWY RG27 134 D2
Chequers Rd BSTK RG21 14 F5
Chequers Wy WODY RG5 5 M6
Cherberry Cl FARN GU14 151 J6 2
Cherbury Cl BRAK RG12 11 M6
Cherington Wy ASC SL5 81 H7 1
Cheriton Av WAR/TWY RG10 46 C6
Cheriton Cl NWBY RG14 13 G8
TADY RG26 126 E2 3
Cheriton Pl CAV/SC RG4 29 G6 1
Cherry Cl CAV/SC RG4 43 K4
HTWY RG27 164 A1
NWBY RG14 12 D1
Cherry Tree Cl SHST GU47 118 E7 1
Cherry Tree Dr BRAK RG12 11 J6
Cherry Tree Gv WWKG RG41 96 C3 1
Chervil Wy THLE RG7 91 G5
Cherwell Rd CAV/SC RG4 43 H6
Cheseridge Rd KSCL RG20 35 G2
Cheshire Pk BNFD RG42 80 B4
Chesilton Crs FLET GU13 167 H7
Chesterblade La BRAK RG12 100 A5
Chester Cl NWBY RG14 13 K9
Chesterfield Rd BSTK RG21 15 H8
NWBY RG14 12 E7
Chesterman St READ RG1 3 J9
Chesterment Wy EARL RG6 75 G5
Chester Pl BSTK RG21 14 C7
Chester St CAV/SC RG4 57 H3
TLHT RG30 2 A5
Chesterton Rd NTHA RG18 85 H2
Chestnut Av CAV/SC RG4 58 B1 3
WWKG RG41 76 D7
WWKG RG41 96 B1
Chestnut Cl FARN GU14 151 K6
HEN RG9 16 C2 1
MLW SL7 19 J3 1
THLE RG7 70 D2 1
Chestnut Crs NWBY RG14 12 E1
WHIT RG2 94 B3
Chestnut Dr TLHT RG30 91 G3
Chestnut Gv FLET GU13 167 J1
GOR/PANG RG8 41 J7
The Chestnuts HEN RG9 45 K1
Cheswell Gdns FLET GU13 167 F5
Chetwode Cl EWKG RG40 97 K1 2
Cheviot Cl KEMP RG22 175 G1
NWBY RG14 103 F3
Cheviot Dr FARN GU14 151 J6
WAR/TWY RG10 60 A1
Cheviot Rd SHST GU47 118 A7
Chichester Pl KEMP RG22 175 K2
Chichester Rd TLHT RG30 55 K5
Chicory Cl EARL RG6 8 F9
Chieveley Cl CALC RG31 55 H5
Chilcombe Wy EARL RG6 75 G4
Child Cl EWKG RG40 77 J6
Childrey Wy CALC RG31 55 G5
Chiltern Cl FLET GU13 167 J6
HEN RG9 30 E3
NWBY RG14 103 F3
Chiltern Ct CAV/SC RG4 43 J6
Chiltern Crs EARL RG6 5 H6
Chiltern Dr WAR/TWY RG10 60 A1
Chiltern Rd CAV/SC RG4 57 K1
HEN RG9 29 F4
SHST GU47 118 A7
Chiltern Vw GOR/PANG RG8 41 J7
Chiltern Wy KEMP RG22 175 F1
Chilton Rdg KEMP RG22 175 G7
Chineham La CHAM RG24 160 B1
CHAM RG24 160 D3
Chineham Park Ct CHAM RG24 160 E3
Chinnock Cl FLET GU13 167 G4
Chippenham Cl EARL RG6 74 C6 3
Chisbury Cl BRAK RG12 100 B4
Chittering Cl EARL RG6 75 F5
Chive Rd EARL RG6 74 D5

Chivers Cl KEMP RG22 175 G1
Chivers Dr EWKG RG40 116 D1 1
Chives Pl BNFD RG42 80 A5 2
Cholmeley Pl READ RG1 4 C6
Cholmeley Rd READ RG1 4 C5
Cholmeley Ter READ RG1 4 C6
Cholsey Cl STHA RG19 86 A4
Chopin Rd KEMP RG22 175 J4
Choseley Cl WAR/TWY RG10 33 K7
Choseley Rd WAR/TWY RG10 33 K7
Christchurch Cl FLET GU13 167 G7 1
Christchurch Gdns WHIT RG2 7 L2
Christchurch Rd READ RG1 7 M2
Christie Hts NWBY RG14 84 A7
Christie Wk YTLY GU46 135 H5
Christopher Ct NWBY RG14 13 H6
Christy Ct TADY RG26 127 F2 1
Chudleigh Gdns WHIT RG2 7 L7
Church Barns Farm THLE RG7 111 J3
Church Brook TADY RG26 126 D3
Church Cl HEN RG9 30 A2
KSCL RG20 102 B2
WWKG RG41 76 B4 1
Church End La TLHT RG30 56 A6
Church Ga STHA RG19 85 J4
Church Gv FLET GU13 167 F2
Church Hams EWKG RG40 116 C2
Church Hl BNFD RG42 78 D1
KSCL RG20 20 D5
WAR/TWY RG10 60 D6
Churchill Av ODIM RG29 180 B3
Churchill Cl HTWY RG27 149 G4
ODIM RG29 180 C4
TADY RG26 127 G2
Churchill Crs CAV/SC RG4 29 G5
Churchill Dr WWKG RG41 76 A4
Churchill Rd ASC SL5 81 J7
Churchill Wy BSTK RG21 14 E4
Churchill Wy East BSTK RG21 15 H4
Churchill Wy West BSTK RG21 14 A5
BSTK RG21 159 K6
KEMP RG22 159 J6
Church Lands TADY RG26 128 E6
Church La BNFD RG42 78 E1
BNFD RG42 80 A1
CHAM RG24 161 J5
DEAN RG23 159 F7
EWKG RG40 96 B6
EWKG RG40 116 D4
GOR/PANG RG8 37 H6
HEN RG9 29 G3
HEN RG9 45 J3
HTWY RG27 131 K3
HTWY RG27 149 J6
KSCL RG20 102 B2
KSCL RG20 120 A1
KSCL RG20 121 K2
NFNM GU10 183 J5
NTHA RG18 51 F4
NWBY RG14 83 G3
OVTN RG25 176 B5
READ RG1 3 J8
STHA RG19 85 J4
TADY RG26 124 E7
THLE RG7 90 A3
THLE RG7 93 J3
THLE RG7 107 G2
THLE RG7 110 D7
THLE RG7 115 G2
TLHT RG30 91 K1
WAR/TWY RG10 46 E7
WHIT RG2 94 A2
WHIT RG2 95 F3
Church Ms GOR/PANG RG8 41 J7 1
WODY RG5 59 J5
Church Rd ASC SL5 80 E6
ASC SL5 101 K2
BRAK RG12 11 G4
EARL RG6 9 J1
FLET GU13 167 F1
FLET GU13 167 G1
KSCL RG20 82 B2
NWBY RG14 83 K2
OVTN RG25 171 H4
SHST GU47 118 A7
SHST GU47 118 E7
TADY RG26 109 H7
TADY RG26 126 E3
THLE RG7 108 D1
THLE RG7 109 F1
THLE RG7 110 B3
WDSR SL4 81 F1
WODY RG5 59 J5
Church Rd East CWTH RG45 118 C3
Church Rd West CWTH RG45 118 C4
Church Sq BSTK RG21 14 E5
Church St BSTK RG21 14 E5
CAV/SC RG4 57 H3
CWTH RG45 118 C3
HEN RG9 31 G2
NFNM GU10 182 D6
NTHA RG18 36 A7
ODIM RG29 180 C2
READ RG1 3 J8
THLE RG7 70 C3
WAR/TWY RG10 46 B2
WAR/TWY RG10 60 C1
Church Vw HTWY RG27 149 H5
HTWY RG27 164 A2
THLE RG7 88 D1
YTLY GU46 135 J2
Churn Cl CHAM RG24 161 J4
Churn Rd KSCL RG20 21 H4
Cibbons Rd CHAM RG24 145 G7
Cinnamon Cl EARL RG6 8 E9
Cintra Av WHIT RG2 7 M2
Circle Hill Rd CWTH RG45 118 D3
Circuit La TLHT RG30 72 D1
City Rd CALC RG31 55 G7
Clacy Gn BNFD RG42 79 H5
Clanfield Crs CALC RG31 55 H3
Clappers Farm Rd THLE RG7 129 F1
Clapps Gate Rd TADY RG26 109 H7
Clare Av EWKG RG40 77 H7
Clare Ct EWKG RG40 77 H7
Clarence Rd FLET GU13 167 G3
HEN RG9 31 G1
Clarence Wy CALC RG31 71 G2
Clarendon Cl WWKG RG41 76 C4
Clarendon Gdns NWBY RG14 12 F2
Clarendon Rd EARL RG6 5 G9
Clares Green Rd THLE RG7 93 J4
Claudius Dr DEAN RG23 159 H4 1
Claverdon BRAK RG12 99 H5
Clay Cl CALC RG31 55 G4
Clayhill Cl BRAK RG12 100 C1
Clay Hill Crs NWBY RG14 84 C2 1
Clayhill Rd THLE RG7 90 E4
Clay La EWKG RG40 98 A1
THLE RG7 88 C1
Claythorpe Rd KEMP RG22 175 G1
Clayton Cl HTWY RG27 149 H5 1
Clayton Gv BRAK RG12 11 L2
Cleeve Down GOR/PANG RG8 25 G4
Cleeve Rd GOR/PANG RG8 24 E4
Clemence Gdns WHCH RG28 169 H7 1
Clements Cl THLE RG7 93 H6
Clements Md CALC RG31 55 G5
Clements Rd HEN RG9 17 F7
Clent Rd WHIT RG2 7 K3
Cleopatra Pl BNFD RG42 80 B5 2
Clere Gdns CHAM RG24 161 G1
Clerewater Pl STHA RG19 85 F4 1
Clevedge Wy ODIM RG29 164 B7
Clevedon Dr EARL RG6 9 H8
Clevedon Rd CALC RG31 55 K5
Cleveland WAR/TWY RG10 60 A1 1
Cleveland Cl KEMP RG22 175 G1
Cleveland Gv NWBY RG14 12 D3
Clevemede GOR/PANG RG8 25 F4 1
Cleves La OVTN RG25 178 E6
Cliddesden Ct BSTK RG21 176 C2
Cliddesden La KEMP RG22 175 J6
Cliddesden Rd BSTK RG21 14 F8
BSTK RG21 176 C2
Clifton Park Rd CAV/SC RG4 57 G2
Clifton Ri WAR/TWY RG10 46 D3
Clifton Rd NWBY RG14 12 A5
WWKG RG41 77 F6
Clifton St READ RG1 2 E7
Clifton Ter BSTK RG21 14 F3
Clintons Gn BNFD RG42 10 D2
Clivedale Rd WODY RG5 75 H2
Clive Gn BRAK RG12 99 J3
Cloister Ms THLE RG7 70 D3 2
The Cloisters CAV/SC RG4 57 H2
The Close ASC SL5 81 G7
BRAK RG12 11 H8
GOR/PANG RG8 26 E3 7
HEN RG9 31 G3
NTHA RG18 36 A7
NTHA RG18 85 G3
TADY RG26 143 G4
THLE RG7 91 F4
WODY RG5 75 H1
Clough Dr NTHA RG18 48 E7 2
Clove Cl EARL RG6 74 C5
Clover Cl EWKG RG40 77 K7
Clover Fld CHAM RG24 161 G3 2
Clover La YTLY GU46 135 F3
Cloves Farm Wd BNFD RG42 78 E7 2
Club La CWTH RG45 118 E3
Coach House Gdns FLET GU13 151 H7
Coachman's Ct NWBY RG14 84 A2 1
Coach Rd ASC SL5 81 H5
Coalport Wy TLHT RG30 55 K4
Coates Cl KEMP RG22 176 A3
Cobbett Gn KEMP RG22 175 K2
Cobham Rd WODY RG5 59 J6
Cochrane Cl STHA RG19 85 K4 1
Cock-a-dobby SHST GU47 118 B7 1
Cock La THLE RG7 68 C4
Cockney Hl TLHT RG30 56 A7
Cody Cl WODY RG5 60 A5
Colbeck FLET GU13 167 J7
Colbred Cnr FARN GU14 151 K6 1
Cold Ash Hl NTHA RG18 65 H6
Coldharbour Cl HEN RG9 31 F3
Coldicutt St CAV/SC RG4 3 L2
Coleman Cl BSTK RG21 160 D4
Colemans Moor La WODY RG5 59 J7
Colemans Moor Rd WODY RG5 60 A6
WODY RG5 75 J1
Coleridge Av YTLY GU46 135 K4
Coleridge Cl CWTH RG45 118 D4 1
WAR/TWY RG10 60 E2 1
Coleridge La GOR/PANG RG8 53 G1
Coley Av READ RG1 2 E9
Coley Hl READ RG1 2 F8
Coley Park Rd READ RG1 2 F8
Coley Pl READ RG1 3 G8
Collaroy Rd NTHA RG18 65 H7
College Piece THLE RG7 110 E2
College Rd BRAK RG12 11 H7
BSTK RG21 14 B4
EARL RG6 4 E8
Colleton Dr WAR/TWY RG10 60 D2
Colliers La HEN RG9 29 F3
Colliers Wy TLHT RG30 56 C6
Collins Cl NWBY RG14 13 J1
Collins Dr NTHA RG18 48 E7
Collis St WHIT RG2 7 J1
Colmore La HEN RG9 29 F3
Colmworth Cl EARL RG6 74 D6 3
Colne Valley Wy WHCH RG28 170 C7
Colne Wy BSTK RG21 15 J5
Colston Cl CALC RG31 71 J2 2
Colthrop La STHA RG19 86 C5
Coltsfoot Cl THLE RG7 91 G4
Coltsfoot Pl HTWY RG27 164 B1 1
Columbia Ct EWKG RG40 116 D1 2
Columbine Rd KEMP RG22 175 F4
Colwyn Cl YTLY GU46 135 G3
Colyer Cl KEMP RG22 175 H1 1
NTHA RG18 49 H5
Colyton Wy GOR/PANG RG8 41 H7
Combe Rd TLHT RG30 56 A6
Comet Wy WODY RG5 59 K6
Comfrey Cl EWKG RG40 77 K6
Commercial Rd WHIT RG2 7 G9
Commonfield La EWKG RG40 96 A7
Common Hl THLE RG7 69 J3
Common Rd STHA RG19 123 K1
Commons Rd WWKG RG41 76 E5
Compass Fld HTWY RG27 164 A2 1
Compton Av CALC RG31 55 G6
Compton Cl BRAK RG12 99 F4 1
EARL RG6 9 M3
FLET GU13 167 J6
HTWY RG27 164 A3
SHST GU47 118 D7
Compton Rd FLET GU13 167 J6
Comsaye Wk BRAK RG12 99 K3 1
Concorde Wy WODY RG5 59 K6 1
Condor Cl CALC RG31 55 H2
Coney Gra BNFD RG42 79 J4
Congreve Cl THLE RG7 108 C1
Conifer Cl FLET GU13 167 G6
TADY RG26 108 B7
Conifer Crest NWBY RG14 103 F4
Conifer Dr CALC RG31 55 G3
The Conifers CWTH RG45 118 B1
Coningham Rd WHIT RG2 93 K1
Coningsby BRAK RG12 11 G7
Conisboro Av CAV/SC RG4 43 F7
Conisboro Wy CAV/SC RG4 43 F7
Coniston Cl STHA RG19 85 F4
WODY RG5 75 H1
Coniston Dr TLHT RG30 56 B5 2
Coniston Rd KEMP RG22 175 G3
Coniston Wy FLET GU13 167 F6
Connaught Cl TLHT RG30 2 B7
YTLY GU46 135 G3
Connaught Rd FLET GU13 167 H3 1
NWBY RG14 13 G4
TLHT RG30 2 B7
Constable Cl BSTK RG21 15 K9
WODY RG5 60 A5 2
Constantine Wy KEMP RG22 175 F6
Constitution Rd TLHT RG30 56 C5 1
Consul Cl WODY RG5 75 K1
Conway Dr NTHA RG18 85 G2
Conway Rd CALC RG31 71 H1
Conygree Cl EARL RG6 74 E5
Cooke Ri BNFD RG42 79 K4 1
Cookham Cl SHST GU47 118 D7
Cookham Rd BRAK RG12 79 F7
Coombe Ct NTHA RG18 85 K4
Coombe Dr FLET GU13 167 K2
Coombehurst Dr BSTK RG21 176 C2
Coombe Pine BRAK RG12 100 A4
Coombe Rd KSCL RG20 36 A2
YTLY GU46 135 G2
Coombes La WWKG RG41 96 B3
Coombe Sq STHA RG19 85 K4
The Coombe GOR/PANG RG8 24 C5
Cooper Cl WHIT RG2 73 K7
Cooper Rd HEN RG9 17 G7
Coopers Ct TADY RG26 129 G6
Coopers Crs NTHA RG18 85 H3
Cooper's Hl HTWY RG27 134 D4
Coopers La TADY RG26 129 F6
Coopers Pightle CAV/SC RG4 42 E1
Cope Hall La NWBY RG14 102 E1
Copenhagen Cl WHIT RG2 73 K7 1
Copes La HTWY RG27 132 D2
Copland Cl KEMP RG22 175 H4
Copperdale Cl EARL RG6 8 E5
Copperfield Av SHST GU47 119 F6
Coppice Cl NWBY RG14 13 G9
TADY RG26 126 A1
Coppice Gdns CWTH RG45 118 A3
YTLY GU46 135 H4
Coppice Gn BNFD RG42 79 G5
Coppice Ms DEAN RG23 159 H5
Coppice Rd KSCL RG20 124 B7
WODY RG5 75 H2
Copse Av CAV/SC RG4 58 A2
Copse Cl CALC RG31 55 J2
Copse Dr WWKG RG41 77 F7
Copse Md WODY RG5 59 J4
Copse Rd OVTN RG25 171 J2
The Copse TADY RG26 126 D1
WAR/TWY RG10 46 D1
Copse View Cl CHAM RG24 145 H6 2
Copse Wy EWKG RG40 116 D1 3
Corbett Gdns WODY RG5 59 H6
Corbridge Rd WHIT RG2 7 M5
Corby Cl WODY RG5 59 K4
Cordale Rd BSTK RG21 14 D8
Cordelia Cft BNFD RG42 11 M1
Corderoy Cl STHA RG19 86 A5 3
Corfe Ms CAV/SC RG4 58 B1
Corfield Cl EWKG RG40 116 D5
Corfield Gn WWKG RG41 76 E6 1
Coriander Wy EARL RG6 74 C5 3
Corinne Cl WHIT RG2 73 J5
Corinthian Cl KEMP RG22 175 H5
Corn Cft BNFD RG42 80 A5 1
Cornfield Rd WODY RG5 59 K5
Cornfields YTLY GU46 135 G5
The Cornfields KEMP RG22 175 H5
Cornflower Cl WWKG RG41 76 C7 3
Cornish Cl KEMP RG22 175 H1 2
Cornwall Cl BNFD RG42 80 C4
WWKG RG41 96 C1 1
Cornwood Gdns WHIT RG2 7 M5
Coronation Cl KSCL RG20 121 J2
ODIM RG29 180 E1 1
Coronation Rd ASC SL5 101 K6
BSTK RG21 15 H2
YTLY GU46 135 J2
Coronation Sq EWKG RG40 77 J7 2
TLHT RG30 72 C2 1
Correlli Rd KEMP RG22 176 A4
Corringway FLET GU13 167 J5
Corsham Rd CALC RG31 72 A3
Corsham Wy CWTH RG45 118 C2
Corwen Rd TLHT RG30 55 J5
Coster Cl NWBY RG14 83 G2 1
Cotswold Cl KEMP RG22 159 G7
Cotswold Rd SHST GU47 118 A7 2
Cotswold Wy CALC RG31 55 H3
Cottage Gn HTWY RG27 149 J5
Cotterell Cl BNFD RG42 79 J5
Cotterell Gdns WAR/TWY RG10 60 E2
Cottesmore BRAK RG12 99 H5
Cottesmore Rd WODY RG5 59 G7
Cottington Cl KSCL RG20 124 B7 1
Cottle Cl BSTK RG21 176 B2
Council Rd BSTK RG21 14 E7
County La BNFD RG42 80 B4
Courage Ct TLHT RG30 72 C1 1
Course Rd ASC SL5 101 K1
Court Dro OVTN RG25 171 G1
Courtenay Dr CAV/SC RG4 43 J5
Courtlands Hl GOR/PANG RG8 54 B1
Courtlands Rd NWBY RG14 13 G8
Courtmoor Av FLET GU13 167 G4
Courts Rd EARL RG6 9 K3
The Courtyard THLE RG7 70 D3
Coventry Cl KEMP RG22 175 G4 2
Coventry Rd READ RG1 4 C6
Cove Rd FARN GU14 151 J7
Covert La BRAK RG12 11 H7
Cowdrey Cl BSTK RG21 160 D4 1
Cowdrey Hts CHAM RG24 15 L3
Cowfold La HTWY RG27 147 K4
Cow La KSCL RG20 20 D4
READ RG1 2 D2
TLHT RG30 2 D4
Cowper Wy TLHT RG30 6 A3
Cowslade NWBY RG14 83 G2 2
Cowslip Bank CHAM RG24 161 G4
Cowslip Crs NTHA RG18 85 J3
Coxeter Rd NWBY RG14 12 A1
Coxheath Rd FLET GU13 167 F5
Coxmoor Cl FLET GU13 167 K6
Cox's La THLE RG7 86 E4
Crabs Hl TADY RG26 140 E1
Crabtree Cl NTHA RG18 48 E7
Crabtree La NTHA RG18 48 E7
Crabtree Wy CHAM RG24 161 J7
Cradock Rd WHIT RG2 7 H4
Craig Av TLHT RG30 56 C5
Crail Cl WWKG RG41 97 F4
Cranbourne Av CALC RG31 71 H2 2
Cranbourne Gdns TLHT RG30 56 A3
Cranbourne La BSTK RG21 176 A2 1
Cranbrook Ct FLET GU13 151 H7
Cranbury Rd TLHT RG30 2 A7
Cranesfield CHAM RG24 143 K6
Cranes Rd CHAM RG24 143 K6
Crane Whf READ RG1 3 K6
Cranford Av FLET GU13 167 F6
Cranford Dr WAR/TWY RG10 60 E5
Cranford Park Dr YTLY GU46 135 J3
Cranmer Cl CALC RG31 55 G2
Craven Dene NWBY RG14 13 H2
Craven Rd NWBY RG14 12 A5
READ RG1 4 A8
Crawford Cl EARL RG6 9 J6
Crawford Pl NWBY RG14 12 D3
Crawley Cha BNFD RG42 80 E4
Crawshay Dr CAV/SC RG4 43 J5
Crawts Rd OVTN RG25 171 H5
Craysleaze CAV/SC RG4 42 E1
Crecy Cl WWKG RG41 96 D1 3
Crediton Cl WODY RG5 59 K7
Cremyll Rd READ RG1 2 E2
Crescent Rd CALC RG31 55 J4
EWKG RG40 97 H2
READ RG1 4 E9
The Crescent BRAK RG12 11 H8
EARL RG6 9 L4
FLET GU13 166 D5
HEN RG9 32 A7
THLE RG7 70 D2
THLE RG7 89 F3
THLE RG7 111 F2
Cressex Cl BNFD RG42 78 D4
Cressida Cha BNFD RG42 80 B5 10
Cressingham Rd WHIT RG2 7 M7
Cresswell Rd NWBY RG14 13 M1
NWBY RG14 84 D3 1
Crest Ct WAR/TWY RG10 46 D6
Creswell Cl WHIT RG2 93 J1
Cricketers KSCL RG20 82 B1
Cricketers La BNFD RG42 80 D3
Cricket Field Gv CWTH RG45 118 E4
Cricket Hl EWKG RG40 116 E6
Cricket Hill La BLKW GU17 135 J6
YTLY GU46 135 K4
Crisp Gdns BNFD RG42 79 F5
Crispin Cl CAV/SC RG4 42 E7
Crisp Rd HEN RG9 17 F7
Crocker Cl ASC SL5 81 H6
Crockford La CHAM RG24 145 F6
CHAM RG24 160 E2
Crockford Pl BNFD RG42 79 G5
Crockhamwell Rd WODY RG5 59 H7
Crocus Md NTHA RG18 85 K3
Crocus Wy WWKG RG41 76 C7 4
Croft Cl WWKG RG41 97 F5
Crofters Meadow
CHAM RG24 161 G3 3
Croft La NFNM GU10 182 D7
NWBY RG14 12 B2
YTLY GU46 135 H2
Crofton Cl BRAK RG12 100 B3
Croft Rd DEAN RG23 173 K2
EWKG RG40 97 F6
GOR/PANG RG8 25 F5
NWBY RG14 12 D9
THLE RG7 93 K5
THLE RG7 110 E2
The Crofts KEMP RG22 175 H6
The Croft BNFD RG42 79 J5 1
Croft Wy GOR/PANG RG8 26 E3
Cromer Cl CALC RG31 55 H4 2
Cromwell Cl CHAM RG24 161 J5
HEN RG9 31 G3 1
Cromwell Rd BSTK RG21 14 D2
CAV/SC RG4 57 J3
HEN RG9 31 H3
NWBY RG14 84 B2
Crondall End YTLY GU46 135 H2
Crondall Rd NFNM GU10 182 D1
Crookham Cl TADY RG26 126 E3 1
Crookham Reach FLET GU13 167 F6
Crookham Rd FLET GU13 167 F5
Cropmark Wy KEMP RG22 175 G5
Cropper Cl STHA RG19 86 B4
Crosby Gdns YTLY GU46 135 F2
Crosfields Cl WHIT RG2 74 B6
Crossborough Hl BSTK RG21 15 H7
Cross Fell BRAK RG12 10 C8
Cross Gates Cl BRAK RG12 100 C1
Crossland Rd READ RG1 3 J7
Cross La THLE RG7 92 B7
THLE RG7 112 E1
Cross St BSTK RG21 14 E6
EWKG RG40 97 H1 2
READ RG1 3 J6
Crowfield Dr STHA RG19 85 G4
Crown Acre Cl STHA RG19 85 H4 1
Crownfields ODIM RG29 180 C2
Crown Gdns FLET GU13 167 J3
Crown La CHAM RG24 161 H5
HTWY RG27 162 E4
THLE RG7 70 D3 3
Crown Pl READ RG1 3 L8
SHST GU47 119 F7 1
Crown Rw BRAK RG12 100 A4
Crown St READ RG1 3 J8
Crowsley Rd HEN RG9 31 K7
Crowsley Wy CAV/SC RG4 29 F6
Crowthorne Rd BRAK RG12 10 C9
BRAK RG12 99 G6
Crowthorne Rd North
BRAK RG12 10 F6
Crutchley Rd EWKG RG40 77 H7
Cuddesdon Cl GOR/PANG RG8 26 E3 3
Cufaude La TADY RG26 145 G4
Cuffelle Cl CHAM RG24 145 H7
Culford Cl EARL RG6 75 G4
Cullen Cl YTLY GU46 135 H4
Culloden Wy WWKG RG41 96 D1
Culver Cft BNFD RG42 79 F5
Culver La EARL RG6 5 H7
Culver Rd BSTK RG21 14 C9
NWBY RG14 83 J7 1
READ RG1 4 E8
SHST GU47 118 E7
Cumberland Av KEMP RG22 175 K3 1
Cumberland Dr BRAK RG12 11 K2
Cumberland Rd READ RG1 4 B6
Cumberland Wy WWKG RG41 96 C1 2
Cumnor Wy BRAK RG12 11 M7
Curlew Cl KEMP RG22 175 F3
STHA RG19 85 H4 2
Curlew Dr CALC RG31 55 H7
Curleys Wy THLE RG7 114 A2 1
Curling Wy NWBY RG14 13 K1
Curl Wy WWKG RG41 97 F2
Curridge Gn NTHA RG18 64 D2
Curridge Rd NWBY RG14 64 B3
Curtis Rd CALC RG31 71 G1
Curzon Dr FLET GU13 167 H6
Curzon St TLHT RG30 2 B5
Cutbush Cl EARL RG6 74 E6
Cutbush La EARL RG6 9 M9
EARL RG6 74 D6
WHIT RG2 94 B1
The Cuttings NTHA RG18 36 A7
Cwmcarn CAV/SC RG4 43 G6
Cygnet Cl STHA RG19 85 G4
Cypress Cl EWKG RG40 97 F7
Cypress Dr FLET GU13 167 K2
Cypress Rd WODY RG5 59 K7
Cyprus Rd KEMP RG22 175 H7
Cyril Vokins Rd NWBY RG14 84 D5

D

Dacre Av CAV/SC RG4 58 B1
Daffodil Cl KEMP RG22 175 F4
Dahlia Cl KEMP RG22 175 F4 1
Dairy La HEN RG9 18 A1
Dalby Cl WAR/TWY RG10 60 E5
Dalby Crs NWBY RG14 13 H9
Dalcross BRAK RG12 100 B4
Dale Rd WHIT RG2 7 J1
Dalewood KEMP RG22 175 F2
Dalton Cl TLHT RG30 55 K5 1
Damar Gdns HEN RG9 31 H3
Damsel Pth BSTK RG21 15 K5
Dancers Meadow CHAM RG24 144 A7
Dances La WHCH RG28 169 H6
Danebury Rd KEMP RG22 175 G6
Daneshill Dr CHAM RG24 161 G3
Dankworth Rd KEMP RG22 175 H4
Danvers Cl STHA RG19 85 J5 2
Danvers Dr FLET GU13 166 E7
Danywern Dr WWKG RG41 76 B4
Daphne Dr FLET GU13 183 F1
Darby La GOR/PANG RG8 38 E7
Darby V BNFD RG42 79 J4
Darell Rd CAV/SC RG4 57 G2
Dare's La NFNM GU10 183 F3
Dark La CALC RG31 55 G3
CHAM RG24 143 K7
THLE RG7 53 F6
WAR/TWY RG10 46 C2
Darleydale Cl SHST GU47 118 E6 1
Darlington Rd BSTK RG21 14 D1
Darset Av FLET GU13 167 H1
Dart Cl EWKG RG40 116 E1
NTHA RG18 85 G2
Dartington Av WODY RG5 75 G2
Dartmouth Cl BRAK RG12 11 M5
Darwall Dr ASC SL5 81 G7
Darwin Cl WHIT RG2 7 H9
Dashwood Cl BRAK RG12 11 J2
Dauntless Rd THLE RG7 91 G4
Davenport Rd BRAK RG12 11 L2
Daventry Ct BNFD RG42 10 E2
Davis St WAR/TWY RG10 76 C2
Davis Wy WAR/TWY RG10 76 C2
Davy Cl EWKG RG40 97 H2
KEMP RG22 159 K6
Dawlish Rd WHIT RG2 7 L7
Dawnay Cl ASC SL5 81 J6
Deacon Cl EWKG RG40 77 H6
Deacons La NTHA RG18 49 H6
Deacon Wy TLHT RG30 56 B3
Deadman's La GOR/PANG RG8 27 H6
GOR/PANG RG8 41 G1
STHA RG19 104 A2
THLE RG7 70 B2
Deadmoor La KSCL RG20 103 H6
Deane's Cl BSTK RG21 15 G2
Deanfield Av HEN RG9 31 G2
Deanfield Rd HEN RG9 31 F2
Dean Gv EWKG RG40 77 H7
Deans Farm CAV/SC RG4 4 A2
Deansgate BRAK RG12 99 H5
Deansgate Rd READ RG1 3 J8

Deanswood Rd TADY RG26 126 D1
De Beauvoir Rd READ RG1 4 C7
De Bohun Rd READ RG1 3 J4
Decouttere Cl FLET GU13 167 F6
Deepdale BRAK RG12 10 C7
Deepdene Cl READ RG1 2 D7
Deepfield Rd BRAK RG12 11 J3
Deep La BSTK RG21 14 A5
Deerhurst Av WWKG RG41 76 B4
Dee Rd TLHT RG30 56 B6
Deer Rock Hl BRAK RG12 99 K4
Deer's La GOR/PANG RG8 27 H1
Delafield Dr CALC RG31 71 H2
Delamere Rd EARL RG6 5 J5
Delane Dr WWKG RG41 76 A4
Delaney Cl TLHT RG30 56 A5
Delft Cl TLHT RG30 56 A5 2
Delibes Rd KEMP RG22 176 A4
Delius Cl KEMP RG22 175 K3
Dellands OVTN RG25 171 H5
Dellands La OVTN RG25 171 G4
Deller St BNFD RG42 79 G5
Dellfield DEAN RG23 174 A1
Dell Rd CALC RG31 55 H3
EWKG RG40 117 F5
The Dell KSCL RG20 124 A7
READ RG1 3 L8
YTLY GU46 135 H4
The Delph EARL RG6 75 G4
De Montfort Rd NWBY RG14 83 G2
READ RG1 3 H3
Denbeigh Pl READ RG1 2 F2
Denbury Gdns WHIT RG2 73 K6 1
Denby Wy TLHT RG30 56 A4
Dene Cl BRAK RG12 11 H1
BRAK RG12 79 K5 5
EARL RG6 9 H6
Dene Wy NWBY RG14 83 J2
Denham Dr KEMP RG22 175 H2
YTLY GU46 135 K4 1
Denham Gv BRAK RG12 99 K4 3
Denman Cl FLET GU13 167 K2
Denmark Av WODY RG5 59 K4
Denmark Rd NWBY RG14 13 G4
READ RG1 4 A7
Denmark St EWKG RG40 97 G2
Denmead Ct BRAK RG12 100 B4
Denmead Rd TADY RG26 126 E1
Denning Cl FLET GU13 167 F4
Dennisford Rd KSCL RG20 20 E6
Dennose Cl EARL RG6 9 H9
Denton Cl STHA RG19 85 H5
Denton Rd EWKG RG40 97 H2
Deptford La ODIM RG29 179 K1
Derby Flds ODIM RG29 164 B5
Derby Rd CAV/SC RG4 57 J2
NWBY RG14 12 D7
Derbyshire Gn BNFD RG42 80 C5
Derby St READ RG1 2 E5
Derrick Cl CALC RG31 71 H2 3
Derwent Cl WWKG RG41 96 D1 6
Derwent Rd KEMP RG22 175 F3
STHA RG19 85 F4
Deveron Dr TLHT RG30 56 B5
Dever Wy DEAN RG23 174 A3
The Devil's Hwy CWTH RG45 117 K3
Devil's Hl HEN RG9 30 A5
De-vitre Gn EWKG RG40 78 A7
Devitt Cl EARL RG6 8 D9
Devon Cha BNFD RG42 80 B4 1
BNFD RG42 80 C4 1
Devon Cl FARN GU14 151 J6
WWKG RG41 96 D1
Devon Dr CAV/SC RG4 58 B1
Devonshire Gdns CALC RG31 55 G1
Devonshire Pk WHIT RG2 8 D7
Devonshire Pl BSTK RG21 14 C7
Dewe La TLHT RG30 71 K4
Dewpond Wk CHAM RG24 161 G3
Dexter Wy FARN GU14 151 J6 3
Diamond Wy WWKG RG41 76 D7 2
Diana Cl KEMP RG22 175 K1
THLE RG7 93 H6
Dianthus Pl BNFD RG42 80 E4
Dibley Cl KEMP RG22 175 H1
Dickens Cl CAV/SC RG4 4 A1
Dickens La CHAM RG24 161 H7
OVTN RG25 177 G2
Dickens Wy YTLY GU46 135 H4
Dieppe Cl WWKG RG41 96 D1 7
Digby Rd NWBY RG14 12 B1
NWBY RG14 83 H2
Dilly La HTWY RG27 149 H6
Dines Wy NTHA RG18 49 G6
Dinorben Av FLET GU13 167 F4
Dinorben Beeches FLET GU13 167 F4
Dinorben Cl FLET GU13 167 G4
Dippenhall St NFNM GU10 182 E6
Ditchfield La EWKG RG40 96 D7
Ditchling BRAK RG12 99 H5
The Dittons EWKG RG40 116 E2 1
Dixon Rd HTWY RG27 145 J2
Dobsons La HEN RG9 17 F1
Doctors La NTHA RG18 49 F7
Doddington Cl EARL RG6 75 F5
Dodsells Well EWKG RG40 96 E7 6
Dog La GOR/PANG RG8 37 H6
HEN RG9 29 H3
Doles Hl WWKG RG41 96 C4
Doles La WWKG RG41 96 D4
Dollis Gn TADY RG26 129 G6
Dolman Rd NWBY RG14 12 E1
NWBY RG14 83 K2 1
Dolphin Cl WWKG RG41 76 B5
Dominica Cl CHAM RG24 160 D1
Domomyclose STHA RG19 85 K4
Donaldson Wy WODY RG5 59 K5
Doncastle Rd BRAK RG12 10 A6
BRAK RG12 99 F1
Don Cl TLHT RG30 56 B5
Donegal Cl CAV/SC RG4 57 K2
Donkin Hl CAV/SC RG4 57 K2
Donnington Cl THLE RG7 67 K6
Donnington Gdns READ RG1 4 B8
Donnington Pk NWBY RG14 83 J1
Donnington Pl WWKG RG41 76 C4 2
Donnington Rd READ RG1 4 B7
Donnington Sq NWBY RG14 83 J2
Donnybrook BRAK RG12 99 H5
Dora's Green La NFNM GU10 183 H6
Dorchester Cl DEAN RG23 159 G6
Dorchester Ct TLHT RG30 56 D7
Dorchester Rd HTWY RG27 163 K2
Dorchester Wy ODIM RG29 163 J7
Dorking Wy CALC RG31 71 F2
Dormer Cl CWTH RG45 118 B3
NWBY RG14 103 H2
Dorothy St READ RG1 3 J8
Dorrel Cl KEMP RG22 175 G6
Dorset St TLHT RG30 56 D5
Dorset V BNFD RG42 80 B4
Dorset Wy WWKG RG41 96 D2
Doswell Wy BSTK RG21 15 G2
Doublet Cl STHA RG19 85 F4
Douglas Gra WAR/TWY RG10 76 C2
Douglas Ride KSCL RG20 120 B1
Dove Cl EARL RG6 74 C6 4
KEMP RG22 174 E3
Dovecote Rd WHIT RG2 73 J7
Dovedale Cl CAV/SC RG4 57 G2
SHST GU47 118 E6
Dove La HEN RG9 28 E3
Dover Cl DEAN RG23 159 J5
Dover St READ RG1 3 G8
Doveton Wy NWBY RG14 13 H1
Dowding Cl WODY RG5 59 K6 2
Dowding Ct CWTH RG45 118 D2 1
Downend La KSCL RG20 48 A2
Downing Rd CALC RG31 55 H5
Down La OVTN RG25 178 D2
Downmill Rd BRAK RG12 10 B4
Downshire Sq READ RG1 2 D8
Downshire Wy BNFD RG42 10 D2
BRAK RG12 10 D4
Downsland Rd BSTK RG21 14 B6
Downs Rd KSCL RG20 22 B7
Downs Wy CALC RG31 55 H3
Doyle Gdns YTLY GU46 135 H4 2
Dragonfly Dr CHAM RG24 161 G3 4
Drake Cl EWKG RG40 116 D1
Draper Cl STHA RG19 85 J5
Draycott BRAK RG12 100 B3
Dray's La HEN RG9 29 H3
Drayton Cl BRAK RG12 11 J4
Drayton Rd TLHT RG30 56 C5
Dresden Wy TLHT RG30 56 A4 1
Drewett Cl WHIT RG2 93 K1
Driftway Cl EARL RG6 75 F5
Driftway Rd HTWY RG27 164 B2
The Drive DEAN RG23 174 A3
EARL RG6 5 G6
NWBY RG14 12 B9
Droitwich Cl BRAK RG12 11 K6
Drome Pth WWKG RG41 75 K3
Drove La NTHA RG18 65 G4
Drovers End FARN GU14 151 K6
Drovers Wy BRAK RG12 100 C1
WODY RG5 75 H1
Droxford Crs TADY RG26 126 D2
Druce Wy STHA RG19 85 J4
Drummond Cl BRAK RG12 80 C6 2
Drury La THLE RG7 111 G4
Dryden BRAK RG12 99 H5
Dryden Cl CHAM RG24 160 D3
NTHA RG18 85 H2
Duchess Cl CWTH RG45 118 C1 1
Duddon Wy BSTK RG21 15 K5
Dudley Cl CALC RG31 55 K4
DEAN RG23 159 G6
Dudley Ms CALC RG31 55 K4 2
Duffield Rd WODY RG5 59 J4
Dukeshill Rd BNFD RG42 10 E1
Dukes Md FLET GU13 166 E2
Duke's Ride CWTH RG45 118 A4
THLE RG7 128 A1
Duke St HEN RG9 31 H1
READ RG1 3 J6
Dukes Wd CWTH RG45 118 C3
Dulnan Cl TLHT RG30 56 B5
Dulverton Gdns WHIT RG2 7 M8
Dumas Cl YTLY GU46 135 H4 3
Du Maurier Cl FLET GU13 183 F1
Dumbarton Wy CAV/SC RG4 44 B7
Dunaways Cl EARL RG6 75 G3
Dunbar Dr WODY RG5 59 K7
Duncan Dr EWKG RG40 97 J2
Duncan Gdns GOR/PANG RG8 55 H1 2
Duncan Rd WODY RG5 59 H7
Dundas Cl BRAK RG12 10 E7
Dundela Cl WODY RG5 59 H7
Dunford Pl BNFD RG42 79 F5
Dungells Farm Cl YTLY GU46 135 J5 1
Dungells La YTLY GU46 135 H4
Dunholme Cl EARL RG6 75 H4 4
Dunkirk Cl WWKG RG41 96 D1 8
Dunley's Hl ODIM RG29 180 B1
Dunluce Gdns GOR/PANG RG8 40 D7 1
Dunmow Hl FLET GU13 167 H1
Dunnock Wy WAR/TWY RG10 46 D1 1
Dunoon Cl CALC RG31 71 K2 2
Dunsfold Rd TLHT RG30 56 A6
Dunsford Crs DEAN RG23 159 H4
Dunsmore Gdns YTLY GU46 135 F4
Dunstall Cl CALC RG31 55 J5 2
Dunstan Rd NTHA RG18 85 K3
Dunstans Dr WWKG RG41 76 A4
Dunster Cl CAV/SC RG4 43 K6
Dunt Av WAR/TWY RG10 76 D2
Dunt La WAR/TWY RG10 76 D1
Durand Rd EARL RG6 9 G9
Durant Wy CALC RG31 55 J2
Durbidges STHA RG19 123 K1
Durham Cl WHIT RG2 73 K6
Durham Rd SHST GU47 119 F6
Durham Wy KEMP RG22 175 G4 3
Durley Md BRAK RG12 100 C3
Durnsford Av FLET GU13 167 H4
Dwyer Rd TLHT RG30 72 A2
Dyer Rd EWKG RG40 77 K7
Dysons Cl NWBY RG14 12 B4
Dysonswood La CAV/SC RG4 43 F4

E

Eagle Cl CWTH RG45 118 B1
KEMP RG22 174 E4 1
WWKG RG41 96 E2 2
Eagle Rd KSCL RG20 105 F6
Eagles Nest SHST GU47 118 B7 2
Earle Cft BNFD RG42 79 K5 3
Earley Hill Rd EARL RG6 9 G2
Earley Pl READ RG1 3 J6
Earlsbourne FLET GU13 167 J7
Earlsfield Cl CAV/SC RG4 58 B1
Earlswood BRAK RG12 99 J5
Easby Wy EARL RG6 75 G5
Easington Dr EARL RG6 75 H4
Eastbury Av CALC RG31 55 G5
Eastbury Pk WWKG RG41 76 C4
Eastcourt Av EARL RG6 5 H8
East Dr CALC RG31 71 K1
Eastern Av READ RG1 4 D9
Eastern La CWTH RG45 119 G4
Eastern Rd BRAK RG12 11 K4
Eastfield Av BSTK RG21 15 G5
Eastfield La GOR/PANG RG8 26 D5
GOR/PANG RG8 40 C5
Easthampstead Rd BRAK RG12 10 C3
EWKG RG40 97 J1
Eastheath Av WWKG RG41 97 F3
Eastheath Gdns WWKG RG41 97 G4 1
East La KSCL RG20 48 A4
Eastlyn Rd TADY RG26 109 H7
East Park Farm Dr
WAR/TWY RG10 60 A1
Eastrop La BSTK RG21 15 G5
Eastrop Rbt BSTK RG21 15 G4
Eastrop Wy BSTK RG21 15 G4
East Stratton Cl BRAK RG12 100 C3 2
East St READ RG1 3 K7
East View Cl WAR/TWY RG10 46 D2
East View Rd WAR/TWY RG10 46 D2
Eastwood Rd WODY RG5 75 H2
Eaton Pl READ RG1 2 F6
Ebborn Sq EARL RG6 75 F6 3
Ecchinswell Rd KSCL RG20 123 J7
Eccles Cl CAV/SC RG4 57 K3 1
Eddington Rd BRAK RG12 99 F4
Edenhall Cl CALC RG31 55 J2
Edenham Cl EARL RG6 75 H4
Edenham Crs READ RG1 6 C1
Eden Wy WWKG RG41 76 A5
Edgar Milward Cl TLHT RG30 56 B4
Edgbarrowhill Star CWTH RG45 118 B5
Edgbarrow Ri SHST GU47 118 B6
Edgcumbe Park Dr CWTH RG45 118 B3
Edgecombe La NWBY RG14 84 B2
Edgedale Cl CWTH RG45 118 C4 1
Edgehill Cl KEMP RG22 175 G1
Edgehill St READ RG1 7 J1
Edgewood Cl CWTH RG45 118 B1 1
Edinburgh Rd TLHT RG30 2 C6
Edmonds Ct BRAK RG12 11 H1
Edney Cl FLET GU13 167 J5
Edward Rd WAR/TWY RG10 46 A7
Edwin Cl STHA RG19 86 A4
Eeklo Pl NWBY RG14 12 F8
Egerton Rd WHIT RG2 74 B5
Eggleton Cl FLET GU13 167 F6 2
Egremont Dr EARL RG6 9 M6
EARL RG6 75 G4 1
Elan Cl TLHT RG30 56 A6
Elbow Cnr BSTK RG21 14 E5
Eldart Cl TLHT RG30 56 C6
Elderberry Bank CHAM RG24 161 G3
Elderberry Wy EARL RG6 75 G5 2
Elder Cl CALC RG31 55 H4
Eldon Pl READ RG1 3 M7
Eldon Rd READ RG1 3 M7
Eldon Sq READ RG1 3 M7
Eldon St READ RG1 4 A7
Eldon Ter READ RG1 3 M7
Elford Cl EARL RG6 9 M9
Elgar Av CWTH RG45 118 C2
Elgar Cl KEMP RG22 175 K4
Elgar Rd WHIT RG2 7 H1
Elgar Rd South WHIT RG2 7 J3
Elgarth Dr EWKG RG40 96 E7 5
Elgin Rd BLKW GU17 151 K1
Eliot Cl CAV/SC RG4 57 H1
NTHA RG18 85 H2
Elizabeth Av NWBY RG14 103 G1
Elizabeth Cl BRAK RG12 11 H8
HEN RG9 30 D2
Elizabeth Dr FLET GU13 167 H6
Elizabeth Rd EWKG RG40 97 J1
HEN RG9 30 E3
KEMP RG22 159 K7
Elizabeth Rout Cl THLE RG7 93 K5
Ellenborough Cl BRAK RG12 11 J2
Ellen Dr FARN GU14 151 K6
Ellen Gdns TADY RG26 129 F6
Ellerton Cl THLE RG7 70 D2 2
Ellesfield Av BRAK RG12 99 F2
Ellesmere Cl CAV/SC RG4 57 J2
Ellington Dr KEMP RG22 175 H5
Elliot Ri ASC SL5 81 G7
Elliots Wy READ RG1 3 J1
Ellison Wy EWKG RG40 97 G1
Ellis Rd CWTH RG45 118 C2
Ellis's Hl WHIT RG2 95 J3
Elm Bank YTLY GU46 135 H2 1
Elm Ct CAV/SC RG4 29 G7
Elmcroft GOR/PANG RG8 25 F6 1
Elm Dr TLHT RG30 91 G2
Elm Farm Gv KSCL RG20 124 A7 1
Elm Gv KSCL RG20 124 A7
NTHA RG18 85 G2
Elmhurst TADY RG26 126 E2
Elmhurst Rd GOR/PANG RG8 25 F4
NTHA RG18 85 F2
READ RG1 8 B2
Elm La EARL RG6 8 F8
Elmleigh Ct CAV/SC RG4 57 K3 2
Elmley Cl WWKG RG41 76 E5
Elm Lodge Av TLHT RG30 2 A5
Elm Park Rd TLHT RG30 2 B7
Elm Rd CAV/SC RG4 42 E5
CHAM RG24 159 J1
EARL RG6 8 E8
OVTN RG25 171 J2
Elms Av STHA RG19 85 K4
Elms Rd EWKG RG40 97 G2
FLET GU13 167 K2
HTWY RG27 163 K1 3
Elmstone Dr CALC RG31 55 H4
Elmwood Wy DEAN RG23 159 H4
Elsley Rd CALC RG31 55 J2
Elstow Av CAV/SC RG4 43 K6
Elstree Cl CALC RG31 55 J3
Eltham Av CAV/SC RG4 44 B7
Elvaston Wy TLHT RG30 56 A6
Elveden Cl EARL RG6 75 H4
Elvendon La GOR/PANG RG8 26 B4
Elvendon Rd GOR/PANG RG8 25 G4
Elvetham Cl FLET GU13 151 G7
Elvetham La HTWY RG27 150 A2
Elvetham Pl HTWY RG27 151 F7
Elvetham Rd FLET GU13 166 E1
Elyham GOR/PANG RG8 41 G7 3
Emblen Crs WHIT RG2 95 H5
Embrook Wy CALC RG31 71 F2 2
Emerald Cl WWKG RG41 76 D7 3
Emery Acres GOR/PANG RG8 38 D6
Emery Down Cl BRAK RG12 100 D1 1
Emma La WAR/TWY RG10 46 D2
Emmbrook Rd WWKG RG41 76 E6
Emmbrook V WWKG RG41 77 F5
Emm Cl WWKG RG41 76 E6
Emmens La GOR/PANG RG8 27 K1
Emmer Green Ct CAV/SC RG4 43 K7
Emmets Nest BNFD RG42 78 D4
Emmets Pk BNFD RG42 78 D4 2
Emmview Cl WWKG RG41 76 E7 1
Empress Rd CALC RG31 71 H1
Enborne Cl CALC RG31 55 H5 1
Enborne Gdns BRAK RG12 80 A5
Enborne Gv NWBY RG14 12 B6
Enborne Pl NWBY RG14 12 B6
Enborne Rd KSCL RG20 83 F6
NWBY RG14 12 B6
Enborne St KSCL RG20 102 D4
Enborne Wy THLE RG7 107 G2
Englefield Rd THLE RG7 70 C2
Englemere Pk ASC SL5 101 G2
Englemere Rd BNFD RG42 79 G5
Ennerdale BRAK RG12 10 C7
Ennerdale Cl KEMP RG22 175 G2
Ennerdale Rd WHIT RG2 8 B5
Ennerdale Wy STHA RG19 85 F4 2
Enstone Rd WODY RG5 59 K5
Enterprise Ct CHAM RG24 160 E4
Enterprise Wy STHA RG19 86 B5
Epping Cl READ RG1 2 F7
Epping Wy BRAK RG12 100 C2
Epsom Ct READ RG1 2 E9
Epsom Crs NWBY RG14 13 H8
Equine Wy NWBY RG14 104 A1
Equinne Wy NWBY RG14 104 A1
Erica Dr EWKG RG40 97 J2
Eric Av CAV/SC RG4 43 H6
Eriswell Cl EARL RG6 75 H4
Erleigh Court Dr EARL RG6 5 H6
Erleigh Court Gdns EARL RG6 5 G6
Erleigh Dene NWBY RG14 12 C8
Erleigh Rd READ RG1 4 A8
Erskine Cl TADY RG26 109 J7
Esher Cl KEMP RG22 175 J3
Eskdale Rd WWKG RG41 75 K2
Eskin Cl TLHT RG30 56 B6
Essame Cl EWKG RG40 97 J1
Essex Ri BNFD RG42 80 C5
Essex Rd BSTK RG21 14 D5
Essex St NWBY RG14 103 G1
WHIT RG2 7 K2
Essex Wy CAV/SC RG4 43 H1
Ester Carling La HEN RG9 28 E3
Eton Cl KEMP RG22 175 F6
Europa Cl TADY RG26 129 G6
Euskirchen Wy KEMP RG22 159 J6
Eustace Crs EWKG RG40 77 J6
Evedon BRAK RG12 99 J5
Evelyn Ct WODY RG5 75 J1
Evendon's Cl WWKG RG41 97 F4
Evendon's La WWKG RG41 96 C4
Everest Rd CWTH RG45 118 C2
Evergreen Dr CALC RG31 72 A2 1
Evergreen Wy WWKG RG41 96 E2 3
Everington La NTHA RG18 50 B4
Eversley Rd WHIT RG2 95 H5
Eversley St HTWY RG27 115 K7
Evesham Rd CAV/SC RG4 43 J7
Evesham Wk SHST GU47 118 D7
Evingar Gdns WHCH RG28 169 H6
Evingar Rd WHCH RG28 169 H6
Evreux Cl STHA RG19 86 A5 3
Ewhurst Rd TADY RG26 142 B3
Ewshot La FLET GU13 183 G1
Exbourne Rd WHIT RG2 73 K6
Exeter Cl KEMP RG22 175 G5
Exeter Gdns YTLY GU46 135 G2
Exmoor Cl KEMP RG22 175 G1
Exmoor Rd STHA RG19 85 H4
Express Wy NWBY RG14 84 D5
Eynsford Cl CAV/SC RG4 44 B7 1
Eynsham Cl WODY RG5 59 H5

F

Fairacre KSCL RG20 120 C1
Faircross BRAK RG12 10 F6
Faircross Quarters NTHA RG18 48 E7
Faircross Rd TLHT RG30 72 D1 1
Fairfax BNFD RG42 10 D2
Fairfax Cl CAV/SC RG4 57 J3
Fairfax Pl NWBY RG14 84 D2 1
Fairfield KSCL RG20 21 J7
WHCH RG28 169 H6
Fairfield Rd GOR/PANG RG8 25 G4
Fairfields Rd BSTK RG21 14 E8
Fairford Rd CALC RG31 55 H3
Fairland Cl FLET GU13 167 J3
Fair Lawn Gn EARL RG6 8 E9
Fairlawn Rd TADY RG26 127 G2
Fairlop Cl CALC RG31 71 J2 3
Fairmead Rd WHIT RG2 94 B2
Fairmile FLET GU13 167 H5
Fair Mile HEN RG9 16 E5
Fair Oak La THLE RG7 129 K2
Fairoak Wy TADY RG26 108 A7
Fairsted Cl TLHT RG30 56 B5 1
Fairthorne Ri CHAM RG24 161 K6 1
Fairview Av EARL RG6 5 J9
Fairview Meadow DEAN RG23 174 A4
Fairview Rd EWKG RG40 97 H2
Fairwater Dr WODY RG5 5 M9
Fairway Av TLHT RG30 55 J7
Fairway Dr WAR/TWY RG10 45 K7 1
Faithfull Cl BNFD RG42 79 J4
Fakenham Cl EARL RG6 74 D6 4
Fakenham Wy SHST GU47 118 E7
Falcon Av WHIT RG2 74 C5
Falcon Cl KEMP RG22 174 E3
Falcon Coppice KSCL RG20 120 C1 1
Falcon Flds TADY RG26 108 E6
Falcon House Gdns KSCL RG20 120 B1
Falcon Wy WWKG RG41 96 E1 2
YTLY GU46 135 G3 1
Falkland Dr NWBY RG14 12 C9
Falkland Garth NWBY RG14 103 G1
Falkland Rd CHAM RG24 160 D1 1
NWBY RG14 103 G2
Falkners Cl FARN GU14 151 K6
Fallowfield FARN GU14 151 K6 2
YTLY GU46 135 G2
Fallowfield Cl CAV/SC RG4 57 J1
Falmouth Rd WHIT RG2 73 K7
Falmouth Wy STHA RG19 86 A4
Falstaff Av EARL RG6 8 E7
Fanes Cl BNFD RG42 10 B2
Fannys La THLE RG7 66 C5
Faraday Cl WHIT RG2 115 H1 1
Faraday Rd CHAM RG24 160 E3
NWBY RG14 13 G3
Faraday Wy EWKG RG40 95 K7
Fareham Dr YTLY GU46 135 G2 1
Faringdon Cl SHST GU47 118 D7
Faringdon Dr BRAK RG12 11 J9
Farleigh Ms CAV/SC RG4 44 B7
Farleigh Ri BSTK RG21 176 D2
Farleigh Rd OVTN RG25 176 C3
Farley Copse BNFD RG42 79 F6
Farman Cl WODY RG5 60 A5
Farm Cl BNFD RG42 10 A1
CWTH RG45 118 D1
GOR/PANG RG8 41 H7
YTLY GU46 135 J4
Farm Dr CALC RG31 55 G7
FARN GU14 151 J6
Farmers Cl WHIT RG2 93 K1 3
Farmers End WAR/TWY RG10 60 A1
Farm Ground Cl HTWY RG27 164 B2 1
Farmhouse Wy FLET GU13 167 F6
Farm La NFNM GU10 182 D7
Farm Rd GOR/PANG RG8 25 F5
Farm Vw YTLY GU46 135 J4
Farm View Dr CHAM RG24 145 H7
Farnham Cl BRAK RG12 11 J4
Farnham Dr CAV/SC RG4 58 B1
Farnham Rd ODIM RG29 180 E1
Farningham BRAK RG12 100 B4
Farnsfield Cl EARL RG6 74 D6 5
Faroe Cl CHAM RG24 160 E2
Farriers Cl TADY RG26 129 G6
WODY RG5 59 H6
Farriers La KSCL RG20 20 D4
Farringdon Wy TADY RG26 126 E2
Far Rd HEN RG9 31 J3
Farrowdene Rd WHIT RG2 73 K6
Fatherson Rd READ RG1 4 A7
Faversham Rd SHST GU47 118 E7 2
Fawcett Crs WODY RG5 59 G7
Fawconer Rd KSCL RG20 124 A7
Fawler Md BRAK RG12 100 C2 4
Fawley Bottom La HEN RG9 16 D2
Fawley Rd TLHT RG30 72 D1
Faygate Wy EARL RG6 74 E5
Fayrewood Cha KEMP RG22 175 G5 2
Feathers La BSTK RG21 14 F6
Feld Wy CHAM RG24 161 H4
Felixstowe Cl EARL RG6 75 G4
The Fells CALC RG31 55 F7 1
Felstead Cl EARL RG6 8 E7
Felthorpe Cl EARL RG6 74 D6 6
Felton Wy CALC RG31 55 H5
Fencote BRAK RG12 100 A5
Fennel Cl CHAM RG24 145 H5
EARL RG6 74 C5 4
NWBY RG14 84 C2
Ferbies FLET GU13 167 H5
Ferguson Cl BSTK RG21 176 B2
Fernbank EWKG RG40 116 C1 1
Fernbank Crs ASC SL5 81 G6
Fernbank Pl ASC SL5 81 F6
Fernbank Rd ASC SL5 81 G7
Fernbrook Rd CAV/SC RG4 42 E7
Fern Cl CALC RG31 71 H1 3
CWTH RG45 118 C1
Ferndale Av TLHT RG30 72 A2
Ferndale Cl CALC RG31 55 K2 1
Ferndale Ct STHA RG19 85 J4
Ferndale Gdns HTWY RG27 163 K1 1
Ferndale Rd FLET GU13 167 G6
Fern Dr FLET GU13 167 F5
Ferne Cl GOR/PANG RG8 25 F4 2
Fern Gln CALC RG31 55 H4 3
Fernhill Cl BNFD RG42 79 G5
Fernhurst Rd CALC RG31 71 H2 2
Ferrard Cl ASC SL5 81 G6
Ferrell Fld HTWY RG27 163 J2
Ferry La HEN RG9 18 C4
MLW SL7 19 G5
WAR/TWY RG10 46 B2
Fidler's La KSCL RG20 20 D4
Fidlers Wk WAR/TWY RG10 46 D2
Field Cl THLE RG7 91 G5
Fielden Pl BRAK RG12 11 K3
The Fielders HTWY RG27 134 D1
Fieldfare Av YTLY GU46 135 F3
Field Gate Dr KSCL RG20 123 K7
Field House Cl ASC SL5 101 K6
Fielding Gdns CWTH RG45 118 B4

Field Pk BRAK RG12 ... 11 K1
Fieldridge NWBY RG14 ... 84 B2 1
Field Rd READ RG1 ... 2 F8
Field Vw CAV/SC RG4 ... 57 J2
Fieldway FLET GU13 ... 166 E3 3
WWKG RG41 ... 76 C4 3
Fifth Rd NWBY RG14 ... 12 A8
NWBY RG14 ... 83 G6
Fifth St STHA RG19 ... 104 E3
Filbert Dr CALC RG31 ... 55 H5
Filey Rd READ RG1 ... 4 D6
Finbeck Wy EARL RG6 ... 74 C6
Fincham End Dr CWTH RG45 ... 118 A4 1
Finchampstead Rd EWKG RG40 ... 97 F6
EWKG RG40 ... 116 E1
EWKG RG40 ... 117 F1 1
Finch Cl TADY RG26 ... 127 F2 2
Finch Rd EARL RG6 ... 9 M4
Finch Wy THLE RG7 ... 91 G4
Finmere BRAK RG12 ... 99 K4
Finstock Cl EARL RG6 ... 75 G5
Finstock Gn BRAK RG12 ... 100 C2 3
Fir Cl FLET GU13 ... 167 G3
Fir Cottage Rd EWKG RG40 ... 96 D7 1
Fircroft Cl CALC RG31 ... 55 H4
Firecrest Rd KEMP RG22 ... 174 E6
Fire Thorn Cl FLET GU13 ... 167 G5
Firglen Dr YTLY GU46 ... 135 J2
Firgrove Rd HTWY RG27 ... 134 D3
YTLY GU46 ... 135 G3
Firlands BRAK RG12 ... 11 H9
Firmstone Cl EARL RG6 ... 75 F5
Firs Cl EWKG RG40 ... 116 E1
Fir's End THLE RG7 ... 91 F5
Firs La ODIM RG29 ... 180 B2
TLHT RG30 ... 6 B2
Firs Rd CALC RG31 ... 55 H7
First Av THLE RG7 ... 109 F6
The Firs NTHA RG18 ... 85 G3
First St STHA RG19 ... 105 F3
Firs Wy DEAN RG23 ... 159 G4
WHCH RG28 ... 169 H7
Firth Cl THLE RG7 ... 128 A1 2
Fir Tree Cl ASC SL5 ... 101 K5
Fir Tree La NWBY RG14 ... 84 D3
Firtree Wy FLET GU13 ... 167 J3
Fisher Gn BNFD RG42 ... 78 C4 1
Fisherman's La THLE RG7 ... 108 D1
Fishers Ct CAV/SC RG4 ... 43 K6
Fisher's La NTHA RG18 ... 65 F5
Fishponds Cl WWKG RG41 ... 97 F2
Fishponds Rd WWKG RG41 ... 97 F3
Fiske Cl KEMP RG22 ... 159 H7
Fitzroy Crs WODY RG5 ... 59 K7
Fitzroy Rd FLET GU13 ... 166 E2
Five Acre CALC RG31 ... 55 G4
Flag Staff Sq STHA RG19 ... 85 K6
Flambards CAV/SC RG4 ... 57 K3
Flamborough Cl EARL RG6 ... 75 H4 3
Flamingo Cl WWKG RG41 ... 96 D2 2
Flaxfield Ct BSTK RG21 ... 14 D5
Flaxfield Rd BSTK RG21 ... 14 D5
Flaxman Cl EARL RG6 ... 8 E8
Flecker Cl NTHA RG18 ... 85 H2 1
Fleet Cl WWKG RG41 ... 96 D1 3
Fleetham Gdns EARL RG6 ... 9 L9
Fleet Hl EWKG RG40 ... 116 B6
Fleet La EWKG RG40 ... 116 A6
Fleet Rd FLET GU13 ... 167 G2
HTWY RG27 ... 150 B5
Fleetwood Cl NWBY RG14 ... 84 C2
Fleming Cl WHIT RG2 ... 115 H1
Fleming Rd NWBY RG14 ... 13 G3
Fletcher Cl BSTK RG21 ... 14 B7
Fletcher Gdns BNFD RG42 ... 78 E6
Flexford Cl KSCL RG20 ... 120 C4
Flexford Gn BRAK RG12 ... 99 F4 2
Flintgrove BRAK RG12 ... 11 J1
Flodden Dr CALC RG31 ... 71 J2 3
Floral Wy NTHA RG18 ... 85 J2
NTHA RG18 ... 86 A3
Floreat Gdns NWBY RG14 ... 12 A7
Florence Cl YTLY GU46 ... 135 H3 1
Florence Portal Cl WHCH RG28 ... 170 C7
Florence Rd FLET GU13 ... 167 J5
Florence Wk READ RG1 ... 4 B6
Florence Wy CHAM RG24 ... 159 H3
Florian Gdns TLHT RG30 ... 72 C1 2
Flower's Hl GOR/PANG RG8 ... 54 B1
Flowers Piece GOR/PANG RG8 ... 37 J6
Fobney St READ RG1 ... 3 H7
Fokerham Rd STHA RG19 ... 86 A5
Folder's La BNFD RG42 ... 79 K5
Folly Cl FLET GU13 ... 167 H4
Folly Gn GOR/PANG RG8 ... 26 D3
Folly La TADY RG26 ... 129 J4
THLE RG7 ... 90 E2
Folly Orchard Rd
GOR/PANG RG8 ... 26 D3
The Folly NWBY RG14 ... 13 G8
Fontwell Dr TLHT RG30 ... 72 A1
Fontwell Rd NWBY RG14 ... 13 H8
Forbury Rd READ RG1 ... 3 J5
The Forbury READ RG1 ... 3 J5
Fordham Wy EARL RG6 ... 75 F5 3
Ford La ODIM RG29 ... 179 J4
THLE RG7 ... 114 D4
Fordwells Dr BRAK RG12 ... 100 C2
The Forehead THLE RG7 ... 112 A4
Forest Cl ASC SL5 ... 101 F1
TADY RG26 ... 108 B7
Forest Dean FARN GU14 ... 151 K6
WHIT RG2 ... 73 K7 2
Forest Dr CHAM RG24 ... 145 G6
Forest End FLET GU13 ... 167 G5
Forest End Rd SHST GU47 ... 118 A7
Foresters Sq BRAK RG12 ... 11 M6
Foresters Wy CWTH RG45 ... 99 F7
CWTH RG45 ... 119 G1
Forest Hl TLHT RG30 ... 56 A3
Forest La TADY RG26 ... 127 G3
Forest Rd ASC SL5 ... 81 G4
BNFD RG42 ... 78 C4
BNFD RG42 ... 79 K3
BNFD RG42 ... 80 C3
CWTH RG45 ... 118 D3
EWKG RG40 ... 77 F4
WWKG RG41 ... 76 E5
Forge Cl CAV/SC RG4 ... 3 M2
TADY RG26 ... 129 H7
Forge Hl NTHA RG18 ... 36 B7
Formby Cl EARL RG6 ... 75 H3
Forndon Cl EARL RG6 ... 75 H4 6
Fosseway CWTH RG45 ... 118 A3 2
Fosters La WODY RG5 ... 59 H7
Fountains Cl CHAM RG24 ... 160 B2
Fountains Garth BRAK RG12 ... 10 C6
Four Acre Coppice
HTWY RG27 ... 164 B1 2
HTWY RG27 ... 164 B2 2
Four Lanes Cl CHAM RG24 ... 145 H7
Four Oaks KSCL RG20 ... 120 C3
Fowler Cl EARL RG6 ... 9 G6
Fowlers La BNFD RG42 ... 10 E2
Foxborough THLE RG7 ... 114 A2
Fox Cl THLE RG7 ... 91 F4
Foxcombe Dr CALC RG31 ... 55 H6
Foxcote EWKG RG40 ... 117 F1
Fox Cft FLET GU13 ... 167 H6
Foxdown OVTN RG25 ... 171 H2
Fox Dr YTLY GU46 ... 135 J2
Foxes Wk WAR/TWY RG10 ... 59 K2
Foxglove Cl BNFD RG42 ... 80 D4
KEMP RG22 ... 175 F5
WWKG RG41 ... 76 C7
Foxglove Gdns READ RG1 ... 2 D5
Foxglove Wy NTHA RG18 ... 85 K2
Foxhays Rd WHIT RG2 ... 74 A6
Foxhill Cl CAV/SC RG4 ... 44 D7
Foxhill La CAV/SC RG4 ... 44 A5
Foxhill Rd READ RG1 ... 4 C9
Foxhunter Wy STHA RG19 ... 84 E4 1
Foxhunt Gv CALC RG31 ... 72 A2
Fox La DEAN RG23 ... 174 B1
HTWY RG27 ... 134 E1
Foxley La BNFD RG42 ... 78 C4
Foxmoor Cl DEAN RG23 ... 174 A1
Fox Rd BRAK RG12 ... 11 H8
Foxs Furlong CHAM RG24 ... 145 J6
Fox's La KSCL RG20 ... 139 K1
Fox Wy NFNM GU10 ... 183 J4
Foxwood FARN GU14 ... 151 K7 1
Foye La FLET GU13 ... 167 J6
Foyle Pk BSTK RG21 ... 176 C2
Framlingham Dr CAV/SC RG4 ... 44 B7 2
Frampton Cl WODY RG5 ... 59 H4
Frances Rd BSTK RG21 ... 14 D7
The Frances NTHA RG18 ... 85 J3
Francis Gdns BNFD RG42 ... 80 A4
Francis St READ RG1 ... 3 J9
Franklin Av HTWY RG27 ... 149 G3 1
TADY RG26 ... 108 D7
Franklin St READ RG1 ... 2 E7
Fraser Av CAV/SC RG4 ... 43 K6
Fraser Cl CHAM RG24 ... 161 K5
Fraser Rd BNFD RG42 ... 10 E1
Frederick Pl WWKG RG41 ... 97 F1
Freeborn Wy BRAK RG12 ... 11 M3
Freelands Dr FLET GU13 ... 167 F6
Freemantle Cl BSTK RG21 ... 160 E4
Freesia Cl WWKG RG41 ... 76 C7 3
Frensham BRAK RG12 ... 100 A4
Frensham Av FLET GU13 ... 167 K6
Frensham Cl YTLY GU46 ... 135 G3
Frensham Gn WHIT RG2 ... 74 C5
Frensham Rd CWTH RG45 ... 118 C1
Frere Av FLET GU13 ... 167 F4
Frescade Crs BSTK RG21 ... 14 C8
Freshfield Cl EARL RG6 ... 75 H3 2
Freshwater Rd READ RG1 ... 4 C5
Freshwood Dr YTLY GU46 ... 135 H5
Friars Keep BRAK RG12 ... 10 F7
Friars Rd NWBY RG14 ... 12 E9
Friar St READ RG1 ... 3 J5
Friday St HEN RG9 ... 31 H2
Friendship Wy BRAK RG12 ... 10 F6
Friesian Cl FARN GU14 ... 151 J6
Frieth Cl EARL RG6 ... 9 G8
Frilsham Rd TLHT RG30 ... 72 C2
Frimley Cl WODY RG5 ... 59 G5 1
Fringford Cl EARL RG6 ... 75 F5
Frithmead Cl BSTK RG21 ... 176 B2
Frobisher BRAK RG12 ... 99 K5
Frodsham Wy SHST GU47 ... 119 F6 2
Frog Hall Dr EWKG RG40 ... 97 K1
Frog La BRAK RG12 ... 10 D5
HTWY RG27 ... 147 G3
OVTN RG25 ... 162 C6
TADY RG26 ... 128 A4
Frogmill MDHD SL6 ... 19 H7
Frogmore Wy TLHT RG30 ... 72 C1
Frogs Hole KSCL RG20 ... 123 K7
Frome Cl BSTK RG21 ... 15 J4
DEAN RG23 ... 174 B3
Fromont Dr STHA RG19 ... 85 J4
Froud Cl HTWY RG27 ... 163 J3 1
Frouds La THLE RG7 ... 88 C5
Froxfield Av READ RG1 ... 6 D1
Froxfield Down BRAK RG12 ... 100 C3 3
Fry's La YTLY GU46 ... 135 K2
Fuchsia Cl CALC RG31 ... 71 H1 4
Fugelmere Rd FLET GU13 ... 167 K1
Fulbrook Wy ODIM RG29 ... 180 C4
Fullbrook Cl WWKG RG41 ... 77 F5
Fullbrook Crs CALC RG31 ... 55 J2
Fuller Cl STHA RG19 ... 86 A5
Fuller's La THLE RG7 ... 92 C3
Fullerton Wy TADY RG26 ... 127 F2
Fulmar Cl KEMP RG22 ... 174 E5
Fulmead Rd TLHT RG30 ... 56 D5
Fulmer Cl EARL RG6 ... 9 G8
Further Vell-mead FLET GU13 ... 167 F7
Furze Hill Crs CWTH RG45 ... 118 D4
Furze Rd TADY RG26 ... 108 C6
Fuzzy Dro KEMP RG22 ... 174 E4
Fyfield Rd STHA RG19 ... 85 J5
Fylingdales STHA RG19 ... 85 H5
Fylingdales Cl KEMP RG22 ... 175 F1

G

Gables Rd FLET GU13 ... 167 G7
Gables Wy STHA RG19 ... 86 C5
The Gabriels NWBY RG14 ... 103 G2
Gage Cl CHAM RG24 ... 161 G4
Gainsborough BRAK RG12 ... 99 K4
Gainsborough Cl WODY RG5 ... 59 K7 1
Gainsborough Crs HEN RG9 ... 31 F3
Gainsborough Dr ASC SL5 ... 101 G1
Gainsborough Hl HEN RG9 ... 31 G3
Gainsborough Rd BSTK RG21 ... 176 D2
HEN RG9 ... 31 F3
TLHT RG30 ... 72 C1
Gairn Cl TLHT RG30 ... 56 B6
Galley La STHA RG19 ... 105 J7
The Gallops KSCL RG20 ... 20 D5
The Gallop YTLY GU46 ... 135 J2
Galloway Cl FARN GU14 ... 151 K6
KEMP RG22 ... 175 G1
Gally Hill Rd FLET GU13 ... 167 G7
Galsworthy Dr CAV/SC RG4 ... 44 A7
Gander Dr CHAM RG24 ... 159 H3
Gannet Cl KEMP RG22 ... 174 E5
Gap Wy GOR/PANG RG8 ... 26 E3
Garden Cl HTWY RG27 ... 163 J2 2
KSCL RG20 ... 124 A7 2
Garden Close La NWBY RG14 ... 103 G4
Gardeners La GOR/PANG RG8 ... 53 F1
Garde Rd CAV/SC RG4 ... 59 H2
Gardners Rd BNFD RG42 ... 80 D4
Garford Crs NWBY RG14 ... 83 G7
Garlands Cl THLE RG7 ... 91 F5
Garnet Fld YTLY GU46 ... 135 F4
Garnet Hl READ RG1 ... 2 F8
Garnet St READ RG1 ... 3 G8
Garrard St READ RG1 ... 3 H5
Garrett Cl KSCL RG20 ... 123 K6
Garrett Rd EWKG RG40 ... 96 D7
Garston Cl TLHT RG30 ... 72 B2 3
Garston Crs CALC RG31 ... 71 G1
Garston Gv EWKG RG40 ... 96 E6 1
Garswood BRAK RG12 ... 100 A4
Garth Cl WWKG RG41 ... 76 B4
Garth Rd THLE RG7 ... 111 F3
Garth Sq BNFD RG42 ... 79 J5
Gaskells End CAV/SC RG4 ... 42 E4
Gas La WAR/TWY RG10 ... 60 C1
Gaston La ODIM RG29 ... 179 J6
Gas Works Rd READ RG1 ... 3 M6
Gatcombe Cl CALC RG31 ... 71 H2
Gatehampton Rd
GOR/PANG RG8 ... 25 F5
The Gates FARN GU14 ... 151 K6
Gayhurst Cl CAV/SC RG4 ... 44 A6
Gaywood Dr NWBY RG14 ... 13 L1
Gazelle Cl WWKG RG41 ... 75 K3
Geffers Ride ASC SL5 ... 101 H1
Gelder Cl EARL RG6 ... 75 G5
Geoffreyson Rd CAV/SC RG4 ... 42 E7 1
Georgeham Rd SHST GU47 ... 118 E6 2
George Rd FLET GU13 ... 167 J2
George St BSTK RG21 ... 14 B5
KSCL RG20 ... 123 K7
READ RG1 ... 2 E5
READ RG1 ... 3 K3
Georgia Gdns TADY RG26 ... 127 H1
Geranium Cl CWTH RG45 ... 98 C7 1
German Rd TADY RG26 ... 129 H7
Gershwin Rd KEMP RG22 ... 175 H4
Gibbins La BNFD RG42 ... 80 A3
Gibbs Cl EWKG RG40 ... 116 D2
Gibbs Wy YTLY GU46 ... 135 G5
Gifford Cl CAV/SC RG4 ... 44 B7 3
Gilbard Ct CHAM RG24 ... 145 H7 2
Gilbert Wy EWKG RG40 ... 96 D7
Giles Rd TADY RG26 ... 127 F1
Gillette Wy WHIT RG2 ... 7 J6
Gillies Dr CHAM RG24 ... 159 H3
Gillotts Cl HEN RG9 ... 30 E4
Gillott's La HEN RG9 ... 30 E4
Gill Ri BNFD RG42 ... 79 K4
Gilroy Cl NWBY RG14 ... 103 F2
Gingells Farm Rd
WAR/TWY RG10 ... 46 A7 1
Gipsy La BRAK RG12 ... 11 J4
EARL RG6 ... 75 G5
EWKG RG40 ... 97 H2
TLHT RG30 ... 55 K4
WWKG RG41 ... 75 J7
Girton Cl SHST GU47 ... 119 F7
Glade Cl CHAM RG24 ... 161 G1
The Glade CALC RG31 ... 55 H1
NWBY RG14 ... 83 J7 2
Gladridge Cl EARL RG6 ... 9 K3
Gladstone La NTHA RG18 ... 65 H6
Glaisdale STHA RG19 ... 85 H5
Glamis Cl DEAN RG23 ... 173 K2
Glamis Wy CALC RG31 ... 71 G2 2
Glastonbury Cl CHAM RG24 ... 160 B3
Glaston Hill Rd HTWY RG27 ... 134 A1
Glebe Cl TADY RG26 ... 127 F2
Glebe Ct FLET GU13 ... 167 G2
Glebefields NWBY RG14 ... 84 A2 2
Glebe Gdns CAV/SC RG4 ... 59 H2
Glebelands STHA RG19 ... 85 H4
Glebelands Rd EWKG RG40 ... 77 G7
Glebe La CAV/SC RG4 ... 59 H2
DEAN RG23 ... 159 F7
HTWY RG27 ... 149 J5
KSCL RG20 ... 82 B2
Glebe Meadow OVTN RG25 ... 171 H4
Glebe Ride GOR/PANG RG8 ... 24 E5
Glebe Rd GOR/PANG RG8 ... 41 G7
NFNM GU10 ... 182 E6
WHIT RG2 ... 7 L2
The Glebe GOR/PANG RG8 ... 37 G1
Glebewood BRAK RG12 ... 11 G9
Glenavon Gdns YTLY GU46 ... 135 J5 3
Glenbeigh Ter READ RG1 ... 2 C8
Glendale Av NWBY RG14 ... 103 F3
Glendale Pk FLET GU13 ... 166 D1
Glendale Rd TADY RG26 ... 108 D7
Glendevon Rd WODY RG5 ... 59 J5
Glen Innes SHST GU47 ... 119 G7
Glenmore Cl STHA RG19 ... 85 J5 3
Glennon Cl TLHT RG30 ... 72 D2 1
Glenrhondda CAV/SC RG4 ... 43 G7
Glen Rd FLET GU13 ... 167 G3
Glenrosa Rd TLHT RG30 ... 56 A5
The Glen TADY RG26 ... 109 H7
Glenwood BRAK RG12 ... 11 K8
Glenwood Dr CALC RG31 ... 55 H6
Gloucester Dr KEMP RG22 ... 175 G5
Gloucester Pl BNFD RG42 ... 80 C5
Gloucester Rd NWBY RG14 ... 12 B5
TLHT RG30 ... 2 A7
Glyncastle CAV/SC RG4 ... 43 G7
Goaters Rd ASC SL5 ... 81 F7
Goat La BSTK RG21 ... 15 G5
Goddard Cl WHIT RG2 ... 94 B2
Goddard Ct WWKG RG41 ... 76 A5 1
Goddard Dr THLE RG7 ... 87 G4
Goddards Cl HTWY RG27 ... 146 A2 2
Goddards Firs DEAN RG23 ... 174 B4
Godstow Cl WODY RG5 ... 59 H5 1
Goldcrest Cl YTLY GU46 ... 135 G3
Goldcrest Wy CALC RG31 ... 55 G7
Gold Cup La ASC SL5 ... 81 G6
Golden Orb Wd BNFD RG42 ... 78 E6
Golding Cl STHA RG19 ... 86 A4 2
Goldsmid Rd READ RG1 ... 2 E7
Goldsmith Cl EWKG RG40 ... 96 D6 1
NTHA RG18 ... 85 H2
Goldsmith Wy CWTH RG45 ... 118 C4
Goldthorpe Gdns EARL RG6 ... 74 C6 3
Goldwell Dr NWBY RG14 ... 12 C2
Gondreville Gdns FLET GU13 ... 167 F7
Gooch Cl WAR/TWY RG10 ... 60 E2
Goodboy's La THLE RG7 ... 92 B6
Goodchild Rd EWKG RG40 ... 97 J1
Goodings Gn EWKG RG40 ... 97 K1
Goodliffe Gdns CALC RG31 ... 55 H1 3
Goodman Cl BSTK RG21 ... 14 A7
Goodrich Ct CAV/SC RG4 ... 44 B7
Goodways Dr BRAK RG12 ... 11 H4
Goodwin Cl CALC RG31 ... 71 K2
Goodwood Cl THLE RG7 ... 90 E5
Goodwood Wy NWBY RG14 ... 13 K8
Goose Gn HTWY RG27 ... 163 J1
Goose Green Wy STHA RG19 ... 85 K4 2
Goose La HTWY RG27 ... 163 K1
Gordon Av FLET GU13 ... 167 J5
Gordon Cl BSTK RG21 ... 15 H2
Gordon Crs KSCL RG20 ... 21 J7
Gordon Pl TLHT RG30 ... 56 D5
Gordon Rd CWTH RG45 ... 118 E5
NTHA RG18 ... 85 F2
NWBY RG14 ... 13 G5
Gordon Wk YTLY GU46 ... 135 K4
Goring La THLE RG7 ... 90 E6
Goring Rd GOR/PANG RG8 ... 26 C4
Gorrick Sq WWKG RG41 ... 97 G4
Gorse Cottage Dr NTHA RG18 ... 65 G5
Gorse Dr WODY RG5 ... 59 K5 1
Gorselands CAV/SC RG4 ... 43 H6
NWBY RG14 ... 103 G3
TADY RG26 ... 127 F1
YTLY GU46 ... 135 H5
Gorse Ride North EWKG RG40 ... 116 D1
Gorse Ride South EWKG RG40 ... 116 D1
Gorseway FLET GU13 ... 167 H4
Gosbrook Rd CAV/SC RG4 ... 3 M1
READ RG1 ... 3 J1
Gosforth Cl EARL RG6 ... 75 G4
Gough Rd FLET GU13 ... 167 F1
Gough's La BRAK RG12 ... 80 A5
Gower Cl BSTK RG21 ... 14 E1
Gower Crs HTWY RG27 ... 164 A2 2
Gower St READ RG1 ... 2 D6
Gracemere Crs KEMP RG22 ... 174 E5
Graces La KSCL RG20 ... 48 A5
Graffham Cl EARL RG6 ... 74 E6 2
Grafton Rd TLHT RG30 ... 55 J6
Grafton Wy KEMP RG22 ... 159 J7
Graham Cl CALC RG31 ... 71 K2 3
Grahame Av GOR/PANG RG8 ... 40 C7
Grainger Cl KEMP RG22 ... 175 K3
Grampian Rd SHST GU47 ... 118 A6
Grampian Wy KEMP RG22 ... 175 G1
Granby Ct READ RG1 ... 4 C7
Granby End THLE RG7 ... 91 G4 2
Granby Gdns EARL RG6 ... 4 C7
Grange Av CWTH RG45 ... 118 C2
EARL RG6 ... 4 F8
HEN RG9 ... 29 H3
Grange Cl GOR/PANG RG8 ... 24 E6
Grange La HTWY RG27 ... 149 G5
Grangely Cl CALC RG31 ... 71 J2
Grange Rd BRAK RG12 ... 11 H2
FLET GU13 ... 167 G6
HEN RG9 ... 31 H2
The Grange NWBY RG14 ... 103 F3
Grantham Cl SHST GU47 ... 119 F7 2
Grantham Rd CALC RG31 ... 72 A2
Grantley Dr FLET GU13 ... 167 G4
Grant Rd CWTH RG45 ... 118 D4
Granville Rd TLHT RG30 ... 72 C1 3
Grasmere Av TLHT RG30 ... 56 A3
Grasmere Cl WWKG RG41 ... 76 A5 2
Grass Hl CAV/SC RG4 ... 57 F2
Grassington Pl STHA RG19 ... 85 J4
Grassmead STHA RG19 ... 86 A5
Gratton Rd WHIT RG2 ... 73 K6 2
Gratwicke Rd TLHT RG30 ... 55 K5
Gravel Hl CAV/SC RG4 ... 43 F6
HEN RG9 ... 29 G5
KSCL RG20 ... 82 B2
Gravel Hill Crs HEN RG9 ... 29 G5
Gravelly Cl TADY RG26 ... 127 F3
Gravel Rd CAV/SC RG4 ... 44 C3
FLET GU13 ... 167 J5
Graveney Dr CAV/SC RG4 ... 57 F2
Gravett Cl HEN RG9 ... 31 F3
Grays Crs WODY RG5 ... 5 M5
Grazeley Rd THLE RG7 ... 93 H3
Great Binfields Crs CHAM RG24 ... 161 G3
Great Binfields Rd CHAM RG24 ... 161 G4
Great Hollands Rd BRAK RG12 ... 99 G4
Great Hollands Sq BRAK RG12 ... 99 G4 1
Great Knollys St READ RG1 ... 2 E5
Great La WHCH RG28 ... 169 H7
Great Lea THLE RG7 ... 93 H2
Great Oaks Cha CHAM RG24 ... 161 F1 1
Great Sheldons Coppice
HTWY RG27 ... 163 K1
Grebe Cl KEMP RG22 ... 174 E5
Greenacre KSCL RG20 ... 124 A7 3
Green Acre Mt TLHT RG30 ... 55 J5 3
Greenacres KSCL RG20 ... 120 B1
Greenacres Av WWKG RG41 ... 75 K4
Greenacres La WWKG RG41 ... 75 K3
Greenbirch Cl KEMP RG22 ... 174 E5
Greenbury Cl DEAN RG23 ... 159 H6
Green Cft EWKG RG40 ... 77 K6
Green Dean Hl CAV/SC RG4 ... 42 C2
Green Dr EWKG RG40 ... 97 J3
Green End YTLY GU46 ... 135 J2 1
Green End Cl THLE RG7 ... 93 J5 1
Greenfields Rd WHIT RG2 ... 73 J6
Greenfield Wy CWTH RG45 ... 118 B1
Greenfinch Cl CALC RG31 ... 55 G7
Green Finch Cl CWTH RG45 ... 118 A2 1
Green Glades FLET GU13 ... 167 G6
Greenham Cl WODY RG5 ... 59 K7
Greenham Rd NWBY RG14 ... 12 F6
Greenham Wd BRAK RG12 ... 99 K5
Greenhaven YTLY GU46 ... 135 G4
Greenhow BRAK RG12 ... 10 C6
Greenidge Cl READ RG1 ... 6 C2
Greenlands KSCL RG20 ... 102 B7
Greenlands Rd KSCL RG20 ... 124 A7
NWBY RG14 ... 13 G9
Green La CAV/SC RG4 ... 29 G6
CAV/SC RG4 ... 44 D3
EWKG RG40 ... 78 B4
GOR/PANG RG8 ... 26 E4
GOR/PANG RG8 ... 40 B7
HEN RG9 ... 31 G3
HTWY RG27 ... 149 H5
KSCL RG20 ... 48 A6
NWBY RG14 ... 12 B5
STHA RG19 ... 85 H4
TADY RG26 ... 127 H5
THLE RG7 ... 68 C3
THLE RG7 ... 90 B5
THLE RG7 ... 130 A1
TLHT RG30 ... 72 B4
WAR/TWY RG10 ... 76 D3
WWKG RG41 ... 76 C5
YTLY GU46 ... 135 G2
Greenleas Av CAV/SC RG4 ... 43 J5
Greenleas Cl YTLY GU46 ... 135 H2
Green Leys FLET GU13 ... 167 G7
Greenmoor GOR/PANG RG8 ... 26 E3
Green Rd EARL RG6 ... 8 F1
Greenside CWTH RG45 ... 118 A3
Green Springs NFNM GU10 ... 182 E5
Greensward La WHIT RG2 ... 95 F4
The Green BRAK RG12 ... 10 F8
OVTN RG25 ... 171 J4
TADY RG26 ... 127 F3
THLE RG7 ... 70 B4
WHCH RG28 ... 169 J7
WWKG RG41 ... 76 D7 4
Greenway HTWY RG27 ... 146 A2
Greenways FLET GU13 ... 167 G5
KSCL RG20 ... 102 B7
SHST GU47 ... 118 C7
Green Wd ASC SL5 ... 81 F6
Greenwood Dr CHAM RG24 ... 145 G6 1
Greenwood Gv WWKG RG41 ... 76 C3
Greenwood Rd CWTH RG45 ... 118 B2
TLHT RG30 ... 72 A1 1
Greenwoods WHCH RG28 ... 169 H6
Gregory Cl BSTK RG21 ... 160 D4
EARL RG6 ... 75 F6 4
Greig Rd KEMP RG22 ... 175 K3
Grensell Cl HTWY RG27 ... 134 D1 3
Grenville Dr FLET GU13 ... 167 F4
Gresham Wy TLHT RG30 ... 56 B3
Gresley Rd BSTK RG21 ... 15 K2
CHAM RG24 ... 15 K1
Greyberry Copse Rd STHA RG19 ... 84 C7
Greyfriars Rd READ RG1 ... 3 H5
Greyhound La OVTN RG25 ... 171 H5
Greys Ct READ RG1 ... 3 L7
Greys Hl HEN RG9 ... 31 G2
Greys Rd HEN RG9 ... 30 D3
Greystoke Ct CWTH RG45 ... 118 B4
Greystoke Rd CAV/SC RG4 ... 57 K1
Greywell Cl TADY RG26 ... 126 D1 2
Greywell Rd CHAM RG24 ... 162 A6
HTWY RG27 ... 163 F7
Griffin Wy North HTWY RG27 ... 148 A7
Griffin Wy South HTWY RG27 ... 148 A7
HTWY RG27 ... 164 B2
Griffiths Cl STHA RG19 ... 86 A5
Grimmer Wy GOR/PANG RG8 ... 26 E3
Grindle Cl NTHA RG18 ... 85 H2
Grosvenor Cl KEMP RG22 ... 175 G7 2
Grosvenor Rd CAV/SC RG4 ... 57 K2
Grove Cl BSTK RG21 ... 15 G9
EWKG RG40 ... 117 K1
Grove Hl CAV/SC RG4 ... 57 H1
Groveland Pl TLHT RG30 ... 56 C5 2
Groveland Rd NWBY RG14 ... 83 G2
Grovelands Av WWKG RG41 ... 76 C4
Grovelands Cl WWKG RG41 ... 76 C3
Grovelands Rd THLE RG7 ... 93 K5
TLHT RG30 ... 56 C5
Grove La BNFD RG42 ... 80 E3
Grove Rd BSTK RG21 ... 15 H9
BSTK RG21 ... 176 D2
CAV/SC RG4 ... 29 G6
CAV/SC RG4 ... 43 H7
FLET GU13 ... 167 J6
HEN RG9 ... 31 H2 1
NWBY RG14 ... 83 G2
Groves Lea THLE RG7 ... 110 E2
The Grove ASC SL5 ... 81 F6
NTHA RG18 ... 85 J3
READ RG1 ... 3 L7
WAR/TWY RG10 ... 46 C7
Guerdon Pl BRAK RG12 ... 100 A5
Guernsey Cl CHAM RG24 ... 160 D1
Guernsey Dr FARN GU14 ... 151 J6
Guildford Rd FLET GU13 ... 167 K2
Guinea Ct CHAM RG24 ... 145 H7 3
Gun St READ RG1 ... 3 H6
Gurney Cl CAV/SC RG4 ... 42 E7
Gurney Dr CAV/SC RG4 ... 56 E1 1
Guttridge La TADY RG26 ... 126 D1
Gwyn Cl NWBY RG14 ... 83 J7
Gwynne Cl CALC RG31 ... 55 J2

H

Hackwood La OVTN RG25 176 C6
Hackwood Rd BSTK RG21 14 F7
BSTK RG21 176 D2
Hackwood Road Rbt BSTK RG21 15 G8
Haddon Dr WODY RG5 59 H5
Hadleigh Pl BSTK RG21 14 D5
Hadleigh Ri CAV/SC RG4 44 B7
Hadrians Wy DEAN RG23 159 H4 2
Hafod CAV/SC RG4 43 G6
Hagbourne Cl GOR/PANG RG8 26 E3 5
Hagley Rd FLET GU13 167 F1
WHIT RG2 7 K3
Haig La FLET GU13 167 J6
Hailsham Cl SHST GU47 118 E7 3
Hailstone Rd BSTK RG21 160 C3
Halcyon Ter TLHT RG30 55 K5 2
Haldane Rd CAV/SC RG4 43 F7
Hale End BRAK RG12 100 C2
Halewood BRAK RG12 99 G4
Halfacre Cl THLE RG7 93 J4
Halifax Pl NTHA RG18 85 H3 1
Hallbrook Gdns BNFD RG42 79 F5
Halley Dr ASC SL5 81 G7
Hall Farm Crs YTLY GU46 135 H4
Halliday Cl BSTK RG21 176 B2
Hall La YTLY GU46 135 H4
Halls La WHIT RG2 74 B5
Halls Rd TLHT RG30 55 H7
Halpin Cl CALC RG31 71 H2
Halstead Cl WODY RG5 59 H6
The Halters NWBY RG14 104 A1 1
Hamble Cl DEAN RG23 174 A3 2
Hamble Ct BSTK RG21 15 K5
Hambledon Cl EARL RG6 75 H5
Hamble Dr TADY RG26 127 G1
Hamborne Ga NWBY RG14 83 G6
Ham Br STHA RG19 84 D4
NWBY RG14 13 M4
Hambridge La NWBY RG14 84 D5
Hambridge Rd NWBY RG14 13 J5
NWBY RG14 84 D4
Hamdens NWBY RG14 103 F2
Hamelyn Rd BSTK RG21 14 C7
Hamilton Av HEN RG9 31 H2
Hamilton Cl NWBY RG14 12 F9
Hamilton Rd FLET GU13 167 J5 1
READ RG1 4 D8
WAR/TWY RG10 46 D2
Ham La TADY RG26 125 J3
Hamlet St BNFD RG42 11 L1
The Hamlet CAV/SC RG4 28 C6
Hammond Cl STHA RG19 85 K5
Hammond Rd BSTK RG21 14 D8
Hammonds Heath THLE RG7 111 G2
Hampden Rd CAV/SC RG4 57 J3
Hampshire Cl KEMP RG22 175 F1
Hampshire Ri BNFD RG42 80 C4 2
Hampshire Wy WWKG RG41 96 C1
Hampstead Norreys Rd
NTHA RG18 49 G6
Hampton Cl FLET GU13 167 H7
Hampton Rd NWBY RG14 12 D7
Hanbury Dr CALC RG31 71 J2 7
Hancombe Rd SHST GU47 118 B6
Handcroft Cl NFNM GU10 182 E4
Handel Cl KEMP RG22 175 K3
Handford La YTLY GU46 135 J4
Hangerfield Cl YTLY GU46 135 H4
Hanger Rd TADY RG26 108 C7
Hanmore Rd CHAM RG24 161 F1
Hannam's Farm NFNM GU10 182 D6 1
Hanningtons Wy THLE RG7 91 H4
Hanover Dr FARN GU14 151 K6
Hanover Gdns BRAK RG12 99 G5 1
BSTK RG21 176 B2
Hanwood Cl WODY RG5 5 M4
Hanworth Cl BRAK RG12 99 K4 4
Hanworth Rd BRAK RG12 99 H5
Harcourt Cl HEN RG9 31 F2
Harcourt Dr EARL RG6 8 E7
Harcourt Rd BRAK RG12 99 J4
Harding Rd WODY RG5 5 M5
Hardings La HTWY RG27 149 J4 3
Hardwell Wy BRAK RG12 11 M7
Hardwick Rd GOR/PANG RG8 40 C5
TLHT RG30 56 A6
Hardy Av YTLY GU46 135 H5
Hardy Cl CAV/SC RG4 3 L1
CAV/SC RG4 57 K3
NTHA RG18 85 H2 2
Hardy Gn CWTH RG45 118 C4
Hardy La BSTK RG21 14 B7
Hardys Fld KSCL RG20 123 K6
Harebell Cl HTWY RG27 149 J3 1
Harebell Dr NTHA RG18 85 K3
Harebell Gdns HTWY RG27 149 J3
Harefield Cl WWKG RG41 76 B4 2
Hare's La HTWY RG27 149 K2
Harewood Dr NTHA RG18 65 H6
Harfield Cl HTWY RG27 163 K2 2
Harlech Av CAV/SC RG4 44 B7
Harlech Cl DEAN RG23 159 H6
Harley Rd READ RG1 3 J1
Harlington Wy FLET GU13 167 F3
Harlton Cl EARL RG6 75 F6 5
Harman Ct WWKG RG41 76 A4
Harmans Water Rd BRAK RG12 11 J9
BRAK RG12 100 A3
Harmar Cl EWKG RG40 97 K1
Harmsworth Rd TADY RG26 126 E1 1
Harness Cl WHIT RG2 93 J1 1
Harpdon Pde YTLY GU46 135 J2 2
Harpsden Rd HEN RG9 31 H3
Harpsden Wy HEN RG9 31 H4
Harpton Cl YTLY GU46 135 J2
Harrier Cl WODY RG5 59 K7
Harrington Cl EARL RG6 9 M7
NWBY RG14 84 C2
Harris Cl WODY RG5 60 A5
Harris Hl KEMP RG22 175 G5
Harrison Cl WAR/TWY RG10 60 E2
Harrogate Rd CAV/SC RG4 57 F1
Harroway WHCH RG28 169 G3
Harrow Ct READ RG1 2 E8
Harrow Wy OVTN RG25 172 E1
The Harrow Wy KEMP RG22 175 K3
Hart Cl BNFD RG42 79 H5
Hart Dyke Cl WWKG RG41 97 G5
Hartford Bridge Flats
HTWY RG27 150 B1
Hartford Ct HTWY RG27 149 H4 1
Hartford Rd HTWY RG27 149 H4
Hartigan Pl WODY RG5 59 K5 2
Hartland Rd WHIT RG2 73 J5
Hartley Court Rd THLE RG7 93 G1
Hartley Gdns TADY RG26 126 E2
Hartley La HTWY RG27 130 C7
Hartley Meadow
WHCH RG28 169 G7 2
Hartleys THLE RG7 127 K1
Hartmead Rd STHA RG19 85 K4
Hartsbourne Rd EARL RG6 9 G6
Harts Cl WHIT RG2 95 H5 1
Harts Hill Rd NTHA RG18 85 K3
Hartshill Rd TADY RG26 126 C1
Harts La KSCL RG20 121 H3
THLE RG7 90 A2
Hartsleaf Cl FLET GU13 167 G3 1
Harts Leap Cl SHST GU47 118 B7
Hartslock Ct GOR/PANG RG8 40 A6
Hartslock Vw GOR/PANG RG8 39 G7
Hartslock Wy CALC RG31 55 H3
Hart St READ RG1 2 D5
Hartswood CHAM RG24 161 F1
Harvard Cl WODY RG5 60 A5
Harvard Rd SHST GU47 119 G7
Harvest Cl CALC RG31 55 G7 2
YTLY GU46 135 G5
Harvest Crs FARN GU14 151 J5
Harvest Gn NWBY RG14 12 B8
Harvest Ride BNFD RG42 79 H4
BNFD RG42 80 A4
BNFD RG42 80 B5
Harvest Wy CHAM RG24 161 G3
Harveys Fld OVTN RG25 171 H4
Harwich Cl EARL RG6 75 G5 3
Harwood Ri KSCL RG20 102 C7
Hastings Cl DEAN RG23 159 G6
TLHT RG30 72 B2 4
Hatch Cl THLE RG7 67 K7
Hatchet La ASC SL5 81 K3
WDSR SL4 81 H2
Hatchets La NTHA RG18 50 D6
Hatchgate Cl NTHA RG18 85 H1
Hatchgate Copse BRAK RG12 99 F4
Hatch Gate La WAR/TWY RG10 32 E4
WAR/TWY RG10 33 F5
Hatchgate Md HTWY RG27 163 K1 3
Hatch La CHAM RG24 161 J6
THLE RG7 87 K1
TLHT RG30 91 J1
Hatch Ride CWTH RG45 118 C1
EWKG RG40 98 A7
Hatchwarren Gdns
KEMP RG22 175 K5 1
Hatchwarren La KEMP RG22 175 H5
Hatch Warren La KEMP RG22 175 K5
KEMP RG22 176 A3
Hatfield Ct CALC RG31 71 G2 6
Hatford Rd TLHT RG30 72 C2
Hathaway Gdns CHAM RG24 160 D3
Hatherley Rd READ RG1 4 C8
Hatton Hl GOR/PANG RG8 37 J5
Haughurst Hl STHA RG19 125 J1
Havelock Rd WWKG RG41 97 F1 1
Havelock St WWKG RG41 97 F1 2
Haversham Dr BRAK RG12 99 J4
Hawkchurch Rd WHIT RG2 74 A6
Hawk Cl KEMP RG22 174 E4 2
Hawkedon Wy EARL RG6 75 G4
Hawker Wy WODY RG5 59 K7
Hawkesbury Dr CALC RG31 71 K3
Hawkes Cl HTWY RG27 149 H3
WWKG RG41 77 F7
Hawkfield La BSTK RG21 14 D7
Hawkins Cl BRAK RG12 80 D7
Hawkins Gv FLET GU13 166 E5
Hawkins Wy EWKG RG40 97 K1
FLET GU13 167 K3 1
Hawk La BRAK RG12 11 J8
Hawkley Dr TADY RG26 127 F2
Hawksworth Rd THLE RG7 91 G4
Hawkwell FLET GU13 167 J7
Haw La GOR/PANG RG8 37 F5
Hawley Cl CALC RG31 71 H2 5
Hawthorn Cl BNFD RG42 10 C1
Hawthorne Rd CAV/SC RG4 58 B2
Hawthornes CALC RG31 55 G3 1
Hawthorn Gdns WHIT RG2 8 C7
Hawthorn Ri HTWY RG27 164 A1 3
Hawthorn Rd NWBY RG14 12 E1
The Hawthorns TADY RG26 126 B1 1
WAR/TWY RG10 59 K2
Hawthorn Wy CAV/SC RG4 59 H3
DEAN RG23 159 H5
Haydn Rd KEMP RG22 175 J4
Haydon La KSCL RG20 20 D4
Hayes La WWKG RG41 96 B3
Hayfield Cl CALC RG31 55 H5
Hayley Gn BNFD RG42 80 C3
Hayley La ODIM RG29 180 A7
Hay Rd READ RG1 6 F2
Haywarden Pl HTWY RG27 149 J3
Haywards Cl HEN RG9 31 F2
The Haywards NTHA RG18 85 J3
Haywood BRAK RG12 99 K5
Haywood Ct EARL RG6 4 E6
Haywood Dr FLET GU13 167 H4
Haywood Wy TLHT RG30 72 A1
Hazelbank EWKG RG40 116 C2
Hazel Cl DEAN RG23 174 A3
TLHT RG30 91 G2
WWKG RG41 96 E2 1
Hazel Coppice HTWY RG27 164 A1 2
Hazel Crs WHIT RG2 8 C7
Hazeldene CHAM RG24 161 G1 1
KSCL RG20 48 A4 1
Hazel Dr WODY RG5 9 M2
Hazeley Cl HTWY RG27 149 H3
Hazel Gdns CAV/SC RG4 29 G5
Hazel Gn TADY RG26 108 A7 1
Hazel Gv NTHA RG18 85 J2
Hazell Hl BRAK RG12 11 G6
Hazelmoor La CAV/SC RG4 28 D7
Hazel Rd CALC RG31 55 H1
Hazelwood Cl CALC RG31 55 H4 4
DEAN RG23 159 J4
Hazelwood Dr DEAN RG23 159 J4
Hazelwood La BNFD RG42 79 H2
Hazely Cl HTWY RG27 149 H3
Heacham Cl EARL RG6 74 D6 7
Headington Cl EWKG RG40 77 J6 1
KEMP RG22 175 J4 1
Headington Dr EWKG RG40 77 J6
Headley Cl WODY RG5 59 K5 3
Headley Rd WODY RG5 59 H6
Headley Rd East WODY RG5 59 J6
Heardman Cl STHA RG19 86 A5
Hearmon Cl YTLY GU46 135 J3
Hearn Rd WODY RG5 75 H1
Hearns La CAV/SC RG4 28 D6
Hearn Wk BRAK RG12 11 L2
Heath Cl WWKG RG41 97 G3
Heath Dr CAV/SC RG4 44 D3
Heath End Rd TADY RG26 108 B7
Heather Cl CAV/SC RG4 29 G6
EWKG RG40 116 D1 4
FARN GU14 151 J7
Heatherden Cl WHIT RG2 73 K7
Heatherdene Av CWTH RG45 117 K4
Heather Dr FLET GU13 167 G6
NTHA RG18 85 J2
TADY RG26 108 C6
Heather Gv HTWY RG27 149 H3
Heather La HTWY RG27 163 F6
Heathermount Dr CWTH RG45 118 A2
Heather Row La HTWY RG27 163 G6
Heatherway CWTH RG45 118 B3
Heather Wy KEMP RG22 175 F5
Heathfield Av HEN RG9 44 E2
TLHT RG30 55 J6
Heathfield Cl HEN RG9 44 E2
Heathfield Ct FLET GU13 167 F4
Heathfield Rd KEMP RG22 175 J5
Heath Hill Rd North
CWTH RG45 118 C3
Heath Hill Rd South
CWTH RG45 118 C3
Heathlands KSCL RG20 120 D1
TADY RG26 108 B7 1
Heathlands Rd EWKG RG40 98 A4
Heath La NFNM GU10 182 E6
NTHA RG18 85 H2
Heathmoors BRAK RG12 99 K3 2
Heath Ride CWTH RG45 117 J4
EWKG RG40 117 F2
Heath Rd EARL RG6 9 H2
TADY RG26 109 H7
THLE RG7 68 D4
Heathrow Copse TADY RG26 126 A1
Heathview HTWY RG27 164 B1 3
Heathway ASC SL5 81 H6
CALC RG31 55 H5 2
Heathwood Cl YTLY GU46 135 J2 3
Hebbecastle Down BNFD RG42 79 J4
Hebden Cl STHA RG19 85 H6
The Hedgerows CHAM RG24 161 H3
Hedgeway NWBY RG14 13 K1
Heelas Rd WWKG RG41 97 F1
Hele Cl BSTK RG21 176 B2
Helksham Cl SHST GU47 118 E7 4
Helmsdale BRAK RG12 100 B3
Helmsdale Cl TLHT RG30 56 C5
Helston Gdns WHIT RG2 7 K9
Hemdean Hl CAV/SC RG4 57 H2
Hemdean Ri CAV/SC RG4 57 H2
Hemdean Rd CAV/SC RG4 57 H1
Hemmyng Cnr BNFD RG42 79 K4 2
Hengrave Cl EARL RG6 75 H4 7
Henley Gdns YTLY GU46 135 J4
Henley Rd CAV/SC RG4 44 D7
CAV/SC RG4 57 J2
HEN RG9 45 F4
WAR/TWY RG10 33 G1
Henley Wood Rd EARL RG6 75 G2
The Henrys NTHA RG18 85 J3
Henry St READ RG1 3 J8
Henshaw Crs NWBY RG14 83 G7
Henwick Cl NTHA RG18 85 F1
Henwick La NTHA RG18 85 F2
Henwood Copse GOR/PANG RG8 38 D6
Hepplewhite Cl TADY RG26 108 B7
Hepplewhite Dr KEMP RG22 175 F5
Herald Wy WODY RG5 59 K7
Herbert Cl BRAK RG12 99 J3
Herbert Rd FLET GU13 167 F2
Hereford Cl ODIM RG29 180 B2 2
Hereford Md FARN GU14 151 J6 4
Hereford Rd DEAN RG23 159 H6
Herewood Cl NWBY RG14 12 C1
Heritage Pk DEAN RG23 175 G7
Hermes Cl FLET GU13 167 K2
Hermitage Dr ASC SL5 81 H7
WAR/TWY RG10 46 C7
Hermitage Rd NTHA RG18 65 G4
Hermits Cl THLE RG7 91 G4
Heroes Wk WHIT RG2 73 J7
Heron Cl ASC SL5 81 G6
FLET GU13 167 K6
Herondale BRAK RG12 99 K5
Heron Dr WAR/TWY RG10 46 D6
Heron Island CAV/SC RG4 3 L2
Heron Pk CHAM RG24 161 G2
Heron Rd WWKG RG41 96 D1
Heron Shaw GOR/PANG RG8 25 F4 3
Heron's Wy EWKG RG40 77 J7
Heron Wy KEMP RG22 174 E4
READ RG1 6 C3
STHA RG19 85 G4
THLE RG7 88 E4
Herriard Wy TADY RG26 126 E2 4
Herriot Ct YTLY GU46 135 H5
Hertford Cl CAV/SC RG4 44 A6
WWKG RG41 96 D2
Hewett Av CAV/SC RG4 56 E1
Hewett Cl CAV/SC RG4 56 E1
Hexham Cl SHST GU47 118 E6
Hexham Rd WHIT RG2 7 M5
Highams Cl KSCL RG20 124 A7
High Beech BRAK RG12 100 C2 6
Highbridge Cl CAV/SC RG4 44 B7
Highbridge Whf READ RG1 3 K6
Highbury Rd CALC RG31 55 F6
Highcliffe Cl WODY RG5 59 J4
Highdown FLET GU13 167 H1
Highdown Av CAV/SC RG4 43 H6
Highdown Hill Rd CAV/SC RG4 43 H5
Highdowns KEMP RG22 175 H6
High Dr KEMP RG22 175 H2
Higher Alham BRAK RG12 100 B5 3
BRAK RG12 100 B5 3
BRAK RG12 100 B5 3
Higher Md CHAM RG24 161 G3
Highfield BRAK RG12 99 G4
EARL RG6 9 J7
Highfield Av NWBY RG14 12 E5
Highfield Cha BSTK RG21 14 B5
Highfield Cl EWKG RG40 97 G1
Highfield Pk WAR/TWY RG10 46 E2
Highfield Rd CALC RG31 55 G1
NWBY RG14 12 D9
Highgate Rd WODY RG5 75 G1
Highgrove St READ RG1 7 L1
Highgrove Ter READ RG1 3 K9
Highland Dr DEAN RG23 173 K2
FARN GU14 151 J7
Highlands Av WWKG RG41 96 B2
Highlands La HEN RG9 30 D4
Highlands Rd KEMP RG22 175 F1
Highmead Cl WHIT RG2 8 C7
High Meadow CAV/SC RG4 56 E2
Highmoor Rd CAV/SC RG4 57 G2
Highmoors CHAM RG24 145 F7
High St ASC SL5 101 J1
BRAK RG12 10 F3
CAV/SC RG4 59 G2
CWTH RG45 118 D4
GOR/PANG RG8 24 D5
GOR/PANG RG8 40 C5
HTWY RG27 149 J4
KSCL RG20 20 D5
KSCL RG20 21 J7
KSCL RG20 48 A4
ODIM RG29 180 C2
OVTN RG25 171 H4
SHST GU47 118 A7
STHA RG19 85 J4
THLE RG7 70 D3
WAR/TWY RG10 46 C3
WAR/TWY RG10 46 C7
High Tree Dr EARL RG6 5 J9
Highview CALC RG31 71 G1
Highway CWTH RG45 118 B3
Highwood Cl NWBY RG14 84 A1
YTLY GU46 135 H5
Highwood Rdg KEMP RG22 175 G6
Highworth Wy CALC RG31 55 G3
Hilary Cl WHIT RG2 73 K7
Hilary Dr CWTH RG45 118 C2
Hilborn Wy EWKG RG40 95 K6
Hilbury Rd EARL RG6 9 H6
Hilcot Rd TLHT RG30 2 A5
Hildens Dr CALC RG31 55 H6
Hillary Rd BSTK RG21 14 B1
Hillberry BRAK RG12 99 K5
Hill Bottom Cl GOR/PANG RG8 40 D1
Hillbrow WHIT RG2 8 C9
Hill Cl NWBY RG14 103 G1
Hill Copse Vw BRAK RG12 11 L2
Hillcrest FLET GU13 151 H7 1
Hillcrest Ct DEAN RG23 159 G5 1
Hillcrest La HEN RG9 29 G4
Hill Gdns GOR/PANG RG8 24 D5
Hillhouse La STHA RG19 106 B7
STHA RG19 124 B1
Hill Lands WAR/TWY RG10 46 C2
Hill Meadow OVTN RG25 171 H2
Hill Rd DEAN RG23 173 K3
NWBY RG14 12 A2
WHIT RG2 95 J6
Hillside GOR/PANG RG8 40 C4
TADY RG26 126 A5
THLE RG7 91 H4
Hillside Cl FLET GU13 166 D5
Hillside Dr BNFD RG42 78 D4
Hillside Pk WHIT RG2 8 E9
Hillside Rd EARL RG6 75 G3
ODIM RG29 180 E3
Hill St READ RG1 3 J9
Hilltop Rd CAV/SC RG4 42 E7
EARL RG6 5 K5
OVTN RG25 171 J2
WAR/TWY RG10 46 D5
Hilltop Vw YTLY GU46 135 G4
Hillview Cl CALC RG31 55 G3
Hill View Rd KEMP RG22 175 K1
Hilmanton EARL RG6 74 C6
Hindhead Rd EARL RG6 9 G6
Hinton Cl CWTH RG45 118 C1
TADY RG26 126 E2
Hinton Dr CWTH RG45 118 C1
Hinton Rd WAR/TWY RG10 60 E5
Hirstwood TLHT RG30 55 K4 3
Hirtes Av WHIT RG2 94 B2 1
Hitches La FLET GU13 166 D4
Hitherhooks Hl BNFD RG42 79 F5 1
Hocketts Cl GOR/PANG RG8 40 D1
Hockford La THLE RG7 107 H5
Hockham Rd KSCL RG20 21 J6
Hodgedale La WAR/TWY RG10 33 J5
Hodge La ASC SL5 81 K3
Hodsoll Rd READ RG1 2 E4
Hogarth Av TLHT RG30 72 A1
Hogarth Cl BSTK RG21 15 L7
Hogmoor La WAR/TWY RG10 60 E4
Hogwood La EWKG RG40 115 K2
Holbeche Cl YTLY GU46 135 F4
Holbeck BRAK RG12 99 G4
Holbein Cl BSTK RG21 15 J9
Holberton Rd WHIT RG2 74 A6
Holborne Cl NWBY RG14 103 F3
Holford Cl CALC RG31 55 H5 3
Holkam Cl TLHT RG30 56 A4 2
Holland Gdns FLET GU13 167 H3
Holland Pines BRAK RG12 99 G5
Holland Rd TLHT RG30 55 J6
The Hollands STHA RG19 85 K4
Hollicombe Cl TLHT RG30 55 K6 2
The Hollies NWBY RG14 103 G3
Hollow La WHIT RG2 94 B2
Hollowshot La KSCL RG20 139 K1
TADY RG26 140 D2
Hollybush La HTWY RG27 134 D1
TADY RG26 126 C7
THLE RG7 90 E5
Hollybush Ride EWKG RG40 117 H3
Holly Cl TADY RG26 129 H7
Hollydale Cl WHIT RG2 74 A5
Holly Dr CHAM RG24 161 K5
Hollyhock Cl KEMP RG22 175 F4
Holly La GOR/PANG RG8 37 J6
NTHA RG18 66 C3
THLE RG7 128 A1
Hollym Cl EARL RG6 75 H4
Holly Orch WWKG RG41 96 E2 5
Holly Rd WODY RG5 59 K7
Holly Spring La BRAK RG12 11 J1
Hollytrees FLET GU13 167 F5
Holmbury Av CWTH RG45 118 B1
Holmdene THLE RG7 91 G4 3
Holme Cl CWTH RG45 118 B1
Holmemoor Dr CAV/SC RG4 59 G3
Holme Park Farm La CAV/SC RG4 5 M2
Holmes Cl KEMP RG22 175 H6 2
WWKG RG41 97 F3
Holmes Crs WWKG RG41 97 F3
Holmes Rd EARL RG6 9 G2
Holmewood Cl WWKG RG41 97 F5
Holmlea Rd GOR/PANG RG8 25 F6
Holmwood Av TLHT RG30 72 A1
Holst Cl KEMP RG22 175 K5
Holsworthy Cl EARL RG6 75 H3 3
Holt Cottages STHA RG19 125 G1
Holt La HTWY RG27 164 B4
TADY RG26 125 G5
WWKG RG41 77 F7
Holton Heath BRAK RG12 100 C2 7
Holt Wy HTWY RG27 164 B1
Holy Barn Cl KEMP RG22 175 F3
Holybrook Crs TLHT RG30 72 B2 5
Holybrook Rd READ RG1 6 E1
Holyhook Cl CWTH RG45 118 B2
Holyrood Cl CAV/SC RG4 44 A6
Holywell Ct STHA RG19 85 J4 1
Hombrook Dr BNFD RG42 79 F6
Home Cft CALC RG31 55 G4
Home Farm Cl WHIT RG2 7 K4
Home Farm Rd HTWY RG27 150 C3
Homelands Wy HEN RG9 31 G2 1
Home Mead Cl NWBY RG14 83 H7
Home Park Rd YTLY GU46 135 H3
Homesteads Rd KEMP RG22 175 F3
Honeybottom Rd TADY RG26 108 E7
Honey End La TLHT RG30 56 B7
Honey Hl EWKG RG40 98 A5
Honeyhill Rd BNFD RG42 10 C2
Honey La MDHD SL6 33 K1
Honey Meadow Cl CAV/SC RG4 4 C1
Honeysuckle Cl CWTH RG45 118 B1
KEMP RG22 175 F4 2
YTLY GU46 135 F3 1
Honister Gdns FLET GU13 167 K1
Honiton Rd WHIT RG2 7 L7
Hook Common HTWY RG27 163 J2
Hookend La GOR/PANG RG8 27 J2
Hook End La GOR/PANG RG8 38 D5
Hook La TADY RG26 125 J3
TADY RG26 157 K3
Hook Rd HTWY RG27 147 K5
HTWY RG27 163 K4
KSCL RG20 124 B7
ODIM RG29 163 J7
ODIM RG29 164 B6
Hoopersmead OVTN RG25 176 B5
Hoopers Wy DEAN RG23 174 A3
Hoops Wy WHIT RG2 73 G6
Hope Av BRAK RG12 100 B5
Hopfield Rd HTWY RG27 149 H5
Hop Gdn FLET GU13 167 F7
Hop Garden Rd HTWY RG27 163 J2
Hop Gdns HEN RG9 31 G1
Hopton Garth CHAM RG24 161 H2
Hopwood Cl NWBY RG14 13 L1
Horatio Av BNFD RG42 11 M1
Horewood Rd BRAK RG12 99 J4
Hormer Cl SHST GU47 118 E7 5
Hornbeam Cl GOR/PANG RG8 41 H7 1
SHST GU47 118 E7 6
WWKG RG41 96 C4
Hornbeam Dr EARL RG6 75 G5
Hornbeam Pl HTWY RG27 164 A1 5
Hornbeams THLE RG7 113 K1
Hornby Av BRAK RG12 100 A5
Horncastle Dr TLHT RG30 72 A1 2
Horndean Rd BRAK RG12 100 C4 1
Horne Rd STHA RG19 85 J5
Hornsea Cl TLHT RG30 55 K4 4
Horn St KSCL RG20 21 K6
The Horse Cl CAV/SC RG4 57 K1
Horse Gate Ride ASC SL5 101 K4
Horsepond Rd CAV/SC RG4 28 C6
Horseshoe Crs THLE RG7 91 F4
Horseshoe End NWBY RG14 104 A1 2
Horseshoe Pk GOR/PANG RG8 40 C7
Horseshoe Rd GOR/PANG RG8 40 C7
Horsham Rd SHST GU47 118 E7
Horsnape Gdns BNFD RG42 78 C4 2
Horsneile La BNFD RG42 10 E1
Horwood Gdns BSTK RG21 176 A2
Hose Hl THLE RG7 71 F7
Hosier St READ RG1 3 H6
Hound Green Cl HTWY RG27 132 A6
Houndmills Rd BSTK RG21 159 K5
Howard Cl FLET GU13 167 K2
Howard Rd BSTK RG21 15 G9
EWKG RG40 97 H2
NWBY RG14 12 E7
Howard St READ RG1 2 F6
Howell Cl BNFD RG42 79 K4
Howes Gdns FLET GU13 167 F5
Howth Dr WODY RG5 59 G6
Hubbard Cl WAR/TWY RG10 60 E2
Hubbard Rd BSTK RG21 14 A1
Hubberholme BRAK RG12 10 D5
Huckleberry Cl
GOR/PANG RG8 55 H1 4
Huddington Gld HTWY RG27 135 F4

Hudson Rd WODY RG5 75 J1
Hudsons Meadow HTWY RG27 132 A6
Hughes Rd EWKG RG40 77 J7
Hugh Fraser Dr CALC RG31 55 H7
Huish La OVTN RG25 177 J2
Hulbert Wy KEMP RG22 175 H2
Hulfords La HTWY RG27 149 K1
Humber Cl NTHA RG18 85 G2
WWKG RG41 76 D7
Hungerford Dr READ RG1 6 D1
Hungerford La THLE RG7 68 B4
WAR/TWY RG10 61 H3
Hunnels Cl FLET GU13 183 F1
Hunters Cha CAV/SC RG4 43 G7
Hunters Cl DEAN RG23 174 A1
Hunter's Hl THLE RG7 90 E4
Hunters Wy THLE RG7 93 H6
Huntingdon Cl EARL RG6 75 H4
Hunts Cl HTWY RG27 164 B2 3
Huntsmans Meadow ASC SL5 81 J6
Huntsmoor Rd TADY RG26 108 D7
TADY RG26 126 C1
Hurricane Wy WODY RG5 59 K6
Hursley Cl TLHT RG30 55 K6 3
Hurst Park Rd WAR/TWY RG10 60 D3
Hurst Rd WAR/TWY RG10 60 D2
The Hurst HTWY RG27 166 A2
Hurst Wy WHIT RG2 73 G6
Hurstwood ASC SL5 101 K4
Huscarle Wy CALC RG31 55 H1 5
Huson Rd BNFD RG42 79 K5
Hutsons Cl EWKG RG40 77 J6
Hutton Cl EARL RG6 9 G8
NWBY RG14 13 G1
Hyacinth Cl KEMP RG22 175 F4 3
Hyde End La STHA RG19 106 E3
THLE RG7 93 K3
Hyde End Rd THLE RG7 93 K5
Hyde La KSCL RG20 123 F3
NFNM GU10 182 C5
Hydes Platt THLE RG7 128 A1
The Hydes CALC RG31 55 H1 6
Hyperion Wy WHIT RG2 7 J5
Hythe Cl BRAK RG12 11 M9

I

Ibstock Cl TLHT RG30 56 C6
Ibstone Av CAV/SC RG4 44 B7
Ibworth La TADY RG26 140 E7
Icknield Pl GOR/PANG RG8 25 G3
Icknield Rd GOR/PANG RG8 25 G3
Ilbury Cl WHIT RG2 94 B2
Ilchester Ms CAV/SC RG4 44 B6 1
Ilex Cl CAV/SC RG4 29 G7
TADY RG26 109 H7
YTLY GU46 135 G3
Ilfracombe Wy EARL RG6 75 H3
Ilkley Rd CAV/SC RG4 57 F2
Ilkley Wy STHA RG19 85 H5
Illingworth Av CAV/SC RG4 44 B7
Illingworth Gv BRAK RG12 80 C6
Ilsley Cl CAV/SC RG4 29 G6 2
Ilsley Rd KSCL RG20 21 H7
Imperial Wy WHIT RG2 73 H7
Impstone Rd TADY RG26 109 J7
Inchwood BRAK RG12 99 K6
Ingle Gln EWKG RG40 117 F1 2
Ingleton BRAK RG12 10 D6
Inglewood Cl CAV/SC RG4 29 G6
Inglewood Ct TLHT RG30 56 D7 2
Inglewood Dr KEMP RG22 175 G6
Inhams Wy THLE RG7 127 K1
Inhurst La STHA RG19 107 K7
Inhurst Wy TADY RG26 108 C7
Inkpen Cl TLHT RG30 72 B2 3
Inkpen Gdns CHAM RG24 161 H3
Innings La BNFD RG42 11 K1
Instow Rd EARL RG6 9 K7
Invergordon Cl CALC RG31 71 K2 4
Iris Cl KEMP RG22 175 F5
Irvine Wy EARL RG6 75 F6 6
Irwell Cl BSTK RG21 15 J5
Isaac Newton Rd WHIT RG2 95 J7
Isis Cl WWKG RG41 76 A5
Island Farm Rd THLE RG7 90 D6
Island Rd WHIT RG2 6 E6
Islandstone La WAR/TWY RG10 61 F7
Itchel La NFNM GU10 182 C5
Itchen Cl DEAN RG23 174 A3
Ivanhoe Rd EWKG RG40 115 K2
Ivar Gdns CHAM RG24 161 H3
Ives Cl YTLY GU46 135 G2
Ivybank CALC RG31 55 H4
Ivydene Rd TLHT RG30 56 D4
Ivy Down La DEAN RG23 173 H1
Ivyhole Hl HTWY RG27 150 C2

J

Jackdaw Cl KEMP RG22 174 E4
Jackson Cl BRAK RG12 99 J3 1
Jacksons La CAV/SC RG4 42 B7
Jacob Cl BNFD RG42 78 E7 3
James Cl BSTK RG21 160 D4
James's La TLHT RG30 91 J3
James St READ RG1 2 E6
Jameston BRAK RG12 99 K6
James Watt Rd EWKG RG40 95 K7
Janson Ct READ RG1 2 E8
Japonica Cl WWKG RG41 96 C3 2
Jaques's La THLE RG7 90 E1
Jarvis Cl HTWY RG27 134 D1
Jarvis Dr WAR/TWY RG10 46 C6
Jasmine Cl WWKG RG41 76 C7 6
Jasmine Rd KEMP RG22 175 G4
Jay Cl EARL RG6 9 K9
EARL RG6 74 E5
Jays Cl KEMP RG22 176 B3
Jedburgh Cl STHA RG19 86 A4
Jefferson Cl CAV/SC RG4 43 K5
Jefferson Rd BSTK RG21 160 C4
Jenkins Cl TLHT RG30 56 D7 3
Jenner Wk CALC RG31 55 F6 1
Jennetts Cl THLE RG7 68 B3
Jenny's Wk YTLY GU46 135 K3
Jerome Cnr CWTH RG45 118 D5
Jerome Rd WODY RG5 59 G7
Jerrymoor Hl EWKG RG40 96 E7 6
Jersey Cl CHAM RG24 160 D1
FARN GU14 151 J6 5
Jesmond Dene NWBY RG14 12 C2
Jesse Ter READ RG1 2 F7
Jessett Dr FLET GU13 167 F7
Jevington BRAK RG12 99 K5
Jibbs Meadow TADY RG26 129 G6 1
Jig's La North BNFD RG42 80 B4 2
Jig's La South BNFD RG42 11 L1
BNFD RG42 80 B5 11
Jobson Cl WHCH RG28 169 H7 2
Jock's La BNFD RG42 79 F6
Joel Cl EARL RG6 9 G6
John Hunt Cl STHA RG19 86 A5 3
John Morgan Cl HTWY RG27 148 A7 1
HTWY RG27 163 K1 6
John Nike Wy BRAK RG12 78 D7
Johnson Dr EWKG RG40 117 G1
Johnson Wy FLET GU13 167 G5
Jonathan Hl KSCL RG20 104 A5
Jones Cnr ASC SL5 81 K7
Jordan Cl CAV/SC RG4 44 B7
THLE RG7 94 A6
Jordan's La THLE RG7 90 E5
Joseph Ct BNFD RG42 80 B4 3
Josephine Ct TLHT RG30 2 B8
Josey Cl CAV/SC RG4 29 G5 1
Jouldings La HTWY RG27 115 G4
Joule Rd BSTK RG21 14 B1
Jubilee Av ASC SL5 81 H6
WWKG RG41 77 F7
Jubilee Cl ASC SL5 81 H6
TADY RG26 109 H7
Jubilee Rd BSTK RG21 14 E7
EARL RG6 5 G9
EWKG RG40 116 E5
NWBY RG14 13 G6
Jubilee Sq READ RG1 3 K8
Juliet Gdns BNFD RG42 80 C5 1
Julius Cl CHAM RG24 159 H3
Julius Hl BNFD RG42 80 C5 2
Julkes La WHIT RG2 75 H7
Junction Rd READ RG1 4 C8
Junction Ter NWBY RG14 13 J5
June Dr DEAN RG23 159 G6
Juniper BRAK RG12 99 K6
Juniper Cl CHAM RG24 145 H6
The Junipers WWKG RG41 96 C3
Juniper Wy CALC RG31 55 J3
Jupiter Wy WWKG RG41 96 E1
Justice Cl STHA RG19 86 A5
Jutland Cl WWKG RG41 96 D1 10

K

Katesgrove La READ RG1 3 H8
Kathleen Cl BSTK RG21 176 B2 2
Kathleen Sanders Ct
THLE RG7 70 D2 3
Kaynes Pk ASC SL5 81 H6
Keane Cl WODY RG5 59 H5
Kearsley Rd TLHT RG30 56 D7
Keates Gn BNFD RG42 10 F1
Keats Cl CHAM RG24 160 D2
WODY RG5 75 H1
Keats Rd WODY RG5 75 H2
Keats Wy CWTH RG45 118 C1
YTLY GU46 135 G5
Keble Wy SHST GU47 119 F6
Keepers Combe BRAK RG12 100 A4
Keephatch Rd EWKG RG40 77 K6
Keeps Md KSCL RG20 123 K6
Keighley Cl STHA RG19 85 H5
Kelburne Cl WWKG RG41 76 B3
Keldholme BRAK RG12 10 D6
Kelmscott Cl CAV/SC RG4 57 F2
Kelsey Av EWKG RG40 116 D2
Kelsey Gv YTLY GU46 135 K4
Kelton Cl EARL RG6 75 H4
Kelvedon Wy CAV/SC RG4 43 F7
Kelvin Cl WHIT RG2 115 H1 2
Kelvin Hl KEMP RG22 175 K2
Kelvin Rd NWBY RG14 13 G2
Kemble Ct CALC RG31 71 J2 3
Kemerton Cl CALC RG31 71 J2 2
Kempshott Gdns KEMP RG22 175 F4 4
Kempshott Gv KEMP RG22 159 F7 1
Kempshott La KEMP RG22 175 F3
Kempton Cl NWBY RG14 13 K8
Kenavon Dr READ RG1 3 L5
Kendal Av CAV/SC RG4 44 A7
WHIT RG2 94 B1 1
Kendal Cl NTHA RG18 85 H3
Kendal Gdns KEMP RG22 175 G3
Kendrick Cl EWKG RG40 97 G2
Kendrick Rd NWBY RG14 103 G3
READ RG1 3 L8
Kenilworth Av BRAK RG12 11 H1
TLHT RG30 6 A2
Kenilworth Crs FLET GU13 167 K1
Kenilworth Rd DEAN RG23 159 G5 2
FLET GU13 167 J2
Kenmore Cl FLET GU13 167 J6
Kennedy Cl NWBY RG14 103 G2
Kennedy Dr GOR/PANG RG8 40 C7
Kennedy Gdns EARL RG6 9 J5
Kennel Av ASC SL5 81 J6
Kennel Cl ASC SL5 81 J4
Kennel Gn ASC SL5 81 H6
Kennel La BNFD RG42 79 J5
Kennel Ride ASC SL5 81 J5
Kennel Wd ASC SL5 81 J6
Kennet Cl BSTK RG21 15 J5
STHA RG19 85 K4
Kennet Ct WWKG RG41 96 E1 3
Kennet Pl THLE RG7 91 G4
Kennet Rd NWBY RG14 12 D5
Kennet Side NWBY RG14 13 J4
READ RG1 3 L6
Kennet St READ RG1 3 L6
Kennet Wy DEAN RG23 174 A3
Kennylands Rd CAV/SC RG4 29 G7
Kensington Cl EARL RG6 74 E5
Kensington Rd TLHT RG30 2 A6
Kent Cl WWKG RG41 96 C2
Kent Folly BNFD RG42 80 C4
Kentigern Dr CWTH RG45 119 F3
Kenton Cl BRAK RG12 11 J4
Kenton Rd EARL RG6 9 M4
Kenton's La WAR/TWY RG10 32 C3
Kent Rd FLET GU13 167 J2
TLHT RG30 2 A7
Kentwood Cl TLHT RG30 55 K4
Kentwood Hl CALC RG31 55 K3
TLHT RG30 55 K4
Kenwith Av FLET GU13 167 K2 1
Kerchers Fld OVTN RG25 171 H5
Kerfield Wy HTWY RG27 164 A2 3
Kernham Dr CALC RG31 55 G3 2
Kerris Wy EARL RG6 74 D5
Kerry Cl FARN GU14 151 J5 1
Kersey Crs NWBY RG14 83 H2
Kersley Crs ODIM RG29 180 B4
Kesteven Wy WWKG RG41 96 D1 11
Keston Cl CAV/SC RG4 57 K2
Kestrel Cl NFNM GU10 183 J5
STHA RG19 85 G4 1
Kestrel Rd KEMP RG22 174 E3
Kestrel Wy THLE RG7 91 G3
TLHT RG30 72 B2
WWKG RG41 96 D1
Keswick Cl TLHT RG30 55 J6
Keswick Gdns WODY RG5 75 H1
Ketcher Gn BNFD RG42 78 D2
Ketelbey Ri KEMP RG22 176 A5
Kettering Cl CALC RG31 71 K2
Kevin Cl KSCL RG20 124 C7
Kevins Dr YTLY GU46 135 K2
Keynes Cl FLET GU13 167 J7
Keynsham Wy SHST GU47 118 E6
Kibble Gn BRAK RG12 99 K4
Kibblewhite Crs
WAR/TWY RG10 46 C6 1
Kidmore End Rd CAV/SC RG4 43 H4
Kidmore La CAV/SC RG4 29 F7
CAV/SC RG4 42 E1
Kidmore Rd CAV/SC RG4 43 F6
Kilburn Cl CALC RG31 71 J2 10
Kildare Gdns CAV/SC RG4 57 K2 1
Kilmington Cl BRAK RG12 100 B5 4
Kiln Cl NTHA RG18 49 G6
Kiln Dr NTHA RG18 64 D1
Kiln Gdns HTWY RG27 149 H4
Kiln Hl THLE RG7 114 E1
Kiln La BRAK RG12 10 C4
CALC RG31 55 F5
HEN RG9 45 F2
TADY RG26 143 F5
THLE RG7 111 H3
Kiln Ride EWKG RG40 97 F7
EWKG RG40 117 F1
GOR/PANG RG8 38 C7
Kiln Ride Extension
EWKG RG40 117 F2
Kiln Rd CAV/SC RG4 43 K5
CHAM RG24 143 K7
NWBY RG14 84 B2
Kilnsea Dr EARL RG6 75 G4
Kiln View Rd WHIT RG2 8 A7
Kilowna Cl WAR/TWY RG10 59 K1
Kimbell Rd KEMP RG22 176 A2
Kimber Cl CHAM RG24 161 G1
Kimberley BRAK RG12 99 K6
FLET GU13 167 J7
Kimberley Cl READ RG1 6 C1
Kimberley Rd KEMP RG22 175 K1
Kimbers Dr NWBY RG14 83 F2
Kimbers La TADY RG26 127 G4
Kimmeridge BRAK RG12 100 B4 1
Kimpton Cl WHIT RG2 74 B6
King Edwards Cl ASC SL5 81 H6 1
King Edwards Ri ASC SL5 81 H6
King Edwards Rd ASC SL5 81 H6
Kingfisher Cl FLET GU13 167 H6
KEMP RG22 174 E3
THLE RG7 89 F4 1
Kingfisher Ct WAR/TWY RG10 60 D2 1
Kingfisher Dr WODY RG5 5 M9
YTLY GU46 135 G3
Kingfisher Pl READ RG1 3 K3
King James Wy HEN RG9 31 F3
King John Rd KSCL RG20 124 A7
King Johns Rd ODIM RG29 164 B7
Kingsbridge Hl THLE RG7 113 H2
Kingsbridge Rd NWBY RG14 12 A7
WHIT RG2 7 K7
Kingsclere Rd BSTK RG21 14 B1
DEAN RG23 158 D1
OVTN RG25 171 H2
Kingscroft FLET GU13 167 H3
Kingsdown Cl EARL RG6 9 J8
Kings Farm La HEN RG9 30 A5
Kingsford Cl WODY RG5 75 K1
Kings Furlong Dr BSTK RG21 14 B8
Kingsgate St READ RG1 4 B7
Kings Keep FLET GU13 167 H5
SHST GU47 118 C7
Kingsland Gra NWBY RG14 83 H7
Kingsley Cl CWTH RG45 118 C5
NWBY RG14 84 A1
WAR/TWY RG10 45 K7
WHIT RG2 73 J7
Kingsley Pk WHCH RG28 169 H6
Kingsley Rd HTWY RG27 134 B1
King's Meadow OVTN RG25 171 H4
King's Meadow Rd READ RG1 3 K4
Kingsmere Rd BNFD RG42 10 A1
Kingsmill Rd BSTK RG21 176 B2
Kings Orch DEAN RG23 174 A4
Kings Pightle CHAM RG24 145 G7
King's Ride ASC SL5 101 F2
King's Rd CAV/SC RG4 3 K1
CWTH RG45 118 C4
FLET GU13 167 J2
HEN RG9 31 G1
HEN RG9 31 G1
KEMP RG22 175 K1
NWBY RG14 12 F5
READ RG1 3 K6
THLE RG7 109 K7
Kings Rd West NWBY RG14 12 F5
Kingston Gdns WHIT RG2 7 L7
Kingston La THLE RG7 90 B1
King St ODIM RG29 180 D1
READ RG1 3 J6
THLE RG7 111 F2
King Street La WWKG RG41 76 A5
Kings Wk WHCH RG28 169 H7
Kingsway CAV/SC RG4 44 B6
Kings Wd MLW SL7 19 J3 2
Kinross Av ASC SL5 101 J3
Kinross Ct ASC SL5 101 J3
Kinson Rd TLHT RG30 56 B4
Kintyre Cl DEAN RG23 173 K2
Kipling Cl NTHA RG18 85 H2
YTLY GU46 135 H5 1
Kipling Wk KEMP RG22 175 K1
Kirkfell Cl CALC RG31 55 H3
Kirkham Cl CAV/SC RG4 44 B6
SHST GU47 118 E6 3
Kirkstall Ct CALC RG31 71 J2 11
Kirkwood Crs THLE RG7 90 E4 2
Kirton Cl TLHT RG30 56 C6
Kirtons Farm Rd TLHT RG30 72 D5
Kittiwake Cl WODY RG5 60 A6
Kitwood Dr EARL RG6 75 H5
Knappe Cl HEN RG9 31 F3
Knapp La TADY RG26 127 G3
The Knapp EARL RG6 9 J3
Knight Cl FLET GU13 166 D5
Knighton Cl CAV/SC RG4 57 H2
Knightsbridge Dr STHA RG19 105 G5
Knight St BSTK RG21 14 A7
Knights Wy CAV/SC RG4 43 J7
Knightswood BRAK RG12 99 J6
Knoll Cl FLET GU13 167 H1
Knoll Rd FLET GU13 167 H1
The Knoll CALC RG31 55 G3 3
Knollys Rd THLE RG7 109 J7
Knossington Cl EARL RG6 9 M8
Knott La THLE RG7 88 E3
Knowle Cl CAV/SC RG4 56 E1
Knowle Crs KSCL RG20 124 A7
Knowle Rd WODY RG5 75 H2
Knowles Av CWTH RG45 118 A3
Knowsley Rd CALC RG31 55 G2
Knox Cl FLET GU13 166 E6
Knox Gn BNFD RG42 78 D3
Kybes La THLE RG7 92 E3
Kyle Cl BRAK RG12 10 E6

L

Laburnum Gdns WHIT RG2 8 C9
Laburnum Gv NWBY RG14 12 E1
Laburnum Rd WWKG RG41 76 B5
Laburnum Wy DEAN RG23 159 J5
Lackmore Gdns GOR/PANG RG8 26 E3
Ladbroke Cl WODY RG5 59 J7
Ladwell Cl NWBY RG14 103 G3
Ladybank BRAK RG12 99 J6
Lady Jane Ct CAV/SC RG4 57 J2
Ladymask Cl CALC RG31 72 A2 2
Laffans Rd ODIM RG29 180 C4
The Laffords THLE RG7 68 D4
Lake End Wy CWTH RG45 118 B4
Lakelands TADY RG26 108 A7 2
Lakeside BNFD RG42 79 K5
EARL RG6 9 J6
Lakeside Ct FARN GU14 151 J7
Lakeside Dr HTWY RG27 133 G5
Lalande Cl WWKG RG41 96 D1 12
Lamb Cl NTHA RG18 85 H2
Lambdens Hl THLE RG7 69 G5
Lambdens Wk TADY RG26 126 E1 2
Lambeth Ct TLHT RG30 56 A6 1
Lambfields THLE RG7 70 C3 2
Lamborne Cl SHST GU47 118 B7
Lambourne Cl CALC RG31 55 J5 4
Lambourne Rd CAV/SC RG4 29 F6
Lambourn Rd KSCL RG20 83 F1
Lambourn Valley Wy KSCL RG20 62 E6
NWBY RG14 12 B4
Lambridge La HEN RG9 16 E7
Lambridge Wood Rd HEN RG9 16 E6
Lambs La THLE RG7 93 H7
Lambs Rw CHAM RG24 161 G4
Lamden Wy THLE RG7 91 G4
Lamerton Rd WHIT RG2 73 J5
Lammas Md BNFD RG42 79 F5
Lamorna Crs CALC RG31 55 H4
Lamp Acres NWBY RG14 84 A2
Lampards Cl HTWY RG27 147 J4
Lanark Cl WODY RG5 59 K7
Lancashire Hl BNFD RG42 80 C4 3
Lancaster Cl NTHA RG18 85 H3
READ RG1 7 M1
Lancaster Gdns EARL RG6 9 J5
Lancaster Rd BSTK RG21 14 C2
Lancing Cl TLHT RG30 2 B7
Landen Ct EWKG RG40 97 G3
Landrake Crs WHIT RG2 7 L9
Landseer Cl BSTK RG21 15 J9
Landsend La WODY RG5 60 A3
Lane End TADY RG26 129 G7
Lane End Cl WHIT RG2 94 B1 2
Laneswood THLE RG7 110 D3
The Lane TADY RG26 126 E1
Langborough Rd EWKG RG40 97 H2
Langdale Dr ASC SL5 81 H7
Langdale Gdns EARL RG6 8 E8
Langford Cl CAV/SC RG4 43 K7
Langhams Wy WAR/TWY RG10 46 C2
Langley Cl FLET GU13 167 G7
Langley Common Rd
EWKG RG40 95 J6
Langley Hl CALC RG31 71 H1
Langley Hill Cl TLHT RG30 55 H7
Laniver Cl EARL RG6 9 J9
Lansdowne Gdns THLE RG7 93 K6
Lansdowne Rd TLHT RG30 55 J6
Lansley Rd BSTK RG21 160 C3 1
Lapin La KEMP RG22 175 G7
Lapwing Cl CALC RG31 55 G7
Lapwing Ri WHCH RG28 169 G6
Larch Av WWKG RG41 77 F7
Larch Cl NWBY RG14 83 G2
TLHT RG30 91 G3
Larch Dr KSCL RG20 124 A7
WODY RG5 75 G1
Larchfield Rd FLET GU13 167 H4
Larchside Cl THLE RG7 93 J5
Larchwood CHAM RG24 145 G7 2
Larges Bridge Dr BRAK RG12 11 H5
Larges La BRAK RG12 11 H4
Larissa Cl CALC RG31 55 K4 5
Lark Cl KEMP RG22 174 E4
Larkes-meade EARL RG6 9 G9
Larkfield CHAM RG24 145 G7
Larks Barrow Hl WHCH RG28 169 H2
Larkspur Cl WWKG RG41 76 C7
Larkspur Gdns NTHA RG18 86 A3
Larkswood Cl CALC RG31 55 J2 3
SHST GU47 118 B7 3
Larkswood Dr CWTH RG45 118 C3
Larmer Cl FLET GU13 166 E4
Lashbrook Rd HEN RG9 32 A7
Latimer BRAK RG12 99 J6
Latimer Dr CALC RG31 71 H2 6
Latimer Rd WWKG RG41 97 G2
Laud Cl NWBY RG14 84 C2
WHIT RG2 7 H1
Laud's Cl HEN RG9 31 F2
Laud Wy EWKG RG40 97 K1
Launceston Av CAV/SC RG4 44 B6 2
Launcestone Cl EARL RG6 9 J7
Laundry La HTWY RG27 132 A4
Lauradale BRAK RG12 10 D7
Laurel Cl ODIM RG29 180 B1
WWKG RG41 96 E2
Laurel Dr CALC RG31 55 G5
The Laurels BSTK RG21 15 H2
FLET GU13 167 H2
GOR/PANG RG8 40 C7 1
Lavell's La THLE RG7 129 H1
Lavender Rd KEMP RG22 175 F5
Lavenham Dr WODY RG5 59 J5
Laverstoke La WHCH RG28 170 D7
Lawford Crs YTLY GU46 135 J3
Lawrence Cl CHAM RG24 160 D2
EWKG RG40 97 J1
Lawrencedale Ct BSTK RG21 14 B6
Lawrence Gv BNFD RG42 78 E6
Lawrence Rd FLET GU13 167 G3
TLHT RG30 56 B5
Lawrences La NTHA RG18 85 J1
Lawson Dr CAV/SC RG4 43 F7
Lay Fld HTWY RG27 163 J2
Layleys Gn NTHA RG18 64 E2 1
Laytom Ri CALC RG31 55 H2
Lea Cl BSTK RG21 15 K4
TLHT RG30 72 B3
Lea Cft CWTH RG45 118 C2
Leafield Copse BRAK RG12 100 C2
Lea Rd CAV/SC RG4 29 G7
Lea Springs FLET GU13 166 E4
The Lea EWKG RG40 96 E7
FLET GU13 166 E4
Leaver Rd HEN RG9 31 F2
Leaves Gn BRAK RG12 100 A4
Leawood Rd FLET GU13 166 E4 1
Le Borowe FLET GU13 167 F7
Ledbury Cl TLHT RG30 56 D5 3
Ledbury Dr CALC RG31 71 J2 12
Ledran Cl EARL RG6 75 F6 7
Lefroy Av BSTK RG21 15 G1
Lefroy's Fld NFNM GU10 182 E4
Leger Cl FLET GU13 167 F6
Lehar Cl KEMP RG22 175 J4
Leicester BRAK RG12 100 A5
Leicester Cl HEN RG9 17 G7
Leigh Fld THLE RG7 110 E2
Leipzig Barracks FLET GU13 183 J2
Leipzig Rd FLET GU13 183 J1
Leiston Cl EARL RG6 75 G5 4
Leith Cl CWTH RG45 118 B1
Lemart Cl TLHT RG30 55 K5 3
Lemington Gv BRAK RG12 99 J4 1
Leney Cl EWKG RG40 77 J6
Lenham Cl WWKG RG41 76 C5
Lennel Gdns FLET GU13 167 K5
Lennon Wy KEMP RG22 175 H5
Lennox Cl CALC RG31 71 G2 7
Lennox Rd EARL RG6 9 H5
Leopold Wk READ RG1 4 A6 1
Leppington BRAK RG12 99 J6
Lesford Rd READ RG1 6 C3
Leslie Southern Ct NWBY RG14 13 G2
Lestock Wy FLET GU13 167 K2
Letcombe Sq BRAK RG12 100 C2
Letcombe St READ RG1 3 J7
Leverkusen Rd BRAK RG12 10 F6
Levignen Cl FLET GU13 166 E6
Lewis Cl BSTK RG21 15 H1
Lewisham Wy SHST GU47 118 E7
Lexington Gv WHIT RG2 93 K1 4
Leyburn Cl WODY RG5 59 K5
Leyland Gdns WHIT RG2 94 B2
Leys Gdns NWBY RG14 12 D2
Leyside CWTH RG45 118 B3
Lichfield Cl EARL RG6 9 M9
Lichfields BRAK RG12 11 M3
Liddell Cl EWKG RG40 116 D5
Liddell Wy ASC SL5 101 J3
Lidstone Cl EARL RG6 75 G5
Liebenrood Rd TLHT RG30 56 D7 4
Lightfoot Gv BSTK RG21 176 C2
Lightsfield DEAN RG23 174 A2
Lightwood BRAK RG12 100 A4
Lilac Cl GOR/PANG RG8 41 J7 2
The Lilacs WWKG RG41 96 B4
Lilac Wy DEAN RG23 159 J5
Lily Cl KEMP RG22 175 F5
Lily Hill Dr BRAK RG12 11 M4
Lily Hill Rd BRAK RG12 11 M3
BRAK RG12 80 C7
Lima Ct READ RG1 2 E8
Limbrey Hl OVTN RG25 178 E7
Lime Cl NWBY RG14 13 M2
WWKG RG41 96 E2
Limecroft YTLY GU46 135 H4
Lime Dr FARN GU14 151 J6 6

Limefield Cl EARL RG6 75 H3 4
Limerick Cl BNFD RG42 10 C1
Limes Av KSCL RG20 121 K2
The Limes TADY RG26 129 J7
Limetree Av KSCL RG20 120 E7
Limetree Rd GOR/PANG RG8 24 E5
Lime Tree Wy CHAM RG24 145 F7
Lime Wk BRAK RG12 11 H7
Limmer Cl WWKG RG41 96 B3 2
Limmerhill Rd WWKG RG41 96 D2
Lincoln Cl KEMP RG22 175 G5
WWKG RG41 75 K4
Lincoln Gdns WAR/TWY RG10 46 C7
Lincoln Rd WHIT RG2 7 L4
Lincolnshire Gdns BNFD RG42 80 B5
Lindberg Wy WODY RG5 60 A4 1
Lind Cl EARL RG6 9 K7
Linden Av CHAM RG24 161 J6
ODIM RG29 164 E7
Linden Cl NWBY RG14 12 C1
WWKG RG41 96 E3
Linden Hill La WAR/TWY RG10 47 H2
Lindenhill Rd BNFD RG42 10 A2
Linden Rd WHIT RG2 8 C8
WODY RG5 75 G2
Lindsey Cl WWKG RG41 96 D1
Lines Rd WAR/TWY RG10 60 D7
WAR/TWY RG10 76 E2
WAR/TWY RG10 77 F2
The Lines KSCL RG20 124 A6
Lingfield Cl CHAM RG24 161 K6
Lingfield Rd NWBY RG14 13 J9
Lingholm Cl TLHT RG30 72 A1
Lingmala Gv FLET GU13 167 J6 2
Lingwood BRAK RG12 99 K4
Link Rd KSCL RG20 124 B7
NWBY RG14 12 E6
Links Dr TLHT RG30 56 B5 2
The Links ASC SL5 81 H7
The Link YTLY GU46 135 H2
Link Wy NTHA RG18 85 G3
DEAN RG23 174 A3
WHIT RG2 95 H5
Linkway CWTH RG45 118 A3
FLET GU13 167 G5
Linnet Cl CALC RG31 55 G7
KEMP RG22 175 F2
Linton Cl TADY RG26 127 F2
Lion Cl OVTN RG25 171 H5
Lion Wy FLET GU13 167 J6
Lipscomb Cl NTHA RG18 49 G7
Lipscombe Cl NWBY RG14 12 A5
Liscombe BRAK RG12 99 J5
Lisle Cl NWBY RG14 83 J2
Lismore Cl WODY RG5 75 H2
Lismoyne Cl FLET GU13 167 G1 1
Lister Cl GOR/PANG RG8 41 H7
Lister Rd KEMP RG22 175 K2
Littington Cl EARL RG6 75 F6 3
Little Aldershot La STHA RG19 107 K6
Little Basing CHAM RG24 161 G4
Little Bowden La
GOR/PANG RG8 39 J7
Little Copse FLET GU13 167 G4
YTLY GU46 135 H2
Little Copse Cha CHAM RG24 161 F1
Littlecote Dr READ RG1 2 D9
Little Croft Rd GOR/PANG RG8 25 F6
Littledale Cl BRAK RG12 11 L5
Little Dean La OVTN RG25 179 H7
Little Fallow CHAM RG24 161 G3
Little Frith EWKG RG40 117 H2
Little Glebe CAV/SC RG4 59 H2
Little Heath Rd CALC RG31 55 F6
Little Hill Rd WAR/TWY RG10 76 C2
Little Hoddington Cl
OVTN RG25 179 F7
Littlejohn's La TLHT RG30 2 A3
Little John's La TLHT RG30 56 D5 4
Little Knowle Hl KSCL RG20 124 C5
STHA RG19 124 E3
Little La THLE RG7 86 D1
Little London Rd THLE RG7 127 K3
Little Moor SHST GU47 118 D7
Little Oak Dr CALC RG31 55 H5 4
Little Ringdale BRAK RG12 11 M8
Littlestead Cl CAV/SC RG4 44 B6 3
Little St READ RG1 2 D5
Little Vigo YTLY GU46 135 G5
Litton Gdns DEAN RG23 174 A3
Litton Rd WHIT RG2 8 A8
Liverpool Rd READ RG1 4 C5
Livery Cl READ RG1 3 K7
Livingstone Gdns WODY RG5 75 H1
Livingstone Rd NWBY RG14 13 G5
Llangar Gv CWTH RG45 118 B3
Llanvair Cl ASC SL5 101 K4
Llanvair Dr ASC SL5 101 J5
Llewellyn Pk WAR/TWY RG10 46 B6
Lloyd's La TADY RG26 141 K5
Lochinver BRAK RG12 99 J5
Lock Pl READ RG1 4 A6
Lockram La THLE RG7 91 H6
Locksbridge La TADY RG26 128 E7
Lockside Ct THLE RG7 89 F4 2
Locks Ride ASC SL5 81 F5
Lockstile Md GOR/PANG RG8 25 F4
Lockstile Wy GOR/PANG RG8 25 F5
Lockton Cha ASC SL5 101 G1
Loddon Br EARL RG6 75 J3
Loddon Bridge Rd EARL RG6 75 J2
WODY RG5 75 J1
Loddon Dr BSTK RG21 15 J5
WAR/TWY RG10 46 A3
Loddon Hall Rd WAR/TWY RG10 46 C7
Lodge Rd WAR/TWY RG10 60 D5
Logan Cl TLHT RG30 56 A6 2
Loggon Rd BSTK RG21 176 B3
Lomond Av CAV/SC RG4 44 B7
Lomond Cl DEAN RG23 173 K3
Londlandes FLET GU13 167 F7
London Rd ASC SL5 100 D1
BNFD RG42 78 D7
BNFD RG42 98 C1
BRAK RG12 11 J3
BSTK RG21 14 F6
CHAM RG24 161 J7
EARL RG6 5 J4
EWKG RG40 97 K1
HTWY RG27 148 D7
HTWY RG27 149 H5 2
HTWY RG27 162 D4
NWBY RG14 12 E2
ODIM RG29 164 E7
ODIM RG29 180 D1
OVTN RG25 171 G5
READ RG1 3 L8
STHA RG19 85 K4
WAR/TWY RG10 46 D6
WHCH RG28 169 K7
London St READ RG1 3 K6
WHCH RG28 169 H7
Longacre NWBY RG14 83 G7
Longacre Ri CHAM RG24 161 F1 2
Long Barn La WHIT RG2 7 K5
Longbridge Cl HTWY RG27 146 B1
Longbridge Rd TADY RG26 129 G6 2
Long Copse Cha CHAM RG24 161 F1
Longcroft Rd KSCL RG20 123 K6
STHA RG19 85 K5
Long Cross La KEMP RG22 175 F6
Longdon Rd WWKG RG41 76 B5
Longdown FLET GU13 167 G5
Longdown Rd SHST GU47 118 B7
Longfield Rd WAR/TWY RG10 46 C6
Long Gv TADY RG26 108 A6
THLE RG7 86 C2
Long Hill Rd ASC SL5 80 E6
BRAK RG12 80 D7
Longhurst Cl CAV/SC RG4 57 K2
Long La CALC RG31 55 G1
CHAM RG24 161 H1
NTHA RG18 64 E4
NWBY RG14 64 B7
ODIM RG29 180 E4
Longleat Dr CALC RG31 55 G2 2
Longmead FLET GU13 167 H5
KSCL RG20 102 C7
Long Mickle SHST GU47 118 B7
Longmoor La THLE RG7 111 F1
Longmoor Rd BSTK RG21 14 C7
Longmoors BNFD RG42 79 F6
Longmore Rd WHIT RG2 94 A1 2
Longridge Cl TLHT RG30 56 C6 2
Longroden La OVTN RG25 177 J5
Longs Ct WHCH RG28 169 H7 3
Longshot La BRAK RG12 79 F7
Longstock Cl CHAM RG24 145 J6
Long's Wy EWKG RG40 77 K7
Long Toll GOR/PANG RG8 27 F6
Longwater La EWKG RG40 116 D6
Longwater Rd BRAK RG12 99 K4
EWKG RG40 116 E6
HTWY RG27 134 E1
Longworth Av CALC RG31 55 G6
Lordsfield Gdns OVTN RG25 171 G4
Lordswood THLE RG7 127 K1
Lorne Pl READ RG1 2 D6
Lorne St READ RG1 2 D6
Loughborough BRAK RG12 100 B4 2
Loundyes Cl NTHA RG18 85 G3
Lovatt Cl CALC RG31 55 G6
Lovedean Ct BRAK RG12 100 B4
Lovegroves CHAM RG24 145 H7
Lovelace Rd BRAK RG12 99 F2
Love La KSCL RG20 124 A7
NWBY RG14 83 J1
ODIM RG29 180 C3
Lovell Cl HEN RG9 31 F3
Lovel Rd ASC SL5 81 J2
Loveridge Cl BSTK RG21 176 B2
Loverock Rd TLHT RG30 2 A3
TLHT RG30 56 D4
Love's Cl THLE RG7 90 E4
Loves Wd THLE RG7 110 E3
Lowbury BRAK RG12 11 M7
Lower Armour Rd CALC RG31 55 J4
Lower Broadmoor Rd
CWTH RG45 118 E4
Lower Brook St BSTK RG21 14 A5
READ RG1 3 H8
Lower Canes YTLY GU46 135 F3
Lower Chestnut Dr BSTK RG21 14 A9
Lower Church Rd SHST GU47 117 K7
Lower Common HTWY RG27 115 H7
Lower Earley Wy EARL RG6 75 H5
Lower Earley Way (North)
EARL RG6 75 J4
Lower Earley Way (West)
WHIT RG2 74 B7
Lower Elmstone Dr CALC RG31 55 H4
Lower Evingar Rd WHCH RG28 169 H7
Lower Farm Ct STHA RG19 84 E6
Lower Field Rd READ RG1 3 G9
Lower Henley Rd CAV/SC RG4 57 K3
Lower Meadow Rd WHIT RG2 8 A7
Lower Moor YTLY GU46 135 J4 3
Lower Mt READ RG1 8 A1
Lower Pool Rd HTWY RG27 133 G5
Lower Sandhurst Rd
EWKG RG40 117 F6
Lower Wy STHA RG19 84 E4
Lower Wokingham Rd
EWKG RG40 117 J2
Lower Wote St BSTK RG21 14 F4
Lowes Cl HEN RG9 32 A7
Lowfield Gn CAV/SC RG4 58 B1
Lowfield Rd CAV/SC RG4 44 A7
CAV/SC RG4 58 A1
Lowlands Rd KEMP RG22 175 F1
Lowther Cl WWKG RG41 76 E6
Lowther Rd WWKG RG41 76 D5
Loxwood EARL RG6 9 L8
Loxwood Av FLET GU13 167 F4
Loyalty La CHAM RG24 161 J5
Lucas Cl YTLY GU46 135 J4
Lucey Cl CALC RG31 55 G2 3
Luckley Pth EWKG RG40 97 H1
Luckley Rd WWKG RG41 97 G4
Luckley Wd WWKG RG41 97 G4
Luckmore Dr EARL RG6 9 H5
Ludlow BRAK RG12 99 J5
Ludlow Cl DEAN RG23 159 J6
NWBY RG14 84 D3 2
Ludlow Gdns DEAN RG23 159 J6
Luker Av HEN RG9 17 F7
Lulworth Rd WHIT RG2 73 K6 3
Lunds Farm Rd WODY RG5 59 K5
Lundy Cl CHAM RG24 160 E2
Lundy La TLHT RG30 56 D6
Lune Cl BSTK RG21 15 J5
Lupin Cl KEMP RG22 175 F4
Lupin Ride CWTH RG45 98 C7
Luscombe Cl CAV/SC RG4 58 A3
Lutman's Hvn WAR/TWY RG10 33 K6
Lutterworth Cl BNFD RG42 79 K5 8
Lutyens Cl CHAM RG24 161 G3
Lycroft Cl GOR/PANG RG8 25 F4
Lydbury BRAK RG12 100 C1
Lyde Cl DEAN RG23 174 A3
Lydford Rd READ RG1 8 C1
Lydney BRAK RG12 99 J5
Lyefield Ct CAV/SC RG4 43 J6
Lyford Rd BSTK RG21 14 F2
Lyme Gv CALC RG31 55 J4
Lymington Av YTLY GU46 135 H4
Lymington Cl KEMP RG22 175 G6
Lymington Ga CAV/SC RG4 43 F7
Lynch Hl WHCH RG28 169 H7
Lynch Hill Pk WHCH RG28 169 J7
The Lynch OVTN RG25 171 F4
WHCH RG28 169 J7
Lyndford Ter FLET GU13 167 G4
Lyndhurst Cl BRAK RG12 100 D1 2
Lyndhurst Dr KEMP RG22 175 H6
Lyndhurst Rd ASC SL5 101 K2
GOR/PANG RG8 25 F5
TLHT RG30 56 A4
Lyneham Rd CWTH RG45 118 C3
Lynmouth Rd READ RG1 3 H3
Lynton Cl WODY RG5 9 M2
Lynwood Cha BRAK RG12 79 K5
Lynwood Gdns HTWY RG27 163 K2
Lyon Cl STHA RG19 86 A5
Lyon Oaks BNFD RG42 79 J4
Lyon Rd CWTH RG45 118 D2
Lyon Sq TLHT RG30 56 B6
Lysander Cl WODY RG5 59 K5
Lytchet Minster Cl
BRAK RG12 100 C3 4
Lytham BRAK RG12 99 F4
Lytham Cl TLHT RG30 72 D2 2
Lytham End CALC RG31 55 G2 4
Lytham Rd WODY RG5 59 H6
Lytton Rd BSTK RG21 15 H5

M

Mabbs La HTWY RG27 149 H6
Macbeth Ct BNFD RG42 11 L1
Mace Cl EARL RG6 74 D5
Mackay Cl CALC RG31 71 K3
Macphail Cl EWKG RG40 77 K6
Macrae Rd YTLY GU46 135 H3
Madeira Cl CHAM RG24 160 E2
Madeley Rd FLET GU13 167 J5
Madingley BRAK RG12 99 J6
Magdalene Rd SHST GU47 119 G6
Magill Cl THLE RG7 93 J5 2
Magnolia Cl SHST GU47 118 E7 7
Magnolia Wy FLET GU13 167 H4
WWKG RG41 96 E2
Magnus Dr KEMP RG22 175 G5
Magpie Cl KEMP RG22 174 E4
NFNM GU10 183 J4 1
STHA RG19 85 G4
Magpie Wy CALC RG31 55 G7
Mahler Cl KEMP RG22 176 A4 1
Maiden Erlegh Dr EARL RG6 9 J3
Maidenhead Rd BNFD RG42 79 J1
EWKG RG40 77 K3
Maiden Pl EARL RG6 75 G4
Main Dr BNFD RG42 80 E5
Mainprize Rd BRAK RG12 11 L2
Main Rd TADY RG26 127 G3
Main St STHA RG19 105 F3
Maitland Rd READ RG1 2 D7
Maiwand Gdns TLHT RG30 55 J6 1
Maize La BNFD RG42 80 A4
Majendie Cl NWBY RG14 83 G2 3
Majestic Rd KEMP RG22 175 F7
Makepiece Rd BNFD RG42 79 J5
Maker Cl TLHT RG30 72 C1
Makins Rd HEN RG9 31 F3
Maldive Rd CHAM RG24 160 E2
Maldon Cl TLHT RG30 2 A8
Malham Fell BRAK RG12 10 D7
Malham Gdns KEMP RG22 175 G7
Malham Rd STHA RG19 85 H4
Mallard Cl EARL RG6 3 G9
KEMP RG22 174 E5
WAR/TWY RG10 60 D2
Mallard Ct NWBY RG14 12 C4
Mallard Rw READ RG1 3 H8
Mallard Wy THLE RG7 88 E4
YTLY GU46 135 G3 2
Mallory Av CAV/SC RG4 43 K6
Mallowdale Rd BRAK RG12 100 B5 3
Malone Rd WODY RG5 59 G7
Malshanger La DEAN RG23 173 K1
Malta Cl CHAM RG24 160 D2
Maltby Wy EARL RG6 74 C6
Malt Hl BNFD RG42 80 B1
Malthouse Cl FLET GU13 167 F6
Malthouse La READ RG1 2 F5
TADY RG26 127 G3
Maltings Pl READ RG1 3 H7
The Maltings TADY RG26 129 G7
Malvern Cl KEMP RG22 175 F1
WODY RG5 59 J7
Malvern Ct NWBY RG14 12 D7
READ RG1 4 B9
Malvern Wy WAR/TWY RG10 46 C5
Managua Cl CAV/SC RG4 58 A3
Manchester Rd READ RG1 4 D5
Mandeville Cl TLHT RG30 72 A1
Manea Cl EARL RG6 75 F6 2
Manley James Cl ODIM RG29 180 D1 1
Manners Rd WODY RG5 59 G6
Mannock Wy WODY RG5 60 A5
Manor Cl BNFD RG42 79 H5
KEMP RG22 175 F6
Manor Ct FLET GU13 167 H7
Manor Crs KSCL RG20 21 J7
Manor Farm La GOR/PANG RG8 54 B3
Manor Farm Rd WHIT RG2 7 J8
Manor House Dr ASC SL5 81 K5
Manor La CHAM RG24 161 J5
NTHA RG18 49 G4
NTHA RG18 84 D3
STHA RG19 106 E1
Manor Park Cl TLHT RG30 55 H7 2
Manor Park Dr EWKG RG40 116 C2 1
EWKG RG40 116 D2 2
YTLY GU46 135 J4
Manor Pl NWBY RG14 83 G2
Manor Rd CHAM RG24 143 K7
GOR/PANG RG8 24 E5
GOR/PANG RG8 40 B5
HEN RG9 31 G3
WWKG RG41 97 F5
Manor Wood Ga HEN RG9 31 K7
Manse La TADY RG26 127 G3
Mansell Ct WHIT RG2 8 D7
Mansell Dr NWBY RG14 103 F3
Mansfield Cl ASC SL5 81 G7 1
Mansfield Crs BRAK RG12 99 J4
Mansfield Pl ASC SL5 81 G7
Mansfield Rd KEMP RG22 175 K2
READ RG1 2 F9
WWKG RG41 96 E2
Man's Hl THLE RG7 91 H4
Mansion Dr HTWY RG27 133 G5
Manston Dr BRAK RG12 99 J4
Maple Cl CAV/SC RG4 29 H7
SHST GU47 118 A7
WWKG RG41 76 C3
Maple Ct GOR/PANG RG8 24 E5
Maple Crs BSTK RG21 160 C4
NWBY RG14 12 E1
Mapledene CAV/SC RG4 57 F2
Maple Dr CWTH RG45 118 D1 1
Mapledurham Dr
GOR/PANG RG8 41 H7
Mapledurham Vw CALC RG31 55 J3 1
Maple Gdns WHIT RG2 8 C7
YTLY GU46 135 J4
Maple Gv TADY RG26 126 E1
Maplehurst Cha KEMP RG22 175 G6
Maple La GOR/PANG RG8 38 E7
Marathon Cl WODY RG5 60 A5
Marbull Wy BNFD RG42 79 J4
Marchant Cl STHA RG19 104 C1 1
Marcheria Cl BRAK RG12 99 J4 2
Marchwood Av CAV/SC RG4 43 K4
Marconi Rd NWBY RG14 13 G2
Marefield EARL RG6 9 L7
Mareshall Av BNFD RG42 79 J4
Marfleet Cl EARL RG6 75 H4 3
Margaret Cl WHIT RG2 73 K7
Margaret Rd KEMP RG22 159 J7
Marigold Cl CWTH RG45 118 A1
KEMP RG22 175 F4
Mariners Cl TADY RG26 127 G3
Mariners La THLE RG7 68 D3
Marino Wy EWKG RG40 115 K2
Markby Wy EARL RG6 75 H4
Market Pl BSTK RG21 14 F6
HEN RG9 31 G1
READ RG1 3 J6
Market St BRAK RG12 10 F3
NWBY RG14 12 E5
Marks Rd WWKG RG41 77 F6
Marlborough Av READ RG1 8 B2
Marlborough Ct READ RG1 2 E9
Marlborough Gdns
DEAN RG23 174 A2 1
Marlborough Wy CALC RG31 71 G2 3
Marling Cl CALC RG31 55 H3 2
Marlowe Cl CHAM RG24 160 D3
The Marlowes NWBY RG14 83 J7
Marlow Rd HEN RG9 17 H7
Marl's La CHAM RG24 144 C6
Marlston Rd NTHA RG18 65 H1
Marmion Rd HEN RG9 31 H3
Marsack St CAV/SC RG4 57 K3
Marsden Ct WHCH RG28 170 D6 1
Marshall Cl GOR/PANG RG8 55 J1
Marshall Gdns BSTK RG21 14 F1
Marshalls Ct NWBY RG14 83 G2 4
Marshcourt CHAM RG24 161 G3
Marshland Sq CAV/SC RG4 43 J7
Marsh La HTWY RG27 134 E2
NTHA RG18 64 C2
NWBY RG14 12 E3
Marsh Rd NTHA RG18 85 K3
Marston Dr NWBY RG14 84 C2
Marston Wy ASC SL5 81 H7 2
Marten Pl CALC RG31 55 G2
Martin Cl BSTK RG21 160 D4
WODY RG5 59 H7
Martineau La WAR/TWY RG10 60 D6 1
Martins Dr WWKG RG41 77 G6
Martins La BRAK RG12 11 L5
Martins St EARL RG6 9 M9
The Martins STHA RG19 86 A5
Martins Wd CHAM RG24 145 G7 3
Maryland EWKG RG40 116 C1
Mary Md BNFD RG42 80 A4 1
Masefield Rd NTHA RG18 85 H3
Mason Cl YTLY GU46 135 K4 2
Mason St READ RG1 2 D5
Master Cl WODY RG5 60 A5
Mathias Wk KEMP RG22 175 J6
Matilda Dr KEMP RG22 175 G5 3
Matlock Rd CAV/SC RG4 57 F1
Matthews Cha BNFD RG42 79 G5
Matthews Cl STHA RG19 85 G4 2
Matthewsgreen Rd WWKG RG41 77 F6
Matthews Wy DEAN RG23 174 B3
Mattock Wy CHAM RG24 145 G7
Mawbray Cl EARL RG6 9 M6
Maw Cl KEMP RG22 176 A4 2
Maxine Cl SHST GU47 118 C7
Maxwell Cl WODY RG5 59 H5
Maybrick Cl SHST GU47 118 A7
Maybrook CHAM RG24 145 G6
May Cl CHAM RG24 161 K5
Mayfair TLHT RG30 55 J6
Mayfair Dr NWBY RG14 12 A7
Mayfield Av CALC RG31 71 G2
Mayfield Ct HTWY RG27 134 C1
Mayfield Dr CAV/SC RG4 57 K2
Mayfield Rdg DEAN RG23 175 G7
May Flds WWKG RG41 75 K5
Mayflower Cl CHAM RG24 161 F1
Mayflower Dr YTLY GU46 135 F2
The Maying WHIT RG2 93 J1 2
Maynard Cl NTHA RG18 85 H2
Maynard's Wd CHAM RG24 161 F1
Mayors La NWBY RG14 12 E5
Mayow Cl STHA RG19 86 A5
May Pk CALC RG31 71 K2
May Pl BSTK RG21 14 F6
Mays Cl EARL RG6 9 J1
Mays La EARL RG6 9 K3
Mays Rd EWKG RG40 97 K1
Mc Carthy Wy EWKG RG40 96 E7
Mccartney Wk KEMP RG22 175 H5
Mccrae's Wk WAR/TWY RG10 46 C2
Mcnair Cl EARL RG6 9 G9
EARL RG6 74 D5 2
Mead Cl CALC RG31 55 G7
Meadham La OVTN RG25 139 J7
Mead La GOR/PANG RG8 39 F6
Meadow Cl GOR/PANG RG8 25 F5 1
STHA RG19 85 H4
Meadow Crs KSCL RG20 21 K6
Meadowcroft Rd WHIT RG2 73 J6
Meadowland CHAM RG24 145 F7
Meadow La HTWY RG27 149 H4
Meadow Pound WHCH RG28 169 J7 1
Meadowridge KEMP RG22 175 H7
Meadow Rd BSTK RG21 176 B3
EARL RG6 75 G3
HEN RG9 31 H2
NWBY RG14 12 D9
READ RG1 2 F3
WWKG RG41 97 F2
Meadowside CALC RG31 55 G4 1
Meadowside Rd GOR/PANG RG8 40 C7
The Meadows HTWY RG27 146 A1
Meadowsweet Cl NTHA RG18 85 K3
Meadow Vw FLET GU13 167 F6 3
WHCH RG28 169 G7
WWKG RG41 76 C3
Meadow Wk WWKG RG41 97 F1
Meadow Wy BNFD RG42 79 H5
THLE RG7 70 C3
WWKG RG41 97 F2
The Mead CHAM RG24 161 J5
The Meadway TLHT RG30 55 K6
The Mearings TLHT RG30 91 K3
Measham Wy EARL RG6 9 L9
Meavy Gdns WHIT RG2 7 K8
Mede Cl OVTN RG25 171 J5
Medill Cl GOR/PANG RG8 26 D3 1
Medina Cl WWKG RG41 96 D1
Medina Gdns DEAN RG23 174 A3 3
Medonte Cl FLET GU13 167 J3 1
Medway Av DEAN RG23 174 A2
Medway Cl NTHA RG18 85 G2
WWKG RG41 76 E7 2
Medway Ct BSTK RG21 15 K5
Meitner Cl TADY RG26 129 G5
Melbourne Av WWKG RG41 76 B5
Meldreth Wy EARL RG6 75 F5
Meldrum Cl NWBY RG14 103 F2 1
Melford Gdns KEMP RG22 175 F2
Melford Gn CAV/SC RG4 44 B6 4
Melksham Cl EARL RG6 74 B6
Melling Cl EARL RG6 75 H3
Melody Cl WWKG RG41 76 B3
Melrose BRAK RG12 99 J6
Melrose Av EARL RG6 9 G2
Melrose Gdns WHIT RG2 95 H5
Membury Wk BRAK RG12 11 M8
BRAK RG12 100 C2 8
Memorial Av HEN RG9 45 H2
Memorial Rd HTWY RG27 163 K3
Mendip Cl KEMP RG22 175 F1
WAR/TWY RG10 60 A1
Mendip Dr CALC RG31 55 F7 2
Mendip Rd BRAK RG12 11 M9
BRAK RG12 100 B3
Menpes Rd CALC RG31 55 H1
Meon Cl TADY RG26 108 D7
Meon Rd DEAN RG23 174 A3
Mercer Cl KEMP RG22 159 H7
Merchants Pl READ RG1 3 H5
Mercury Av WWKG RG41 96 D1 13
Mereoak La THLE RG7 93 H2
Merivale FLET GU13 166 E3
Merlewood BRAK RG12 11 J9
Merlin Clove BNFD RG42 80 E4
Merlin Md KEMP RG22 174 E6
Mermaid Cl WWKG RG41 76 A4
Merriatt Cl BSTK RG21 176 C2
Merrileas Gdns KEMP RG22 175 F4
Merrivale Gdns WHIT RG2 7 K9
Merron Cl YTLY GU46 135 H4 4
Merrydown La CHAM RG24 161 H1 1
Merryfield CHAM RG24 145 F7
Merryhill Green La
WWKG RG41 76 C3 1
Merryman Dr CWTH RG45 118 A2
Merryweather Cl EWKG RG40 96 E6 2
Mersey Wy NTHA RG18 85 G2
Merthyr V CAV/SC RG4 43 H6
Merton Cl SHST GU47 119 G6
Merton Rd BSTK RG21 14 B2
Merton Rd North WHIT RG2 7 K9
Merton Rd South WHIT RG2 73 J5
Meteor Cl WODY RG5 59 K6
The Mews READ RG1 4 D8
TADY RG26 129 J7
Meyrick Dr NWBY RG14 103 F3
Michaelmas Cl YTLY GU46 135 J5
Micheldever Wy BRAK RG12 100 C4
Micklands Rd CAV/SC RG4 58 A1
Mickle Hl SHST GU47 118 B7
Middle Cl NWBY RG14 103 G1
Middlefields WAR/TWY RG10 46 D6
Middle Md HTWY RG27 163 K2 3
Middleton Ct NWBY RG14 84 D2
Middleton Gdns BSTK RG21 14 F1
Midlane Cl BSTK RG21 176 B2

Midsummer Meadow
CAV/SC RG4 43 G6 1
Midwinter Cl TLHT RG30 55 K5 1
Milbanke Ct BRAK RG12 10 B3
Milbanke Wy BRAK RG12 10 B3
Mildmay Ct ODIM RG29 180 D2
Milestone Av WAR/TWY RG10 45 J6
WAR/TWY RG10 59 K1
Milestone Crs WAR/TWY RG10 59 K1
Miles Wy WODY RG5 59 K6
Milkhouse Rd KSCL RG20 82 A1
Milkingpen La CHAM RG24 161 J4
Millard Cl BSTK RG21 160 A4
Millbank Crs WODY RG5 59 J7
Millbridge Rd YTLY GU46 135 G1
Mill Cl HEN RG9 16 C2
WWKG RG41 76 E7
Mill Cnr FARN GU14 151 K5 1
Milldown Av GOR/PANG RG8 25 F4
Milldown Rd GOR/PANG RG8 25 F4
Millers Cl GOR/PANG RG8 24 E4
Millers Gv CALC RG31 71 K2
Millers Rd TADY RG26 126 E1
Milley La WAR/TWY RG10 47 G4
Millford Rd READ RG1 2 F3
Mill Gn BNFD RG42 79 F5
CAV/SC RG4 3 L2
Millgreen La STHA RG19 106 A6
Millins Cl SHST GU47 118 E7
Mill La BRAK RG12 99 H3
CALC RG31 71 K2
CAV/SC RG4 42 D3
EARL RG6 75 H3
HEN RG9 31 J3
HEN RG9 45 K2
HTWY RG27 146 E3
KSCL RG20 123 F5
NWBY RG14 12 F4
ODIM RG29 164 A7
READ RG1 3 J7
TADY RG26 129 K6
THLE RG7 89 F4
THLE RG7 129 K4
WWKG RG41 75 J5
YTLY GU46 135 J1
Millmead WWKG RG41 77 F7
Millmere YTLY GU46 135 J2
Mill Reef Cl STHA RG19 84 E4
Mill Ride ASC SL5 81 G6 1
Mill Rd CAV/SC RG4 3 L2
CHAM RG24 159 H3
GOR/PANG RG8 25 F4
HEN RG9 46 A1
TLHT RG30 71 K4
Millworth La WHIT RG2 94 B3
Milman Cl BRAK RG12 80 D7 1
Milman Rd WHIT RG2 7 K2
Milsom Cl WHIT RG2 94 B2 2
Milton Cl BRAK RG12 99 J4
CHAM RG24 160 D3
HEN RG9 31 G1
Milton Ct EWKG RG40 77 G7
Milton Dr EWKG RG40 77 G7
Milton Gdns EWKG RG40 77 G7
Milton Rd EARL RG6 5 G7
EWKG RG40 97 G1
WWKG RG41 77 G7
Milton Wy WAR/TWY RG10 46 E7 1
Milward Gdns BRAK RG12 78 D7
Minchens La TADY RG26 129 F4
Minchin Gn BNFD RG42 78 D3 1
Minden Cl CHAM RG24 161 F1 3
WWKG RG41 96 D1 14
Ministry Rd STHA RG19 105 F3
Minley Gv FARN GU14 151 J7 1
Minley Rd FARN GU14 151 J6
Minstead Cl BRAK RG12 100 C1
TADY RG26 126 E3
Minstead Dr YTLY GU46 135 H4
Minster St READ RG1 3 H6
Mint Cl EARL RG6 8 F9
Minton Cl TLHT RG30 56 A5 3
Mire La WAR/TWY RG10 61 J1
Mistletoe Rd YTLY GU46 135 J5
Mitcham Cl WHIT RG2 7 K2
Mitchell Av HTWY RG27 149 H5
Mitchell Gdns KEMP RG22 175 H5 1
Mitchell Wy WODY RG5 59 K6
Mitford Cl WHIT RG2 74 A6
Moat Cl TADY RG26 129 F5
Modbury Gdns WHIT RG2 7 M7
Mohawk Wy WODY RG5 60 A6
Mole Rd WHIT RG2 95 J2
WWKG RG41 75 K6
Moles Cl EWKG RG40 97 J2
Mollison Cl WODY RG5 60 A5
Molly Millar Br WWKG RG41 97 G3
Molly Millar's La WWKG RG41 97 F2
Monachus La HTWY RG27 149 J3
Monarch Cl KEMP RG22 175 F6
Mongers Piece CHAM RG24 145 H6
Monksbarn WHIT RG2 8 B7
Monk Sherborne Rd
TADY RG26 142 C3
Monkshood Cl EWKG RG40 77 K7
Monks La NWBY RG14 103 H1
Monks Ri FLET GU13 166 E2 1
Monks Wy TLHT RG30 6 A2
Monkswood Cl NWBY RG14 103 G1 1
Monks Wood Crs TADY RG26 126 E2 5
Monktons La THLE RG7 111 H3
Mons Cl WWKG RG41 96 D1 15
Montacute Dr STHA RG19 86 A5 6
Montague Cl EWKG RG40 77 K7
Montague Pl BSTK RG21 14 F8
Montague St CAV/SC RG4 3 L1
READ RG1 4 A7
Montague Ter NWBY RG14 12 E9
Monteagle La YTLY GU46 135 G4
Montgomery Dr THLE RG7 93 J5
Montgomery Rd NWBY RG14 12 A9
Montpelier Dr CAV/SC RG4 44 B7 4
Montrose Cl FLET GU13 167 J3
Montserrat Pl CHAM RG24 160 D1 2
Montserrat Rd CHAM RG24 160 D1
Monument Cl NWBY RG14 103 G1 2
Moor Cl EWKG RG40 116 D1
SHST GU47 119 F7
Moor Copse Cl EARL RG6 9 K5
Moordale Av BNFD RG42 10 B1
BNFD RG42 79 F6
Moore Cl FLET GU13 167 H6
Moore Rd FLET GU13 167 H6
Moores Gn EWKG RG40 77 K6
Moorfoot Gdns KEMP RG22 175 G1
Moorhams Av KEMP RG22 175 F6
Moorhen Dr EARL RG6 74 E5
The Moorings BSTK RG21 15 K4
Moorlands Cl FLET GU13 167 J3 2
The Moors GOR/PANG RG8 40 C7
STHA RG19 85 J5
Moor Vw CHAM RG24 161 J4
Morden Cl BRAK RG12 100 C2 2
Morecambe Av CAV/SC RG4 43 F7
Moreleigh Cl WHIT RG2 73 K6 4
Moreton Cl FLET GU13 167 G7
Morgan Rd READ RG1 7 L1
Morgaston Rd TADY RG26 144 A3
Moriston Cl TLHT RG30 56 C5
Morlais CAV/SC RG4 43 G7
Morlands Av TLHT RG30 72 B1 1
Morley Cl YTLY GU46 135 G4
Morley Rd BSTK RG21 176 B3
Mornington Av EWKG RG40 96 E7
Mornington Cl TADY RG26 108 A7
Morpeth Cl WHIT RG2 7 M5
Morris St HTWY RG27 163 H3
Morse Rd KEMP RG22 159 K7
Mortimer Cl HTWY RG27 149 G6 1
WHIT RG2 73 K7
Mortimer Gdns TADY RG26 127 F2
Mortimer La BSTK RG21 14 D5
THLE RG7 111 J1
THLE RG7 129 J1
Moss Cl CAV/SC RG4 57 K2
Moulsham Copse La YTLY GU46 135 G2
Moulsham La YTLY GU46 135 G2
Moulshay La HTWY RG27 145 K5
Mountbatten Cl NWBY RG14 84 B2 2
Mountbatten Ri SHST GU47 118 A7
Mount Cl KSCL RG20 120 C3
NWBY RG14 12 E8
Mountfield GOR/PANG RG8 25 F4 1
Mount La BRAK RG12 11 G5
Mount Pleasant BRAK RG12 11 H5
HTWY RG27 149 J4
READ RG1 3 K9
SHST GU47 118 B7 4
TADY RG26 126 D1
WWKG RG41 97 F1
Mount Pleasant Gv READ RG1 3 K9
Mount Rd KSCL RG20 120 C2
NTHA RG18 85 J3
Mount St WHIT RG2 7 J1
The Mount CAV/SC RG4 57 G2
FLET GU13 167 H1
READ RG1 7 M1
Mount Vw HEN RG9 17 G7
Mourne Cl KEMP RG22 159 G7
Mowbray Dr TLHT RG30 56 B5
Mower Cl EWKG RG40 78 A7 1
Mowforth Cl GOR/PANG RG8 26 D2 1
Mozart Cl KEMP RG22 175 K4
Mud La HTWY RG27 115 J7
Muirfield Cl READ RG1 4 A7
Mulberry Cl CWTH RG45 118 D4
WODY RG5 59 H7
Mulberry Wy CHAM RG24 145 G7
THLE RG7 70 D4
Mulfords Hl TADY RG26 108 E7
TADY RG26 127 F1
Mull Cl DEAN RG23 173 K2
Mullins Cl BSTK RG21 160 C3
Mumbery Hl WAR/TWY RG10 46 D3
Munday Ct BNFD RG42 79 F5 2
Mundesley St READ RG1 3 J8
Munkle Marsh STHA RG19 86 B4 2
Munnings Cl BSTK RG21 15 J9
Munro Av WODY RG5 75 J2
Murdoch Rd EWKG RG40 97 H2
Murray Rd WWKG RG41 97 F1
Murrell Green Rd HTWY RG27 148 D5
Murrellhill La BNFD RG42 78 D6
Musgrave Cl KEMP RG22 175 J4 2
Mushroom Castle BNFD RG42 80 E4
Musket Copse CHAM RG24 161 H5
Mustard La CAV/SC RG4 59 H4
Muswell Cl THLE RG7 70 D3 4
Mutton Oaks BNFD RG42 78 E6
Myland Cl BSTK RG21 160 D3 1
Mylne Sq EWKG RG40 97 J1 1
Mylum Cl WHIT RG2 93 K1 5
Myrtle Cl CALC RG31 55 H2 1
THLE RG7 91 G4
Myton Wk THLE RG7 70 D3

N

Nabbs Hill Cl CALC RG31 71 H1 5
Napier Cl CWTH RG45 118 D4
Napier Rd CWTH RG45 118 D4
READ RG1 3 M4
Napoleon Dr DEAN RG23 159 H4
Napper Cl ASC SL5 81 F7
Narromine Dr CALC RG31 72 A2
Naseby BRAK RG12 99 J6
Naseby Ri NWBY RG14 84 C2
Nash Cl BSTK RG21 15 G1
EARL RG6 9 G5
Nash Gdns ASC SL5 81 G7
Nash Grove La EWKG RG40 96 D5
Nash Pk BNFD RG42 78 C4
Nately Rd OVTN RG25 179 G1
The Naylors THLE RG7 114 A2
Neals La CAV/SC RG4 28 C1
Neath Gdns TLHT RG30 56 A6 3
Neath Rd BSTK RG21 15 J4
Nelson Cl BRAK RG12 11 M3
Nelson Rd CAV/SC RG4 3 L1
Nelson's La WAR/TWY RG10 77 G1
Neptune Cl WWKG RG41 96 D1 16
Netherhouse Moor
FLET GU13 166 E4 2
Netherton BRAK RG12 10 D7
Netley Cl CAV/SC RG4 44 B6
Nettlecombe BRAK RG12 100 A3
Nevelle Cl BNFD RG42 78 E6
Neville Cl BSTK RG21 176 C2
Neville Dr STHA RG19 85 K4
Nevis Rd CALC RG31 55 J2 1
Newalls Ri WAR/TWY RG10 46 D2
Newark Rd BLKW GU17 151 K1
Newark St READ RG1 3 K8
New Barn Cl FLET GU13 166 E4 3
New Bath Rd WAR/TWY RG10 46 A7
WAR/TWY RG10 59 K1
Newbery Cl CALC RG31 55 J4 3
Newbold Rd NWBY RG14 83 G2 5
Newbolt Cl NTHA RG18 85 H2
New Bright St READ RG1 3 H8
Newbury Cl WAR/TWY RG10 60 A1
Newbury Hl NTHA RG18 36 A7
Newbury La KSCL RG20 21 J7
Newbury Rd KSCL RG20 123 K6
NTHA RG18 49 F7
WHCH RG28 169 J3
Newbury St WHCH RG28 169 H7
Newcastle Rd WHIT RG2 7 M4
Newchurch Rd TADY RG26 108 D7
Newell Gn BNFD RG42 79 K3
Newell's La CAV/SC RG4 42 C5
Newfield Rd CAV/SC RG4 29 G5
New Forest Ride BRAK RG12 100 B5
New Hl GOR/PANG RG8 41 H7
Newhurst Gdns BNFD RG42 80 A3
Newlands FLET GU13 167 H5
Newlands Av CAV/SC RG4 57 J2
Newlands Cl YTLY GU46 135 J4
New Lane Hl TLHT RG30 55 K7
TLHT RG30 72 A1
Newlyn Gdns WHIT RG2 7 K9
Newmarket Cl EARL RG6 75 G4
New Meadow ASC SL5 81 G6
New Mill La HTWY RG27 115 H6
New Mill Rd HTWY RG27 115 H6
Newnham La CHAM RG24 162 A3
HTWY RG27 163 F2
Newnham Pk HTWY RG27 163 J3 2
Newnham Rd HTWY RG27 163 G3
Newport Cl NWBY RG14 13 H2
Newport Rd NWBY RG14 13 H1
READ RG1 3 G2
New Rd ASC SL5 81 J5
BRAK RG12 11 K3
BSTK RG21 14 F6
CWTH RG45 118 D3
FLET GU13 167 J5
HEN RG9 45 K1
HTWY RG27 134 D2
HTWY RG27 149 H4
HTWY RG27 163 K2
NWBY RG14 13 G7
ODIM RG29 164 B7
READ RG1 8 B2
STHA RG19 104 C1
TADY RG26 126 E2
TADY RG26 127 H6
THLE RG7 91 J7
WAR/TWY RG10 46 C5
WAR/TWY RG10 46 E6
WWKG RG41 75 K6
New Road Hl THLE RG7 87 J4
New St BSTK RG21 14 E6
HEN RG9 31 H1
THLE RG7 130 B1
Newton Av CAV/SC RG4 44 A7
Newtown TADY RG26 108 D7
TADY RG26 126 D1
Newtown Gdns HEN RG9 31 H3
Newtown Rd HEN RG9 31 J3
NWBY RG14 12 E8
NWBY RG14 103 K2
New Wy THLE RG7 68 D4
New Wokingham Rd
CWTH RG45 118 B1
Niagara Rd HEN RG9 31 H3
Nicholas Rd HEN RG9 30 E3
Nideggan Cl STHA RG19 85 J4
Nightingale Crs BRAK RG12 11 H9
Nightingale Gdns CHAM RG24 159 H3
HTWY RG27 163 K2
Nightingale La THLE RG7 111 J2
Nightingale Ri OVTN RG25 171 J5
Nightingale Rd WODY RG5 9 M3
WODY RG5 75 G2
The Nightingales NWBY RG14 12 F9
Nightjar Cl NFNM GU10 183 J4
Nimrod Cl WODY RG5 59 K6
Nimrod Wy WHIT RG2 7 J2
Nine Mile Ride CWTH RG45 99 H6
EWKG RG40 116 C2
Nire Rd CAV/SC RG4 58 B2
Noakes Hl GOR/PANG RG8 37 J5
Norcot Rd TLHT RG30 55 K5
Norden Cl BSTK RG21 14 F2
Nores Rd WHIT RG2 74 A7
Norfolk Cha BNFD RG42 80 C5
Norfolk Cl WWKG RG41 96 D1
Norfolk Rd TLHT RG30 56 D6
Norlands NTHA RG18 85 H2
Norman Av HEN RG9 31 H2
Norman Keep BNFD RG42 80 C6
Norman Pl READ RG1 3 J3
Norman Rd CAV/SC RG4 57 K1
Normanstead Rd CALC RG31 55 H5
BSTK RG21 160 C3 2
Normanton Rd BSTK RG21 160 C4 3
Normay Ri NWBY RG14 103 F3
Normoor Rd THLE RG7 90 E6
Norn Hl BSTK RG21 15 H2
Norn Hill Cl BSTK RG21 15 H2
Norreys Av EWKG RG40 77 J7
Norris Rd EARL RG6 4 F8
Northam Cl EARL RG6 75 H3
Northampton Cl BRAK RG12 11 K6
Northbourne Cl EARL RG6 9 J8
Northbrook Copse
BRAK RG12 100 C4 2
Northbrook Rd CAV/SC RG4 44 A7
Northbrook St NWBY RG14 12 E3
Northbury Av WAR/TWY RG10 46 D7
Northbury La WAR/TWY RG10 46 D6
Northcott BRAK RG12 99 H6
Northcourt Av WHIT RG2 8 A3
Northcroft La NWBY RG14 12 B3
North Dr THLE RG7 70 C7
Northern Av NWBY RG14 83 K1
Northfield Av HEN RG9 31 K7
Northfield Cl FLET GU13 167 J5 2
Northfield End HEN RG9 17 G7
Northfield Rd FLET GU13 167 J5
HEN RG9 32 A7
HTWY RG27 146 A1
NTHA RG18 85 G3
READ RG1 3 G3
North Fryerne YTLY GU46 135 J1
North Gn BRAK RG12 11 K2
Northington Cl BRAK RG12 100 C4 3
North Lodge Dr ASC SL5 81 F7
North Rd ASC SL5 80 E6
North St CAV/SC RG4 57 J3
KSCL RG20 124 A7
READ RG1 2 F5
WDSR SL4 81 J1
Northumberland Av WHIT RG2 7 L4
WHIT RG2 73 K6
Northumberland Cl
BNFD RG42 80 C5 3
North View Rd TADY RG26 127 G2
North Wk THLE RG7 70 D2 4
North Warnborough St
ODIM RG29 180 A1
Northway NTHA RG18 85 H2
NWBY RG14 13 G6
WWKG RG41 76 D7
Northwood Dr NWBY RG14 13 J1
Norton Cl NWBY RG14 103 F2 2
Norton Ride CHAM RG24 161 G4
Norton Rd EWKG RG40 97 H2
READ RG1 4 D6
THLE RG7 113 K6
WODY RG5 75 J1
Norwich Dr WODY RG5 5 M5
Norwood Rd READ RG1 4 B6
Notton Wy EARL RG6 74 C6
Novello Cl KEMP RG22 175 J5
Nuffield Dr SHST GU47 119 G7
Nuffield Rd WHIT RG2 115 J1
Nugee Ct CWTH RG45 118 C3 1
Nuneaton BRAK RG12 100 B4
Nunhide La GOR/PANG RG8 54 E4
Nun's Acre GOR/PANG RG8 24 E4
Nursery Cl CHAM RG24 145 H7 4
HEN RG9 31 K7
HTWY RG27 163 K1 7
WAR/TWY RG10 60 D5
Nursery Gdns GOR/PANG RG8 41 G7
Nutbean La THLE RG7 114 C3
Nuthatch Cl NFNM GU10 183 J5
Nuthatch Dr EARL RG6 9 K3
Nuthurst BRAK RG12 11 L9
BRAK RG12 100 B3
Nut La WAR/TWY RG10 47 K6
Nutley BRAK RG12 99 H6
Nutley Cl YTLY GU46 135 J4
Nutmeg Cl EARL RG6 8 F9
Nutter's La WHIT RG2 94 D6

O

Oak Av SHST GU47 118 E7
Oak Cl DEAN RG23 174 A3
OVTN RG25 171 H5
Oakdale BRAK RG12 100 A4
Oakdale Cl CALC RG31 55 H5
Oakdene GOR/PANG RG8 26 E4 1
THLE RG7 91 F4
Oakdown Cl GOR/PANG RG8 40 D1
Oak Dr NWBY RG14 12 C6
THLE RG7 90 E5
WODY RG5 59 K7
Oaken Copse FLET GU13 167 J7
Oak End Wy THLE RG7 89 F3
Oakengates BRAK RG12 99 H6
Oaken Gv NWBY RG14 83 G7
Oakfield Rd TADY RG26 109 H7
Oakfields Cl KSCL RG20 122 E5
Oakham Cl CALC RG31 55 J3 2
Oak Hanger Cl HTWY RG27 164 A2 1
Oakland Rd WHCH RG28 169 H7
Oaklands NTHA RG18 64 B3
YTLY GU46 135 J3
Oaklands Cl ASC SL5 81 J5
Oaklands Dr ASC SL5 81 K5
WWKG RG41 97 F3
Oaklands La CWTH RG45 118 B2
Oaklands Pk WWKG RG41 97 F3
Oaklands Wy DEAN RG23 159 H5
Oaklea Dr HTWY RG27 115 H6
Oaklea Gdns TADY RG26 129 J7
Oakley Dr FLET GU13 167 H3
Oakley La DEAN RG23 173 K3
Oakley Rd CAV/SC RG4 57 G1
NWBY RG14 13 L1
TADY RG26 140 C7
Oakmead TADY RG26 129 F5
Oakridge Rd BSTK RG21 160 B4
Oakside Wy WHIT RG2 74 B6
Oaks Rd HEN RG9 31 K7
The Oaks BRAK RG12 11 J3
FLET GU13 166 E2
TADY RG26 126 D1
YTLY GU46 135 J4
Oak Tree Cl TADY RG26 108 E7 1
Oak Tree Copse CALC RG31 55 K2 2
Oak Tree Dr HTWY RG27 164 A1
Oak Tree Rd CALC RG31 55 J3
STHA RG19 85 K5
Oak Tree Wk GOR/PANG RG8 41 J7
Oaktree Wy SHST GU47 118 B7
Oak Vw CALC RG31 55 H5
Oak Wy WODY RG5 75 G2
Oakwood CHAM RG24 145 G7
FLET GU13 167 H7
Oakwood Rd BRAK RG12 11 M3
Oareborough BRAK RG12 11 M9
Oareborough La NTHA RG18 49 F3
Oasthouse Dr FARN GU14 151 K6
Oatlands Rd WHIT RG2 94 C2
Oban Cl DEAN RG23 173 K2
Oban Gdns WODY RG5 75 H2
O'bee Gdns TADY RG26 108 B7
Ochil Cl KEMP RG22 175 G1
Octavia BRAK RG12 99 H6
Octavian Cl KEMP RG22 175 G5
Oddfellows Rd NWBY RG14 12 D5
Odell Cl EARL RG6 74 E6
Odette Gdns TADY RG26 108 E7
Odiham Av CAV/SC RG4 44 B7
Odiham Rd HTWY RG27 114 A7
HTWY RG27 165 F4
NFNM GU10 183 G4
THLE RG7 113 K5
Officers Rw TADY RG26 129 J7
Ogmore Cl TLHT RG30 55 K6 4
Okingham Cl SHST GU47 118 E7 8
Old Acre La WAR/TWY RG10 46 A7
Old Barn Cl CAV/SC RG4 43 H6
Old Bath Rd CAV/SC RG4 5 M3
CAV/SC RG4 59 H3
NWBY RG14 12 C2
WAR/TWY RG10 59 K1
Oldberg Gdns KEMP RG22 176 A4 3
Old Bracknell Cl BRAK RG12 10 E5
Old Bracknell La East
BRAK RG12 10 E5
Old Bracknell La West
BRAK RG12 10 D5
Oldbury BRAK RG12 10 B5
Old Common Rd BSTK RG21 15 J7
Old Copse Gdns HEN RG9 29 G5
Oldcorne Hollow HTWY RG27 135 F4
Old Cove Rd FARN GU14 151 J7
Old Down Cl KEMP RG22 175 F3
Old Elm Dr TLHT RG30 55 J5 3
Old Farm Crs CALC RG31 55 H3 3
Old Farm Dr BRAK RG12 79 K5
Oldfield Cl EARL RG6 5 J8
Oldfield Vw HTWY RG27 149 H5 3
Old Forest Rd WWKG RG41 77 F4 1
Old Kempshott La KEMP RG22 175 F1
Old Lands Hl BRAK RG12 11 J1
Old La STHA RG19 107 F7
The Old La READ RG1 6 E2
Old Mill Ct WAR/TWY RG10 46 C7
Old Newtown Rd NWBY RG14 12 D7 1
The Old Orch CALC RG31 71 K2
Old Pharmacy Ct
CWTH RG45 118 D4 2
Old Potbridge Rd HTWY RG27 165 F2
Old Priory La BNFD RG42 80 A4
Old Pumphouse Cl FLET GU13 167 J1
Old Reading Rd BSTK RG21 15 G4
Old Sawmill La CWTH RG45 118 D2
Old School Cl FLET GU13 167 H2 1
HTWY RG27 149 J4 4
Old School La YTLY GU46 135 H3
Old School Rd HTWY RG27 163 H3
Oldstead BRAK RG12 100 A3
Old St KSCL RG20 34 B7
NTHA RG18 48 C4
NTHA RG18 48 E5
Old Vyne La TADY RG26 142 C1
Old Welmore YTLY GU46 135 K4
Old Whitley Wood La WHIT RG2 93 K1
Old Wokingham Rd
CWTH RG45 118 D1
EWKG RG40 98 C5
Old Woosehill La WWKG RG41 76 E7
Old Worting Rd KEMP RG22 159 H7
Oleander Cl CWTH RG45 118 A1
Oliver Dr CALC RG31 71 G1
Oliver Rd ASC SL5 101 K2
Olivers Cl TADY RG26 129 H7
Oliver's La TADY RG26 129 H5
Oliver's Wk CHAM RG24 161 G4
Ollerton BRAK RG12 99 H6
Omer's Ri THLE RG7 90 E4
Onslow Cl CHAM RG24 161 F2
Onslow Dr ASC SL5 81 K5
Onslow Gdns CAV/SC RG4 57 K2
Opal Wy WWKG RG41 76 D7 5
Opladen Wy BRAK RG12 99 K3
Oracle Pkwy EARL RG6 4 F4
Orbit Cl EWKG RG40 116 E2
Orchard Av CAV/SC RG4 29 F6
Orchard Cha WAR/TWY RG10 60 E6
Orchard Cl CALC RG31 55 G1
EWKG RG40 97 J1
HEN RG9 31 H2
HEN RG9 45 H2
NTHA RG18 49 H5
NWBY RG14 84 B2
THLE RG7 87 K5
THLE RG7 93 J5
Orchard Coombe
GOR/PANG RG8 40 C1
Orchard Ct BRAK RG12 11 G4
Orchardene NWBY RG14 13 H2
Orchard Est WAR/TWY RG10 46 D7
Orchard Fld CAV/SC RG4 28 D6 1
Orchard Gv CAV/SC RG4 58 B1
Orchard Pl EWKG RG40 97 H1
Orchard Rd KEMP RG22 159 H7
THLE RG7 111 G3
WAR/TWY RG10 60 E6
Orchard St READ RG1 3 H8
The Orchard OVTN RG25 171 H4
TADY RG26 127 G1
THLE RG7 70 D2 5
Oregon Av CALC RG31 55 H2
Oregon Wk EWKG RG40 116 C1 2
Orion BRAK RG12 99 H6
Orkney Cl CALC RG31 71 K2
CHAM RG24 160 E2
Ormathwaites Cnr
BNFD RG42 80 B5 12
Ormonde Rd WWKG RG41 97 F2
Ormsby St READ RG1 2 D6
Orrin Cl TLHT RG30 56 B5
Orts Rd READ RG1 3 M6
Orville Cl WODY RG5 59 K6
Orwell Cl CAV/SC RG4 57 G1
Osborne Cl BSTK RG21 14 C1
BSTK RG21 160 B4
Osborne Dr FLET GU13 167 J4

Osborne La BNFD RG42 79 K3
Osborne Rd EWKG RG40 97 H1
TLHT RG30 56 C5
Osborn Wy HTWY RG27 164 A3
Osler Cl TADY RG26 129 G6
Osman's Cl BNFD RG42 80 E5
Osprey Cl KEMP RG22 174 E3
Osprey Rd KEMP RG22 174 E3
Osterley Cl EWKG RG40 98 A2 1
Osterley Dr CAV/SC RG4 44 B6
Oswald Cl BNFD RG42 80 A4 2
Otterbourne Crs TADY RG26 126 E3
Otter Cl CWTH RG45 118 B1
Overbridge Sq NWBY RG14 13 M4
NWBY RG14 84 D5 1
Overbury Av WWKG RG41 76 E5
Overdown Rd CALC RG31 55 J2
Overlanders End CALC RG31 55 K2 3
Owen Rd NWBY RG14 84 A1
Owl Cl WWKG RG41 96 D2 3
Owston EARL RG6 9 L7
Oxenhope BRAK RG12 10 C8
Oxford Rd CALC RG31 41 H7
CALC RG31 55 J1
KSCL RG20 48 B4
NWBY RG14 12 D1
NWBY RG14 83 J2
READ RG1 2 F6
SHST GU47 119 F6
TLHT RG30 2 B5
TLHT RG30 56 C5
WWKG RG41 97 F1
Oxford St CAV/SC RG4 57 H3
NWBY RG14 12 D2
Oyster Cl KEMP RG22 175 F5

P

Pack And Prime La HEN RG9 31 F1
Packenham Rd BSTK RG21 14 B7
Pack La DEAN RG23 174 A1
KEMP RG22 175 F2
Packman Dr WAR/TWY RG10 46 C6 2
Paddick Cl CAV/SC RG4 59 H2
Paddick Dr EARL RG6 75 G5
Paddock Ct HTWY RG27 149 H5 4
Paddockfields CHAM RG24 161 J4
Paddock Hts WAR/TWY RG10 60 D1
Paddock Rd CAV/SC RG4 4 A2
KEMP RG22 175 J1
NWBY RG14 12 D8
The Paddock BRAK RG12 11 H6
CWTH RG45 118 B2
HTWY RG27 149 J3
KSCL RG20 123 K7
NWBY RG14 13 K5
Padstow Gdns WHIT RG2 7 K9
Padwick Cl BSTK RG21 14 C7
Padworth La THLE RG7 89 H4
Padworth Rd THLE RG7 90 D7
Page's Cft EWKG RG40 97 J2
Pages Orch CAV/SC RG4 29 F6
Paice Gn EWKG RG40 77 J7
Paices Hl THLE RG7 108 D4
Painters Pightle HTWY RG27 163 J2
Pakenham Rd BRAK RG12 100 A5
Palace Ga ODIM RG29 180 C1
Pale La HTWY RG27 150 C6
HTWY RG27 166 B1
Palmera Av CALC RG31 71 H2 7
Palmer Cl BSTK RG21 160 D3
EWKG RG40 98 B7
Palmer Park Av EARL RG6 4 F8
Palmer School Rd EWKG RG40 97 H1
Palmer's La THLE RG7 91 F5
THLE RG7 92 B4
Palmerstone Rd EARL RG6 5 H7
Pamber Heath Rd TADY RG26 127 G1
Pamber Rd THLE RG7 109 K7
Pangbourne Hl GOR/PANG RG8 40 B7
Pangbourne Rd GOR/PANG RG8 39 H7
GOR/PANG RG8 53 F1
Pangbourne St TLHT RG30 56 C5
Pankhurst Dr BRAK RG12 100 A3
Pankridge St NFNM GU10 182 E5
Pantile Dr HTWY RG27 164 B2
Pantings La KSCL RG20 120 C3
Papermakers OVTN RG25 171 J5
Paprika Cl EARL RG6 8 F9
The Parade TADY RG26 108 E7 2
WODY RG5 59 J5
Paradise Rd HEN RG9 31 F2
Paradise Wy THLE RG7 67 K7
Pardown DEAN RG23 174 A5
Park Av CHAM RG24 161 J6
NTHA RG18 85 J3
Park Cl CAV/SC RG4 29 H5
DEAN RG23 173 K2
Parkcorner La WHIT RG2 95 J1
Park Crs TLHT RG30 56 B7
Park End NWBY RG14 12 F2
Parker's La BNFD RG42 80 E1
Parkfields YTLY GU46 135 J4
Park Gdns BSTK RG21 15 H8
Park Hl FLET GU13 167 G7
Parkhill Dr CALC RG31 55 J3 3
Parkhouse La TLHT RG30 2 A8
Parkland Dr BRAK RG12 11 M2
Park La BNFD RG42 79 F5 3
CALC RG31 55 H6
CHAM RG24 161 J6
EWKG RG40 115 K5
GOR/PANG RG8 27 K5
NTHA RG18 85 J2
THLE RG7 111 H6
THLE RG7 112 C6
WAR/TWY RG10 60 A2
Park Pl FLET GU13 167 G6
Park Rd BRAK RG12 11 J2
EWKG RG40 97 G1
HEN RG9 31 H2
Parkside HEN RG9 31 F1
Parkside Rd BSTK RG21 15 G8
NTHA RG18 85 J2
TLHT RG30 2 A8
Park St NWBY RG14 12 E2
Park View Dr North
WAR/TWY RG10 45 K6
Park View Dr South
WAR/TWY RG10 45 K7
Park Wk GOR/PANG RG8 41 J7 3
Park Wall La GOR/PANG RG8 38 E4
Park Wy NWBY RG14 12 E2
Parkway CWTH RG45 118 B3
Parkway Dr CAV/SC RG4 59 G2
Parkwood Cl CHAM RG24 145 G6 2
Parsley Cl EARL RG6 8 F9
Parsons Cl FLET GU13 167 G6
NWBY RG14 12 A5
WHIT RG2 115 K1
Parthia Cl READ RG1 3 H8
Part La THLE RG7 113 K5
Partridge Av YTLY GU46 135 G3
Partridge Cl NFNM GU10 183 J4 2
Partridge Dr CALC RG31 55 G7
Pasture Cl EARL RG6 74 E6
Paterson Cl KEMP RG22 175 H5
Patrick Gdns BNFD RG42 80 B5
Patrick Rd READ RG1 3 J1
Patriot Pl READ RG1 3 M6
Patten Ash Dr EWKG RG40 77 K7
Patten Av YTLY GU46 135 H4
Pattinson Rd WHIT RG2 94 A1 3
Paulet Pl CHAM RG24 161 J5
Paul's Fld HTWY RG27 134 D1
Pavenham Cl EARL RG6 74 D6
Pavy Cl STHA RG19 86 A5
Pawmers Md FLET GU13 183 F1
Paxton Cl KEMP RG22 175 G5 5
Payley Dr EWKG RG40 77 K6
Paynes Cl STHA RG19 123 K1
Paynesdown Rd STHA RG19 85 G4
Peachey Dr STHA RG19 86 A5
Peach St EWKG RG40 97 H1
Peacock La BRAK RG12 98 E2
Pearce's Orch HEN RG9 17 G7
Pearson Rd CAV/SC RG4 59 G2
Pearson Wy WODY RG5 75 H1
Pear Tree Av FLET GU13 167 G1 2
Pear Tree La NWBY RG14 84 B2
Pease Hl THLE RG7 67 G6
Peatmoor Cl FLET GU13 167 F1
Peat Moor Cl FLET GU13 167 F1 1
Peddlars Gv YTLY GU46 135 K3
Peel Cl CAV/SC RG4 58 A3
Peel Ct HTWY RG27 149 H4 2
Peel Gdns KSCL RG20 123 K6
Pegasus Cl STHA RG19 85 F3
Pegasus Ct CALC RG31 55 H6 2
Peggotty Pl SHST GU47 119 F6 3
Peg's Gn TLHT RG30 56 C6 3
Peg's Green Cl TLHT RG30 56 C7 1
Pelham Cl CHAM RG24 161 J6
Pelican La NWBY RG14 12 E2
Pelican Rd TADY RG26 109 H6
Pell St READ RG1 3 J9
Pelton Rd BSTK RG21 14 B3
Pemberton Gdns CALC RG31 71 J2
Pembroke BRAK RG12 99 G5
Pembroke Cl THLE RG7 91 H4
Pembroke Pl CAV/SC RG4 57 K2
Pembroke Rd DEAN RG23 159 G6 1
NWBY RG14 12 D3
Pemerton Rd BSTK RG21 15 H1
Pendals Cl NTHA RG18 36 A7
Pendennis Av CAV/SC RG4 44 B6
Pendennis Cl DEAN RG23 159 G5
Pendine Pl BRAK RG12 99 J3 2
Pendlebury BRAK RG12 99 H5
Pendred Rd WHIT RG2 93 K1
Penn Cl CAV/SC RG4 43 H6
Pennfields WAR/TWY RG10 46 D6
Pennine Cl CALC RG31 55 G7 3
Pennine Wy KEMP RG22 175 G1
WAR/TWY RG10 60 A1
Penn Rd NWBY RG14 83 G2
Pennypiece GOR/PANG RG8 25 F4
Pennyroyal Ct READ RG1 3 G9
Penny's Hatch KSCL RG20 124 B7
Penrith Rd BSTK RG21 14 C6
Penroath Av TLHT RG30 56 D7
Penrose Av WODY RG5 59 H7
Penrose Cl NWBY RG14 83 J2
Pensford Cl CWTH RG45 118 C1
Pentland Cl KEMP RG22 175 G1
TLHT RG30 72 A1 3
Penwood Gdns EWKG RG40 98 E4
Penwood Hts KSCL RG20 120 D1
Penwood Rd KSCL RG20 103 F5
Peppard Hl HEN RG9 29 G3
Peppard La HEN RG9 31 G4
Peppard Rd CAV/SC RG4 29 H6
CAV/SC RG4 43 K5
CAV/SC RG4 57 K1
Pepper La EARL RG6 8 C4
Peregrine Cl BRAK RG12 10 F9
BRAK RG12 99 J3 3
WWKG RG41 96 E2 3
Periam Cl HEN RG9 31 F3
Perkins Wy WWKG RG41 97 F2
Perry Dr FLET GU13 166 E2
Perryhill Dr SHST GU47 118 A7
Perry Oaks BRAK RG12 11 M4
Perry Wy BRAK RG12 11 M3
Perseverance Hl HEN RG9 30 D6
Pershore Rd CHAM RG24 160 C2
Perth Cl WODY RG5 59 K4
Peterhouse Cl SHST GU47 119 G6
Petersfield Cl CHAM RG24 145 J6 1
Petrel Cl WWKG RG41 96 D2 4
Petrel Cft KEMP RG22 175 F4 5
Petty's Brook Rd CHAM RG24 145 G6
Petunia Cl KEMP RG22 175 F4
Petworth Av CALC RG31 72 A3 2
Petworth Cl KEMP RG22 175 G6 1
Pevensey Av CAV/SC RG4 44 B7
Pewsey V BRAK RG12 100 C3
Pheaben's Fld TADY RG26 129 F6 1
Pheasant Cl KEMP RG22 174 E4
WWKG RG41 76 B5
Pheasant Copse FLET GU13 166 E1
Pheby Rd KEMP RG22 175 J2
Phillimore Rd CAV/SC RG4 43 K4
Phillips Cl WODY RG5 60 A4
Phoebe Ct READ RG1 3 H9
Phoenix Cl WWKG RG41 96 D1 7
Phoenix Ct HTWY RG27 149 G6
KSCL RG20 124 A7
Phoenix Park Ter BSTK RG21 14 E3
Phoenix Ter HTWY RG27 149 G6
Phyllis Court Dr HEN RG9 17 H7
Pickering BRAK RG12 10 D8
Picket Post Cl BRAK RG12 100 D1 3
Picketts La GOR/PANG RG8 53 H1
Pickwell Cl EARL RG6 9 M8
Picton Wy CAV/SC RG4 57 J1
Piercefield CALC RG31 71 G2
Pierce's Hl CALC RG31 55 H4
Pigeon Cl TADY RG26 129 H7
Pigeonhouse La WDSR SL4 81 H1
Pigeons Farm Rd STHA RG19 104 C1
Piggott's Rd CAV/SC RG4 3 M2
Pigott Rd EWKG RG40 77 J6
Pikeshaw Wy CALC RG31 55 H3 4
Pike St NWBY RG14 13 H1
Pilcot Rd HTWY RG27 166 C5
Pimento Dr EARL RG6 8 F9
Pimpernel Pl NTHA RG18 86 A3 1
Pimpernel Wy CHAM RG24 161 G4
Pincents La CALC RG31 71 F2
THLE RG7 71 F1
Pinchcut THLE RG7 91 F4
Pinchington La NWBY RG14 103 K1 1
Pindar Pl NWBY RG14 84 D2 2
Pine Croft Rd WWKG RG41 97 F5
Pine Dr EWKG RG40 117 F1
THLE RG7 110 E2
Pinefields Cl CWTH RG45 118 C3 2
Pine Gv FLET GU13 167 J6
WAR/TWY RG10 46 C7
Pinehill Rd CWTH RG45 118 C4
Pinehurst TADY RG26 126 E2
Pine Rdg NWBY RG14 84 B2
Pine Ridge Rd THLE RG7 91 F5
Pines Rd FLET GU13 167 G1
The Pines WAR/TWY RG10 46 D5
Pinetree Ct CAV/SC RG4 43 H7 1
Pinewood Av CWTH RG45 118 D2
Pinewood Cl TADY RG26 108 A7
Pinewood Dr KSCL RG20 103 K6
Pinewood Hl FLET GU13 167 H1
Pingewood Cl TLHT RG30 72 B5 1
Pingewood Rd North TLHT RG30 72 B4
Pingewood Rd South
TLHT RG30 72 C7
Pinkerton Rd KEMP RG22 175 H2
Pinks La TADY RG26 108 B7
Pinnell Cl KEMP RG22 175 F6
Pintail Cl KEMP RG22 174 E5 2
Pipers Cft FLET GU13 167 H7 1
Pipers La STHA RG19 86 A6
Pipers Wy STHA RG19 86 B5
Pipit Cl STHA RG19 85 G4
Pipsons Cl YTLY GU46 135 J3
Pitcairn Cl CHAM RG24 160 D1
Pitch Pl BNFD RG42 78 E3 2
Pitcroft Av EARL RG6 5 G9
Pitfield La THLE RG7 111 H4
Pitford Rd WODY RG5 59 J5
Pither Rd ODIM RG29 180 B4
Pitman Cl KEMP RG22 175 G2
Pittard Rd BSTK RG21 14 B8
Pitts Cl BNFD RG42 78 D4 3
Pitt's La EARL RG6 5 K6
Plantagenet Pk BNFD RG42 80 C6 3
Plantation Cl NTHA RG18 64 E1
Plantation Rd TADY RG26 108 B6
Players Gn WODY RG5 75 H1 1
Playhatch Rd CAV/SC RG4 44 D7
Play Platt THLE RG7 70 C2
Pleasant Hl TADY RG26 126 E1
Ploughlands BNFD RG42 10 A1
Plough La EWKG RG40 78 A7
HEN RG9 45 H3
HTWY RG27 132 E6
Plough Rd YTLY GU46 135 K2
Plover Cl KEMP RG22 175 F3
WWKG RG41 96 E2 7
Plowden Wy HEN RG9 45 H3
Plumpton Rd NWBY RG14 13 J8
Plumtrees EARL RG6 9 K8
Plymouth Av WODY RG5 9 M1
Plympton Cl EARL RG6 75 H3
Pocket Cl BRAK RG12 78 E7 4
Poffley Pl STHA RG19 86 B4 3
Pointers Cl KSCL RG20 48 A3 1
Poland La ODIM RG29 164 D5
Polehampton Cl WAR/TWY RG10 60 C1
Polkerris Wy FLET GU13 167 J7 1
Pollardrow Av BNFD RG42 10 A2
Pollards Wy CALC RG31 71 H2
Polmear Cl FLET GU13 167 J7
Polsted Rd CALC RG31 55 J4
Polyanthus Wy CWTH RG45 98 C7
Pond Cl NWBY RG14 103 G1
OVTN RG25 171 H6
Pond Cft YTLY GU46 135 K3
Pond End Rd CAV/SC RG4 29 H5
Pond Head La WODY RG5 75 G2
Pond La CAV/SC RG4 42 A6
NTHA RG18 49 H6
Pond Moor Rd BRAK RG12 10 E9
Pond Rd TADY RG26 129 H7
Pondtail Cl FLET GU13 167 K3
Pondtail Gdns FLET GU13 167 K3
Pondtail Rd FLET GU13 167 K3
Pondview Cl FLET GU13 167 K1
Poole Cl TLHT RG30 56 A6
Pool Rd HTWY RG27 149 H3
Poors Farm Rd CHAM RG24 162 B3
Popes Hl KSCL RG20 123 K7
Popeswood Rd BNFD RG42 78 E6
Popham Cl BRAK RG12 100 C3 5
Poplar Av TLHT RG30 72 A1 4
Poplar Cl HTWY RG27 146 A1
TADY RG26 126 A1
Poplar Gdns WHIT RG2 8 D9
Poplar La WAR/TWY RG10 76 D3
WWKG RG41 76 C3
Poplar Pl NWBY RG14 83 K1
The Poplars ASC SL5 101 K3
Popley Wy CHAM RG24 160 D2
Poppy Dr NTHA RG18 86 A3
Poppy Flds CHAM RG24 161 H3
Poppy Pl EWKG RG40 97 G1
Poppy Wy CALC RG31 71 H1
Porchester ASC SL5 101 K2
Porchester Rd NWBY RG14 12 E8
Porchfield Cl EARL RG6 9 H9
Porlock Cl STHA RG19 85 J5 4
Porlock Pl CALC RG31 71 H2 3
Portacre Ri BSTK RG21 14 A8
Porter Cl EARL RG6 75 F6 10
ODIM RG29 180 B4 2
Porter End NWBY RG14 13 H9
Porter Rd KEMP RG22 176 A3
Portia Gv BNFD RG42 11 M1
Portiswood Cl TADY RG26 127 G1 2
Portland Dr FLET GU13 167 G7
Portland Gdns TLHT RG30 55 H6
Portman Cl BNFD RG42 10 C2
Portman Rd TLHT RG30 56 C4
Portmeirion Gdns TLHT RG30 56 A4 3
Portrush Cl WODY RG5 59 G7
Portway TADY RG26 108 A7
THLE RG7 113 K6
Portway Cl READ RG1 2 D9
Portway Pl DEAN RG23 159 G6
Post Horn La HTWY RG27 147 H5
Post Horn Pl CALC RG31 72 A2 3
Posting House Ms NWBY RG14 12 B1
Post Office La TLHT RG30 91 H2
Potbridge Rd ODIM RG29 164 E3
Potkiln La GOR/PANG RG8 26 D5
Pot La CHAM RG24 162 C3
Potters La HTWY RG27 130 C6
Pottery Rd TLHT RG30 55 K4
Poultons Cl OVTN RG25 171 H6
Poultons Rd OVTN RG25 171 H5
Pound Cl TADY RG26 129 F6
Poundfield Wy WAR/TWY RG10 60 E2
Pound La CAV/SC RG4 59 G2
KSCL RG20 121 H3
NWBY RG14 83 G3
STHA RG19 85 F4
WAR/TWY RG10 77 G1
Pound Meadow HTWY RG27 146 B2
Pound Rd OVTN RG25 171 J5
Pound St NWBY RG14 12 D6
Poveys Md KSCL RG20 124 B7
Poyle Gdns BRAK RG12 11 J1
Poynings Crs BSTK RG21 176 D2
Poyntz Rd OVTN RG25 171 H4
Prescott BRAK RG12 99 G5
Preston Pl NWBY RG14 84 C2 2
Preston Rd WHIT RG2 7 J2
Price Gdns BNFD RG42 79 J4 1
Prides Crossing ASC SL5 81 K5
Priest Av EWKG RG40 98 A2
Priest Hl CAV/SC RG4 57 H2
Priestley Rd CHAM RG24 159 K4
Priestwood Av BNFD RG42 10 A1
Priestwood Court Rd
BNFD RG42 10 B1
Primrose Cl GOR/PANG RG8 41 H7 2
Primrose Dr HTWY RG27 149 H3
Primrose Gdns KEMP RG22 175 G7
Primrose La WWKG RG41 76 B3
Primrose Wk BRAK RG12 99 K3
Primrose Wy SHST GU47 118 C7
Prince Albert Dr ASC SL5 101 G2
Prince Andrew Wy ASC SL5 81 G7
Prince Consort Dr ASC SL5 101 G2
Prince Dr SHST GU47 118 B7
Prince Hold Rd STHA RG19 85 F4
Prince of Wales Av TLHT RG30 2 A6
Princes' Crs KEMP RG22 175 K1
Princess Marina Dr EWKG RG40 95 K6
WHIT RG2 95 J7
WHIT RG2 115 J1
Prince's St READ RG1 3 M7
Prince William Dr CALC RG31 55 H4
Priors Cl KSCL RG20 124 A7 4
Prior's Ct READ RG1 3 J8
Priors Court Rd NTHA RG18 65 H5
Priors Keep FLET GU13 167 K3
Priors Rd TADY RG26 108 D7
Priors Wd CWTH RG45 117 J4
Priory Av CAV/SC RG4 57 H3
Priory Cl FLET GU13 166 E3
Priory Ct WWKG RG41 76 B3
Priory Gdns CHAM RG24 161 J4
Priory La BRAK RG12 79 K5
HTWY RG27 149 H6
WHCH RG28 170 B5
Priory Pl NWBY RG14 104 A2
Priory Rd ASC SL5 80 E6
NWBY RG14 12 E8
The Priory WWKG RG41 76 B3 1
Priory Wk BRAK RG12 100 C2 10
Pritchard Cl STHA RG19 104 C1 2
Privet Cl EARL RG6 74 E5
Privett Cl CHAM RG24 161 H3
Proctors Rd EWKG RG40 98 A1
Promenade Rd READ RG1 3 G1
Prospect Pl NWBY RG14 12 E7
Prospect St CAV/SC RG4 57 H3
READ RG1 2 E7
Provident Wy BSTK RG21 14 E4
Pudding Hl WAR/TWY RG10 33 J5
Puffers Wy NWBY RG14 12 A5
Puffin Cl KEMP RG22 174 E6
Pump La THLE RG7 92 D5
Purbrook Ct BRAK RG12 100 B4
Purbrook Rd TADY RG26 126 D1
Purcell Cl KEMP RG22 176 A3
Purcell Rd CWTH RG45 118 C1
Purfield Dr WAR/TWY RG10 46 D2
Purley La GOR/PANG RG8 41 H7
Purley Ri GOR/PANG RG8 40 E7
Purley Village GOR/PANG RG8 41 H7
Purley Wy GOR/PANG RG8 40 D7
Pursers Farm THLE RG7 93 J4 1
Purslane EWKG RG40 97 J2
Puttenham Rd CHAM RG24 145 H7
Pyegrove Cha BRAK RG12 100 B5 6
Pyotts Copse CHAM RG24 161 H2
Pyotts Ct CHAM RG24 161 H2
Pyotts Hl CHAM RG24 161 H2

Q

Quadrant Ct BRAK RG12 11 L5
Qualitas BRAK RG12 99 G6
Quantock Av CAV/SC RG4 44 A7
Quantock Cl WAR/TWY RG10 60 A1 2
The Quantocks STHA RG19 85 J5
Quarrington Cl STHA RG19 85 K5
Quarry La HEN RG9 31 K7
YTLY GU46 135 K4
Quartz Cl WWKG RG41 76 C7
Queen Annes Ga CAV/SC RG4 57 K2
Queen Cl HEN RG9 31 H2
Queen Mary Av BSTK RG21 14 F2
Queen Mary Cl FLET GU13 167 G1
Queensborough Dr CAV/SC RG4 43 F7
Queen's Cottages READ RG1 3 K6
The Queen's Dr EARL RG6 8 B3
Queens Pine BRAK RG12 100 B4
Queen's Pl ASC SL5 101 K1
Queens Ride CWTH RG45 118 B1
Queen's Rd BSTK RG21 14 B4
CAV/SC RG4 3 K2
FLET GU13 167 H4
KSCL RG20 124 B7
NWBY RG14 13 G6
ODIM RG29 180 B1 1
READ RG1 3 K6
Queen St CAV/SC RG4 57 H2
HEN RG9 31 H2
Queensway CAV/SC RG4 44 A6
Queen Victoria St READ RG1 3 J6
Quelm La BNFD RG42 79 J4
Quentin Rd WODY RG5 59 G7
Quilter Rd KEMP RG22 175 J3
Quince Tree Wy HTWY RG27 164 A2
Quintilis BRAK RG12 99 G6

R

Rachaels Lake Vw
BNFD RG42 80 B5 13
Rackstraw Rd SHST GU47 118 E7
Radbourne Rd CALC RG31 71 J2
Radcliffe Wy BNFD RG42 79 F6
Radcot Cl WODY RG5 59 H4
Radford Gdns BSTK RG21 176 A2
Radical Ride EWKG RG40 116 E1
Radnor Cl HEN RG9 31 H1
Radnor Rd BRAK RG12 100 C1
EARL RG6 9 L5
Radstock La EARL RG6 9 J7
Radstock Rd READ RG1 4 D6
Ragdale THLE RG7 91 F4
Raggleswood Cl EARL RG6 9 L5
Raghill THLE RG7 109 G2
Raglan Gdns CAV/SC RG4 57 K1
Ragley Ms CAV/SC RG4 44 A6 1
Railside THLE RG7 88 C5
Railton Cl WHIT RG2 74 A7 1
Railway Rd NWBY RG14 13 G5
Rainbow Cl CHAM RG24 161 K6
Rainbow Pk WWKG RG41 76 A5
Rainham Cl KEMP RG22 174 E5
Rainworth Cl EARL RG6 74 D6 3
Raleigh Cl WODY RG5 75 H1
Ralphs Ride BRAK RG12 11 L5
Ram Aly STHA RG19 124 D1
Ramptons La THLE RG7 110 A2
Rampton's Meadow
TADY RG26 127 G2
Ramsbury Cl BRAK RG12 99 F4 3
Ramsbury Dr EARL RG6 9 H4
Ramsdell Cl TADY RG26 126 E2
Ramsdell Rd TADY RG26 141 F1
TADY RG26 143 G1
Ramsey Cl EARL RG6 75 H4
Ramslade Rd BRAK RG12 11 J8
Rances La EWKG RG40 97 K1
Randall Md BNFD RG42 78 C4 3
Randolph Rd READ RG1 3 G2
Ranelagh Crs ASC SL5 81 F6
Ranelagh Dr BRAK RG12 11 H5
Range Rd EWKG RG40 117 G1
Rangewood Av CALC RG31 72 A3
Raphael Cl BSTK RG21 15 K8
Rapley Gn BRAK RG12 99 K4
Ratby Cl EARL RG6 9 L8
Ravel Cl KEMP RG22 175 K3
Ravelin Cl NFNM GU10 182 E7 1
Raven Cl YTLY GU46 135 G3 3
Ravenglass Cl EARL RG6 9 M7
Raven Rd HTWY RG27 163 K2
Ravensbourne Dr WODY RG5 59 H5
Ravens Cft HTWY RG27 164 B2 4
Ravenscroft Rd HEN RG9 31 G1
Ravensdale Rd ASC SL5 101 K3
Ravenswood Av CWTH RG45 117 K3
Ravensworth Rd THLE RG7 110 D2
Rawlings Rd HTWY RG27 164 A3
Rayleigh Rd BSTK RG21 14 D5
Reade's La CAV/SC RG4 28 D6
Reading Rd CAV/SC RG4 28 A7
CHAM RG24 145 H7
CHAM RG24 160 E3
EWKG RG40 115 J4
GOR/PANG RG8 24 D5
GOR/PANG RG8 37 H2
GOR/PANG RG8 40 C7
HEN RG9 31 H3
HTWY RG27 134 C1
HTWY RG27 146 A2
HTWY RG27 148 B2
HTWY RG27 163 K1 3
HTWY RG27 164 A1
THLE RG7 90 E7
THLE RG7 109 J3
TLHT RG30 91 H3
WHIT RG2 95 F3
WODY RG5 5 M4
WODY RG5 59 G5
WWKG RG41 76 A4
YTLY GU46 135 F2
Reading Rd North FLET GU13 166 E1

Reading Rd South FLET GU13 167 H4
Rebecca Cl FLET GU13 183 F1
Recreation La THLE RG7 93 J5
Recreation Rd ODIM RG29 180 B2
THLE RG7 91 F5
TLHT RG30 55 K5
WAR/TWY RG10 46 D2
Rectory Cl BRAK RG12 11 G7
EWKG RG40 97 H1
NWBY RG14 12 C7
TADY RG26 127 F3
Rectory La BRAK RG12 10 E9
TADY RG26 140 D2
Rectory Rd CAV/SC RG4 57 H3
DEAN RG23 173 H3
EWKG RG40 97 H1
GOR/PANG RG8 23 K4
HTWY RG27 163 K3
THLE RG7 109 J1
Redberry Cl CAV/SC RG4 44 A7
Redbridge La CHAM RG24 15 M5
Red Cottage Dr CALC RG31 71 H2 8
Red Cross Rd GOR/PANG RG8 25 F5 2
Redditch BRAK RG12 100 A5
Redfield Ct NWBY RG14 13 M2
Redfields La NFNM GU10 183 F3
Redgauntlet EWKG RG40 116 D2 3
Redhatch Dr EARL RG6 8 F7
Red Hl HEN RG9 30 C6
HTWY RG27 148 D1
Red House Cl EARL RG6 74 E6
Red House Dr CAV/SC RG4 29 G6
Redlake La EWKG RG40 98 A4 1
Redlands La NFNM GU10 182 E5
Redlands Pl WWKG RG41 96 E5
Redlands Rd READ RG1 8 A2
Red La GOR/PANG RG8 26 D2
THLE RG7 109 G3
Red Lion La BSTK RG21 14 F6
OVTN RG25 171 H4
Red Rose BNFD RG42 78 D3
Redruth Gdns WHIT RG2 7 K9
Red Shute Hl NTHA RG18 65 F2
Redvers Rd BRAK RG12 99 J3
Redwing Cl KEMP RG22 174 E5
Redwood Av WODY RG5 75 K1
Redwoods Wy FLET GU13 167 J7
Redwood Wy CALC RG31 55 J2
Reeds Av EARL RG6 8 F6
Reed's Hl BRAK RG12 99 J3
Reeves Wy WWKG RG41 97 F3
Regent Cl EARL RG6 75 F5
FLET GU13 167 H3
Regent Ct READ RG1 3 G4
Regent St FLET GU13 167 H3
READ RG1 4 D6
Regis Cl WHIT RG2 74 A7
Regnum Dr NWBY RG14 84 A2
Rembrandt Cl BSTK RG21 15 K8
WWKG RG41 96 C1 3
Rembrandt Wy READ RG1 6 D1
Rememberance Gdns
CHAM RG24 161 G1 2
Remembrance Rd NWBY RG14 12 A6
Remenham Church La HEN RG9 17 K6
Remenham La HEN RG9 31 J1
Renault Rd WODY RG5 59 K7
Renoir Cl BSTK RG21 15 K9
Renown Wy CHAM RG24 145 G6 3
Repton Rd EARL RG6 9 M4
Restormel Cl DEAN RG23 159 G5
Restwold Cl TLHT RG30 72 D2 3
Retford Cl WODY RG5 59 J4
Reuben's Crs TADY RG26 126 E2
Reynards Cl TADY RG26 126 E1
WWKG RG41 76 B4
Reynolds Cl BSTK RG21 15 K7
Reyntiens Vw ODIM RG29 180 D1 2
Rhigos CAV/SC RG4 43 G6
Rhine Cl CAV/SC RG4 58 A3
Rhodes Cl EARL RG6 75 H3
Rhododendron Cl ASC SL5 81 H5
Rhododendron Wk ASC SL5 81 H5
Ribbleton Cl EARL RG6 75 H3 3
Ribble Wy BSTK RG21 15 J5
Richard Cl FLET GU13 167 F4
Richborough Cl EARL RG6 9 J8
Richfield Av READ RG1 2 E2
Richfield Pl READ RG1 2 E2
Richmond Cl FLET GU13 167 G5
Richmond Ri WWKG RG41 76 D7 3
Richmond Rd BSTK RG21 14 D2
CAV/SC RG4 57 F1
TLHT RG30 56 D5
Rickman Cl BRAK RG12 99 K4 3
WHIT RG2 95 H6
WODY RG5 75 G1
Riddings La STHA RG19 106 D6
Rider's La THLE RG7 92 B3
Ridge Cl KEMP RG22 175 H7
Ridge Hall Cl CAV/SC RG4 57 F2
Ridge La HTWY RG27 163 H1
Ridgemount Cl CALC RG31 55 G3 4
The Ridge GOR/PANG RG8 39 J4
NTHA RG18 65 H5
Ridge Wy WAR/TWY RG10 46 C2
Ridgeway DID OX11 21 F1
DID OX11 22 B3
GOR/PANG RG8 25 F3
Ridgeway Cl NTHA RG18 49 G6
The Ridgeway BRAK RG12 11 G6
CAV/SC RG4 57 H2
WODY RG5 75 J1
The Ridings CAV/SC RG4 43 K4
Riding Wy WWKG RG41 96 C1 4
Ridley Cl FLET GU13 167 G4
Ridlington Cl EARL RG6 75 H4
Righton Cl WAR/TWY RG10 60 A2 1
Riley La CHAM RG24 161 J4
Riley Rd TLHT RG30 56 A5
Rimes's La TADY RG26 126 C3
Ringmead BRAK RG12 99 F5
Ringshall Gdns TADY RG26 129 F6
The Ring BRAK RG12 10 F4
Ringway North CHAM RG24 159 K4
Ringway South BSTK RG21 14 D9
BSTK RG21 176 B2
Ringway West DEAN RG23 159 K4
KEMP RG22 159 K7
Ringwood BRAK RG12 99 G5
Ringwood Rd TLHT RG30 56 A4
Ripley Rd TLHT RG30 56 B4
Ripplesmere BRAK RG12 11 K9
The Rise CAV/SC RG4 57 J1
CWTH RG45 118 A3
EWKG RG40 115 K6
NTHA RG18 65 H6
WWKG RG41 77 F7
Rissington Cl CALC RG31 55 K2
Rivacres GOR/PANG RG8 40 D1
Riverdene Dr WWKG RG41 75 J3
River Gdns GOR/PANG RG8 41 J7
Rivermead Rd WODY RG5 75 J1
River Pk NWBY RG14 13 H3
River Rd CAV/SC RG4 56 E2
READ RG1 3 H9
YTLY GU46 135 G2
Riversdale Ct READ RG1 4 C5
Riverside Cl CHAM RG24 161 J4
OVTN RG25 171 J4
Riverview Rd GOR/PANG RG8 40 B6
Robert Mays Rd ODIM RG29 180 B2 3
Robertsfield STHA RG19 84 E4
Roberts Gv WWKG RG41 96 E4
Robertson Cl NWBY RG14 84 A7 2
Robin Cl KEMP RG22 175 F4
THLE RG7 91 G4 4
Robindale Av EARL RG6 75 G3
Robinhood La WWKG RG41 76 B4
Robin Hood Wy WWKG RG41 76 B3
Robins Cl NWBY RG14 103 J1
Robins Grove Crs YTLY GU46 135 G3
Robinson Ct EARL RG6 9 G9
Robin Wy CALC RG31 55 G7
Roby Dr BRAK RG12 100 A5
Rochester Av WODY RG5 59 H4
Rochester Cl KEMP RG22 175 G4 4
Rochester Gv FLET GU13 167 G3
Rochford Rd BSTK RG21 14 C5
Rockbourne Gdns TLHT RG30 56 B4 1
Rockingham Rd NWBY RG14 12 C5
Roding Cl BSTK RG21 15 J5
Rodway Rd TLHT RG30 55 K4
Roebuck Est BNFD RG42 78 D5
Roebuck Ri CALC RG31 55 J2
Roebuts Cl NWBY RG14 83 J7
Roentgen Rd CHAM RG24 15 M1
CHAM RG24 161 G5
Rokeby Cl BRAK RG12 11 J3
NWBY RG14 103 K1
Rokeby Dr CAV/SC RG4 42 E4
Roke La ODIM RG29 181 F3
Rokes Pl YTLY GU46 135 F3
Roman Ride CWTH RG45 117 J3
Roman Rd DEAN RG23 159 G6
Romans Fld THLE RG7 110 A7 1
THLE RG7 128 A1
Romans Ga THLE RG7 109 J7
Roman Wy BNFD RG42 80 C6
DEAN RG23 159 F6
EARL RG6 75 G3
NTHA RG18 85 F3
Romany Cl TLHT RG30 56 B4
Romany La TLHT RG30 56 B4
Romeo Hl BNFD RG42 80 C6 4
Romsey Cl CHAM RG24 160 B2
Romsey Rd TLHT RG30 56 B4
Rona Ct TLHT RG30 56 C5
Rook Cl WWKG RG41 96 D2
The Rookery WHCH RG28 169 H7 4
Rooksdown Av CHAM RG24 159 H3
Rooksdown La CHAM RG24 159 H2
Rooksfield KSCL RG20 105 F6
Rookswood BNFD RG42 79 J5 2
KSCL RG20 82 C1
Rookswood Cl HTWY RG27 164 A2 3
Rookwood Av SHST GU47 119 F7
Rope Wk STHA RG19 85 H4
Ropley Cl TADY RG26 126 D2
Rosary Gdns YTLY GU46 135 J3 1
Rosebay EWKG RG40 77 K6
Rose Bay Gdns HTWY RG27 164 B1 4
Roseberry Cl KEMP RG22 175 G7
Rosebery Rd CAV/SC RG4 42 E5
Rose Cl KEMP RG22 175 G4
WODY RG5 60 A6
Rosecroft Wy WHIT RG2 94 B2
Rosedale BNFD RG42 78 D3
Rosedale Crs EARL RG6 5 H4
Rosedale Gdns BRAK RG12 10 D9
STHA RG19 85 H5
Rosedene Gdns FLET GU13 167 G1
Rose Hl BNFD RG42 78 D3
Rosehill Pk CAV/SC RG4 43 K5
Rosehip Wy CHAM RG24 161 G4
Rose Hodson Pl DEAN RG23 159 H4
Rose Kiln La WHIT RG2 7 G1
Rose La WAR/TWY RG10 33 F3
Rosemary Av EARL RG6 74 C5
Rosemary Dr TADY RG26 126 E3
Rosemead Av CALC RG31 55 G2 2
Rose St EWKG RG40 97 H1
Rose Wk FLET GU13 167 G1
READ RG1 3 H7
Rosewood WODY RG5 75 G2
Rosier Cl STHA RG19 86 A5
Roslyn Rd WODY RG5 59 G7
Ross Cl BSTK RG21 176 B2 3
Rossendale Rd CAV/SC RG4 58 A2
Rosset Cl BRAK RG12 10 E8
Rossington Pl WHIT RG2 73 K6 3
Rossini Cl KEMP RG22 175 K4
Ross Rd READ RG1 2 F3
Rothay Ct BSTK RG21 15 J5
Rotherfield Av WWKG RG41 77 F7
Rotherfield Cl THLE RG7 70 E2 2
Rotherfield Rd HEN RG9 31 G4
Rotherfield Wy CAV/SC RG4 57 H1
Rotherwick La HTWY RG27 146 E2
Rotherwick Rd TADY RG26 126 E2
Rothwell Gdns WODY RG5 59 J4
Rotten Green Rd HTWY RG27 151 F4
Rotten Hl OVTN RG25 170 E6
Rotten Row Hl THLE RG7 68 C3
Roughgrove Copse BNFD RG42 78 C4
Roundabouts La WWKG RG41 76 C6
Round End NWBY RG14 103 G3
Roundfield THLE RG7 86 C1 1
Roundhead Rd THLE RG7 70 C3
Roundmead Rd BSTK RG21 14 C6
Roundshead Dr BNFD RG42 80 A5
Rounton Rd FLET GU13 167 H6
Routh La TLHT RG30 55 K7
Rowallan Cl CAV/SC RG4 44 A6
Rowan Cl CAV/SC RG4 29 G7
FLET GU13 167 K2
WWKG RG41 96 E2
Rowan Dl FLET GU13 167 G6
Rowan Dr CWTH RG45 118 D1
NWBY RG14 83 K2
WODY RG5 59 H5
Rowan Rd TADY RG26 127 F2
Rowan Wy TLHT RG30 91 G3
Rowcroft Rd WHIT RG2 115 J1
Rowdell Dr WHIT RG2 74 A5
Rowe Ct TLHT RG30 56 C5
Rowland's Cl THLE RG7 110 B3
Rowland Wy EARL RG6 8 E7
Row La CAV/SC RG4 44 B4
Rowley Cl BRAK RG12 11 M5
Rowley Rd WHIT RG2 7 K3
Royal Av CALC RG31 71 G2
Royal Cl DEAN RG23 175 F7
Royal Oak Dr CWTH RG45 98 C7
Royal Wy WHIT RG2 73 G6
Roy Cl NTHA RG18 48 E7 3
Roycroft La EWKG RG40 96 D7
Royston Cl TLHT RG30 56 A6
Rubens Cl BSTK RG21 176 E2
Ruby Cl WWKG RG41 76 D7 7
Rudland Cl STHA RG19 85 J5
Rufford Cl FLET GU13 167 H5
Rufus Isaacs Rd CAV/SC RG4 57 J3
Rugby Cl SHST GU47 119 F7 3
Rupert Cl HEN RG9 17 H7
Rupert Rd NWBY RG14 83 J7
Rupert St READ RG1 4 B7
Ruscombe La WAR/TWY RG10 46 D7
Ruscombe Pk WAR/TWY RG10 46 D7
Rushall Cl EARL RG6 74 B7
Rushbrook Rd WODY RG5 5 M7
WODY RG5 59 G6
Rushden Dr WHIT RG2 74 B5
The Rushes BSTK RG21 15 K5
Rushey Wy EARL RG6 9 K9
EARL RG6 74 D5
Rushmoor Cl FLET GU13 167 H4
Rushmoor Gdns CALC RG31 71 G2
Ruskin Cl BSTK RG21 15 L8
Ruskin Ct CWTH RG45 118 A4 2
Ruskin Wy WWKG RG41 96 C1
Russell Cl BRAK RG12 100 A6
Russell Rd BSTK RG21 14 F8
CAV/SC RG4 42 E5
NWBY RG14 12 B5
Russell St READ RG1 2 F7
Russell Wy WWKG RG41 76 A5
Russet Cl CAV/SC RG4 29 F6
Russet Gld CAV/SC RG4 43 K5
THLE RG7 91 G5
Russetts Dr FLET GU13 167 H3
Russley Gn EWKG RG40 97 F6
Rustic Gln FLET GU13 167 G6
Rustington Cl EARL RG6 74 E5 2
Ruston Wy ASC SL5 81 H7
Rutherford Rd CHAM RG24 160 E3
Rutland Rd TLHT RG30 2 A7
Rydal Av TLHT RG30 56 A3
Rydal Dr FLET GU13 167 F6
STHA RG19 85 F4
Ryebeck Rd FLET GU13 167 H6
Rye Cl BRAK RG12 80 A5
FARN GU14 151 K5
Rye Cft FLET GU13 167 F7
Ryecroft Cl WAR/TWY RG10 46 D2
WODY RG5 59 H4
Ryehurst La BNFD RG42 79 G1
Ryeish La THLE RG7 93 K4
Ryeland Cl FARN GU14 151 K5 3
Ryelaw Rd FLET GU13 167 H6
Ryemead La WDSR SL4 81 F1
Ryhill Wy EARL RG6 74 B6
Rylstone Rd TLHT RG30 2 A4
Ryves Av YTLY GU46 135 F4

S

Sackville St READ RG1 3 G5
Saddleback Wy FARN GU14 151 J6
Sadler's Ct WWKG RG41 76 C5 1
Sadlers End WWKG RG41 76 A7
Sadler's La WWKG RG41 76 C6
The Sadlers CALC RG31 55 G4
Saffron Cl CHAM RG24 145 G6
EARL RG6 9 M4
NWBY RG14 12 D3
Saffron Rd BRAK RG12 10 E8
Sage Cl EARL RG6 74 D5 4
Sagecroft Rd NTHA RG18 85 H2
Sage Rd CALC RG31 55 H2 2
Sage Wk BNFD RG42 80 A5 3
Sainfoin La DEAN RG23 174 A4
St Andrews BRAK RG12 99 F4
St Andrews Cl CWTH RG45 118 A2
St Andrew's Rd CAV/SC RG4 57 G1
HEN RG9 31 G3
KEMP RG22 175 J1
St Anne's Cl HEN RG9 31 G2
St Anne's Rd CAV/SC RG4 57 H3
St Anthonys Cl BNFD RG42 10 D1
St Barbara's Cl TADY RG26 129 J7
St Barnabas Rd CAV/SC RG4 43 H6
WHIT RG2 8 E9
St Bartholomews Rd EARL RG6 4 E6
St Birinus Rd CALC RG31 71 H1 3
St Catherine's Cl WWKG RG41 75 K5
St Catherine's Hl THLE RG7 110 D3
St Christophers Cl
KEMP RG22 175 H1 3
St Christophers Gdns ASC SL5 81 G6
St Cross Rd NFNM GU10 182 E7
St David's Cl CAV/SC RG4 43 G7
ODIM RG29 180 B2 4
St David's Rd KEMP RG22 175 K1
NWBY RG14 12 D5
St Donats Pl NWBY RG14 12 F6
St Edward's Rd EARL RG6 5 G8
St Elizabeth Cl WHIT RG2 73 J7 2
St Gabriels Lea CHAM RG24 145 H7
St George's Av NWBY RG14 12 B6
St George's Rd TLHT RG30 56 C5
St Giles Cl READ RG1 3 J8
St Giles Ct READ RG1 3 J8
St Helier Cl WWKG RG41 97 G4
St Ives Cl THLE RG7 70 C3
St James Cl GOR/PANG RG8 40 B6
WAR/TWY RG10 46 D7
St James Rd EWKG RG40 96 D7
FLET GU13 167 G3
St John Cl TADY RG26 129 H7
St Johns Cl HTWY RG27 164 A2 6
WODY RG5 59 J5
St John's Hl READ RG1 3 M6
St John's Piece DEAN RG23 174 A4
St John's Rd ASC SL5 81 J5
CAV/SC RG4 3 L1
CAV/SC RG4 57 K3
DEAN RG23 174 A2
HTWY RG27 149 J5
NWBY RG14 12 E7
READ RG1 3 M7
STHA RG19 85 H4
THLE RG7 111 F3
St John's St READ RG1 3 M6
St Joseph's Crs CHAM RG24 161 G1 3
St Katherine's Rd HEN RG9 31 G4
St Leonard's Av CHAM RG24 145 H7
St Lukes Wy CAV/SC RG4 57 J1
St Marks Cl STHA RG19 85 H4
St Mark's Rd BNFD RG42 78 D6
HEN RG9 31 G3
St Mary's Av GOR/PANG RG8 41 H7
TADY RG26 129 J7
St Mary's Butts READ RG1 3 H6
St Mary's Cl HEN RG9 30 D3
St Mary's Ct BSTK RG21 15 G5
St Marys La WDSR SL4 81 G1
St Mary's Rd HTWY RG27 149 H5
KSCL RG20 124 A7
NWBY RG14 12 F2
THLE RG7 111 F3
WWKG RG41 76 A5
St Mary's Wy THLE RG7 91 H4 1
St Michaels Cl FLET GU13 167 K3
St Michaels Ct WAR/TWY RG10 46 D6
St Michaels La THLE RG7 90 C2
St Michael's Rd KEMP RG22 175 H1
NWBY RG14 12 C6
TLHT RG30 55 K6 3
St Neot's Rd HTWY RG27 133 J2
St Nicholas Cl FLET GU13 167 G2
St Nicholas Ct KEMP RG22 159 J7
St Nicholas' Rd NWBY RG14 12 D5
St Patrick's Av WAR/TWY RG10 45 K7
St Patrick's Rd KEMP RG22 175 K1
St Paul's Ct READ RG1 3 G9
St Paul's Ga WWKG RG41 97 F1
St Paul's Rd KEMP RG22 175 K1
St Peter's Av CAV/SC RG4 57 F1
St Peter's Gdns YTLY GU46 135 J3
St Peter's Hl CAV/SC RG4 57 G2
St Peter's Rd EARL RG6 5 G9
KEMP RG22 175 H1
St Richards Rd NWBY RG14 84 A2
St Ronans Rd TLHT RG30 56 C5
St Saviour's Rd READ RG1 6 E2
St Sebastian's Cl EWKG RG40 97 K7
St Stephens Cl READ RG1 3 H1
St Thomas' Cl BSTK RG21 14 D1
Salamanca CWTH RG45 117 K3 1
Salcombe Dr EARL RG6 9 K3
Salcombe Rd NWBY RG14 12 A7
WHIT RG2 8 A6
Saleby Cl EARL RG6 75 H4
Salford Cl WHIT RG2 73 K7
Salisbury Cl ODIM RG29 180 B2 5
WWKG RG41 97 F5
Salisbury Gdns KEMP RG22 159 H7
Salisbury Rd TLHT RG30 2 C4
Salmon Cl THLE RG7 93 J5
Salmond Rd WHIT RG2 93 K1
Salmons Rd ODIM RG29 180 B2
Saltersgate Cl EARL RG6 75 G4 2
Salters Heath Rd TADY RG26 143 G4
Salwey Cl BRAK RG12 99 J4 3
Samian Pl BNFD RG42 79 F5
Sampage Cl WHIT RG2 93 K1
Sampson Pk BNFD RG42 78 E6
Sanctuary Cl TLHT RG30 55 K5
Sandbanks Dr KEMP RG22 175 G5 3
Sandcroft Rd CAV/SC RG4 43 F6
Sandford Cl GOR/PANG RG8 26 E3 10
KSCL RG20 124 C7
Sandford Down BRAK RG12 100 C3 6
Sandford Dr WODY RG5 59 J4
Sandford La WODY RG5 60 A6
Sandford Rd TADY RG26 126 D1
Sandgate Av TLHT RG30 56 A3 1
Sandhills WAR/TWY RG10 47 J1
Sandhurst Rd CWTH RG45 118 C5
EWKG RG40 97 G7
YTLY GU46 135 K3
Sandleford Cl WHIT RG2 93 K1 3
Sandleford Ri NWBY RG14 103 K1
Sandown Av CALC RG31 71 G2
Sandown Wy NWBY RG14 13 J8
Sandpiper Wy KEMP RG22 174 E5
Sandpit Hl KSCL RG20 103 F5
Sandpit La CAV/SC RG4 44 B3
THLE RG7 114 E3
Sandringham Wy CALC RG31 71 G2 3
Sandstone Cl WWKG RG41 76 B5
Sandy Cl NTHA RG18 64 E2
Sandy La ASC SL5 81 F6
BRAK RG12 11 G1
FLET GU13 167 H7
HTWY RG27 149 J5
NTHA RG18 64 E2
SHST GU47 118 A7
TADY RG26 127 G1
WWKG RG41 96 B3
Sandys Cl KEMP RG22 175 K1
Sandys Rd KEMP RG22 159 K7
Sapley La OVTN RG25 171 H5
Sapphire Cl WWKG RG41 76 C7
Sargood Cl STHA RG19 85 K5 1
Sarisbury Cl TADY RG26 126 D1
Sarum BRAK RG12 99 F6
Sarum Crs EWKG RG40 77 J7
Sarum Hl BSTK RG21 14 D6
Sarum Rd TADY RG26 108 D7
Saturn Cl WWKG RG41 96 D1 13
Saturn Cft BNFD RG42 80 E4
Savernake Cl TLHT RG30 56 A6 3
Savernake Wy BRAK RG12 100 C4
Savory Wk BNFD RG42 78 D4
Sawmill Rd NTHA RG18 65 F2
Sawpit Rd WAR/TWY RG10 60 D6
Sawtry Cl EARL RG6 75 H4 5
Sawyers Ley THLE RG7 91 J7
Saxby Cl THLE RG7 91 G4
Saxon Ct STHA RG19 85 F4 3
Saxon Dr BNFD RG42 80 C6
Saxon Wy CHAM RG24 161 G4
Sayers Cl NWBY RG14 84 A7
Scafell Cl CALC RG31 55 G3
Scania Wk BNFD RG42 80 E4 1
Scarlatti Rd KEMP RG22 176 A4
Scarletts La WAR/TWY RG10 47 G4
Scholars Cl CAV/SC RG4 57 G2 1
School Hl CWTH RG45 118 E4
SHST GU47 118 B7
WAR/TWY RG10 46 C3
School La CAV/SC RG4 43 J7
KSCL RG20 62 A2
MLW SL7 19 G4
READ RG1 3 H1
THLE RG7 90 E5
THLE RG7 110 A7
THLE RG7 114 B5
WAR/TWY RG10 46 C2
YTLY GU46 135 G3
School Rd CALC RG31 55 J5
EWKG RG40 97 J1 2
KSCL RG20 21 K7
THLE RG7 89 J6
THLE RG7 114 B4
TLHT RG30 91 H1
WAR/TWY RG10 60 E6
WHIT RG2 95 J5
School Ter READ RG1 4 B5
Schroeder Cl BSTK RG21 176 B2
Schubert Rd KEMP RG22 175 K4
Scotney Rd BSTK RG21 160 C4
Scots Dr WWKG RG41 76 D7
Scottalls La NTHA RG18 36 A7
Scott Cl CAV/SC RG4 43 H7
WODY RG5 59 K6
Scott Ter BNFD RG42 11 M1
Scours La TLHT RG30 56 C4
Scratchface La NTHA RG18 52 A6
Scrivens Md STHA RG19 86 A4
Scures Rd HTWY RG27 163 J2
Seaford Gdns WODY RG5 59 H7
Seaford Rd EWKG RG40 97 J1
Seagull Cl KEMP RG22 174 E4 3
Seal Rd BSTK RG21 14 F5
Searing Wy TADY RG26 108 D7
Searles Farm La TLHT RG30 72 C5
Searl's La HTWY RG27 148 A6
Seaton Gdns WHIT RG2 7 M7
Second Av THLE RG7 109 F6
Second St STHA RG19 104 E4
Seddon Hl BNFD RG42 79 J4 2
Sedgefield Cl CAV/SC RG4 29 G5
Sedgefield Rd NWBY RG14 13 J9
Sedge Gv NTHA RG18 85 K3
Sedgewell Rd CAV/SC RG4 29 G6
Segsbury Gv BRAK RG12 11 M7
Selborne Cl HTWY RG27 164 A2
Selborne Gdns TLHT RG30 56 B4
Selcourt Cl WODY RG5 59 G5
Sellafield Wy EARL RG6 9 M7
Selsdon Av WODY RG5 59 J5
Selsey Wy EARL RG6 74 E6
Selva Ct READ RG1 3 L9
Selwyn Dr YTLY GU46 135 G3
Sen Cl BNFD RG42 79 K4 3
Send Rd CAV/SC RG4 3 M2
Setley Wy BRAK RG12 100 C1
Seton Dr CALC RG31 72 A1 3
HTWY RG27 163 J3 3
The Sett YTLY GU46 135 G4
Sevenoaks Dr THLE RG7 93 H4
Sevenoaks Rd EARL RG6 9 K5
Seventh St STHA RG19 104 E3
The Severals CHAM RG24 143 K7
Severn Cl NTHA RG18 85 G2
Severn Gdns DEAN RG23 174 A3
Severn Wy BSTK RG21 15 K5
TLHT RG30 56 A7
Sewell Av WWKG RG41 77 F6
Sewell Cl NTHA RG18 65 H5
Seymour Av WHIT RG2 94 B2
Seymour Rd KEMP RG22 175 H2
Shackleton Wy WODY RG5 59 K6
Shaftesbury Cl BRAK RG12 11 J9
Shaftesbury Rd TLHT RG30 56 C5
Shakespeare Cl CAV/SC RG4 44 A7 1
Shakespeare Rd CHAM RG24 160 D3
NTHA RG18 85 H3
Shakespeare Wy BNFD RG42 11 M1
BNFD RG42 80 B5 14
BNFD RG42 80 C5 4
Shaldon Wy FLET GU13 166 E3 4
Sharnwood Dr CALC RG31 72 A1
Sharpethorpe Cl EARL RG6 74 E5 3
Shaw Farm Rd NWBY RG14 84 A2
Shaw Hl NWBY RG14 84 A2
Shaw La TADY RG26 126 C3
Shaw Pk CWTH RG45 118 C5
Shaw Pightle HTWY RG27 163 J2 3
Shaw Rd NWBY RG14 13 G1
READ RG1 2 F9
Sheep Wk CAV/SC RG4 57 J1
Sheepwash La KSCL RG20 103 K6
TADY RG26 142 C4
Sheepways La CAV/SC RG4 42 C4

Sheerlands Rd EWKG RG40 ...... 115 H2
Shefford Crs EWKG RG40 .... 77 J6
Sheldon's La HTWY RG27 .... 163 K2
Sheldon's Rd HTWY RG27 .... 163 K2
Shelley Av BRAK RG12 .... 11 M5
Shelley Cl CHAM RG24 .... 160 D3
 FLET GU13 .... 167 H3
 MLW SL7 .... 19 J3
 WODY RG5 .... 75 H2
Shelley Ri NTHA RG18 .... 85 H3
Shelley Wk YTLY GU46 .... 135 G4
Shenstone Cl EWKG RG40 .... 97 F7
Shenstone Rd WHIT RG2 .... 7 K3
Shepherds Av EARL RG6 .... 5 K4
Shepherds HI BRAK RG12 .... 11 H1
 EARL RG6 .... 5 L4
 KSCL RG20 .... 35 K1
Shepherd's House La EARL RG6 ... 5 G4
Shepherds La BNFD RG42 .... 79 H5
 CAV/SC RG4 .... 42 E6
 MDHD SL6 .... 19 J6
Shepherds Mt KSCL RG20 .... 35 K1
Shepherds Ri KSCL RG20 .... 21 K7
Shepherds Wk EARL RG6 .... 5 M4
Shepherds Wy CWTH RG45 .... 117 K4
Shepley Dr TLHT RG30 .... 72 D2
Sheppard Rd BSTK RG21 .... 176 B2
Sheraton Av KEMP RG22 .... 175 C5
Sheraton Dr CALC RG31 .... 55 G4
Sherborne Rd BSTK RG21 .... 14 C1
 CHAM RG24 .... 160 A1
Sherbourne Dr WODY RG5 .... 59 J5
Sherfield Cl WHIT RG2 .... 8 A4
Sherfield Dr WHIT RG2 .... 8 A4
Sherfield Rd TADY RG26 .... 129 C6
Sheridan Av CAV/SC RG4 .... 57 C1
Sheridan Crs TADY RG26 .... 108 B7
Sheridan Wy WWKG RG41 .... 96 D2
Sherlock Lea HTWY RG27 .... 134 D2
Sherman Rd READ RG1 .... 3 J8
Sherrardmead NWBY RG14 .... 84 A2
Sherring Cl BNFD RG42 .... 79 K5
Sherwood Cl BRAK RG12 .... 80 D7
 KEMP RG22 .... 175 H6
Sherwood Gdns HEN RG9 .... 31 F3
Sherwood Ri GOR/PANG RG8 .... 55 G1
Sherwood Rd WWKG RG41 .... 76 B4
Sherwood St TLHT RG30 .... 56 D5
Shetland Rd CHAM RG24 .... 160 D2
Shetland Wy FARN GU14 .... 151 J6
Shilling Cl TLHT RG30 .... 56 C7
Shinfield Ri WHIT RG2 .... 8 D9
Shinfield Rd WHIT RG2 .... 8 D9
 WHIT RG2 .... 74 B5
 WHIT RG2 .... 94 B1
Shiplake Bottom HEN RG9 .... 29 F4
Shipley Cl WODY RG5 .... 59 K4
Shipton Cl CALC RG31 .... 55 H2
Shipton Wy KEMP RG22 .... 175 H2
Shire Av FARN GU14 .... 151 K7
The Shires WWKG RG41 .... 96 D3
Shires Wy YTLY GU46 .... 135 J1
Shirley Av WHIT RG2 .... 73 K7
Shirvell's HI GOR/PANG RG8 ..... 26 C4
Shooter's HI GOR/PANG RG8 ...... 39 J4
Shooters Wy BSTK RG21 .... 15 C1
 WHIT RG2 .... 73 G6
Shop La NWBY RG14 .... 83 J1
Shorland Oaks BNFD RG42 .... 79 K4
Shortheath La THLE RG7 .... 90 C4
Short St CAV/SC RG4 .... 57 J3
 GOR/PANG RG8 .... 40 C7
 READ RG1 .... 3 K9
The Short GOR/PANG RG8 .... 41 J7
Shropshire Gdns BNFD RG42 ...... 80 C5
Shrubland Dr TLHT RG30 .... 72 B2
Shute End EWKG RG40 .... 97 C1
Shyshack La TADY RG26 .... 108 B7
Sian Cl FLET GU13 .... 167 J6
Sibelius Cl KEMP RG22 .... 175 K5
Sibley Park Rd EARL RG6 .... 9 G8
Sibson EARL RG6 .... 9 L7
Sidestrand Rd NWBY RG14 .... 83 G7
Sidlaw Cl KEMP RG22 .... 175 F1
Sidmouth Grange Cl EARL RG6 .... 5 J6
Sidmouth Grange Rd EARL RG6 .... 5 J6
Sidmouth St READ RG1 .... 3 H7
Silbury Cl CALC RG31 .... 71 G2
Silchester Rd TADY RG26 .... 108 E7
 TADY RG26 .... 127 K4
 TADY RG26 .... 128 C6
 TLHT RG30 .... 72 D2
Silk Mill La OVTN RG25 .... 171 G4
Silver Birch Cl FLET GU13 ...... 167 G6
Silver Birches WWKG RG41 .... 96 B4
Silverdale FLET GU13 .... 167 H5
Silverdale Rd EARL RG6 .... 9 K5
 TADY RG26 .... 108 D7
 WAR/TWY RG10 .... 46 C3
Silver Fox Crs WODY RG5 .... 59 G7
Silverglades YTLY GU46 .... 135 H5
Silver La THLE RG7 .... 89 K7
Silver Park Cl FLET GU13 .... 167 J5
Silver St READ RG1 .... 3 K8
Silverthorne Dr CAV/SC RG4 ..... 42 E6
Silvester Cl BSTK RG21 .... 15 H1
Silvester Wy FLET GU13 .... 167 F7
Silwood BRAK RG12 .... 99 F6
Simkins Cl BNFD RG42 .... 80 E4
Simmonds Cl BNFD RG42 .... 79 F6
Simmonds St READ RG1 .... 3 H7
Simmons Cl BRAK RG12 .... 86 A3
Simmons Flds WAR/TWY RG10 ...... 60 A2
Simmons Rd HEN RG9 .... 17 C7
Simms Farm La THLE RG7 .... 110 E4
Simons Cl CALC RG31 .... 55 H1
Simon's La WWKG RG41 .... 76 C6
Simons Rd CHAM RG24 .... 161 G1
Sims Cl TADY RG26 .... 129 J7
Sindle Cl WWKG RG41 .... 76 A4
Sindlesham Rd WHIT RG2 .... 95 H4
Singers Cl HEN RG9 .... 31 H3
Sirius Cl WWKG RG41 .... 96 E1
Sixth St STHA RG19 .... 104 E3
Skarries Vw CAV/SC RG4 .... 42 E4
Skates La TADY RG26 .... 127 G4
Skeffling Cl EARL RG6 .... 75 H4
Skelmerdale Wy EARL RG6 .... 75 H3

Skelton Flds BNFD RG42 .... 79 K5
Skerritt Wy GOR/PANG RG8 .... 55 J1
Skilman Dr STHA RG19 .... 86 A4
Skilton Rd CALC RG31 .... 55 H2
Skimpedhill La BRAK RG12 .... 10 E3
Skinner's Green La KSCL RG20 ... 102 C2
Skippetts La East BSTK RG21 .... 176 C2
Skippetts La West BSTK RG21 .... 176 C2
Skippons Cl NWBY RG14 .... 103 F2
Skye Cl CALC RG31 .... 71 K2
Skylark Ri WHCH RG28 .... 169 G6
Skyllings NWBY RG14 .... 13 J2
Slaidburn Gn BRAK RG12 .... 100 B5
Slanting HI NTHA RG18 .... 65 G1
The Slopes CAV/SC RG4 .... 58 A3
Smallfield Dr HTWY RG27 .... 164 B2
Smallmead Rd WHIT RG2 .... 6 F9
 WHIT RG2 .... 72 E5
Smallridge KSCL RG20 .... 103 F4
Smith Cl CAV/SC RG4 .... 29 G6
Smith Sq BRAK RG12 .... 11 J3
The Smithy TADY RG26 .... 129 G6
Snake La KSCL RG20 .... 82 D1
Snowberry Cl WWKG RG41 .... 96 E2
Snowden Dr CALC RG31 .... 55 F7
Snowdon Cl STHA RG19 .... 85 J5
Snowdrop Cl KEMP RG22 .... 175 F4
Snowdrop Copse NTHA RG18 .... 86 A3
Snowdrop Gv WWKG RG41 .... 76 B3
Soane End CAV/SC RG4 .... 43 H6
Soham Cl EARL RG6 .... 75 F6
Soke Rd THLE RG7 .... 109 H4
Solby's Rd BSTK RG21 .... 14 C5
Soldiers Ri EWKG RG40 .... 117 J1
Solent Dr KEMP RG22 .... 175 G5
Somerset Cl WWKG RG41 .... 96 C1
Somerset Gv BNFD RG42 .... 80 C5
Somerstown Ct READ RG1 .... 2 E7
Somerton Gdns EARL RG6 .... 9 H7
Somerton Gv STHA RG19 .... 85 H5
Somerville Cl WWKG RG41 .... 96 C3
Somerville Crs YTLY GU46 .... 135 K3
Sonning Cl KEMP RG22 .... 174 E5
Sonning La CAV/SC RG4 .... 5 M2
 CAV/SC RG4 .... 59 G3
Sonning Mdw CAV/SC RG4 .... 5 L2
Soper Gv BSTK RG21 .... 14 E2
Sopwith Cl WODY RG5 .... 59 K6
Sorrel Cl EWKG RG40 .... 77 K6
 NWBY RG14 .... 84 C2
 THLE RG7 .... 91 G4
Sorrell's Cl CHAM RG24 .... 145 G7
Southampton St READ RG1 .... 3 J8
South Av HEN RG9 .... 31 H3
Southbury La WAR/TWY RG10 ...... 46 E7
 WAR/TWY RG10 .... 61 F1
Southby Dr FLET GU13 .... 167 J2
South Cl EWKG RG40 .... 97 H2
 MLW SL7 .... 19 J3
Southcote Farm La TLHT RG30 .... 6 A2
Southcote La TLHT RG30 .... 72 B2
Southcote Rd TLHT RG30 .... 2 B9
Southdown Rd CAV/SC RG4 .... 43 J7
 STHA RG19 .... 84 E3
 TADY RG26 .... 108 D7
South Dr CAV/SC RG4 .... 5 M3
 EARL RG6 .... 8 E8
 EWKG RG40 .... 97 H2
 THLE RG7 .... 70 C7
 WHIT RG2 .... 8 D8
Southend NTHA RG18 .... 85 H1
Southend Rd BSTK RG21 .... 14 C5
South End Rd THLE RG7 .... 68 E4
Southerndene Cl CALC RG31 ...... 55 J3
Southern Haye HTWY RG27 .... 149 H5
Southern HI READ RG1 .... 8 A2
Southern Rd BSTK RG21 .... 14 E7
Southglade WHIT RG2 .... 74 A6
South Gv FARN GU14 .... 151 K6
South Ham Rd KEMP RG22 .... 159 K7
South Hill Rd BRAK RG12 .... 99 J4
Southington Cl OVTN RG25 .... 171 F4
Southington La OVTN RG25 .... 171 G4
South Lake Crs WODY RG5 .... 75 H1
Southlands CHAM RG24 .... 145 F7
Southlands Cl EWKG RG40 .... 97 J2
Southlands Rd EWKG RG40 .... 97 J3
South Lynn Crs BRAK RG12 .... 99 J3
South Meadow CWTH RG45 .... 118 E5
South Rdg ODIM RG29 .... 180 D2
South Rd CWTH RG45 .... 119 F5
 EWKG RG40 .... 99 F6
 HEN RG9 .... 28 C2
 KSCL RG20 .... 124 B7
South St READ RG1 .... 3 K7
 READ RG1 .... 57 J3
South View Av CAV/SC RG4 .... 57 J3
Southview Cl WAR/TWY RG10 ...... 46 D6
South View Cottages
 WHCH RG28 .... 170 B5
South View Pk CAV/SC RG4 .... 57 K3
Southwark Cl YTLY GU46 .... 135 H3
Southwick Ct BRAK RG12 .... 100 B4
Southwold BRAK RG12 .... 99 F6
Southwold Cl EARL RG6 .... 75 G4
Southwood EWKG RG40 .... 97 J3
Southwood Gdns THLE RG7 .... 91 F4
Southwood Rd FARN GU14 .... 151 K1
Sovereign Wy CALC RG31 .... 71 H7
Spackman St STHA RG19 .... 85 J5
Span HI HEN RG9 .... 44 E5
Sparrow Cl WWKG RG41 .... 96 D2
Sparrowhawk Cl NFNM GU10 .... 183 J4
Sparvells HTWY RG27 .... 134 D1
Speckled Wood Rd CHAM RG24 ... 160 C2
Speedwell Wy NTHA RG18 .... 86 A3
Speen Hill Cl NWBY RG14 .... 12 A1
Speen La NWBY RG14 .... 12 B2
Speen Lodge Ct NWBY RG14 .... 12 A1
Speen Pl NWBY RG14 .... 12 A1
Spencer Cl FLET GU13 .... 167 J6
 TADY RG26 .... 109 H7
 WWKG RG41 .... 96 C1
Spencer Rd BNFD RG42 .... 10 B2
 NWBY RG14 .... 103 G2
 WHIT RG2 .... 73 J7
Sperrin Cl KEMP RG22 .... 175 G1
Spey Rd TLHT RG30 .... 56 B5

Spiers Cl TADY RG26 .... 127 G1
Spinis BRAK RG12 .... 99 F6
Spinner Gn BRAK RG12 .... 10 D9
Spinney Cl CAV/SC RG4 .... 43 J5
The Spinney EWKG RG40 .... 96 E7
 FLET GU13 .... 166 E3
 HTWY RG27 .... 163 K1
 YTLY GU46 .... 135 H2
Spitfire Wy WODY RG5 .... 59 K6
The Splash BNFD RG42 .... 79 J4
Spode Cl TLHT RG30 .... 55 K5
Sprat's Hatch La HTWY RG27 ..... 165 K4
 ODIM RG29 .... 165 J6
Spriggs Cl STHA RG19 .... 85 J5
Spring Cl CHAM RG24 .... 143 K6
 GOR/PANG RG8 .... 39 G7
Springdale EARL RG6 .... 9 J7
 EWKG RG40 .... 96 D7
Springfield
 GOR/PANG RG8 .... 25 F3
Springfield La FLET GU13 .... 167 F2
 NWBY RG14 .... 83 K7
Springfield Pk WAR/TWY RG10 .... 60 D1
Springfield Rd BRAK RG12 .... 78 D7
 TADY RG26 .... 109 H7
Springfield End
 GOR/PANG RG8 .... 25 F3
Spring Gdns THLE RG7 .... 93 J6
Spring Gv READ RG1 .... 3 G9
Springhill GOR/PANG RG8 .... 25 F3
Spring La CAV/SC RG4 .... 44 E6
 KSCL RG20 .... 121 J5
 NTHA RG18 .... 65 H6
 THLE RG7 .... 109 F2
 THLE RG7 .... 111 F1
 THLE RG7 .... 113 J3
Spring Meadow BRAK RG12 .... 11 K1
The Springs THLE RG7 .... 129 J1
Spring Wk WAR/TWY RG10 .... 46 C5
Springwell La HTWY RG27 .... 149 J2
Springwood La HEN RG9 .... 29 G3
Spring Wood La THLE RG7 .... 91 F5
Spring Woods FLET GU13 .... 167 G4
 SHST GU47 .... 118 D7
Spruce Cl WODY RG5 .... 59 K7
Spurcroft Rd STHA RG19 .... 85 J5
The Spur WAR/TWY RG10 .... 46 D1
Squarefield Gdns
 HTWY RG27 .... 164 B1
The Square THLE RG7 .... 93 J5
Squirrels Drey CWTH RG45 .... 118 A5
Squirrels Wy EARL RG6 .... 9 K8
Stable Cl HTWY RG27 .... 163 J2
 THLE RG7 .... 91 F4
Stable Vw YTLY GU46 .... 135 J2
Staddlestone Cl CALC RG31 ...... 55 H3
Stadium Wy TLHT RG30 .... 56 C4
Stafford Cl WODY RG5 .... 59 J6
Staffordshire Cl TLHT RG30 ..... 56 A4
Staffordshire Cft BNFD RG42 .... 80 C4
Stag HI KEMP RG22 .... 175 J2
Stanbrook Cl THLE RG7 .... 68 D5
Stanfield TADY RG26 .... 126 E1
Stanford Rd KEMP RG22 .... 175 J5
Stanham Rd TLHT RG30 .... 56 A5
Stanhope Rd WHIT RG2 .... 7 M5
Stanlake La WAR/TWY RG10 .... 60 E1
Stanley Gv READ RG1 .... 2 D5
Stanley Rd EWKG RG40 .... 97 K1
 NWBY RG14 .... 13 G6
Stanley St READ RG1 .... 2 E5
Stanmore Cl ASC SL5 .... 101 K7
Stanmore Gdns THLE RG7 .... 110 E3
Stanmore Rd KSCL RG20 .... 20 D4
 KSCL RG20 .... 34 A2
Stanshawe Rd READ RG1 .... 3 G4
Stanton Cl EARL RG6 .... 9 L3
Stanton Dr FLET GU13 .... 167 F3
Stapleford Rd TLHT RG30 .... 72 D2
Staplehurst BRAK RG12 .... 99 F5
Stapleton Cl NWBY RG14 .... 103 F2
Star HI HTWY RG27 .... 166 D7
Star La KSCL RG20 .... 120 C3
 WAR/TWY RG10 .... 33 H5
Starling Cl KEMP RG22 .... 174 E4
 WWKG RG41 .... 96 E2
Starlings Dr CALC RG31 .... 55 G7
Starmead Dr EWKG RG40 .... 97 J2
Starting Gates NWBY RG14 .... 13 J8
Statham Ct BNFD RG42 .... 79 F6
Station Ap READ RG1 .... 3 H4
Station HI ASC SL5 .... 101 K1
 OVTN RG25 .... 171 J2
 READ RG1 .... 3 H4
Station Rd BRAK RG12 .... 10 F4
 DEAN RG23 .... 173 J2
 EARL RG6 .... 9 M3
 EWKG RG40 .... 97 G1
 GOR/PANG RG8 .... 25 F5
 HEN RG9 .... 31 H2
 HEN RG9 .... 31 K7
 HTWY RG27 .... 163 K2
 KSCL RG20 .... 102 D5
 NWBY RG14 .... 12 E6
 NWBY RG14 .... 83 G2
 OVTN RG25 .... 171 J4
 OVTN RG25 .... 176 C5
 READ RG1 .... 3 H5
 STHA RG19 .... 85 K4
 THLE RG7 .... 70 D3
 THLE RG7 .... 87 K5
 THLE RG7 .... 111 K3
 WAR/TWY RG10 .... 46 E6
 WAR/TWY RG10 .... 60 C1
 WHCH RG28 .... 169 H6
Staverton Cl EWKG RG40 .... 98 A1
Steeple Wk EARL RG6 .... 74 C6
Steerforth Copse SHST GU47 ... 119 F6
Steggles Cl WODY RG5 .... 59 G5
Stephanie Chase Ct
 EWKG RG40 .... 77 J7
Stephen's Cl WAR/TWY RG10 ...... 60 E2
Stephen's Cl THLE RG7 .... 110 E2
Stephens Firs THLE RG7 .... 110 D2
Stephenson Rd NTHA RG18 .... 85 H3
Stephenson Rd WHIT RG2 .... 115 K1

Stephens Rd TADY RG26 .... 127 F1
 THLE RG7 .... 110 E2
Sterling Wy TLHT RG30 .... 56 B4
Stevens HI YTLY GU46 .... 135 K4
Stevens La HEN RG9 .... 28 E3
Stevenson Dr BNFD RG42 .... 78 D3
Stilton Cl EARL RG6 .... 75 H4
Stilwell Cl YTLY GU46 .... 135 K3
Stirling Cl CAV/SC RG4 .... 44 A6
Stirling Wy NTHA RG18 .... 85 H3
Stirrup Pightle NWBY RG14 ...... 104 A1
Stockbridge Cl CHAM RG24 .... 145 J6
Stockbridge Wy YTLY GU46 .... 135 J5
Stockbury Cl EARL RG6 .... 9 J9
Stocker Cl BSTK RG21 .... 176 B2
Stockton Av FLET GU13 .... 167 G1
Stockton Pk FLET GU13 .... 167 G1
Stockton Rd WHIT RG2 .... 73 K5
Stockeford Cl BRAK RG12 .... 100 C3
Stoken La HTWY RG27 .... 148 E3
Stoke Row Rd HEN RG9 .... 29 F3
Stokes Cl STHA RG19 .... 107 K7
Stokes Vw GOR/PANG RG8 .... 40 B7
Stonea Cl EARL RG6 .... 75 F6
Stone Copse NTHA RG18 .... 64 D7
Stoneham Cl TLHT RG30 .... 56 B7
Stonehaven Dr WODY RG5 .... 59 K7
Stone St TLHT RG30 .... 56 C4
Stoney Cl YTLY GU46 .... 135 J5
Stoneyfield THLE RG7 .... 88 D1
Stone La NWBY RG14 .... 84 C1
 STHA RG19 .... 85 K4
Stoney Rd BNFD RG42 .... 10 C2
Stookes Wy YTLY GU46 .... 135 G5
Stour Cl TLHT RG30 .... 56 B5
Stour Rd DEAN RG23 .... 174 A3
Stow Rd HEN RG9 .... 31 J3
St Patrick's Br WAR/TWY RG10 ... 45 G6
Strachey Cl GOR/PANG RG8 .... 54 B2
The Straight Mile
 WAR/TWY RG10 .... 61 J5
Strand Wy EARL RG6 .... 74 E5
Stratfield BRAK RG12 .... 99 F6
Stratfield Av YTLY GU46 .... 135 H2
Stratfield Cl BSTK RG21 .... 160 C3
Stratfield Saye Rd TADY RG26 ... 129 H4
Stratford Wy CALC RG31 .... 55 F7
Stratheden Pl READ RG1 .... 2 E6
Strathmore Dr WAR/TWY RG10 ..... 59 K1
Strathy Cl TLHT RG30 .... 56 C5
Stratton Gdns WHIT RG2 .... 73 K5
Stratton Rd BSTK RG21 .... 176 A2
Strauss Cl KEMP RG22 .... 175 H4
Stravinsky Rd KEMP RG22 .... 176 A4
Strawberry Flds TADY RG26 ...... 129 G6
Strawberry HI BNFD RG42 .... 80 B4
 NWBY RG14 .... 12 D2
Streamside FLET GU13 .... 167 H3
Streatley HI GOR/PANG RG8 ...... 24 B5
Street End HTWY RG27 .... 150 C6
The Street CHAM RG24 .... 161 H5
 FLET GU13 .... 166 E6
 HTWY RG27 .... 147 H5
 ODIM RG29 .... 179 J1
 TADY RG26 .... 128 E7
 THLE RG7 .... 70 A1
 THLE RG7 .... 108 D1
 THLE RG7 .... 111 G3
 THLE RG7 .... 113 K2
Stretton Cl THLE RG7 .... 68 D5
Strokins Rd KSCL RG20 .... 124 A6
Stroud Cl CHAM RG24 .... 161 F1
Stroud La HTWY RG27 .... 166 D6
Stroudley Rd CHAM RG24 .... 161 F4
Strouds Meadow NTHA RG18 .... 86 A3
The Strouds THLE RG7 .... 88 C1
Stuart Cl CAV/SC RG4 .... 43 J7
Stuart Rd NWBY RG14 .... 103 F2
Stubbs Rd BSTK RG21 .... 176 D2
Studland Cl WHIT RG2 .... 73 K7
Stukeley Rd BSTK RG21 .... 14 B7
Sturbridge Cl EARL RG6 .... 9 M9
Sturges Rd EWKG RG40 .... 97 H2
Suck's La GOR/PANG RG8 .... 52 A3
Suffolk Cl WWKG RG41 .... 96 C1
Suffolk Combe BNFD RG42 .... 80 C5
Suffolk Rd TLHT RG30 .... 2 A7
 TLHT RG30 .... 56 D6
Sulham La GOR/PANG RG8 .... 54 D1
Sulhamstead HI THLE RG7 .... 90 B1
Sulhamstead Rd THLE RG7 .... 90 C3
Sullivan Rd KEMP RG22 .... 175 K3
Summer Down La DEAN RG23 ...... 157 H8
Summerfield Cl WWKG RG41 .... 76 E5
Summerfield Ri GOR/PANG RG8 ... 25 G4
Summerfields CHAM RG24 .... 145 H6
Summit Cl EWKG RG40 .... 116 E2
Sunderland Cl WODY RG5 .... 60 A5
Sunderland Pl NTHA RG18 .... 85 H3
Sundew Cl EWKG RG40 .... 77 K7
Sundial Cl TLHT RG30 .... 56 B7
Sunflower Cl KEMP RG22 .... 175 F5
Sun Gdns THLE RG7 .... 91 F6
Sun La THLE RG7 .... 113 J6
Sunley Cl NWBY RG14 .... 103 G2
Sunnybank ASC SL5 .... 101 K2
Sunny Md DEAN RG23 .... 174 A4
Sunnyside FLET GU13 .... 167 F1
Sun St READ RG1 .... 4 B6
Surley Rw CAV/SC RG4 .... 43 H7
Surrey Ct BNFD RG42 .... 80 C5
Surrey Rd WHIT RG2 .... 7 K4
Sussex Gdns FARN GU14 .... 151 J6
 WODY RG5 .... 59 H6
Sussex La THLE RG7 .... 93 K6
Sutcliffe Av EARL RG6 .... 75 G3
Sutherland Cha ASC SL5 .... 81 H7
Sutherland Gv CALC RG31 .... 71 K2
Sutherlands Av READ RG1 .... 103 H1
Sutherlands Av READ RG1 .... 7 M2
Sutton Cl BSTK RG21 .... 14 E1
 NWBY RG14 .... 83 G2
Suttons Park Av EARL RG6 .... 4 E5
 READ RG1 .... 4 E5
Swains Cl TADY RG26 .... 126 E1
Swains Rd TADY RG26 .... 126 E1
Swainstone Rd WHIT RG2 .... 7 K2
Swaledale BRAK RG12 .... 99 H3

Swaledale Gdns FARN GU14 .... 151 J6
Swallow Cl CALC RG31 .... 55 H7
 KEMP RG22 .... 174 E4
 YTLY GU46 .... 135 G2
Swallowfield Dr WHIT RG2 .... 93 J1
Swallow Field Gdns THLE RG7 .... 70 D2
Swallowfield Rd THLE RG7 .... 114 D2
Swallow Wy WWKG RG41 .... 96 D2
Swancote Gn BRAK RG12 .... 10 E9
Swan Ct HTWY RG27 .... 149 J4
Swan Dr THLE RG7 .... 88 E4
Swan Ms ODIM RG29 .... 164 B7
Swanmore Cl EARL RG6 .... 75 H5
Swan Pl READ RG1 .... 3 H7
Swans Ct WAR/TWY RG10 .... 60 D2
Swansea Rd READ RG1 .... 3 G3
Swansea Ter CALC RG31 .... 55 J4
Swanston Fld GOR/PANG RG8 ...... 40 C5
Swan St KSCL RG20 .... 139 K3
Swan Wy FLET GU13 .... 166 E4
Swedish Houses TADY RG26 .... 127 F2
Sweetbriar CWTH RG45 .... 118 B3
Sweet Briar Dr CALC RG31 .... 71 H2
Sweetzer's Piece THLE RG7 ...... 110 D2
Swepstone Cl EARL RG6 .... 9 M8
Swift Cl WWKG RG41 .... 96 D2
Swinbrook Cl CALC RG31 .... 55 J2
Swing Swang La CHAM RG24 .... 161 G4
Swinley Rd ASC SL5 .... 101 F2
Swiss Cottage Cl CALC RG31 ..... 55 H5
Swithin Cha BNFD RG42 .... 80 B5
Sycamore Cl TLHT RG30 .... 91 G2
 WODY RG5 .... 9 M2
Sycamore Crs FLET GU13 .... 167 F5
Sycamore Dr WAR/TWY RG10 .... 46 C7
Sycamore Ri BRAK RG12 .... 11 K5
 NWBY RG14 .... 84 B1
Sycamore Rd WHIT RG2 .... 8 C7
Sycamore Wy DEAN RG23 .... 159 J4
The Sydings NWBY RG14 .... 83 G2
Sydney Cl CWTH RG45 .... 118 D1
Sylvan Rdg SHST GU47 .... 118 B7
Sylvanus BRAK RG12 .... 99 G5
Sylvan Wy FLET GU13 .... 167 G6
Sylverns Ct BNFD RG42 .... 80 A5
Sylvester Cl NWBY RG14 .... 83 H2
 WAR/TWY RG10 .... 76 C3
Symondson Ms BNFD RG42 .... 78 D2
Sympson Rd TADY RG26 .... 109 G7

Tadham Pl STHA RG19 .... 85 H5
Tadley Common Rd TADY RG26 ... 109 F7
Tadley HI TADY RG26 .... 127 F2
Tadpole La NFNM GU10 .... 183 J3
Taff Wy TLHT RG30 .... 56 B6
Tag La WAR/TWY RG10 .... 47 F3
Talbot Cl NWBY RG14 .... 83 G1
Talbot Ct READ RG1 .... 3 G7
Talbot Wy CALC RG31 .... 55 H2
Talfourd Av EARL RG6 .... 9 G2
Talisman Cl CWTH RG45 .... 117 J3
Tallis Gdns KEMP RG22 .... 175 K3
Tallis La TLHT RG30 .... 6 A3
Talmey Cl CHAM RG24 .... 145 F7
Tamar Dr DEAN RG23 .... 174 A3
Tamar Gdns WHIT RG2 .... 7 M6
Tamarind Wy EARL RG6 .... 8 F9
Tamarisk Av WHIT RG2 .... 8 C9
Tamarisk Cl KEMP RG22 .... 175 H7
Tamarisk Ri NTHA RG18 .... 86 A5
Tamarisk Rd WHIT RG2 .... 77 H7
Tamar Wy WWKG RG41 .... 96 D1
Tamworth BRAK RG12 .... 100 A5
Tamworth Cl EARL RG6 .... 9 M9
Tamworth Dr FARN GU14 .... 151 J6
Tanglewood EWKG RG40 .... 117 F1
Tangley Dr WWKG RG41 .... 97 G3
Tangway CHAM RG24 .... 145 G6
Tanhouse La WWKG RG41 .... 97 F2
Tanners Cl THLE RG7 .... 90 E6
Tanners La CAV/SC RG4 .... 43 G4
Tanners Wy DEAN RG23 .... 174 A2
Tape La WAR/TWY RG10 .... 60 E5
Taplin's Farm La HTWY RG27 ..... 149 K7
Target HI BNFD RG42 .... 79 G6
Targett Ct WWKG RG41 .... 76 A4
Tarlton Ct TLHT RG30 .... 55 K7
Tarnbrook Wy BRAK RG12 .... 100 B5
Tarn La NWBY RG14 .... 12 C9
Tarragon Cl EARL RG6 .... 8 F9
Tarragon Wy THLE RG7 .... 91 G4
Tarrant Gn BNFD RG42 .... 79 K5
Tasmania Cl CHAM RG24 .... 160 D1
Tattersall Cl EWKG RG40 .... 97 K2
Taverner Cl BSTK RG21 .... 15 J1
Tavistock Cl FLET GU13 .... 166 E3
 WHIT RG2 .... 7 K6
Tawfield BRAK RG12 .... 99 F5
Taylor Dr TADY RG26 .... 129 H7
Tay Rd TLHT RG30 .... 56 B6
Tazewell Ct READ RG1 .... 2 E9
Teal Crs KEMP RG22 .... 174 E5
Tebbit Cl BRAK RG12 .... 11 J4
Telford Crs WODY RG5 .... 59 J4
Temple Ms WODY RG5 .... 59 J6
Temple Pl READ RG1 .... 3 H8
Templeton Gdns WHIT RG2 .... 7 L9
Tenaplas Dr GOR/PANG RG8 .... 38 C7
Tenby Av CAV/SC RG4 .... 44 A7
Tennyson Rd NTHA RG18 .... 85 H3
 WODY RG5 .... 59 H6
Tennyson Wy KEMP RG22 .... 175 K1
Teresa V BNFD RG42 .... 80 B4
Tern Cl TLHT RG30 .... 56 B6
Terrace Rd North BNFD RG42 ..... 78 D3
Terrace Rd South BNFD RG42 ..... 78 D4
The Terrace CWTH RG45 .... 118 E3
 EWKG RG40 .... 97 G1
Tesimond Dr YTLY GU46 .... 135 F4
Tessa Rd READ RG1 .... 2 E2
Test Cl TLHT RG30 .... 56 B5
Test Wy BSTK RG21 .... 15 J5
Teviot Rd TLHT RG30 .... 55 K6

Tewkesbury Cl *CHAM* RG24 **160** C2
Thackham's La *HTWY* RG27 **148** E5
The Thakerays *STHA* RG19 **85** J5 8
Thames Av *GOR/PANG* RG8 **40** C6
READ RG1 **3** H2
Thames Ct *BSTK* RG21 **15** J4
READ RG1 **2** D3
Thames Dr *WAR/TWY* RG10 **45** J6
Thames Pth *GOR/PANG* RG8 **24** E7
GOR/PANG RG8 **39** K3
GOR/PANG RG8 **41** H7
HEN RG9 **19** F7
HEN RG9 **32** A5
READ RG1 **57** F3
Thames Reach *GOR/PANG* RG8 **55** J1
Thames Rd *GOR/PANG* RG8 **24** E5
NTHA RG18 **85** G2
Thames Side *HEN* RG9 **31** H1
Thames Side Prom *READ* RG1 **2** F1
Thames St *CAV/SC* RG4 **59** G1
Thanington Wy *EARL* RG6 **9** J8
Theale Rd *TLHT* RG30 **91** G1
Theobald Dr *CALC* RG31 **55** J1
Thetford Ms *CAV/SC* RG4 **44** A6 2
Thicket Rd *TLHT* RG30 **55** K5
Third St *STHA* RG19 **104** E3
Thirlmere Av *TLHT* RG30 **56** A4
Thirlmere Crs *FLET* GU13 **167** F6 4
Thirtover *NTHA* RG18 **65** G5
Thistledown *CALC* RG31 **55** H4 5
Thistleton Wy *EARL* RG6 **75** H4
Thomas Dr *BNFD* RG42 **80** B5 10
Thomas La *EWKG* RG40 **96** D7
Thompson Cl *NTHA* RG18 **48** E7 4
Thompson Dr *STHA* RG19 **85** K5 2
Thomson Wk *CALC* RG31 **71** K2
Thornbers Wy *WAR/TWY* RG10 **46** A7
Thornbridge Rd *WHIT* RG2 **73** J6
Thornbury Cl *CWTH* RG45 **118** C3
Thorne Cl *CWTH* RG45 **118** B1 3
WWKG RG41 **96** C4
Thorneley Rd *KSCL* RG20 **124** A7 3
Thorney Cl *EARL* RG6 **75** H4
Thornfield *STHA* RG19 **105** J5 1
Thornford Rd *STHA* RG19 **105** J6
Thornhill *BRAK* RG12 **11** L8
Thornhill Wy *CHAM* RG24 **145** H6
Thorn La *READ* RG1 **3** J6
Thorn St *READ* RG1 **3** G6
Thornton Ms *TLHT* RG30 **56** D5 3
Thorp Cl *BNFD* RG42 **78** D3 2
Thorpe Cl *WWKG* RG41 **97** F4
Thrale Ms *TLHT* RG30 **56** C5
Three Acre Rd *NWBY* RG14 **83** J7
Three Castles Pth *ASC* SL5 **101** F1
HTWY RG27 **133** K4
HTWY RG27 **135** F2
ODIM RG29 **164** A7
ODIM RG29 **179** J2
OVTN RG25 **178** D3
Three Firs Wy *THLE* RG7 **90** D6
Three Gables La *GOR/PANG* RG8 **24** D4
Threshers Cnr *FARN* GU14 **151** K6 3
Threshfield *BRAK* RG12 **10** C9
Throgmorton Rd *YTLY* GU46 **135** F4
Thrush Cl *THLE* RG7 **91** G4
Thumwood *CHAM* RG24 **145** G7 1
Thurlestone Gdns *WHIT* RG2 **7** L7
Thurnscoe Cl *EARL* RG6 **74** C6 1
Thurso Cl *TLHT* RG30 **56** B5
Thurston Pl *BSTK* RG21 **176** A3
Thyme Cl *CHAM* RG24 **145** H6
EARL RG6 **74** C5
Tiberius Cl *DEAN* RG23 **159** H4
Tickenor Dr *EWKG* RG40 **116** E1
Tickhill Cl *EARL* RG6 **74** C7 1
Tidmarsh La *GOR/PANG* RG8 **53** K3
Tidmarsh Rd *GOR/PANG* RG8 **54** B1
Tidmarsh St *TLHT* RG30 **56** C5
Tidmore La *GOR/PANG* RG8 **26** E2
Tiffany Cl *WWKG* RG41 **96** C1
Tiger Cl *WODY* RG5 **60** A6
Tigerseye Cl *WWKG* RG41 **76** C7 2
Tilbury Cl *CAV/SC* RG4 **57** K2
Tilebarn Cl *HEN* RG9 **31** F2
Tilehurst La *BNFD* RG42 **78** E3
Tilehurst Rd *READ* RG1 **2** D7
TLHT RG30 **2** A7
TLHT RG30 **56** C7
Tilling Cl *CALC* RG31 **55** G3
Tilney Wy *EARL* RG6 **74** C6 7
Timberlake Rd *BSTK* RG21 **14** E5
Timberley Pl *CWTH* RG45 **117** K4 2
Timline Gn *BRAK* RG12 **80** C7
Tindal Cl *YTLY* GU46 **135** J3
Tinsley Cl *EARL* RG6 **74** C6
Tintagel Cl *DEAN* RG23 **159** H5
Tintagel Rd *EWKG* RG40 **97** F7
Tintern Cl *CHAM* RG24 **160** A3
Tintern Crs *READ* RG1 **6** E2
Tinwell Cl *EARL* RG6 **75** H4
Tippet Gdns *KEMP* RG22 **176** A4
Tippett Ri *WHIT* RG2 **7** J1
Tippings La *WODY* RG5 **59** K4
Tippits Md *BNFD* RG42 **78** E7
Tiptree Cl *EARL* RG6 **74** C6 3
Titchfield Cl *TADY* RG26 **127** F2 3
Tithebarn Gv *CALC* RG31 **72** A2 4
Tithe Meadow *KEMP* RG22 **175** H7 2
Tiverton Cl *WODY* RG5 **59** H4
Tiverton Rd *DEAN* RG23 **159** H6
Tobago Cl *CHAM* RG24 **160** C2
Tocker Gdns *BNFD* RG42 **79** J4 3
Tofrek Ter *TLHT* RG30 **56** D6
Tokers Green La *CAV/SC* RG4 **42** E3
Tollgate Cl *DEAN* RG23 **174** A1
Tollway *CHAM* RG24 **145** H7
Tomlin Cl *STHA* RG19 **85** K5 3
Tomlins Cl *TADY* RG26 **126** E2
Tomlinson Dr *EWKG* RG40 **117** F2
Topaz Cl *WWKG* RG41 **76** D7
Top Common *BRAK* RG12 **80** A5
Tope Rd *WHIT* RG2 **95** J7
The Topiary *CHAM* RG24 **161** H3
Torcross Gv *CALC* RG31 **71** G2
Torrington Rd *WHIT* RG2 **7** M8
Toseland Wy *EARL* RG6 **75** H3
Totale Ri *BNFD* RG42 **79** J4 3
Totnes Rd *WHIT* RG2 **7** M8
Tottenham Cl *TADY* RG26 **129** G5
Tottenham Wk *SHST* GU47 **118** E7
Totterdown *THLE* RG7 **90** E6
Totters La *HTWY* RG27 **164** E2
Toutley Cl *WWKG* RG41 **76** D5
Toutley Rd *WWKG* RG41 **77** F5
Tower Cl *CAV/SC* RG4 **43** K5
Towers Dr *CWTH* RG45 **118** C4
Town Mill La *WHCH* RG28 **169** J7
Townsend Cl *BRAK* RG12 **11** M9
BSTK RG21 **14** B6
Townsend Rd *GOR/PANG* RG8 **24** D4
GOR/PANG RG8 **37** F1
Trafalgar Cl *WWKG* RG41 **96** D1 11
Trafalgar Ct *TLHT* RG30 **2** B9
Trafford Rd *READ* RG1 **2** D3
Tredegar Rd *CAV/SC* RG4 **43** G7
Tree Cl *TLHT* RG30 **55** J5 3
Treeton Cl *EARL* RG6 **74** C6 3
Trefoil Cl *EWKG* RG40 **77** K7
HTWY RG27 **149** H3
Trefoil Dro *NTHA* RG18 **86** A3
Treforgan *CAV/SC* RG4 **43** G7 1
Trelawney Dr *CALC* RG31 **55** G4
Trelleck Rd *READ* RG1 **6** F2
Trellis Dr *CHAM* RG24 **161** H3
Trent Cl *WWKG* RG41 **76** D7
Trent Crs *NTHA* RG18 **85** G2
Trent Wy *BSTK* RG21 **15** K5
Tresham Crs *YTLY* GU46 **135** F3 2
Trevelyan *BRAK* RG12 **99** F5
The Triangle *NWBY* RG14 **104** A1
Trindledown *BNFD* RG42 **79** H5
Tring Rd *CALC* RG31 **55** H2
Trinidad Cl *CHAM* RG24 **160** C2
Trinity *SHST* GU47 **119** F6
Trinity Ct *THLE* RG7 **70** C3 3
Trinity Pl *READ* RG1 **2** F6
Triumph Cl *WODY* RG5 **75** J1 1
Trotwood Cl *SHST* GU47 **119** F6 5
Troutbeck Cl *WAR/TWY* RG10 **46** C6
Trout Cl *EARL* RG6 **5** G4
Trout Wk *NWBY* RG14 **84** A2
Trowe's La *THLE* RG7 **112** E4
THLE RG7 **114** A3
Trumbull Rd *BNFD* RG42 **79** H5
Trust Cl *HTWY* RG27 **163** J2 4
Trust Cnr *HEN* RG9 **31** H3
Trusthorpe Cl *EARL* RG6 **75** H4
Tubb's La *KSCL* RG20 **120** C3
TADY RG26 **143** F2
Tudor Av *KSCL* RG20 **48** B1
Tudor Cl *EWKG* RG40 **98** A2
Tudor Dr *YTLY* GU46 **135** J4 4
Tudor Rd *NWBY* RG14 **12** F7
READ RG1 **3** G4
Tudor Wy *FLET* GU13 **167** H7
Tulip Cl *KEMP* RG22 **175** F5
Tuns La *HEN* RG9 **31** H1
Tunworth Ms *TADY* RG26 **127** F1
Tunworth Rd *OVTN* RG25 **162** B7
OVTN RG25 **178** A3
Tupsley Rd *READ* RG1 **6** E2
Turbary Gdns *TADY* RG26 **108** E7
Turk's La *THLE* RG7 **110** E4
Turmeric Cl *EARL* RG6 **8** F9
Turnberry *BRAK* RG12 **99** F4
Turnbridge Cl *EARL* RG6 **74** E6
Turner Cl *BSTK* RG21 **15** L7
Turners Dr *STHA* RG19 **85** K4
Turner's Green La *HTWY* RG27 **150** D6
The Turnery *STHA* RG19 **85** H4 3
Turnfields *STHA* RG19 **85** J4
Turnpike Rd *BNFD* RG42 **78** E7
NTHA RG18 **84** D3
NWBY RG14 **13** M1
Turnpike Wy *DEAN* RG23 **173** K2
Turnstone Cl *WWKG* RG41 **75** K3
Turnstone End *YTLY* GU46 **135** G3 4
Tuscan Cl *TLHT* RG30 **55** K5
Tuxford Ms *TLHT* RG30 **56** C6 4
Tweedsmuir Cl *KEMP* RG22 **159** G7
Tweseldown Rd *FLET* GU13 **167** J7
Twin Oaks *CAV/SC* RG4 **43** J6
Twisell Thorne *FLET* GU13 **167** F7
Two Gate La *OVTN* RG25 **171** J5
Two Gate Meadow *OVTN* RG25 **171** J4
Two Rivers Wy *NWBY* RG14 **13** M3
Two Tree Hl *HEN* RG9 **30** E3
Twycross Rd *EWKG* RG40 **77** K7
Twyford Rd *EWKG* RG40 **77** G6
WAR/TWY RG10 **47** K6
Tyberton Pl *READ* RG1 **6** E2
Tydehams *NWBY* RG14 **103** H1
Tyfield *CHAM* RG24 **143** K7
Tyler Cl *CAV/SC* RG4 **43** F7
Tyler Dr *WHIT* RG2 **115** H1
Tyle Rd *TLHT* RG30 **55** J5 7
Tyler's La *THLE* RG7 **66** C4
Tylers Pl *TLHT* RG30 **56** A5 3
Tylney La *HTWY* RG27 **163** G2
Tylorstown *CAV/SC* RG4 **43** G6
Tyne Wy *NTHA* RG18 **85** G2
Tytherton *BRAK* RG12 **11** H4

U

Uffcott Cl *EARL* RG6 **74** C6 10
Uffington Cl *CALC* RG31 **55** H5
Uffington Dr *BRAK* RG12 **11** M7
Ullswater *BRAK* RG12 **99** F5
Ullswater Cl *STHA* RG19 **85** F4
Ullswater Dr *CALC* RG31 **55** J2
Ulster Cl *CAV/SC* RG4 **44** A7
Underwood *BRAK* RG12 **99** F4
Underwood Rd *TLHT* RG30 **72** A2
Union Cl *SHST* GU47 **119** F6
Union La *KSCL* RG20 **124** A4
Union Rd *THLE* RG7 **69** F3
Unity Cl *CAV/SC* RG4 **43** J6
Upavon Dr *READ* RG1 **6** D1
Upavon Gdns *BRAK* RG12 **100** C3
Upfallow *CHAM* RG24 **161** H4
Uplands Rd *CAV/SC* RG4 **43** F7
Upper Broadmoor Rd
CWTH RG45 **118** E3
Upper Chestnut Dr *BSTK* RG21 **14** A8
Upper Crown St *READ* RG1 **3** K8
Upper Farm Rd *DEAN* RG23 **173** K4
Upper Meadow Rd *WHIT* RG2 **8** A7
Upper Red Cross Rd
GOR/PANG RG8 **25** F4
Upper Redlands Rd *READ* RG1 **8** B1
Upper Sherborne Rd
BSTK RG21 **160** B4
Upper St *FLET* GU13 **167** G2
Upper Warren Av *CAV/SC* RG4 **56** D2
Upper Woodcote Rd
CAV/SC RG4 **42** E7
Uppingham Dr *WODY* RG5 **59** J4
Uppingham Gdns *CAV/SC* RG4 **44** A6 3
Upron Field Cl *KEMP* RG22 **175** G5
Upshire Gdns *BRAK* RG12 **100** C2
Upton Cl *HEN* RG9 **31** H2
Upton Crs *BSTK* RG21 **160** B4
Upton Grey Rd *OVTN* RG25 **179** G3
Upton Rd *TLHT* RG30 **56** B6
Urquhart Rd *STHA* RG19 **85** J6
Usk Rd *TLHT* RG30 **56** A7

V

Vachel Rd *READ* RG1 **3** G5
Vale Crs *TLHT* RG30 **55** K4
Valentia Rd *TLHT* RG30 **2** B5
Valentine Cl *WHIT* RG2 **74** B5
Valentine Crs *CAV/SC* RG4 **57** K1
The Vale *DEAN* RG23 **173** K3
Vale Vw *WAR/TWY* RG10 **60** A1
Vale View Dr *THLE* RG7 **112** E3
Valley Cl *CAV/SC* RG4 **57** H1
GOR/PANG RG8 **25** F5 3
Valley Crs *WWKG* RG41 **77** F6
Valley Rd *HEN* RG9 **30** E3
NWBY RG14 **12** A9
NWBY RG14 **83** G7
THLE RG7 **91** F4
Valley Wy *TADY* RG26 **109** H7
Valmeade Cl *HTWY* RG27 **164** A2 7
Valon Rd *WHIT* RG2 **95** H6
Valpy St *READ* RG1 **3** J5
Vanburgh Gdns *KEMP* RG22 **175** G5
Van Dyck Cl *BSTK* RG21 **15** L8
Vandyke *BRAK* RG12 **99** F4
Vanlore Wy *CALC* RG31 **71** H1 3
Vanners La *KSCL* RG20 **102** A3
Vastern Rd *READ* RG1 **3** H3
Vauxhall Dr *WODY* RG5 **59** J7
Velmead Cl *FLET* GU13 **167** J4
Velmead Rd *FLET* GU13 **167** H4
Venetia Cl *CAV/SC* RG4 **43** K5
Venning Rd *WHIT* RG2 **95** J7
Ventnor Rd *CALC* RG31 **55** J4 4
Verbena Cl *WWKG* RG41 **75** K3
Verdi Cl *KEMP* RG22 **175** J4
Verey Cl *WAR/TWY* RG10 **60** E2
Vermont Woods *EWKG* RG40 **116** D1
The Verne *FLET* GU13 **167** H6
Verney Ms *TLHT* RG30 **56** D6
Vernon Crs *WHIT* RG2 **73** J7
Vernon Dr *ASC* SL5 **81** G7
Veronica Cl *KEMP* RG22 **175** F5
Veronica Dr *FLET* GU13 **166** E6
Vespasian Gdns *CHAM* RG24 **159** H3
Vetch Flds *HTWY* RG27 **164** B2
Viables La *BSTK* RG21 **176** C3
Vicarage Cl *EWKG* RG40 **116** E2 2
Vicarage Gdns *ASC* SL5 **101** K3 1
FLET GU13 **167** G7
Vicarage Hl *HTWY* RG27 **149** J5
Vicarage La *HTWY* RG27 **147** J1
NTHA RG18 **65** H6
YTLY GU46 **135** H2
Vicarage Rd *HEN* RG9 **31** H3
WHIT RG2 **7** M2
YTLY GU46 **135** H2
Vicarage Wood Wy
CALC RG31 **55** G4 2
Victoria Gdns *NWBY* RG14 **12** F2
Victoria Hill Rd *FLET* GU13 **167** F2
Victoria Rd *ASC* SL5 **101** K3
CALC RG31 **55** J5
CAV/SC RG4 **57** H2
FLET GU13 **167** F2
SHST GU47 **119** F7
THLE RG7 **110** E2
WAR/TWY RG10 **46** D2
Victoria St *BSTK* RG21 **14** E6
READ RG1 **4** A7
Victor Pl *THLE* RG7 **87** K5
Victor Rd *STHA* RG19 **85** K4
Victor Wy *WODY* RG5 **59** K6
Victory Rbt *BSTK* RG21 **14** D4
Vigo La *YTLY* GU46 **135** H4
Viking *BRAK* RG12 **99** F3
Village Cl *WHIT* RG2 **93** J1 3
The Village *EWKG* RG40 **116** D5
Village Wy *YTLY* GU46 **135** J2
Villiers Md *WWKG* RG41 **97** F1
Villiers Wy *NWBY* RG14 **103** F2
Vincent Cl *WODY* RG5 **59** J7
Vincent Ri *BRAK* RG12 **11** L5
Vincent Rd *NTHA* RG18 **85** K3
Vine Crs *TLHT* RG30 **72** B2
The Vines *WWKG* RG41 **96** B4
Vine Tree Cl *TADY* RG26 **127** G2
Vinns La *OVTN* RG25 **171** G5
Viola Cft *BNFD* RG42 **80** C6 3
Violet Cl *KEMP* RG22 **175** F5
Violet Gv *NTHA* RG18 **85** K2
Violet La *TADY* RG26 **125** K3
Virginia Wy *TLHT* RG30 **72** C1
Viscount Wy *WODY* RG5 **59** J6
Vivaldi Cl *KEMP* RG22 **175** K5
Vivian Cl *FLET* GU13 **167** J5
Voller Dr *CALC* RG31 **55** H7
Volunteer Rd *THLE* RG7 **70** C3
Vulcan Cl *WODY* RG5 **60** A4
Vyne Meadow *CHAM* RG24 **144** A6
Vyne Rd *BSTK* RG21 **14** E2
CHAM RG24 **144** A6

W

Wade Rd *CHAM* RG24 **161** F3
Wadham *SHST* GU47 **119** G7
Wagbullock Ri *BRAK* RG12 **99** K4 6
Wagner Cl *KEMP* RG22 **175** K4
Wagon La *HTWY* RG27 **164** A1
Wagtail Cl *WAR/TWY* RG10 **60** D1
Waingels Rd *WODY* RG5 **59** K3
Wakeford Cl *TADY* RG26 **109** H7 2
Wakefords Copse *FLET* GU13 **183** J1
Wakefords Pk *FLET* GU13 **183** J1
Wakemans *GOR/PANG* RG8 **53** G1
Walbury *BRAK* RG12 **11** M8
Waldeck St *WHIT* RG2 **7** J1
Walden Av *WHIT* RG2 **95** F4
Waldron Hl *BRAK* RG12 **80** C6
Walker Cl *GOR/PANG* RG8 **26** D2 2
Walkers Pl *TLHT* RG30 **56** D6 3
Wallace Cl *WODY* RG5 **75** G1
Wallcroft Cl *BNFD* RG42 **79** F5 4
The Walled Gdn *WAR/TWY* RG10 **46** C2
Waller Ct *CAV/SC* RG4 **57** J3 1
Waller Dr *NWBY* RG14 **84** D2
Wallingford Cl *BRAK* RG12 **11** M8
Wallingford Rd *GOR/PANG* RG8 **24** D3
KSCL RG20 **21** K6
Wallins Copse *CHAM* RG24 **161** G1 4
Wallis Dr *TADY* RG26 **129** J7
Wallis Rd *BSTK* RG21 **14** E8
Wall La *THLE* RG7 **110** B6
Wallner Wy *EWKG* RG40 **97** J2
Wallop Dr *KEMP* RG22 **175** F6
Walmer Cl *CWTH* RG45 **118** D3
TLHT RG30 **56** B7 2
Walmer Rd *WODY* RG5 **59** J4
Walnut Cl *CAV/SC* RG4 **29** F6
WWKG RG41 **96** E2 9
YTLY GU46 **135** J5
Walnut Tree Cl *WAR/TWY* RG10 **46** D6
Walnut Tree Ct
GOR/PANG RG8 **25** F5 4
Walnut Wy *TLHT* RG30 **55** J5
Walrus Cl *WODY* RG5 **60** A6
Walsh Av *BNFD* RG42 **80** B5
Walter Rd *WWKG* RG41 **76** D6
Walters Cl *NTHA* RG18 **65** H6
Waltham Cl *SHST* GU47 **118** E7 9
Waltham Ct *OVTN* RG25 **171** J4 1
Waltham La *OVTN* RG25 **172** A7
Waltham Rd *OVTN* RG25 **171** J5
WAR/TWY RG10 **47** G7
WAR/TWY RG10 **60** D1
Walton Av *HEN* RG9 **31** H3
Walton Cl *WODY* RG5 **5** M6
Walton Dr *ASC* SL5 **81** J6
Walton Wy *NWBY* RG14 **13** J1
Wandhope Wy *CALC* RG31 **55** H3
Wansey Gdns *NWBY* RG14 **84** C2
Wanstraw Gv *BRAK* RG12 **100** B5 7
Wantage Cl *BRAK* RG12 **11** L9
Wantage Rd *GOR/PANG* RG8 **24** C2
TLHT RG30 **56** D6
Warbler Cl *CALC* RG31 **55** G7 4
Warbler Dr *EARL* RG6 **9** K9
Warbleton Rd *CHAM* RG24 **145** H7 5
Warblington Cl *TADY* RG26 **127** F2
Warborough Av *CALC* RG31 **55** G6
Warbreck Dr *CALC* RG31 **55** G2
Warbrook La *HTWY* RG27 **133** K1
Ward Cl *EWKG* RG40 **77** J6
Wardle Av *CALC* RG31 **55** J4
Wards Stone Pk *BRAK* RG12 **100** B5 8
Wareham Rd *BRAK* RG12 **100** C3
Warehouse Rd *STHA* RG19 **104** E3
Warfield Rd *BNFD* RG42 **79** K4
Warfield St *BNFD* RG42 **79** K3
Wargrave Hl *WAR/TWY* RG10 **46** C2
Wargrave Rd *HEN* RG9 **31** K3
WAR/TWY RG10 **46** C5
Waring Cl *EARL* RG6 **75** F6 13
The Warings *THLE* RG7 **68** D7
Warley Ri *CALC* RG31 **55** G1
Warnford Rd *TLHT* RG30 **56** A6
Warnham La *KSCL* RG20 **35** G2
Warnsham Cl *EARL* RG6 **74** E5
Warren Cl *FLET* GU13 **167** J4
HTWY RG27 **149** J5
THLE RG7 **91** F5
Warren Cnr *NFNM* GU10 **183** H5
Warren Down *BNFD* RG42 **79** F6 2
Warren House Rd *EWKG* RG40 **77** J6
Warren La *EWKG* RG40 **116** C3
Warren Rd *NWBY* RG14 **103** G2
WODY RG5 **59** G4
Warren Rw *ASC* SL5 **81** G7
Warren Row Rd *WAR/TWY* RG10 **32** E4
WAR/TWY RG10 **33** K7
The Warren *CAV/SC* RG4 **56** D2
READ RG1 **57** G3
TADY RG26 **126** D1
Warton Rd *BSTK* RG21 **15** G2
Warwick *BRAK* RG12 **100** B5
Warwick Dr *NWBY* RG14 **13** H8
Warwick Rd *DEAN* RG23 **159** H5
WHIT RG2 **7** L3
Wasdale Cl *SHST* GU47 **118** E6
Wash Brook *HTWY* RG27 **163** K1 3
Washington Gdns *EWKG* RG40 **97** F7
Washington Rd *CAV/SC* RG4 **57** J3
Wash Water *KSCL* RG20 **102** D5
Wasing La *THLE* RG7 **108** A2
Watch La *WHCH* RG28 **170** B3
Water End La *CHAM* RG24 **162** C4
Waterford Wy *EWKG* RG40 **97** H1 3
Waterham Rd *BRAK* RG12 **99** J4
Wateridge Rd *BSTK* RG21 **160** D3
Water La *STHA* RG19 **104** B1
Waterlily Cl *BSTK* RG21 **15** K5
Waterloo Av *DEAN* RG23 **159** H4
Waterloo Crs *EWKG* RG40 **97** K3
Waterloo Ri *WHIT* RG2 **7** J3
Waterloo Rd *CWTH* RG45 **118** B4
EWKG RG40 **97** K3
WHIT RG2 **7** J2
Waterman Pl *READ* RG1 **3** G2
Waterman's Rd *HEN* RG9 **31** H3
Watermans Wy *WAR/TWY* RG10 **46** B3
Water Rede *FLET* GU13 **183** F1
Water Ridges *DEAN* RG23 **174** A4
Water Rd *TLHT* RG30 **56** C6
Watersfield Cl *EARL* RG6 **74** E5 4
Waterside Ct *FARN* GU14 **151** J7
Waterside Dr *GOR/PANG* RG8 **41** J7
THLE RG7 **70** E3
Waterside Gdns *READ* RG1 **3** H7
Watersplash La *BNFD* RG42 **79** J4
Water St *NTHA* RG18 **36** A6
Water Wy *BSTK* RG21 **15** K4
Watery La *FLET* GU13 **183** F1
Watling End *KEMP* RG22 **175** G5
Watlington St *READ* RG1 **3** L6
Watmore La *WWKG* RG41 **76** C3
Watson Wy *DEAN* RG23 **159** J4
Wavell Cl *KEMP* RG22 **175** K2
WHIT RG2 **74** C5
Waverley *BRAK* RG12 **99** F3 1
Waverley Av *BSTK* RG21 **176** B2
FLET GU13 **151** G7
Waverley Cl *ODIM* RG29 **180** E1
Waverley Rd *TLHT* RG30 **56** C6
The Waverleys *NTHA* RG18 **85** J3 1
Waverley Wy *EWKG* RG40 **96** D6
Waybrook Crs *READ* RG1 **4** E9
Wayfarer's Wk *KSCL* RG20 **139** G4
Wayland Cl *BRAK* RG12 **100** C2
Waylands *THLE* RG7 **69** F2
Waylen St *READ* RG1 **2** F6
Wayside Gn *GOR/PANG* RG8 **26** D3
GOR/PANG RG8 **26** D3 2
Wayside Rd *DEAN* RG23 **159** G6
Wealden Wy *TLHT* RG30 **55** K5
Weald Ri *TLHT* RG30 **56** A3
Weatherby Gdns *HTWY* RG27 **149** J4 6
Weavers Wy *WAR/TWY* RG10 **60** C1
Webb Cl *BNFD* RG42 **79** F5
CHAM RG24 **161** F1
Webb Ct *EWKG* RG40 **77** K6
Webbs Acre *STHA* RG19 **86** A5
Webbs La *THLE* RG7 **68** E7
Wedderburn Cl *WWKG* RG41 **76** C4
Wedgewood Wy *TLHT* RG30 **56** A4 5
Wedman's La *HTWY* RG27 **147** J3
Weighbridge Rw *READ* RG1 **2** F3
Weir Cl *CALC* RG31 **72** A2 5
Weir Rd *HTWY* RG27 **149** G6
Welbeck *BRAK* RG12 **99** F3
Welby Crs *WWKG* RG41 **76** A5
Weldale St *READ* RG1 **2** F5
Weldon Cl *FLET* GU13 **167** J6
Welford Rd *WODY* RG5 **59** K5
Welland Cl *CALC* RG31 **55** H4
Wella Rd *KEMP* RG22 **176** A2
Weller Dr *EWKG* RG40 **115** K2
Weller's La *BNFD* RG42 **79** K1
Wellesley Dr *CWTH* RG45 **117** K3
Wellfield Cl *CALC* RG31 **55** H6 3
Well House La *HTWY* RG27 **114** E5
Wellhouse La *NTHA* RG18 **49** J7
Wellington Av *FLET* GU13 **167** J1
WHIT RG2 **8** B4
Wellington Cl *NWBY* RG14 **84** B2 3
Wellington Crs *TADY* RG26 **108** A7
Wellington Dr *BRAK* RG12 **11** K9
Wellington Gdns *THLE* RG7 **68** C5
Wellingtonia Av *EWKG* RG40 **117** G4
Wellington Rd *CWTH* RG45 **118** D4
EWKG RG40 **97** G1
Wellington Ter *DEAN* RG23 **159** H4
Wellmans Meadow *KSCL* RG20 **123** K6
Well Meadow *NWBY* RG14 **84** A2
Well Rd *NFNM* GU10 **182** D6
Well St *KSCL* RG20 **121** K3
Welsh La *THLE* RG7 **113** H6
Welshman's Rd *THLE* RG7 **110** A3
Welton Ct *BSTK* RG21 **14** C4
Welwick Cl *EARL* RG6 **75** H4 12
Wendan Rd *NWBY* RG14 **12** D9
Wendover Wy *TLHT* RG30 **55** J6
Wenlock Edge *WAR/TWY* RG10 **60** A1
Wenlock Wy *STHA* RG19 **85** J5 7
Wensley Cl *WAR/TWY* RG10 **46** C7
Wensley Dr *FLET* GU13 **151** H7 2
Wensley Rd *READ* RG1 **6** E2
Wentworth Av *ASC* SL5 **81** F7
WHIT RG2 **74** A6 2
Wentworth Cl *CWTH* RG45 **118** A2
YTLY GU46 **135** J4 5
Wentworth Ct *NWBY* RG14 **13** G7
Wentworth Wy *ASC* SL5 **81** F7
Wescott Rd *EWKG* RG40 **97** J1
Wessex Av *ODIM* RG29 **180** C3
Wessex Cl *BSTK* RG21 **14** C9
Wessex Crs *ODIM* RG29 **180** C3
Wessex Dr *ODIM* RG29 **180** C3
Wessex Gdns *WAR/TWY* RG10 **60** D2
Westbourne Ter *TLHT* RG30 **56** D6
West Brook Cl *DEAN* RG23 **174** A4
Westbrook Gdns *BRAK* RG12 **11** H2
Westbrook Rd *TLHT* RG30 **56** D4 3
Westbury Cl *CWTH* RG45 **118** C2
FLET GU13 **167** K3
Westbury La *GOR/PANG* RG8 **41** F6
West Chiltern *GOR/PANG* RG8 **26** D3 3
Westcombe Cl *BRAK* RG12 **100** A5
Westcote Rd *TLHT* RG30 **2** A8
Westcotts Gn *BNFD* RG42 **80** A5
West Ct *CAV/SC* RG4 **59** H3
Westdean Ct *BSTK* RG21 **14** B6
Westdeane Ct *BSTK* RG21 **14** B6
Westdene Cresent *CAV/SC* RG4 **57** F1
West Dr *CALC* RG31 **71** K1
CAV/SC RG4 **59** G4
West End *TADY* RG26 **143** J5
West End La *BNFD* RG42 **79** J3
West End Rd *THLE* RG7 **110** D3
Westerdale *STHA* RG19 **85** H4
Western Av *HEN* RG9 **31** H3
NWBY RG14 **12** E1
WODY RG5 **59** G5
Western Elms Av *TLHT* RG30 **2** C7

Western End NWBY RG14 12 A6 1
Western La ODIM RG29 180 C2
Western Oaks CALC RG31 55 K3
Western Rd BNFD RG42 79 F6
BRAK RG12 10 A3
HEN RG9 31 H3
READ RG1 2 C8
Western Wy KEMP RG22 175 J2
West Field Cl TADY RG26 127 G1
Westfield Crs HEN RG9 46 A1
NTHA RG18 85 G3
Westfield Rd BSTK RG21 15 H9
NTHA RG18 85 F2
WWKG RG41 76 A4
Westfields KSCL RG20 21 J7
Westfield Wy NWBY RG14 12 A6
West Fryerne YTLY GU46 135 J2
Westgate Rd NWBY RG14 12 A6
West Gn YTLY GU46 135 G2
West Green Rd HTWY RG27 148 E4
West Ham Cl KEMP RG22 159 H7
West Ham La KEMP RG22 159 G7
Westhatch La BNFD RG42 79 K2
West Hl READ RG1 3 J9
Westland NTHA RG18 85 G3 1
Westlands Rd NWBY RG14 12 F9
West La HEN RG9 31 G1 3
Westleigh Dr CAV/SC RG4 29 H7
Westlyn Rd TADY RG26 109 H7
Westmead Dr NWBY RG14 83 J7
West Mills NWBY RG14 12 D4
Westminster Cl FLET GU13 167 H1 1
KEMP RG22 175 G5 6
Westminster Wy EARL RG6 9 L9
Westmorland Cl WWKG RG41 96 C1 3
Westmorland Dr BNFD RG42 80 C4
Westonbirt Dr CAV/SC RG4 57 F2 1
Weston's KSCL RG20 34 C4
Westover Rd FLET GU13 167 J2
Westray Cl BSTK RG21 15 J1
Westridge KSCL RG20 120 B4
Westridge Av GOR/PANG RG8 41 H7 3
West Rd EWKG RG40 98 D5
HEN RG9 28 C1 1
Westside Cl KEMP RG22 175 J1 1
West St HEN RG9 31 G1
KSCL RG20 121 H4
NWBY RG14 12 D3
ODIM RG29 180 B2
READ RG1 3 G5
TADY RG26 127 G1
Westview Dr WAR/TWY RG10 46 C6
Westward Rd WWKG RG41 76 E7
Westway GOR/PANG RG8 25 F3 2
Westwood Gln CALC RG31 55 H5
Westwood Rd CALC RG31 55 J4
NWBY RG14 13 H9
Westwood Rw CALC RG31 55 H3
Wetherby Cl CAV/SC RG4 43 K6
Weybridge Md YTLY GU46 135 K2
Weybrook Ct TADY RG26 143 J6
Weycrofts BNFD RG42 79 G5
Weyhill Cl TADY RG26 126 E2
Weysprings Cl BSTK RG21 15 J4
Whaley Rd EWKG RG40 77 J6
Wharfedale Rd WWKG RG41 75 K3
Wharfe La HEN RG9 31 H1
Wharf Rd NWBY RG14 12 F4
Wharfside THLE RG7 89 F4
Wharf St NWBY RG14 12 E4
Whatley Gn BRAK RG12 99 J4 3
Wheatfields Rd WHIT RG2 94 B2
Wheatlands Cl CALC RG31 71 K2
Wheatlands La NWBY RG14 102 E2
Wheatley BRAK RG12 99 F3
Wheatley Cl WHIT RG2 74 B5
Wheble Dr WODY RG5 59 G5
Wheeler Cl THLE RG7 91 G4 3
Wheeler Ct CALC RG31 55 K4
Wheeler Hl HTWY RG27 164 B2
Wheelers Green Wy STHA RG19 85 K5
Wheelton Cl EARL RG6 75 H3 6
Whinchat Cl HTWY RG27 149 H3
Whin Holt FLET GU13 167 H5
Whistler Cl BSTK RG21 15 J8
Whistlers La THLE RG7 110 A7
Whistley Cl BRAK RG12 11 L6
Whitby Dr READ RG1 7 M1
Whitby Gn CAV/SC RG4 44 A6
Whitchurch Rd GOR/PANG RG8 40 C6
Whitebeam Cl WWKG RG41 96 C4
White City CWTH RG45 118 E3
White Cl NTHA RG18 48 E7
Whitedown Rd TADY RG26 126 C1
Whitegates La EARL RG6 5 H6
Whitehall Dr WHIT RG2 95 H7
Whiteham Cl THLE RG7 70 D2 7
White Hart La BSTK RG21 15 G6
TADY RG26 142 D2
Whitehead Cl CHAM RG24 161 G4 2
White Hl GOR/PANG RG8 38 A6
HEN RG9 30 D6
HEN RG9 31 K1
KSCL RG20 121 G7
KSCL RG20 122 E6
Whitehills Gn GOR/PANG RG8 25 F5
White Horse La EWKG RG40 116 B3
White House Cl KEMP RG22 175 J2
White House Gdns
YTLY GU46 135 H2 2
Whitehouse Rd GOR/PANG RG8 26 D3
Whiteknights Rd EARL RG6 9 H3
Whitelands Dr ASC SL5 81 G6
Whitelands Rd NTHA RG18 85 H3
White La HEN RG9 16 B3
OVTN RG25 179 G2
TADY RG26 157 F5
White Lion Wy YTLY GU46 135 J2
White Lodge Cl CALC RG31 55 G2
Whitemoor La GOR/PANG RG8 38 B7
Whitenights Rd READ RG1 8 E1
Whites Cl HTWY RG27 163 J2 3
White's Hl THLE RG7 90 D3
White's La THLE RG7 68 E6
Whitestone Cl EARL RG6 75 H3 7
Whitestones KEMP RG22 175 H6 3
Whitewalls Cl KSCL RG20 21 J6
Whitewater Ri HTWY RG27 164 B1 6
Whitewater Rd ODIM RG29 164 B7
Whitewell Cl WHIT RG2 95 H5 3
Whitewood CHAM RG24 145 G7
Whitley Park La WHIT RG2 8 A3
Whitley Rd YTLY GU46 135 J5
Whitley St READ RG1 7 K1
Whitley Wood La WHIT RG2 73 K7
Whitley Wood Rd WHIT RG2 74 B5 1
WHIT RG2 93 J1
Whitmarsh La CHAM RG24 145 J7
Whitney Rd CHAM RG24 15 L1
Whitstone Gdns WHIT RG2 7 L9
Whittle Cl EWKG RG40 116 D1
SHST GU47 118 B7 3
Whitton Cl EARL RG6 75 G4
Whitton Rd BRAK RG12 100 C1
Whitworth Rd WHIT RG2 115 K1
Whynstones Rd ASC SL5 101 K3
Wickers Cl WHIT RG2 94 C3 1
Wickford Wy EARL RG6 74 C6 11
Wickham Cl FLET GU13 167 F6
TADY RG26 126 E1
Wickham Pl FLET GU13 167 F5
Wickham Rd EARL RG6 75 H5
FLET GU13 167 F5
Wickham V BRAK RG12 99 F4 4
Wick Hill La EWKG RG40 117 F3
Wicklow Cl KEMP RG22 175 G1
Wick's Gn BNFD RG42 78 C3
Wicks La WAR/TWY RG10 61 K3
Widmore La CAV/SC RG4 29 H5
Widmore Rd KEMP RG22 175 H2
Wield Ct EARL RG6 75 H5 1
Wiggett Gv BNFD RG42 78 D4
Wights Wk KEMP RG22 175 G5 7
Wigmore La THLE RG7 70 B4
TLHT RG30 56 C4 1
Wigmore Rd TADY RG26 108 C7
Wilberforce Wy BRAK RG12 100 A3 2
Wild Briar EWKG RG40 116 E1
Wild Cl EARL RG6 75 F6 14
Wildcroft Dr EWKG RG40 97 F6
Wilder Av GOR/PANG RG8 40 D7 2
Wilderness Ct EARL RG6 9 G5
Wilderness Rd EARL RG6 8 F6
Wilders Cl BNFD RG42 79 H5
Wild Herons HTWY RG27 164 B2 5
Wildmoor La HTWY RG27 145 K4
Wildridings Rd BRAK RG12 10 D5
Wildwood Gdns YTLY GU46 135 H5
Wilfred Wy STHA RG19 86 A4
William Cl STHA RG19 85 J5
William Sim Wd BNFD RG42 80 E4
William St READ RG1 2 E5
Williams Wy FLET GU13 167 K2
Willis Cl NTHA RG18 65 G3
Willoughby Rd BRAK RG12 10 A6
Willoughby Wy DEAN RG23 159 J5
Willow Cl NWBY RG14 12 D8
TLHT RG30 91 G2
Willowdale EWKG RG40 96 E7 7
Willow Dr BRAK RG12 11 H2
WAR/TWY RG10 46 C6
Willowford YTLY GU46 135 J3
Willow Gdns CALC RG31 55 G3 3
WHIT RG2 8 B9
Willowherb Cl EWKG RG40 77 K7
Willow La HEN RG9 32 B7
Willowmead Cl NWBY RG14 103 F3
Willow Rd KSCL RG20 104 E6
TADY RG26 126 E1
Willowside WODY RG5 59 H4
The Willows READ RG1 3 H1
Willow St READ RG1 3 G7
Willow Tree Gld CALC RG31 71 H2 11
Willow Wy DEAN RG23 159 J4
HTWY RG27 146 A1
SHST GU47 118 A7
Wilmington Cl WODY RG5 59 H5
Wilmot Cl BNFD RG42 78 D4 3
Wilmott Wy DEAN RG23 159 J5
Wilsford Cl WHIT RG2 74 B7
Wilson Av HEN RG9 31 H3
Wilson Cl KSCL RG20 21 K7
Wilson Ct WWKG RG41 76 A5 3
Wilson Rd TLHT RG30 56 D6
Wilstrode Av BNFD RG42 79 G5
Wilton Pl BSTK RG21 14 B5
Wilton Rd TLHT RG30 56 D5
Wiltshire Av CWTH RG45 118 C2
Wiltshire Dr EWKG RG40 77 J7
Wiltshire Gv BNFD RG42 80 C4
Wiltshire Rd EWKG RG40 77 H6
EWKG RG40 97 H1
Wilwood Rd BNFD RG42 79 F5 3
Wilwyne Cl CAV/SC RG4 57 K2
Wimblington Dr EARL RG6 74 E6
Wimborne Gdns TLHT RG30 56 B4 2
Wimbushes EWKG RG40 116 C2
Wincanton Rd WHIT RG2 73 K7
Winch Cl BNFD RG42 78 D3 3
Winchcombe Cl FLET GU13 167 H2
Winchcombe Rd BSTK RG21 14 C6
NWBY RG14 12 F5
WAR/TWY RG10 60 D2
Winchester Rd BSTK RG21 14 B9
KEMP RG22 175 J3
KSCL RG20 139 K3
WHIT RG2 7 K4
Winchester St BSTK RG21 14 E6
OVTN RG25 171 J4
Winchfield Ct HTWY RG27 166 B2 1
Winchgrove Rd BNFD RG42 79 H5
Wincroft Rd CAV/SC RG4 43 F7
Windermere Av KEMP RG22 175 F2
Windermere Cl WWKG RG41 76 B3 2
Windermere Rd WHIT RG2 8 A5
Windermere Wy STHA RG19 85 F4
Windlesham Rd BNFD RG42 10 B1
Windmill Av WWKG RG41 76 D7
Windmill Cnr THLE RG7 111 F2
Windmill La THLE RG7 87 H2
Windmill Rd BNFD RG42 10 B1
THLE RG7 111 F2
Windrush Wy TLHT RG30 56 C6 3
Windsor Gdns KEMP RG22 175 F6
Windsor Ride ASC SL5 100 E3
BFOR GU20 100 B6
EWKG RG40 117 F1
Windsor Ri NWBY RG14 13 J9
Windsor Rd ASC SL5 81 J7
Windsor Wy CALC RG31 71 G2 11
Wingate Rd WODY RG5 59 H7
Wingrove Rd TLHT RG30 56 D7
Winkfield BNFD RG42 80 E3
Winkfield Cl WWKG RG41 97 G4
Winkfield Rd ASC SL5 81 K4
Winklebury Wy DEAN RG23 159 J4
Winkworth La THLE RG7 109 F6
Winnersh Ga WWKG RG41 76 C4
Winnersh Gv WWKG RG41 76 B5
Winscombe BRAK RG12 99 F3
Winser Dr TLHT RG30 6 A3
Winston Av TADY RG26 127 G2
Winston Cl THLE RG7 94 A5
Winston Wy STHA RG19 84 E3
Winterberry Wy CAV/SC RG4 43 F6
Winterbourne Rd KSCL RG20 62 B2
Winterthur Wy BSTK RG21 14 D4
Winterton Dr NWBY RG14 83 G2
Winton Crs YTLY GU46 135 J4
Winton Rd WHIT RG2 74 B5
Wintringham Wy
GOR/PANG RG8 41 J7
Wise's Firs THLE RG7 90 C4
Wispington Cl EARL RG6 75 G4
Wistaria La YTLY GU46 135 H4
Wisteria Cl WWKG RG41 96 E2 10
Wiston Ter READ RG1 3 J5
Witan Ct WHCH RG28 169 G6
Witcham Cl EARL RG6 75 G6 1
Wither Ri DEAN RG23 173 K2
Withybed Wy NTHA RG18 85 K2
Withy Cl CALC RG31 71 H1
The Withys NTHA RG18 51 F4
Wittenham Av CALC RG31 55 G5
Wittenham Cl
GOR/PANG RG8 26 E3 11
Wittenham Rd BRAK RG12 80 C6
Woburn Cl CAV/SC RG4 57 F1
Wokefield Rw THLE RG7 91 J7
Wokingham Rd BNFD RG42 10 E2
CWTH RG45 117 K5
EARL RG6 4 D7
EARL RG6 9 K3
WAR/TWY RG10 60 E5
Wolseley St READ RG1 3 G9
Wolsey Rd READ RG1 3 H1
Wolsingham Wy STHA RG19 85 J5 3
Wolverton La TADY RG26 141 G1
Wolverton Rd TADY RG26 125 H4
Wondesford Dl BNFD RG42 78 D2
Woodbine Cl EARL RG6 9 M9
EARL RG6 75 F5 8
Woodbine La KSCL RG20 103 J7
Woodbourne Cl YTLY GU46 135 J3 2
Woodbridge Rd CALC RG31 55 G7 3
Woodbury Rd KEMP RG22 175 G6
Wood Cl KEMP RG22 175 G6
Woodcock Ct THLE RG7 93 H3
Woodcote Gn FLET GU13 166 E3
Woodcote Pl ASC SL5 81 J6
Woodcote Rd CAV/SC RG4 57 F1
Woodcote Wy CAV/SC RG4 42 E7
Wood End CWTH RG45 118 A4
Woodenhill BRAK RG12 99 F5
Woodfield Wy THLE RG7 70 D2 3
Woodford Cl CAV/SC RG4 57 F1
Woodford Gn BRAK RG12 100 C2
Woodgarston Dr KEMP RG22 175 F6
Woodgate FARN GU14 151 K7 2
Wood Gn GOR/PANG RG8 26 D3 4
Wood Green Cl TLHT RG30 2 C7
Woodhouse La STHA RG19 107 F5
Woodhouse St BNFD RG42 79 F5 3
Woodhurst La WWKG RG41 76 E5 2
Woodies Cl BNFD RG42 78 D5
Woodland Av WWKG RG41 76 D6
Woodland Crs BNFD RG42 79 K5
Woodland Dr TADY RG26 129 J7
TLHT RG30 55 J6
Woodland Ri FLET GU13 167 F6
Woodlands CHAM RG24 145 H6 3
CWTH RG45 118 C5
FLET GU13 167 G1
KSCL RG20 120 D2
OVTN RG25 171 H4
YTLY GU46 135 J6
Woodlands Av EARL RG6 5 K7
THLE RG7 91 F4
WODY RG5 59 G6
Woodlands Cl ASC SL5 101 J4
NTHA RG18 64 C1
Woodlands Ct SHST GU47 119 G7
Woodlands Gv CAV/SC RG4 58 A1
Woodlands Ride ASC SL5 101 J4
Woodlands Rd CAV/SC RG4 29 F5
HEN RG9 31 H5
TADY RG26 108 A7
The Woodlands WWKG RG41 96 C3
Wood La CAV/SC RG4 28 C7
CAV/SC RG4 42 D1
FLET GU13 167 K2
GOR/PANG RG8 26 C3
HTWY RG27 163 F6
THLE RG7 113 F3
WHIT RG2 95 J5
Wood Lane Cl CAV/SC RG4 29 G6
Woodleigh FLET GU13 167 H3
Woodley Gn WODY RG5 59 J5
Woodman Cl WHIT RG2 93 K1 2
Woodmancott Cl BRAK RG12 100 C3
Woodman's La THLE RG7 90 E4
Woodmere BRAK RG12 11 L8
Woodmere Cl EARL RG6 9 J7
Woodmere Cft KEMP RG22 174 E5
Wood Moor EWKG RG40 116 E6
Woodpecker Cl KEMP RG22 174 E4
NFNM GU10 183 J4 3
WAR/TWY RG10 60 D2
Wood Rdg NWBY RG14 103 H1
Woodridge Cl BRAK RG12 11 G6
Woodroffe Dr KEMP RG22 175 H3
Woodrow Dr EWKG RG40 97 K1
Woodsend Cl EARL RG6 74 B6
Woodside NTHA RG18 65 H5
NWBY RG14 103 G1
Woodside Cl EWKG RG40 96 D7 2
THLE RG7 86 D2
THLE RG7 111 F2 1
Woodside Dr NTHA RG18 49 G7
Woodside Gdns CHAM RG24 145 G6
FLET GU13 167 K1
Woodside La CAV/SC RG4 28 D6
Woodside Wy WHIT RG2 74 A7
Woods La OVTN RG25 176 A5
Woods Rd CAV/SC RG4 58 A1
Woodstock St READ RG1 4 B6
Woodview Rd GOR/PANG RG8 40 C7 3
Woodward Cl WWKG RG41 76 C5
Woodwaye WODY RG5 59 G6
Woodyer Cl WODY RG5 75 H1
Woolacombe Dr EARL RG6 8 D8
Wooldridge Crs ODIM RG29 180 B4
Woolford Cl BNFD RG42 80 E5
Woolford Wy DEAN RG23 159 J5
Woolhampton Hl THLE RG7 87 K5
Woolhampton Wy BRAK RG12 11 K9
Woolton Lodge Gdns
KSCL RG20 102 C6 1
Woosehill WWKG RG41 76 E7
WWKG RG41 96 D1
Woosehill La WWKG RG41 96 E1
Wootton Cl CALC RG31 55 H5 6
Wootton Rd HEN RG9 31 F3
Worcester Av KEMP RG22 175 G4
Worcester Cl TLHT RG30 72 B1
Worcestershire Lea
BNFD RG42 80 C5 8
Wordsworth BRAK RG12 99 G3
Wordsworth Av YTLY GU46 135 G5
Wordsworth Cl CHAM RG24 160 D3
Wordsworth Rd NTHA RG18 85 H3 3
Worlds End Hl BRAK RG12 100 C4
Wormersley Rd STHA RG19 104 C1
Worrall Wy EARL RG6 74 C6
Worsley Pl THLE RG7 70 D3
Worting Rd BSTK RG21 14 B6
DEAN RG23 158 D7
KEMP RG22 159 J7
Worton Dr WHIT RG2 73 H6
Wote St BSTK RG21 14 F6
Wrekin Cl KEMP RG22 175 G1
Wren Cl THLE RG7 91 G4 7
WWKG RG41 96 D2
YTLY GU46 135 G3 5
Wrenfield Dr CAV/SC RG4 43 G7
Wrenswood Cl WHIT RG2 93 J1
Wroxham BRAK RG12 10 A9
Wroxham Rd WODY RG5 59 G5
Wurford Dr STHA RG19 86 A4
Wychcotes READ RG1 57 G3
Wychelm Rd WHIT RG2 94 B2
Wychwood Av BRAK RG12 100 C2
Wychwood Cl EARL RG6 8 F7
Wychwood Crs EARL RG6 8 F6
Wye Cl TLHT RG30 56 A7
Wyfold La CAV/SC RG4 28 B4
HEN RG9 29 F3
Wykeham Ct ODIM RG29 180 C4
Wykeham Dr DEAN RG23 159 F7
Wykeham Rd EARL RG6 5 G8
Wylam BRAK RG12 10 B9
Wyld Court Hl NTHA RG18 36 C7
Wyncote Cl WHIT RG2 8 E9
WHIT RG2 74 C5
Wyndale Cl HEN RG9 31 H2
Wyndham Cl YTLY GU46 135 J2
Wyndham Crs WODY RG5 5 M4
WODY RG5 59 G4
Wyndham Rd NWBY RG14 84 C2
Wynford Cl TLHT RG30 72 D2 5
Wynne Gdns FLET GU13 167 J6
Wyre Ct CALC RG31 55 H2
Wyresdale BRAK RG12 100 C5 1
Wythemede BNFD RG42 78 C4 3
Wyvern Cl BRAK RG12 10 D7

Y

Yale Cl SHST GU47 119 G6
Yardley BRAK RG12 99 G3
Yarnold Cl EWKG RG40 78 A7 2
Yarnton Cl CAV/SC RG4 43 K6
Yates Copse NTHA RG18 84 D2
Yattendon La NTHA RG18 51 H4
Yattendon Rd NTHA RG18 49 H6
Yellowhammer Rd KEMP RG22 174 E6
Yelverton Rd WHIT RG2 7 L6
Yeomans HTWY RG27 134 D2
Yeomans La KSCL RG20 103 K7
Yeovil Rd SHST GU47 119 F7
Yew Cl KSCL RG20 124 B7
WWKG RG41 96 E2
Yew Ga NWBY RG14 83 J1
Yewhurst Cl WAR/TWY RG10 46 B6
Yew La READ RG1 6 E3
Yew Tree Cl DEAN RG23 174 A4
TADY RG26 129 H7
Yew Tree Ct GOR/PANG RG8 25 F5 3
Yew Tree Ri CALC RG31 71 H1
Yew Tree Stables KSCL RG20 21 K7
Yield Hall La READ RG1 3 J6
Yield Hall Pl READ RG1 3 J6
Yoreham Cl EARL RG6 75 H5 2
York Cl KEMP RG22 175 G4
NWBY RG14 13 G6
York La HTWY RG27 149 H5
York Rd BNFD RG42 78 E3
HEN RG9 31 G1
NWBY RG14 13 G6
READ RG1 3 G3
Yorkshire Pl BNFD RG42 80 B5 17
Young Crs STHA RG19 13 M9

Z

Zinnia Cl KEMP RG22 175 F6
WWKG RG41 76 C7 3
Zinzan St READ RG1 2 F6

Index - featured places

The AA-Fanum House
BSTK RG21 15 K3
The Abbey School
READ RG1 3 L9
Acre Business Park
WHIT RG2 73 J6
Addington School
WODY RG5 59 J7
AFC Newbury Football Ground
NWBY RG14 13 G3
Aldermaston C of E School
THLE RG7 108 C1
Alfred Sutton Primary School
EARL RG6 4 F9
All Saints C of E Junior School
FLET GU13 166 E3
All Saints Infants School
READ RG1 2 D7
Ambulance Station
READ RG1 2 F5
Animal Care College
ASC SL5 101 K1
The Anvil Concert Hall
BSTK RG21 14 E4
Arborfield C of E School
WHIT RG2 95 J4
Arcade Gallery
GOR/PANG RG8 24 E5
The Argyle Clinic
READ RG1 2 D6
The Ark School
THLE RG7 89 J6
Arlington Business Park
BRAK RG12 11 G3
Art Gallery
HEN RG9 31 H1
The Art Gallery
READ RG1 3 H7
Arthur Hill Memorial
Swimming Baths
READ RG1 4 B7
Ascot Heath Junior School
ASC SL5 81 H5
Ashford Hill Primary School
STHA RG19 107 F7
AsHMead School
READ RG1 7 L9
Auction Market
READ RG1 2 F4
The Avenue School
WHIT RG2 7 L3
Badgemore CP School
HEN RG9 31 F1
Bartley Wood Business Park
HTWY RG27 164 B3
Basildon House
GOR/PANG RG8 39 H3
Basildon School
GOR/PANG RG8 38 D6
Basing County Infants School
CHAM RG24 161 J5
Basingstoke Business Centre
KEMP RG22 175 K2
Basingstoke College
of Technology
BSTK RG21 14 C5
Basingstoke County Court
BSTK RG21 15 H4
Basingstoke & Deane
Borough Council
CHAM RG24 161 F3
Basingstoke Ice Rink
KEMP RG22 159 J6
Basingstoke & North
Hants Cricket Club
BSTK RG21 14 E8
Basingstoke Rugby Club
KEMP RG22 175 G3
Basingstoke Sports Centre
BSTK RG21 14 E4
Basingstoke Town
Football Club
KEMP RG22 175 K2
Battle Farm Trading Estate
TLHT RG30 2 A3
Battle Primary School
TLHT RG30 2 A6
Bearwood College
WWKG RG41 76 A7
Bearwood Primary School
WWKG RG41 76 A6
Beech Down County
Primary School
KEMP RG22 175 J4
Beechwood County Junior
& Infant School
WODY RG5 59 H6
Beedon Primary School
KSCL RG20 34 C4
The Bell Surgery
HEN RG9 31 G1

Benham Park
KSCL RG20 .... 82 D3
Berkshire Business Centre
STHA RG19 .... 86 B5
Berkshire County Council
NWBY RG14 .... 12 E7
Berkshire County Council
NWBY RG14 .... 12 B8
Berkshire County Council
NWBY RG14 .... 12 D3
Berkshire County Council
READ RG1 .... 3 K6
The Berkshire Golf Club
ASC SL5 .... 101 F2
Bilton Industrial Estate
CHAM RG24 .... 160 E2
Bilton Industrial Estate
CHAM RG24 .... 161 F2
Binfield Primary School
BNFD RG42 .... 78 D4
Binfield Surgery
BNFD RG42 .... 78 D3
Birch Copse Primary School
CALC RG31 .... 55 H5
Birch Hill Medical Centre
BRAK RG12 .... 99 J5
Birch Hill Primary School
BRAK RG12 .... 99 K6
Bishop Challoner RC Secondary
School
KEMP RG22 .... 175 H1
Bishopswood Co Junior School
TADY RG26 .... 126 E1
Bishopswood Co Infant School
TADY RG26 .... 126 E2
Blakes Lock Museum
READ RG1 .... 4 A5
Blands Infant School
THLE RG7 .... 90 E5
Blue Mountain Golf Club
& Conference Centre
BNFD RG42 .... 78 E4
Boathouse Surgery
GOR/PANG RG8 .... 24 E5
Bohun Gallery
HEN RG9 .... 31 H2
Borocourt Hospital
CAV/SC RG4 .... 28 B2
Boundary House Surgery
BRAK RG12 .... 11 H4
Bracknell Business Centre
BRAK RG12 .... 10 B4
Bracknell College
BRAK RG12 .... 11 G1
Bracknell College
BRAK RG12 .... 11 H4
Bracknell Forest
Borough Council
BRAK RG12 .... 11 G3
Bracknell Rugby Football Club
BRAK RG12 .... 11 M4
Bracknell Sports Centre
BRAK RG12 .... 99 K3
Bracknell Town Council
BRAK RG12 .... 10 F3
Bracknell Town Football Club
BRAK RG12 .... 11 H4
Bradfield C of E Primary School
THLE RG7 .... 68 E4
Bradfield College
THLE RG7 .... 53 F7
Brakenhale School
BRAK RG12 .... 10 F8
Bramley C of E Primary School
BRAK RG12 .... 129 G5
Brickfields Industrial Park
BRAK RG12 .... 10 C4
Brick Kiln Industrial Estate
TADY RG26 .... 109 F7
Brighton Hill
Community School
KEMP RG22 .... 175 J3
Brimpton School
THLE RG7 .... 107 G2
Broadmoor County
Primary School
CWTH RG45 .... 118 E4
Broadmoor Hospital
CWTH RG45 .... 118 E4
Brockhurst Preparatory School
NTHA RG18 .... 66 A2
Brookfields School
CALC RG31 .... 55 H2
Brookside Business Centre
THLE RG7 .... 114 A2
The Brookside Group Practice
EARL RG6 .... 75 G3
Bucklebury C of E
Primary School
THLE RG7 .... 86 D1
Building Design School
WHIT RG2 .... 94 C3
The Bulmershe School
WODY RG5 .... 5 M6
Burdwood Surgery
STHA RG19 .... 85 K5
Burghclere CP School
KSCL RG20 .... 121 K3
Burghfield Aqua Sports Club
TLHT RG30 .... 72 B5
Burghfield Health Centre
THLE RG7 .... 91 G4
Burma Hills Surgery
EWKG RG40 .... 77 J7
Burnham Copse Junior School
TADY RG26 .... 108 D7
Burnside Surgery
FLET GU13 .... 167 F2
Buryfields Infant School
ODIM RG29 .... 180 D2
Bus Depot
READ RG1 .... 2 E5
The Business Centre
BSTK RG21 .... 15 G5
The Business Centre
THLE RG7 .... 107 G2
The Business Centre
WWKG RG41 .... 97 F3
Calcot Junior and Infant School
CALC RG31 .... 71 G2
Calleva Roman Antiquity
and Museum
THLE RG7 .... 110 A7
Calthorpe Park School
FLET GU13 .... 166 D3
Castle Hill Clinic
READ RG1 .... 2 E7
Castle Hill Junior School
DEAN RG23 .... 159 H4
Castle Industrial Park
NWBY RG14 .... 84 B2
Castle Royle Golf Club
WAR/TWY RG10 .... 47 J2
Castle School
NWBY RG14 .... 83 J1

Caversham Park Primary School
CAV/SC RG4 .... 44 B6
Caversham Primary School
CAV/SC RG4 .... 57 H2
Cedar Park School
WAR/TWY RG10 .... 46 B7
Cedars School
THLE RG7 .... 108 D1
Centenary Business Park
HEN RG9 .... 31 J2
Central Swimming Pool
READ RG1 .... 2 E5
Century Galleries
HEN RG9 .... 31 H1
Century Galleries
HTWY RG27 .... 149 J4
Chalfont Surgery
EARL RG6 .... 74 D5
Chalkridge School
KEMP RG22 .... 175 K3
Chapel Hill Surgery
CALC RG31 .... 55 H5
Chapel Row Surgery
THLE RG7 .... 67 K6
Charles Kingsley School
HTWY RG27 .... 134 E1
Chatham Street Surgery
READ RG1 .... 2 F6
Chiltern Edge Secondary School
CAV/SC RG4 .... 29 F7
Chineham Park Primary School
CHAM RG24 .... 160 E3
Christchurch Primary School
WHIT RG2 .... 7 J2
Christ the King School
READ RG1 .... 73 K6
Church Grange & Bramblys
Grange Health Centre
BSTK RG21 .... 14 D6
Church Grange Lychpit Surgery
CHAM RG24 .... 161 G4
Church Hill House Hospital
BRAK RG12 .... 99 H3
Church of England School
THLE RG7 .... 88 A3
The Clere Secondary School
KSCL RG20 .... 121 K2
Cliddesden Primary School
OVTN RG25 .... 176 B7
Clift Surgery
TADY RG26 .... 129 F5
Club House
BRAK RG12 .... 100 A6
Coley Park School
READ RG1 .... 6 D2
Coley Park Surgery
READ RG1 .... 6 D1
Coley Primary School
READ RG1 .... 3 G8
Colleton CP School
WAR/TWY RG10 .... 60 D2
Comprehensive
YTLY GU46 .... 135 H5
Compton C of E Primary School
KSCL RG20 .... 21 K7
Coombe Infants School
WHIT RG2 .... 95 H4
Court Moor School
FLET GU13 .... 167 G4
Coxmoor Farm Light
Industrial Estate
RENHAM GU10 .... 182 C2
Cranbourne School
ASC SL5 .... 81 K2
Cranbourne Secondary School
BSTK RG21 .... 14 B9
Crazies Hill Primary School
WAR/TWY RG10 .... 32 E5
Crondall CP School
NFNM GU10 .... 182 E6
Crookham C of E
Infants School
FLET GU13 .... 167 G7
Crookham County
Junior School
FLET GU13 .... 167 J7
Crosfields School
WHIT RG2 .... 74 B6
Crown Wood CP School
BRAK RG12 .... 100 A4
Crowthorne Business Centre
CWTH RG45 .... 118 D1
Crowthorne C of E
Primary School
CWTH RG45 .... 118 C3
Curridge CP School
NTHA RG18 .... 64 C2
Curtain Gallery
WWKG RG41 .... 76 B5
Danesfield County
Combined School
MLW RG7 .... 19 K3
Daneshill East Industrial Estate
CHAM RG24 .... 15 L2
Daneshill Industrial Estate
CHAM RG24 .... 15 M1
Daneshill School
HTWY RG27 .... 131 G5
David Lloyd Sports Centre
EARL RG6 .... 5 H2
Delwood Hospital
TLHT RG30 .... 56 D7
Diva Gallery
ODIM RG29 .... 180 D1
Dogmersfield C of E
Primary School
HTWY RG27 .... 166 B4
The Dolphin School
WAR/TWY RG10 .... 61 F3
Donnington Castle
NWBY RG14 .... 63 H7
Douai School
THLE RG7 .... 88 A2
Dove House School
BSTK RG21 .... 14 F1
Downe House School
NTHA RG18 .... 65 F3
Downlands Sports Centre
KSCL RG20 .... 21 J7
The Downs School
KSCL RG20 .... 21 J7
Downs Way School
CALC RG31 .... 55 H2
Dryleas Sports Ground
HEN RG9 .... 17 G7
Duffield Road CP School
WODY RG5 .... 59 J4
Dunston Park Primary School
NTHA RG18 .... 85 J3
Eagle House School
SHST GU47 .... 118 B6
East Barn Surgery
CHAM RG24 .... 161 G3
East Berkshire Golf Club
CWTH RG45 .... 117 K3

Eastern Business Centre
BRAK RG12 .... 11 K4
Eastfield House Surgery
NWBY RG14 .... 12 E6
Easthampstead Park School
EWKG RG40 .... 98 E4
Ebony Health Centre
WAR/TWY RG10 .... 46 C7
Edgebarrow School
CWTH RG45 .... 118 C5
Edgebarrow Sports Centre
CWTH RG45 .... 118 D5
Elstree School
THLE RG7 .... 88 A3
Emmbrook County Junior
& Infant School
WWKG RG41 .... 76 E5
The Emmbrook School
WWKG RG41 .... 76 E6
Emmer Green Clinic
CAV/SC RG4 .... 43 J7
Emmer Green CP School
CAV/SC RG4 .... 43 J6
Emmer Green Surgery
CAV/SC RG4 .... 43 H6
Enborne C of E School
KSCL RG20 .... 102 B3
Enborne Lodge
NWBY RG14 .... 102 E3
Englefield Estate Yard
THLE RG7 .... 70 A1
Englefield School
THLE RG7 .... 70 A2
English Martyrs RC
Primary School
TLHT RG30 .... 56 B6
E P Collier School
READ RG1 .... 3 G3
Eversley Cricket Club
HTWY RG27 .... 134 E1
Evingar Industrial Estate
WHCH RG28 .... 169 G6
Fairfields Primary School
BSTK RG21 .... 14 E7
Fairview Trading Estate
HEN RG9 .... 31 J3
Falkland CP School
NWBY RG14 .... 103 G2
Family Planning Clinic
READ RG1 .... 3 M8
Farley Hill Primary School
THLE RG7 .... 115 F3
Farmhouse Gallery
KSCL RG20 .... 120 E2
Finchampstead C of E
Primary School
EWKG RG40 .... 116 C3
Finchampstead Sports Club
EWKG RG40 .... 116 D5
Finns Industrial Park
NFNM GU10 .... 182 C2
Fireplace Gallery
EWKG RG40 .... 97 H1
FireStation
READ RG1 .... 3 G3
Fir Tree CP School
NTHA RG18 .... 84 D3
Fleet Business Park
FLET GU13 .... 183 J1
Fleet Community Hospital
FLET GU13 .... 167 F1
Fleet Police Station
FLET GU13 .... 167 G3
Food Gallery
READ RG1 .... 4 B6
Football Club
HEN RG9 .... 31 J3
Forbury Retail Park
READ RG1 .... 3 L5
The Forest Comprehensive
School
WWKG RG41 .... 76 A4
Forest End Medical Centre
BRAK RG12 .... 99 J4
Fort Hill School
DEAN RG23 .... 159 H5
Forthill Surgery
DEAN RG23 .... 159 H5
Fosters Business Park
HTWY RG27 .... 163 G4
Foxhill Primary School
BRAK RG12 .... 10 F9
Francis Bailey School
STHA RG19 .... 85 K4
Friar's Walk Shopping Centre
READ RG1 .... 3 H5
The Gallery
CAV/SC RG4 .... 44 E7
Garlands County Junior School
THLE RG7 .... 91 F4
The Garth Hill School
BRAK RG12 .... 11 G1
George Palmer Junior School
WHIT RG2 .... 7 L3
Gillies Health Centre
KEMP RG22 .... 175 J4
Gillotts School
HEN RG9 .... 30 E4
Golf Course
STHA RG19 .... 104 C1
Goring C of E Primary School
GOR/PANG RG8 .... 25 F4
Goring & Streatley Golf Club
GOR/PANG RG8 .... 24 B4
Gorse Ride Junior School
EWKG RG40 .... 116 D1
Grazeley School
THLE RG7 .... 93 F5
Great Hollands County
Infant School
BRAK RG12 .... 99 F3
Great Hollands County
Junior School
BRAK RG12 .... 99 F3
Great Hollands Health Centre
BRAK RG12 .... 99 G4
Great Hollands
Recreation Centre
BRAK RG12 .... 99 F6
Greenfields Junior School
HTWY RG27 .... 149 H5
Greenham Road Retail Park
NWBY RG14 .... 12 F6
Green Meadows Surgery
ASC SL5 .... 81 J4
Green Road Surgery
EARL RG6 .... 4 F7
Gresham Way Industrial Estate
TLHT RG30 .... 56 B3
Grey House Private School
HTWY RG27 .... 149 J4
Greys Gallery
HEN RG9 .... 31 H2
Grimsbury Castle
NTHA RG18 .... 65 H1

Grovelands Surgery
TLHT RG30 .... 56 C5
Gun Street Gallery
READ RG1 .... 3 H6
Hackwood Ho
OVTN RG25 .... 176 E4
The Hampshire Clinic
CHAM RG24 .... 15 M2
Hampshire County Council
BSTK RG21 .... 14 F5
Hampshire County
Council - Basing House
CHAM RG24 .... 161 H5
Hampshire County
Council - Chute House
BSTK RG21 .... 14 E4
Hampstead Norreys
Primary School
NTHA RG18 .... 36 A7
Harmans Water Infant
& Junior School
BRAK RG12 .... 11 L9
Harriet Costello School
BSTK RG21 .... 15 H6
Hart Sports Centre
FLET GU13 .... 166 D3
The Hart Surgery
HEN RG9 .... 31 G1
Hassocks Wood
Industrial Estate
CHAM RG24 .... 161 F4
Hatch Ride Primary School
CWTH RG45 .... 118 C1
Hatch Warren County
Infant School
KEMP RG22 .... 175 H5
Hatch Warren County
Junior School
KEMP RG22 .... 175 H5
Hatch Warren Retail Park
KEMP RG22 .... 175 F6
Hatch Warren Surgery
KEMP RG22 .... 175 H5
Hawkedon Primary School
EARL RG6 .... 75 H4
Hawthorns Primary School
WWKG RG41 .... 76 D7
The Hawthorns School
KEMP RG22 .... 175 H3
Haymarket Theatre
BSTK RG21 .... 14 E6
Headmaster Bradfield College
THLE RG7 .... 53 F7
The Health Centre
WHIT RG2 .... 8 D6
Heatherwood Hospital
ASC SL5 .... 101 H1
Heathfield School
ASC SL5 .... 80 E7
Heath Hill Surgery
CWTH RG45 .... 118 C4
Hemdean House School
CAV/SC RG4 .... 57 H2
The Henley College
HEN RG9 .... 31 F2
Henley District Indoor
Sports Centre
HEN RG9 .... 30 E4
Henley Golf Club
HEN RG9 .... 31 G5
Henley Town Football Club
HEN RG9 .... 31 J3
Hermitage Primary School
NTHA RG18 .... 49 G5
Hernes Estate
HEN RG9 .... 30 C3
Heron Industrial Estate
THLE RG7 .... 93 H7
The Hexagon
READ RG1 .... 3 G6
Highclere Castle
KSCL RG20 .... 120 E7
Highdown School
CAV/SC RG4 .... 43 H7
Highwood Primary School
WODY RG5 .... 5 M8
The Hill Primary School
CAV/SC RG4 .... 43 K7
Hillside Primary School
EARL RG6 .... 74 C6
H M Prison
READ RG1 .... 3 L5
Hollyspring Junior
& Infants School
BRAK RG12 .... 11 L3
Hollywood Bowl
BRAK RG12 .... 10 E3
Holme Grange School
EWKG RG40 .... 98 A4
Holmwood Health Centre
TADY RG26 .... 108 D7
The Holt School
WWKG RG41 .... 77 G7
Home Farm School
THLE RG7 .... 88 A4
Hook County Junior School
HTWY RG27 .... 164 A2
Hook Infant School
HTWY RG27 .... 164 A2
Horris Hill Preparatory School
KSCL RG20 .... 103 H5
Houndmills Industrial Estate
BSTK RG21 .... 159 K4
Humphries Industrial Estate
BRAK RG12 .... 11 G8
The Hurst Community School
TADY RG26 .... 108 A7
Ian Walker Odiham Gallery
ODIM RG29 .... 180 D1
Ibis Sports Club
CAV/SC RG4 .... 56 C3
Inhurst House School
STHA RG19 .... 107 K7
John Hunt of Everest
Community School
CHAM RG24 .... 160 D2
John Rankin County
Infants School
NWBY RG14 .... 83 G7
John Rankin Junior
NWBY RG14 .... 83 G7
The Junior School
GOR/PANG RG8 .... 39 J7
Katesgrove Primary School
READ RG1 .... 3 H8
Keep Hatch County
Junior School
EWKG RG40 .... 77 J7
Kempshott County
Infant School
KEMP RG22 .... 175 F4
Kempshott County
Junior School
KEMP RG22 .... 175 F4
Kendrick Girls School
READ RG1 .... 3 K7

Kennet Secondary School
STHA RG19 .... 85 K4
Kennet Surgery
READ RG1 .... 4 D6
Kennet Valley Primary School
TLHT RG30 .... 72 A2
Kenton Theatre
HEN RG9 .... 31 H1
Kidmore End Primary School
CAV/SC RG4 .... 42 E1
Kingsclere Health Centre
KSCL RG20 .... 124 A7
Kingsclere Primary School
KSCL RG20 .... 124 A7
Kings Furlong Infant School
BSTK RG21 .... 14 A8
Kings Furlong Junior School
BSTK RG21 .... 14 B8
Kings School
BSTK RG21 .... 14 D6
Laffords Industrial Estate
THLE RG7 .... 71 F4
Lambrook Haileybury School
BNFD RG42 .... 80 D3
Lambs Farm Business Park
THLE RG7 .... 93 H7
Lambs Lane CP School
THLE RG7 .... 93 H7
Lambwood Industrial Estate
THLE RG7 .... 92 D6
Langtree Secondary School
GOR/PANG RG8 .... 26 E3
Lavender Golf Club
ASC SL5 .... 101 F1
Leighton Park School
WHIT RG2 .... 8 C4
Leighton Park School
WHIT RG2 .... 8 D6
The Licensed Victuallers School
ASC SL5 .... 81 F7
Limington House School
KEMP RG22 .... 175 J1
Loddon Business Centre
CHAM RG24 .... 15 M1
Loddon County Infants School
EARL RG6 .... 75 G3
Loddon County Junior School
EARL RG6 .... 75 G3
The Loddon Vale Practice
WODY RG5 .... 59 K6
Loddon Valley Leisure Centre
EARL RG6 .... 74 D5
London Road School
ODIM RG29 .... 180 D1
Long Barn Lane Surgery
WHIT RG2 .... 7 K5
Longfellow Parade Clinic
CHAM RG24 .... 160 D3
Long Lane Primary School
GOR/PANG RG8 .... 55 G5
Longshot Industrial Estate
BRAK RG12 .... 99 F1
Luckley Oakfield School
WWKG RG41 .... 97 G4
Ludgrove Preparatory School
EWKG RG40 .... 97 J4
Madejski Stadium
WHIT RG2 .... 73 G6
Maiden Erlegh School
EARL RG6 .... 9 K4
The Malls/The Walks
Shopping Centre
BSTK RG21 .... 14 F4
Manor County School
TLHT RG30 .... 72 B2
Manorfield Infant School
KEMP RG22 .... 175 K5
Mansbridge House School
READ RG1 .... 4 E8
MapledurhamHouse
CAV/SC RG4 .... 41 K6
Maple Ridge School
BSTK RG21 .... 14 E1
Marnel Infant & Junior Schools
CHAM RG24 .... 160 D2
Marsh Farm Business Centre
NFNM GU10 .... 182 E3
Mary Hare Grammar School
NWBY RG14 .... 63 J3
Mayhill County Junior School
ODIM RG29 .... 180 D4
May's Bounty
BSTK RG21 .... 14 E8
Meadow Vale CP School
BNFD RG42 .... 10 B1
Meadway
Comprehensive School
TLHT RG30 .... 56 A6
Meadway Sports Centre
TLHT RG30 .... 56 A7
Melrose Surgery
READ RG1 .... 3 M7
Merton County Junior School
CHAM RG24 .... 160 B3
Micklands CP School
CAV/SC RG4 .... 58 A1
The Micro Centre
WHIT RG2 .... 7 H6
Milestone Transport Museum
KEMP RG22 .... 159 H6
The Mill at Sonning
CAV/SC RG4 .... 59 F1
Mill Ride Golf Club
ASC SL5 .... 81 G6
Milman Road Health Centre
WHIT RG2 .... 7 K2
Moorlands Primary School
TLHT RG30 .... 55 K6
Morland Surgery
TADY RG26 .... 126 E2
Mortimer Surgery
THLE RG7 .... 110 E2
Mulberry Business Park
WWKG RG41 .... 97 J3
Murrell Green Business Park
HTWY RG27 .... 164 D2
The Museum
of Berkshire Aviation
WODY RG5 .... 60 A7
The Natural Health Centre
NWBY RG14 .... 103 G2
Newbold College
BNFD RG42 .... 78 E5
Newbold School
BNFD RG42 .... 78 E5
Newbury Business Park
NWBY RG14 .... 13 G2
Newbury College of Further
Education
NWBY RG14 .... 12 C1
Newbury District Council
NWBY RG14 .... 13 G6
Newbury District Council
WHCH RG28 .... 169 G6
Newbury District Hospital
NWBY RG14 .... 12 D7

Newbury District Museum
& Tourist Information Centre
NWBY RG14 .... 12 F4
Newbury Retail Park
NWBY RG14 .... 104 A1
Newbury Rugby Football Club
NWBY RG14 .... 103 J2
Newbury Town Council
NWBY RG14 .... 12 E4
The New Chineham Surgery
CHAM RG24 .... 161 G1
New Greenham Park
Leisure Centre
STHA RG19 .... 105 F4
Newlands CP School
YTLY GU46 .... 135 H4
New Scotland Hill CP School
SHST GU47 .... 118 B6
Newtown Junior
& Infant School
READ RG1 .... 4 B5
Nimrod Industrial Estate
WHIT RG2 .... 7 J2
Northcroft Surgery
NWBY RG14 .... 12 D4
North Hampshire Hospital
CHAM RG24 .... 159 K3
North Hants Golf Club
FARM GU14 .... 151 H6
The Norton Practice
READ RG1 .... 3 L7
Oaklands Business Centre
WWKG RG41 .... 97 F4
Oaklands County Junior
& Infant School
CWTH RG45 .... 118 B2
Oakley C of E Junior School
DEAN RG23 .... 173 K3
Oakley County Infant School
DEAN RG23 .... 173 K3
Oak Park Golf Club
NFNM GU10 .... 183 F6
Oakridge County Junior School
BSTK RG21 .... 160 B4
Oakwood School
HTWY RG27 .... 149 J5
Odiham Castle
ODIM RG29 .... 164 A7
Odiham Cottage Hospital
ODIM RG29 .... 180 D2
The Odiham Health Centre
ODIM RG29 .... 180 C1
Old Art Gallery
EWKG RG40 .... 98 A5
Old Basing Surgery
CHAM RG24 .... 161 J6
Oracle Shopping Centre
READ RG1 .... 3 J6
The Oratory
Preparatory School
GOR/PANG RG8 .... 26 C7
The Oratory School
GOR/PANG RG8 .... 27 F3
Osborn Way Industrial Estate
HTWY RG27 .... 163 K3
Our Ladys Preparatory School
CWTH RG45 .... 118 B3
Overbridge Surgery
KEMP RG22 .... 159 K7
Overton C of E Primary School
OVTN RG25 .... 171 G3
Overton Gallery
OVTN RG25 .... 171 H4
Overton Surgery
OVTN RG25 .... 171 J4
Owlsmoor Primary School
SHST GU47 .... 119 F7
Oxford Rd Surgery
READ RG1 .... 3 G6
Oxford Road Primary School
READ RG1 .... 2 D6
Paddock Road Industrial Estate
CAV/SC RG4 .... 4 A2
Paddock Road Industrial Estate
CAV/SC RG4 .... 4 A1
Padworth College
THLE RG7 .... 89 H6
Palmer C of E Junior School
EWKG RG40 .... 77 J7
Pangbourne College
GOR/PANG RG8 .... 53 J2
Pangbourne Infants School
GOR/PANG RG8 .... 40 D7
Pangbourne Medical Centre
GOR/PANG RG8 .... 40 B6
Papplewick School
ASC SL5 .... 81 J6
Park House School
NWBY RG14 .... 103 H2
Park Lane Primary School
CALC RG31 .... 55 H5
Parkside Business Park
WODY RG5 .... 59 H5
Park View Infant School
KEMP RG22 .... 175 H2
Park View Junior School
KEMP RG22 .... 175 H1
Parsons Down Infant School
STHA RG19 .... 85 G4
Parsons Down Junior School
STHA RG19 .... 85 F4
Peppard C of E School
HEN RG9 .... 29 H3
Perborough Castle
KSCL RG20 .... 35 K4
Phoenix Business Park
BRAK RG12 .... 78 D7
Phoenix Plaza Bowling Alley
EWKG RG40 .... 97 G2
Physiotherapy Surgery
GOR/PANG RG8 .... 40 C6
The Piggott C of E School
WAR/TWY RG10 .... 46 B4
The Pines Junior
& Infant School
BRAK RG12 .... 99 H5
Pinewood Leisure Centre
EWKG RG40 .... 98 C7
Pipers Industrial Estate
STHA RG19 .... 86 A6
P M S Health Centre
READ RG1 .... 3 L9
Polehampton County
Infant School
WAR/TWY RG10 .... 46 C7
Polehampton Junior School
WAR/TWY RG10 .... 46 C6
Presentation College
TLHT RG30 .... 6 A1

Princess Marina College
EWKG RG40 .... 95 J7
Priors Court School
NTHA RG18 .... 48 C5
The Priory Primary School
TADY RG26 .... 143 G1
Progress Theatre
READ RG1 .... 7 M2
Prospect Foot Clinic
CAV/SC RG4 .... 57 H2
Prospect School
TLHT RG30 .... 72 B1
Purley C of E School
GOR/PANG RG8 .... 41 H7
Queen Annes School
CAV/SC RG4 .... 57 J2
Queen Marys College
BSTK RG21 .... 14 F9
Raceview Business Centre
NWBY RG14 .... 13 H5
Radstock CP School
EARL RG6 .... 9 J8
Ranelagh School
BRAK RG12 .... 11 G5
Ranikhet Primary School
TLHT RG30 .... 56 B5
Reading Adult College
READ RG1 .... 56 D5
Reading Adult
& Community College
READ RG1 .... 3 H1
Reading Blue Coat School
CAV/SC RG4 .... 59 F2
Reading Borough Council
READ RG1 .... 3 G7
Reading Business Centre
READ RG1 .... 3 K7
Reading Clinic
READ RG1 .... 3 M7
Reading College
READ RG1 .... 4 B6
Reading College of Technology
READ RG1 .... 4 F9
Reading County Court
READ RG1 .... 3 K5
Reading Girls School
WHIT RG2 .... 7 M5
Reading Retail Park
TLHT RG30 .... 56 C4
Reading School
READ RG1 .... 4 A8
Reading Superbowl
CALC RG31 .... 71 F2
Reading University
EARL RG6 .... 9 H3
Redfields Industrial Estate
FLET GU13 .... 183 G1
Redfields Industrial Park
FLET GU13 .... 183 F2
Redlands Primary School
READ RG1 .... 8 C1
Red Shute Hill Industrial Estate
NTHA RG18 .... 65 F1
Register Office
READ RG1 .... 2 F8
Reme Museum
EWKG RG40 .... 95 K7
Retail Park
NWBY RG14 .... 13 K3
Retail Park
READ RG1 .... 3 M5
Richard Aldworth
Community School
KEMP RG22 .... 175 J2
Richmond Surgery
FLET GU13 .... 167 G5
Ridge House School
NTHA RG18 .... 65 J6
Rivermead CP School
WODY RG5 .... 59 J7
Rivermead Leisure Centre
READ RG1 .... 2 E1
Riverpark Industrial Estate
NWBY RG14 .... 13 J3
The River & Rowing Museum
at Henley
HEN RG9 .... 31 J2
Robert Cort Industrial Estate
WHIT RG2 .... 7 J2
Robert Mays School
ODIM RG29 .... 180 B1
Robert Piggott C of E
Infant School
WAR/TWY RG10 .... 46 D3
Robert Piggott C of E
Junior School
WAR/TWY RG10 .... 46 C3
Rosedale Clinic
READ RG1 .... 8 A1
Royal Ascot Golf Club
ASC SL5 .... 81 K7
Royal Berkshire
& Battle Hospital
TLHT RG30 .... 2 B5
Royal Berkshire Hospital
READ RG1 .... 3 M8
Ruckstall County Primary School
BSTK RG21 .... 15 J8
Rupert House School
HEN RG9 .... 17 H7
Russell Street Surgery
READ RG1 .... 2 F7
Ryeish Green
Comprehensive School
THLE RG7 .... 93 J3
Sacred Heart RC School
HEN RG9 .... 31 G2
St Andrews School
GOR/PANG RG8 .... 53 F4
St Annes Catholic
Primary School
KEMP RG22 .... 175 J1
St Annes RC Primary School
CAV/SC RG4 .... 57 J3
St Bartholomews
NWBY RG14 .... 12 B7
St Bartholomews School
NWBY RG14 .... 12 B8
St Bedes Catholic
Primary School
CHAM RG24 .... 160 B2
St Crispins Secondary School
EWKG RG40 .... 97 K1
St Crispins Sports Centre
EWKG RG40 .... 97 K1
St Dominic Savio RC
Primary School
WODY RG5 .... 59 G5

St Edwards School
TLHT RG30 .... 2 C7
St Finians School
NWBY RG14 .... 65 J6
St Francis RC School
ASC SL5 .... 101 K4
St Gabriels School
KSCL RG20 .... 104 A2
St Johns C of E School
TLHT RG30 .... 3 M7
St Johns School
BSTK RG21 .... 14 D9
St Johns School
NWBY RG14 .... 12 D9
St Johns School
THLE RG7 .... 111 F3
St Josephs Convent School
READ RG1 .... 8 C1
St Josephs RC Primary School
BRAK RG12 .... 11 J4
St Josephs RC Primary School
NWBY RG14 .... 13 H1
St Margaret Clitherow
Primary School
BRAK RG12 .... 99 G5
St Marks C of E School
NTHA RG18 .... 65 H5
St Marks Primary School
KEMP RG22 .... 175 G6
St Martins RC Primary School
CAV/SC RG4 .... 44 B6
St Marys All Saints C of E
Primary School
READ RG1 .... 6 D2
St Marys C of E Junior School
CHAM RG24 .... 161 G3
St Marys C of E Junior School
NTHA RG18 .... 85 J3
St Marys C of E Primary School
BNFD RG42 .... 80 E3
St Marys Preparatory School
HEN RG9 .... 31 H1
St Marys Primary School
TLHT RG30 .... 91 H1
St Marys School
THLE RG7 .... 111 J3
St Michaels C of E
Primary School
SHST GU47 .... 135 K1
St Michaels School
BRAK RG12 .... 99 H3
St Michaels Primary School
TLHT RG30 .... 56 B7
St Michaels School
KSCL RG20 .... 121 J3
St Neots Preparatory School
HTWY RG27 .... 133 H1
St Nicholas C of E
Primary School
WAR/TWY RG10 .... 60 E5
St Nicholas C of E School
NWBY RG14 .... 12 D6
St Nicholas School
NFNM GU10 .... 183 F2
St Pauls C of E Junior School
WWKG RG41 .... 97 F1
St Pauls RC Primary School
CALC RG31 .... 55 H6
St Peter C of E School
EARL RG6 .... 9 J2
St Peters CM C of E School
YTLY GU46 .... 135 J3
St Sebastians Primary School
EWKG RG40 .... 97 K7
St Teresa RC Primary School
EWKG RG40 .... 97 J2
St Thomas Infant School
KSCL RG20 .... 120 B1
Sandford Springs Golf Club
TADY RG26 .... 124 D7
Sandleford Hospital
NWBY RG14 .... 83 K7
Sandmartins Golf Club
EWKG RG40 .... 97 G6
Sandy Lane County
Infant School
BNFD RG42 .... 79 K5
Saxonwood School for the
Handicapped
DEAN RG23 .... 159 G3
Shaw-cum-donnington School
NWBY RG14 .... 83 K1
Sherborne St. John
Primary School
CHAM RG24 .... 143 K6
Shinfield C of E Junior School
WHIT RG2 .... 94 C3
Shinfield Infant School
WHIT RG2 .... 94 B3
Shiplake C of E Primary School
HEN RG9 .... 45 H2
Shiplake College
HEN RG9 .... 45 J3
Showcase Cinemas Reading
WODY RG5 .... 75 J2
Shute End Medical Practice
WWKG RG41 .... 97 G1
Silchester Primary School
THLE RG7 .... 110 A7
Sindlesham School
WWKG RG41 .... 75 J7
Skimped Hill Health Centre
BRAK RG12 .... 10 F3
Sonning Church of
England Primary School
CAV/SC RG4 .... 59 G2
Sonning Common CP School
CAV/SC RG4 .... 29 G6
Sonning Common Health Centre
CAV/SC RG4 .... 29 G6
Southcote Clinic
TLHT RG30 .... 72 C2
Southcote CP School
TLHT RG30 .... 72 D2
Southfields Special School
EWKG RG40 .... 97 J3
South Ham Medical Centre
KEMP RG22 .... 175 H1
Southlake County Junior School
WODY RG5 .... 75 G1
Southlake Primary School
WODY RG5 .... 75 H1
South Reading Leisure Centre
WHIT RG2 .... 7 M9
21 South Street Arts Centrel
READ RG1 .... 3 K7
Speenhamland CP School
NWBY RG14 .... 12 D1

Springfield Primary School
CALC RG31 .... 55 G6
Spurcroft Primary School
STHA RG19 .... 85 J5
Stadium Industrial Estate
NWBY RG14 .... 56 C4
Station Industrial Estate
FLET GU13 .... 151 J7
Station Industrial Estate
WWKG RG41 .... 97 G1
Sterling Industrial Estate
NWBY RG14 .... 13 G5
Stockcross School
KSCL RG20 .... 82 B1
Strathfield Saye
THLE RG7 .... 130 E2
Streatley School
GOR/PANG RG8 .... 24 C5
Surrey Hampshire Borders
NHS Trust
BSTK RG21 .... 15 C5
Suttons Business Park
EARL RG6 .... 5 G4
Suttons Business Park
READ RG1 .... 4 D5
Swallowfield Medical Practice
THLE RG7 .... 113 K1
Swallowfield Park
THLE RG7 .... 94 B7
Swinley CP School
ASC SL5 .... 101 K3
Swinley Forest Golf Club
ASC SL5 .... 101 J5
Tadley CP School
TADY RG26 .... 127 F3
Tadley Police Station
TADY RG26 .... 108 E7
Tavistock County Infant School
FLET GU13 .... 166 E3
Tavistock Industrial Estate
WAR/TWY RG10 .... 46 E7
Temple
READ RG1 .... 3 H7
Tempus Business Centre
BSTK RG21 .... 14 A1
Tennis Club
FLET GU13 .... 183 G1
Thames Gallery
HEN RG9 .... 31 H1
Thameside School
READ RG1 .... 3 J1
Thatcham Bowling Club
NTHA RG18 .... 85 J3
Thatcham Health Centre
NTHA RG18 .... 85 H3
Thatcham Town Council
NTHA RG18 .... 85 H3
Thatcham Town Football Club
STHA RG19 .... 86 A7
Theale C of E Primary School
THLE RG7 .... 70 C3
Theale Green School
THLE RG7 .... 70 C3
Theale Medical Centre
THLE RG7 .... 70 C3
Theatre & Arts Centre
WHIT RG2 .... 74 A7
THMaes Valley Business Park
EARL RG6 .... 5 H2
Thorneycroft Industrial Estate
BSTK RG21 .... 14 A6
Thorngrove School
KSCL RG20 .... 120 B2
Tilehurst Medical Centre
CALC RG31 .... 55 K5
Tilehurst Parish Council
CALC RG31 .... 71 G1
Tilehurst Village Surgery
CALC RG31 .... 55 J4
Toutley Industrial Estate
WWKG RG41 .... 76 E4
Town Hall & Museum
READ RG1 .... 3 J5
Townlands Hospital
HEN RG9 .... 31 F1
Trinity Primary School
HEN RG9 .... 31 H2
Trinity School
NWBY RG14 .... 84 A2
Tunworth Ho
OVTN RG25 .... 178 A4
Tweseldown Infant School
FLET GU13 .... 167 J7
Twyford Business Park
WAR/TWY RG10 .... 60 C1
Twyford Health Centre
WAR/TWY RG10 .... 46 D7
Tylney Park Golf Club
HTWY RG27 .... 147 G6
U C I Cinema
BRAK RG12 .... 10 E3
Ufton Nervet Parochial
Primary School
THLE RG7 .... 90 B3
University Health Centre
WHIT RG2 .... 8 B3
University of Reading
EARL RG6 .... 5 K8
University of Reading
EARL RG6 .... 8 E4
University of Reading
READ RG1 .... 3 L8
University of Reading
READ RG1 .... 8 C1
University of Reading
WHIT RG2 .... 8 A3
Upcroft Primary School
TLHT RG30 .... 56 A5
Upton Grey Ho
OVTN RG25 .... 178 D6
Valley Road Primary School
HEN RG9 .... 31 F3
Viables Industrial Estate
KEMP RG22 .... 176 B3
Vickers Business Centre
CHAM RG24 .... 159 K3
Waingels Copse School
WODY RG5 .... 59 K3
Walter County Infant School
WWKG RG41 .... 97 F1
Warfield C of E
Controlled Primary School
BNFD RG42 .... 80 B5
Watermill Theatre
STHA RG19 .... 104 A3
Watermill Theatre
& Restaurant
KSCL RG20 .... 62 E7

Waverley School
EWKG RG40 .... 96 E6
Welfare Clinic
TLHT RG30 .... 55 J5
Wellington Business Park
CWTH RG45 .... 117 K4
Wellington College
CWTH RG45 .... 118 B5
Wellington Industrial Estate
THLE RG7 .... 93 H4
Wellington Sports Centre
CWTH RG45 .... 118 A4
Wescott County Infants School
EWKG RG40 .... 97 J1
Wessex Bowl
KEMP RG22 .... 159 H6
Wessex Downs Golf Club
THLE RG7 .... 88 B3
West Berkshire Council
NWBY RG14 .... 12 D5
West Berkshire District Council
NWBY RG14 .... 12 E5
West Berkshire District Council
NWBY RG14 .... 12 E4
West Berkshire District Council
NWBY RG14 .... 13 G2
West Berkshire District Council
THLE RG7 .... 70 D3
Westende County Junior School
EWKG RG40 .... 97 J1
Western Elms Surgery
TLHT RG30 .... 2 C6
Westfield County Junior School
YTLY GU46 .... 135 G4
The West Street Practice
HEN RG9 .... 31 G1
Westwood Farm County Junior
School
CALC RG31 .... 55 H2
Westwood Road Health Centre
CALC RG31 .... 55 J4
Whitchurch Medical Centre
WHCH RG28 .... 169 G2
Whitchurch Primary School
GOR/PANG RG8 .... 40 D5
White County Infants School
EWKG RG40 .... 77 J7
White Hart Gallery
OVTN RG25 .... 171 H4
White House School
WWKG RG41 .... 97 F4
Whiteknights Park CP School
EARL RG6 .... 8 E8
Whitelands Park CP School
NTHA RG18 .... 85 J3
Whitewater C of E
Primary School
HTWY RG27 .... 147 H1
Whitley Park School
WHIT RG2 .... 7 K8
Whitley Villa Surgery
READ RG1 .... 7 L1
Whitley Wood Surgery
WHIT RG2 .... 73 J7
Wildridings CP School
BRAK RG12 .... 10 C8
Willink Leisure Centre
THLE RG7 .... 90 E5
Willink School
THLE RG7 .... 90 E5
Willis Museum
BSTK RG21 .... 14 F6
Willowdene Play School
CHAM RG24 .... 161 G1
Wilson Junior & Infant School
TLHT RG30 .... 56 D6
Winchcombe CP Infant School
NWBY RG14 .... 83 K2
Winchcombe Junior School
NWBY RG14 .... 12 E1
Winklebury Infant School
DEAN RG23 .... 159 J5
Winklebury Junior School
DEAN RG23 .... 159 J5
Winklebury Medical Centre
DEAN RG23 .... 159 H5
Winnersh CP School
WWKG RG41 .... 76 C3
Winterbourne House Clinic
READ RG1 .... 2 C6
Wokingham Child
Guidance Clinic
EWKG RG40 .... 97 G1
Wokingham Cricket Club
WWKG RG41 .... 97 G2
Wokingham Hospital
WWKG RG41 .... 97 F1
Wokingham Theatre
EWKG RG40 .... 77 G6
Wokingham Town Council
EWKG RG40 .... 97 H1
Woodcote CP School
GOR/PANG RG8 .... 26 D2
Woodley Centre Surgery
WODY RG5 .... 59 H6
Woodley C of E Primary School
WODY RG5 .... 60 A5
Woodley Park Estate
WODY RG5 .... 59 G5
Woodley Town Council
WODY RG5 .... 59 H5
Woodside Business Park
WHIT RG2 .... 73 J7
Woolton Hill County
Junior School
KSCL RG20 .... 120 B2
Woosehill Surgery
WWKG RG41 .... 76 E7
Worting County Infant School
DEAN RG23 .... 159 F7
Worting County Junior School
KEMP RG22 .... 159 G2
Yateley County Infant School
YTLY GU46 .... 135 J3
Yateley Health Centre
YTLY GU46 .... 135 J3
Yateley Manor
Preparatory School
YTLY GU46 .... 135 J2
Yateley School
YTLY GU46 .... 135 H4
Yattendon C of E
Primary School
HEN RG9 .... 51 F3
Youngs Industrial Estate
THLE RG7 .... 108 C4

Page 31
G3
1 Cromwell Cl

Page 41
J7
2 Lilac Cl
3 Park Wk

Page 43
H7
1 Pinetree Ct

Page 55
K2
1 Ferndale Cl
2 Oak Tree Copse
3 Overlanders End

K4
1 Brendon Cl
2 Dudley Ms
3 Hirstwood
4 Hornsea Cl
5 Larissa Cl

K5
1 Dalton Cl
2 Halcyon Ter
3 Lernart Cl
4 Midwinter Cl

K6
1 Cadogan Cl
2 Hollicombe Cl
3 Hursley Cl
4 Ogmore Cl
5 St Michael's Rd

Page 70
D2
1 Chestnut Cl
2 Ellerton Cl
3 Kathleen Sanders Ct
4 North Wk
5 The Orchard
6 Swallow Field Gdns
7 Whiteham Cl
8 Woodfield Wy

Page 71
G2
1 Bamford Pl
2 Caistor Cl
3 Camden Pl
4 Charlville Dr
5 Glamis Wy
6 Hatfield Ct
7 Lennox Cl
8 Marlborough Wy
9 Sandringham Wy
10 Silbury Cl
11 Windsor Wy

Page 75
F5
1 Bourn Cl
2 Elford Cl
3 Fordham Wy
4 Martins St
5 St Clements Cl
6 Sturbridge Cl
7 Tamworth Cl
8 Woodbine Cl

F6
1 Bassett Cl
2 Bottisham Cl
3 Ebborn Sq
4 Gregory Cl
5 Harlton Cl
6 Irvine Wy
7 Ledran Cl
8 Littington Cl
9 Manea Cl
10 Porter Cl
11 Soham Cl
12 Stonea Cl
13 Waring Cl
14 Wild Cl

H4
1 Barholm Cl
2 Barkwith Cl
3 Burniston Cl
4 Dunholme Cl
5 Flamborough Cl
6 Forndon Cl
7 Hengrave Cl
8 Marfleet Cl
9 Sawtry Cl
10 Skeffling Cl
11 Stilton Cl
12 Welwick Cl

Page 80
B5
1 All Saints Rl
2 Augustine Wk
3 Barley Mead
4 Bartholomew Pl
5 Benedict Gn
6 Bernadine Cl
7 Burnthouse Gdns
8 Caesars Ga
9 Cleopatra Pl
10 Cressida Cha
11 Jig's La South
12 Ormathwaites Cnr
13 Rachaels Lake Vw
14 Shakespeare Wy
15 Swithin Cha
16 Thomas Dr
17 Yorkshire Pl

C5
1 Juliet Gdns
2 Julius Hl
3 Northumberland Cl
4 Shakespeare Wy
5 Shropshire Gdns
6 Suffolk Combe
7 Surrey Ct
8 Worcestershire Lea

C6
1 Beswick Gdns
2 Drummond Cl
3 Plantagenet Pk
4 Romeo Hl
5 Viola Cft

Page 85
J5
1 Cairngorm Rd
2 Danvers Cl
3 Glenmore Cl
4 Porlock Cl
5 Snowdon Cl
6 The Thakerays
7 Wenlock Wy
8 Wolsingham Wy

Page 91
F4
1 Horseshoe Crs

G5
1 Burdock Cl
2 Field Cl

H4
1 St Mary's Wy

Page 93
J4
1 Pursers Farm

Page 95
H5
1 Anderson Crs
2 Brants Cl
3 Chamberlain's Gdns
4 Harts Cl
5 Whitewell Cl

Page 96
C1
1 Cornwall Cl
2 Cumberland Wy
3 Rembrandt Cl
4 Riding Wy
5 Somerset Cl
6 Spencer Cl
7 Suffolk Cl
8 Westmorland Cl

D1
1 Agincourt Cl
2 Bedfordshire Wy
3 Blenheim Cl
4 Cambridgeshire Cl
5 Crecy Cl
6 Derwent Cl
7 Dieppe Cl
8 Dunkirk Cl
9 Fleet Cl
10 Jutland Cl
11 Kesteven Wy
12 Lalande Cl
13 Mercury Av
14 Minden Cl
15 Mons Cl
16 Neptune Cl
17 Phoenix Cl
18 Saturn Cl
19 Trafalgar Cl

E7
1 Burchett Coppice
2 Burnt Oak
3 Charlton Cl
4 Dodsells Well
5 Elgarth Dr
6 Jerrymoor Hl
7 Willowdale

Page 97
G1
1 Alderman Willey Cl
2 Bell House Gdns
3 Bird Ms
4 The Terrace

Page 100
B5
1 Burn Moor Cha
2 Cabin Moss
3 Higher Alham
4 Kilmington Cl
5 Mallowdale Rd
6 Pyegrove Cha
7 Wanstraw Gv
8 Wards Stone Pk

Page 118
E7
1 Cherry Tree Cl
2 Faversham Rd
3 Hailsham Cl
4 Helksham Cl
5 Hormer Cl
6 Hornbeam Cl
7 Magnolia Cl
8 Okingham Cl
9 Waltham Cl

Page 129
H7
1 Beech Cl

J7
1 Oaklea Gdns

Page 145
G7
1 Birchwood
2 Larchwood
3 Martins Wd
4 Thurnwood

Page 149
H4
1 Hartford Ct
2 Peel Ct

Page 160
B7
1 Devonshire Pl

E2
1 Crockford La

E6
1 Buckby La
2 The Butty
3 Colne Wy
4 Duddon Wy
5 Hamble Ct
6 Medway Ct
7 Ribble Wy
8 Roding Cl
9 Rothay Ct
10 Severn Wy
11 Thames Ct
12 Trent Wy
13 Weysprings Cl

Page 161
G3
1 Bracken Bank
2 Clover Fld
3 Crofters Meadow
4 Dragonfly Dr

Page 163
K1
1 Broad Leaze
2 Chalky Copse
3 Elms Rd
4 Ferndale Gdns
5 Hatchgate Mead
6 John Morgan Cl
7 Nursery Cl
8 Reading Rd
9 Wash Brook

Page 175
F5
1 Berewyk Cl
2 Bunting Ms
3 Sunflower Cl